MANIFESTATIONS OF MASCULINE MAGNIFICENCE

MANIFESTATIONS OF MASCULINE MAGNIFICENCE

DIVINITY IN AFRICANA LIFE, LYRICS, AND LITERATURE

TERESA N. WASHINGTON

OYA'S TORNADO

Copyright © 2014, 2015
Teresa N. Washington
All rights reserved

This book is a publication of
ỌYA'S TORNADO
Books To Blow Your Mind
oyastornado@yahoo.com

ỌYA'S TORNADO™, Books To Blow Your Mind™, and all associated tornado logos are trademarks of Ọya's Tornado.

All rights reserved

No part of this book may be reproduced or utilized in any form or by any means, electronic or mechanical, including photocopying and recording, or by any information storage and retrieval system, without permission in writing from the author and/or publisher.

Washington, Teresa N.,
Manifestations of Masculine Magnificence: Divinity in Africana Life, Lyrics, and Literature / Teresa N. Washington.
p. cm.
Includes bibliographical references and index.
ISBN 978-0-9910730-0-9 (pbk); ISBN 978-0-9910730-2-3 (cloth)
1. American literature—African American authors—History and criticism. 2. Men in literature—United States. 3. Masculinity and divinity in literature. 4. African American men in popular culture. 5. Masculinity and divinity in music. 6. Religion in music. 7. African Americans—Music—Religion—History and criticism. 8. African Gods. 9. African religions. 9. Indigenous African technology. 10. African American culture—African influences. I. Title.

Revised Edition
Third Printing 2016

Manufactured in the United States of America

For Odùduwà

For

Tekena Elkanah, Chidiaka Biringa Lordson, Ugonna Obuzor, and Lloyd Michael Toku

Your only crime was
Shining
amidst the dull and damned who rallied and
beat the life and light out of you

Your skulls exploded
showering your divinity, power, and potential
onto the Earth
into the oceans and
throughout the universe
where

You glow forever

You are evidence
of the truth most evident:

It is the nature
of the
Sun
to
Shine

May your radiance
eternally project
the brilliance
and the vengeance
of the
Gods

TABLE OF CONTENTS

Acknowledgements / ix
Notes on Style / xi

Cipher   1

PART ONE:
MASCULINE MAGNIFICENCE
IN AFRICANA LIFE AND LYRICS

1. Divinity and Divine Technology in the African Continuum   17

2. High John and His Conquering Suns: Re-Developing Divinity and Re-Determining Destiny   65

3. "I Call My Brother Sun 'Cause He Shine Like One": The Divine, the Shining, and the Poetics of Rap   101

The Bridge: Shining Lords of the Singing Soul-Piece: A Three Part Harmony   137

PART TWO:
MASCULINE MAGNIFICENCE
IN AFRICANA LITERATURE

4. Resurrecting the Shining Self in August Wilson's *Joe Turner's Come and Gone* and Bill Harris' *Robert Johnson: Trick the Devil*   151

5. "Meet Me In Another World": The Middle Passages Within Walter Mosley's *47*, Amos Tutuola's *My Life in the Bush of Ghosts*, and Malidoma Somé's *Of Water and the Spirit*   182

6. The Saline Solutions and Winged Revolutions of Toni Cade Bambara and Toni Morrison   226

7: Warriors, Writers, Revolutionaries: Africana Secret
Societies and Spiritual-Political Imperatives in the
Literature of Ayi Kwei Armah, Toni Morrison,
Ishmael Reed, and Ngugi wa Thiong'o   257

360°   319

Notes / 339
Bibliography / 380
Index / 397

ACKNOWLEDGEMENTS

All rise for the Warrior Gods! I am eternally thankful for the wisdom, courage, and dedication of my Husbands, my Fathers, and my Brothers of the Struggle who forever gird me with their power: Òrìṣà Olufela Anikulapo Kuti, Boukman, Fred Hampton, James Baldwin, Mutabaruka, Ali Farka Toure, Patrice Lumumba, Thomas Sankara, Ayi Kwei Armah, Ben Okri, El Hajj Malik El Shabazz, Amiri Baraka, Ngugi wa Thiong'o, Sembene Ousmane, and Miles, Miles, Miles Davis. Send forth the Suns! We need many more of you . . . many many more of you.

I extend special praise to Sly who, before I was even conceived, whispered to me a warning, "Jealous people like to see you bleed," and prepared me for the challenges of existence with the reminder, "Dying young is hard to take / Selling out is harder."[1]

I am grateful to myself, My Divine Self, for never selling out, for never giving up, for fighting for and defending me, for protecting and perfecting me, for standing firm on my square no matter the costs, threats, circumstances, or perils. I am grateful to myself for keeping this book safe from the vapidity and viciousness of racist editors and the sizzling brands of neoenslaving petty egomaniacs. Without my fortitude this book would be exactly what they wanted it to be—a mockery of itself and of you. I insisted on presenting you with the womb-deep powers that are your birthright because you need and deserve your truths.

I extend to myself most perfect praise because without my temerity and tenacity the struggles, attacks, and outrages that I have faced in this world—from degenerate negroes bent on determining how low down they can go without being buried, to the vile, hypocritical, racist mutants who are this world's living atrocities—would have moved me to adhere to the demand of my paternal grandmother who concluded one of her vicious ritual beatings of my naked six-year-old body with the demand that I stop breathing. . .

I am not only breathing—I am shining. The one deemed unworthy of life, the one casually condemned, is glowing, and every breath I take is a confirmation of my numinosity. The power that destitute mortals see, despise, and attempt to manipulate, delimit, or destroy is as unconquerable and as resplendent as the Sirius system. So, look up at us and marvel! Yes, "us," for attempts to obliterate me merely multiply my divinity: I, The One Who Becomes Two. Majesty manifest as You:

Odùduwà

I am so honored that you chose to build a new world with me. You taught me more than a million professors by simply growing in my womb. Your emergence through my vagina was a revelation. You suckling my breasts is the most ancient covenant kept. Every day you shower me in wisdom and crown me with divinity.

My goal in life is to ensure that you know precisely who you are—from the perfection that shimmers in your soul, to the power that radiates your visage, to the riches of the Cosmos that wait in your womb. No matter how they try, relatives who are morally bankrupt enough to steal from an infant can never hurt you: You are the child of Miles; you will never suffer. The tears that I shed will never dampen your eyes. There will be no raping brother in your bed. There will be no father hurling words of hate at you until your soul shatters. There will be no spiritually bereft aunt marinating you in the bile of her barren womb's bitterness. And never will you ever wonder or doubt if I love you.

You are the tiny warrior who sprang from my womb fighting injustice. Together we will continue to fight, and we shall conquer because you have taught me that together we can do not only the impossible, we can accomplish the unimaginable.

NOTES ON STYLE

African words are italicized in the first usage only. Proper nouns are not italicized unless they are italicized in a direct quotation.

African languages are extraordinarily complex and fluid. To avoid unintended insult or error and to maintain consistency, with the exception of direct quotations, the proper names of academics and authors are not tone marked unless such marks are necessary to avoid confusion.

CIPHER

"Do the lords still talk? Do the lords still walk? Are they writing this book?"
~ Ishmael Reed, *Flight to Canada*

A cipher is a circle that has neither beginning nor end. The circle that is a cipher could be a zero, which could be considered either a starting point or the nothingness with which Africana men are often associated. A cipher could symbolize the unending ever-revolving power of a God. A cipher, in and of itself, constitutes a riddle, and all over America, Africans who have been dislocated from their Continent for more than 570 years gather in circular groups that they call ciphers and create linguistic riddles in rap that encode, decode, and recode English into their own language, the language of the Gods.

The curvilinear existence and divine continuum that undergirds Africana identity is mired in ciphers of varying degrees. Africana peoples, especially those associated with the United States of America, are casually and routinely associated with the concept of "nigger," a term (along with all of its phonemic and international derivatives and equivalents) that signifies a worthless, useless, reprehensible person; it is a term that signifies the dehumanized. That dehumanization is the intended purpose of this word is intimated in its etymology. The word "nigger" originates with "negro," the Spanish and Portuguese word for the color black. With the adjective "black" replacing a proper noun befitting human beings and supplanting the history, culture, and geography that informs ethnic identity, Africans became, to objectifiers, adjectival non-entities.[1]

The concept of relating human beings to colors and then to arbitrary values can be traced to Caucasian pseudoscience. In 1775 a physician named Johann F. Blumenbach devised a racial schema in which he associated various peoples with colors that were assigned values rooted in Eurocentrism, racism, and objectification: Caucasian: white (pure, holy, clean); Mongolian: yellow (cowardly, sneaky); Native American: red (savage, blood thirsty); Malayan: brown (irritated, angry, filthy, dingy); Negro: black (evil, hostile, destitute).[2]

While every ethnic group who has ever been associated with a color has felt the blow of the Blumenbachean assault, the two peoples arguably the most affected by false color designations are those who occupy the lowest and highest positions on Blumenbach's spectrum of humanity

Blumenbach stationed "Negro" at the bottom of his racial scale and decreed that Africans, with their rich melanin, embodied the fabricated and subjective concepts of evil, dishonor, sin, and other notions that Caucasians decided to associate with the word "black." The association of Africana people with the Caucasian definition of "black" gave birth of the myth of inherent "black" inferiority which, in turn, fomented the rise of one of the most destructive words ever uttered, "nigger."

Blumenbach positioned "Caucasian" as the polar opposite in every respect to "Negro," and he brought the reification of ludicrous equivalents to its apex by associating Caucasians with "white" which was linked to such notions as being without blemish or stain, holy, pure, clean. Blumenbach got so carried away by the "science" he was concocting that he claimed that his group was "the most beautiful race of men."[3] So impassioned are Blumenbach's attempts at reifying his constructs of "Caucasian" and "white" that Nell Irvin Painter describes Blumenbach as using the word "beautiful" compulsively.[4] Perhaps he thought that if he made the associations often and vigorously enough they would be mistaken for truth—by many accounts he was correct.

Blumenbach's glorification of the Caucasian self and denigration (pardon the pun) of international others was embraced by Caucasian politicians, scientists, psychologists, historians, and writers. Blumenbach's hierarchy was especially useful to Caucasian conquerors, missionaries, enslavers, and colonizers, because it supplied them with a "scientific" rationale with which to justify their slaughter, rape, and oppression of millions of innocent people all over the world. One could argue that Blumenbach did not merely create the construct of race but that he fomented the institutionalization of racism.

Caucasian editors of dictionaries and encyclopedias embraced, formalized, and trumpeted Blumenbach's color-coded fictions. The 1884 edition of the *Encyclopedia Britannica* asserts that the Negro "occupies . . . the lowest position in the evolutionary scale, thus affording the best material for the comparative study of the highest anthropoids and the human species."[5] According to this erudite assessment, Africana people are just *barely* human beings—a cipher indeed.

Although the Blumenbach's color scheme is insulting, childish, in no way universal, and the antithesis of scientific, its simplicity seems to have given it international appeal. Various peoples with rich cultures, deep ancestries, and expansive geographical scopes casually describe themselves as colors that are loaded with false, racist, and arbitrary values. The impact that color associations exert on identity is most evident in adjectival "white" and "black" people. Many Caucasian people despise the use of the term "Caucasian," as they seek to erase their ethnic and historical origins with the solipsistic, presumably normative, and (un)consciously glorified construct of "white." Conversely, while "black" has been embraced as beautiful and pumped up with pride-pounding fists, its racist definition and connotation have much more staying power and prominence.[6] Apparently, Africana people are still stymied by the lesson that schoolteacher of Toni Morrison's *Beloved* tried to beat into Sixo: "definitions belonged to the definers—not the defined."[7]

Despite the rallying cries, slogans, and anthems, being at the bottom of Caucasia's evolutionary scale has taken such a psychological toll on Africana people that a rhyme was devised to help African Americans prepare for and acquiesce in racism as well as intracommunal casteism:

> If you're white, you're all right
> If you're yellow, you're mellow
> If you're brown, stick around
> If you're black, get back!

This little ditty even crossed the oceans to find a home in Australia.[8] Whether or not they know the rhyme, peoples all over the world follow the code—even unconsciously.

No matter the hipness in which the construct is dressed, no one wants to be what Western culture casually defines as "a black" or "a nigger." Toni Morrison and El Hajj Malik El Shabazz (also known as Malcolm X) both opined that the first word that immigrants to America learn is "nigger" because no matter what horrific social, cultural, or economic conditions they had escaped or would face at least they could not be placed as low as "niggers."[9] As is all too well known, centuries of savage oppression have placed some African Americans in the paradoxical position of attempting to disassociate from one construct of "nigger" while clamoring and crying for the right to embrace another "nigger" construct. Many will even attempt to prohibit Caucasians from uttering the word when it and all of its derivatives (including negar, niggah, nigga, *ad nauseum*) are the linguistic and cultural brainchildren of Caucasians.

The stupidity, intractability, laziness, and barbarity of "niggers" is the subject of nearly every disquisition on Africana peoples written by Caucasians during the era of slavery and quite a few afterward; however, British, Portuguese, French, Spanish, American, and German governments, businessmen, and fortune seekers did not invest millions of dollars in natural and human resources and risk their own lives and abandon their families to travel to Africa and abduct, dislocate, and fill their homelands and the lands they were colonizing with uncivilized subhuman savages. No one would expect beasts to use their architectural skills to fortify existing and build new civilizations; to use their agricultural ingenuity to introduce to foreign lands and successfully cultivate such indigenous African staples as okra, black-eyed beans, watermelon, rice, peanuts, indigo, and cotton; to use their bodies, compassion, and intellect to administer—preferably straight from the African breast—nourishment to Caucasian children and oversee their care. How could entities of dubious humanity fight valiantly in their nations' wars; undertake the surveying and settling of cities and uncharted territories; paint portraits, navigate ships, build roads, lay rails, and write poetry, novels, inspirational *Appeals*, and autobiographies, *ad infinitum*? These are not the activities that useless animals could or would perform. Furthermore, no entrepreneur would make an investment in "nigger." No one would want "the missing link" rocking, soothing, and teaching their children or cleaning their homes, cooking their food, and building their nation's Capitol.

The stereotype does not fit the reality. But if "niggers" aren't and "black" isn't, what lies beneath the façade of niggerdom? That may be the deepest cipher of all.

The Greeks are credited with having developed one of the world's most advanced and enviable civilizations, and in their art, letters, religion, and philosophy they herald the African geniuses who civilized, educated, and directed them. The respect and reverence that the Greeks held for Africans is evident in Homer's *Iliad*:

> For Zeus had yesterday to Ocean's bounds
> Set forth to feast with Ethiopia's faultless men,
> And he was followed there by all the gods[10]

The fact that Greeks describe their "gods," led by no less august a figure than Zeus, as traversing time and space to dine and worship with Ethiopian "men" speaks volumes about the consideration and regard that ancient Greeks held for Africans. Indeed, both the *Iliad* and *Odyssey* are rich with tributes to Africans.

Respect for African genius and divinity is not limited to creative works. The theorem associated with Pythagoras is the product of ancient African holistic wisdom, as is illustrated in the tomb of Ramses VI.[11] Herodotus, the so-called "Father of History," and Hippocrates, the would-be "Father of Medicine," both credit the African Imhotep with making the discoveries with which they have come to be associated. Herodotus' high regard for Africans is clear in his writings which also detail the source of Greek culture and philosophy:

> Almost all of the names of the gods came into Greece from Egypt. . . . the Egyptians were the first to introduce solemn assemblies, processions, and litanies to the gods, all of which the Greeks were taught to use. It seems to me sufficient proof of this that in Egypt these practices have been established from remote antiquity, while in Greece they are only recently known.[12]

The findings of Herodotus are better appreciated when contextualized by the research of Sicilian historian Diodorus, who discerned that Kemet (Ancient Egypt) was founded as a colony of Ethiopia and that the Kemites (Ancient Egyptians) acknowledge the Ethiopians as the originators of their social and moral laws, funeral rites, architectural advances, and educational systems.[13]

From Kemet, which means "Land of the Blacks"; to Sudan, which also means "Land of the Blacks"; to Ethiopia, a Greek word that signifies a people enriched by the Sun; it is clear that, for Herodotus, Diodorus, and other ancient historians, "Black" relates to Africans, including the Egyptians, the Ethiopians, and the Sudanese, and that "Blackness" signifies wealth, wisdom, perfection, and Divinity.

Just as the Nile flows from Uganda to Ethiopia to Egypt, so too did literacy, philosophy, science, mathematics, spirituality, wisdom, architectural knowledge, and methods of state governance and defense flow from Ta Ntr, the Land of God (Uganda), to the Land of Gold (Nubia), to the Land of the Blacks (Kemet).[14] And Africans protected the worlds that they built. Rather than assuming stances of nonviolent martyrdom when violent, hate-filled, jealous adversaries sought to destroy their creations and civilizations, Africans fought: Indeed, Africans are some the world's most ancient and revered warriors. Not only does the Bible repeatedly discuss the prowess of Ethiopia and Kush (modern-day Sudan), but the Bible reveals that Kush is the home of Kush, the empire builder, and his progeny Nimrod, the master architect and mighty warrior. Alexander of Macedonia and Augustus Caesar encountered more recent progeny of Kush: the shining Nubian Kandake (Queen Rulers) who overawed Alexander and Augustus and made a mockery of their claims of unequalled greatness and world domination.

Although some African Americans have been miseducated to believe that learning and using language correctly are "white" preoccupations, university education is of African origin. From the ancient universities of Kush and Kemet, which foreigners like Herodotus, Moses, and Pythagoras called "mystery schools" because they were not made privy to or inclined to understand all of the knowledge disseminated among the Africans, to the University of Sankore in Timbuktu, Mali which was built in the 900s and become a magnet for international wisdom seekers in the 14th and 15th centuries, Africans' love for the acquisition and respect for the dissemination of knowledge is unrivalled.

The fact that many Americans think that Timbuktu is a mythical concept as opposed to an actual place offers evidence of the degree to which racist anti-intellectualism undergirds every level of the American educational system as well as of the success of the global agenda to replace African wisdom keepers with mythically ubiquitous "ignorant niggers." But Timbuktu's significance to knowledge dissemination is eternal and cannot be erased. The proverb of ancient intellectuals, "Salt comes from the north, gold from the south, and silver from the country of the white men, but the word of God and the treasures of wisdom are only to be found in Timbuktu," rings with resounding truth to this day, as every family in Timbuktu maintains its own library.[15]

The Africans who created and disseminated genius know that wisdom's treasures, the words of the Gods, and the Gods, themselves, can be found throughout the Continent. This is evident in the storied empires of stone and gold and the unique inventions for which Africa is known. There are more pyramids in modern-day Sudan than there are in Egypt. One can find ancient *tekhens* (also known by the Greek term obelisks) all over East and West Africa. Ancient writing systems and architectural wonders abound on the Continent.

The knowledge of astronomy displayed in the celestial maps and through the wisdom of the ancient Africans of Nabta Playa, Kenya, Mali, Kemet, and Nubia make clear Africans' cognizance of their divine technological faculties and of their cosmic identities, relationships, and destinies. Ancient Africans also logically exerted themselves as global entities. One finds Africans' influence all over the world, including, but not limited to, the Coburg and Freising Moors of Germany, the flag of Corsica, and the massive Olmec heads and pyramids of Mesoamerica. Perhaps the most stunning example of international African influence is the bevy of Black Madonnas that are worshipped in Spain, Germany, Mexico, Italy, Poland, and France, to name but a few countries. These revered and adored icons give honor to the African God Ast and her son Heru who was divinely conceived after the death of Ausar, The Lord of Perfect Blackness. If this story sounds familiar that is because the Greeks borrowed the history and changed the African names of Aset, Heru, and Ausar to Isis, Horus, and Osiris before the Christians made the event the cornerstone of their religion and changed the Gods' African names to Mary, Jesus, and Yahweh.

These few examples reveal that, historically, the terms Black, African, Ethiopian, Nubian, Kemite, Kushite, Abyssinian and others that signify African peoples and ethnic groups, indicate power, beauty, correctness, wisdom, and, most of all, divinity. Originally, the people considered "African" or "Black" were in no way associated with wickedness, evil, turpitude, or degeneracy. Africans' Greek, Roman, Arab and other neighbors looked upon them with awe, respect, and admiration. There is no mention of "niggers" or anything akin to that construct in ancient documents about Africans. There are no complaints about the laziness of "darkies" or pontifications on the whimsy of Negro frolics. Far from being intellectually inferior, according to French historian Count Constantine Francis Chassebeuf de Volney, the words "African" and "Black" signify the people who created the "arts, sciences, and even the use of speech!"[16]

Africans are the world's first nation-builders, educators, seafarers, philosophers, and architects, but when Caucasian imperialists usurped the power to define, African accomplishments were ignored or attributed to others, and Africans went from being shining and divine beings to being humanity's dregs. Beneath *persona non grata*, Africans became, thanks to the power of linguistic reification, *non persona*. By turning "Black" into "black," the humanity of Africans was negated by an adjective that Caucasians used to signify all manner of negativity. Furthermore, as non-human "blacks" Africans became irresistibly enslavable.

In their efforts to control, economize, and industrialize the talents of others, in 1441 the Portuguese began kidnapping West Africans. In their attempt to legalize the atrocities that they were committing, Portuguese and Spanish invaders requested from the Vatican permission to enslave Africans. The Vatican offered its hearty Christian approval with not one but three papal bulls issued in 1442, 1444, and 1452.[17] With the downgrade in humanity having been sanctioned by the Catholic church again and again and again, the enslavement and exile of Africans thrived to the extent that Caucasian enslavers made the term "slave" synonymous with "black." This association served many purposes: it helped other ethnic groups forget their inglorious pasts; it furthered the goals of Blumenbach and gave teeth to his hierarchical schemata; and it prepared Africana people for an eternity of oppression.

In *Slavery and Social Death: A Comparative Study*, Orlando Patterson defines slavery as "the permanent, violent domination of natally alienated and generally dishonored persons."[18] To ensure perpetual servitude, the mind must be enslaved. To facilitate mental enslavement in the United States of America, those who created speech, arts, and the alphabet were forbidden education: In fact, African Americans are the only people in America for whom it was illegal to read and write. It is not necessary to outlaw literacy if the entities to be disenfranchised are animals that are incapable of reading, writing and "ciphering"; such laws are only necessary when an oppressor seeks to replace innate intelligence with a vacuity and self-hatred that will perpetuate erroneous definitions and perpetual servitude—both mental and physical.

Oppressors filled the gaps left by their mandate of ignorance with propaganda. Christians launched a relentless global colonizing crusade to convince Africana people to love their enemies and to hate themselves. This misplaced adoration also served to bolster the myth that the "white" other was superior to the "inferior," "black," "nigger" self.

As they hefted genitals, peered into mouths, raped with vengeance, marveled at ironwork as fine as lace, posed for portraits, enjoyed sweetmeats, rocked on porches, picked banjos, and feasted on watermelon, Caucasian oppressors made no mention of the monumental investments that they made to put African ingenuity to work for their agendas. They did not discuss the African inventiveness and creativity that made their lives richer; they omitted mention of their ancestors who had risked life and limb to travel halfway around the world to take, by any and all means, the people who had the skills, knowledge, and technology that they knew they could not live or advance without. Those gentlemen and gentlewomen of ease chuckled, relaxed, and enjoyed the way the word "nigger" rolled off of their tongues.

There is no need to abduct people, drag them to distant lands, and force them to do work that one can do oneself or that one can hire or compel citizens of one's own nation to do. Such an investment is made only when the coveted captives possess something the captors do not.

Despite the strenuous efforts of the Vatican, Blumenbach, and various planters, pastors, pseudo-academics, and fortune seekers, there were and are many Africana people who refuse to believe that they are "niggers" and that slavery and colonization were blessings bestowed upon their poor heathen souls. They re-member their "ancient properties."[19] They see in their melanin the perfection of the Cosmos, and in their bones they feel the glories of the Gods. They read to their children, spouses, and siblings from the book of ages that is inscribed in each of their souls. They hold up the truth of the self as a mirror so that Divinity can be reflected, magnified, and proliferated.

How is it, one might ask, that a people placed so low that their humanity was measured in mere fractions, that a people grown so confused that they rally in support of the very slurs and institutions created to destroy them, would find in themselves the power, skills, and will to re-determine their destinies and in the process discover their inherent divinity and resurrect the God of Self? Some would say that the answer to the cipher is the Self which is also known as the Arm, Leg, Leg, Arm, Head.

The assertion that Africana people are divine is not new. Inherent divinity is a cornerstone of ancient African cosmologies, and many contemporary African rulers are considered divine. Recognition of humanodivinity is also not restricted to Africans. Two biblical scriptures assert outright that human beings are Gods, and numinosity is implied in other scriptures. The inherent divinity of humanity is also intimated in the Qur'an. While divinity knows few ethnic bounds, it is significant that African Americans, those deemed the lowest of the low, carried within the tools to fully access, activate, and actualize divinity.

Formal acknowledgements of inherent divinity in African America appear as early as 1900 when Samuel H. Morris proclaimed himself to be "God in a body" as well as "Father Jehovia, God in the Fathership degree."[20] More recently, Bishop Carlton D. Pearson preached the gospel of innate numinosity at the 2010 Harlem Book Fair panel on religion. Holding a God-reflecting mirror up to his audience, Pearson revealed a profound and elemental truth: "The best God you may ever know is the God you are."[21]

In *God is Not a Christian, Nor a Jew, Muslim, Hindu. . . : God Dwells with Us, in Us, Around Us, as Us,* Pearson asserts that human beings are not merely made in the image of God, but are "Divine in nature."[22] Pearson goes on to situate humanity within a divine continuum that spans from Moses on Mount Horeb to before and beyond: "[T]he true essence of who we are is 'I AM,' and that is eternal and unchanging.[23] Pearson encourages his audience to disabuse their minds of myths, fairy tales, and religious terrorism, and expand their vision and consciousness to a full 360° for, "From this clearer vantage point of wholeness and accuracy, you will know 'I Am God,' or that indeed you are god."[24]

African American Gods and the institutions they founded have been the subject of many academic studies, including Michael A. Gomez's *Black Crescent*; Jill Watts' *God, Harlem U.S.A.: The Father Divine Story*; Jeffrey Louis Decker's essay, "The State of Rap: Time and Place in Hip Hop Nationalism"; Ted Swedenburg's essay, "Islam in the Mix: Lessons of the Five Percent"; Dasun Allah's article, "The GODS Of Hip-Hop: A Reflection On The Five Percenter Influence On Rap Music & Culture"; Felicia Miyakawa's *Five Percenter Rap: God Hop's Music, Message, and Black Muslim Mission*; The RZA's *The Wu-Tang Manual* and *The Tao of Wu*; Michael Muhammad Knight's *The Five Percenters: Islam, Hip Hop, and the Gods of New York*; and Lord Jamar's groundbreaking concept album, *The 5% Album*, which includes a 90 page booklet about the history, codes, and obligations of the "True and Living" Gods of the Five Percent

Nation. Lord Jamar is also featured in an insightful National Public Radio report titled "God, the Black Man and the Five Percenters" by Christopher Johnson.[25]

The Gods are much closer, accessible, and responsible than one might have imagined. This is especially true of the Gods of the Five Percent Nation, also known as the Nation of Gods and Earths. These Gods have never been cloistered in churches, secluded in synagogues, or trapped in temples. These Gods have always been throbbing in the hearts of their communities and inspiring elevation. Indeed, the Five Percent Nation's preferred method of knowledge dissemination is the most ancient: sharing wisdom in their communities in a circular formation called a cipher. When Gods began formalizing their artistic intellectual exhibitions as rap music, citizens of the Five Percent Nation increased exponentially, and today they can be found on every continent.

It is fitting that rap music serves as both a stage upon which Africana divinity shines and a megawatt sub-woofer that reverberates divinity through to the core of the speaker's and listener's beings because rap has its genesis in the Wolof word "Raap." Raap, also known as Rab, are Gods of Water who are praised through sacred hymns that it takes more than a decade to memorize.[26] The relationship of Raap to water is significant because the reverence that Raap enjoy and the resonance of their songs survived the horrors of the Middle Passage and the atrocities of slavery, lynch law, segregation, rape, social degradation, and humiliation to be reborn in Gods of Rap. When one realizes that Digable Planets, Busta Rhymes, Erykah Badu, X Clan, De La Soul, Red Man, Wu-Tang Clan, Sunz of Man, Brand Nubian, Big Daddy Kane, King Sun, Poor Righteous Teachers, and Rakim Allah (to name but a few) are all Gods and are consciously and unconsciously sowing the seeds that will proliferate divinity in their lyrics, the impact of Wolof Raap and the power of their divine progeny, rappers and rap, are better appreciated.

The objective of this study is to contextualize and analyze the myriad elaborations and manifestations of Africana divinity in life, lyrics, and literature, from ancient Africa to contemporary Pan-Africa, with the goal of revealing the revolutions of a divine continuum in which the Africana man is central. This line of inquiry is not a new one for me. My books *The Architects of Existence: Àjẹ́ in Yoruba Cosmology, Ontology, and Orature* and *Our Mothers, Our Powers, Our Texts: Manifestations of Àjẹ́ in Africana Literature* analyze the power called Àjẹ́, which is an inherent biological-spiritual force of Africana women that endows them with so much power that Àjẹ́ are known as the Gods of Society, and that is not hyperbole or fawning praise.[27] Women—who give birth to the world and also have the power to do and undo, create and destroy, and heal or harm as politically, socially, and personally necessary—are, indeed, Gods.

While there are males with Àjẹ́, and I elaborate on them in the aforementioned books, Àjẹ́ is owned and controlled by Africana women. Africana men have their own unique and complex relationship to divinity, and I elucidate the intricacies of that relationship in *Manifestations of Masculine Magnificence: Divinity in Africana Life, Lyrics, and Literature* (*Manifestations of Masculine Magnificence*).

The subject matter of *Manifestations of Masculine Magnificence* is compelling to me for important reasons. Since I was a child reciting and revising others' and composing my own raps, I was fascinated by the references to humanodivinity that ranged from subtle to resolute. Equating the human body with Allah (Arm-Leg-Leg-Arm-Head) and the three-tiered categorization of human beings as five percenters, ten percenters, and eighty-five percenters have been part of my consciousness for so long that I do not know when this information was first conveyed to me—and I am not from Mecca (New York) or Medina (Newark); I was born in "corn country" in the heart of Illinois.

It became clear to me early on that in addition to being forms of entertainment, many rap songs are lyrical maps and signposts that direct listeners to the ultimate destination: their inherent divinity. The drive toward numinosity is not restricted to rap music; it pulses in certain reggae, jazz, and soul songs as well. If one knows what to listen and look for, the messages to and from the Divine can be found in every Africana artistic genre. Summonses to resurrect the buried God within resonate in the ink of some of the greatest and most heralded literary works and shimmer in the oils, acrylics, and sculptures of celebrated fine artists. These messages are not coincidental or erroneous: Renowned wordsmiths do not have to write certain passages or depict certain powers; so-called gangs do not have to adopt particular signs, stances, and phrases; noted activists need not make telling political and spiritual proclamations—but they do. An impressive body of verbal and visual art stands as a testament to Africana humanodivinity, and it keeps growing. In my effort to better understand the source and force motivating these artists, I submerged myself into the study of the masculine and divine. My research took me to the beginning of time and catapulted me into the Cosmos. Along the way, this book, a guide of the Gods, if you will, was born.

Manifestations of Masculine Magnificence is a book of two interconnected parts. Part one, "Masculine Magnificence in Africana Life and Lyrics," establishes the spiritual, lyrical, and historical foundation for this study. Chapter one, "Divine Powers and Powerbrokers in the Africana

Continuum," analyzes historical examples of Africana spiritual technologies and humanospiritual power wielders. Through comparative analysis of African and African American philosophies, technologies, and wisdom workers, the force of Pan-African continuity becomes apparent. This chapter reveals the seamless manner by which divinity is transmitted and transferred despite space, time, and unflagging attempts at physical, spiritual, and cultural genocide.

The spiritual systems and technologies elucidated in chapter one provide striking examples of Africana Divinities in action, and those ancient and historical exhibitions of power find continued expression in contemporary Africana life and orature. Chapter two, "High John and His Conquering Suns: Re-Developing Divinity and Re-Determining Destiny," examines how African Americans folded the communal wisdom, skills, powers, and technologies into the womb of recreation to create High John the Conqueror, who could be considered the tutelary Deity of African America. The multiplicity of High John the Conqueror, as extolled by millions of African Americans and gently molded to literary perfection by Zora Neale Hurston, forms the foundation for the development and proliferation of divinity in such leaders as George Hurley, Marcus Garvey, Father Divine, W. D. Fard, and Allah, the Father. My study of these and other leaders' philosophies, commandments, and creeds reveals the diversity, flexibility, and invincibility of Africana divinity.

Chapter three, "'I Call My Brother Sun 'Cause He Shine Like One': The Divine, the Shining, and the Poetics of Rap" undertakes an in-depth analysis of the creation and proliferation of Africana male divinity in contemporary Africana life, lyrics, and literature. This chapter analyzes manifestations of divinity in Africana music, especially rap, and looks specifically at the lyrics, revelations, and proclamations of such influential artists as Goodie Mob, Digable Planets, Sunz of Man, The RZA, Erykah Badu, Rakim Allah, Killarmy, and Gravediggaz, all of whom extol humanodivinity in their art for the education and elevation of their audiences.

Similar to the function a bridge in a musical composition, "The Bridge: Shining Lords of the Singing Soul-Piece: A Three Part Harmony" connects the analysis of Africana divinity in life and lyrics with the exploration of numinosity in Africana literary arts. Divinity knows no bounds and boasts interdisciplinary influence; these facts are evident in Souleymane Cisse's film *Yeelen*, John McCluskey's novel *Look What They Done to My Song*, and Arthur Flowers' novel *De Mojo Blues: De Quest of HighJohn de Conqueror*. The Bridge examines how Cisse, McCluskey, and Flowers harness ancient and contemporary musical traditions and spiritual technologies, symbols, and codes to further the proliferation of divinity in cinema, in literature, and in the souls of their audiences.

The ancient and historical powers and powerbrokers that I discuss in Part One find revivification in the literary works that I analyze in "Part Two: Masculine Magnificence in Africana Literature." The second part of this book focuses on how contemporary Africana writers of both genders infuse the concepts of masculine magnificence, inherent divinity, and the powers of the Ancients into literature of various genres including satirical, historical, and science fiction novels; drama; autobiography; and books that defy categorization.

Chapter four explores the powers of song, self-actualization, and divine shining in August Wilson's *Joe Turner's Come and Gone* and Bill Harris' *Robert Johnson: Trick the Devil*. These plays are veritable siblings that share symbolism, subject matter, and objectives. *Robert Johnson: Trick the Devil* reveals the shining divinity of Johnson and seeks to demystify and liberate his legacy which has been hijacked by a Faustian myth. *Joe Turner's Come and Gone* also explores a battle for the soul: To protect his divinity from Joe Turner, Herald Loomis buried it so deeply within himself that he cannot find his shining or illuminate his path in life. With help from two-headed doctors, Stokes and Bynum Walker, Robert Johnson and Herald Loomis, respectively, liberate themselves from destructive myths and reclaim and burnish their spiritual shine for their sakes and for the benefits of Wilson's and Harris' audiences.

Chapter five explores the travels and interactions between cosmic and terrestrial worlds and entities in Walter Mosley's *47*, Amos Tutuola's *My Life in the Bush of Ghosts*, and Malidoma Somé's *Of Water and the Spirit*. These three works challenge the concept of a heaven of leisure and luxury that one must die to visit. These writers depict the spiritual realm as a world that is as intricate and accessible as our own. The protagonists of these works make it clear that to survive in the spiritual realm a human must have the flexibility and divinity of High John the Conqueror. And these protagonists are literary sons of High John who use their wits and spiritual and technological skills to combat physical, mental, and religious slaveries. Rather than an enclave of eternal bliss, the spiritual realm is revealed to be a most intense finishing school where prepared human beings are transformed into Gods.

Chapter six undertakes an in-depth study of a skill that only the Gods can master: human flight. To understand the science involved in the phenomenon, chapter six focuses on the complex relationship between salt and human flight in Africana life, technology, and literature. Using the biochemical and spiritual properties of sodium chloride and its impact on African divinity and divine technology as its foundation, this chapter explores the connection between salt and flight in Toni Cade Bambara's short story "Broken Field Running" and novel *The Salt Eaters* and Toni Morrison's novel *Song of Solomon*.

Many scholars dismiss the concept of African flight altogether; others describe it as a metaphor. However, a significant number of academics understand what traditional African scientists have always known: that African flight is one of many African technologies, and it has various means of actualization. The literature of Bambara and Morrison, in distinct but intricately connected ways, reveals the significance of salt to human flight and the sociopolitical, psychological, and cultural influence of human flight on the Africana community.

The recognition of divinity without its purposeful application is an exercise in ego-inflation. In other words, if the Gods are not going to come in handy, they might as well not come in (to recognition or to being) at all. Rather than being secluded in a gold-embossed and pearl-encrusted heaven, Ayi Kwei Armah's *Two Thousand Seasons* and *Osiris Rising*, Toni Morrison's *Song of Solomon*, Ishmael Reed's *Mumbo Jumbo*, and Ngugi wa Thiongo's *Matigari* and *The Wizard of the Crow* depict the Gods sharing knowledge at chittlin' switches, planning insurrections on slave ships, escaping from prisons, and seeking solutions in rubbish heaps. In these seemingly ignominious settings, the Gods are doing the most work where it is most needed. Using the methodologies set forth by the world's most ancient sacred and secret societies, these literary Deities labor devotedly to erect a world that is worthy of True and Living Gods.

From their creative contributions it is evident that the writers, filmmakers, and lyricists under study and countless other verbal, visual, and literary artists are not striving to merely entertain; they are creating art to inspire change. Using their ink as reflecting pools and their lyrics as blinding political and evolutionary jewels, Africana artists lead their audiences into the curvilinear continuum of divine power. The goal of *Manifestations of Masculine Magnificence* is a simple but revolutionary one—to elucidate what has always been inscribed in the ink of the leaves, the curve of the spine, the pulse of the beat, the power of the rhymes: those multidimensional properties that lie dormant or burst forth with irrepressible ebullience from the masculine and divine.

PART ONE

MASCULINE MAGNIFICENCE IN AFRICANA LIFE AND LYRICS

"Now the journey to Gods begins"

~ X Clan, "Verbal Milk"

CHAPTER ONE

Divinity and Divine Technology in the African Continuum

"There are a people, now forgotten, who discovered, while others were yet barbarians, the elements of the arts and sciences. A race of men, now ejected from society for their sable skin and frizzled hair, founded on the study of the laws of nature, those civil and religious systems which still govern the universe."
~ Count Constantine C. F. de Volney, *The Ruins of Empires*

The Power of the Cosmos Within

Recognition of human divinity is as ancient as the Earth and as evident as the Cosmos. The vast majority of Africana cosmological and ontological systems, including those of the Kemites, Kushites, BaKongo, Dogon, Dahomey, and Yoruba, contend that the Gods travel from the Cosmos and spiritual realm to Earth to assist in the creation and fortification of the world and human existence. Africana cosmologies also describe human beings' ability to travel to and from the Cosmos and spiritual realm with ease. Such fluidity is indicative of a seamless and holistic relationship between human beings, Divinities, and the Cosmos. Indeed, it is because African cosmologists recognize the Earth's roles as a part of—as opposed to being thought of as apart from—the Cosmos, that African technologists can readily harness cosmic powers and celestial wisdom. The interactivity and interconnectivity between African wisdom workers, the Earth, and the Cosmos is essential to the activation and proliferation of Africana divinity.

Africana spiritual systems recognize that there is a curvilinear continuum that connects human beings to their divinity and to the galaxy and that there are divine guides available to help human beings who seek to heal, balance, and harmonize themselves, their communities, and the world. The Yoruba God Èṣù Ẹlẹ́gbára, who resides at the literal and metaphysical crossroads and ushers human beings through or misdirects them at crossroads as necessary to manifest destiny, is an example of a guiding God. Among the Dagara, spiritual entities called Kontombili dialogue with human beings who have the ability to listen. Unborn children can also reveal human beings' divine nature and celestial obligations; consequently, Dagara elders converse with *in vitro* souls just prior to their births so that they can discern the mission, needs, and goals of the divine *arrivant* and prepare the tools necessary for her full self-actualization. Across the African continuum, the ancestors are recognized as some of the most easily accessible and faithful guides for human beings.

Collaboration between humans and divine guides is crucial, for Africana cultures from Kemet to the Kongo confirm that when ancient properties, skills, and technologies are purposefully applied for personal and communal evolution and elevation, immortality is attained. The Ancients would submit that rather than working for a paycheck or for a living and instead of fearing death or hell, one should be working for one's immortality, for, as a Yoruba proverb reveals, "*Àikú parí ìwà*," literally, "Immortality completes existence,"[1] or one might say that immortality is the result of a complete and perfect existence. From the Africana worldview, not only is divinity within the grasp of human beings, but one could argue that human beings' ultimate challenge is to become Divine Immortals.

That divinity is the most appropriate outcome of a self-actualized existence is as central to African cosmology as the fact that immortality is often only an utterance away. The second stanza of an incantation from a Coffin Text from Kemet begins with an important revelation: "*The dead speaks*."[2] Rather than being "dead," the speaker uses his innate and eternal Power of the Word to speak his divinity into being for all eternity:

> I shall shine and be seen every day as a dignitary of the All-Lord, having given satisfaction to the Weary-hearted.
> I shall sail rightly in my bark, I am lord of eternity in the crossing of the sky.
> I am not afraid in my limbs, for Hu and Hike overthrow for me that evil being.[3]

After a full and fulfilled terrestrial existence, "the dead" embarks on a new life that is a journey of the righteous undertaken in the manner of Ra. "The dead" is revealed to be an Immortal: a God who rejoins the Gods. The conclusion of the Coffin Text confirms that the ability to attain immortality is not limited to any particular individual, and it invites everyone to enter the realm of the Gods: "As for any person who knows this spell, he will be like Re in the eastern sky, like Osiris in the netherworld. He will go down to the fire, without the flame touching him ever!"[4]

In the Coffin Text, divinity is catalyzed by utterance; the speech of "the dead" is as organic and empowered as "the dead's" knowledge that Hu and Heka (offered as Hike, above) provide him eternal protection. Hu and Heka in their multitudinous Pan-African forms, names, and manifestations are central and essential to Africana divinity. According to Molefi K. Asante, Heka is translated as "the activating of the Ka."[5] Ka can be defined as spirit, soul power, life energy. In addition to empowering humans and Gods, Heka, as the God of medicine, health, and healing, ensures physical wholeness and longevity. Hu is Power of the Word, and Hu is manifest in triplicate in the Coffin Text: The "dead" verbalizes through Hu; Hu is invoked as a protector; and Hu is activated through incantation.

In *The Priests of Ancient Egypt*, Serge Sauneron makes important observations about the powers of language and speech that elucidate the layered power of Hu:

> The Egyptians never considered their language—that corresponding to the hieroglyphs—as a *social* tool; for them, it always remained a resonant echo of the vital energy that had brought the universe to life, a *cosmic* force. Thus, study of this language enabled them to "explain" the cosmos.
>
> It was word-play that served as the means of making these explanations. The moment one understands that words are intimately linked to the essences of the beings or objects they indicate, resemblances between words cannot be fortuitous; they express a natural relationship, a subtle connection that priestly erudition would have to define.[6]

Sauneron's assertions about the power of the Kemetic language, called Medu Netcher (literally, Language of the Gods), is also manifest in other African languages including Dogon, Bambara, Igbo, KiKongo, and Yoruba. The dynamic interrelationship between words and speech described by Sauernon is evident upon merely hearing Yoruba spiritual orature whether or not one understands the language. Yoruba *itàn* (historical accounts), *oríkì* (praisenames), and especially the *ẹsẹ* of Odù Ifá (sacred divination verses) are rich with the same cosmic, physical, and causal associations, and puns, riddles, and raw power that are manifest in Medu Netcher. Similar to the various manifestations and applications of Hu, in Yoruba language, "Ọ̀rọ̀" is the divine embodiment of Power of the Word, while "ọ̀rọ̀" is translated as "word."[7] When Ọ̀rọ̀ and ọ̀rọ̀ unite with *àṣẹ*, which, similar to Ka, signifies force, authority, and the power to bring thought into existence, the tools of the Gods are born.

It is logical that the earliest evidence of humanodivinity comes from the world's first civilizations—the East African empires of Nubia, or Kush, and Kemet—which are also heralded as the points of origin of many West and Central African peoples. Such studies as J. Olumide Lucas' *The Religion of the Yorubas*, Cheikh Anta Diop's *The Cultural Unity of Black Africa: The Domains of Patriarchy and of Matriarchy in Classical Antiquity*, Ayi Kwei Armah's *The Eloquence of the Scribes: A Memoir on the Sources and Resources of African Literature*, and Laird Scranton's *The Science of the Dogon: Decoding the African Mystery Tradition* offer profound evidence of linguistic, cultural, spiritual, and socio-political continuity between Ancient East and contemporary West African ethnic groups.

While Kush has not been as extensively researched as other African civilizations, and research is now forever impeded as a result of systematic geopolitical assaults, Kush is regarded by many archeologists and historians as the source and "lifeline" of Kemetic philosophy, hieroglyphics, religion, and architecture.[8] Sicilian historian Diodorus details the impact of Kush, known then as Ethiopia, on Kemet:

> The Ethiopians say that the Egyptians are one of their colonies which was brought into Egypt by Osiris. They even allege that this country was originally under water, but that the Nile, dragging much mud as it flowed from Ethiopia, had finally filled it in and made it a part of the continent. . . . They add that from them, as from their authors and ancestors, the Egyptians get most of their laws. It is from them that the Egyptians have learned to honor kings as gods and bury them with such pomp; sculpture and writing were invented by the Ethiopians.[9]

Diodorus' findings are echoed centuries later by Flora L. Shaw who draws the following conclusion about Meroë, one of Kush's most storied capitals: "This remarkable spot is regarded by the ancients as the 'cradle of the arts and sciences, where hieroglyphic writing was discovered, and where temples and pyramids had already sprung up while Egypt still remained ignorant of their existence.'"[10]

The anthropomorphism that is prevalent in Africana spiritual systems finds its source in Kush. Shape-shifting technology, which has been documented throughout the African continuum, also has its roots in Kushite technology. Ancient Nubians heralded myriad Gods and held that Deities took the forms of human beings as well as animals.[11] With a worldview rooted in holism and empowered by dynamic terrestrial and cosmic technologies, Nubian rulers were not only regarded as protectors and administrators of the God Amun but were also considered Gods in their own rights.[12] For example, Queen Amenirdis, whose name means That Which Amun Creates, She Gives, ruled in 740 BCE, and "[a]lthough she could never marry a mortal man, she served as 'God's Wife' for about forty years. Her position was that of a queen and living goddess."[13]

Kemet, Kush's geopolitical daughter, boasts a well-documented heritage of numinosity. The influential Kemetic Gods Ausar and Aset are at once siblings, spouses, historical figures, and elemental forces. Heru is Ausar and Aset's divinely conceived son who is immortalized as the Heru-em-akhet.[14] Heru-em-akhet literally means "Heru of the horizon" or "Heru, where the sun rises and sets" because the Sun appears to navigate the circumference of the anterior portion of Heru's head.[15] Anthony T. Browder describes Heru-em-akhet as "the physical symbol of the spiritual concept of the power of God manifested in man."[16]

Heru's divine conception, inherent divinity, and immortality are articulated in the concept of time. The Greeks called Heru "Horus," and that name is the origin of the words "hour" and "horoscope." In order for ancient African astronomers to create the calendar and zodiac and master the science of agriculture, they had to watch the constellations and be "watchers of the hours" or "horus-scope."[17] By deciphering Heru's codes, it is possible for human beings to access astronomical knowledge and enjoy agricultural fecundity as well as cosmic immortality.

Harnessing the power of such Kemetic predecessors as Aset and Heru, Queen Hatshepsut of Kemet proclaimed her divinity to all and inscribed praises to both her earthly and divine fathers, Thutmose I and Amun, respectively, on one of the tekhens (obelisks) she had hewn during her reign:

> I have done this with a loving heart for my father Amun;
> Initiated in his secret of the beginning,
> Acquainted with his beneficent might,
> I did not forget whatever he had ordained.[18]

In addition to confirming that she is a faithful daughter of and dutiful administrator for her father, Amun Re, The Hidden One, Hatshepsut celebrates a reign and a Divinity that is as expansive as the Cosmos:

> As I wear the white crown,
> As I appear with the red crown,
> As the Two Lords have joined their portions for me,
> As I rule this land like the son of Isis,
> As I am mighty like the son of Nut,
> As Re rests in the evening bark,
> As he prevails in the morning bark,

> As he joins his two mothers in the god's ship,
> As sky endures, as his creation lasts,
> As I shall be eternal like an undying star,
> As I shall rest in life like Atum[19]

Not only does the Queen detail her natural and supernatural lineage in language similar to the speaker of the Coffin Text, but she is also clearly cognizant of the importance of being a gender-inclusive humanospiritual political force, and she adorns herself in the masculine gender with confidence. Whether she styles herself the son of Aset (Isis) and Nwt (Nut) or the daughter of Amun (the source of the word "amen"), or envisions a peaceful and eternal rest with Atum (the source of the word "atom"), Hatshepsut celebrates the fact that she has attained immortality during her lifetime and is a God.

The concept of the Ruler God is not restricted to the eras of the Ancients; in many lands, contemporary African rulers are deified in the same manner as their historical counterparts. In *African Religions and Philosophy*, John S. Mbiti describes African kings and queens as "divine or sacral rulers, the shadow or reflection of God's rule in the universe."[20] Mbiti finds that, because of their divinity, these rulers must adhere to specific regulations:

> Some rulers must not be seen in ordinary life—they wear a veil, take meals alone . . . their eating and sleeping may not be mentioned; in some societies . . . the king must not touch the ground with his feet, and has either to be carried or walk on a special mat; parts of the ruler's body (like saliva, faeces, hair, and nails) are buried lest they should be seen by ordinary people or used in malicious ways against them. . . . The spirit of the departed king may also continue to play an active part in the national affairs of his people (by being re-incarnated, possessing the successor or recognized medium, and being consulted or having sacrifices and offerings given to it).[21]

The departed king may also be immortalized in the manner of Heru-em-akhet and the *Atal*, the latter of which are elegantly and elaborately carved stone monoliths of the Ejagham and Ekoi people of Cross River, Nigeria that commemorate the *Ntoon*, who are "divine kings."[22]

The matrix of divinity that empowers rulers can be even more pronounced in those who make and coronate kings. As I detail in chapter four of *The Architects of Existence: Àjẹ́ in Yoruba Ontology, Cosmology, and Orature*, the divinity of Yoruba rulers is due to Àjẹ́,[23] and these divine Mother Creators are not only recognized as Gods, they are also considered to be superior to other Gods.[24] As the Mothers of the

World and the Gods of Society, Àjẹ́ ensure the survival and evolution of humanity, and they are the only beings capable of selecting, creating, and guiding the rulers of the Yoruba nation. Àjẹ́ literally make the kings, and they determine how and how long they will rule. When aberrant rulers must be dethroned, it is the Mothers who introduce them to oblivion. When compared to that of the creating and making Mothers, the divinity and power bestowed on Yoruba kings is clearly that which a son can only be granted by his God Mother.

Other terrestrial beings who are recognized as divine are diviners, as the root-word of the vocation signifies. Yoruba diviners are called *babaláwo* or *iyaláwo*, fathers of mysteries or mothers of mysteries, respectively. Igbo wisdom keepers are called *dibia*, and their place in the cosmological plane is indicated by the truism that "after God is dibia."[25] The Fon *bokono* (diviner) is addressed as "God."[26] Luke Turner, the diviner who carried on the mantle of African American Voodoo Queen Marie LaVeau, said of his mentor: "She is a god, yes. Whatever she say, it will come so."[27]

As Ulli Beier reveals, it is necessary for certain human beings who work with the Gods and distribute their wisdom to become those Gods:

> To *be orisha* is an equally correct translation of the word *olorisha*. The worshipper offers his body as a vehicle to [*orisha*], he allows the *orisha* to "mount his head," to ride him, and he strives to become *for brief moments*, the personification of the *orisha*.
>
> Only very few and very powerful priests could really represent the *orisha* all the time. But every *olorisha* must become the *orisha* some time.[28]

While becoming Òrìṣà is essential for certain individuals, what is arguably more important is the human being attaining divine status in her own right. Yoruba proverbs make it clear that human beings can attain divinity: *"Ẹnì ó gbọ́n mà l'òrìṣà*, One who is wise is a deity"; *"Ẹnì ó gbọ́n ni ẹ jẹ́ a máa bọ*, One who is wise is the one who should be worshipped."[29] Proverbs, the horses of communication in Yoruba language, swiftly transport us to the gateway of the Gods. Yoruba proverbs also reveal that it is one's Orí, one's personal God and the director of one's destiny, who makes one wise: *"Ẹni t'ó gbọ́n Orí ẹ̀ l'ó ní ó gbọ́n* (He who is wise is made wise by his Orí)."[30]

Orí is literally the human head, and it is comprised of cosmological components that include Orí-Inú, one's Inner or Spiritual Head, and Orí Àpéré, "Head-the ruler."[31] In "Verbal and visual metaphors: mythical allusions in Yoruba ritualistic art of *Orí*," Rowland Abiodun reveals that Orí, as a multiply empowered amalgamation, is not only a God but is "the first and most important Òrìṣà in heaven, Ọrun."[32] In Yoruba cosmology, the human soul chooses its Orí with its attendant Orí Inú and Orí Àpéré in the spiritual realm before birth. Once born, human beings worship Orí because this destiny-directing God, with knowledge of the material realm augmented by divine spiritual vision and power, is "crucial to a successful life."[33] The concept of Orí offers one of many rich examples of the profound complexities that Yoruba humanodivinity neatly encapsulates.

Cornelius O. Adepegba makes an important observation in "Associated Place-Names and Sacred Icons of Seven Yorùbá Deities: Historicity in Yorùbá Religious Traditions": "Ifá, the God of Divination, is said to emphasize that Yorùbá deities, including himself, were originally humans who displayed extraordinary wisdom, skill or power."[34] Because Africana divinity exists as a continuum, the Gods do not elevate, transmigrate, and gaze on humanity from afar; they thrive and guide on the Earth, and they clear and illuminate the paths that human beings can follow to arrive at the threshold of their own divinity.

Even missionaries had to acknowledge the numinosity permeating Yoruba culture. From the research he conducted in the 1800s, Abbé Pierre Bouche found that "[e]very object becomes an Òrìṣà as soon as it has got the appropriate consecration. . . . the Òrìṣà object acquires a kind of personality; what was only earth, wood, or iron becomes Òrìṣà, i.e. superhuman power. In reality it is not the mere material that receives the respects of the black; he directs them toward a higher power."[35] To create and direct the Gods, one must be a God. Given the fluidity and vastness of Africana numinosity, it is not illogical to assert that many contemporary human beings are on their way to becoming Divinities and that there are Gods among us who are busy creating new Gods. Indeed, it appears to be the case that certain human beings are obligated to fully manifest their divinity and continue the curvilinear work of the Ancient Immortals.

Stephen W. Boston encourages people of all religions and ethnicities to discover and acknowledge their divine potential with a narrative titled "And God Said. . ." The story focuses on a wisdom seeker who asks his mentor to explain who the Christian God is speaking to when he says, "Let us make man in our image, after our likeness" (Genesis 1:26 *King James Version*). This scripture constitutes both a riddle and a mirror, as the questioner is the answer to the question. The seeker and his guide use wisdom gleaned from Buddhism, Sikhism, Hinduism, and Judaism to decipher the riddle, but their primary source is the Bible. Their theological search includes the spiritual-familial assertion in Romans 8:17, that human beings are "heirs of God and joint-heirs with Christ," which is echoed in Psalms 82:6, which describes human beings as "children of the most High" and also includes the Christian God's acknowledgement to humanity: "I have said, Ye *are* gods," which is confirmed by Jesus in John 10:34: "Is it not written in your law, I SAID, YE ARE GODS?" Boston's narrative confirms that it is logical that a divine impetus drives humanity because human beings are, in fact, the creating Gods who are mentioned in Genesis 1:26.[36]

Boston's exposition echoes African philosophy. Dagara cosmology, for example, holds that every newborn is a divine being returning to undertake specific duties. Malidoma Patrice Somé expounds on this process in his autobiography, *Of Water and the Spirit: Ritual, Magic, and Initiation in the Life of an African Shaman*: "Our errand on this planet is informed by a decision to partake in the building of the Earth's cosmic origin, and to promote awareness of our celestial identity to others who are less evolved."[37] This essential work of revealing to others their divinity and divine obligations would be so simple as to be unnecessary if not for the fact that the majority of human beings do not know who they are or what their purpose is. In addition to forgetting one's divine objectives, most earthlings are indoctrinated with organized religions' master myths of inherent human inferiority, fallibility, and mortality. Indeed, the training is so pervasive and terroristic that persons seeking to manifest their divinity risk being shunned, institutionalized, or killed. However, these social, psychological, and organized religious impediments make the acquisition of divinity all the more rewarding.

Similar to matter, divinity cannot be created or destroyed; furthermore, divinity is not restricted to a particular person or era. The data that I analyze in this chapter confirm that divinity is a transferable force that has many modes of transmission—from the womb to shared wisdom. Hatshepsut accessed numinosity through Thutmose I and Amun. Marie LaVeau taught her divine wisdom and skills to Luke Turner. Turner, and such wisdom keepers as Father Watson, Eulalia, Mother Catherine, and Dr. Duke, shared divine knowledge and technology with Zora Neale Hurston who earned the crowns of the Gods and used her wisdom to revolutionize Africana studies. Bakhye bestowed his numinosity on his grandson Malidoma Somé who uses his gifts to repair our disjointed world. When divine elders find worthy receptacles for their wisdom and technology, they pour forth their knowledge to ensure cosmic continuity.

Hurston and Somé sought and found numinosity; other individuals are bestowed with divinity from birth and use their gifts to facilitate collective elevation. Some people understand the languages that unlock the principles and powers of flora and fauna. Some individuals simply listen to and summon from their bodies the tools and technologies necessary to even the odds. In addition to living beings who are divine or who boast divine powers, the ancestors are essential to Africana spiritual elevation because they assist human beings in their quests to understand their destinies and to attain divinity. As Somé reveals, "The ancestors are the real school of the living. They are the keepers of the very wisdom the people need to live by."[38]

In African cosmology and ontology, humanity does not conflict with, stand in opposition to, or lie subordinate to numinosity; humanity and divinity are complementary and symbiotic. This open exchange and equilibrium ensures the eternal development and proliferation of Africana Divinities and divine powers.

Marked and Signified Behind the Veil

In the Africana worldview, vision is not limited to the range of one's physical eyesight. Some people also have spiritual vision. What the Yoruba refer to as *ojú inú* (inner eyes) and what is also known as the third eye is considered the source of spiritual vision. Ojú inú are open from birth in certain individuals, but those whose inner eyes are closed can have them opened through any number of methods.

Many African American elders hold that pigs can see the wind, and that after introducing sow's milk into the eyes, human beings can see the wind too.[39] Ellis Strickland of Georgia asserts that with the Black Cat Bone, "You can even see de wind which is like a red blaze of fire."[40] In *The Practice of Witchcraft in Ghana*, Gabriel Bannerman-Richter discusses twin sisters who purchase a preparation that endows them with the ability to see inside of the human body.[41] Among the Igbo, certain flora are combined and given to worthy initiates so that they can *ifu mmuo* or see the spirit.[42]

There is also great diversity among those who are born with spiritual vision. Among the Yoruba, individuals known *emèrè* are able to "detect what a person has done in secret," which implies the ability to read minds and to see past actions and events; *àlùjànún* can gain knowledge of things that occur in distant areas and alter those events if necessary.[43] Àjẹ́ may boast various gifts, including spiritual vision. A proverb reveals that Àjẹ́ *arínú rode*: they see the inside and the outside.[44] Àjẹ́'s spiritual vision is the result of their being both human and Divine and their need to oversee human birth, growth, death, and rebirth.

As it relates to the Mothers' guardianship of existence, the Yoruba say, "The sack tied by the gods cannot be untied by anyone" (*Ọ̀kẹ́ ti òrìṣà di ọmọ ar'aiyé ò le tù*).[45] The Gods in question are Àjẹ́, who are logically heralded as Àwọn Ìyá Wa, Our Mothers: The sack is the amnion which supports all *in vitro* human lives. In Yoruba culture, children born with the amnion (*òkẹ́*) over their faces are recognized as the divine and divinely empowered progeny of Àjẹ́.

A Deity of Àjẹ́ who boasts a unique link with veiled children is Ọya. She is the God of Transformation who oversees the transmigration from human being to ancestor and who keeps open the communicative channels between spiritual and material realms and beings. One of the primary implements Ọya uses to connect human beings with their spiritual identity is the caul. One of Ọya's praisenames is "Ìyánsàn, mother of nine—who bore small children in a caul."[46] The caul that encased Ọya's nine divine children and that covers the heads and faces of other newborns accentuates their relationships with spiritual powers, ancestors, and divine beings.

The significance of children born with veils and the rituals that accompany such births are well-known in African America. Elders hold that a child who is born with the amnion covering her face has a direct connection with the divine and can see spirits. While many spirits educate and guide their charges, there are also discontented spirits who can harm. To keep the child from being constantly harassed and possibly driven insane by capricious spiritual forces, she must drink a tea made from the caul. Some customs demand that the caul be preserved so that when the child grows older she can have a tactile as well as spiritual connection with the power-giving caul. In other rituals, the caul, like the umbilical cord, is buried at the foot of a significant tree.

Rituals that relate to cauls and veiled births were once staples of Africana obstetrics, but they have been largely forgotten with the advent of Western obstetrical mandates, cultural discrimination, and spiritual ignorance. With the foresight of the ancestors, Tina McElroy Ansa immortalizes Africana caul-related rituals in her novel *Baby of the Family*. Rich information about spiritual sight can also be found in the testimonies of individuals who were born with and protected by their cauls. Carrie Nancy Fryer of Augusta, Georgia discusses the gifts afforded her by her caul: "Hunh! My mother said [the caul covered] my head, shoulders and all! I kin see ghosts."[47] Fryer is able to both observe spiritual entities and interact with them. As is the case with many West and Central African wisdom keepers, Fryer's ancestors teach her cures for high blood pressure, worms, rheumatism, headaches, and bad blood through her dreams.[48]

Fryer's link to the spiritual realm goes beyond communication; the caul endows Fryer with spiritual knowledge and power. Fryer uses Ọya's signature number nine to protect her children and ensure their physical strength and development: "All my babies growed straight cause I swept em nine times for nine mornings from de knees down an out dataway."[49]

Because Oya connects human beings to their transmigrated ancestors, it is fitting that her earthly abode is the cemetery and that she and the ancestors can be found protecting children at graves. At one time, African American tradition demanded elders pass a surviving infant back and forth over his mother's grave. With this custom, elders acknowledge and protect the child's eternal spiritual relationship with his deceased mother while concretizing the child's bond with the living.[50] A community elder expands this ritual to cure Fryer's daughter, who had developed a growth on her neck. The elder uses the spiritual power and compassion of a recently deceased person whose body is still warm and the dynamism of Oya to cure the child. After the elder passed Fryer's daughter "nine times across, nine times straight" over the corpse, the child was cured.[51] Similarly, in *Mules and Men*, to cure "general afflictions," Zora Neale Hurston suggests visiting the corpse of someone who had been kindly disposed to you, whispering their name, and asking them to take your illness along with them to the other side.[52]

The divine sight and skills acquired as a result of being born with a caul multiply when one is born with two cauls. Braziel Robinson of Georgia was born with a "double caul" over his face, and, as a result, he is the recipient of a multilayered spiritual endowment:

> I have two spirits, one that prowls around, and one that stays in my body. The reason I have two spirits is because I was born with a double caul. People can see spirits if they are born with one caul, but nobody can have two spirits unless they are born with a double caul, very few people have two spirits. . . . My two spirits are good spirits, and have power over evil spirits, and unless my mind is evil, can keep me from harm. If my mind is evil my two spirits try to win me, if I won't listen to them, then they leave me and make room for evil spirits and then I'm lost forever, mine have never left me, and they won't if I can help it, as I shall try to keep in the path.[53]

Although Robinson states that "very few people have two spirits," having multiple spirits is widely recognized in continental African cosmology and ontology.[54] However, few human beings boast such a dynamic relationship with their souls as Robinson and Africana Ancients.

The spirit that remains in Robinson's body is akin to the Kemetic Ka, the foundation of human beings' creative power and the "activator of cosmic forces."[55] Robinson's prowling spirit, which explores the world, is the equivalent of the Ba, the Kemetic "world soul" which represents the "soul's ability to move between heaven and Earth."[56] A Kemetic text titled "The Dispute Between A Man and His Ba" concerns a man's lamentation to his Ba, who initially threatens the man with silence, which foretells oblivion. The man responds to his Ba's silence with anguish and outrage: "This is too great for me today, / My *ba* will not converse with me! / . . . . / It is like [it is] deserting me! / My *ba* shall not go, / It shall attend to me in this!"[57]

The man longs to produce an heir so as to solidify his immortality before entering eternity with his Ba, so he counsels his Ba: "Be patient, my *ba*, my brother."[58] The man also reminds his Ba of the symbiotic nature of their relationship: The only way these "comrades" and "brothers" can attain immortality is if they work together, as do Robinson and his two spirits.

Robinson's spirits also act similarly to the Igbo *chi* and the Yoruba *enikejì*, both of which are defined as divine comrades or spiritual doubles with whom human souls make covenants before being born.[59] While most people forget their pacts upon birth and must struggle to find their destinies, it appears that twins,[60] Àjẹ́, and individuals born with two cauls have direct access to their guiding souls and knowledge of their cosmic covenants. Robinson, with his double veil—which could indicate that early in his *in vitro* development he was a twin—boasts an intimate relationship with his souls and, thus, his destiny.

Robinson's description of his spiritual-terrestrial obligations to and relationships with his spirits is at one with the traditional African ethos. In traditional African cosmology and ontology, human beings are not offered facile routes to immortality by professing belief in an entity. Indeed, the "belief" upon which organized religions are dependent is irrelevant in Africana spiritual systems, which are rooted in empirical knowledge acquisition. In the African ethos, one's ability to self-actualize, manifest one's destiny, and attain immortality and divinity hinges directly on how one treats everyone and everything in one's environment. Robinson must strive to attain harmonic balance and exude exemplary character every day in every way. If Robinson decides to live a life of willful deceit and treachery, his being will become inhospitable to his spirits, and, like the Igbo chi, the Yoruba enikejì, and the Kemetic Ba, his spiritual guides will abandon him.

Emefie Ikenga Metuh asserts that among the Igbo, one's *chi* "is good and goads a person on to good conduct by admonitions, rewards and punishments"; however, the chi may "get tired" and refuse to assist someone "who is always doing wrong."[61] As it relates to the Yoruba enikejì, Lawal finds that "offending one's spirit double or heavenly comrade may cause it to withdraw its spiritual protection."[62] In the Kemetic text, the Ba's threatening silence is enough to spur its human complement to redemptive action. Robinson strives to live his life in such a way that he and his spirits are always in harmony. The Kemetic, Yoruba,

Igbo, and African American elaborations on the human's relationship with the spirit stress the fact that it is not enough to profess divinity: One must *live* it consistently.

While the caul offers the most obvious connection to spiritual sight, it is not the only way spiritual vision is obtained. In her 2007 autobiographical essay titled "I Wore No Veil. . . I Have No Caul," African American Rochelle Williams discusses her unsettling and edifying spiritual encounters with various entities, including living relatives, ancestors, and the unborn. Williams describes what appears to involve telepathic communication between herself and her grandfather when he was on his deathbed. When it was her turn to watch over her dying progenitor, Williams was terrified: "I prayed a silent prayer that he would not die while I was with him. And as if he heard me, he sat up and smiled at me. He told me not to be scared. He said that he would stay as long as I was there. He talked and laughed as if he had never been sick. He kept his promise. He died after I left the hospital."[63]

Williams' relatives appear to her at various times to share important news with her, to offer guidance and reassurance, and to confirm the covenant of power she inherited. Williams' son conveys an especially resonant message to his mother:

> My son introduced himself to me two years before he was born. I'd fallen asleep at a friend's house and was awakened by a child's laughter. When I opened my eyes, the whole room was dark except for one bright spot. I sat up to see a beautiful little boy reach out to me. This time I wasn't afraid and reached back. I knew that he was mine. Two years later, I gave birth to him.[64]

Many Africana wisdom systems hold that children choose the parents they wish to be born to. Given the cosmic directives and objectives of Orí and ẹnikejì, such a selection process is crucial to the full manifestation of destiny and divinity. In *Home*, Toni Morrison writes of the anguish that ensues when this union cannot be made physically manifest.[65] Williams' testimony not only verifies that the souls of the unborn are sentient, active, and seeking, but it also describes the bliss that these divinely appointed unions bring.

It could be the case that Williams' gifts are inherited and biologically transmitted, for her son is also able to communicate with his ancestors. When Williams heard her two-year-old son giggling and talking in his bedroom and she asked him what he was doing, he replied, "I'm talking to my Diddy. . . . He was playing with my ears and making me laugh."[66] The child had been playing with his "deceased" great-grandfather.

Similar to Fryers' educational interactions with her ancestors, Williams' grandfather, affectionately known as "Diddy," continued to visit her and provide her with important information. For example, when her uncle was impaled while dismantling a rollercoaster, he was not expected to live, and the family began planning his funeral. However Diddy came to Williams and told her that her uncle would survive, and he recovered fully.

Another contemporary example of the spiritual realm's influence on the physical realm comes from African American Sharen Rawls who described her family's amazement when, on his first trip to the family's Jamaican homestead, Rawls' younger brother knew everything about Jamaica. He confidently led his relatives through towns and down streets that he had never seen before—in his terrestrial lifetime—but was intimately familiar with. He also instantly knew relatives he had never met before. Rawls' grandmother, who orients all the beds in her house to the East, signifying ascension, immortality, and spiritual-terrestrial unification, said of her grandson what almost any Africana elder would have said, that "he has been here before" in a previous life.[67]

Spiritual and terrestrial beings communicating and providing one another with assistance is indicative of a worldview centered on curvilinear time and cosmic-terrestrial reciprocity. However, the world is complex, and events from the seemingly mundane to the definitely otherworldly can have profound influences and repercussions. Marking provides a wonderful example of cosmic-terrestrial interaction. Marking occurs when an unborn child is physically affected by her expecting mother's exposure and/or reaction to an event. Marking can range from the innocuous lines and discolorations of "birthmarks" to psychological or more serious physical indicators.

African American midwife Easter Sudie Campbell issues a stern warning: "Mothers oughter be more careful while carrying dey chilluns not ter git scared of enthing for dey will sho mark dar babies wid turrible ugly things."[68] The most serious marks apparently result from a mother finding amusement in someone's pain or deformity or from her being shocked or traumatized. Fryer, the owner of the veil, marked three of her children. Below she describes how she marked her son:

> My sister-in-law made me ruin't my other child. Twas an old man coming along. He was ruptured [had a herniated or traumatized scrotum[69]]. He had on a white apron, and she bus' out laughin' and say: "Look at dat!" I jus' young gal, ain' be thinkin' and I bus' out laughin' too, he did look funny. I ruin't my boy. He was in de same fix and when I look at him I feel so bad, and think "dat didn' have to be."[70]

Dye Williams of Old Fort, Georgia did not laugh at anyone; when she was pregnant she walked over a hole that bore a bottle of conjure designed to kill her. After she was cured, she gave birth to twins, one of whom was marked with a small hole on his left side which mirrored Williams' injury. The child died after nine days.[71]

Flora Nwapa's novel *Efuru* includes a number of prenatal restrictions and precautions for expectant mothers, including that they should not venture out at night, because heightened spiritual energies increase the potential for marking and miscarriage, and that they should not go on excursions without a companion.[72] Although the opposite occurs with Fryer, the companion is supposed to protect the mother and fetus from natural and supernatural phenomena that can lead to marking.

The theories about and physical realities of marked children could be related to another African phenomenon: the Yoruba *àbíkú* or Igbo *ogbange*. Àbíkú means, born to die, and àbíkú children are born, live a short while, and die only to return to the mother's womb and continue this cycle. One could hypothesize that the mother's womb is marked to attract àbíkú. Babatunde Lawal posits that Àjẹ́ punish women who have committed offenses by having àbíkú enter their wombs.[73]

When parents, elders, and doctors recognize that a woman has given birth to an àbíkú and the child dies, he will be marked before burial. The marks, often slashes and cuts about the face and arms, are meant to discourage the spirit's return, but a "stubborn" spirit will be reborn with his scars.[74] As depicted in Lawal's *The Gẹ̀lẹ̀dẹ́ Spectacle: Art, Gender, and Social Harmony in African Culture*, the living àbíkú child is given unique facial marks that are designed to "scare away its spirit companions."[75] Living àbíkú children are considered Divinities because of their evident and overwhelming cosmic connections.

Because the àbíkú's desire to return to the spirit realm is so great, in addition to rituals and supplication, parents use empowered naming to try to persuade àbíkú children to remain on Earth and also to shield them from harm. Àbíkú children are adorned with names such as Dúrójayé (Stay-and-enjoy-this-world) and Dúró-o-rí-kẹ́ (Wait-and-see-how-you-will-be-pampered).[76] With every lullaby, summons or greeting, the àbíkú is reminded of his earthly obligations and the joys that come with terrestrial life.

The scarring rituals that are used to shun and protect àbíkú are used in diverse capacities throughout Pan-Africa. Some continental Africans ritually marked their progeny so that they would be rejected by enslavers and escape exile and enslavement, and some exiled Africans ritually marked their children to re-member them to their African culture and identity.[77]

Africana families also employ protective ritual naming or linguistic marking to great effect. The names given Africana children in infancy are chosen with great care. Children may bear names that reflect significant events or inventions or forebears who may be living or dead.[78] Because African naming practices reflect the fluidity of identity and identity formation, it is not uncommon in African America for a person to have a legal name that is entirely different from the one that appears on his birth certificate. After the legal name is logged it is immediately supplanted by at least one other name. For example, a mother may name her daughter Zula at birth but never use the name. Zula is called Ba as an unconscious heralding of the child's Ba.[79] As she grows and manifestations of ancestors are evident in her character, Dona, the name of a great-grandmother, supplants Zula. While Zula continues to be called Ba among close relatives, she enters school, the employment arena, and marriage as Dona.[80]

In addition to protecting them, sacred and multiple names empower their bearers. Among the Yoruba, one's sacred name is called *ipǫnri*, and one's ipǫnri is the signifier of one's destiny, lineage, identity, and divinity. As J. A. A. Ayoade explains:

> A name is the neatest encapsulation of a man's being. In a large number of cases it is believed that a man's name and the names of his parents are most essential to the control of the man because these names are regarded as the total summary of the person's being since they indicate his origin [*ipǫnri*].[81]

An even more complex concept is *ìtàn ipǫnri* which signifies one's complete history and ancestry. Ipǫnri and ìtàn ipǫnri are carefully safeguarded because knowledge of them "gives one the power to kill a person by summoning his ancestral guardian soul, and some elders hold that one will die if he even talks about his *ipǫnri*."[82]

Because of the power it contains, there are some instances when one's ìtàn ipǫnri must be uttered. In "Àṣẹ: Verbalizing and Visualizing Creative Power through Art," Rowland Abiodun discusses how àṣẹ, or divine authority, works in concert with ipǫnri and Ọ̀rọ̀ to galvanize and solidify the power and glory of Yoruba rulers:

> An important part of the installation ceremony of an *ǫba* is the voicing of his given and secret names (usually unknown to strangers), for the purpose of imbuing them with the newly conferred *àṣẹ*. On such occasions, the air and space between the one who vocalizes *àṣẹ* and the recipient of the *àṣẹ* is believed to be

so powerfully charged that it is considered unsafe for anyone to obstruct it. This is understandable because the verbal complex of àṣẹ is made up of potent sacred oratory which makes heavy and esoteric use of metaphors in distinctive language patterns and poetic structures.[83]

The same dynamic melding of àṣẹ, ipọnri, and Òrò that is essential to the creation of rulers is also vital to the identity formation of children. Names, from the attributes they describe to the power contained in their utterance, are signifiers of destiny and repositories of power.

In modern America with computerized record keeping, African American ipọnri are threatened. However, African Americans, constituting a melding of various African peoples and powers and boasting a vast repertoire of signifying abilities, are not daunted by technology. In some African American families, one's sacred identity is concealed (or, ironically, revealed) through a parade of day-names, crib-names, and pet-names, such as Zula's nickname, Ba, in the previous example.[84] It may also be the case that one's day-name, nickname, or title is so fitting that it replaces one's legal name altogether.[85] In Africa, in this contemporary era, it is not unusual to meet elders who are known exclusively by such titles as "The Old Man" or "The Old Woman": Their longevity, wisdom, and importance to their communities are reflected in these seemingly understated encomia.[86]

The assumption that human beings must be limited to one name and identity is a Western concept mandated to facilitate capitalistic control, usurpation, and taxation. In the African purview, as one enters deeper stages of self-actualization and character development, one is honored with and can adopt new properly reflective names or titles (i.e. Sojourner Truth from Isabella Baumfree; El Hajj Malik El Shabazz from Malcolm X, Malcolm Little, Big Red, Satan, et al.; and Prince from Prince R. Nelson and ⚥). Africana signifiers and protective naming practices move from tomb to womb and also across the Ethiopic (misnamed Atlantic) Ocean with ease.

The force that empowers names and human beings is Òrò, and Òrò can also be used to activate the àṣẹ of flora, fauna, and seemingly inanimate objects. Ayoade explains the process:

> The second and more difficult level [in invoking spirit forces] is that in which the spirit forces still remain dormant until they are called forth through the utterance of words of power. The knowledge of the secret names of spirits and of incantations is of special importance in concretizing the inner essence of an object.[87]

By using their sacred names as catalysts, African wisdom keepers work with flora and fauna to create perfect medicines and astounding technological devices.

Western medicine focuses on the treatment of symptoms, and this results in recurrent ailments, the development of new ailments or death from medicinal side effects, and consistent profits for physicians and insurance and pharmaceutical companies. By contrast, in *African Philosophy, Culture, and Traditional Medicine*, Moses Akin Makinde reveals that the goal of Yoruba oníṣègun is to achieve a "complete cure," and this is done by giving the ailment what it is forbidden to take and by invoking the ailment by "its original but secret name."[88] With this two-tiered approach, the source of the ailment is treated with its pharmacological antidote, and the spirit or ẹmí of the ailment is identified, invoked, and banished.

The power of names and naming also extends to that which cannot be named. In *Of Water and the Spirit*, Somé reveals that, similar to the Yoruba injunction against mentioning one's ipọnri, the Dagara recognize certain plants as having sacred properties and inner essences that are so potent and important that they cannot be named "because naming them would kill them. Among the Dagara, some things are known not for what they are, but for what they do. The Dagara avoid naming them in order to ensure that their magical properties stay alive."[89] John Umeh reveals that flora may impose additional restrictions as well: "Some of the herbs and Ogwu [medicines and medicinal preparations] shown to one in the dream must not be made public property or revealed to unauthorized, uninitiated persons."[90] Rather than inanimate objects awaiting manipulation, certain plants, animals, stones, rivers, and spaces boast both the same spiritual identifiers as human and divine beings and the power to purposefully direct their invocation, application, and dissemination.

"See How He Flies!"

Knowledge of the secret names and pharmacological and spiritual properties of flora and fauna is central to African technology, and this wisdom may be the key to understanding certain facilitators of one of the most well documented and most discredited African skills: human flight. By activating ipọnri, Ọ̀rọ̀ (Power of the Word), and the material and spiritual properties of flora, fauna, and the Cosmos, many enslaved Africans created technologies that enabled them to fly away from their oppressors.

African American testimonies about physical flight boast great diversity. Some individuals describe farm implements being used to facilitate flight; in other instances, rivers and creeks are used as runways. Some African Americans utter sacred words to fly; others shift shapes and transform themselves into buzzards. Some wisdom workers use spiritual technology to free themselves of gravity's pull. It is important to note that no single utterance or device facilitates flight: The methods are as diverse as the ethnic groups harnessing the power. What is more, witnesses of human flight include Spanish enslavers, Caucasian American oppressors, and devastated Africana relatives.

Esteban Montejo, an African of Yoruba and BaKongo ancestry who liberated himself from enslavement in Cuba, describes Spanish enslavers as refusing to acquire Africans from certain ethnic groups because so many flew away that "it was bad for business."[91] African American Priscilla McCullough describes Africans who, while working in a field, ran around in a circle with increasing speed until one by one, "[D]ey riz up an take wing an fly lak a bud."[92] McCullough states that the overseer "run an he ketch duh las one by duh foot jis as he was bout tuh fly off."[93] In a most poignant testimony, Rosa Grant describes how her great-grandmother, Theresa, emancipated herself from a plantation in Georgia:

> Theresa . . . wuz caught too an . . . wuz brought tuh dis country. Attuh dey bin yuh a wile, duh mothuh git to weah she caahn stan it an she wannuh go back tuh Africa. One day muh gran Ryna wuz standin wid uh in duh fiel. Theresa tun roun—so. . . . She stretch uh ahms out—so—an rise straight up an fly right back tuh Africa. Muh gran say she wuz standin right deah wen it happen. She alluz wish dat uh mothuh had teach uh how tuh fly. She try an try doin duh same way but she ain nubuh fly. She say she guess she jis wuzn bawn wid duh powuh.[94]

Perhaps the most stunning evidence of African flight lies in the sorrow of those who saw their loved ones soar but were unable to join them.

While in some instances flying away could be interpreted as selfish, flying Africans left a phenomenal gift in the recollections of those left behind to document a successful levitation and liberation. In Carriacou and Cuba, those who were grounded but witnessed flight danced the power into the annals of history.[95] Montejo recalls the grace of the Yuka dance: "Sometimes they swooped about like birds, and it almost looked as if they were going to fly, they moved so fast."[96] African American dancers of the Buzzard Lope also mimic the precision and grace of human transformation and flight.

The "Crow Song" and its accompanying dance, both recorded by Zora Neale Hurston, also celebrate the feat of flight:

> Oh, my mama, come see that crow
> See how he flies!
> Oh, my mama, come see that crow
> See how he flies!
> This crow, this crow gonna fly tonight
> See how he flies!
> This crow, this crow gonna fly tonight
> See how he flies!
> Oh, my mama, come see that crow
> CAAWW!!
> Oh, my mama, come see that crow
> CAAWW!![97]

The singer is not singing about such a mundane event as a crow flying. She is singing about a human being who has outwitted gravity. She calls her mother so that she too can bear witness to the spectacle. In anticipation of emancipation, the singer chants, "This crow, this crow gonna fly tonight!" and the seeing singer, the human subject, and the crow become one. With the exultant crow call, "CAAWW!!" the singer could be cheering on a flying human, or she may have undergone transformation herself. Ironically, racist Caucasian Americans called African Americans "crows" as an insult, but rather than a hateful epithet, the crow's relationship to African Americans intimates divine transformation, transportation, and liberation.

In her discussion of the "Crow Song," Hurston states that the bird in question is not actually the crow but the buzzard. This assertion is logical in that the birds most commonly associated with human transformation and flight are vultures and buzzards because they are birds of divine judgment. However, given the color association made between the crow and the African and the belief that if one catches a crow and splits its tongue the crow will be able to speak,[98] it could well be the case that the song heralds a unique spiritual relationship between birds that are divine messengers and Africana peoples.

The kinship between African Americans and birds as expressed in "Crow Song" is comparable to the relationship described in the Igbo song to Ayolo, a bird akin to a swallow:

> *Ayolo* I have come to your home
> *Ayolo* I have come to your home
> Your head is like the head of my child

Your eyes are like the eyes of my child
Your nose is like the nose of my child
Your legs are like the legs of my child[99]

Ayolo so closely resembles a human child that Ayolo may be the speaker's progeny. Such transmutability is evident in Africana testimonies about human transformation and flight and when in the Crow Song the speaker declares she will fly and then offers a "CAAWW" as validation of transformation.

John Umeh offers important information about the ode to Ayolo and the era when human beings and birds shared gifts of soul and flight: "The arrival of man in Ayolo's tree-top residence is . . . indicative of the astral travel and levitations of that age which man practiced with the greatest ease and at will. And to equate Ayolo's parts of the body with those of human beings is indicative of the high degree of feeling of oneness between them."[100] Umeh's analysis not only elucidates the consonance between human beings and Ayolo, but it also reveals that at one time flight and levitation—far from stupendous feats or magic acts—were as common as strolling down a path. Umeh describes an era in which Africans' relationship to the Earth and its flora and fauna and the Cosmos is so harmonious that they possess the transformative, communicative, and regenerative properties of the universe.

To better understand the relationships and technologies that freed humans from gravity in the Western Hemisphere, it is necessary to examine flight and other feats on the Continent. In addition to *kánàkò*, which shortens distances while walking; *òògùn egbé*, which can be used to immediately transport a person from one place to another; and *ọfẹ*, which is a technological device that can remove its bearer from a site of impending death, Yoruba wisdom keepers are knowledgeable about which fauna and flora to combine to facilitate human flight. In Barry Hallen and J. Olubiyi Sodipo's *Knowledge, Belief and Witchcraft: Analytic Experiments in African Philosophy*, a Yoruba oníṣègun (physician and wisdom worker) reveals: "If the 'powerfuls' want to travel to somewhere like Lagos, they will be making a lot of preparation [spiritual and medicinal implements] in the afternoon. And when it is night time, they will tie all the medicine on their body. Then they will rise from the earth to the sky and they will be moving."[101] In an ẹsẹ Ifá (divination verse) included in Bascom's *Ifa Divination: Communication between Gods and Men in West Africa*, the technology to facilitate flight is òògùn egbé, a term that translates as medicine or technology (òògùn) of the whirlwind (egbé), and it is effective for a limited time and must be reactivated.[102] An ẹsẹ Ifá recorded by Wande Abimbola in *Sixteen Great*

Poems of Ifá recounts how, when Ọrúnmìlà needed to return home because of an emergency, he "put Èṣù's àṣẹ in his mouth, / And he got up in haste, / And turned himself into wind" and instantaneously arrived at his home.[103]

A complex Igbo technology called *ikwu ekili* uses power of the word to transform the dibia and all she seeks to transport, including other humans, into a beam of light which can fly to any destination. In *After God is Dibia: Igbo Cosmology, Divination & Sacred Science In Nigeria*, John Umeh describes how the dibia begins the process of "jumping through the animalness of man and attaining spiritual union" with the Cosmos by uttering a counting chant that links the stars in the sky to the grains of sand on the Earth.[104] When nine, the number of completion, is uttered, the dibia commands, "*Onunu M bulu binie*!!! (My Onunu take off go!!!)," and with this, the transformation occurs: "All one would see is a stick of pure white light speeding across the sky. . . . at a speed several times greater than the speed of sound. The *Dibia* had gone to the desired destination."[105] Discussions of African flight in the Western Hemisphere often mention sacred words that have been forgotten. In some cases words are recorded, but without translation, context, or accompanying rituals, they are of little use.[106] Umeh's work fills in the gaps created by centuries of dislocation and attempts at cultural genocide, and his research confirms that the catalyst for human flight is African science, not African imagination.

The Igbo activate and become one with the energies of the Earth and Cosmos to fly; the BaKongo do the same through the *prenda* which Esteban Montejo describes as the source of the power of flight and many other technologies.[107] Lydia Cabrera elaborates on the prenda's intricacies: "The prenda is like the entire world in miniature, a means of domination. The ritual expert places in the kettle all manner of spiritualizing forces: there he keeps the cemetery and the forest, there he keeps the river and the sea, the lightning-bolt, the whirlwind, the sun, the moon, the stars—forces in concentration."[108] Not only must the wisdom keeper be in complete harmony with the Earth and Cosmos, but he must have intimate knowledge of the physical, chemical, astronomical, and biological properties of everything.

A mastery of holistic knowledge that includes the mysteries of the Cosmos is evident in the construction of a prenda called Seven Stars, which Cabrera also discusses: "They celebrate this prenda not in the house but in the forest. . . . the stars come down to this charm. There is an hour in the night when the nkisi is left by itself in the forest, so that the stars may come down, to enter into its power. When you see something brilliantly coming down—it is a star, entering an nkisi."[109] When one views the video recordings of NASA's space shuttle missions STS-63, STS-64, STS-75, and STS-80, to name a few, and witnesses various glowing, throbbing, self-directed entities thriving in space, moving at various rates of speed, and leaving and entering the Earth's atmosphere at their leisure, one may very well be observing the forces that activate prenda and ekili.[110]

With their intimate and extensive knowledge of the Cosmos, Africana scientists and technologists exist in a realm of possibility that is much wider than most humans can fathom. Rather than outstanding feats, the ability to summon the stars, transform one's self into light, and literally become time and space are common technologies among African scientists. In *Of Water and the Spirit*, Malidoma Somé describes how his Dagara elders open a portal into the space-time continuum that Dagara males must enter during their initiation into manhood. When Somé enters the portal, he finds that he has no breath to hold and no body to touch or see, as his material being has been completely transformed. He has entered a realm of raw undulating power in which he exists as pure energy. According to Somé, the transformation the human body undergoes upon returning to the material realm is the reverse of that which occurs through ekili. When the initiates reenter the terrestrial plane, their form is initially that of a ball of light that shoots through the air. As the transformation continues, that which was pure energy and then light regains its human form and characteristics. Somé says of a returned initiate: "His body was violet colored at first, then it became green, and then dark as usual."[111]

Westerners often relegate such phenomena as these to the realm of the magical or unbelievable, but they are best defined as examples of African technology, science, and Divinity-at-work. When discussing *satulmo*, the ability to cook upside down on the ceiling to prepare the last meal of an elder who is entering the spiritual realm, Somé reveals: "There are secret plants in nature that are very powerful. By using some of these plants, known only by healers and men and women in touch with the great medicine of Mother Earth, our cooks were able to produce, for a short time, an area free of gravity."[112] Far from being the work of witches, magicians, and sorcerers or the products of active imaginations, Africana technologists are accessing scientific knowledge that simply exceeds that lauded in the West.

Shaping the Shifting Self

An understanding of the interdependence and interrelatedness of all the forms, forces, and entities who share this planet and the Cosmos is central to Africana spiritual systems and the diverse abilities and technologies harnessed by Africana peoples. When a person understands his relationship to the dandelion, the saw palmetto, the fly, the lizard, the Sirius system, and the sea, and recognizes that he is each of these things and more, he is able to harness infinite powers, skills, and knowledge. Africana cosmology makes it clear that human beings can access their inherent divinity and do what many deem impossible, including disappear, assume other shapes, move through walls, and become invisible.

John Umeh describes several Igbo transportation devices and transformative abilities that are comparable to those of ancient Nubian Gods and to the technologies described by African Americans of the late 19th and early 20th centuries. An Igbo technology called *Ikwu eli* gives one the ability to move through time and space or disappear from one place and reappear in another, and *igho* allows a human being to transform into an inanimate object.[113] Jack Wilson of Georgia discusses his uncle's power which is comparable to ikwu eli: He "could disappeah lak duh win, jis walk off duh plantation an stay way fuh weeks at a time."[114] Wilson's uncle could use an igho-like technology to turn himself into the wind or enter a tree: "One time he git cawnuhed by duh putrolmun an he jis walk up to a tree an he say, 'I tink I go intuh dis tree.' Den he disappeah right in duh tree."[115] Similarly, Evans Brown recalls the police arresting a man and handcuffing him to a wagon only to find seconds later that they had in custody not a man but an "ole gray mule!"[116]

Other Igbo skills include *ndena*, the ability to pass through solid objects, such as walls, and *ishi eshishi*, a technology that allows the soul the ability to seep out of the body and inhabit another body, such as that of a leopard, cat, or donkey.[117] Ishi eshishi could be the power used by individuals who "step out of their skin" and "ride" other individuals.[118] There are also accounts of individuals using technology similar to ishi eshishi to remove the souls of and retaliate against their oppressors. In *The Practice of Witchcraft in Ghana*, Bannerman-Richter describes how school children teach a lesson to an overzealous instructor by removing his head while he sleeps and using it as a kickball.[119] Similarly, an enslaved African American father and son turn their oppressor and his son into a bull and a bull yearling. The enslaved Africans mount the pair "and spend the night riding and whipping them."[120]

In *After God is Dibia*, Umeh discusses how such technology as *ibi iboo* and *igba isaa* helped Africans outwit enslavers. Ibi iboo gives its user "the ability to appear physically in two places simultaneously."[121] Igba isaa is an Igbo technology also found among the Yoruba that allows one to divide one's being into "seven identical selves."[122] Umeh reveals that dibia used igba isaa "to baffle slave-traders and kidnappers in Igboland in those days and some indeed deliberately arranged for their relations to sell them to the slave-traders and obtain money from them."[123] Once the money had been obtained, the captive dibia would "split into seven identical selves, thereby confounding and escaping the slave traders."[124] The ability to transform and make invisible the self is not restricted to human beings. During Nigeria's Biafra War (1967–1970) a dibia named Ogbujaba used his skills to hide entire towns so that war planes could not find their intended targets.[125]

Another skill that helped people avoid enslavers and other threats is the ability to disappear. A Yoruba preparation called àfẹ̀ẹ̀rí enables a person "to elude their pursuers or to be unseen."[126] James Moore of Tin City, Georgia discusses the phenomenon in African America: "I seen folks disappeah right fo muh eyes. Jis go right out uh sight. De do say dat people brought frum Africa in slavery times could disappeah an fly right back tuh Africa. Frum duh tings I see mysef I blieb dat dey could do dis."[127] The power to disappear is not restricted to the bearer. Some spiritualists can make other people disappear. As Martha Page's grandfather informed her: "Some ub em [Africans] could make yuh disappeah . . . an some could fly all roun duh elements an make yuh do anyting dey wants yuh to do."[128]

Closely related to the power to disappear is the power of invisibility. African American elders hold that the Black Cat Bone is the technological device sure to endow one with the power of invisibility. Ellis Strickland asserts that with the Black Cat Bone one has the ability to do "all kinds of magic. You can talk to folks an' dey can't see you. You can even disappear an' come right back."[129] George W. Little confirms, "Not long ago I see a man vanish intuh tin eah by snappin his finguhs. Hab yuh heahd uh duh man wut wuz in prison in Springfield? He jis flied away frum duh jail an wuz nebuh caught agen. Yes, ma'am, I know wut yuh hab tuh hab in awduh tuh fly aw vanish away, but it is mighty hahd tuh git. It's duh bone ub a black cat."[130] Little is not fully forthcoming with his interviewer. It is not difficult to get a bone of a black cat, but it takes great courage and fortitude to obtain the technology known as the Black Cat Bone.

One of the highlights of her study with Father Watson, the "Frizzly Rooster," is Zora Neale Hurston's acquisition of the Black Cat Bone. Many variations on the methodology have been recorded, but the following description from Hurston is the richest account to date:

> When a big rain started, a new receptacle was set out in the yard. It could not be put out until the rain actually started for fear the sun

might shine in it. The water must be brought inside before the weather faired off for the same reason. If lightning shone on it, it was ruined. . . .

When dark came, we went out to catch a black cat. I must catch him with my own hands. Finding and catching black cats is hard work, unless one has been released for you to find. Then we repaired to a prepared place in the woods and a circle drawn and "protected" with nine horseshoes. Then the fire and the pot were made ready. A roomy iron pot with a lid. When the water boiled I was ready to toss in the terrified trembling cat.

When he screamed, I was told to curse him. He screamed three times, the last time weak and resigned. The lid was clamped down, the fire kept vigorously alive. At midnight the lid was lifted. Here was the moment! The bones of the cat must be passed through my mouth until one tasted bitter.

Suddenly, the Rooster and Mary rushed in close to the pot and cried, "Look out! This is liable to kill you. Hold your nerves!" They both looked fearfully around the circle. They communicated some unearthly terror to me. Maybe I went off in a trance. Great beast-like creatures thundered up to the circle from all sides. Indescribable noises, sights, feelings. Death was at hand! Seemed unavoidable! I don't know. Many times I have thought and felt, but I always have to say the same thing. I don't know. I don't know.

Before day I was home, with a small white bone for me to carry.[131]

The black cat is the logical choice for a technology that is created at night to endow one with invisibility. The cat's bone is consecrated by the power of Oya, who is most active in stormy overcast weather, and the unifying principles of Oya's number nine. The fearsome entities who converge on Hurston, Rooster, and Mary before entering and infusing the Black Cat Bone with their powers appear to be the products of fiction until one compares Hurston's account to Malidoma Somé's description of the fearsome terrestrial and cosmic forms and forces who attend his grandfather's funeral. Somé says of the spectacular visitors: "Because my grandfather had been a very great medicine man and the leader of our family, it was fitting that the supernaturals who had befriended him and aided him in his work would come and pay their last respects."[132] The manner by which the divine forces introduce themselves to a newly-initiated spirit worker, as is recounted by Hurston, is identical to the manner in which they gather to celebrate a wisdom keeper whose terrestrial reign has ended.

The Yoruba have a preparation to make a person invisible that utilizes elements and principles similar to those necessary to empower the Black Cat Bone. The Yoruba process is not as arduous as obtaining the Black Cat Bone, but the Black Cat Bone imparts more than invisibility. The Yoruba preparation uses certain leaves, black pepper, the skin of a small brown monkey, and a whole partridge. These items are activated by the Odù of Ìrẹtẹ̀ọ̀bàrà and the following incantation:

> Darkness is an attribute of *ibó*
> Darkness is the character of *ijòkùn*
> We see the monkey only when he wants us to see him
> If the monkey says we should not see him, we cannot see him
> Wherever *àparò* [the partridge] hides, the farmer can never see her[133]

After the ingredients have been prepared and spiritually charged, the medicine is poured into a gourd which is covered with a blue cloth and wrapped in leather. This gourd is hung around the neck. When the bearer wants to be invisible she needs only open the gourd. To be visible, she closes the gourd.[134] Because it is activated by the characteristics of particular diurnal and nocturnal flora and fauna, the preparation can impart invisibility day or night. In the preparation of both the Yoruba and the African American technologies, knowledge of the exoteric and esoteric properties of flora and fauna and material and astronomical agents is essential, as is the activating force of Power of the Word.

African power wielders do not merely use the forces of the Earth to satisfy their needs. They understand the àṣẹ, or life force, of flora and fauna, and they listen to and respect it. That respect, coupled with the understanding that the human being is a part of the world's flora and fauna, and adherence to the laws of reciprocity and harmony, results in holistic relationships as well as knowledge transmission and power sharing. Somé describes a blind healer who "would speak to Mother Nature in a strange language, giving her a list of illnesses. She would respond in a buzzing language, telling him which plants he needed to gather."[135] Umeh echoes Somé's recollection, confirming that "herbs talk particularly at certain hours in the night."[136] In African America, the aptly-named Divinity of Mississippi is a "tree-talker" who hails from a family of individuals who communicate with trees.[137]

Western scientists are finally witnessing communicative skills that Africana wisdom workers have been applying since the dawn of existence. Researchers in Bonn, Germany have recorded the diverse communications of plants and have documented their defense mechanisms as well.[138] But the Africana spiritualist's relationship with flora and fauna extends far beyond documentation and manipulation; the relationship between wisdom keepers, plants, and animals is so fluid that two-headed doctors can transform themselves into flora and fauna. Umeh avers that "very knowledgeable Igbo *Dibias* change themselves mystically into animals in order to win some very valuable knowledge of herbs and their uses and applications."[139] Umeh reveals that some dibia transform themselves into animals every four years to remain current in the healing arts.[140]

By understanding the interdependent dynamics that connect humans, flora, fauna, the Earth, astronomical bodies, and the Cosmos, Africana wisdom workers obtain skills that are infinite and seemingly phenomenal but are actually extraordinarily logical. Carlos Moore's *Pichón: A Memoir: Race and Revolution in Castro's Cuba* offers two examples of wisdom keepers at work. When Moore's father contracts tuberculosis and Western-trained doctors try and fail to cure him, an Àjẹ́ named Tecla, without masks, gloves, or fear, quietly cures his father with combinations of distilled and smudged flora.[141] Millions of lives have been lost because racism, ignorance, and capitalism prevent the wisdom of the world's Teclas from being respected and disseminated.

It is also the case that millions of people all over the world live lives of pain and shame because their eyes are crossed. Moore's crossed eyes were a source of devastation for him until he sought treatment from Mr. Heath, a Jamaican two-headed doctor whose mouth gleams with thirty-two gold teeth. Mr. Heath uses the Sun to correct Moore's crossed eyes: "Mr. Heath's therapy consisted of having me 'travel' around the sun, starting from its center, out to the sides, then in circles."[142] Mr. Heath's cure is in complete consonance with BaKongo works that harness the power and movement of the Sun. Mr. Heath directs Moore to create, with his eyes, the Yowa sign, which is the "Kongo sign of the cosmos and the continuity of human life."[143] By harnessing the "four moments of the sun"[144] and the Sun's radiant power, Moore's crossed eyes straighten.

Once Moore becomes one with the wisdom of the world, his fear of Mr. Heath is replaced with affinity and excitement: "In time, I was able to look at what he called the sun's equator. Every noon, Mr. Heath explained about planets and stars. I could not wait for nightfall. I did the eye exercises on my own at night, using the moon as my reference."[145] Moore shows the initiative and passion of an individual who is developing a second head and who is a worthy vessel for Mr. Heath's immense body of knowledge.

When Mr. Heath reaches the end of his terrestrial life he tells Moore, "When me dead, me no really go dead."[146] As Mr. Heath prepares to begin his next life in the Cosmos as an astronomical force, he informs Moore that, just as he can access the Sun for healing power, when Moore wants to speak to Mr. Heath he need only "look at the moon, the stars, and speak to him. I would hear his reply in my own mind."[147]

In addition to astral bodies facilitating communication and healing, Africana wisdom workers also use fauna to transmit messages, to heal, and to carry souls to the afterlife. Birds in particular are central to ways of knowing, doing, and healing. According to Braziel Robinson of Georgia, "When a person is sick and meets good spirits near enough to feel the air from their bodies, or wings, he generally gets well."[148] Researcher Ruth Bass also documented the use of spirit birds in healing: "The strangest cure I think I ever heard of in Mississippi was when Overlea, a seventh son and born double-sighter, loosed five white pigeons that had never known freedom, for a sick child. When the pigeons crossed water, the child was cured."[149]

In *Jambalaya: The Natural Women's Book of Personal Charms and Practical Rituals*, Luisah Teish provides her readers with specific ways to harness the healing power of birds:

> If there has been too much illness and/or insanity in your home, purchase a pigeon or dove and talk to it about the problem. Let it fly around the house at will for nine days (of course you must feed and care for it). Then release the bird in a park or other open space.
>
> For a particular illness, press the bird gently to the appropriate spot while visualizing blood flowing from you to it. If you find the bird dead, give it a proper burial and say a prayer of thanks.[150]

The African American use of birds to facilitate healing and spiritual renewal originates in Africa. In *Yoruba Beliefs and Sacrificial Rites*, J. Omosade Awolalu discusses how birds can be used to assist human beings in Yoruba culture, and his data is markedly similar to Teish's:

> At times, a live pigeon is used as a sponge, to which special soap is applied, for washing the head and the whole body. When used in this way, the bird is squeezed and weakened in the process. In some cases, it is expected that the bird must die and be thrown into the river to carry away the supplicant's impurities and misfortunes as the river flows away. And, in some other cases or circumstances, the bird is released alive to fly away, thus carrying with it the supplicant's unhappiness, misfortunes, disease, or death.[151]

The similitude between Awolalu's and Teish's recommendations provides clear evidence of African continuity in understanding and harnessing birds' cosmic and terrestrial curative abilities across the Pan-African continuum.

Perhaps by intentionally introducing a bird into one's home and life, as Awolalu and Teish suggest, a person can prevent the bird's independent arrival and its accompanying omen. A bird flying into one's house, a screech owl's cry, a woodpecker pecking on one's house, and a hawk flying over one's house are well known death signs. As Camilla Jackson testifies, "My daughter and I were ironing one day and a bird flew in the window right over her head. She looked up and said, 'mama that bird came after me or you, but I believe it came for me.' One month later my daughter took sick with pneumonia and died."[152] In this capacity, birds could be considered ambassadors of Àjẹ́, "the mysterious bird in the center of the boundary between heaven and earth" who "knows-when-man-would-cease-to-exist."[153] The birds also embody the Kemetic Ba, the "world soul" who moves between the spiritual realm and the Earth and also leaves the human body at the time of death.[154]

Cosmic Signs and Spiritual Literacy

To find one's destiny and attain immortality and divinity, it is necessary to protect one's terrestrial life from physical death. Numerous spiritually charged objects can be used to protect one's body, home, and property. In addition to the defense they provide, these avenging elements are so resplendent that they enjoy wide appreciation and dissemination. It would be unusual to drive through a southern town in America and not see trees with white rings emblazoned on their trunks, front doors sparkling with mirrors, and bottle trees of myriad colors and styles glistening in the yards of peoples of various ethnicities. These signs and symbols, which are routinely and mistakenly classified as "southern," are African in origin and signify the presence and protection of the Gods.

The white painted trees of America are the offspring of the African custom of adorning trees that are the sacred abodes of spirits or Deities with white or red cloths.[155] Given the significance of trees in Pan-Africa— as portals of the Loa in Haiti, as talking companions in African America, and as sentinels and worship sites in general—it is fitting that sacred trees are ritually designated and decorated. A tree's inherent protective force can be further amplified with bottles, medicines, spiritual script, and mirrors. By the same token, the protective power of trees that have been processed and used to build homes can be expanded by mirrors, bottles, pots, and other visible and buried devices. Among the Yoruba, the Baálẹ̀ of Ogbomoso, Nigeria has protective Gods surrounding his home and a barrier of protective tools or "roots" buried in the ground "from one side of his compound to the other."¹⁵⁶ One can find dazzling reproductions of the Baálẹ̀'s protected compound all over the American South.

The southern United States is famous for its resplendent bottle trees. But traditionally the sparkle of the bottles is not meant to attract tourists but to empower protective ancestral spirits. The graves of Africana peoples are often adorned with the last objects they touched or the items they cherished the most. These objects absorb the energy of the ancestor and become charged with power. The ancestor's progeny can visit the grave and stroke these items—often bottles, china, pitchers and pots—and communicate with their ancestor. A survivor can also relocate pieces of these objects to her home and hang them in trees, plant them in the earth, or station them at doorways and porches to obtain her ancestor's protection.¹⁵⁷ A sibling of this custom is the Yoruba ààlè, which often take the form of bottles filled with powerful medicines that are used to protect wares, property, and crops from thieves. Depending on its components, ààlè can kill, maim, or derange a miscreant.¹⁵⁸ A contemporary African American reconceptualization of ààlè is the plastic bag filled with water. While it is said that the glint of sunlight on water repels flies, the water may be dressed with liquid soap to purify the intentions of visitors, coins to attract wealth, or honey to sweeten the disposition of guests.¹⁵⁹ Flies cannot appreciate these ingredients, which are sealed in plastic, but the spirits certainly can.

Ritual adornment and protection also serve the human body. Nation sacks are small cloth bags filled with the protecting and empowering signifiers of one's identity, such as hairs, fabric, and coins, and such flora as High John the Conqueror Root and Life Everlasting. Nation sacks are dressed with perfume and positioned close to the groin where they charge and are recharged by the host. Until the mid-1900s many African American parents protected their children with jewelry that consisted of black thread knotted nine times. But one of the most ancient protective tools is the glint and gleam of precious metals, and this befits a people whose displays of wealth are legendary.

The original African adornment and signifier of wealth and power is gold; this is evident in the material wealth of such ancient empires as Nubia, which means "Land of Gold," and the Golden Empires of Ghana, Mali, and Songhai. Gold also signifies spiritual, genetic, and indestructible wealth, as is apparent in the Yoruba saying "Ìyá ni wúrà" which means "Mother is gold." In addition to denoting eternal maternal, material, and spiritual wealth, in African America, gold is said to strengthen vision. Consequently, wearing gold earrings reflects inner and outer treasures and serves a practical purpose. Silver money also used to be a popular form of adornment among African Americans, but the goal was not to flaunt wealth but to protect life: Silver wards off conjure, and tarnished silver indicates that one has been conjured.

In *Yoruba Beliefs and Sacrificial Rites*, Awolalu reveals some of the sources for African American spiritual adornment in a discussion that emphasizes the degree to which technological preparations are part of the collective consciousness, ritual protection, and external adornment of the Yoruba:

> In consequence of belief in magical power, many Yorùbás are found wearing all kinds of charms—copper rings (òrùkao [sic] bàbà), amulets (ifúnpá), preparations sewn up in leather (oǹdè). In homes we sometimes find a broom hanging from the door post, a small gourd shining bright from which some liquid is apparently dropping, an enchanted chain partly buried in the ground or some cowries arranged in [symmetrical] order on the floor. Some babies wear coils round their necks and waists; men and women have some black powder injected into their bodies through incisions (gbẹ́rẹ́).[160]

George Boddison, the mayor of Tin City, Georgia, appears to have retained the Yoruba customs of using òrùka bàbà and ifúnpá for protection. Boddison was interviewed in the 1930s, and his interviewers offer a stunning portrait of the mayor and his ritual and technological protection and adornment:

> His wrists and arms were encircled by copper wire strung with good luck charms; his fingers were covered with several large plain rings. A copper wire was bound around his head and attached to this wire were two broken bits of mirror which, lying flat against his temples with the reflecting side out, flashed and glittered when he moved his head. . . . a brass ring had been inserted in his mouth in the place of a lower jaw tooth.[161]

Just as Mr. Heath's golden smile attracts the sun's rays and the attention of anyone in his vicinity, the WPA interviewers are dazzled by Boddison's sparkling adornments, and the mesmerism of his accoutrement is wherein Boddison's protection lies. He reveals that nothing can harm him as long as he is girded in his brilliant totems of power.[162]

The use of spiritual implements augmented by mirrors and other reflective, sparkling, and shielding objects for protective adornment is evident in ancient and contemporary West African warriors, Mande historian-musicians known as *djeli*, and Yoruba royalty. Ayanna Gillian finds that the beaded crowns of Yoruba rulers are similar to Boddison's in style and purpose: "The wearing of the sacred crown or adenla is a symbol of his spiritual power and authority. The crown is veiled to protect his subjects for no one can see the face of a God. Possibly the most important element of his crown is the presence of the Ashe from which his power is derived."[163] Boddison's crown, which is constructed from power-conducting copper and flashing mirrors, performs the same function as the Adénlá: It protects Boddison from harm while shielding others from the power of his visage. Boddison—in the glory of his survival and his careful harnessing of the powers of the Ancients—is his own àṣẹ, or activating spiritual agent, in the flesh.

The protective implements known as oǹdè among the Yoruba and as *minkisi* among the BaKongo are called *mojos* and *tobies* in African America. The words mojo and toby are of African origin, as are the devices. The elements of and ritual processes behind most African American concepts of "working roots" to personal advantage and "putting roots on someone" to alter their destiny can be traced to Africa, with the BaKongo of Central Africa being the biggest contributors of this technology, as is elucidated by Robert Farris Thompson in *Flash of the Spirit*.[164] While primary spiritual elements, such as graveyard dirt, eggs, and blood, remain constant in African America, given the differences of their terrain, African Americans freestyle and create neo-minkisi using whatever speaks to their souls.

Spirit work is cyclical: External spiritual adornment protects and charges internal cosmic gifts. Internal gifts can then be used to help one understand external forces and foretell future events. One of the most reliable ways of knowing is interpretation of signs. Itching palms or feet, twitching eyes, howling dogs, burning ears, and dreams of fish, weddings, funerals, and raw meat are just a few of numerous well-known signs in African America. These twitches, pangs, and dreams are the ẹnikejì's or Ba's way of informing the human counterpart about future events. These signs are so reliable in African America that they spawned a cottage industry of "Dream Books" that associate events in dreams with numbers that one can play in hopes of hitting the lottery.

It is possible that the roots of African American semiology can be traced to an aspect of spiritual vision that the Igbo call *icheku oku*. In addition to the physical eyes and the third eye, which the Igbo call *akpa uche*, the human body also has icheku oku, which are metaphysical receptors that react to spiritual stimuli and impending events with twitches, itches, tingles, and dreams that human beings can interpret.

According to Umeh: "The relevant spots located in the various parts of the body are all psychic seeing spots which receive appropriate messages from *uche* ["Universal Consciousness"] as soon as it lands at *akpa uche* [the third eye] and [is] decoded by *ako*, the intellect or cognitive faculty."[165] This spiritual process results in "*okwudu* such as twitchings on the eyes (*anya odudo*) which may be a sign that one will weep or will enjoy happy scenery or dance; *ukwu okpukpo* and *ukwu odudo* which may stand for a . . . looming good or bad journey as the case may be."[166]

The ability to receive and interpret signs manifests itself in various ways. An important skill, especially to an agrarian people, is the ability to read and interpret meteorological signs and phenomenon and control the weather. Henry Rogers of Georgia boasts such gifts:

> Regarded highly as the local weather prophet. . . Henry gets up every morning before daybreak and scans the heavens to see what kind of weather is on its way. He guards all these "signs" well and under no consideration will he tell them. They were given to him by someone who has passed on and he keeps them as a sacred trust. If asked, upon making a prediction, "How do you know?" . . . Henry shakes his wise old head and with a wave of the hand says, "Dat's all right, you jess see now, it's goin' ter be dat way". And it usually is![167]

Rogers guards the source of his knowledge as closely as the Igbo do. If Rogers were to betray this living wisdom, it would withdraw its power and cease communication.

Some individuals have the ability to read the skies; others have the power to control the weather. In some African societies, wisdom keepers who can initiate and stop rain are hired for these skills and can be punished if they fail to control the weather.[168] The means by which weather controllers do their work are diverse and can range from elaborate rituals to incantations rich with Òrò. Pierre F. Verger's *Ewé: The Use of Plants in Yoruba Society*, includes Yoruba preparations to stop and produce rain. The ritual to make rain fall calls for wild lettuce and salt. The lettuce is cooked and the water is squeezed from it. When the sky is clear, salt is poured on the ground and Odù Òbàrà òṣẹ́ is written in it. The following incantation is recited:

> Vegetables always arrive at the market drenched in water
> Salt cannot be wrapped without turning to water
> Òbàrà òṣẹ́ go and direct the rain to the earth
> Òbàrà òṣẹ́ go and direct rain to the ground.[169]

The catalysts for this technology are the interconnected forces of weather, agriculture, human sustenance, and economics. Salt is a widely utilized Pan-African catalyst for rainfall, and while his methodology differs from that of the Yoruba, Overlea, a wisdom worker from Mississippi, "can produce rain by crossing two matches and sprinkling salt on them."[170] Overlea combines his spiritual power with sodium chloride and the phosphorous of matches to produce nucleation. His use of salt is similar to that employed in Western hydroscopic cloud seeding, in which certain chemicals, including salt, are introduced into clouds to cause particles of water and dust to develop until they result in precipitation.[171] However, with their knowledge of and effective application of salt, Africana wisdom keepers have been doing for millennia what Western scientists began experimenting with mere decades ago.

The Yoruba also have a medicine to stop rain that "involves tying some seeds of alligator pepper and some other objects in a handkerchief or tying palm-fronds into knots and swinging these overhead swiftly as incantations are uttered."[172] African American methods of cloud splitting seem simpler but can be devastating if used casually or dishonorably. Lenell Harris of Mississippi describes two ways to split a storm cloud. With the first, an individual positions herself before the storm cloud and throws an axe into the ground under the cloud. Just as the axe splits the ground, so too will the storm cloud split. The other method of cloud splitting involves the Bible, known by many wisdom workers as "the greatest conjure book in the world."[173] To split a cloud using the Bible, one simply opens the Bible while standing under the thunderhead and it will split. While these works seem simple and harmless, Harris makes it clear that splitting clouds is for emergencies only, for if the split cloud reunites, "You got yourself a cloud"[174]—one that could kill its splitter.

Evening the Odds

Controlling the elements is an essential skill for an agrarian people. For a displaced and disenfranchised people who are targeted by the tireless minion of an unjust judicial system, controlling the elements often translates into ensuring the most fundamental right: freedom. In addition to the obvious profits made off of African intellect during the institution of slavery, the Thirteenth Amendment to the Constitution, which holds that slavery is illegal except as a punishment for a crime, has made it possible for America to eternally profit off of Africana people by criminalizing, incarcerating, and *legally* enslaving them in perpetuity. The song "No More Prisons" by Hurricane G and featuring Rishi offers a succinct elucidation of how American capitalists and police officers use the prison industrial complex to convert Divinities into dividends: "If Gods ain't locked, no jobs for cops / If blocks ain't hot, stock options drop."[175] However, no matter where in the world they occur, attempts to cage Africana Gods have always been and will always be met with resistance.

The Yoruba have many preparations for extrication from judicial entanglements. *Ewé* offers two works for *afọ̀ràn*, avoiding a judicial procedure. In the first, a practitioner pulverizes *gbẹ́gi* (crabgrass), *ewé àgbọn* (cocoanut tree leaves), and *ewé èèsún funfun* (elephant grass) and mixes them with black soap while chanting:

> *Ogbè alárá*, help me dismiss this case
> *Gbẹ́gi* says it will be forgotten
> Cracking is the destiny of *àgbọn* [coconut]
> *Gbẹ́gi* is meant to be uprooted
> The vibration of *èèsún* is harmless.[176]

The plants of this preparation are specifically chosen so that the client's case will be uprooted like crabgrass, cracked like a cocoanut, and rendered as innocuous as elephant grass. The soap made with these ingredients is fortified with the power to literally scrub the court case from the client's life.

Another medicine for afọ̀ràn uses roasted flora because

> Roasted beans can never grow if planted
> My case should not surface again
> Roasted maize can never grow if planted
> My case shall not come to light again
> Roasted peppers can never grow if planted
> My case should not come to light again
> *Ogbè alárá* says that the case should be forgotten.[177]

With the same logic, ease, and ingredients that one can use to create a satisfying meal, one can prepare and serve a complete exoneration.

The criminal injustices that Africans in America face call for liberation technologies that are culture-specific and diverse. *Mules and Men* includes a number of rituals for success in court battles that Hurston learned while studying with Dr. Duke. For a defendant to control the courtroom and his adversaries, he can have his shoes or his entire body, depending on the severity of the charges, "dressed with the court" to ensure victory.[178] One can also enlist the aid of High John the Conqueror to win one's case by steeping nine pieces of High John the Conqueror Root in whiskey for thirty-eight hours and mixing the extract with Jockey Club cologne.[179]

The defendant who is "dressed" with High John's power is dressed for spiritual and judicial success.

Dr. Duke also teaches Hurston how to silence opposing witnesses:

> We took a beef tongue, nine pins, nine needles, and split the beef tongue. We wrote the names of those against our man and cut the names out and crossed them up in [the] slit of tongue with red pepper and beef gall, and pinned the slit up with crossed needles and pins. We hung the tongue up in a chimney, tip up, and smoked the tongue for thirty-six hours. Then we took it down and put it in ice and lit on it from three to four black candles stuck in ice. Our client read the Twenty-second Psalm and Thirty-fifth also, because it was for murder. Then we asked the spirits for power more than equal to man.[180]

It is important to note that spirit workers use the Bible without compunction because there is no conflict. As a holistic system, Hoodoo—like Vodun, Ifá, Fa, and other Africana spiritual systems—has neither limitations nor boundaries; it accesses spirit and power wherever they are.

In addition to galvanizing rituals with spiritually empowered fauna and flora and verses from the Book of Fa, the Bible, the Qur'an, the Odù Ifá, or other texts, spirit workers infuse common objects with power. A technology that Awolalu shares in *Yoruba Beliefs and Sacrificial Rites* involves "locking an enchanted padlock [on an effigy] to make it impossible for an accuser to speak against one in the law court."[181] Similarly, Father Watson teaches Hurston how to use a key, a deep bowl, red and black pepper, a one penny nail, vinegar and ammonia to keep in jail a person who is already incarcerated.[182]

Yoruba and African American rituals for spiritual stultification and death also share similarities. Hurston describes the ritual she and Father Watson enact to prevent a prominent pastor from gaining more prestige:

> We wrote the preacher's name on a slip of paper with black ink. We took a small doll and ripped open its back and put in the paper with the name along with some bitter aloes and cayenne pepper and sewed the rip up again with the black thread. The hands of the doll were tied behind it and a black veil tied over the face and knotted behind it so that the man it represented would be blind and always do things to keep himself from progressing. The doll was then placed in a kneeling position in a dark corner where it would not be disturbed. He would be frustrated as long as the doll was not disturbed.[183]

Watson's antidote for success is comparable to the following Yoruba work to bring about death. The Yoruba ritual calls for certain herbs and seven pigeons to be charred, mixed with clay, and molded into the form of the victim and dressed in his clothes. "The Ifá priest should wear rags and sit with the figure at night singing thus: '*Ìdìn àìsùn* that never sleeps, do not allow this person to sleep. *Ìdìn àìsùn* that never sleeps.' The Ifa priest must not sleep until the *sìgìdì* [soul] of the figure has arrived back from its mission."[184] While the sìgìdì's target is specified by the clothes of the intended which contain his spiritual DNA, the care that must be taken when invoking and directing the sìgìdì is evident in the fact that the babaláwo's vigil is parallel to the sìgìdì's mission. If the sìgìdì returns and finds the babaláwo asleep, the sìgìdì may very well prevent him from waking up.

Til WhoDo(?) Us Part

Many of the ingredients in African technological preparations are harmless by themselves, but combined and directed by the hand and mind of the Divine, they are potent and can be lethal. One must "carry power" or be a spiritually aligned person—a babaláwo, iyaláwo, dibia, nganga, or two-headed doctor—to successfully enact many spiritual technologies. But with Africana divinity being a timeless force that flows effortlessly through generations, genders, African ethnic groups, and classes, one does not need extensive knowledge to "work roots" on someone.

Women have a natural gift and advantage over men that many use to get, keep, or summon lovers: That gift is the Àjẹ́ resident in their menstrual blood. One of the most common Pan-African works involves a woman putting her menstrual blood in her beloved's food. Another work involves a woman tying raw meat to her inner thigh so that her menstrual blood will marinate in the meat before she prepares it for her mate to eat.

A Yoruba medicine to "win the heart of a man" also employs blood, but the methodology differs from African American preparations. The worker grinds together the feathers of a vulture and a partridge. The Odù of Òfúnọ̀ṣẹ́ is drawn and the following incantation is recited,

> Female and male partridges do not dare part from each other
> If they fly together, they perch together
> Both the male and the female vulture lay in the same place
> May so-and-so be unable to part with me.[185]

The practitioner cuts her body and mixes her blood with the ground feathers and the Odù. She then gives her beloved this medicine in food or drink. A similar methodology is employed by an African American conjurer named Menthy who binds couples through symbolic flora: "Menthy gets some hair from the head of each. She takes this to the woods and finds a young sapling that has grown up in a fork. She splits the tree a little at this fork and puts the hair in the split place. When this tree grows up the two will be eternally united."[186]

What is put together via Hoodoo is difficult to tear asunder—unless another powerful hand is at work. There are as many preparations to foment love as there are works to sow seeds of discord. A Yoruba medicine for upheaval calls for gunpowder and a broken clay pot. After placing the powder in the pot, the practitioner lights the concoction while taking great care to avoid the smoke, because if the smoke reaches the practitioner's eyes, he "too will take part in the fight."[187] The work is activated with the following incantation:

> The day that fire set eyes on gunpowder
> That day it will explode
> Èjìogbè, this very day you must carry evil to them
> Èjìogbè, fire and gunpowder always fight till they part.[188]

Hurston and a two-headed doctor named Eulalia also use gunpowder to end a relationship. Hurston inserts a paper with the couple's names written nine times into a lemon along with gunpowder.[189] At the couple's vacant home, Eulalia consults the Sun in the tradition of her Kemetic and BaKongo forebears, and she and Hurston bury the conjure in accord with the astronomical sentinel so that the setting Sun will usher the end of love. Hurston and Eulalia salt and pepper the couple's home while Eulalia chants: "Just fuss and fuss till you part and go away."[190] The Yoruba and African American medicines both employ spiritually symbolic agents: the setting sun, gunpowder, a broken pot, salt, lemons, and pepper, and both include similar commands to fight until separation ensues.

Once the quarrelling begins, it may be necessary to banish one's antagonist from one's home and even from existence. There are numerous works for such eradications. The Yoruba have a work "to make a person get lost" that is similar to African American "running feet." The Yoruba work uses such materials as *iyerosùn* (camwood powder), red pepper, male and female pigeons and the divination sign of *Òbàrà 'wòrì*. Once the objects have been charred and bound and set in a moving body of water, the following incantation is uttered:

> The river does not look backwards when it is running
> Ifá help me destroy their sense totally

Ọparum oko destroy their sense
Ọ̀bàrà kòṣì, Ifá help me remove their sense to make them stray
May so-and-so get lost and never return
A pigeon flies about restlessly in the bush
A pigeon dies while flying from one bush to another
So-and-so should die while roaming strange places.[191]

To enact "running feet," the rootworker takes the unwanted person's right footprint and parches it in a frying pan along with a dirt dauber's nest and cayenne pepper. The entire concoction is wrapped in the offender's sock and taken to a river at noon. When coming within forty feet of the river's edge, the rootworker must run to the shore, "[w]hirl suddenly and hurl the sock over [the] left shoulder into the water and never look back and say, 'Go and go quick in the name of the Lord.'"[192]

The shared elements in a "medicine to make a person get lost" and "running feet" are running water, fauna affiliated with flight, red pepper, and incantation. Both medicines are logical: The Yoruba prescription, galvanized by the victim's name, will cause the person to flit about aimlessly like a pigeon; the pepper will derange the mind; the river will impel the victim forward until he or she dies. "Running feet" utilizes the àṣẹ of the victim's footprint, which is heated to cause rapidity of action and laced with deranging pepper. Wandering like a dirt dauber and running like the river, this victim will also run to death. Although in African America the incantation is truncated due to religious imposition, Ọ̀rọ̀ is essential to the activation of both works.

Firing Forwards and Backwards

Yoruba babaláwo say there is an ẹsẹ Ifá for each of life's dilemmas. Igbo dibia hold that there is ogwu, or medicine, for every illness.[193] There is also a medical or technological work of Hoodoo for all of life's predicaments. But it is important to understand that combining various herbs and roots is not the same as making an effective medicine. Doctors and diviners train for decades. They must know the laws of nature, the chemical and spiritual properties of flora and fauna, the rules of the Ancients, and the words of power. Africana spirit workers and technologists are also expected to use their powers responsibly and share wisdom only with conscientious people who are mentally and spiritually balanced. An Igbo proverb issues a clear warning: "Herb is a gun / It fires frontwards / It fires backwards."[194] Herbs can be used to kill or cure, and misdirected preparations can boomerang back on the preparation's creator. It is also important to note that the works described in this book are taken out of context for the purposes of comparative analysis. One may never know what odds were evened and which wrongs were righted by the padlocks, running feet, and beef tongues employed in these works.

The metaphorical association of flora with a gun becomes literal when discussing one of Pan-Africa's most compelling powers: The ability to summon someone's spirit and kill or heal the spirit's human bearer. In *African Philosophy, Culture and Traditional Medicine*, Makinde describes a power known as *apeta*, which means summon (*pè*) and shoot (*ta*), which is related to *apepa*, which means summon and kill (*pa*). Apeta involves the construction of a representative mud image of the intended victim. The victim is called by name three times, which causes the person's spirit to enter the image. With the victim's spirit installed, the mud image is shot and the victim dies. Makinde emphasizes apeta's relationship to the intended's ipǫnri and spiritual identity stating that "use of this kind of power demands the knowledge of an enemy's real name and other important details."[195] Once the name has been invoked and the spirit summoned, distance, religion, and ethnicity are irrelevant and pose no barriers to apeta. Apeta, like the foregoing Yoruba works to kill someone, debilitates the intended's spirit which results in the death of the physical body. What is more, as Makinde reveals, "Apeta presents a problem to modern doctors because, although the symptoms of gun shots are seen, there are no visible marks to assist diagnosis."[196]

Among members of the Egbo secret society in Eastern Nigeria, the equivalent of apeta is "shadow calling," and its method of actualization involves smoke. In his book, *In the Shadow of the Bush*, P. Amaury Talbot, who finds that the mysteries of the Egbo are linked to "ancient Egyptian mysteries," describes shadow calling as he had witnessed it:

> Within the open space in the center of the compound a fire was burning. On this from time to time medicine was thrown, which caused clouds of smoke to rise. These died down, save for isolated puffs, which after a time assumed definite shape. . . . [A]gainst the background of the moonlit sky, dark silhouettes began to pass, each clearly recognizable as that of some person known to be absent at the time.[197]

In *The Man-Leopard Murders*, David Pratten discusses a technology called soul trapping, which is used by the Ibibio and Anang of Eastern Nigeria:

> [D]iviners and specialists in the preparation of medicines . . . could "trap" a bush soul by attracting it with familiar food, catching it in a wooden dish . . . and then spearing it in order to kill the soul's human form. Variations of this process relate ways in which a

person's soul is drawn out and imprisoned within a pot, which is then hung over a slow fire so that the body of the victim withered.[198]

While the methodologies of this science in Eastern Nigeria vary, the power and its results are similar. To understand the neutrality, fluidity, and flexibility of this technology, it is helpful to compare the preceding accounts to the power of Malidoma Somé's grandfather, Bakhye, who defended his community with technology called Pintul. As Somé reveals, "If he wished to destroy an enemy, he would retire to the quiet of his chambers place an arrow upside down on his bow, and magically hit his target. The arrow would kill whomever or whatever he named, then rematerialize in his chamber ready for more."[199] While the technology is related to apeta, Pintul actually has more in common with a power that the Yoruba call *àkàtàmpó* which allows the user to kill hundreds of adversaries with one arrow.[200] Bakhye was so proficient with Pintul he was known as "the upside-down arrow shooter," and he used his technology to battle the French who sought to rape, pillage, and colonize the Dagara.[201]

Bakhye also had a complex security system that was undergirded by a clay pot that was filled with water that never touched the ground in its descent from the clouds. Somé reveals that Bakhye "saw everything that happened throughout the community by looking into this water," and if animals were raiding the crops, he could throw a pebble at the offending animal's image in the water and kill it.[202]

Using spiritually-charged objects to see, control, or kill is also found in African America. In *The Sanctified Church*, Hurston describes how Uncle Monday uses apeta to exact revenge for Mrs. Bradley, whose daughter was seduced, impregnated, and abandoned by John Wesley. Uncle Monday sits Bradley before a mirror and places a pistol and a dagger before her:

> As soon as the water passed over her tongue she seized the gun. He pointed towards the looking-glass. Slowly the form of John Wesley formed in the glass and finally stood as vivid as life before her. She took careful aim and fired. She was amazed that the mirror did not shatter. But there was loud report, a cloud of bluish smoke and the figure vanished.[203]

As she makes her way home, Bradley learns that Wesley "dropped dead."

Another African American variant comes from Kentucky and features Henry Coulter who harnesses apeta through a glass pistol. A woman identified as Mrs. Duncan witnesses Coulter's apeta in action and describes its versatility. When Duncan's husband was suffering from a back ailment, he sought treatment from Coulter who "just shot him in the back with a glass pistol, and cured him. Of course there was not any bullet in the pistol, but it cured him. He [Coulter] could draw a picture of a chicken on a paper and shoot it, and a chicken would fall dead in the yard."[204]

The methods for calling shadows, viewing distant regions, and killing or healing at a distance are nearly as varied as methods of flight. While forms of apeta-like technology share similarities, they are also culturally and geographically distinct. It appears to be the case that the power is able to conform itself to the tools most efficacious to the era and environment of the spirit worker. Coulter does not have Bakhye's charged water to view and protect his farm, but he can heal community members, kill offenders, and put food on the table with his glass pistol. Uncle Monday, Bakhye, Coulter, and other Africana wisdom workers with apeta-like technology could have terrorized and decimated their communities, but they used their powers for community protection, healing, and empowerment.

Duncan, who discusses Henry Coulter's technology, further emphasizes the neutrality and flexibility of Hoodoo and the African origin of African American spiritual, medicinal, and technological works when she describes how Africana medicinal technology was used to harm and later to heal and restore her daughter, Della. When Della's leg is paralyzed as a result of Hoodoo, Duncan does not sink to her knees and pray. Knowing that it takes power to combat power, Duncan consults a two-headed doctor named Linda Woods. Duncan's decision to employ Woods is not only common sense given Della's ailment and Wood's two heads of wisdom, but it is also part of the process of knowledge acquisition. The importance of matching skills, wills, and strengths— spiritual and physical—recurs in Africana life, lyrics, and literature because contests between wisdom workers deepen and develop intellect.

The depth of Linda Woods' intellect is evident in her medicines, which include a revered herb and a force so important that it became an internationally recognized brand. Seven African Powers candles, soaps, incense and oils can be purchased commercially in modern America. These syncretized spiritual facilitators boast seven colors and are packaged with pictures of Catholic saints who bear the names and powers of seven Yoruba Deities: Òrúnmìlà, Òṣun, Ṣàngó, Ògún, Ọbàtálá, Èṣù, and Yemọja. Linda Woods is at least one African American source for the proliferation of the Seven African Powers products commercially marketed today, for in the early 1900s she was making her own Seven African Powers oil. Duncan recalls Woods' effective medicines and prescriptions:

She come with a bottle of something, all striped with all colors, but when you shake it up it was all the same color. She rubbed [Della's] leg with it and told me to get all the life everlasting [an herb also known as rabbit tobacco] that I could carry in my arms, and brew it for tea to bathe her leg in. Then pour it in a hole in the ground, but not to cover it up. Then not to go down the road for nine days.[205]

In Woods' cure, the Seven African Powers work in conjunction with the oft-unmentioned but indispensable eighth and ninth powers: Onílè, the Yoruba Earth Deity, receives and neutralizes the conjure, and the entire ritual is aligned with Oya's number nine which demarcates the closing of the cycle. Baths in the aptly named Life Everlasting ensure Della's full recovery. Just as Life Everlasting continues to flourish in America, so too do the Seven African Powers continue to assist dislocated Africans in their quests for spiritual expansion and holistic evolution.

The Rainbow Serpent and the Radar

The Seven African Powers brand offers irrefutable evidence of continuity, but it also establishes a false hierarchy and omits important Gods. Not only does Yoruba cosmology boast innumerable Gods, but without such elemental Deities as Onílè, there is no Earth and no life; without Oya, human beings cannot breathe let alone transform, evolve, and become ancestors; and without Òṣùmàrè, human beings have no covenant with the Divine and no path to attain immortality and divinity.

Òṣùmàrè is a profoundly important but often overlooked Òrìṣà. Òṣùmàrè is the Rainbow Serpent who emerges from the Womb of Origins to ensure humanity's continuous life, death, and rebirth. Òṣùmàrè delivers "a covenant between Olódùmarè and the people of Earth" and represents human beings' ability to "become transformed and experience rebirth."[206] Òṣùmàrè is symbolized cosmically by a serpent biting its tail or a serpent encircling the Earth, signifying immortality. Terrestrially, Òṣùmàrè takes the form of the Nigerian Rainbow Boa. These sacred serpents have "power of vision" in the form of a stone, and this stone is rich with power, as Awo Fa'lokun Fatunmbi reveals:

> There exists in Nigeria a real snake known as the Rainbow Python [sic], and this snake is used as one of the symbolic images that represents *Olódùmarè*. When the live Rainbow Python [sic] gets old, it loses its eyesight. At the same time that the snake goes blind, it discharges a small florescent stone that radiates with the colors of the rainbow. The sightless snake is able to sense the radiations from the stone and will strike anything that blocks its perception of them

This gives the Rainbow Python [sic] the ability to survive after it can no longer see. Hunters who locate the stone use it as a charm for invoking abundance.[207]

In *Olódùmarè: God in Yorùbá Belief*, E. Bolaji Idowu divulges more information about Òṣùmàrè, her earthly emissaries, and their sacred stones:

> The Yoruba believe, generally, that the rainbow is produced by a very large boa: the reptile discharges from its inside the sulphurous matter which sets all its surroundings aglow and causes a reflection, which is the rainbow (Òṣùmàrè), in the sky. The matter which is so discharged is known as Imi Òṣùmàrè ("rainbow excrement") and is considered valuable for making people wealthy and prosperous.[208]

Given that Òṣùmàrè symbolizes and facilitates rebirth and immortality, it is logical that the God and her divine terrestrial emissaries survived the Middle Passage. In *The Sanctified Church*, Hurston discusses a serpent in Florida who is an obvious sibling of the Nigerian Rainbow Boa, and Hurston details how one can obtain the serpent's "diamond of diamonds":

> The singing stone . . . is the greatest charm, the most powerful "hand" in the world. It is a diamond and comes from the mouth of a serpent (which is thought of as something different from any ordinary snake) and it is the diamond of diamonds. It not only lights your home without the help of any other light, but it also warns its owner of approach.
> The serpents who produce these stones live in the deep waters of Lake Maitland. There is a small island in this lake and a rare plant grows there which is the serpent's only food. She comes only to nourish herself in the height of a violent thunderstorm, when she is fairly certain that no human being will be present.
> It is impossible to kill or capture her unless nine healthy people have gone before to prepare the way with The Old Ones, and then more will die in the attempt to conquer her. But it is not necessary to kill or take her to get the stone. She has two. One is embedded in her head, and the other she carries in her mouth. The first one cannot be had without killing the serpent, but the second one may be won from her by trickery.[209]

Hurston goes on, in great detail, to explain the means by which the stone may be obtained without violence, and, by doing so, she puts in her readers' hands ancient tools of empowerment.

Hurston's disquisition is one of the most profound examples of African continuity ever recorded. In addition to detailing rituals of acquisition that rely on the forces of Òrìṣà Ọya and Àjẹ́, Hurston's exposition describes a serpent that is identical in form, function, and facilitators to the sacred Nigerian Rainbow Boa. What is more, while both Hurston and Idowu explain how difficult it is to obtain Imí Òṣùmàrè because of the serpent's vigilance; only Hurston gives an exact location for the serpent and *two* methods for procuring the stone. Most significant is the fact that Hurston is, to my knowledge, the first person to publish information about divine serpents with powerful and empowering stones. Her findings were published in 1934—twenty-eight years *before* those of Idowu. That Hurston's rural Floridian community heralds the same serpent and stone as their ancient and contemporary Yoruba kin provides stunning evidence of the continuum of the Divine—from Gods to technologies.

The Sacks Tied by the Gods Cannot be Untied

The spiritual technologies discussed in this chapter—including the ability to fly, to disappear, to shapeshift, to manipulate minds, to heal, and to harm—are feats that only divine and divinely balanced entities can accomplish, and evidence of the magnitude of these powers may lie in the fact that there are few Gods who can enact these skills in this era. Elders who are now ancestors saw internal fragmentation and the disease that is capitalism beginning to infect Africana communities and minds, and they refused to share wisdom that could be misused. Similar to Henry Coulter, whose trunk of spiritual implements was buried when he died, Esteban Montejo recalls that many BaKongo elders "died so sad" because they found no one worthy of inheriting their prendas or the knowledge of how to make them, and the tools and wisdom were buried with the elders.[210] Somé's Dagara elders did not share the secrets of satulmo with Somé's generation, and anti-gravity technology remains lodged in the leaves of sacred plants.

That the contemporary era has produced few individuals worthy of receiving spiritual knowledge is a constant refrain in *After God is Dibia*. Umeh describes the anguish that the elders' reticence causes contemporary wisdom seekers:

> On one occasion Joseph Mbanaso broke down and wept bitterly that when my father passed on, his knowledge would be lost the way that . . . his own father's got lost. My father consoled him and explained that the age and the generation were not right. He added that Ikwu Ekili may be used by criminals to escape arrest, and Ishi Agu would

be used . . . to harass or kill their opponents for very flimsy reasons.[211]

In addition to the fact that some medicines can be shared between dibia only after a blood oath "forbidding the negative use of herbs" has been made,[212] the force of modernization moves elders to impose additional restrictions. When Umeh begged his father to share his technological repertoire with him, his father refused because Umeh was "too young" and "would not be able to keep all the rules."[213] Admitting that it would be impossible for him to ensure the purity of the food he would ingest in the foreign lands to which he would travel in the future, Umeh deferred to his father's authority.

The wisdom keepers understood the changes being wrought in the world. With the globalization of currency and capitalism, those who believe that "everything has a price" seek to purchase that which is priceless. P. Amaury Talbot attempted to buy knowledge of Nsibidi and was rebuffed by an Egbo elder. Talbot recalls, "He refused point blank, though a good remuneration had been offered for his services. He added as an aside to another member of the society. . . 'If I taught him Nsibidi, he would know all the Egbo signs, and the secrets of the animals.'"[214] Although many try, it is not possible to buy or sell wisdom and knowledge of the Gods. If such an exchange is attempted, it will net useless objects, dead ends, and destruction.

. . .

Just as divinity cannot be bought or sold or created or destroyed, the powers of the Divine have not been lost or erased; they cannot be. Some forces are lying dormant in bodies and books awaiting rebirth; others are bursting through wombs, penises, pens, and fingertips seeking recognition. It could very well be the case that the elders did not share their technologies because the Gods of each generation are responsible for fashioning divine tools unique to their needs, environments, oppressions, and conundrums. And, yes, the Gods are still among us. While their powers may range from the understated to the unbelievable, they are always readily identifiable for they all boast two heads and they all shine like new money.

CHAPTER TWO

High John and His Conquering Suns:
Re-Developing Divinity and Re-Determining Destiny

"Before and after
I be Self Lord And Master"
~ Wu-Tang Clan, "Heaterz"

The Africana two-headed doctors, babaláwo, dibia, and wisdom keepers may have taken some secrets of their technologies with them to the other side for safe-keeping, but they did not keep their divinity to themselves: They could not. Africana numinescence is such that it *must* regenerate, proliferate, and disseminate. Furthermore, Gods are always available to help human beings re-member their spiritual origins and fulfill their cosmic obligations. The Gods invest readily in human beings because, through the Gods' assistance, human beings become Gods who become human beings who become Gods in an endless cycle of wisdom acquisition and divine actualization. The transmission of divinity can occur in myriad ways, including through the biological seeds of life and the Womb of All, through knowledge sharing and initiation, and through the empowered ink, galvanizing lyrics, and catalyzing characters that leap off of pages, spring from loins, shoot from tongues, and land in shimmering souls.

This chapter explores the transference and proliferation of divinity from the dibia, two-headed doctors, babaláwo, and innumerable other Africana Gods to High John the Conqueror and his immortal Suns. This exploration begins where the resurrection of the Gods began, in the bowels of slavery. Following an elucidation of how enslaved Africans reached into the infinite depths of African cosmology and fashioned a high and conquering God of their own, this discussion will turn to historical figures including, but not limited to, Zora Neale Hurston, Father Divine, C. M. Bey, Noble Drew Ali, W. D. Fard, Elijah Muhammad, and Allah, the Father, who reached within their souls, found their waiting Divinities, and used their literature, pulpits, and sermons to introduce multitudes to knowledge of the divine Africana self.

High John the Conqueror—Everyone and EveryGod

The Africans who stepped onto the lands of oppression toting countless Deities in their bodies and infinite powers in their empty hands were often forced to renounce their Gods and acknowledge the supremacy of four Christian figures: "the Father, the Son, the Holy Ghost," and the devil; and one earthly figure: the plantation owner. Given the great hypocrisy that Christianity represented to the enslaved African, not to mention its parochial belief system and sanctioning of slavery, Christianity and its five figureheads were neither sufficient nor appropriate for enslaved Africans.

Christianity differs from Africana spiritual systems in many fundamental and profound ways. The ontological and cosmological centrality of woman and the gender balance that is the foundation of the Africana ethos reflect the fact that, logically and biologically, without mother, there can be no life of any kind, let alone any father or son. Such reverence for women and their fundamental and essential roles in creation are nowhere present in Christianity. Indeed, while Christianity shuns the genitals and their functions as filthy and defiling, in the African worldview, the reproductive organs, especially the womb, are correctly revered as the storehouses of existence.

Traditional African spiritual systems do not recognize an inherently evil entity or original sin; consequently, the Christian devil, a dubious construct at best, makes no sense and does not exist in the traditional African worldview which is centered on reciprocity, balance, and the acquisition and purposeful application of knowledge. Especially hypocritical and unconscionable is the idea that no matter the heinous acts and atrocities one has committed, one can enter paradise as long as one professes certain beliefs and/or receives a sprinkling of certain waters immediately prior to death. Because of the vast differences in worldviews and Christianity's stunning contradictions, early African Americans made important revisions to the religious concepts Caucasians introduced them to.

The first Deity that Africans restyled was the Christian God. When reading or hearing African American orature, one encounters a God who has the trappings of the Christian Deity but who is fully at one with the Africana community and who shares its ethnicity, language, and mores. The African American God's consonance with his Africana community is logical in that the archetypal reference for the African American God is the Yoruba Creator, Olódùmarè. Both Deities are generous and give Earth's inhabitants exactly what they ask for. Both Gods also consistently overlook and forget things and regularly go back and refashion their creations—often at the creations' demand. Africana Gods are not omniscient, omnipotent, and infallible, and it is essential that they are not because the spaces they leave in the work of creation facilitate the proliferation and multiplication of divinity in human beings and in flora, fauna, and the Earth, as well.

As is depicted in the ęsę Ifá (Yoruba divination verses) and in African American orature (much of which finds its source in the ęsę Ifá and other forms of African orature[1]), Olódùmarè and the African American God both create entities who initially do not appear to fit properly into the Grand Design, but the very reason the design is grand is because, like Africana orature, it is malleable and open to rewrites, revisions, repositioning, deletions, and additions. Ole Maker is also not too proud to stand a straightening. In the orature recorded in Zora Neale Hurston's *Mules and Men*, God struggles three days and nights to catch a porpoise that swims too fast; he is unable to catch the Jew who steals the soul-piece; and because he creates snakes without a system of defense, God must revise his work twice.[2] Similarly, in the ęsę Ifá recorded by C. Osamaro Ibie in *Ifism: The Complete Works of Orunmila*, Olódùmarè forgets to give Boa the ability to defend himself and must revise his efforts, and Olódùmarè is unable to stop Ejioko from stealing the symbol of a king, and Ejioko is able to "prosper immensely on earth" with the stolen icon.[3] Both God and Olódùmarè are described as leaving women defenseless and later assisting in their supreme empowerment.[4] In all of these instances and more, the "mistakes" of these Africana Gods provide their creations with the opportunities and abilities to attain complete self-actualization and divine manifestation by directing their own destinies. When God tells Brer Rabbit that from the 1960s to 1970s he "ain't gon' be nowhere to be found" and he "ain't answering no prayers during that time,"[5] it is clear that God expects Africana peoples to be their own Gods, design their own destinies, and raise their own hell as necessary.

The devil also received a spiritual and cultural makeover. In a holistic worldview, one must learn from trials and tribulations, including and especially those that are self-generated. When human beings can lay blame on an inherently evil scapegoat, they will be disinclined self-educate, self-evaluate, and self-correct. Because belief in the Christian concept of the devil makes it impossible for human beings to undertake the necessary effort to become Gods, African Americans infused the empty devil construct with the tricksterian properties of Èṣù Ęlęgbà and other African Trickster Gods; their own wit, intelligence and cunning; and their holistic worldview. Displaced Africans transformed the concept of "the devil" into Devil, a master trickster. Rather than being feared and shunned or blamed for everything, Devil is a favorite and a hero who is sought out for card games, contests of strength, and intellectual challenges because he is the standard by which one can measure one's divine and intellectual development: If one can out-trick the Trickster, one's skills are highly evolved indeed.[6]

Devil plays an integral part in African American ontology and numinosity, and his contributions impart social, gender, and spiritual balance.[7] Extolling Devil's virtues in *The Sanctified Church*, Hurston avers that he "can outsmart everyone but Jack [also known as John]. *God is absolutely no match for him.* [Devil] is good-natured and full of humor. The sort of person one may count on to help out in any difficulty."[8] Hurston's assessment of Devil's relationship with God points directly to Africans' ability to expand a narrow and parochial ethos to fit their flexible, expansive, holistic one. In Africana orature, Devil and God enjoy a congenial relationship as they create animals together and exchange presents.[9] Devil was even astute enough to give the world the linguistic gift of "unh hunh."[10] While God often speaks to Devil with an air of condescension, it is Devil's actions, words, and creations that give God and humanity new concepts to ponder and richer arcs of expression to explore: This why God is "no match" for him.

Displaced Africans needed Deities and philosophies that were logical, complex, rich, and relevant, and rather than pray that the oppressors' Deities would miraculously reverse their static, racist, and stultifying positions and become warriors, liberators, and political strategists on their behalves, enslaved Africans reached within themselves, into the deep and inexhaustible pot of divinity and creativity, and found infinite materials to invoke, create, or become the Gods they needed. With the power to name and claim their destinies bursting from their souls, African Americans undertook their most important work—the creation of a ubiquitous God to whom they would have immediate and unlimited access in the horrific lands of slavery. The Deity would have to be innocuous to the oppressor and charming enough to put his rabid mind at ease. This God would have to positively influence everything and everyone. Using their command of power and paradox, the beings who were not even considered human in America used their oppressors' ignorance and the cloak of anonymity to create the most powerful God of all—the collective communal Self who is known as High John the Conqueror and who also goes by the deceptively simple name "John."

High John the Conqueror stands at the crossroads of holistic African technology, orature and literature (including biographies, folktales, songs), and manifest human divinity. High John is able to unify these seemingly disparate forms and forces because he is, has, and informs all of them. Very much an ancient Nubian God returned, High John the

Conqueror takes any of many forms. He is a root of multifold spiritual-technological power; he is the subject of one of the world's richest and most diverse libraries of lore; and he is a God who is composed of every Africana man and woman forced to draw breath in America. If it were possible to amalgamate and distil all of the wonder workers and the wondrous works of chapter one, the result would be High John the Conqueror.

The Conqueror's role as a repository of African American numinosity where biographies of Divinities are stored and disseminated is of the utmost importance, for the tricksterian skills, wisdom, and wit he displays are not those of one man but of a vast Pan-African nation. The "tales" that feature John include fictionalized accounts of historical events, modified ancient African orature (including ęsę Ifá), and uniquely African American folktales. High John the Conqueror is able to perform impossible feats for the Devil, con Ole Massa out of shoats and financial fortunes, and convince the oppressor to free all Africans and then kill himself because John's successes are those of an ancient porpoise, a resourceful mother in Mississippi, a cunning father in Alabama, a Maroon community in South Carolina, and any number of African Gods who have always used the trials, triumphs, and tribulations of their earthly existences to hone, recharge, and modify their inherent divinity. John was essential to enslaved and impoverished African Americans not merely as a figure to inspire or emulate but as a reflection of the best possible Self—the magnificent diversity of Divinity. John is much more than a folk hero, High John the Conqueror is the heroic folks themselves.

Some of the most significant volumes in the African American cultural library are the "John and Massa" tales. While there are customs, events, and motifs that were retained from Continental lore and while African orature has a strong tradition of critiquing and castigating oppressive and nearsighted rulers, the majority of the "John and Massa" tales are born of the sufferings, triumphs, oppressions, and liberations experienced by Africans dislocated in America. The fact that there is no extensive body of continental African orature dedicated to enslaved peoples routinely outwitting and outshining their oppressors helps elucidate some of the differences between American chattel slavery and forms of African debt and caste systems.

While the majority of the "John and Massa" tales are African American creations, John is indeed African. A comprehensive study of etymology elucidates John's Continental origins. While from a Eurocentric perspective, "John" would be defined as a masculine name of Hebrew origin and "Massa" appears to be a truncation of Master, "John" and "Massa" are two of many notable contributions from the Wolof and Mande languages of West Africa.

There are numerous African words presently in use in American English, and Joseph Holloway and Winifred K. Vass' *The African Heritage of American English* offers an impressive list that includes such words as booty, poontang, juke, bukrah, moola, jiffy, bamboozle, donie, and jon and massa, among many others. The Mande peoples, who are geographical and cultural neighbors of the Wolof, call their rulers *Masa* or *Mansa*. Apropos this discussion of divine humanity, the title Mansa denotes a ruler who is both human and divine.[11] The Mande peoples enslaved in the United States were cognizant of the similarity between the title Mansa and the noun "master." The convergence of meanings, coupled with the fact that some enslavers made the term "master" exclusive to themselves, forbidding Africans to use the term master for God, made "massa" a smooth verbal and social fit. For the enslaved African to style "massa" as the dominating authority figure was logical; taking "jon" from disenfranchised enslaved person to master of African language, culture, destiny, and existence was revolutionary.

Rather than a proper noun, "John" in the African American lexicon is derived from the Wolof terms *jon* and *jaam*, both of which mean "slave."[12] In African America, "jaam" means a boisterous revel or a celebration. Jaam is the source of the African American verb "jam," meaning to get on down, and the noun "jam," signifying a favorite song. The Wolof term for freeperson is *jaambuur*, and this is the origin of the word "jamboree." Before the term was adopted by boy scouts, jamborees signified the plantation dances organized by enslaved Africans and the Juneteenth festivals that Africans held to celebrate their freedom.[13] To understand the development of jaam is to truly comprehend the power of the African ethos, because the jaam, the most downtrodden members of society, would come together in jaam sessions that involved using the power of words and music to invoke ancestors and Gods for freedom and elevation. Once enslaved Africans gained their freedom, the jaam sessions became *jam* sessions where liberated jaam gave rebirth to indigenous African American musical genres such as jazz, blues, rap, and rock and roll which helped them better navigate the oppression wrought by neoslavery and also chronicle their tragedies and triumphs. Most significantly, as evidence of their inherent power and divinity, the jaam recreated themselves as John.

Similar to the Wolof words "jaam" and "jon," the African American concept of "John" includes both genders. In African America, women did not resign themselves to merely hearing and repeating the exploits of John; they were active agents who also incorporated their experiences into the revolutionary storehouse of John. John's skills, abilities, and powers have as many female as male sources as the entire community freely added to and accessed the collective pot of power that is High John.

Lawrence Levine's *Black Culture and Black Consciousness: Afro-American Folk Thought from Slavery to Freedom* includes a testimony that provides a clear example of the ease with which historical events can become secularized and attributed to the wisdom and wiles of John. Josie Jordan's mother told her about enslaved Africans who were starving and suffering because of a greedy enslaver. On the morning of the annual butchering of hogs, the heartless plantation owner was awakened by the wailing and weeping of enslaved Africans who exclaimed that all the hogs had died of a mysterious disease called "malitis." The oppressor figured that the African constitution could survive whatever maladies malitis might cause and ordered the diseased hogs be butchered, smoked, salted, and served to the enslaved Africans that year. The oppressor and his family could easily make do with beef and chicken. Jordan's mother then revealed the origin of malitis: When one of "the strongest Negroes" awoke before dawn and tapped those hogs between their eyes with a mallet, "malitis set in mighty quick."[14]

The enslaved Africans on this plantation were able to literally eat "high on the hog"—enjoying chops, tenderloin, rump roast, and ham hocks—instead of struggling to choke down the innards and offal that Africans were usually allotted. What is more, with Africans capitalizing on their ability to encode revolutionary and secularize historical events, diseases like malitis could become pandemic and strike from plantation to plantation and feed chuckling multitudes. All one need do is substitute "John" for "the strongest [Negro]" and a revolutionary strategy takes on the appearance of a harmless folktale. Through African wisdom systems and knowledge sharing, the simple and plantation-approved act of telling folktales offered ample opportunities to share tactics for liberation and elevation.

The development of John's identity as humorist, conjurer, master of destinies, and force superior to God and kissing kin with the Africana-constructed Devil is also evident in the song "Promises of Freedom," which is a revolutionary treatise in disguise:

> My ole Mistiss promise me,
> W'en she died, she'd set me free,
> She lived so long dat 'er head got bal',
> An' she give out'n de notion a-dyin' at all.
>
> My ole Mistiss say to me:
> "Sambo, I'se gwine ter set you free."

[But] w'en dat head git slick an' bal',
De Lawd couldn't a' killed 'er wid a big green maul.

My ole Mistiss never die,
Wid' er nose all hooked an' skin all dry.
But my ole Miss, she's somehow gone,
An' she lef' Uncle Sambo a-hillin' up co'n.

Ole Mosser lakwise promise me,
W'en he died, he's set me free.
But ole Mosser go an' make his will
Fer to leave me a-plowin' ole Beck still.

Yes, my ole Mosser promise me;
But "his papers" didn't leave me free.
A doze of pizen he'ped 'm along.
May de Devil [p]reach 'is funer'l song.[15]

In this orature it is not the promises that are relevant; such duplicity on the part of oppressors was standard. It is the longevity of the female enslaver that is baffling. Even "de Lawd" armed with a cudgel, cannot kill her! This is a powerful critique of the Christian God and prayers to him. Indeed the plantation mistress does not die; she just evils away but leaves "Uncle Sambo" enslaved. Sambo learns from the lesson Mistiss teaches him, and rather than trust Mosser to issue him a paper freedom, he utilizes his knowledge of flora and poisons his oppressor. After finding liberating knowledge, resources, and strength within, Sambo takes the initiative to invoke the Devil so that he can prepare for Mosser a proper place in the afterlife. Although the term "Sambo" is associated with racist buffoonery in America, Sambo is a proper name of both the Wolof and Hausa peoples of West Africa.[16] Boasting a self-effacing tricksterian methodology identical to that of High John, Sambo emerges as a revolutionary with a repertoire so complete that everything from his name to his song camouflages and encodes power.

As is apparent in Seven African Powers products, the spiritual wares of botanicas, and the shrines to Ṣàngó, Ògún, and Yemọja that grace African American homes, graves, and businesses, many dislocated Africans invoked the Òrìṣà outright. And while many converted to organized religions, many more consciously and unconsciously syncretized Christianity with their African spiritual systems. But the force that transcended all religions, ideologies, and doctrines is High John the

Conqueror. As a "character" conveniently ensconced in the "secular" realm, Africans could safely catalog, access, and add to a vast library of liberating tools and skills. Caucasians saw Africana orature as harmless humor; indeed, Hurston describes the tales as "big ole lies." But High John comprises the collective character and characteristics (ìwà) and divinity of African identity. So while Caucasian American minds were locked by their dichotomous concepts of the secular and the sacred, Africans had created a new God who was at once very African and every African.

Hurston captures the mutability and mastery of John's many manifestations in her essay "High John de Conquer," which is included in *The Sanctified Church*. Hurston's power as an authorizing agent is clear in her exposition for she reaches within herself, grasps the signifying power of the Ancients, and recreates High John the Conqueror's origin and his origin text:

> He had come from Africa. He came walking on the waves of sound. Then he took on flesh after he got here. The sea captains of ships knew that they brought slaves in their ships. They knew about those black bodies huddled down there in the middle passage, being hauled across the waters to helplessness. John de Conquer was walking the very winds that filled the sails of the ships. He followed over them like the albatross.[17]

In the manner of an iyaláwo reciting an ęsę Ifá, Hurston reveals John to be the spiritual and physical twin of Ọ̀rọ̀, Power of the Word, which arrived on Earth groaning with sound and throbbing with power because it was filled with ọgbọ́n (wisdom), ìmọ̀ (knowledge), and òye (understanding).[18] Enslaved Africans may have been dislocated, weighted with chains, and decorated with whip scars, but they carried within their sacred beings the components of Ọ̀rọ̀ which are the keys to liberation, elevation, and deification.

Yoruba cosmology holds that there are 600 + 1 Òrìṣà: 400 Gods on the right, 200 Gods on the left, and one that, according to Hurston and Yoruba wisdom-keepers, indicates the ability to create another God when necessary.[19] One could posit that Èṣù Ẹlẹ́gbà, Divine Linguist, Mediator, Trickster; guardian of àṣę; and Determiner of Destinies, compiled the Àję́, àṣę, ìwà, and orí of the 600 Yoruba Gods, including Ṣàngó, Ògún, Yemọja, Ọbalúayé, Ìyàmi Òṣòròngà, and welcomed that of other African Gods, such as Ausar, Mani, Ast, Olisabuluwa, Nzambi, and Anyanwu, and combined that diverse Pan-African power to create High John the Conqueror who, like many of his divine siblings, is cloaked in human garb and bursting with numinosity. Hurston further elucidates the conqueror's origin:

High John de Conquer came to be a man, and a mighty man at that. But he was not a natural man in the beginning. First off, he was a whisper, a will to hope, a wish to find something worthy of laughter and song. Then the whisper put on flesh. His footsteps sounded across the world in a low but musical rhythm as if the world he walked on was a singing-drum. . . . High John de Conquer was a man in full, and had come to live and work on the plantations, and all the slave folks knew him in the flesh.[20]

Enslaved Africans knew John intimately because they were him. Consequently, High John the Conqueror lived wherever Africana people did:

Old Massa couldn't know, of course, but High John de Conquer was there walking his plantation like a natural man. He was treading the sweat-flavored clods of the plantation, crushing out his drum tunes, and giving out secret laughter. He walked on the winds and moved fast. Maybe he was in Texas when the lash fell on a slave in Alabama, but before the blood was dry on the back he was there. A faint pulsing of a drum like a goat-skin stretched over a heart, that came nearer and closer, then somebody in the saddened quarters would feel like laughing, and say, "Now, High John de Conquer, Old Massa couldn't get the best of him. That old John was a case!" Then everybody sat up and began to smile.[21]

High John heals, comforts, and protects. He uplifts and inspires his enslaved kin who, were it not for his abiding presence, might have chosen to forego this life for the next.

An important aspect of High John's genius is his malleability. John not only boasts expert knowledge of flora and fauna, he *is* the flora and fauna. In addition to being a God, High John the Conqueror is also the root of the *Ipomoea jalapa* plant. The bearer of this root can escape any scrape and can wield power to be more than a conqueror in any situation. As fauna, John enjoys taking the forms of those who are most vulnerable and defenseless, such as Signifying Monkeys and Brother Rabbits, but who rule the animal kingdom with their superior intellect:

Old Massa met our hope-bringer all right, but when Old Massa met him, he was not going by his right name. He was traveling, and touristing around the plantations as the laugh-provoking Brer Rabbit. So Old Massa and Old Miss and their young ones laughed with and at Brer Rabbit and wished him well. And all the time, there was High John de Conquer playing his tricks of making a way out of no-way. Hitting a straight lick with a crooked stick. Winning the jack pot with no other stake but a laugh. Fighting a mighty battle without outside-showing force, and winning his war from within. Really winning in a permanent way, for he was winning with the soul of the black man whole and free.[22]

Hurston stresses the fact that High John the Conqueror represents Africana peoples' inherently divine and liberated state of existence. Hurston also avers that while High John may have risen to prominence on the plantation, his origin, like that of Africana peoples, is not in slavery and oppression. High John is an Eternal Immortal who Hurston finds is descended from "the 'Be' class. Be here when the ruthless man comes and be here when he is gone."[23] What is more, rather than support the heinous institution of slavery like Jewish, Christian, and Muslim Gods, scriptures, surahs, and prophets, John and the Africana Gods are unwavering opponents of slavery: "John knew that it is written where it cannot be erased, that nothing shall live on human flesh and prosper. Old Maker said that before He made any more sayings."[24] John and Ole Maker are clearly very different Divinities from the Gods of organized religions.[24]

The chosen people bearing wisdom teeth from the East and boasting gleaming souls, Africana peoples *are* time, the essence of *be*-ing. Consequently, High John does not indoctrinate his kin with lessons about how to be good slaves; he re-members his progeny to the truth of their inherent divinity so that they can enjoy, not merely freedom, but the numinescence that is their birthright.

The diverse ways in which High John overcame the seemingly insurmountable odds posed by slavery are remarkable and remarkably funny, and some of his richest and most humorous exploits are included in Hurston's *Mules and Men*. An orature titled "Ole Massa and John Who Wanted to Go to Heaven" finds John praying every night for God to descend and take him to heaven so that he can be free of Massa and soul-crushing oppression. This type of prayer is certainly understandable given the conditions to which Africana people were subjected. However, it is not John's orí to escape through prayer, for to whom does God pray? After hearing John's prayer, Massa dresses up in a sheet to adopt the identity of a heavenly "master" and to terrorize John (this orature may lend insight as to the origin of the Ku Klux Klan and its costumes).

Massa may have sheets but John has the advantage of inherent divinity. When numinosity is coupled with intelligence, cunning, and speed, High John cannot be beaten. With the masquerading oppressor completely unawares, John takes off running. When her child asks if God can catch John, John's wife Liza exclaims, "Shet yo' mouf, talkin' foolishness! .... You know de Lawd can't outrun yo' pappy—specially when he's barefooted at dat."[26]

While John appears to have joined ranks with the porpoise who could outrun God, John is outrunning the Caucasian myth of God; which is a rather easy feat to accomplish. Indeed, it is not John's warp speed but his self-effacement that is the key to his success in this orature. While John heaps effusive glories on the egos of both of his oppressors (Massa and Massa's master) and swaddles himself in the humility of the unworthy, he is preparing to show and prove his divinity before the imposter. By outwitting and outrunning his oppressors, John lays bare the fallacies of the Christian God's claims of omniscience and omnipotence, and he debunks the myths of "white superiority" and "black inferiority."

In "Praying for Rain," John, like his Africana progenitors and peers, shows himself to be knowledgeable of the spiritual language and power necessary to cuss up a storm. John S. Mbiti refers to rainmakers and rainstoppers as being of supreme importance in African societies because they "know the words of God . . . that is their work."[27] With his linguistic virtuosity, John can easily summon storms, and because his Ọ̀rọ̀ is layered with power, John uses his prayer to signify, once again, on both Massa and Massa's master. Rather than risk losing his tongue by using it to invoke Òrìṣà whose worship has been banned, John cloaks his message in his oppressor's arrogance:

> Lord, first thing I want you to understand that this ain't no nigger talking to you. This is a white man and I want you to hear me. Pay some attention to me. I don't worry and bother you all the time like these niggers . . . so when I do ask a favor, I want it granted. Now, Lord, we want some rain. Our crops is all burning up and we'd like a little rain. But I don't mean for you to come in a hell of a storm like you did last year—kicking up racket like niggers at a barbecue. I want you to come calm and easy. Now, another thing, Lord, I want to speak about. Don't let the niggers be as sassy as they have been in the past. Keep 'em in their places, Lord, Amen.[28]

John's prayer is one of pure and potent African signifying.

The Africana God and Olódùmarè welcome interaction with their creations, and the exchanges are mutually respectful and bespeak equality. These African Gods have nothing in common with the Deity Massa reveres. The Caucasian God is identical to Massa but boasts "a heap more hair," as Shug Avery of *The Color Purple* observes.[29] With masterful encoding and signifying, including a nod to his "sassy" self,

John highlights the dubious status of the Caucasian God and challenges his power with language that a superior would use when addressing an inferior. John's prayer will result in a storm, just as it did the year before. It may even rain like Africans at a jamboree and precipitate Africans who can rest and act sad about water-ruined crops.

One of the most popular religious sentiments is that there is only one God but different peoples and cultures have different names for that being. As is evident in "Praying for Rain" and many other orature, not to mention various cosmologies, this was not a belief held by dislocated Africans or their oppressors. "The First Colored Man in Heaven" offers an illuminating critique of the Caucasian God. John tricks his way into heaven and is allowed to stay only because the Caucasian God is afraid that if John's cavorting is disturbed he may destroy something: "The Lord said . . . 'Just leave that nigger alone before he tear up heaven.'"[30] Such portraits of the Christian heaven reveal what awaited the mentally enslaved African who prayed to the God of the oppressor and longed sojourn in his heaven. This is why an elder named Silas of Virginia interrupted a racist pastor's sermon to inquire, "Is us slaves gonna be free in Heaven?"[31] With this query, such maxims as the White man's heaven is the Black man's hell come to mind. John and Silas use humor and righteous outrage, respectively, to remind their communities not to be misled or deceived.

Another orature that offers a resounding critique of Christianity while remaining firmly grounded in Yoruba ontology and cosmology is the biography of Big Sixteen, who is a reserved and reticent manifestation of John. His name reflects the facts that he wears size sixteen shoes and is huge. Big Sixteen's biographers could have designated his size with any digits, but sixteen has spiritual significance. Sixteen is the prime number of Ifá: sixteen cowries or palm nuts are used to divine; sixteen is the number of roads of worship for Ọbàtálá; Àjẹ́ usher sunrise and sunset into being while meeting at the crossroads of sixteen roads and holding sixteen long livers or sixteen long Ẹdan, both of which signify their control over time, destiny, and humanity.[32]

Big Sixteen's long liver and cosmic umbilical cord are connected to those of an entity named Father of the Gods Who Could Do Everything In This World (Father of the Gods), who is the protagonist of Amos Tutuola's *The Palm-Wine Drinkard*. With a few exceptions,[33] most academics ignore the protagonist's name and refer to him as The Palm-Wine Drinkard, this is despite the facts that his name fuels the plot of the narrative and that his identity and power as a "god and juju man" are essential to his survival and success.[34] With Father of the Gods we have a clear example of an African man who is fully manifesting his divinity and an academic community that refuses to acknowledge his numinosity and chooses to focus on the God's mundane enjoyments—drinking palm wine—instead. Òrìṣà Ọbàtálá learned a powerful lesson through the consumption of palm wine and so too does the Father of the Gods.

Father of the Gods' search for his palm wine tapper leads him to God who demands Father of the Gods prove that he is as powerful as his name by completing seemingly impossible tasks. The relationship between God and Father of the Gods provides a rich example of the balance, interplay, and exchanges among Gods in the holistic African worldview. In this meeting of two Gods, Father of the Gods, as his name confirms, is God's superior in every way, including spiritual prowess, wisdom, and technology. While Father of the Gods could easily scoff at God's challenges and refuse to show and prove his divinity, Father of the Gods relishes the opportunity to match skills, wits, and wills because by doing so he verifies and strengthens his powers and acquires new wisdom. The works of the Gods and their passion for wisdom acquisition are unending. By contrast, while the challenges that Massa gives Big Sixteen are similar to those that Father of the Gods accomplishes, Massa's tasks, including asking Big Sixteen to capture Devil, are rooted in Massa's awe of Big Sixteen's over-abundant divinity. Massa is not part of the divine continuum.

Important differences are also evident in the afterlives of Big Sixteen and Father of the Gods. While Father of the Gods moves freely between the material and spiritual realms, when Big Sixteen dies and goes to heaven, he is denied admittance because he has too much power and glory. Big Sixteen goes to hell for lodging, and while Devil's wife refuses to allow the man who killed her husband to enter her domain, the spirit of African hospitality moves her to offer a compromise and a gift: "Here, take dis hot coal and g'wan off and start you a hell uh yo' own."[35] With his gift, Big Sixteen ends his association with Father of the Gods and begins his association with Death. Father of the Gods reveals, "Since the day that I had brought Death out from his house, he has no permanent place to dwell or stay, and we are hearing his name about in the world."[36] Big Sixteen is in a similar predicament: "When you see a Jack O'Lantern in de woods at night you know it's Big Sixteen wid his piece of fire lookin' for a place to go."[37] Jack O'Lanterns are the colorful flames that dance in swampy phosphorous-rich areas at night. With his final manifestation, Big Sixteen becomes the eternal fire-shine of the divine.

While John and his alter egos, Jack and Big Sixteen, are known for their cunning, wit, and cool dispositions, it is important to remember that these Gods are Nathaniel Turners, Boukmans, Sojourner Truths, Harriet

Tubmans, and Jean-Jacques Dessalines: They are liberators. In African American orature, as in reality, it is not Jesus, Massa, or Abraham Lincoln who freed enslaved Africans: The liberator is the Africana collective also known as High John the Conqueror. This is confirmed in such orature as "Ah'll Beatcher Makin' Money," "Member Youse a Nigger," and "The Fortune Teller/How the Negroes Got Their Freedom."[38] The roles that African Americans played in their liberation are also evident in the routinely overlooked battles they fought against oppression long before, during, and long after the Civil War.

Hurston reveals that when slavery was abolished, "High John de Conquer went back to Africa," but he left his power in the High John the Conqueror root: "Possess that root, and he can be summoned any time."[39] High John the Conqueror Root is easily the most esteemed tool in African American pharmacopoeia; and as it summons High John's eternal power, the root may be singing in KiKongo language: "According to Kongo mythology, the very first nkisi given to man by God was Funza, distributor of all minkisi, himself incarnate in unusual twisted root formations."[40] Intricately twisted roots are repositories of the profound powers that make medicines, mojos, and or tobies supremely potent. Perhaps as a testament to its strength, dried John the Conqueror Root is said to resemble Africana testicles. High John also funneled an aspect of his power into the root of the galangal plant which is called Little John to Chew and is used for success in legal matters. Perhaps the most popular actualization of the memory and activation of the power of High John is the custom of carrying a rabbit's foot for good luck, which, like so many African customs and cultural outgrowths—especially those involving rabbits (Bugs Bunny and the Trix cereal rabbit come immediately to mind)—was co-opted by Caucasian capitalists.

High John de Conqueror boasts many of the divine technologies and powers that I discuss in chapter one, including flight, invisibility, shape-shifting, rainmaking, and splitting the self into multiple selves. While the Òrò of the Gods is his trademark, he also scampers in signifying fauna, and his testicular flora steadily inseminate the Earth. High John is the Liberator, the Truth, the Answer. Melding all categories, embracing both genders, and defying definitions, He is She is God. High John the Conqueror represents African America's most politically, culturally, and spiritually astute act of neo-Òrìṣà re-creation and worship, and High John is a Deity of Reciprocity. Just as everyone contributes to and takes from the pot of wisdom that is High John, so too are all community members able to access numinosity and become conquering Gods in their own rights.

"I Found God In Myself"[41]

The more one reads the writing of Zora Neale Hurston the more one comes to appreciate the insight, depth, and wisdom of her lifework. In her autobiography, *Dust Tracks on a Road*, Hurston includes a chapter titled "Religion" that elucidates her personal path to the power of High John and to the recognition of the Deity of the Self. As a child, Hurston had no formal education in African philosophy, but she did have the intelligence to question the inconsistencies in Christianity. She pondered the contradictory concept of sin that claimed on one hand that "Christ died to save the world from sin" and on the other that "people were prone to sin, that they sinned with every breath they drew."[42] Hurston also questioned the paradoxical Christian articulation of death, for if Jesus' execution resulted in everlasting life, why did death cause such anguish and lamentation? When Hurston asked her father, who was a pastor, and his colleagues about these issues, they subjected her to religious terrorism. She stopped voicing her doubts and concerns aloud, but Hurston continued critically analyzing religion:

> Neither could I understand the passionate declarations of love for a being that nobody could see. Your family, your puppy, and the new bull-calf, yes. But a spirit away off who found fault with everybody all the time, that was more than I could fathom. When I was asked if I loved God, I always said yes because I knew that that was the thing I was supposed to say. It was a guilty secret with me for a long time.[43]

The invisible, fault finding, implacable God to whom Hurston refers is the Christian God, not the folksy Olódùmarèan Deity who peppers the pages of *Mules and Men* with wit, humor, mistakes, and excuses and who resembles her aptly named father, John, as well as Hurston, herself. While Hurston found wisdom, power, and culture reflected in the orature of the Ancients, she could find neither herself nor any logic in Christianity.

Hurston was not able to find the answers to her queries in the church or its elders, so she went inside of herself and into the world in search of truth. She shares what she found in a stunning treatise:

> As for me, I do not pretend to read God's mind. If He has a plan of the Universe worked out to the smallest detail, it would be folly for me to presume to get down on my knees and attempt to revise it. That, to me, seems the highest form of sacrilege. So I do not pray. I

accept the means at my disposal for working out my destiny. It seems to me that I have been given a mind and will-power for that very purpose. I do not expect God to single me out and grant me advantages over my fellow men. Prayer is for those who need it. Prayer seems to me a cry of weakness, and an attempt to avoid, by trickery, the rules of the game as laid down. I do not choose to admit weakness. I accept the challenge of responsibility. Life, as it is, does not frighten me, since I have made my peace with the universe as I find it, and bow to its laws. . . . It seems to me that organized creeds are collections of words around a wish. I feel no need for such. . . . Somebody else may have my rapturous glance at the archangels. The springing of the yellow line of morning out of the misty deep dawn is glory enough for me. I know that nothing is destructible; things merely change form. When the consciousness we know as life ceases, I know that I shall still be part and parcel of the world. I was a part before the sun rolled into shape and burst forth in the glory of change. I was, when the earth was hurled out from its fiery rim. I shall return with the earth to Father Sun, and still exist in substance when the sun has lost its fire, and disintegrated in infinity to perhaps become a part of the whirling rubble of space. Why fear? The stuff of my being is matter, ever changing, ever moving, but never lost; so what need of denominations and creeds to deny myself the comfort of all my fellow men? The wide belt of the universe has no need for finger-rings. I am one with the infinite and need no other assurance.[44]

Hurston begins her elucidation with a reassuring, for the Christian, acknowledgement of "God" and "His" infinite wisdom and master plan. But she deftly undercuts his power with her own. Hurston describes herself as another manifestation of High John who is making her own ways out of no way and doing the impossible with elegance. As a divine and empowered being, Hurston does not fear life because she is Life. She is equipped with the skills to manifest her destiny—or, to be plain, she is God. Hurston does not pray because she is the answer to her prayers. She has no fear of death because in the Africana worldview there is no death. In full possession of what Toni Morrison calls "ancient properties,"[45] and in complete harmony with her Ba and Ka, Hurston was enjoying her immortality long before her body took its last breath. Decades before she became a celebrated canonized literary icon, Hurston knew she was divine.

Following the directive of High John the Conqueror, Hurston used her literary genius to illuminate the power of the God within for all. The majority of Hurston's publications, especially *Mules and Men*, can and should be read as manuals for activating and actualizing one's divinity.

Hurston's literature certainly served that purpose for her. She did not merely record orature and observe rituals; she strode the moonlit paths to the crossroads, bared her soul to the Cosmos, and earned the crowns of the Gods. Hurston's recognition of her divinity and her embracing the weighty responsibilities that come with that acknowledgement was an organic personal and literary articulation of ontological reality with deep African American roots.

August Wilson, master playwright and dramaturgical genius, makes it clear: "When you look in the mirror, you should see your god. If you don't, then you have the wrong god."[36] Renowned historian John Henrik Clarke makes the same point and adds that if the God you envision looks like another people, you are the spiritual prisoner of those people.[47] The wisdom that Wilson, Clarke, and others were sharing in the 1980s and 1990s extends formally at least as far back as 1900. The first documented instance of an African American formally embracing his divinity was in 1900 when Samuel H. Morris' theological study led him to the realization that he was "God in a body."[48] His revelations and pontifications earned the man called Father Eternal many followers, but his most well-known acolyte is the aptly named Father Divine.

Father Divine was named George Baker, Jr. when he was born in 1876 in Rockville, Maryland. When he met Father Eternal, Baker became his divine son. Father Eternal adopted the title "Father Jehovia, God in the Fathership Degree," and while under Jehovia's tutelage, Baker was "Messenger, God in the Sonship Degree."[49] The duo became a trinity when John A. Hickerson, also known as "Reverend Bishop Saint John the Vine," joined their ministry. The trio that was enlightened and empowered by I John 4:15 parted company in 1912. That God, Messenger, and Bishop dissolved their union is not surprising. Each man read the Bible and found a Divinity-reflecting mirror therein.

Father Divine embarked on a mission to use his gift to preach women's empowerment.[50] As is the case for nearly every Africana person who openly acknowledges his or her divinity, Father Divine was declared insane. However, his flock was unwavering in their support, and when asked what Father Divine's "real" name was, his followers confirmed, "[H]e ain't named nothing but God!"[51]

While many early Gods found eager audiences in the North, the southern soil of Georgia was especially fecund for divinity. In 1899 Dupont Bell acknowledged that he was the "son of God," and founded a movement in Savannah, Georgia.[52] George Hurley of Reynolds, Georgia is especially significant because he used a holistic approach to infuse the power of divinity within the people. Perhaps inspired by the enslavement, subjugation, rape, and, later, glorification of the biblical Hagar, who

Hurston, among others, recognizes as the grand progenitor of Africana peoples,[53] Hurley founded the Universal Hagar's Spiritual Church (UHSC) in 1923, and the church is thriving at the time of this publication. Hurley introduced the masses to his divinity as well as to their own. He was revered as "God Incarnate" and the "black God of this Age," and Hurley taught his followers that they were "minor gods and goddesses."[54] Hurley led his parishioners to embrace Ethiopian as their ethnic identity and to understand their biblical and historical heritage as the "original Hebrews and creators of civilization."[55]

As God Incarnate, it is only fitting that Hurley crafted commandments to fit the needs of his world. His commandments include the following directives:

> Thou shall believe in Spirit (God) within matter.
> Thou shall ignore a sky heaven for happiness and a downward hell for human punishment.
> Thou shall believe in heaven and hell here on earth.
> Thou shall believe in what you sow, you shall also reap.
> Thou shall believe that the Ethiopians and all nations will rule the world in righteousness.
> Thou shall not pray for God to bless your enemies.
> Thou shall ask God to give you power to overcome them. Thou shall believe that our relatives and friends whose [spirits]
>   have departed from their bodies, are within our own bodies to help us overcome all difficulties in life.[56]

Perhaps the only truly holy doctrine is one that is flexible enough to encompass the changes, discoveries, inventions, and innovations of each age. The UHSC displays not only the flexibility of the Divine, but through its commandments it champions ancient African principles, such as recognizing the curvilinear nature and work of humanodivinity.

The only way that human beings can manifest their inherent numinosity is if they know, understand, and love themselves. Christian Caucasian oppressors commanded that the people that they had raped, enslaved, colonized, exiled, disenfranchised, and mutilated love their enemies because those oppressors stood to reap immense and eternal benefits from that love. The UHSC is cognizant that the people who invest in their enemies the love that they should be investing in themselves and their progeny, their communities, their educations, and their nations, are a damned people. Likewise, the people who allow their enemies to choose their heroes, leaders, and ways of life for them are a demolished people. With their commandments, the UHSC offers not indoctrination but wisdom to be applied for holistic Africana liberation and elevation in this lifetime.

The UHSC's multipoint creed adds further definition and dimension to its commandments and emphasizes the holistic nature of the organization:

> WE BELIEVE that God is Spirit.
> WE BELIEVE that our bodies are matter, and a dwelling place for God.
> WE BELIEVE that man is spirit just like God.
> WE BELIEVE that man is the name given by God to His creation (man).
> WE BELIEVE our real selves are God (spirit) clothed with matter (body).
> WE BELIEVE that all life is God.
> ....
> WE BELIEVE that whatsoever good we need is within us at all times.
> WE BELIEVE that when we have realized Christ we can draw all good from within us.
> WE BELIEVE that the Christ is the wisdom and power of God.
> ....
> WE BELIEVE in mental telepathy and thought force.
> WE BELIEVE that thoughts are spirit and to think of a thing is the prophecy of its fulfillment.
> WE BELIEVE that all men are equal regardless of their color.[57]

The principles outlined in the creed aver that "Christ" is a degree of wisdom and a state of mind that human beings can attain and be empowered by. The UHSC's definition of God is especially relevant for, rather than a supernatural or invisible being or force, God is defined as "our real selves" and "all life." Human beings, flora and fauna, molecules, ions, and atoms that are unseen and often unappreciated; the planets, nebula, and galaxies of the Cosmos, all this and much more constitute God.

The UHSC's all-encompassing definition of God is identical to that revealed in Alice Walker's *The Color Purple*.[58] And similar to Hurston's revelation on religion, the UHSC Creed leaves little if any room for prayer because "whatsoever good we need is within us." Just as the Yoruba can bring utterance and thought to fruition through ọfọ̀ àṣẹ, the UHSC uses the spirit manifest in thought to direct destiny. The importance of revering one's spirit and journeying inward into the self to better know one's Self and one's divine inheritance is also evident in

Hurley's charge to humanity: "Man Know Thyself! When you know yourself then you will know God or Elohim."[59]

Booker T. Washington is often dismissed as a "sell out" or "Uncle Tom," but his Tuskegee University produced two divine revolutionary warriors who knew and extolled the truth about themselves and their people: George Hurley is one, and Marcus Mosiah Garvey is the other. Like Hurley, Garvey understood self-cognition's relationship to self-actualization especially for a dislocated, discredited, and often discarded people. Garvey was very well aware that the power of divinity is exponentially magnified when married to pragmatic political purpose. So while Garvey created the Universal Negro Improvement Association (UNIA) as a nondenominational organ, he knew that the displaced Africans he sought to awaken and spur to evolution and elevation would need to see the divine in themselves and know themdivineselves to properly direct their destinies.

Steeped in knowledge augmented by Tuskegee, Garvey was prepared to inspire Africana masses with historical, political, and spiritual truths:

> Yet honest students of history can recall the day when Egypt, Ethiopia and Timbuctoo towered in their civilizations, towered above Europe, towered above Asia. When Europe was inhabited by a race of cannibals, a race of savages, naked men, heathens and pagans, Africa was peopled with a race of cultured black men, who were masters in art, science, literature; men who were cultured and refined; men who, it was said, were like the gods.[60]

While some may consider his words incendiary, Garvey is merely paraphrasing Homer's *Iliad* (and he goes on to refer directly to the *Iliad*) and expounding on the research that French historian Constantine C. F. de Volney includes in *The Ruins of Empires*.[61]

Referencing the biblical description of Jesus and the centrality of Africa and Africans in the Bible, Garvey asserted, quite logically, that "God made black skin and kinky hair because he desired to express Himself in that type"; consequently, Garvey insisted that the UNIA depict God, Jesus, and Mary as African.[62] While some African Americans were "revolted" by a God who looked like them (which speaks volumes about the impact of Christianity on the Africana psyche and the self-destruction fomented by loving one's enemy), Alexander McGuire, the UNIA's Chaplain General, revealed that an African American elder gave him a five dollar offering after McGuire preached a sermon on the African Christ. The elder also uttered a truth that was shamefully ignored but abundantly apparent during America's Red Era of lynchings, rapings, and mass expulsions of Africana citizens: "No white man would ever die on the cross for me."[63]

Having awakened the masses to the Gods in themselves and their attendant political obligations, Garvey embraced his own divinity. When *Champion Magazine* asserted in 1917 that "The Negro is crying for a Mohammed to come forth and give him the Koran of economic and intellectual warfare,"[64] Marcus Garvey knew that he was the requested Mohammed. Indeed, Garvey was compared to the prophet Muhammad and called a "child of Allah."[65]

Noble Drew Ali, who founded the Moorish Science Temple of America (MSTA) in 1926, is another one of Allah's influential offspring. Because Ali associated conventional Islam with the "slave master's orientation,"[66] possibly because of the Arab participation in the enslavement and exile of Africans and because the popular name "Abdul" or "Abd" means "servant" or "slave," he took the initiative to craft his own religion which he named "Islamism." Ali melded Buddhist, Hindu, and other Asian philosophies with the tenets of Islam and Christianity with the hopes of offering his followers a universal religion. Ali's teachings survive in many texts including *The Holy Koran of the Moorish Science Temple of America Circle 7 Koran*, which is popularly known as the *Circle 7 Koran*.

The *Circle 7 Koran*, despite its title, is a heavily Christian-inspired and -influenced text, and this foundation impedes the development of divinity. Chapter two, verse eighteen of the *Circle 7 Koran* teaches that "Allah and man are one," but man "debased himself" with "carnal thoughts and words and deeds."[67] This reification of a sacred/secular dichotomy reveals the influence of a Caucocentric and Christocentric pseudo-puritanical worldview—not a scientific and holistic African understanding of the human body, biological creation, the world, and the universe. In chapter seven, verse thirty-one of the *Circle 7 Koran*, Jesus reveals that "man is saved when he has reached deific life; when he and Allah are one."[68] Although still couched in dichotomous rhetoric, Jesus' assertion here is similar to that expressed in John 10:34 of the Bible.

Verses ten through twelve of chapter eight of the *Circle 7 Koran* also contain veiled references to inherent divinity that are similar to those in the Bible:

> 10. But in their image man was made, and he who looks into the face of man, looks at the image of the Allah who speaks within.
> 11. And when man honors man, he honors Allah, and what man does for man he does for Allah.
> 12. And you must bear in mind that when man harms in thought or word or deed another man, he does a wrong to Allah.[69]

With these verses, Ali introduces his audience to the force of divine reciprocity and to the power of the continuum. Chapter twelve, verse nine of *the Circle 7 Koran* offers simple scientific truths: "Allah never made a heaven for man; He never made a hell; we are creators and we make our own."[70] However rather than use these verses as a springboard for the recognition and actualization of personal power and divinity, Ali seeks solace in the master myth of monotheism. Chapter thirty-five, verse one asserts: "There is but one Allah, the author, the creator, the governor of the world; almighty, eternal, and incomprehensible."[71]

Despite the contradictions in the *Circle 7 Koran*, Noble Drew Ali's teachings contributed mightily to the proliferation of divinity in African America. Indeed, his death resulted in the births of many Gods including Allah El, the "son of the most High God-Allah,"[72] and Charles Mosley, who later became known as C. M. Bey, whose approach to divinity was refreshingly pragmatic.

C. M. Bey revealed his motivations and objectives with a powerful declaration: "I am not interested in religion and the 'GOD' no one has ever seen. I am interested only in the solving of my economic problems and helping others to solve their problems in the most reasonable and intelligent manner."[73] Bey took the power of humanodivinity to its logical and biological roots by making it clear that the Africana woman is God. Unlike the invisible, amorphous, and mysterious male Gods of organized religions, Bey asserted that God is "not a secret nor mystery. She is a reality—the living God of humanity."[74] Relying on the actual facts evident in biology, science, and ontology, and arguing that man finds divinity within woman, Bey challenges men with a rhetorical question: "Do you know of any being that is superior to you and your mother?"[75] Bey extended the biological supremacy and Divinity of the Africana woman to the origin of existence, arguing that the Great Mother "declared some thirteen hundred and sixty-seven years ago: 'Inni Anallahum La Illaha Illa Ana' – Truly I am God-Allah, Besides Me There is no Other."[76]

Bey's wisdom continues to be disseminated through the Moorish-American Institute, which he founded in 1965, and his numerous publications. Many scholars have built on Bey's cosmic and scientific studies, including Rahsmariah V. Bey who argues in *She Redeems* that the Africana woman is the architect of existence. R. V. Bey goes on to assert that the arc of the covenant is actually the perfect arc that the womb creates in a mother's body when she is molding human life.[77] R. V. Bey avers that the Africana woman is the "womb of the universe. All beings come to life through the womb."[78] R. V. Bey emphasizes the fact that without woman, man cannot exist at all, let alone comprehend his divinity.

In *All Hail the Great Moabite Moorish Woman: Matriarch of the Human Family*, R. V. Bey recognizes Woman as "All Law (Allah), and her children (male and female), are the manifestation of All Law into the physical as Arm, Leg, Leg, Arm, Head."[79] R. V. Bey's revolutionary treatise on the Divine is at one with Yoruba, Igbo, Kemetic, Masonic, and MSTA philosophies and with science, geology, ontology, cosmology, and spiritual-etymology. But it is important to note that R. V. Bey's elaboration on the Mother springs forth from the foundation built by a son, C. M. Bey. The ability to not only appreciate but to encourage holistic gender-balanced growth and to boast the flexibility necessary to encompass contemporary scientific, astronomical, and biological revelations is why Africana divinity remains a powerful and attractive force.

The influence of the teachings Noble Drew Ali and the Moorish Science Temple are evident in numerous organizations and philosophies, most notably, the Nation of Islam. W. D. Fard, who is also known as W. D. Fard Muhammad,[80] founded the Nation of Islam (NOI) in 1922, and one of the cornerstones of the religion is recognition of inherent Africana divinity. In the following quotation, Elijah Muhammad, the NOI's legendary leader and Fard's acolyte, explains to his congregation their divine inheritance:

> All praise is due to Allah. Allah is all of us. But we have a Supreme One that we can throw this name "Holy" upon. He is Allah, The One over all of us; The Most Supreme One, the Wisest One, the Mightiest One; The One that Sees and Hears that which we can't see and hear. That Is He. He is rooted in all of us. Every righteous person is a god. We are all God. When we say "Allah" we mean every righteous person.[81]

In *The Theology of Time*, Muhammad is even more forthright as he declares, "I am Allah and you are Allah. . . . We are all Allah."[82] Muhammad's assertions about the multiplicity of Allah are rooted in the most logical sources including such Qur'anic surah as Al-Baqarah 49–58 where the plural pronoun "we" is used in reference to Allah, and Genesis 1:26, Psalms 82:6, and John 10:34 of the Bible.

Fard and Muhammad insisted that the only religion worthy of consideration is one rooted in fact as opposed to faith. They also stressed that the only God or Allah suitable for reverence is one whose existence is actual as opposed to imaginary. What makes Fard and Muhammad's apologia on divinity more empowering than those found in surahs and scriptures is that through the cultivation of righteousness, divinity can be developed and expanded infinitely: God is not restricted to any individual or era. God is always present in the limitless potential of the Self.

In addition to introducing his congregants to their numinosity, Elijah Muhammad, like George Hurley and Noble Drew Ali, debunked myths about the Gods and devils and heavens and hells of organized religions:

> God is not a mystery today; He is not something invisible. He is not a spirit. He is not something other than flesh and blood; He is in the flesh and in the blood. God is a human being! God would have no joy or pleasure in humans (us) if He himself were something other than a human being. God would have no joy or pleasure in the material universe if He Himself were other than material. . . . There is no such thing as seeing God or the devil after you die. There is no such thing as a heaven up in the sky or a hell down in the ground. All of that is fantasy, false stories made up by your slave master to further enslave you. God is a man! The devil is a man! Heaven and hell are two conditions, and both are experienced in this life right here on this earth. You have already suffered the worse kind of hell in the hands of the only real devil.[83]

Muhammad's demystifications and revelations extend beyond the texts and beliefs of organized religions. They find their source in the holistic spiritual systems of the Kemites, Kushites, Yoruba, Dogon, Mande, and other African groups. Far from being self-righteous demagogues, Muhammad and Fard were reminding their followers of the ancient birthright and ontological reality of which slavery, racism, and natal alienation sought to rob them.

The power and logic of their teachings earned them many followers, but in terms of the direct proliferation of divinity, it could be said that Fard and Muhammad placed the seeds of divinity in fertile soil and dared them to grow. Similar to Samuel Morris and George Hurley, Fard and Muhammad followed the hierarchy typical of organized religions and placed a "supreme" masculine God over "minor" Gods. The supreme living Allah to whom Elijah Muhammad refers is W. D. Fard. While some charge that he ran the Nation of Islam in a totalitarian fashion akin to the Christian God, Muhammad did not embrace the power and responsibility of a Divinity. The reluctance of members of the Nation of Islam to transfer textual and verbal proclamations on numinescence into their flesh could be the result of members thinking that divinity was beyond them. What is more, in addition to being labeled crazy, Muslims who were bold enough to admit to being divine would likely face disciplinary measures that could range from being silenced, to being excommunicated, to facing the NOI's infamous enforcement wing nicknamed the "Doom Squad."[84] However, a tsunamic force was stirring in the Nation of Islam that would bring Africana divinity to the world stage, and the transformation from mortal to visionary to God was the result Elijah Muhammad's careful guidance and his unfettered wrath.

The enlightenment of Malcolm Little began when his brothers, Philbert and Reginald, started introducing him to knowledge of self. Although his father was a staunch follower of Marcus Garvey and was lynched because of his activism, Malcolm Little chose the flash of criminality over the struggle for liberation. While Malcolm was incarcerated, his brothers began "civilizing" or dropping jewels of enlightenment on him, and it did not take long for his buried activist roots to sprout new growth.

Reginald informed Malcolm that "God is a man. . . . His real name is Allah," and Allah has 360° of knowledge, which is the sum total of all knowledge.[85] This full spectrum of knowledge eclipses the "devil's" 33°. Reginald further signified on the Freemasons by charging that "[t]he devil uses his Masonry to rule other people."[86] Reginald told his brother that Allah came to America and revealed himself to Elijah Poole (later Elijah Muhammad) so that they could build a nation and end the devil's rule.

Such is the beginning of building process that sparked the mental, physical, and spiritual awakening that transformed Malcolm Little into Malcolm X. Malcolm revealed that, when the tree of enlightenment had taken firm root in his soul, he was visited in his prison cell by a suited, nonthreatening, silent entity. After he and Malcolm gazed at one another, the figure vanished. Malcolm understood he had been visited by "Master W. D. Fard, the Messiah."[87] It is significant that this visitation occurred when Malcolm was meditating on the fate of his brother Reginald who had been excommunicated from the NOI at the behest of Elijah Muhammad. Reginald had committed the crime of proclaiming his divinity. First, he asserted that he had "divine power"; later, he admitted that he was Allah; finally, Reginald proclaimed himself to be "greater than Allah."[88] While Malcolm and many others considered Reginald to be insane, it is likely that Reginald was struggling to reconcile the NOI's doctrine that "[t]he black people, God's children, [are] Gods themselves" with the attempt of another God to condemn him.[89]

Reginald's plight also offers evidence as to how quickly adherents of organized religions dismiss manifestations of divinity as insanity. At one point during his excommunication, Reginald walked 722 miles from Roxbury, Massachusetts to Detroit, Michigan. On another occasion, during a visit with Malcolm, Reginald observed that "each hair" of Malcolm's beard "was a snake."[90] Malcolm initially ascribed his brother's ability to walk unimaginable miles to "Allah's chastisement."[91] He went on to assert that "[t]here is a dimension of time with which we are not familiar here in the West" and that Reginald's punishment catapulted him into that dimension and into derangement.[92] However, in retrospect, Malcolm realized that Reginald walked over 700 miles and used his prophetic vision to warn Malcolm about the slithering and nesting enemies who were, indeed, as close to Malcolm as the whiskers of his beard.[93]

Despite his abiding fear that he would suffer the same fate as Reginald,[94] Malcolm X, through a roller coaster ride of enlightenment, ostracism, humiliation, world travel, and personal, political, and spiritual revelation, manifested his destiny as El Hajj Malik El Shabazz, and it is important to note the definitive spiritual growth that accompanies this name. "X" represents the unknown while "Shabazz" signifies a mighty and glorious people.[95] El Shabazz devoted his entire life to ensuring his people knew their might and glory.

El Shabazz knew that fighting for justice was an essential aspect of the elevation of dislocated Africans, and he was prepared to take the United States to war for justice:

> I slipped in on the reporters something they hadn't been expecting. I said that the American black man needed to quit thinking what the white man had taught him—which was that the black man had no alternative except to beg for his so-called "civil rights." I said that the American black man needed to recognize that he had a strong, airtight case to take the United States before the United Nations on a formal accusation of "denial of human rights"—and that if Angola and South Africa were precedent cases, then there would be no easy way that the U.S. could escape being censured, right on its own home ground.[96]

With his refocused political agenda and method of attack and his expanding Pan-African consciousness, El Shabazz posed a serious threat to the United States and all forces of imperialism. Another threatening aspect of his transformation was his recognition of the divisive and destructive nature of organized religion. Having come into his own as a divine revolutionary, during his famous "The Ballot or The Bullet" speech, delivered 12 April 1964, El Shabazz told his audience that he would refrain from discussing his religion so as to better facilitate his work as "Black Nationalist Freedom Fighter" and to further the Pan-African world's fight against its common enemies.[97] Free of the shackles of dogma, El Shabazz was poised to unify revolutionary organizations across America and the world.

El Shabazz was a political whirlwind who evolved and grew and moved all in his path toward growth and evolution. He was a man in full possession of his divinity, and during his final transformation he exhibited the focus, dedication, and isolation with which Gods are often beset; indeed, he found himself walking a path similar to that Reginald was condemned to tread a decade and a half earlier. But rather than derange or derail him, El Shabazz's vicissitudes deepened what Sonia Sanchez describes as his "God Conscious Activism."[98] At the 2011 Harlem Book Fair, Sanchez described El Shabazz's manifestation and proliferation of divinity in the following way: "His eyes looked back to Africa and the Caribbean and America and told us to take God out of the sky and put God in our hearts, our feet, our hands, and we did. And we are forever grateful."[99]

Because the Nation of Islam is founded on and grounded in the principles of inherent Africana divinity, it is not surprising that it gave birth to many Gods. A peer of El Shabazz's who built a Nation of Gods by simply teaching Africana youths the truth about themselves is fittingly known as Allah or Allah, the Father. Allah was born as Clarence Smith, and he was known as Clarence 13X when he was a member of the Nation of Islam. Clarence 13X was excommunicated from the NOI in 1963 for reasons that are unknown.[100] However, with his expulsion came the ultimate transformation, because Clarence 13X claimed his divinity outright. Using Elijah Muhammad and W. D. Fard's own lessons as his ultimate validation, in 1964 Clarence renamed and proclaimed himself Allah. Rather than establish himself as an overlord, Allah did something that is unimaginable and unpardonable in organized religions: He taught every Africana person he could reach that they were Allah too.

One of the most significant lessons crafted by Fard and Muhammad that illuminated the path to divinity for Allah, the Father, is "Lost-Found Muslim Lesson No. 2" which describes three categories of human beings:

> 14. **Who [are] the 85%?**
> ANS. The uncivilized people; poison animal eaters; slaves from mental death and power, people who do not know the Living God or their origin in this world, and they worship that they know not what --- who are easily led in the wrong direction, but hard to lead into the right direction.
>
> 15. **Who [are] the 10%?**
> ANS. The rich; the slave-makers of the poor; who teach the poor lies --- to believe that the Almighty, True and Living God is a spook and cannot be seen by the physical eye.
> Otherwise known as: The Blood-Suckers Of The Poor.

16. **Who [are] the 5% in the Poor Part of the Earth?**
ANS. They are the poor, righteous Teachers, who do not believe in the teachings of the 10%, and are all-wise; and know who the Living God is; and Teach that the Living God is the Son of man, the supreme being, the (black man) of Asia; and Teach Freedom, Justice and Equality to all the human family of the planet Earth.
Otherwise known as: Civilized People.
Also are: Muslim and Muslim Sons.[101]

The way of life that Allah, the Father, instituted finds its root in number 16, above. The Five Percent, who are also known as the Five Percenters and the Nation of Gods and Earths, are the True and Living Gods, and they are the actualization of one of the world's most influential, flexible, and enduring articulations of humanodivinity.

The impact, longevity, and appeal of the Five Percent are due in large part to the fact that their acknowledgment and actualization of divinity is not rooted in vanity, egotism, or megalomania. The Five Percent articulation of numinosity is at one with that of Ifá the Yoruba God of Divination who sang, "I am humble, hence I have become a spirit (a god)," and the Sufi Muslim poet Farid ud-Din Attar who extolled, "I am free from spite, arrogance and greed, / I am God, I am God, I am God."[102] Humility is a necessary characteristic of True and Living Gods because divinity is inextricably bound to infinite responsibilities.

Just as Allah introduced the youths that he met to their divinity and educated them about their power, every God, every person with knowledge of self divine, must educate and help elevate—or "civilize"—members of the lost 85% of the world. This work is the Gods' obligation, and if Five Percenters refuse to civilize the uncivilized, "They should be punished with a severe punishment."[103] The harshness of the penalty reflects the fact that one who could and should be building is facilitating destruction, and this is a grave offense. The Gods are the poor righteous teachers, and, as that term indicates, their passion is to enlighten and to participate in the uplift of the masses. The Gods know that the true measure of divinity lies in the number and the power of the Gods that the Gods bring into being.

Lessons 14–16 of "Lost-Found Muslim Lesson No. 2" comprise the cornerstone of the ethos of the Five Percent Nation. These knowledge seekers and wisdom keepers take it upon themdivineselves to manifest, analyze, and reinterpret NOI texts and definitions as part of their eternal quest for holistic development. Similar to the way in which Hurston weaves High John the Conqueror's origin text and adorns him with revelatory myths, history, and secrecy, so too do the Five Percent find proof of their Divinity in the catechisms of W. D. Fard and then "build" and "add on" or expand his teachings for personal and communal evolution. Rather than adhere to a lock-step curriculum, the Five Percent use their agency and divinity to create and embrace socially and culturally appropriate definitions of God and Self that are realistic, empowering, and reflective of their identity. For example, Five Percenters cannot be "Muslim Sons" or "sons of man," as is indicated in number 16 of "Lost-Found Muslim Lesson No. 2," because these terms signify hierarchy and subservience. The Gods embrace the term "Suns of Man," which signifies their similitude to the Sun and their ability to generate light, life, and consciousness. Likewise, Five Percenters cannot be Muslims who submit to the will of Allah because they *are* Allah: Each person is God—a creator and master and controller of his universe.

Allah's consciousness-raising, nation-building, and curriculum-designing efforts resulted in the births of innumerable Gods, but Allah was not the first Muslim to graduate to God and take his message to the grassroots. Clarence Cooper, Jr. undertook the same path through literature in a work published in 1962. Cooper's short story "Not We Many" is a masterful critique of the NOI that includes an articulation of divine mathematics, political empowerment, and discovery of divinity.

The protagonist is David, a member of the NOI who, similar to El Shabazz's brother Reginald, is suffering a crisis of conscience for which he has been censured and suspended. In addition to questioning the "current-day Allah's" refusal to wage war against racist ten percenters and the blind obedience and ignorance of the Muslim masses, David also critiques the Nation of Islam's rhetoric as well as the divinity of the Africana man. David muses that "[s]omewhere, during his various metamorphic stages, Original Man lost his originality"; David further surmises that after eons of replicating perfection, God ended up creating a God who was "more man than God."[104] David's searing critique of divinity as understood by the NOI is most compelling because he appears to appropriate the NOI's mythistorical origin text of Yacub, the scientist who grafted the melanin and all other dominant genotypic and phenotypic attributes out of Africana people and created Caucasians, and apply it to displaced Africana Gods who grafted away their divinity.

While excommunicated from the NOI, David does in literature, what Allah, the Father, and El Hajj Malik El Shabazz did in life: He submerges himself into the study of ontology, history, science, mathematics, and divinity. He and his complement Famat use a numerological computation system that melds "Ax, orthodox Islam, and theory" to understand the meaning of life and interpret the mysteries of the universe. The "Ax Muslim mathematical equations" are as follows:

One: - The Beginning.
Two: - A Nation: man and woman.

Three: - The light of the world: the sun, moon and stars.
Four: - The square by which all things are equal, i.e., 4 x 9 = 36, which points to 9 as the beginning of One.
Five: - The number of Allah, Who is just to the obedient.
Six: - The Dragon's number – the number of a man who was six hundred years in the making, has six thousand years to rule, at which time his cycle of life will be complete – and he will die forever from the face of the Earth.
Seven: - Is complete in itself, causing the first to last and the last to come first.
Eight: - Yacub's number, signifying the maker and the tamed.
Nine: - Is exact and the beginning of One.[105]

The Ax mathematical equations boast correlations to the Igbo numerological sciences that are used by dibia to catalyze the properties of the Earth and the Cosmos and fly.[106] Evidence of Ax mathematics is also apparent in some of the speeches included in Elijah Muhammad's *The Theology of Time: The Secret of Time*. Although there are differences in some equations, Ax mathematics' most obvious sibling is the Supreme Mathematics of the Five Percent.

The Ax mathematical equations are supposed to serve as a "panacea for all the black man's ills."[107] After a seemingly fruitless analysis of science, numerology, ontology, and cosmology, frustration gives way to illumination, and David and Famat realize that they have "discovered God."[108]

Through the Ax equations it becomes clear that "Two: - A Nation: man and woman" plus "Three: - The light of the world: the sun, moon and stars" (which signifies human beings' astronomical equivalents, as man symbolizes the sun, woman is associated with the moon, and children are equated to stars) equals "Five: - The number of Allah, Who is just to the obedient." The association of the number five with Allah in the Ax mathematical equations correlates to God being represented in the human body synecdochically as Arm-Leg-Leg-Arm-Head: The initials of these five major extremities reveal A-L-L-A-H. The divine significance of the number five is also apparent in the understanding that five percent of the world's population are Gods. In Supreme Mathematics, seven is related to God because G is the seventh letter of the alphabet, but to equate five with Allah is equally right and exact.

To continue the computations of the Divine as revealed in "Not We Many," two plus five equals seven, and seven "[i]s complete in itself, causing the first to last and the last to come first." This would imply that the central element and cornerstone of all existence and its continuity is Man and Woman knowing that they are Gods and creating Gods—and, consequently, a microcosmic Cosmos—through their children who understand that they are Gods who must create Gods. The computations grow even deeper: Two (Man and Woman) plus seven (the principle of completion) equals nine, which is "exact and the beginning of One." One signifies "The Beginning" which alludes to the conception and birth of a child, who is Allah reborn.

According to Ax Mathematics, true divinity is found in when two Gods—male and female—unite in successful sexual bliss and create another God. The reverence of children is also a central pillar of Five Percent ontology. Allah simply said, "*The Babies are the Greatest*," and he encouraged the Gods to have as many children as possible "because the only way you will find God is by reproducing."[109] The logic of his assertions is evident in the Supreme Mathematics in which Children are associated with "Understanding," and Knowledge/Man:1 plus Wisdom/Woman:2 equals Understanding/Child:3.

Whether or not Allah and Cooper shared wisdom with one another is unknown, but Allah and Cooper's protagonist, David, share the same objective: to educate the masses and introduce them to the numinous Self. Allah and his colleague Justice revised and built upon Fard's Lost-Found lessons with their creation of the Supreme Alphabets and Supreme Mathematics. Their goal was to create a curriculum worthy of living Gods—a curriculum based in "actual facts" as opposed to a system of indoctrination rooted in belief, faith, and religious terrorism. Allah and Justice did what would be unimaginable in the American public school system; they planted the wisdom of holistic education into the wise domes of African American youths and facilitated personal elevation and social-cultural evolution.

The Gods' curriculum is comprised of W. D. Fard's *Supreme Wisdom Lessons*, which include, but are not limited to, Lost-Found Muslim Lesson No. 1, Lost-Found Muslim Lesson No. 2, Student Enrollment, English Lesson No. C1, and the Actual Facts.[110] The curriculum also includes the Solar Facts, which provide data about the solar system, and the Supreme Mathematics and Supreme Alphabet. With the latter two systems, numbers and letters are associated with particular concepts that serve to both decode and encode Five Percent science and philosophy depending on whether or not one is deep enough to understand the *w*ise *c*ipher *r*egulating *d*ivine *s*elf (words).

The Supreme Alphabet

A   Allah
B   Be or Born
C   Cee

D   Divine
E   Equality
F   Father
G   God
H   He or Her
I   Eye, I, or Islam
J   Justice
K   King or Kingdom
L   Love, Hell, or Right
M   Master
N   Now, Nation, or End
O   Cipher
P   Power
Q   Queen
R   Ruler
S   Self or Savior
T   Truth or Square
U   You or Universe
V   Victory
W   Wise or Wisdom
X   Unknown
Y   Why
Z   Zig-Zag-Zig

The Supreme Mathematics

1. Knowledge
2. Wisdom
3. Understanding
4. Culture/Freedom
5. Power/Refinement
6. Equality
7. God
8. Build/Destroy
9. Born
0. Cipher

In *Five Percenter Rap: God Hop's, Music, Message, and Black Muslim Mission*, Felicia Miyakawa asserts that "[f]or Gods and Earths, numbers not only unlock the mysterious scientific workings of the universe, but also provide a way to understand the 'true' meanings of words."[111] Examples of revealing a word's alternate or encoded meaning include my breakdown of "words" (above) and this chapter's epigraph in which "I be Self Lord And Master" is code for "I.S.L.A.M." Supreme Alphabetic associations also apply synecdoche and puns effectively. For example, the letter "U" represents "you," and it symbolizes the microcosmic encapsulation of the "universe," which is also represented as "U-N-I-Verse," and can signify the Cosmos as centered on a male-female dyad or two individuals dropping knowledge in a cipher as they decipher the mysteries of existence. When Posdenus of De La Soul raps that he "graduated from the U-N-I-Versity" he is making an assertion that resonates on intellectual, communal, and cosmological levels but has little to do with Western academic institutions.[112] Indeed, rather than a paper certificate from a college, the Gods of the Five Percent are, themselves, universities. And not only do they not charge tuition for the wisdom that they share, but each God's lifework is to provide the tools, bricks, and mortar for the erection universities of divinity in every righteous soul they meet.

Every aspect of the Five Percent curriculum boasts a flexibility and dynamism that is spiritually, lyrically, and politically empowering. In her analysis of the Supreme Alphabets, Miyakawa observes that "Five Percenters do not limit themselves only to the original meanings ascribed to each letter but instead creatively apply the spirit of the system to find meaning."[113] The operative phrase is "creatively apply the spirit." As each God is the master and controller of her universe, creative ingenuity is expected, and Gods are encouraged to "build" or contribute new philosophies, theories, and data to the comprehension and development of divine existence. The Supreme Mathematics and Alphabet apply the same principles employed by such Gods as Nzambi, Olódùmarè, MawuLisa, and High John the Conqueror. These Deities leave spaces and openings throughout Creation for human beings, flora, and fauna to purposefully apply their àṣẹ and enrich the world with meaning, power, spirit, and depth.

Armed with the Supreme Understanding of his and all Africana people's divinity, Allah began awakening and educating his Nation who, in turn, took the lessons of Allah and expounded upon, expanded, and shared them in gatherings called ciphers. In addition to being a circular forum where Five Percent wisdom is conveyed, cipher also means 0 (zero), to put in secret writing or encode, to solve problems or decode, a system for decoding encrypted messages, and encrypted messages. To the Gods, cipher also signifies perfection, completion, and 360°: 120° of knowledge, 120° of wisdom, and 120° of understanding.[114] The Five Percent combine and take from all of these meanings as they share encoded lessons, decode them, and recode them with the goal of educating, civilizing, and birthing and welcoming more Gods to the Nation.

Allah, the Father, stunned and appalled the members of the Nation of Islam, for in contrast to their uniforms—dark suit and tie—rigidity and lengthy list of prohibitions, here was God holding court at the Universal Parliament while smoking a cigarette.[115] There was Allah incarcerated in a mental institution but standing firm on his square and transforming eighty-fives into fives. Here was God proclaiming that there was no devil because he had not made one.[116] There was Allah networking with the mayor of New York and other Caucasian city officials.[117] Here was God shooting craps in an alleyway.[118] There was Allah sipping a drink in the Glamour Inn. Verily, this God was unlike any who had come before him—except for Gods like Ṣàngó, Father of the Gods Who Can Do Everything in this World, Marie LaVeau, Ọbàtálá, Ausar, Zora Neale Hurston, and High John the Conqueror. Allah, the Father, was not isolated on a throne in the mesosphere. Like his many progenitors, Allah could always be found with his Suns, on the streets, in a cipher, building on the Earth because that was where he was needed. Allah wanted to ensure he planted the seeds of divinity in fertile ground: and to determine the ground's fecundity Allah had to know it, walk it, feel it, taste it.

A Five Percenter offers the following analysis of Allah's pedagogy and methodology and why they proved so effective:

> You couldn't go to the movies and see a Muslim. Muslims didn't go to the movies. They didn't go to discotheques. That's where our people who . . . need knowledge of self is. They in the movies, they in the discotheques, you see what I'm saying? They in the dice holes, they in the drug dens. Who's going to teach them people? Who's gonna teach them? He was a leader who made leaders, he wouldn't make no followers. He told us to be leaders who make leaders because . . . you got to stand out and be the Arm, Leg, Leg, Arm, Head. That's nothing but A-L-L-A-H.[119]

While Allah was not a showbiz leader who basked in a media spotlight, he could always be found shining and inspiring numinosity where illumination was needed most.

The building process that the Father undertook with the Five Percent was so successful and revolutionary that enemies of progress assassinated him in 1969. Like the slayings of many other visionary Africana activists, his murder remains unsolved. Unlike other leaders who were assassinated and were unable to prepare those who would come after them and those who refused to prepare their followers to lead out of selfishness, Allah equipped and armed each God of the Five Percent with knowledge of their divinity and power from the moment of their awakenings. In the words of Beloved Allah: "Allah had told his Five Percenters before he left them that his death would born the Nation of Gods and Earths. That they did not need a leader because they were all leaders of themselves and their family."[120] Some members of the Nation doubt that Allah, the Father, actually made this proclamation, but the possibility that Allah did not make this statement does not change the fact that the prophecy Beloved Allah attributes to Allah did indeed occur.

Seven bullets from an assassin's gun did not kill Allah; they dispersed his infinite numinosity. As did High John the Conqueror before him, Èṣù before him, and Ausar before him, Allah manifested his destiny in life, death, and the afterlife by successfully undertaking the most difficult, important, and sacred work of all—ushering more Gods into existence. The young men and women who had been miseducated to believe that they were worthless, who had been written off by professors, pimped by parents, and prostituted by pastors found in Allah a Father of divine and dynamic proportions who was as nurturing as the Earth and as resplendent as the Sun.

CHAPTER THREE

"I Call My Brother Sun 'Cause He Shine Like One":
The Divine, the Shining, and the Poetics of Rap

"When niggers turn into Gods, walls come tumbling . . ."
~ Erykah Badu, "The Healer"

Manifestations of masculine magnificence in African America spring from a foundation that is as deep as it is wide. Whether inspired by biblical scriptures, Qur'anic surah, the fire of Şàngó, the water of Yemọja, the tricksterian skills of High John the Conqueror, or the Supreme Mathematics, there are infinite sources from whence to develop, reflect, and project Divinity. This chapter explores the expansiveness and diversity of Africana masculine magnificence and analyzes the myriad properties of numinosity that abound in and are disseminated through Africana music, especially rap music and hip hop culture. In an era in which most popular music celebrates the vapidity and depravity mandated by the deadening nexus of blind consumerism and clutching capitalism, some artists eschew the art for cash's sake mandate and make not only art for life's sake but art for Gods' sake so that they can awaken and vivify new Gods and welcome them into a divine continuum that is as ancient and as sure as the revolutions of the Earth.

U-N-I-Verses of the Living Gods

High John the Conqueror has manifested himself across time, space, geography, and gender with the grace that only the progeny of Èṣù can boast. But High John's recent and most renowned manifestation may well be that of rap artist. Rappers and members of the hip hop generation are easily the most successful tricksters of this era. These artists routinely go from being society's dregs—drug pushers and addicts, convicts, hustlers, pimps, prostitutes, strippers—to being millionaires who dictate culture, style, fashion, and influence language and economies around the world. The impact that rap, rappers, and hip hop have on the world is not surprising given these arts forms' ancient provenance and social, political, and cosmic imperatives.

Rap and hip hop are said to have begun in the Bronx in the 1970s, but this is incorrect. Scholars who are familiar with the African epics of Sundiata, Ozidi, and Sarraounia and such works as the Yoruba Odù Ifá and the Kemetic Book of the Coming Forth by Day know that rap is an ancient African art form.[1] Indeed, in 2010, Yoweri Museveni, the Head of State of Uganda, showcased his freestyling abilities while revealing to his constituency rap's deep East African roots.[2]

Given that rapping is a classic African art, it is not surprising that the word "rap" is of African origin. In Wolof language and cosmology, Raap are important and potent Gods "of the sea and waters" to whom particular hymns are sung.[3] Just as it takes true emcees years to master the lyrical artistry of rap, Molara Ogundipe reveals, "It takes eleven years of apprenticeship to learn all the hymns to be sung to a *Raap*."[4] When one considers the two-month long journey that enslaved Africans were forced to make across the Ethiopic Ocean—a body of water that August Wilson calls "the largest unmarked grave in the world"[5]—one could assert that the powerful Wolof Raap ensured African ancestors' survival and encouraged their progeny to rap so as to communicate, document, and spread knowledge of—and make the world hip to—their ancient and modern trials and triumphs.

Hip hop also originated with the Ancients. "Hip," also pronounced "hep," is a Wolof word that means to have knowledge or insight; "to open one's eyes, to be aware of what is going on."[6] Hip hop's original meaning and function can be best articulated as the artistic collection and dissemination of genealogical, historical, social, cultural, and political feats, facts, issues, and intricacies for the purpose of cultural, social, and political enlightenment, evolution, and elevation. The individuals who are entrusted with the wisdom and enlightenment of the nation are called *djeli* in Mande language. Djeli means blood, which signifies the fact that the djeli "are repositories of the tradition and collective life, that is the memory of their people. They become the encyclopedia of the history of the peoples, the transmitter of usages and customs. In short, the djeli are to society what blood is to the body."[7] The meaning of djeli emphasizes the terrestrial and ontological significance of the force known as hip hop.

While a great deal of modern commercial rap focuses on individual success, hedonism, and violence, rap was originally, and in many articulations remains, a communal art designed to educate and uplift in the same way that Raap are Gods who fortify the bonds that connect humans to their Divinity and to their communities.[8] The impact of communality is evident in the original method by which verbal arts were transmitted. Traditionally, Africana orature, from the exploits of Anancy to the victories of High John the Conqueror, was shared among a group of individuals who were positioned in a circle. As is evident in *Mules and Men*, everyone in the circle has the opportunity to contribute legends to the library of High John, to critique the texts being shared, and to add relevant recollections, testimonies, and poetry to the communal library.

The circle—the locus of creative continuity where wisdom is exchanged and consciousness is elevated—also serves as the preferred format for exchanging such toasts as the "Signifying Monkey," "Shine and the Titanic," and "Stagolee." Contemporary rap is the direct descendant of these rhyming toasts, and rap and break dancing are both born of the same circular communal format. The ascension of Gods of Jazz like Charlie Parker, Sun Ra, Miles Davis, and John Coltrane can also be attributed to the power of the circle, for jazz is often performed in rotation. With this format, two central artistic principles are highlighted: the mastery of theme and the artistic ingenuity and virtuosity of improvisation, which could be considered the defining ìwà (character, identity) of the Gods—the ability to riddle a simple melody with labyrinthine riffs and take it to unimaginable, even "Dizzy"ing, heights.

The Five Percenters share wisdom with one another in circles called ciphers where Gods exhibit their mastery of the curriculum established by Allah, the Father. After revealing the scientific foundation and cosmological significance of the day by translating the day, month, and year into Supreme Mathematics, the Gods pontificate on the established cosmic, spiritual, and scientific wisdom revealed in the divine curriculum and then "build" and "add on" to that knowledge base with their own observations and revelations. The cipher is literally the University of the Gods. It is where wisdom and knowledge are born, where understanding is proliferated, and where new doors of comprehension and routes of analysis are opened. In the cipher, Gods "show and prove" that they are, in fact, Allah, and they use dexterous articulations and manifestations of Òrò, Power of the Word, to catalyze and further disseminate divinity.

It is important to recall Rowland Abiodun's observation that when a new Yoruba ruler is being enthroned and his ìtàn ipọnri are uttered, "[T]he air and space between the one who vocalizes àṣẹ and the recipient of the àṣẹ is believed to be so powerfully charged that it is considered unsafe for anyone to obstruct it."[9] As the locus of power and empowerment that is activated by stupendous exhibitions of Òrò, the cipher of the Gods becomes a "powerfully charged" space, identical to that described by Abiodun, which solidifies the divinity of some Gods and galvanizes the divine potential of others. Contemporary rap transfers the wisdom and power of the cipher to the studio, backs it with pulsating beats and rhythms, and immortalizes it through recordings that reach multitudes. Despite its myriad negative outgrowths, the commercialization of rap fomented the internationalization of the Five Percent Nation.

High John is a master wordsmith, and Allah was so smooth that his nickname was Puddin'; it stands to reason that their progeny, the Five Percenters, would also have silken tongues. Hip hop mogul Russell Simmons describes the Five Percenters' "slick, smooth-talking, crafty" manner as being made for mass appeal: "A true Five Percenter could sit on a stoop or stand out on a street corner and explain the tenets of the sect for hours on end—and be totally entertaining!"[10] Thanks to their mastery of Power of the Word, the Gods have had a massive influence on rap music and hip hop culture.

The RZA, a Five Percenter who is easily one of the most versatile, prolific, and respected forces in the music industry, asserts that "[a]bout 80 percent of hip-hop comes from the Five Percent."[11] The RZA is referring not only to the myriad artists who are Gods, as is he, but also to the fact that some of the most commonly used phrases in rap and, now, popular culture, are from the Five Percent, including demands to "break it down," "show and prove," and "drop science," and salutations and conclusions of "peace." The impact that the oral tradition and Power of the Word, specifically, have on Five Percenters is obvious in some of their most popular phrases: "word is bond," "word life," "word up," and, simply, "word." But what the Five Percenters have most in common with High John is also where they diverge from him.

High John the Conqueror is a Deity of myriad power and profound importance, but neither High John nor his collective could honor him with his proper designation of God without fear of violent reprisals from various communities. By contrast, members of the Five Percent Nation acknowledge their divinity outright and greet each other with salutations of "Peace, God" or "Peace, G." In communities where the codes of the Gods thrived through their music but were disconnected from divine knowledge and understanding, many came to associate "G" with "gangster." It is not surprising that many people and institutions are more supportive of Africana men living brief and destructive lives as gangsters than manifesting their destiny as Gods. However, as is apparent in the Supreme Alphabet and Supreme Mathematics, the letter "G" represents God, and it is the seventh letter of the alphabet; consequently the letter G and the number seven have places of prominence and recur in Five Percenter lingo and iconography and rap lyrics.

Recognition of the Gods abounds in hip hop. Jay Z, who bears the praisename Jehovah, begins "Heaven" by praising the "Arm Leg Leg Arm Head" that comprises his "God body" before he drops nine of the

Gods' twelve jewels on his audience.[12] In "Run This Town," Jay Z proclaims his numinescence and that of his elders and peers, especially Rakim Allah, with the lines, "It's the return of the God / Peace, God."[13] That reciprocal recognition and respect circulate among divine peers is also evident in Redman's simple utterance, "God bless the God," which he delivers in De La Soul's song "Oooh."[14] At the conclusion of "Whatever Happened," The RZA informs his audience that "Black God exists in physical form."[15] Wise Intelligent of the Poor Righteous Teachers proclaims, "Praises are due to Allah, that's me."[16] And if his telling surname does not offer sufficient identification, Rakim Allah in "No Competition" informs his audience of his divinity in the simplest of terms: "I'm God."[17]

In addition to outright identification with the divine, some Gods use the methodology of the trickster and articulate their divinity through encoded ciphers. In the chorus of his appropriately titled song "I.S.L.A.M.," Lord Jamar uses the Supreme Alphabet to both reveal and conceal his message:

> I be the Arm Leg Leg Arm Head
> Here to drop bombs on the mentally dead
> I.S.L.A.M. will keep you properly fed
> And to the four devils: Yo, I'm choppin' your head.[18]

In the chorus' first and second lines, Lord Jamar informs his listeners that he is Allah and is undertaking the work of a God: educating and civilizing the "mentally dead" eighty-five percent of the population and enlightening them to the fact that I.S.L.A.M. will provide them with abundant spiritual, physical, and intellectual nourishment. In Arabic, "Islam" means peace, but to the Five Percent, Islam is another affirmation of inherent divinity. Because no God can submit to a religion or to another God, and because they are responsible for determining their own destinies, "Islam" becomes "I.S.L.A.M.," an acronym that can stand for I Self Lord Am Master, or I Sincerely Love Allah's Mathematics, or I Stimulate Life And Matter, or any other relevant phrase depending on the God and the context. The soul food that will nourish Lord Jamar's listeners is the harvest that will come from them embracing their divinity as articulated through "I.S.L.A.M." In the last line of the chorus of "I.S.L.A.M.," Lord Jamar extends a warning to ten percenters: He will exterminate them—lyrically if not physically.

The song "I.S.L.A.M." appears on Lord Jamar's *The 5% Album* which is crafted in the traditions of both Raap and djeli to serve as an educational tool, a biography of Allah, the Father, and a lyrical magnum opus. Each of the songs on *The 5% Album* explicates particular aspects of the Five

Percent way of life and discusses the difficulties that the Gods face in a corrupt, capitalistic, racist, materialistic world. For example, in the song "Supreme Mathematics," Lord Jamar breaks down divine numerology while emphasizing his vocation and his motivation:

> Supreme Mathematics, this ain't black magic
> I do my work amongst dope fiends and crack addicts
> Civilize the savage; eighty-fives run rampant
> I'm tryin' to save these babies' lives, god damn it![19]

Rather than preaching to the choir of a gilded megachurch, Lord Jamar follows in the footsteps of his progenitor, Allah, the Father: Lord Jamar is in the trenches, the drug dens, and the "traps" struggling to share knowledge of self with those who need it most. For the Five Percent, recognition of one's divinity is inextricably tied to educating and liberating the masses, and protecting and glorifying the young Gods, or children. The Gods must also be prepared to accept their divine responsibilities which are innumerable, weighty, and include war.

The concerns of the Five Percent are vast and varied, but one of the most recurrent and important themes in the lyrics of the Gods is war. When one juxtaposes Africans' historical accomplishments and contributions to humanity and world civilization with their inglorious exile to foreign lands and the physical and mental slaveries to which Africans on the Continent and in the Ìtànkálẹ̀ have been and continue to be subjected, it is easy to understand the Gods' focus on war.

Elijah Muhammad repeatedly stressed to his congregation the importance of proper priorities and political consciousness. He averred that rather than fighting for America in any of its cyclically fomented wars,

> the American Negro should be saving his energy and ammunition for "The Battle of Armageddon," which will be waged in the wilderness of North America. This battle—and this is one of the central teachings of the Nation of Islam—will be for freedom, justice, and equality. It will be waged to success or under death.[20]

While entertainers are gyrating into oblivion, the Gods are oiling and loading lyrical and literal machine guns.

In "Universal Soldiers," Dom Pachino echoes the commandments of Hurley's Universal Hagar's Spiritual Church and affirms that he invests no love on his enemies. And rather than leaning and depending on the God of his enemies, Pachino emphasizes that it is "in us we trust."[21] In "Last Poet," Islord of the group Killarmy warns that "there's no exit and no such thing as three men / You only got one man in this game that we play for keeps."[22] Islord's lines inform his audience that that there is no logic in praying to a Caucasian male trinity or waiting for assistance from a mystery God in a mythical heaven: The only God one can rely on is one's self. Islord reiterates these points in "Allah Sees Everything":

> We in the middle of a war zone, Black
> Politically, word life, you better open
> Your eyes and realize the game plan
> That the Caucasian man got mastered
> And you only plan with one man left on the battlefield

After stressing the need for self-reliance and self-determination, Islord extols the virtues of armed self-defense:

> So grab a steel and ya shield and stand firm
> With your God U Now to God you right now
> Cock back with off safety one in the head
> Enough said[23]

The phrase "God U Now" is a Supreme Alphabetical representation for the word "gun."[24] Consequently, in addition to championing the Second Amendment, Islord uses elision to meld the words "guard" and "god" and verbalize and make active one of the most powerful nouns in the English language.[25] The phrase "God you right now" serves as a confirmation that protection and salvation are the ever-ready attributes of every individual and every Warrior God, from Ṣàngó to High John the Conqueror to Islord.

Africana history is replete with Warrior Gods: Ramses the Great of Kemet; the Kandake, or Divine Queen Rulers, of Kush who protected their empire from Alexander of Macedonia and Augustus Caesar; Yaa Asante Waa of Ghana, Ṣàngó and his wife Ọya, who is heralded as "the wife who is fiercer than the husband" and the "woman who grows a beard on account of war";[26] Niger's Sarraounia Aben Soro; Mali's Sundiata; the Maji Maji of East Africa; the Black Panthers; Nyabinghi; Black Liberation Army; and Revolutionary African Movement are just a few of the legendary figures and forces that used their power and divinity to fight for justice, freedom, and elevation. The descendants of these and other African Warrior Gods find themselves in foreign lands fighting wily foes.

Gil Scott-Heron describes the nebulous nature of the war currently being waged in his song "Winter in America":

> It's winter, winter in America
> And all the healers done been killed or put in jail

It's winter, winter in America
And ain't nobody fighting 'cause nobody knows what to save[27]

Winter is the perfect symbol for the West's literal and figurative relationship to Africana peoples as even the climate is hostile to African existence. In Goodie Mob's "Black Ice," Andre 3000 muses, "There's even lower levels you can go / Take Sun People put 'em in the land of snow,"[28] and provides a poignant reminder that the concept of the "African American" is a creation born largely of forced exile. One could argue that African Americans are not and cannot be fully at home in America and that living in the West constitutes a perpetual assault against the nature, humanity, and divinity of Africana peoples.

Social psychologist Wade W. Nobles describes Africana peoples' relationship to America as analogous to a hostage crisis, and he argues that if one calculates from the mid-1700s, when it is thought that enslaved Africans were first brought to America, to the mid-1990s when Nobles was writing, "African American families have been held hostage for more than 89,000 days."[29] Nobles provides a sobering tally and a stunning definition of Caucasian America's relationship to its Africana citizens. As disturbing as Nobles' assessment of this monumental tragedy is, the reality is more chilling. According to William Loren Katz, the first enslaved Africans arrived in America in 1526 courtesy of Luis Vasquez de Ayllon.[30] That would make the hostage crisis one of 177,325 days . . . and counting. The Battle of The American Winter has been lengthy indeed.

In the past, the enemy was easier to spot and revolutions and revolutionaries were multitudinous. The present war is elastic and fluid in structure, and this can make strategizing and fighting difficult. However, some warriors have *Silent Weapons for Quiet Wars*[31]: This is both the title of a Killarmy album and it is a code for the covert battle being fought against Western world domination. The title reassures listeners that African Gods are eternally equipped with weaponry that protects, defends, educates, and elevates.

In "Dangerous Mindz," Too Poetic of the Gravediggaz informs his audience that oppressors will be annihilated by an army of poor righteous teachers armed with divine truth:

But evil men will soon be on the receiving end
of Universal Law
I'm callin' on the meek and the poor
to fight back and never forfeit
the day you have to go to war[32]

In the same song, The RZA heralds biblical African warriors and reveals his knowledge of and ability to revise Caucasian pagan rites: "[I] cause war like the grandson of Kush / I'm hangin' devils' heads on a evergreen bush."³³ The RZA's couplet references Nimrod, the African who is described in the Bible as a hunter, warrior, ruler, master architect, and progeny of Kush, the African empire-builder. The RZA is aware that holidays like Easter and Christmas have no historical relation to the Christian religion; they are holdovers from pagan European rites. Consequently, after harnessing the power of Nimrod to destroy ten percenters, The RZA takes the Christmas tree back to it pagan roots, so to speak, with a twist: He decorates the tannenbaum with the heads of vanquished ten percenters.

The cultural awareness, lyrical genius, and political depth of the Gravediggaz's lyrics cannot be found in commercial rap, but the philosophies of the Gods are evident in various Africana cosmologies, worldviews, and artistic genres. A resounding example of shared philosophy and political directive is apparent in the reggae classic, "Get Up, Stand Up," by Bob Marley and Peter Tosh. The entire song constitutes an attack on the "heavenly father" myth and a demand for the listener to stop praying and fully self-actualize. In the second verse, Marley chastises people who think a "great God will come from the skies" to liberate and glorify humanity.³⁴ He urges his listeners to manifest their own divinity in their lifetimes. Peter Tosh is even more forthright: In the third verse, he compares Christianity to a con game designed to obfuscate the fact that "Almighty God is a living man."³⁵ By calling out Christian grift, Tosh's lyrics serve as a wake-up call to listeners who may have been lulled to sleep by the lies of ten percenters and the mewling of eighty-fivers.

"Get Up, Stand Up" is one of the most popular, beloved, and well-known songs in the world, and it is a song that is in complete consonance with Five Percent philosophy and politics. Although Jah of Rastafari is routinely associated with either a supernatural being or Emperor Haile Selassie, Mutabaruka, the renowned Jamaican actor, poet, philosopher, and activist, reveals that those correlations are erroneous and the result of Christianized misinterpretations and political machinations.³⁶ In an interview with Ian Boyne of "Religious HardTalk," Mutabaruka demystifies the concept of Jah and avers: "Man is really a divine being in Earth. There is no entity outside of himself that is signaling him."³⁷ Mutabaruka goes on to assert that not only does religion impede human beings from becoming divine, but that the world would be a healthier place without the Bible and religion, "because the search for self does not lie in a supernatural connection with any being outside of yourself."³⁸

The RZA echoes Mutabaruka's assertions on the corrupting nature of religion. The RZA reveals that the objective of religion is evident in the word's root, for religion "basically means to rely on something."[39] The RZA goes on to state the obvious for the oblivious: "If you're relying on anything other than yourself you're always gonna have a problem."[40] To avoid the problem of being dependent on any person, place, or thing, Five Percenters are emphatic about the fact that they are not a religious organization or religious offshoot but a way of life: That way of life is I.S.L.A.M. In the holistic worldview of the Five Percent and Mutabaruka, the very concept of religion is antithetical and opposed to the manifestation of divinity.

The philosophies espoused by the Five Percent are part of a rich continuum that encompasses ancient history, countless Africana ethnic groups, and various artistic genres. The continuity expands to envelop and elucidate some of the most electrifying musicians to ever mount a stage. The knowledge, wisdom, and understanding of the Gods' are found in the philosophies of Sun Ra, the great jazz composer, philosopher, and creator of the intergalactic Arkestra; Pharaoh Sanders, the tenor saxophonist who was named by Sun Ra; and George Clinton, the indefatigable leader of Parliament Funkadelic. Sun Ra was originally named Herman Poole Blount. His mother named him after the great prestidigitator, Black Herman, and Sun Ra speculated that he was related to Elijah Poole, who is better known as Nation of Islam's Elijah Muhammad. Whether or not they were related in fact, Sun Ra was certainly related to Muhammad in ideology, as the NOI incorporated Sun Ra's wisdom into their philosophies, and Sun Ra learned from the teachings of the NOI.[41]

Sun Ra's broadsides, which were distributed to the masses from street corners, contained his unique philosophical pontifications as well as paths to knowledge of self. In "Negroes are not Men," Sun Ra uses the 82nd Psalms to elucidate the divinity and paradox of Africana peoples. In "MESSAGE TO THE SPOOK. . . ." (a title which either inspired or was inspired by Muhammad's *Message to the Blackman*) and in "Jacob in the Land of U.S.," Sun Ra defines Africana peoples as Divinities: "I WILL SPEAK OF THE NEGRO AS A MAN ALTHOUGH HE IS NOT OF THIS WORLD, HE IS IN THE FORM OF A MAN BUT IN REALITY HE IS THE SPOOK, THE HOLY GHOST."[42] With his assertion, Sun Ra recalls Yoruba, Dogon, Dagara, Fon, and many other African cosmologies that describe Africans as traveling to the Earth from the Cosmos to undertake divine labors. Sun Ra enlightens his audience about the inherently spiritual nature of Africana peoples, and he describes how Africana powers went from being revolutionary tools of liberation to being jokes that were used to malign and mock. The degradation of Africana powers and peoples is evident in the fear, shame, and disdain with which many Africana people greet discussions of Africana technologies and spiritual systems and in such terms as "shine," "mumbo jumbo," and "zombie" being divorced from their original meanings—the latter two concepts are African terms—and being infused with racism, superstition, and general negativity.

Sun Ra was a revolutionary-philosopher-artist in the tradition of his Kemetic and Kushite forebears, and he dispensed wisdom through broadsides, music, and members of his Arkestra. The spiritual-genealogical tie that connects Sun Ra, which means God of the Sun, to his Pharaoh (Sanders) is similar to bond between Hatshepsut and Amun Re. George Clinton, not unlike a young brother to Sun Ra, adopted the fitting moniker of "Star Child" to represent his astronomical lineage. Clinton is also the captain of the intergalactic Mother Ship, which may have come from the same galaxy as Elijah Muhammad's "mother plane." While many may dismiss Clinton, Ra, and Muhammad as eccentrics, there are multitudes who understand the men, their artistry, and their messages. What is more, these Gods understand, respect, and celebrate each other. Star Child said of Sun Ra: "This boy was definitely out to lunch—same place I eat."[43]

Sun Ra may have died in the Western sense of the word on 30 May 1993, but, just as Fard visited El Shabazz, so too does Sun Ra communicate with the members of his Arkestra, none of whom are surprised or frightened by his visits and messages.[44] Furthermore, he appears to communicate to and through younger warrior-philosophers such as Prodigal Sunn and through such songs as Goodie Mob's "Sky High."

Goodie Mob could be considered direct heirs of Sun Ra's cosmological teachings, as they come from a Christian oriented, as opposed to a Five Percent, background. Their aesthetic is less cosmic and more earthy-southern-soul, but the rhetoric, political analysis, and urgency are the same. In the song "Fighting," Cee-Lo reveals the meanings of his group's name: "Goodie Mob means, 'The Good Die Mostly Over Bullshit.' You take one 'o' away and it will let you know that 'God is Every Man Of Blackness.'"[45]

In "The Experience," released three years after "Fighting," Cee-Lo calls out "jive pretenders," a term used to identify Five Percenters who live in ways far less than righteous, with the chant: "I thought you said you was the G. O. D. / Sound like another nigger to me."[46] Leaving it up to his audience to determine if he is calling out wayward members of his own group, or other misdirected Gods, or both, Cee-Lo defines and deconstructs the "nigger" concept and all its attendant myths and fallacies. In the song, Cee-Lo recounts his meeting with a wisdom keeper who reveals to him important facts. She informs him that "a great deal of the Black man's downfall / Is not knowing that we were never niggers at all."[47] The wise woman deepens and broadens the knowledge she shares with Green with the following revelation: "Brother don't you know / You complain about being Black / When they mad cuz they can't be Black no mo'."[48] The wisdom keeper leaves Green to ponder the tragic irony of men so confused that they are not only "*trying* to be niggers" but "keeping it real to the point that they *dying* to be niggers."[49] Cee-Lo's lyrical exposition also serves as a reminder that while there are many Gods strolling this Earth, the seductive "nigger" construct is also strutting, tempting, lying, and taking Gods through the changes that test mettle and either obfuscate or magnify numinosity.

The magnificent thing about the Gods is that they are not perfect. They can fall victim to the tinseled traps and velvet ditches that line Babylon's boulevards. The Gods of the Nation compare favorably to Olódùmarè and the African American God, who both forgot to arm snakes; Olódùmarè, who forgot to bring kola nuts, which symbolize life, to a meeting of the Gods; and Ìyá Ayé, the Mother of the Earth, who was improperly interred because she breached her own rules of reciprocity.[50] The ultimate lesson conveyed by these Gods is that a perfect world is one that is dead and useless. The things that Gods forget or overlook become spaces that make room for new revelations to unfold and for new Gods to be born. Our "perfect imperfections," to quote a Cee-Lo Green subtitle, give this world, the Cosmos, and human beings texture and complexity. This is why tricksters play such important roles in Africana life and art. In African American orature, the Devil assists human beings in turning mistakes into miracles and converting tragedy to triumph: High John the Conqueror is definitely divine, but it is the Devil who keeps him perpetually sharp.

The devils that populate Five Percenter lyrics serve similar purposes but on a more sinister level because the trickery of these devils results in spiritual and physical genocide. Witness the chorus of Gravediggaz's "The Night the Earth Cried":

> At night time you can hear the Earth cry:
> How many more Black Gods got to die
> Before we realize there's no God in the sky?
> The devil tricked us, that's the worst lie[51]

With these lyrics, the Gravediggaz chant simple truths with such clarity that they cannot but spur critical analysis and divine awakening.[52] The lyrics reveal that while the devil's trick may have led to indoctrination and death, it is the responsibility of the individual to stop participating in his own religious oppression and to find and utilize his divine inheritance.

Given the historical and contemporary atrocities and injustices that Caucasian ten percenters have inflicted on Africana peoples, it is logical that in most liberation movements the word and concept of "devil" would be code for Caucasians. Early Nation of Islam rhetoric even popularized the concept with the expression "blond-haired blue-eyed devil." However, the Five Percent Nation denounces racism in any form; and while it is not possible for a Caucasian to be a God, there are many Caucasian fans of Five Percent rap, there are Caucasian Five Percent rappers, and there are Caucasian Five Percenters. Allah personally brought at least two Caucasians into the Five Percent way of life.

Barry Gottehrer was the assistant of New York Mayor Michael V. Lindsay and the creator of the Urban Action Task Force of New York; these associations brought Gottehrer into the sphere of Allah and the Gods. Lindsay and Allah respected and supported one another, but Gottehrer was completely mesmerized by Allah and spent nearly as much time with him as Allah's Suns did, whether the venue was a Universal Parliament, a picnic for the Gods, a local tavern, or a basement dice game.[53] Gottehrer was so devoted to Allah that his colleagues began to question his priorities. For his part, Allah thought so much of Gottehrer that he called him "Moses."[54] After Allah was assassinated, Gottehrer could not help but see the world through the lens of the Five Percent.[55]

A few months before he met and began building with Gottehrer and Lindsay in 1967, Allah was housed in a literal hell on Earth. As one might imagine, the American institution most befitting a God is either a prison or a mental hospital: New York had one institution that served both purposes. While incarcerated at the Matteawan State Hospital for the Criminally Insane for twenty months, Allah earned the respect of both inmates and staff, and he gained a devout follower in a sixteen-year-old Caucasian named John Kennedy. After Kennedy adopted the Five Percent way of life, Allah renamed him Azreal, after the "death Angel" who "is in charge of inhabitants of Hell, the only one with the key to both Heaven and Hell, who can come and go as he pleases, [whose] job it is to get the wrong doers to reveal who they are."[56] Decades after Allah's assassination, Azreal remains a Five Percenter whose loyalty to Allah is unimpeachable.

While it may seem odd or contradictory that Caucasians would embrace the Five Percent way of life, they have been part of the Nation for several decades. Michael Muhammad Knight's *The Five Percenters: Islam, Hip Hop and the Gods of New York* includes photos of Five Percenters gathered around Allah in the 1960s, and some of those Five Percenters are Caucasian.

The negative reputation that shadows the Five Percent and Allah is the result of a character assassination program initiated by American authorities. The FBI has a history of discrediting and destroying progressive and consciousness-raising Africana organizations that dates back to its inception. In its attempts to undermine Allah's efforts, the FBI defined a Nation that acknowledges and disseminates Divinity as a racist gang. Despite myriad and unrelenting attacks, peoples of various ethnicities have always been attracted to the Five Percent; indeed, one could posit that wisdom, knowledge, and understanding, three of the twelve jewels of the Five Percent, are naturally attractive to people, no matter their ethnicity.

During an interview with David Hunter, Knight, a Caucasian who rose to prominence because of his stated affiliation as a Five Percenter,[57] offers a compelling explanation as to why he is both a "devil" and a Five Percenter:

> To me, being a devil means what you've inherited. Like me, I am who I am. I'm in control of my actions. I have free will. But I didn't decide my bloodline. That's something I got handed to me. And, to be white and American, your bloodline is devil. I have Confederate captains in my ancestry. My dad is all into Hitler. Just from talking to my dad, I'm like, "Yeah, I'm the son of the devil." So, I get that. The best I can do is try to slay that devil that's in my blood.
>
> That's what I get out of the Five Percenters. The Five Percenters are an offshoot of the Nation of Islam. They study the same lessons as the Nation. The difference is that the Five Percenters will "teach the devil." The Five Percenters will make the devil a righteous man. There's a place in that culture that the Nation of Islam doesn't allow that the Five Percenters will allow to a certain extent.[58]

Rather than being attracted to the Five Percent *despite* his ethnicity, Knight claims to be drawn to the Nation *because* of it. Equally significant is Knight's acknowledgement that the Five Percenters are motivated to teach and that he is receptive and willing to learn.

However, Knight is incorrect about the Nation of Islam's position on "the devil": "Lost-Found Muslim Lesson No. 1" reveals that the Nation of Islam will also "teach the devil," to use Knight's phrase. However, Fard, who crafted the lesson, was highly cognizant of the fact that one's stated desire to learn does not indicate a desire or the ability to be righteous. Cognizant of certain "devils'" objectives to infiltrate and destroy the Nation while acknowledging other "devils'" genuine motivations, number nine of "Lost-Found Muslim Lesson No. 1" offers "devils" something akin to a trial period: "After he has devoted thirty-five or fifty years trying to learn and do like the original man, he [the Devil] could come and do trading among us and we would not kill him as quick as we would the other Devils – that is, who have not gone under this Study."[59] The lesson goes on to reveal that after decades of study, a "devil" can wear the Flag of the Nation; however, "He must add the sword on the upper part. The sword is the emblem of Justice and it was used by the original man in Muhammad's time. Thus, it was placed on the upper part of the Flag so that the Devil can always see it, so he will keep in mind that any time he reveals the Secrets, his head would be taken off by the sword."[60] While "devils" may undertake decades of study and revise their way of life, they cannot attain the status of "Muslim" and certainly not that of "God." The "devil" can only hope to "clean himself up."[61]

For "devils" who are beyond redemption, death awaits. The Battle of Armageddon, to which Elijah Muhammad refers, and the duties of the Gods therein are further specified in lesson ten of "Lost-Found Muslim Lesson No. 1," which asserts that the prophet Muhammad "learned that he could not reform the devils, so they had to be murdered."[62] The lesson goes on to aver that "[a]ll Muslims will murder the devil[;] they know he is a snake, and also, if he be allowed to live, he would sting someone else."[63] The lesson declares, "Each Muslim is required to bring four devils."[64] While it is not specified, the logical inference is that those "four devils" will be executed.

While murdering "devils" may sound extreme, it is actually a rather measured response to the genocide, whippings, torture, rape, and innumerable violations to which African Americans were routinely subjected in the 1930s, when Fard finalized and formalized his *Supreme Wisdom Lessons*. Marcus Garvey, Noble Drew Ali, W. D. Fard, Elijah Muhammad and all of the forerunners mentioned in this book witnessed the horrors of lynching, which was America's favorite national pastime. America sent these men clear messages through the charred, impaled, castrated, raped, decapitated bodies of their kin which Caucasians used as confounding community decorations. The Gods could not offer themselves, their families, and their congregations for sacrifice on America's altar to savagery and submission. They had to offer protection, and they were perfectly justified in offering vengeance.

Because America's terrorist attacks on its Africana citizens have not abated but now stand as the proudly polished cornerstone of the American Dream, Fard's mandates regarding "devils" recur in the Gods' rap lyrics. The last line of the chorus of Lord Jamar's "I.S.L.A.M." finds him meeting his quota of four devils. The RZA's act of decorating an evergreen with the heads of devils offers surviving Caucasians the opportunity to pick their own strange fruit from trees. In the song "Terrorist," Killa Sin describes an adversary as "slithering," not unlike a snake, after being beaten for breaking "the code of honor."[65] Killa Sin ultimately resolves to "dust . . . off" and behead the "two devils" who have betrayed him.[66] Killa Sin's lyrics are important because the ethnicity of his "devils" is ambiguous, and, from what his verse describes, they could be African Americans.

Just as the seeds of evolution can grow in any fertile soil, the ten percent of the population who stand in opposition to the five percent can be of any ethnicity, including Africana. Reflective of the Rastafarian chant "Nyabinghi," which means "Death to all oppressors [of all ethnicities]," the Gods oppose anyone who would disfranchise, miseducate, or oppress any other human being. In social-political terms, the association of oppressors with devils is clear. As it concerns religion, the association is a bit more complex. Stephen Boston's philosophical narrative "And God Said..." asserts, similar to the findings of Noble Drew Ali, that God created human beings so that they could attain "God consciousness" or become Gods and that Lucifer rebelled "[b]ecause he discovered that God was creating God beings that would forever be more glorious than even he was."[67] From this perspective, the "devil" is anyone who or anything that attempts to prevent a person from manifesting her divinity. The "devil," then, could be one's pastor, parents, priest, or professor. The "devil" could be the God one worships or even one's self. In the light of this, killing the "devil" becomes a more complex and delicate task, especially for those who have mastered the practice of loving one's enemy at the expense of the self and those who are living lives of social death.

While slaying literal and figurative devils is a central trope in Five Percent lyrics, the Gods actually appear to be much more concerned with awakening sleeping Gods. At the beginning of the song "Twelve Jewelz," The RZA explains the meaning of one of his praisenames, "RZArector," and the purpose of the group called "Gravediggaz":

> As long as you got mentally dead people who are living in a . . . mental grave, you need somebody to dig that grave up and bring them back to life. There's no chance for [revivification after] physical death, but there is a chance for the mentally dead. So we gon come and resurrect them. That's why they call me the RZArector. I'm bout to resurrect the mental dead. . . .[68]

What, the reader may ask, gives Africans displaced and discredited in America the authority to revise and create meaning, to name and claim, to be so bold as to resurrect the dead and rebirth them in divinity? The answer is the fact of their existence. The Gods are born with unlimited creative abilities, and it is their responsibility to purposefully apply them. As a result, the Gods are constantly learning, elevating, and evolving their wisdom. The desire to have one's knowledge mirror the infinitude of the Cosmos is, perhaps, the secret of the Five Percent's relevance. Rather than championing one text that will be rendered obsolete with new scientific discoveries or establishing a precarious perch on the fallacy of infallibility, the Gods, themselves, are the texts, and they are constantly revising, updating, editing, and deepening their masterpieces.

One of the most important revisions that the Gods made was to truthfully acknowledge their ethnicity. Originally, many Five Percenters, like many members of the NOI, referred to themselves as being "Asiatic," a term coined by Noble Drew Ali. "Asiatic" was a comforting concept to individuals who had been programmed to avoid associations with Africa and to be ashamed of their African identity, culture, and origin. However, in the late eighties and early nineties, hip hop turned to its African geographical, intellectual, and phenotypical roots and found there infinite sources of political empowerment, philosophical depth, and pride. One group of hip hop Gods who held up to African Americans a mirror that reflected their rich heritage, history, and divinity is X Clan.

Eschewing the dubious concept of Asiatic ethnicity, Brother J, the group's wordsmith, proclaims his ethnicity and power to be "African," in fact, "*very* African," and in the song "Grand Verbalizer, What Time Is It?" he invites listeners to "step in Brother's temple see what's happenin'."[69] X Clan knew that before Africana peoples could manifest their divinity they would need to know and love the African Gods who had come before and were thriving inside of them. Consequently, X Clan's songs regularly invoke Èṣù Ẹlẹ́gbára, the Yoruba Trickster Deity, and honor the God with praisesongs. Indeed, the "X" of the Clan is not a reference to unknown African identity; it is homage to the home of Èṣù Ẹlẹ́gbára, who resides at the literal and metaphysical crossroads of existence.[70]

When X Clan and Èṣù Ẹlẹ́gbára meet at the crossroads, they are joined by a multitude of Gods. In the song "Do It Like You?!," Brother J pours lyrical libation to the Yoruba Gods Ẹlẹ́gbára, Ọ̀ṣun, Ṣàngó, Ògún, Ọbàtálá, and Yemaya before welcoming himself into the circle of Gods as the Seventh African Power.[71] Cognizant that divine African progenitors constitute an eternally interconnected collective, X Clan also invokes such East African Gods as Ptah, Ra, Atum, Amen, Ausar, and Aset in their songs. The group emphasizes the curvilinear continuity of Africana wisdom workers and freedom fighters by heralding revolutionary activists and ancestors such as Patrice Lumumba, Marcus Garvey, El Hajj Malik El Shabazz, and Sonny Carson, the Brooklyn activist who fathered Lumumba Carson, who is known as Professor X, X Clan's Overseer.

"Protected by the red, black, and green" of African unity and liberation and armed with the ankh, the Kemetic key of life and symbol of the mysteries of the universe, X Clan's music enlightens multitudes. Most significantly, they impart upon Blackness something deeper than mere beauty. By incorporating the tenets of the Five Percent Nation with traditional African spiritual systems, science, and cosmology, X Clan makes it clear that the inherent divinity of Africana peoples is not a neoreligious idea of eccentric demagogues, but a reality that is as ancient and abiding as the African Self. By embracing their African roots, X Clan does precisely what Allah, the Father, did with the teachings of Fard and Muhammad: The group builds upon and expands the lessons of those who preceded them. What is more, the charge that is arguably the most important for the Gods remains intact, as X Clan is ever-traveling "to the East," with the essential goal of

> Teaching Gods to be
> What it was
> What it is
> And again shall be[72]

The simplicity of the lyric and the cyclical nature of the goal give these lines a powerful political resonance and offer a concrete elucidation of the purpose of their art. No matter how many lifetimes it may take, X Clan is devoted to the arduous work of giving birth to Gods. Brother J concludes the song "Dark Sun Riders" by emphasizing the curvilinear nature of his mission: "If the mortals don't get it and it don't seep in / resurrect me with my mic I'll go at it again."[73]

It is only within the context of the African worldview, with curvilinear time, ancestor reverence, immortality, holism, and inherent divinity at its foundation, that the wisdom of Brother J conveys its intended meaning. Because of Five Percent rap groups such as X Clan, De La Soul, Jungle Brothers, and Lakim Shabazz, who embraced their African origin and identity, African culture, philosophy, science, and technology became central to the Gods' divine curricula and lyrics. Rather than the outlandish displays of savagery created and popularized by racist ideologues and propagandists, African American Gods found African Gods who resembled them in appearance and also boasted identical philosophies, technologies, cultural foundations, and political motivations.

The impact of African Gods, philosophies, religions, and cultures, while not often acknowledged, is so profound and global that Judaism, Christianity, and Islam would not exist without them: The Five Percent are aware of this because their study includes world religions. Furthermore, in addition to embracing the biblical confirmations of inherent divinity in Psalms 82:6 and John 10:34, the Gods are knowledgeable about the Africanity of Jesus Christ. The omnipresent Europeanized images of Jesus do not confuse the Five Percent. The Gods know that they share genotypic, phenotypic, and divine attributes with Yashua ben Yoseph.

The RZA begins his verse in the song "Dangerous Mindz" by revealing that the description of Jesus in Revelations 1:14–15 describes him as well: "Rotate your head like a gyro / My hair grows in knotty spirals / Feet resemble Christ's description from the Bible."[74] The RZA and Jesus do not merely share physical attributes; they share technologies as well. The RZA confirms that, like Jesus and the Igbo, he, too, can walk on water.[75]

As he continues rapping, it becomes clear that The RZA's abilities surpass those of Jesus in important ways. The RZA's divinity will not condemn him to betrayal, agony, and immortalization as lynching victim *par excellence*. Not only is he "immune to all physical torture," but having mastered contemporary technology along with ancient tools, rather than submit to suffering, The RZA can simply "[p]ull off fast in a Porsche / Upon a double-crosser."[76] Perhaps The RZA's most important revelation is that he is not a neutered God. Like Èṣù, Ṣàngó, Ògún, High John the Conqueror, Ausar, and other African Gods, The RZA's physical disseminator of divinity reminds him every morning that a God's duties include creating more Gods not only spiritually but also physically: "My penis rise up in the morning like a Phoenix / And blast iron cells into a low-blooded anemic."[77] The RZA is a whole and holistic God who imparts sensual bliss as well as sexual healing and biological creation as effortlessly as the Earth rotates.

Too Poetic's verse in "Dangerous Mindz" describes his ancient lineage and, in the process, reveals that some concepts thought to be Christian are of ancient African origin:

> Had my photographs etched inside of pyramids
> To laugh at this revelation
> Without 365 days of concentration
> And twenty-four hour meditation
> Would be foolishly pagan
> I'm ancient as Amen[78]

The narrator of Ayi Kwei Armah's *Two Thousand Seasons* avers that Africana people "are not a people of yesterday."[79] The narrator instructs those who wish to know when Africana people began to exist to count the stars in the sky and the grains of sand on the Earth. Although they could next count the drops of rain that have fallen, numbering the stars and grains of sand will suffice to help the inquisitive comprehend what "ancient" truly means. Too Poetic is cognizant that he is part of this timeless continuum, and in addition to informing his audience that his visage is immortalized in the eternal masterpieces of Kemet—a truth that any Africana person touring the ruins of Kemet can also behold—Too Poetic dates the origin of his existence not to "amen," the borrowed closing of a prayer, but to the primeval source of the borrowing, the African God, Amen, whose name means "The Hidden One."

In "Guess Who's Back," Rakim Allah uses the wisdom of the Supreme Mathematics to reveal that he is not only God, but God to the third power who was "born with three sevens in [his] head."[80] Rakim's three honorable names—William Michael Griffin—all have seven letters; consequently, the supreme mathematics of his birth designate him not only as God but as God cubed. The fact that Rakim Allah is the bearer of magnified and compounded divinity and its necessary component, wisdom, is apparent in his lyrics:

> In time no one can seem to blow your mind as far as this
> To find you'll need philosophers and anthropologists
> Astrologists, professors from your smartest colleges
> With knowledge of scholarships, when Ra be droppin' this[81]

That Rakim's intellect is as versatile as it is deep and wide is evident in his elaboration on his name and its meanings. In an interview with Wakeel Allah, Rakim Allah reveals that, while the Arabic meaning of the name Rakim, "writer," fits his occupation as a wordsmith, he defines the name Rakim as a compound construction of "Ra," the Kemetic God of the Sun, and "Kim," as in Kemet, the Land of the Blacks.[82]

As he raps, it is clear that Rakim is fully cognizant of the eternal nature of his divinity and his literary, lyrical, spiritual, political, and intellectual responsibilities:

> Some of the things that I know will be in your next Bible
> When I die go bury me and my notebook in Cairo
> With the great God from Egypt
> Manifest was write rhymes
> Align with the stars
> I come back to bless the mic[83]

Zora Neale Hurston is lauded for her ability to weave history with myth and create sacred texts; in this, Rakim Allah is her spiritual son. Not only does he inform his audience that a new Bible is being written, but he confirms that his knowledge will infuse its pages.

Rakim's Bible has a source much more ancient and authentic than Judaism or Christianity. Some of the most revered Kemetic texts are erroneously grouped under the name "Book of the Dead." This mistranslation reveals the inability of Westerners to comprehend the African ethos and worldview, let alone divinity and immortality. Those who are dead have no need for books. The Kemites were interred with Books of the Coming Forth By Day.[84] These scrolls, incantations, scriptures, and inscriptions ensured the immortality of the soul. With his notebook as his Book of the Coming Forth By Day, Rakim will journey into the galactic womb and join his Kemetic and Nubian forebears before being reborn so that he can continue enlightening the masses and expanding soul power exponentially through his Ọrọ̀, Power of the Word.

African cosmology, ontology, philosophies, and Gods offer ample proof of the fact with which Rakim concludes "Guess Who's Back": that for the divine, there is no death. Rakim's pontification on resurrection is reminiscent of Brother J's lyric in "Grand Verbalizer, What Time Is It?":

> Come into the darkness, path is light
> Death meaning life as the pharaohs take flight
> Too much degrees for a silly pale thief
> You can't define what direct from the East[85]

Brother J mocks Caucasian Egyptologists and Africanists who, stymied by the depth and holism of the African ethos, have been unable to understand and unwilling to admit the profundity of African science and technology.

While X Clan is not the first hip hop group to meld Five Percent philosophy with African consciousness, their consistent lauding of their African identity made it both easy and necessary for rappers like Rakim Allah to journey lyrically and spiritually to Africa. X Clan is the first rap group, to my knowledge, to herald ancient and contemporary female Gods as being equal to male Gods. Such recognition, while logical, is groundbreaking because the patriarchally-skewed gender hierarchy that is standard in organized religions abounds in Five Percent lyrics and philosophies.

Subordination of women is evident in the cosmological interpretation of the Sun, as giver of life, representing man, and the Earth, which rotates around and is illuminated by and dependent on the Sun, symbolizing woman. The Moon is also used to represent woman, not only because of its impact on menstruation, but also because of its seeming lack of significance as compared to the Sun. The linking of genders to hierarchically scaled astrological bodies reveals a patriarchal desire to infuse subservience and subordination into both an inherently egalitarian way of life and worldview and on the Cosmos itself.

Knight's *The Five Percenters* includes an important discussion about certain Gods' attempts to reify misogyny and patriarchal supremacy:

> Prince A Cuba believes that since Allah's murder, the Five Percenters have grown consumed by a "preoccupation with male supremacy" manifesting in all aspects of the culture. Gods altered their Universal Flag to make the 7 dominate the crescent moon, he argues, to assuage their "inferiority complexes about the Black woman." In Cuba's reading of the original flag, the 7 appeared within the crescent to "show man entering the womb or Equality of the Woman." For Cuba, the movement's adopted name, "Nation of Gods and Earths" also reflects inequality when compared to other options such as "Gods and Goddesses" or "Suns and Earths."[86]

The original design of the Universal Flag and Prince Allah Cuba's analysis of it have clear African antecedents. The Mande cosmological and ontological articulation of humanodivinity reveals that Tasi, the "creative spirit of the universe," "is represented in the number 7," and seven is comprised of three and four: "3 is the male symbol (penis and testicles); 4, the female (the labia); and, added together, these two numbers make the ideal androgynous pair of twins."[87] Mande cosmology and ontology make it clear that neither the number seven nor the cosmic and biological power that seven signifies can exist without Woman.

The Mande articulation of the significance of the female principle to the work of creation is comparable to that of Yoruba cosmology which holds that the Moon, especially the crescent Moon, relates to not only women, but women's essential roles as the creators of existence. In "*À Yà Gbó, À Yà Tó*: New Perspectives on Edan Ògbóni," Babatunde Lawal reveals that "[t]he Yoruba refer to menses as a 'sign of the moon' (nkan osù)," and the "sign of the moon" is truly the sign of life because women use the moon to time their menstrual cycles and periods of ovulation so that they can conceive.[88] Cognizant of their personal relationship with the Moon as it relates to the creation and continuity of life, Lawal asserts that Yoruba "maidens and newly married women pray to the moon to make them fertile and give them the strength with which to carry a baby on the back."[89]

When a woman ovulates and attains a Moon-like fullness, and man, to quote Prince Allah Cuba, "[enters] the womb or Equality of the Woman," he releases the sperm that fertilizes the ovum that is embedded in and nourished by the rich Motherblood that comprises the foundation of human existence. However, man not only enters and inseminates the crescent of Creation, he is born of that crescent as well. The existence of every man and every God is dependent on Woman, who is The Mother of All the Gods and All Living Things Without Whom Life Ceases to Exist.[90]

Prince Allah Cuba's assertions are important for many reasons, including the fact that he reveals the process by which a spiritual system becomes an organized religion and, thus, a tool of oppression. Once biases and insecurities supplant biology, logic, and science, a way of life becomes twisted into an ideological weapon at best, a path to social death at worst. However, because the Five Percent is not an organized religion and because it is rooted in such principles as growth, fluidity, and intellectual exchange and dynamism, misogynistic rhetoric and imagery can be revised or ignored at any time by any God.

Because wisdom, knowledge, and understanding are at their nadir when miseducation and instant gratification are at their apex, it is easy to assume that there is one single Five Percent doctrine. But the secret of the Nation's longevity and vitality is that it revolves around the acknowledged and respected autonomous power of the Divine and the ability of the Divinities to reason and exchange information to facilitate intellectual growth and philosophical and scientific enlightenment. The cipher is central to the Gods because it where knowledge is continually and holistically born. The resilience and relevance of the Gods is a direct result of the fact that they are not a monolithic group with a corpus of edicts and beliefs. In the universe of the Gods, Lord Jamar's assertion that woman is "secondary but most necessary" coexists alongside Divine Prince's revelation that "Earth is God in female form," and Justice's confirmation that a Five Percenter named Tawanna was not only a God but "more God than some of the men."[91] Consequently, just as a group of Gods decided to try to reduce the significance of woman, so too are many male and female Gods standing firm on the science of biological and divine equality.

A great deal of the insecurity and jealousy that women inspire in some men revolves around the fact that man's existence and continuity are dependent on woman. Woman's ovum, menses, womb, and vagina constitute the source of man's existence. Another interpretation of the number seven's position within the crescent moon of the original Universal Flag is that man can only be born of and cannot experience life without woman. One could also interpret the original flag as reflecting the fact that man's life has its literal foundation in the ovum and menstrual fluid that reside in the core of woman's being and that are controlled by the Moon. While technology can store sperms indefinitely and any of many tools can facilitate insemination, there is no technological equivalent for the elegant magnificence of the womb. While many men may seek comfort in misogyny, many others know that Woman provides them with the surest protection and with the promise of immortality.

Celestial bodies also impress upon the scientifically-minded observer the importance of interdependence, interconnectedness, balance, and harmony. Sun, Earth, and Moon, like man, woman, and child, work in a complementary fashion to ensure existence and proliferation: Without the Sun, the Earth and its beings perish; without the Earth, the Sun is irrelevant to humanity for humanity cannot exist. The Moon's relationship with woman results in a magnetic resonance and rhythm that is essential to existence. The significance of woman to creation and existence both on Earth and in the Cosmos is evident in the fact that only woman bears a womb, and without the womb there can be no sons; likewise, without the cosmic womb, known as the universe, there can be no astronomical suns and no life.

Brother J of X Clan understands well the actual cosmological, biological, and historical facts as they relate to the power that is Woman. Woman is equated with Wisdom in Supreme Mathematics, and in the aptly titled song "Wiz Degrees," Brother J offers an ode of reverence to the Africana woman. He opens his song asking, "In how many words can I express / My respect for Wisdom and the Goddess manifest?"[92] After nearly two decades of grand verbalizing, Brother J remains consistent in his recognition of the Africana woman as his "equal" and the complement with whom he builds homes as well as universes.[93] Rather than lounging in the recliner of unearned domestic patriarchal privilege, Brother J's divinity is so evolved that he fortifies his family's constitution for the necessary work of building and battling by cooking breakfast.[94]

With lyrics that emphasize the need for balance and cooperation in relationships—"If we both do our homework, the home will be free"[95]— Brother J makes it clear that the division of labor in the sphere of the Gods is as logical as it is biological: Brother J's complement bestows their children with the breath of life and he protects those children "to the death."[96] Brother J encourages members of his audience to "research the swing and the swagger of queens / . . . / that can civilize kings,"[97] so that they can better appreciate the dynamism of Woman. Brother J offers eloquent confirmation of the fact that respect for woman does not diminish but exponentially accentuates a man's "God body gangster lean."[98]

Lyrics from female Gods are not as plentiful as those of males, but the women who represent their divinity in their artistry offer verses that reverberate with power. Medusa, "Tha Gangsta Goddess" and "God Mother" of hip hop, consistently emphasizes the equality and unity of Gods of both genders in her lyrics. Heralding herself as the "female Tupac," Medusa raps in X Clan's "Keys to Ur City": "God said, 'Let lead be spit,' / You know the Gangster Goddess gone represent it / 'Til they arms outstretch like white Jesus."[99] With these lyrics, Medusa gives a nod to Brother J, who asked her to spit lead (rap) on his track, and she reveals that she is the Great Mother God whose verses are so powerful that they render mediocre rappers as immobile and useless as the "white Jesus" who reigns over the destitution soaked "City of God" in Rio de Janeiro. Medusa goes on to inform her divine male peers that they cannot compare to her for she is the Source from whence they spring: "You spit flames? / I'm the light that jumpstarts the heart and motivates the game."[100]

One of the most successful artists to infuse Five Percent philosophy in song is Erykah Badu. Her hit song "On and On" awakened many to the knowledge of the Nation. Singing, "Peace and blessings manifest with every lesson learned / If your knowledge were your wealth then it would be well earned,"[101] Badu's lyrics constitute clear nods to Five Percenters, who gather in ciphers to recite, expound, and build upon lessons in the Gods' curriculum.

In one of the song's more esoteric verses, Badu divulges her origin:

> I was born under water
> With three dollars and six dimes
> Yeah, you might laugh
> 'Cause you did not do your math[102]

The unschooled would interpret these lyrics as evidence of a new-age or impoverished birth, but, in addition to punning on her astrological sign of Pisces, Badu is actually informing her audience that when she was frolicking in the amniotic perfection of the womb—both the maternal womb and the primordial womb of the Earth's creation—she had knowledge of self, was divine, and was manifesting 360° of wisdom, knowledge, and understanding. With her sparse but deftly encoded lyrics, Badu does with her verses precisely what Toni Morrison does with her literature, which is what Olódùmarè does with creation and what Five Percenters do daily: She leaves spaces for her audience to enter, interpret, and "do the math" themselves and thereby awaken their own latent numinosity.

Badu is a master of encoding, and in her efforts to help her audience better understand not only her lyrics but also themselves, Badu forms an interactive cipher with her audience and explains the chorus of "On and On":

> Y'all know what a cipher is? It's all kinds of ciphers. But a cipher can be represented by a circle, which consists of how many degrees? What? 360 degrees. And my cipher keeps moving like a rolling stone. So, in my song when I say that, my cipher represents myself or the atoms in my body and the rolling stone represents the Earth. The atoms in the body rotate at the same rate on the same axis that the Earth rotates, giving us a direct connection with the place we call Earth; therefore, we can call ourselves Earth.[103]

Like a true Five Percenter, Badu "adds on" to or expands on established Five Percent wisdom. Rather than promote cosmological and ontological gender bias, Badu initiates every member of her audience, males and females without distinction, into the Earth, which is the cipher that effortlessly supports all.

Badu's recognition of her divine nature and that of her Africana audience is also evident in the lines that repeatedly introduce the chorus:

> If we were made in his image
> Then call us by our names
> Most intellects do not believe in God
> But they fear us just the same[104]

Badu makes resonant points about the fear that holistic power and ìtàn ipǫnri inspire in those who do not have them. Perhaps Badu has read *The Palm-Wine Drinkard*, for the misnaming and lack of respect given Father of the Gods by literary critics is identical to that which Africana people in general are subjected. Badu's lyrics intimate that the disrespect shown Africana people is rooted in fear which is born of the fact that Africana people are, indeed, Gods. It is also significant that other than the reference to the biblical scripture that much of her audience will recognize, Badu uses the gender neutral pronoun "we" and "us" to emphasize the fact that Divinity is a characteristic of a collective that includes both genders. Badu does not divide men from women in her statements about Africana divinity, and she does not adhere to the patriarchal hierarchy that places women in the position of subordinate Earth to superior male God/Sun. Her cipher reinforces the fact of equality.

Another God of note is Mecca, who rose to fame as the female lyricist of Digable Planets. She describes her suzerainty in understated and undeniable ways. With the name "Mecca" the God equates herself with Islam's holiest city and intimates that it is to her that all Muslims prostrate and pray. But there is an astronomical complement to her terrestrial dominion. In the song "9th Wonder," Mecca offers the following description of herself: "Now, you see that I'm 68 inches above sea level / 93 million miles above these devils."[105] Mecca stands five feet eight inches tall physically, but her astronomical equivalent is the Sun, which is ninety-three million miles from the Earth. When she drops these jewels there is no music save a minimalist bass line which serves to emphasize and highlight Mecca's assertion and ascendancy. Refusing subordinate designations and heralding the life-giving powers of her womb, Mecca claims her rightful identity and place as a female Sun whose brilliance is equal to, if not greater than, that of any male Sun.

When male Gods stand up and fully embrace their divine perfection and the source of their existence and continuity they will find themselves shoulder to shoulder with female Gods. Mecca advocates the recognition of the fact that existence and knowledge are born of balance:

> We need to know that there is a feminine and masculine [principle] or consciousness that is considered the God or the Creator. It's not a male, like religion will tell you. It's a mother/father principle, a masculine/feminine principle.
> The feminine principle is what gives birth to the universe. It's what brings creation forth, so there has to be an acknowledgement and respect for her in order to bring back the balance.[106]

Mecca's wisdom is rooted in logical and biological fact. Her explication also recalls Elijah Muhammad's and R. V. Bey's assertion that God cannot make that which God is not and C. M. Bey's query: "Do you know of any being that is superior to you and your mother?"[107] As if in response to C. M. Bey, in "Warrior's Song," rapper Nas confirms, "Your mother's the closest thing to God that you'll ever have."[108] The veracity of Nas' statement is apparent in the fact that all human beings exist as a result of the choices made by their mothers.

The primordial and eternal divinity of woman as the source of life must be acknowledged, because without woman—her vulnerable vulva, her wondrous womb, her millions of shimmering eggs, and her resilience—Gods, life, cipher, and wisdom all cease to exist. While I understand that the quest for African American patriarchal supremacy is a response to centuries of racist oppression and emasculation, Africana men cannot both claim to respect actual facts and ignore and/or devalue the elemental power of Woman. Because the actual facts are apparent and because my inherent divinity leads me to do so, for the rest of this book I will not use the term "Nation of Gods and Earths"; I will use the term "Nation of Gods." This term uses the gender-neutral word "God" to signify, as it should, male and female Deities of the Nation who exist as a cooperative collective, as a partnership of equals. This usage is right and exact.

As is apparent in the lyrics of Mecca and as is logical given the cosmic origins and holistic spiritual systems of Africana people, references to astronomical forces and to the relationship of stars and planets to Divinities and divinity abound in the Nation of Gods' verbal artistry. Not surprising given its significance to earthly existence, the Sun is the most often invoked celestial body in hip hop, and solar invocations of praise are logically extended to the Gods: For those who think that the widely used hip hop term of endearment is "son," indicating a quasi-biological affiliation, Method Man's lyric in "Wu-Gambinos" is illuminating: "I call my brother Sun 'cause he shine like one."[109]

Hip hop is teeming with glowing Gods. The aptly named group Sunz of Man collaborated with Mood on a song titled "Illuminated Sunlight" in which they proclaim their nature to be "Genuine / Everlasting light / Sunshine."[110] In Wu Tang Clan's appropriately titled "Sunlight," The RZA confirms his identity: "I'm the seven in the center of the Sun."[111] The RZA's seemingly simple statement is a delicately layered acknowledgment of his divinity. Not only is The RZA the "7," signifying "G" or God, which is stationed in the center of the Nation of God's sign, but The RZA avers that he is the God who created and maintains the Sun and its solar system.

The most glorious ode to the shining self may well be Lord Jamar's "The Sun" which describes the God as being indistinguishable from the star:

> Well, here come the Sun; here come the One
> It's Lord Jamar; a new day has begun
> Just look at me shining as I rise in the East
> I welcome you with the Universal greeting of "Peace"[112]

If Lord Jamar's listeners have difficulty comprehending his relationship to the Sun and the Sun's relationship to the Earth, he spells it out—"G – O – D"—repeatedly in the song's chorus.[113] Grounded in science, astrophysics, and cosmology, "The Sun" is a resonant praisesong to the numinous self that is offered with the same precision as Hatshepsut's speech and Nikki Giovanni's classic poem "Ego-Tripping (There Must Be a Reason Why)."

Knowledge of astronomy is an important part of the Gods' curriculum, and it reflects the holistic nature of Africana spiritual systems and the knowledge that Africana people are a cosmic people. Indeed, the origin of existence in Yoruba ontology and cosmology begins not on Earth but in the Cosmos with a vast spectrum of Gods who began life as constellations.[114] These celestial forces came to the Earth countless millennia ago to undertake the building of this planet, and they continue their work on Earth to this day, for they are cyclically reincarnated as the rappers, djeli, writers, dibia, jazz masters, philosophers, and wisdom keepers discussed in this book. Most important, these wonder workers *know* who they are.

The Gods also know that the human body is a microcosmic encapsulation of every element that exists on the Earth and in the Cosmos, and their lyrics describe their association with the infinite and eternal. In the song "9th Wonder," Cee Knowledge of Digable Planets describes how his Five Percent way of life—"rollin' with the seven and a crescent"—coupled with his purposeful use of flora—"puffin' some expression"—help him acquire knowledge on a daily basis and apply it to attain curvilinear intergalactic wisdom:

> Manifestin' today's lesson
> Stressin' the fact that I'm solar
> Guaranteed to go far
> 'Cause the mind is interstellar.[115]

The fact that his name signifies that whenever you behold him, you Cee (or See) Knowledge is a powerful motivator for the God who also refers to himself as an "Afronaut" and "Cosmic Funkateer."[116]

In his appropriately titled song "Deep Space," Lord Jamar boasts about his intimate relationship with the Cosmos and invites his listeners to join him on an intergalactic journey to the realm of the Gods:

> Enter the seventh dimension
> Witness my ascension into the heavens
> Like Christ on the third day
> I'm nice with the wordplay
> Master of all that I survey[117]

Lord Jamar continues to celebrate his cosmic origin and knowledge while challenging his audience with powerful truths. With a simple couplet: "Let's take a trip through the galaxy / Mystery god is a fallacy," Lord Jamar demystifies the myths and antiscientific assertions upon which the Gods of organized religion rely. Following his revelation, Lord Jamar asks his audience to examine the documented evidence about cosmic entities who have visited Earth: "Celestial beings / Mother Ship over the White House / Had your president shook."[118] Lord Jamar is likely referring to the fact that in July 1952, during successive weekends, objects from the Cosmos flew at close range over Washington D.C., befuddling the Truman administration.[119]

When he encourages his audience to "take a self-evident look" into the universe and at the Earth's relationship to it, Lord Jamar could well be asking his audience to view the video that NASA recorded during space shuttle missions STS-48, STS-63, STS-75, and STS-80[120] so that they can see what Lord Jamar knows and appreciate the depth of the ancestral and cosmic connections that he boasts and that move him to proclaim: "Lord Jamar, I got a constellation of stars / You only did your observation from afar."[121]

The relationship of the Five Percent to the Cosmos is a modern articulation of an ancient Pan-African association. While every schoolchild is made to learn the stages in Caucasian history when they believed that the Earth was flat and that the Sun rotated around the Earth, no mention is made of the ancient African astronomers, who, far beyond understanding the Earth's shape and rotation, had astrophysical knowledge of the planets and constellations that modern Western scientists have yet to fully understand. The celestial maps found in Namoratunga, Kenya and Nabta Playa in Northern Sudan reveal the fact that African knowledge of the galaxy is *at least* 16,000 years old and extraordinarily precise.[122] The Nubians and Kemites used their astronomical and astrophysical knowledge to build perfectly constructed massive pyramids and temples and harness the energy of the Earth and the Cosmos to enrich life and ensure immortality.[123]

The ancient Dogon of Mali discerned that Sirius B is literally the Mother of the Earth, and they celebrate with a grand festival called *sigui* when the Mother's orbit brings her closest to her offspring.[124] Igbo cosmologists have always known that the planets rotate counterclockwise around the Sun, and the movement of the planets is reproduced in ritual ceremonies and dances. The Igbo hold that "there are as many stars up in the sky/space as we have grains of sands on earth."[125] With this knowledge, they unite the properties of the Earth with those of the Cosmos and fly. Among the Igbo, travel through the galaxy is a common and necessary reality given the rigors of spiritwork. However, it is not the case that only dibia engage in galactic travel; the Igbo consider Afa divination to be a sentient being who, after seeking wisdom from "the solar system and all its planets," shares with the dibia information that, given its source, must be taken "very seriously."[126]

Africana knowledge of and association with the Cosmos is as ancient as African peoples. The complex relationships that ancient and many contemporary Dogon, Fon, Igbo, Nubian, Kemite, Yoruba, Fanti, Bachwezi, and Dagara peoples have with the Cosmos is logical and natural considering the number of African spiritual systems that state that Africans came to the Earth from other celestial bodies. Having come from the stars it is not surprising that many Africana people describe themselves as shining and associate themselves with stars. Celestial references abound in music. Sly & the Family Stone croon, "Everybody is a star / I can feel it when you shine on me."[127] Earth, Wind & Fire commands listeners, "Keep your head to the sky," for the keys to destiny and divinity there lie: "Shining star for you to see / What your life can truly be."[128]

These references to the celestial are not metaphorical; they are literal. In Dagara cosmology, the shining that manifests itself in human beings' material and cosmic selves is equated to God, stars, and fire:

> [T]he rising part, the fire, [is] the god that makes us do, feel, see, love, and hate. The fire has power, a great power of motion both within us and without. Outside of us, it drives us toward one another, toward the execution of our respective duties, toward the planning of our lives. We act and react because this rising power is in us and with us. Inside of us the fire pulls the spiritual forces beyond us toward us. This fire within us is what causes our real family—those we are always drawn to when we see them—to identify us. *From the realm where the ancestors dwell this fire can be seen in each and every one of us, shining like the stars that you see above your heads.*[129]

Hip hop lyrics offer abundant odes to shining and bling, but for some people, these references go beyond jewelry; they bespeak the composition of the soul and signify immense responsibilities. For people such as U-Allah, the concept of shining brings divinity to mind. U-Allah describes Allah, the Father, as having vibrant luminosity and numinosity: "He stood smiling and shining, with an aura so thick it [appeared] to float though the atmosphere with scintillating colors."[130] In Ishmael Beah's autobiography *A Long Way Gone*, an acquaintance recalls that when Beah was a child, his forehead "used to glow naturally," and when he was being mischievous, the glowing intensified.[131] Malidoma Somé recalls that during the elaborate rituals and exchanges that took place during his grandfather's transition from the material to the spiritual realm, his "dead" grandfather shared the wisdom of the Ancients with Somé, and "[a]s he continued to speak, a glow, first yellow then green, came out of the crown of his head and spread throughout the tiny room."[132]

Africana soulshine has both biochemical and spiritual sources. In Kemetic philosophy, Khu is "the shining part of man which bridges the gap between human (man) and superhuman (God) beings; and the body Khat."[133] Khu is closely related to Ba, the world soul, and Ka, the activator of cosmic forces, and Khu is manifest biochemically through melanin and serotonin. The Kemites of Ancient Egypt called the pineal gland the "eye of Heru," and the pineal gland secretes melatonin, which is a combination of melanin and serotonin.[134] Marimba Ani describes melanin's role in the human body as analogous to the role of chlorophyll in plants; the validity of this comparison is further substantiated by the fact that sunlight is a key stimulus for both chlorophyll and melanin. Richard King asserts that sunlight also acts as a point of divergence, because, while the growth of plants is toward sunlight, the growth of human beings is "directed toward higher states of consciousness."[135] King finds that melanin and serotonin are essential for allowing "human beings to learn from their ancestors."[136] Africana peoples' profusion of melanin may facilitate communication with other spiritual entities as well. Africana wisdom workers across the continuum state that one of the most effective ways to learn pharmacology, astronomy, cosmogony, and other sciences is through dreams, and melanin and serotonin are secreted at night, and can lead to vivid dreams. The biochemical and spiritual properties of melanin and serotonin have yet to be fully understood, but it could be the case that the pineal and pituitary glands house an aspect of the power that results in a distinct spiritual shining.

Khu's attributes and actualities are biochemical, physiological, and physical. The Kemites state that they originally came from Ta Ntr, "The Land of God," and Ta Ntr is in present day Uganda.[137] The original inhabitants of Ta Ntr include the Bachwezi, who founded the empire of Kitara. The Bachwezi's divinity endowed them with many skills. They had the ability to communicate with each other across vast distances, and they were master hunters, agriculturalists, and metallurgists.[138] The Bachwezi are thought to be the source of Kemetic and Nubian astronomy, cosmology, religion, philosophy, agriculture, and architecture. While some hold that the Bachwezi vanished and others state that they "disappeared into the underworld";[139] others argue that the historical and contemporary African inhabitants of Uganda, Sudan, Ethiopia, and Egypt are the direct descendants of the Bachwezi.[140] The Bachwezi offer a powerful example of Khu and the gifts and abilities that accompany it. Witnesses describe the Bachwezi as being so full of Khu that it was literally bursting from their eyes: "One could not look them in the face because their eyes were so bright that it hurt one's own eyes to look at them. It was like looking at the sun."[141]

Khu takes myriad forms in African physiognomy, and although some of its manifestations are not readily discernable to the average contemporary human being, Western science is finally able to detect what the spiritual vision of African wisdom keepers has always been able to see. Contemporary scientists have discerned that "the human body literally glows" and emits a "visible light" albeit in "extremely small quantities."[142] Scientists also found that one body part glowed more than others, and the place and possible reason are both significant:

> Faces glowed more than the rest of the body. This might be because faces are more tanned than the rest of the body, since they get more exposure to sunlight — the pigment behind skin color, melanin, has fluorescent components that could enhance the body's miniscule light production.[143]

It would be logical to surmise that Africana people, especially those with profuse melanin and routine exposure to the sun, would glow more than other ethnic groups. This correlates to the contention that the more melanin one has, the more spiritual and technological access and power one commands.[144] While more research must be done in this area, it seems evident that melanin, shining, and soulpower are all interconnected.

Shining has an important relationship to soul. African American, Kemetic, Igbo, and Yoruba philosophies confirm that human beings can be endowed with two souls. But soul can manifest itself in various ways in human beings—including not at all. There some human beings who are devoid of soul. Their spiritual bankruptcy is evident in their abominable nature and acts. Pedophiles, racists, enslavers, serial killers, and ethnic cleansers fall into this category. There are people whose souls are like tiny pebbles or dried peas. These atrophied souls rattle around in the human frame and are unable to blossom due to various social and cultural impediments designed by the creators of capitalism, patriarchy, and religious orders to keep human beings dependent, confused, and docile. Some individuals who are branded luminaries actually have souls that are about the depth and dimension of stick figures. These individuals often wield great power that they routinely misuse. The rarest human beings are those who have fully manifested their destiny and whose souls fill their bodies multidimensionally so much so that, at times, their souls shine through their bodies. These are the Gods whose external and internal perfection is magnified by 360° of cosmic-terrestrial knowledge. Their evolution is so complete that their soulshine is blinding.

Spiritual shining can be present from birth, as is the case with the Bachwezi and Beah. Shining can also be developed over time or be shared as a gift with the prepared. August Wilson's play *Joe Turner's Come and Gone*, which I analyze in chapter four, and Ben Okri's novel *Infinite Riches* both offer striking examples of the development of soulshine. In *Infinite Riches*, after the protagonist's patriarch, known simply as Dad, is wrongfully incarcerated and beaten, he takes a lesson from Igbo wisdom workers and "dissolves into seven selves" in his search for resilience.[145] Despite being broken by torture, Dad invokes his ancestors, especially Ozoro, the son of Ògún, the Òrìṣà of iron, technology, and creativity. After Ozoro is conscripted into the Caucasian colonizer's military, he realizes that "the white man's power was both real and an illusion."[146] When he returns to Nigeria, his consciousness begins to expand. As is befitting a son of the God of Technology, Ozoro is the first man in his village to build a radio. But he informs his community that "in the spirit-world we had already gone past the age of technology and entered their era of pure power, the power that moves the volcanic planets, the distant constellations, the wind, the moon, the heart and all destiny."[147] Ozoro's description of the spirit world and its inhabitants' mastery of power are in consonance with the detailed expositions of the spirit realm offered by Malidoma Somé in his autobiography *Of Water and the Spirit*.

After comparing the vast knowledge, power, and technologies of the Cosmos to the primitive, ecology killing, soul crushing machinations of the Earth's capitalist-imperialists, Ozoro becomes a disillusioned God amongst stymied mortals:

> Dad cried out the name of the legendary Ozoro who died an enlightened man, who saw the world being made smaller, who saw his people worshipping alien dreams, exiled from the mighty spirit world where the atom had been split thousands of years ago: and whose last cry to the world, the essence of his legacy, was "CATCH UP WITH YOURSELVES!"[148]

Ozoro will not let his community be satisfied with fractions of power. He will not encourage them to make do with atrophied souls or stick figure spirits. He wants his people full to bursting, expanding and overflowing with the creative potential and power that waits within.

After invoking Ozoro, Dad travels into and catches up with himself. In his prison cell, Dad is visited by a boy whose head is emblazoned with a golden crown. Following this, Dad encounters a force that is "darker than darkness," and this entity takes Dad to the origin and end of time. The Deity of Darkness, perhaps Ausar the Lord of Perfect Blackness or the Cosmos, Herself, literally burns words of power into his being, and Dad becomes the Word. A new consciousness is created within him, and its imprint is visible. In the morning, his jailers find the walls of Dad's prison cell streaked with aquamarine, gold, and red, "as if a goldsmith had patterned the walls in rough medieval splendour."[149] And the man is more bedazzled than his cell: "They found Dad's hair matted with gold dust. Diamond powder clung to his face."[150] Dad's soul has burst forth from his mind, pineal gland, and spirit and has infused his outer being as well as his surroundings with its tangible magnificence. Everything he could ever want and many powers he never imagined he could wield had always been within Dad.

Human beings are microcosmic Cosmoses and many have unlimited potential to shine. Education and elevation are essential to shining because illumination without elevation is useless glorification. According to the Dagara, many human beings have come to Earth with the recuperative, empowering, and deifying tools necessary to bring the collective Self to the highest evolutionary state possible. This attainment of "pure power" is what Dad, the Dagara, and the Five Percent work to develop in everyone. In the song "Wake Up," by Killarmy featuring the Sunz of Man, Hell Razah describes what will occur when the Africana world catches up to itself:

> Soon as we unite the sky crack
> A group of UFOs form the seven in the heavens
> Gods celebrated devils' death day signal
> Jail let loose the criminals
> Bystanders die
> Waiting for miracles we giving you[151]

Hell Razah foresees the perfect melding of the cosmic and political. The Pan-African unification he envisions is one that is intergalactic in scope, and the seven that is formed in the heavens is a reference to Gods uniting across time and space. The women of *Infinite Riches* unite and liberate their incarcerated husbands; likewise, Hell Razah prophesies that the unification of Africana people will have such a resounding impact on the world that it will prompt the emancipation of male and female Gods from the shackles and pens of America's sprawling prison industrial complex. Hell Razah prophesies that when complete cosmic expansion occurs, ten percenters will be destroyed as will eighty-fivers who refuse to elevate.

The Gods will take their building, growth, and development to the next level.

Continuing the exploration of divine cosmic inheritance and empowerment, in his verse on "Wake Up," Prodigal Sunn chants:

> My forty-third conviction
> incarcerated in hell for eternity
> But my mentality and chemistry
> made me celestial through the galaxy[152]

Forty-third is another reference to divinity, as 4 + 3 = 7, and the seventh letter of the alphabet is G which represents God. Despite having been condemned to the hell created by the ten percenters, Prodigal Sunn, similar to Hurston, has attained his immortality and his Khu, biochemical composition, and cosmic physiognomy eternally unite him with the universe its power and its organisms. Prodigal Sunn goes on to signify on his shining surname and proclaim: "I be that star from afar / illuminating through the dark!"[153] With these lines, Sunn re-members his kinship with Hatshepsut who is "eternal like an undying star" and his origin in the Sirius B constellation. Prodigal Sunn's lyrics reveal him to be at the center of a grand celestial continuum.

With their cipher giving birth to wisdom, evolution, and divinity, the Gods of the Five Percent are identical to their Ancient African forebears in that they embody the Gift. And these God do precisely what the Divine should do with their inheritance: They disseminate the gift to the masses to facilitate the conception of new Gods.

THE BRIDGE

Shining Lords of the Singing Soul-Piece: A Three Part Harmony

"The people can be their own gods."
~ John A. Mccluskey, *Look What They Done to My Song*

Zora Neale Hurston's *Mules and Men*, easily one of the most important books ever written, includes a profoundly important but intentionally inconspicuous work of Africana orature. Hurston does not give the folktale a title but I call it "The Song of the Soul-Piece."[1] As I analyze in detail elsewhere,[2] the text concerns the creation and distribution of soul. After God creates the soul-piece he realizes that it is too strong for the human body, so he sets it aside until he can establish the perfect balance. The "white man," the "Indian," and the "Negro" see the soul-piece's diamond-shine and hear its thunderous song, and they leave it alone; the "Jew," however, steals the soul-piece.[3] The soul-piece fights its antagonist, and this battle results in the soul-piece being broken, shattered, and scattered and the Jew being burned, bruised, and marked by his theft. God mixes shattered soul-pieces with feelings and gives the compound to everyone but the Jew, who remains locked in battle with the enraged soul-piece.

"The Song of the Soul-Piece" is the most recent version of a gem of the Africana continuum that is retold in different forms in various ancient and contemporary works,[4] some of which I analyze in *Manifestations of Masculine Magnificence*. The recastings of the saga of the soul-piece in Africana verbal, visual, and literary arts are prompted by the desire to determine both "who stole the soul" (a question also asked in song by Public Enemy) and how Africana people can reclaim and revitalize their soul power. In this Bridge I analyze three works that offer unique perspectives on Africana men's activation and actualization their soul-pieces and soul power: Souleymane Cisse's film *Yeelen*, John A. Mccluskey's *Look What They Done To My Song*, and Arthur R. Flowers' *De Mojo Blues: De Quest of HighJohn de Conqueror*. As a testament to the significance of music in the Africana ethos, the soul-piece's signature attributes are its Khu—shine of the Divine—and the summoning power of its songs, and each of the works in this Bridge emphasizes the role that music plays in invoking and catalyzing divinity.

Souleymane Cisse's *Yeelen* is a recasting of an ancient Mande mythistory that is a progenitor of "The Song of the Soul-Piece." Mande wisdom-keepers reveal that Mangala, the Great Creator, implanted twins Pemba and Faro in the Womb of Origins. Although the twins were supposed to represent gender balance, harmony, and unity, while in the womb, Pemba, the male twin, stole and devoured his sister's placenta in hopes of dominating creation and surpassing Mangala. In order to reinstitute balance, Mangala cut Faro's body into sixty pieces and scattered them throughout the Cosmos.[5] Human beings are instructed to consult Faro who, as a result of having been deified, divided, and multiplied, resides everywhere and acts as an intermediary between human beings and the Divine. By contrast, Pemba, like the Jew character, comes to signify inherent incompletion and is forever marked by his theft, deviousness, and treachery.

Yeelen is a film fashioned in curvilinear time that revisits the struggle between Pemba and Faro and the Jew and the soul-piece. The film, which could be set in any of many eras, centers on the conflict dividing the Diarra family. Nianankoro and his mother, Ma Diarra, have been running and hiding from Soma, their father and husband, respectively, since just before Nianankoro was born. It was prophesied that Nianankoro would take sacred Bambara wisdom and technology and put them to use for all of humanity. Soma and the elders of the Komo seek to kill Nianankoro to prevent holistic human elevation and illumination from occurring. While the primary action in *Yeelen* centers on the father-son dynamic, the battle between Soma and Nianankoro is a recasting of a confrontation that Djigui, Soma's twin brother, had with their father. When Djigui suggested to his father that they share their wisdom and technology so that all humanity can benefit, his father used his power to blind his son. Pemba's minion will do everything they can to maintain power and dominate existence.

Nianankoro is a reincarnation of Faro, and, like his ancient predecessor, Nianankoro seeks to facilitate human beings' divine development. In order to undertake his work, Nianankoro must be divine, himself. When watching *Yeelen* one realizes that Gods do not need velvet cloaks, gold crowns, or trumpeted announcements. Nianankoro, garbed in a simple homespun cloth, has melanin so resplendent that he shines, and his glow is from the soul to the skin and beyond. At the beginning of Nianankoro's journey, a hyena spirit prophesies the following for him: "Your road will be good; your destination happy. Your future is grand; your life radiant; your death luminous."[6] The use of shine-related adjectives is not coincidental. The word *yeelen* means brightness; and, in addition to the enriching rays of the Sun, yeelen signifies the melanin that attracts, absorbs, and catalyzes the power of sunlight as well as that of stars and other astronomical bodies.

Similar to the Dogon, Kemites, Kushites, Namoratungans, Igbo and other African ethnic groups with impressive knowledge of astronomy, the Bambara are cognizant of their cosmic origins and their relationship to their cosmogonic source. This is apparent in the prophecy that Djigui shares with his nephew: "If I were to die today and you were too, our family would not perish. Your wife is pregnant. The child will shine. It's a boy and predestined to be a bright star."[7] The yet unborn star who found a home in Atou's womb only a few days prior to Djigui's utterance is the twin of a star that spoke to Djigui the night before Nianankoro and Atou's arrival: "But last night I saw a bright star cross the sky and stop before me. It said, 'Djigui, the threat hovering over the Bambaras will strike the country but spare your family. . . . Your descendants will undergo a great change. They'll be slaves and deny their race and faith.'"[8] This knowledge-bearing star is referring to the Africans forcibly exiled from Bambara, Dogon, and Peul lands as a result of Caucasian and Arab enslavers. These enslaved Africans or "jons," in Mande language, became the high conquering Johns of African America. Furthermore, Gods such as Nianankoro and Djigui are reborn in the Nation of Gods, just as Soma and the corrupt Komo elders are forerunners of the ten percenters. These two groups remain locked in struggle, as one faction seeks to raise the consciousness of eighty-fivers while the other strives to keep the masses mired in ignorance.

Djigui and Nianankoro possess the Kore wing which symbolizes the vulture and represents knowledge, space, and discernment. Soma and his brother Bafing wield the Kolonkolanni, a wooden pylon that is used to "find lost things and to expose and punish thieves, traitors, and perjurers."[9] The Kolonkolanni is no passive stationary phallic symbol; this pylon quite literally rapes homes, lives, and villages in its search for Nianankoro. The phallic power and single-mindedness of the Kolonkolanni is symbolic of the all-male Komo society of which Soma and Bafing are members.

Midway through the film, the Komo elders gather under a sacred baobab tree that is emblazoned with the signs of divine knowledge. Soma is the cantor of the Komo, and just as High John the Conqueror is the library of oral literature, Soma is a living repository of ancient and cosmic wisdom. He is the djeli, the blood of the Bambara who summons the Gods with his voice. And Soma's voice, from its pitch, to its pleas, to its long-held gritty howls, is the grandfather of the blues. In this scene, Cisse reveals the original form, power, and use of the blues, and Cisse's audience is able to understand why this musical genre in particular was embraced, revivified, and invoked by Africans dislocated in America. Far from being "the devil's music" or ballads of depression, the blues, in its original form, is communication from one God to another. In a scene that could easily take place in Mississippi, the Komo elders sit in a cipher, pour libation, sip liquor, and put their concerns into song to facilitate the re-determination of destinies.

In contrast to the patriarchal order of Soma and the Komo elders, which, save for oft-invoked Mother Gods, is bereft of the power of woman, when the viewer first encounters Nianankoro he is with Ma Diarra, who has endured decades of pain and humiliation to protect her son and who guards him with her own technological devices and her milk-rich prayers to the "Goddess of the Waters" the "Mother of mothers."[10] While in Peul country, the ancestors and Gods place Nianankoro in the path of Atou, who becomes his wife and who ensures his immortality by bearing Nianankoro's son. Unlike his father, Nianankoro is consistently allied with the force of Woman; consequently, he has the balance essential for holistic universal evolution. He also differs from his father in that he does not pray to or invoke any Deity. He is the source of his divine shining, and he harnesses his numinosity and luminosity to maximum effect.

Similar to the Georgia conjure man who could draw a ring around and immobilize a person for as long as he wished,[11] Nianankoro can suspend human animation. He can start fires from miles away and can send bees to do his bidding. But unlike Soma and Bafing who use their power to cow and subjugate humanity, Nianankoro's use of technology is balanced and humane. When Nianankoro does battle, he harms as few people as possible; for example, when his uncle Bafing closes in on him, Nianankoro simply makes him disappear.

The patriarchal Komo society and Soma's and Bafing's blindly destructive Kolonkolanni offer arresting displays of power that actually signify decay, decadence, and inner defeat. Confirming the fact that many spiritual implements are not only sentient but are also divine entities themselves, after enduring centuries of misuse, the Kolonkolanni divorces itself from the Komo and explains its decision in the following monologue:

> Soma, your ancestors were priests of the Komo, but for centuries they've misused their powers. I've left only ruin in my wake. I've been faithful to the Diarra. Now it's over. Your lust for revenge, your contempt and hate for humanity have gone too far. I'm going to

disappear. You won't survive, Soma, for you are those who use their power only for evil and injustice.[12]

That Cisse uses the ultimate phallic symbol, the Kolonkolanni, to reprimand keepers of the patriarchal order is a cultural and cinematic masterstroke. However, while the Kolonkolanni vanishes, smaller but similarly potent pylons rest between the legs of all men. How will they choose to use their power? What lives will spring forth from their seeds?

At the film's climax, the opposed but ever-interconnected forces of Nianankoro and Soma engage in a shapeshifting battle that generates so much energy that the eyes embedded in the Kore wing and Kolokolanni spew forth rays that emblazon the landscape with light and the squealing roaring tumult of a world being reborn. It is significant that the first figure present in the revised world is Atou. She stands before the Kore wing, as did Nianankoro before he was transformed from human to light to egg. While the role of woman appears to be limited in this male-driven film, understated Atou represents Mangala, the Great Mother God. She is the bearer of life: her eggs ensure the continuity of the Diarra, and she is the positioner of the sacred eggs of power and their totems, which hold the mysteries of the universe. Atou is also both a manifestation of Ma Diarra, and she is the literal answer to Ma Diarra's prayers. As did Ma Diarra, Atou, alone, makes the choice to bear her son and provide him with protection, sustenance, education, and the wisdom of his father. Atou is the custodian of Nianankoro's legacy and his immortality; she is also the architect of their son's existence. She is the library who will teach her progeny his truth so that he can know his fathers and himself. Atou is the God of Eternity who ensures the continuity of a mission that finds its origins in the beginning of time.[13]

During his meeting with Nianankoro, Djigui muses, "I think one can die without ceasing to exist":[14] Soma and Nianankoro both achieve this feat, as they are transformed into and await rebirth as resplendent white eggs that reflect all possibilities and probabilities. The cyclic fates of Nianankoro and Soma are eternally overseen by the silently watching ever-present Ancestor who resides at the Komo shrine and symbolizes the intensity and the immensity of Bambara power and technology. The Ancestor shows no favoritism and offers no assistance; he bears silent witness to all that is occurring, that has occurred, and that will occur. On the Ancestor's forehead, parallel to the pineal gland which is the seat of spiritual cognition, is a green pyramidal crystal that represents the third eye and spiritual vision. As the embodiment of rememory as well as wisdom, knowledge, and understanding, the Ancestor introduces the battles, answers the prayers, provides the weapons, and presents an open-ended conclusion to an ever-cycling text.

Cisse's *Yeelen* forces one to reconsider the significance of the Western ages of enlightenment and industrialization and contemporary technological advances and devices, because the spiritual-technological knowledge that can create Kolonkolanni, that can give one the ability to observe what is happening miles away through a pot of water, that can make it possible to control time and the movements of living entities, and that can give a human being the ability alter his or other people's matter are the skills of a tremendously enlightened and numinous people. These technologies are light years ahead of modern surveillance and communication devices, drones, airplanes, and artillery; and, unlike Western machinery, traditional African technology is not tied to capitalism. Most important, not only have multitudes—especially enslaved Africans—benefitted from these technologies, as Djigui and Nianankoro intended, but also, these skills are still in use today throughout the Pan-African world.

Human beings' concepts of reality and possibility relate directly to the science, technology, and knowledge of their eras and communities. In *Yeelen*, the skills of Soma, Bafing, and Nianankoro are considered customary forms of technology. Similarly, discussions about spiritual skills and technologies in *Drums and Shadows*, *After God is Dibia*, *Mother Wit From the Laughing Barrel*, and *The Autobiography of a Runaway Slave* are not whispered in shame, laced with ridicule, or dismissed as unbelievable any more than an American would laugh at a Nigerian's ability to communicate with a Russian via email or mobile phone. Africana divinity and its scientific and technological advances were, at one time, norms, and, in addition to being comfortable with their divine powers, Africana peoples were originally at ease with their own divinity and technology. However, the rise of the West and its violent religious and cultural indoctrination campaigns coupled with a tireless anti-African propaganda agenda resulted in a vilification and repudiation of the African and divine so successful that rather than using skills and technologies to further evolution, many Africana people struggle to remember and re-member their "ancient properties." Such personal and communal struggles are the focus of McCluskey's *Look What They Done to My Song* and Flowers' *De Mojo Blues*.

McCluskey's novel begins with an epilogue that is written in a style that could be defined as fragment-unified poetic prose. In addition to marrying dichotomy and melding genre, the epilogue is a praisesong to the powerful confluence of author, protagonist, narrator, and God:

Mack-on-Mack. I am the juju priest to Shango, knower of black magic eternal. Understand that it is no lost art and did not vanish when black people buried their bones in southern yards and trusted to luck in great cold cities or huddled here along the sea. Words and needs—these tools, yes, for blues and roots. In quiet dawns I seek the sea and ponder black magic. Create chants to destroy the curse sealed with the first native betrayal when slaves, though it was long before the captive knew the real stink of submission, were exchanged for bracelets and rusty guns and the Bible.[15]

Mack has full knowledge of his identity and the depth and breadth of his African ancestry: He inherited the power of Ṣàngó as surely as he did the blood of the djeli. Foremost in Mack's mind are the labyrinthine tragedies that beset African Americans, but he does not sink into apathy; he channels the power of his ancestors. Mack describes himself as *"ageless Du Bois stilled in thought."*[16] The narrator invokes W. E. B. Du Bois, the legendary Pan-Africanist, sociologist, and historian, as his guiding ancestor. Mack tempers the intellectual zeal of Du Bois with the curvilinear vision and power of High John: *"I am frozen by responsibilities for futures not birthed. I make possibilities of thin suns above me. I rap out a gift of love along the way."*[17] A True and Living God, Mack acknowledges his responsibility to resurrect and perfect as well as his vulnerabilities.

Ṣàngó is the Òrìṣà of divine retribution who exacts justice with lightning or with his oṣé Ṣàngó, which is a double-headed axe. Mack bears an oṣé Ṣàngó befitting his mission and manifestation of divinity: the saxophone. A love interest describes Mack as a musician with "a crazy idea about music saving the world."[18] Mack's mission leads him into the center of a cipher, a gathering of men who are all on the path to divinity. With his self-effacing demeanor and still-water passions, Mack bonds with Omowale, the Pan-African revolutionary; GA, the disillusioned GI; The Right Reverend C. E. Fuller; Antar, the poet; Henry, the elder; and Ugbangi, Mack's brother of the struggle who totes the same mojos as Mack and kicks cops' asses alongside him.[19]

A recurrent theme in the lives of and literature by and about Africana men is that to make sense of and overcome certain impediments, it is important to share knowledge, histories, and strategies in groups that are composed of persons of the same ethnicity and gender: Gender and ethnic exclusivity lie at the core of *Look What They Done to My Song* and its characters' evolution. Some wisdom is best transferred through like minds or "A-alikes," to use Nation of Gods terminology, and the sharing of information, art, and power among McCluskey's men is as graceful as a Miles Davis–John Coltrane composition.

Gods do not need to boast or shout. They can simply ponder and produce perfection; such is the case for Mack who has an epiphany: "We need a better religion that brings the best of everything together. *The people can be their own gods.*"[20] Mack converts Reverend Fuller, pastor of the aptly-named Crumbly Church, to the Gospel of the God of Self, and in the novel's finale, Fuller's church is converted to a bastion of divine communal awakening. As Mack's jazz band plays, prostitutes, pimps, and players rub elbows with the sanctified and the sanctimonious. At the conclusion of what will be his final sermon, Reverend Fuller initiates his congregation into themholyselves: "For the young ones, there's a world waiting. All I can say is go and get it. *Be your own gods.*"[21] Reverend Fuller, a literary figure who has real-world brothers in Bishop Carlton D. Pearson, George Hurley, and Allah, the Father, stands courageous on the Word—Psalms 82:6 and John 10:34 of the Bible—and allows the church to crumble so the Gods can thrive. No mention is made in McCluskey's novel of Sun Ra or the Five Percenters or their philosophies, and McCluskey may or may not be familiar with them. But he need not be furthering any worldview besides that which common sense bestowed upon him. The paths that lead to recognition of personal power and Divinity are infinite and ever-present.

The charge that Reverend Fuller issues to his congregants in *Look What They Done to My Song* is taken up by Tucept HighJohn, the protagonist of Flowers' *De Mojo Blues*. After being court-martialed during the Vietnam War, Tucept HighJohn reenters American society a fragmented man with a shattered concept of self. McCluskey's Mack has knowledge of his power and of his responsibility as part of a collective of emergent Africana Gods. He also has a rabbit's foot, a mojo tooth, a nation sack filled with goober dust, and Ugbangi, who is his ẹnikeji.[22] Similarly, HighJohn has his empowered name and lineage, and he has a mojo bag filled with potent bones that was given to him by Jethro, a Mississippi two-headed doctor who introduces HighJohn to his namesake.

While it would be logical to posit that HighJohn's mojo blues is the result of his court-martial and the atrocities of war, that would be a misreading of both mojo and blues. Mojo signifies African technology: The prenda and egbé used to fly, the nkisi that distil and galvanize soul power, and the ààlè that protect goods are all mojos. The blues, as is evident in its Bambara geographical home, is not a coping mechanism for depression, it is communication from and to the Gods. As his name signifies, HighJohn is a walking mojo, a strolling toby, a taproot of soul-deep power, but he does not know this. Ọ̀rọ̀, Power of the Word, marinates in his larynx, and he is incognizant of it. Rather than access his divinity and marshal that of other Gods, Tucept HighJohn dismisses his surname as a silly myth. Jethro decodes and encodes for HighJohn, as a Trickster God should:

> HighJohn de Conqueror is more than a slavery myth, said Jethro heatedly, it's just that slavery was the last time blackfolks needed him, but his spirit rests right there in that there root of his and wherever blackfolk's backs are pressed up against the wall, then old HighJohn he get to walking this earth like a natural man, kicking ass 'n taking names, overcoming all obstacles in his path. Blackfolks just can't lose when the spirit of HighJohn is walking with them. Hell ole HighJohn might get to walking over here in Nam, tough as it's been 'round here. According to the Lost Book of Hoodoo, the spirit of HighJohn gon be walkin soon.[23]

Tucept responds the way many mortals would when faced with the wisdom of a God: "Fuck Jethro with his wild riddle-talking ass."[24] Jethro responds as a true Trickster—with laughter and an additional riddle: "I was told to wake you up."[25]

Although Jethro is killed in Vietnam, he is reborn in America as Spijoko, the hoary-headed elder who leads HighJohn in his search to find The Lost Book of Hoodoo. In the course of his quest, HighJohn discovers and finds himself for he is the latest chapter to be written in the Lost Book of Hoodoo. Spijoko introduces HighJohn to his embryonic divinity:

> We talking masterwork here, a master hoodoo needs no tools other than hisself, his will and his mojo. . . . Other traditions call it different, ki, mana, prana, the force, etheric, even god or laws of nature, on and on, all kinds of names for the power. Different traditions approach it different too. Some looks for nothingness, or to be one with the cosmos, or the perfect existence, all kinds of things. The hoodoo thing is to be a conduit of the power. The way is to align yourself so precisely in the dynamic of the natural laws that you become one with the power. You are the power. The strongest force on the board. De mojo. The center of the universe and thereby its rulemaker, A Master of Destiny.[26]

This elaboration of intrinsic and extrinsic power is the verbal milk, to borrow a phrase from rapper Brother J, that Spijoko feeds a thirsty HighJohn. He also teaches his charge how to harness such technologies as spiritual vision and power of the word.

HighJohn learns what the Five Percenters know, that his divinity must be used for community elevation and evolution. However, he does not understand how arduous his task is until he peers into the souls of a group of Africana youths:

> Tucept shifted into spirit vision with more confidence and less power shed this time. Even though he was braced and ready for it, the line of people become suddenly a line of spirits brought a surprised grunt from him. . . . He frowned, most all of them ailed, lackluster, ill, tattered, some stunted and stilted, cramped into low horizons. Some were half alert, asleep. Tucept frowned, thoroughly shocked. . . . Before he walked a block he was demoralized. So many black spirits crippled and cramped if not out-and-out dead. Tucept began to hurt for them, his eyes full and trying to blink back the tears that threatened to fall from them.[27]

America's endless winter has taken a great toll on the Sun People. Children and adolescents who should be filled with light, power, and vitality are drained, grey, and spiritually dead. Confronted with living victims of social death, Tucept cries—but the tears of a God do not heal, they merely fall. Gods must work to achieve change, and HighJohn has a great deal of work to do because he is "responsible for the survival and destiny of the Tribe."[28] HighJohn's mission is similar to that of the Gravediggaz's RZArector: He must dig up the graves of the mentally dead and revivify them with the divinity lodged in the cores of their beings.

As a newly initiated Master of the Word, Tucept finds that he is merely one member of a grand continuum:

> Tucept sat motionless in his high back chair. The bones lay on the floor in front of him, the 4 shouldered cross. Shadowed figures stood around him, their voices a low murmuring babble of languages and dialects that only he heard. The voices of Ol' Prophet Nat. Gullah Jack. O Baliol. uMlenghi. Doc John. D. Walker. Boukman. O. L. Young. LaBas. And on. And on. Shadows in shadows in shadows. The Hoodoo Brotherhood. Sorcerers all. Our Games have been many. These are our victories, these are our defeats, these are your lessons as written in the Great Book of Hoodoo. Listen young hoodoo and grow in power.
>
> Tucept listens and is born again. HighJohn stands. Hoodooman. I am The Way.[29]

Voices, powers, warriors, and Gods merge into One. The third person omniscient narrator becomes part of a plural possessive collective that is fully unified in the being of Tucept HighJohn who accepts his mission and his position in the ancient continuum.

The gender solidarity that is central to *Look What They Done To My Song* is also apparent in *De Mojo Blues*. It is imperative that Africana men bond, build, collaborate, and elevate; but following such knowledge sharing, Man must recognize his equal and complement in Woman. After the male God gathering, HighJohn meets the Council of Elders, the head of which is "a striking nutbrown woman of indeterminate age."[30] After the council accepts HighJohn as the giver of the Call to the tribe, he returns home to find Mother Divine awaiting him: She is Àjẹ. When he opens his cosmic, spiritual, intellectual, and physical self to her, he discovers, "There is no greater pleasure."[31] Nothing compares to being recognized by and making love with one's equal.

Flowers' respect for and understanding of women is also apparent in his literary relationship with Zora Neale Hurston. Not only does Flowers pay homage to Hurston through Jethro's elucidation of High John the Conqueror, which is a clear recasting of Hurston's origin text, but he also critiques Hurston's attempt to redirect the Conqueror's power. Scholars of Hurston's work are aware of the questionable addition she made to her seminal essay "High John de Conquer" when she republished it during World War II. In the essay's conclusion, Hurston informs Caucasians that the God who fought against everything that they represent and everything that they lied, raped, and enslaved to erect is "working for all America now," and Hurston offers a gift: "White America, take a laugh out of our black mouths, and win! We give you High John de Conquer."[32]

Hurston's bequest reveals how difficult it is to write for three audiences: racist Caucasian patrons and publishers, the bourgeois Harlem "niggerati" (Hurston's term), and the "folks of the tales" (my term) who basked in the power of their roots, soul, Hoodoo, and High John. Perhaps in an attempt to inspire, cater to, or coddle members of her Caucasian audience, Hurston presents them with a gift that cannot be given.

Forty-two years later, Flowers undertakes the literary reclamation of High John:

> Zora did a sweet Highjohn riff. Only problem was that she goes through this "and now we give him to you America" bit and I was offended. It was at the start of WWII and she was trying to make the country feel good. I wanted to take the myth back. Zora's was the most definitive work on Highjohn so I decided that I would try to work him into a myth that would replace hers.[33]

Flowers does not attack the Ancestor: With understanding, grace, and dexterity, he returns African conquering power to its rightful owners and creators who are most in need of it.

At the novel's conclusion, a fully self-actualized HighJohn stands before his people in their full Pan-African glory and issues the Call. Killarmy, Ògún, Elijah Muhammad, and Ausar would recognize it, for it is a call for war by a self-determined Warrior God. Vietnam veteran Tucept HighJohn comes to embody the truth that Elijah Muhammad preached to his congregation: If Africana people must fight, the battle must be waged against the enemies of progress and destroyers of Divinity. High John the Conqueror usually triumphs with wit, cunning, intelligence, and humor, but a new era and a new war necessitate new weaponry. Tucept HighJohn, with the technologies of Nianankoro bursting from his soul and the artillery of Ògún lodged in his palms, calls for "Holywar of the Blacks. Demoja."[34] High John the Conquering God is reclaimed and resurrected both by and within his chosen and shining Suns for the correct cause and the right reasons.

PART TWO

MASCULINE MAGNIFICENCE IN AFRICANA LITERATURE

"This life of ours is a strange story that only the gods can read."

~ Ben Okri, *Starbook*

CHAPTER FOUR

Resurrecting the Shining Self in August Wilson's *Joe Turner's Come and Gone* **and Bill Harris'** *Robert Johnson: Trick the Devil*

"To look straight into the center of the sun was a hell of a thing."
~ Carlos Moore, *Pichón*

"Acknowledge that you are God."
~ Miguel Pinero, *Short Eyes*

The struggle to acquire knowledge of self and the dexterity necessary to properly harness soul power can lead one to the crossroads where absurdity, insanity, and divinity meet. At this crossroads, men are left confused, neutralized, or deified. In *Joe Turner's Come and Gone* (*JTCG*) and *Robert Johnson: Trick the Devil* (*RJTD*) Herald Loomis and Robert Johnson, respectively, journey to that crossroads and emerge with the glow of the Gods. But the protagonists are not alone: As we traverse August Wilson's pages of power and navigate Bill Harris' labyrinths of ink, the playwrights fully intend for us, the intended audience, to join their protagonists in the quest for divinity and find our own shining along the way.

Harris' and Wilson's plays are siblings in many respects. *JTCG*, which was published in 1988, is the elder of *RJTD*, which was written in 1995. Wilson's play is set approximately sixteen years before Harris' so it is fitting that when the lights go down on Herald Loomis he is "shining like new money," and when the lights come up on Robert he is described as "a shining star": One would expect nothing less from the sons of High John the Conqueror.

The soul power that shimmers through Harris' and Wilson's plays is resplendent, but these works have not received much critical attention. While there are some intriguing analyses of *JTCG*, to date, only Sandra Richards' "Yoruba Gods on the American Stage: August Wilson's *Joe Turner's Come and Gone*" is able to effectively enter and analyze the play's Africana ethos and appreciate the roles of High John the

Conqueror, Ògún, and Èṣù therein. Most other analyses are so skewed by Eurocentric and Christocentric ideology that they fail to adequately interpret the genius of Wilson's art and the magnificence of Loomis' transformation. While many of the reviews of *RJTD* extol the power of Harris' craft, at the time of this writing there are no published analyses of *RJTD*. The paucity of research on these plays may be due to their revolutionary themes, for these works not only offer scathing critiques of Western hypocrisy, miseducation, and mythmaking, but they also offer complex perspectives on and representations of Africana people, history, and divinity.

With *RJTD*, Bill Harris seeks to right the historic wrong done to Robert Johnson. He is motivated by the fact that "in most people's minds, Johnson was more a myth than a man. [And] the nature of the myth — that he sold his soul to the devil — seemed, to me, to serve a community other than the one from which Johnson came."[1] With Harris properly positioning Robert Johnson at the center of his life and history, we find Robert comfortably seated as a divine self-authorizing agent, and this will infuriate the many individuals who have substantial financial and ideological investments in "devil" and "nigger" worship.[2] Furthermore, it is important to note that while Robert's divinity is articulated through and complemented by his artistry, his guitar playing did not make him a God; the fact of his existence did that. By contrast, Herald Loomis is not a musician, and he has precious little respect in his community. Although Loomis appears to have lost contact with his song, its magnetic pull has actually led him to the doorway of divinity which is where he stands upon his initial appearance in the play.

Fertile Foundations, Two-Headed Doctors, and Culture Vultures

JTCG and *RJTD* are both set in spaces of cosmic-terrestrial power. The primary space of interaction in *JTCG* is Seth Holly's boardinghouse, and the point of spiritual-material convergence in *RJTD* is Georgia Mayberry's Colored Jook Joint. Seth's house and Georgia's jook are both symbolic of the crossroads; the literal and metaphorical space where all entities, issues, humans, and spirits meet. The boarding house and jook are as essential to the characters of *JTCG* and *RJTD* as 124 Bluestone Road is to the characters of Toni Morrison's *Beloved*. These edifices are way-stations, praisehouses, makeshift shrines to the love, sex, sadness, and souls of newly born Gods and their powers. Seth's house is a magnet that draws "[f]rom the deep and the near South the sons and daughters of newly freed African slaves." Wilson goes on to describe the spiritual malaise that plagues these entities: "Isolated, cut off from memory, having forgotten the names of the gods and only guessing at their faces they arrive dazed and stunned, their heart kicking in their chest with a song worth singing." Described as "[f]oreigners in a strange land," these "marked men and women" are searching for the dismembered elements of their souls and selves so that they might be fully re-membered. They seek the ink of signification necessary to leave their marks on life, inscribe their songs in the Earth. The pens of self-inscription, the sticks with which one can hit impossible licks, and the ability to access the divine all reside within and are catalyzed at the crossroads.

Wilson sets the foundation for his play in an uncommon way, as the quotes above are included in the introductory section titled "The Play" which has no page numbers. The absence of page numbers seems to reflect the absence of so many truths from the annals of what is presumed to be history. Like much of Africana history, the play's foundation represents knowledge that has been intentionally ignored and left undocumented by some but has been life-altering, maiming, and psyche-scarring to others. This floating foundation rocks, pitches, and reels like the millions of ancestral bones that nestle and wrestle at the bottom of the Ethiopic Ocean. Wilson's morphing base yearns, bucks, and rends the air like the wails of Memphis' finest who lost their lovers to another in a long line of American experiments in greed, depravity, and casual barbarity.

As is befitting a floating foundation that will also serve as the meeting place for all textual forms and forces, *JTCG* opens with an uneasy alliance between Hoodoo and Christianity. Seth describes Bynum's work as "mumbo jumbo nonsense" and "heebie-jeebie stuff."[3] However Bertha reminds Seth that he benefits from the spiritual works that both she and Bynum use to protect their home and ensure prosperity. Seth stands at the same crossroads' junction that many African Americans occupied when their spiritual systems were assaulted by Christianity and Christians. In *Black Culture and Black Consciousness*, Lawrence Levine offers a wonderfully contradictory testimony from Anthony Dawson who confirms, "We all knowed about the Word and the unseen son of God and we didn't put no stock in conjure. 'Course we had luck charms and good and bad signs, but everybody got dem things."[4] Similarly, Seth struggles to balance Hoodoo's comprehensiveness and Christianity's quest for ideological domination.

The judgmental, often acerbic, and tireless Seth represents middle-class values and the nearly joyless quest to attain the American dream. He is a fitting contrast to Bynum Walker who has neither financial wealth nor property but who is the master of fates and controller of destinies. While Seth's discussions with every resident of his house center on money and much of his time is spent bargaining and exchanging goods for cash with Rutherford Selig, Bynum is motivated by Spirit.

Piet Meyer's "Divination among the Lobi of Burkina Faso" offers a direct Continental reference for Bynum's economic and spiritual ethics. Meyer reveals that, among the Lobi, "a diviner is not allowed to refuse a client who wants a consultation."[5] If he does refuse, his personal God, or *Wathil*, will censure him. Not only does a diviner have little time to engage in work other than divination, as he may see from four or five to as many as twenty clients a day, but the number of individuals the diviner assists has no impact on his finances because

> the diviner earns practically nothing for his divinatory services. . . . He receives five cowries (about half a cent) per consultation when he divines at home and twenty cowries at another location chosen by the client. Furthermore, a diviner enjoys neither high social status nor any particular privileges; *he gains prestige only if his divination is particularly good.*[6]

The relationship that Lobi diviners have with money was standard throughout Pan-Africa before the globalization of capitalism and the Caucasian fetishization of Africana spiritwork. While it is becoming increasingly apparent in the 21st century that a capitalist economy is one that is grounded in artifice and doomed to failure,[7] true spiritualists have always followed the laws of the universe which hold that wisdom, knowledge, and understanding are not commodities and cannot be commoditized.

Bynum's Hoodoo Economics manifest themselves in significant and tellingly paradoxical ways throughout the play. For example, the proceeds Bynum derives from his binding work are minimal: The only money he makes in the course of the play is fifty cents, which he earns after divining for Mattie Campbell and accepting whatever she happens to have handy. However, Bynum can afford to pay Seth two dollars a week for rent and purchase from Reuben the pigeons that are essential to his work. In one of the play's most important exchanges, Bynum even pays Rutherford Selig a dollar to find his shiny man.

Selig calls himself a People Finder, and Bynum adds the approbation "first class" to Selig's designation, but what sounds like high praise is mockery. As Bynum reveals, Selig is a peddler, a tracker, and an opportunist:

> Rutherford Selig. He go around selling pots and pans and every house he come to he write down the name and address of whoever lives there. So if you looking for somebody, quite naturally you go

and see him . . . 'cause he's the only one who know where everybody live at. (16)

In addition to his ability to actually find people being an obvious distortion, Selig's information about a person's whereabouts hinges on his knowledge of a person's name. This seems logical until one considers the fluidity of African naming practices and the unique relationships that Africans in America have had with names. In *RJTD*, Stokes and Georgia analyze the differences in naming in Caucasian and Africana communities: "White man get a name he keep it forever"; "We ain't knowed our real name since we been here" (16).

The unknown is not necessarily an impediment; it can become a space that empowers and endows one with the ability to define one's self and determine one's destiny and also impact the destinies of others. Bynum, for example, calls the shiny man "John" only because he met him in Johnstown; and yet, this name connects him with a "High" progenitor. Being named after a Divinity and having the glow of the Gods makes John one of the most easily identifiable people in the world—but only to those who can see. Bynum knows Selig does not have the ojú inú (spiritual vision) necessary to see, so by "hiring" him, Bynum signifies on the People Finder and issues to Wilson's audience an ophthalmological challenge.

Although he knows he cannot locate a man called John whose most distinguishing characteristic is spiritual shine, Selig accepts Bynum's money because that is his nature—to profit by all means. During his nickel and dime negotiations with Seth, Selig beats him out of a nickel per sheet of sheet metal (7, 39), and he surely marks up the price of the implements that Seth makes and that he sells. Selig's history of dislocating, disenfranchising, and dismembering Africana peoples has deep roots. In his advertising pitch to Loomis, Selig outlines his credentials which extend to ancestors he describes as "bringers and finders":

> My great-granddaddy used to bring Nigras across the ocean on ships. [That] wasn't no easy job either. Sometimes the winds would blow so hard you'd think the hand of God was set against the sails. But it set him well in pay and he settled in this new land and found him a wife of good Christian charity with a mind for kids and the like and well . . . here I am, Rutherford Selig. You're in good hands, mister. Me and my daddy have found plenty of Nigras. My daddy, rest his soul, used to find runaway slaves for the plantation bosses. He was the best there was at it. Jonas B. Selig. Had him a reputation stretched clean across the country. After Abraham Lincoln give you all Nigras your freedom papers and with you all looking all over for

each other ... we started finding Nigras for Nigras. Of course, it don't pay as much. But the People Finding business ain't so bad. (41)

"Selig" is a word of German/Yiddish origin than means "blessed." The Seligs' blessings result from them terrorizing and devastating Africans. From the theft of Africans on the Continent, to the capture of Africans who had liberated themselves from slavery in America, to the dislocation of Africans who have had their familial roots severed by the buying and selling of their relatives, a Selig has been on the scene orchestrating separation and reaping the financial benefits of geographical and familial upheaval. Even in the 1900s, a Selig is present to continue the work of taking people away (for a fee, of course) and logging their names so that he can find them for some seeking party (for a fee, of course). Bertha sheds additional light on the duplicitous nature and motivations of Selig: "You can call him a People Finder if you want to. I know Rutherford Selig carries people away too. He done carried a whole bunch of them away from here. Folks plan on leaving plan by Selig's timing. They wait till he get ready to go, then they hitch a ride on his wagon. Then he charge folks a dollar to tell them where he took them" (42). Selig is a clear example of a ten percenter.

Cash may rule everything around Seth and Selig, but Bynum rules cash and everyone around him. Bynum's Hoodoo Economics further his binding and healing work, as the dollar he pays Selig is a sacrifice in inverse. The dollar alerts the reader to the fact that Bynum, who seems to be the poorest and most dubious of characters, is so wealthy that he can literally throw money away—or use it as spiritual facilitator. In paying Selig to find the shiny man, Bynum marks Selig with what he loves most, the almighty dollar, and because Selig will never find a shiny man, he will be in Bynum's employ forever. While Seth and Selig haggle over money, Bynum is investing in and reaping the rewards of spiritwork for the enrichment of the community.

Bynum knows the rule of the Gods: It is not enough to simply be Divine; a God's divinity is measured by the Gods he or she creates—through the womb and/or through wisdom. Gods must introduce others to their powers and welcome more Gods into the continuum. To fully self-actualize and manifest his divinity, Bynum must lead another God to the mirror of numinous recognition. Because he is not working for a living or for a salary, but for his immortality and that of others, Bynum can afford to use money as the tool it is. By paying Selig to locate the shiny man, Bynum offers a riddle to Selig and to Wilson's audience. But by encouraging Loomis to hire Selig, Bynum accomplishes three things: 1) he concretizes in the terrestrial sphere the force of the Spirit, 2) he keeps his emergent shiny man in his immediate vicinity, and 3) he uses Selig to summon the bound and seeking parties who are essential for Loomis' revelation.

While his primary concern is Herald Loomis, Bynum helps to heal and make whole three other fragmented people: Mattie, Martha, and Zonia. The only questionable act Bynum commits is that he may have bound Reuben to Eugene's pigeons. Pigeons are spiritual messengers, and, as such, they are important sacrificial animals in Africana spiritual systems.[8] Bynum needs the pigeons and their àṣẹ rich blood to bind individuals, draw them to the boarding house, and keep destabilizing influences at bay. The pigeons are necessary for Bynum's work, but they are also essential for Eugene's transmigration. Before Eugene died he told his friend, "Reuben, promise me when I die you'll let my pigeons go" (29). Although Reuben promises to release the birds, his grief (and possibly some binding) moves him to keep the birds: "I ain't never gonna let them go. Even when I get to be grown up. I'm just always gonna have Eugene's pigeons" (29). Despite this proclamation, Reuben sells the pigeons to Bynum who uses them in his spiritwork.

The night before the play's dénouement, Reuben thinks he hears Bynum talking to the wind, but Bynum is conversing with Miss Mabel, a community ancestor. After her discussion with Bynum, Miss Mabel visits Reuben. She is wearing a white dress, her hands and feet are huge, and "[s]he had this light coming out of her" (79). The shining Miss Mabel demands Reuben release the pigeons so that Eugene can fully transmigrate. The pigeons are Eugene's Ba, the Kemetic spirit bird that leaves the human body at the time of death to journey to the spiritual realm, and Eugene cannot embark on his journey into the afterlife without his Ba.

Although his acts, such as possibly stalling Eugene at the crossroads, may not be understood initially, everything that Bynum does is for the benefit of the community. What is more, Bynum does not insult anyone in the course of the play; he does not preach, proselytize, mystify, or demystify; he also does not knock anyone's hustle. He watches as events unfold, and he folds, creases, wrinkles and irons events accordingly. A perfect example of a member of that rare five percent, who are "poor righteous teachers" and "living god(s)," Bynum does not take advantage of a lost and fragmented people seeking wholeness; in fact, he fronts the cost on behalf of his clients. As his name indicates, Bynum is a unifier, but he only binds what clings, and it costs him a piece of himself every time he undertakes the work of unification (10). The most exorbitant fees and the richest rewards are often those with no dollar amount.

The foundation of *RJTD* is as spiritually rich and flexible as that of *JTCG*. The play is set in the summer of 1938 on the eve of Robert Johnson's assassination. However when Stokes, the narrator, speaks he does so to the play's contemporary audience, making the play a curvilinear revelation. *RJTD's* prologue has dual introductions as well: The first thing heard is Robert Johnson singing. As the lights go up on him in San Antonio, Texas in 1937, Robert is facing a corner and making one of the recordings that made him famous. This is a fitting opening as it reveals the duality of Johnson and the susceptibility of his persona to mythmaking. For example, while no one argues that Johnson recorded songs while facing a corner, the reason he faced the corner is the subject of debate. Some argue that Johnson faced the corner so no one could see how he coaxed screams, moans, and exultation from his guitar. Others assert that Johnson was simply trying to get the best acoustics possible from the hotel room in which he was recording. Johnson could have been accomplishing both of these feats at once.

When Johnson finishes playing and sits "intensely still," Harris gives his audience the impression that his play will simply be flashback.[9] Harris does in fact take us to that fateful day in 1938, but he does this through the eyes of Stokes, the blind elder, who makes his authority and agency clear: "Robert Johnson? Yeah I knowed him. And he was a shining star. Met him in the flesh not too long before he died" (5). Stokes' description of Robert's numinosity is not metaphorical; it is spiritual and literal fact. With the same vision employed by Stevie Wonder, creator of *Inner Visions*, and harnessed by Djigui, the blind wisdom worker of Souleymane Cisse's *Yeelen*, Stokes can see the Khu that suffuses Johnson's being. Stokes' role in *RJTD* is also analogous to that of Bynum in *JTCG* in that Stokes binds Robert Johnson to his truth, history, and divinity.

With his opening monologue, Stokes establishes the fact that he is the authorized knowledge bearer and truth teller: "Died right over there. Now it's plenty of folks say they was here and what not. Tell you everything that happened. What all he did, how he died and everything. Lies. They wasn't here. I was" (6). Stokes continues to directly educate his audience throughout the course of the play—and so do all of the characters, including Robert Johnson and Kimbrough, the academic who is hunting Robert to learn about the origin of his "Satan songs." At the play's conclusion, Stokes tells Robert that he has fulfilled his destiny: "You done struck your lick for the people to hear. . . . Now they got the listen, each for theyself, 'cause you sure done put it out there for them to hear" (45). Stokes is referring to both the lyrics of Johnson's songs and the manner by which he came about his guitar-playing skills. While it may seem confusing, Harris' play is not an example of the classic African dilemma tale. The truth is as simple and plain as The Secret of Life that Bynum shares with Selig in *JTCG*.

Rutherford Selig of *JTCG* does not appear to have much in common with *RJTD's* Kimbrough. Selig is a poor hustler, a jackleg informer, and a profiteer. Kimbrough is an English professor who specializes in Shakespeare, whom he is fond of quoting: He even speaks in iambic pentameter. But Kimbrough and Selig have two things in common. They do not have the ability to comprehend Africana spiritual systems and technologies, and they profit off of the enslavement of Africans. Similar to Selig, Kimbrough owes quite a debt to his forbearers, and they owe the ultimate debt to the Africans they victimized. Kimbrough remarks that his grandfather died a multi-millionaire because "the Kimbrough family fortune came from the trafficking in slaves. Selling human flesh. . . . I wanted nothing to do with him, his world—nothing—nothing except his money—which makes me a coward and a hypocrite, and as ineffectual as Hamlet. I try to sleep, but have nightmares filled with blues" (42). Kimbrough needs Robert to help him assuage his nightmares because if he can attribute Robert's genius to the devil, Kimbrough can also compartmentalize and justify the evil that conceived and nourished him.

Kimbrough reveals that he first heard Robert Johnson the day his grandfather died, and his family's servant, "Dear old Auntie Bell," played Johnson's music. Kimbrough gushes about the uniqueness of the music, but Stokes remarks, "Probably heard it every day and just wasn't listening" (22). Stokes makes it clear that Robert is part of the same continuum to which Auntie Bell belongs and that Auntie Bell had been singing her own gutbucket blues to survive laboring in the Kimbrough home. Stokes' aside also reveals that Kimbrough is not merely oblivious to the blues' holistic truth; he is resistant to it.

Rather than recognize that Johnson is part of the whole, Kimbrough, like the Caucasian musicians who have made a Deity out of the Robert Johnson myth they created, sets Johnson apart. By doing this, Johnson can be considered exceptional, supernatural, extraordinary. Critics use terms like these not to praise but to mythologize the Africana artist: By attributing talents to some mythical entity, the hard work, practice, dedication, and struggle that gives birth to genius can be conveniently ignored. As Kimbrough reveals, musicians like Robert Johnson create additional problems for academics: "How does he—this unschooled black Orpheus / produce songs as universal and complex / as the intellectual love of my life?" (23–24). If Robert Johnson can better the Bard with wisdom gained in the humble backwaters of the Delta, what is the point of attending Julliard, Harvard, Oxford, and the Sorbonne? Like the dibia who came before and the hip hop artists who came after him, Robert Johnson is one of many graduates of the University of Africana Wisdom. Robert was born with what Joe Turner sought when he enslaved thousands of African American men and what Colonel and Elvis hoped to find when they went out song stealing: the inherent divinity and power that comprises Africana soul.

Although Kimbrough's purpose and foundation are dubious, Stokes does not dismiss him. African hospitality moves him to see if there is fragment of soul in Kimbrough that can be coaxed into righteousness. Stokes offers Kimbrough a riddle that compares the professor to Brer Fox chasing Brer Rabbit, but Kimbrough rejects Brer Rabbit's wisdom:

> KIMBROUGH: My Auntie Belle told me those as a child.
> Nonsense tales, anthropomorphized critter
> stories with trite cautionary morals
> for kids. Diversionary, but little more.
> STOKES: Might've found who you think you looking for by now
> you'd've listened about that cunning bunny rabbit. Lives lean
> and tricks his way along. Them stories, you take so light, come
> with us from Africa, carry the Black wisdom like my Ma Ruth
> used to heal. They don't just tickle, they teach. And you might
> be the fox amongst them school girls, but you in Robert
> Johnson's briar patch now. (24)

In addition to highlighting the pseudo-erudition that characterizes Kimbrough's every utterance, Kimbrough's refusal to open his mind to African wisdom-working ways confirms for Stokes that he need not fluff the pillows on Zora Neale Hurston's fabled "feather bed [of] resistance" to smother Kimbrough; he is already dead to the culture. However it is ironic that, as Kimbrough dismisses didactic orature as childish folktales, he puts his career on hiatus and risks his life to associate Johnson with the Caucasian folktale of Faust and fiction of Satan.

Perhaps the most significant information about the character and motivations of Kimbrough is revealed when he threatens to scream rape if Robert is not brought out for inspection: "[C]onjure him, or I will set up an alarm that there is a wild nigger on the loose; / create heinous crimes for him: murder, rape, / and unleash those mindless redneck dogs" (29). Kimbrough, the would-be high-minded northerner, shows himself to be indistinguishable from the vilest stereotypical southern racist. Kimbrough is prepared to have innocent people mauled, lynched, incarcerated, and enslaved, so that he can lay claim to knowledge of the genesis of Robert's art. Kimbrough is very much the literary brother of Joe Turner who would steal up to eighty African American men at a time so that he could benefit from their free labor while attempting to steal their songs.

Herald Loomis met Joe Turner when he was a happily married man and a deacon at the Abundant Life Church. One day Loomis stopped to preach to a group of gamblers, and Joe Turner's men converged on them. Deacon Loomis and the gamblers, without distinction, were arrested and ultimately relocated to Joe Turner's farm where they were enslaved for seven years. Lem of *RJTD* astutely observes that a "[d]irt hauling negro same as a blues hollering one far as [Caucasians] concerned" (26). Verily, Joe Turner does not care about the occupations, faiths, or economic or social statuses of his Africana captives. He wants shiny laborers with strong backs and rich songs. But perhaps the deepest irony and the issue central to *JTCG* is that Herald Loomis is captured while he is trying to mind those gamblers' business; while proselytizing for the "lord" Loomis winds up enslaved under the "lord's" auspices.

Unlike Deacon Loomis, Robert Johnson is a wind-free roamer and a lover of many women. He clears the path for himself and others with his artistry, but he does not proselytize to, enable, or cripple anyone. He honors his own and others' independence and free will in literature, lyrics, and life. In the documentary *"Can't You Hear the Wind Howl?": The Life and Music of Robert Johnson*, Johnny Shines, Johnson's friend, colleague, and traveling companion, recounts how when he and Johnson were traveling and playing together, Johnson told Shines that they should split up so that Johnson could make his money in one part of town while Shines could make his money in another.[10] This is great entrepreneurship. Why should two men struggle on four legs when each can be "blues-walking like a man" on his own three? At one point, as Shines recalls how he and Johnson traveled all over America and to Canada, Shines states matter-of-factly: "He would leave you."[11] Perhaps by periodically abandoning his friend, Johnson was encouraging Shines to be his own source of empowerment so that he would never be dependent on or enslaved to anyone.

Agents of Degradation and Forces of Restoration

Both *RJTD* and *JTCG* reveal the methodologies by which Gods give birth to Gods. While the deifications of Bynum, Stokes, Robert, and Herald are unique, examples of similar transferences and transformations can be found throughout Africana life and history. Bynum recounts his initiation into Divinity when he shares the Secret of Life with Selig.

Because Selig has not been educated, or, more accurately, miseducated, to the same degree as Kimbrough, Selig is able to glimpse the Divine. Although he makes the statement in jest, when Bynum probes him about the shiny man, the People Finder tells Bynum, "The only shiny man I saw was the Nigras working on the road gang with the sweat glistening on them" (8). Selig is looking at the sweat and confused by slurs so he is oblivious to the fact that he has witnessed Divinity-in-the-making. Bynum knows that Selig has glimpsed God, and he tells him so, but Bynum reveals this in such a way that Selig would need the superior interpretive skill that the Yoruba call *iluti* to understand. After asserting that the shiny man does not glow from sweat but from manifest divinity, Bynum offers a riddled agreement to Selig's mockery: "I ain't even so sure he's one special fellow. *That shine could pass on to anybody. He could be anybody shining*" (8, emphasis added). Selig, confused by abundant visual evidence, asks, "Well, what's he look like besides being shiny? There's lots of shiny nigras" (8). Bynum and Selig are discussing the same phenomenon, but what to Selig is superficial luminosity Bynum knows is intrinsic numinosity.

The exchange between Bynum and Selig is not designed to reveal Selig's myopia as much as stimulate the latent and buried divinity of Bertha and Seth, respectively, and catalyze the divinity Wilson's intended audience. What is more, Bynum's shining friend, the one he tellingly calls "John," the one who "could be anybody," is a manifestation of the African American God, High John the Conqueror. The communal God is present in Wilson's play because slavery was never actually abolished. In addition to lynching becoming America's favorite national pastime and convict leasing swallowing people whole, "free" Africana people found themselves scattered, lost, threatened, and fragmented; High John the Conqueror was needed just as much, if not more, after the so-called abolition of slavery as before.

Bynum reveals that his encounter with John is initiated with African rituals of reciprocity and balance: Bynum shares both his knowledge and his food with John, and in return, John shares with Bynum the Secret of Life. It is significant that part of the process involves the shiny man leading Bynum back the way Bynum had come; this implies that Bynum had walked right past his destiny, right past the cosmic tools and technologies he needs to fully manifest his divinity. The shiny man tells Bynum that "a voice inside him [tells] him which way to go" (9). This voice could be Bynum's father who watches his son navigate through life and awaits the most opportune time to introduce his son to his power. Bynum's encounter with the shiny man confirms that the spiritual realm is always present and accessible; however, so many people lack spiritual vision and/or are so consumed with the rigors and distractions of terrestrial existence that they are blind to and unable to receive assistance from ubiquitous cosmic entities and elements. However, because of his giving character and respect for reciprocity, the spiritual realm and spiritual forces are eager to interact with Bynum.

In order for Bynum to behold the Secret of Life, his ojú inú (spiritual eyes) must be opened. As Bynum recalls, the shiny man initiates Bynum into his divinity so that he is able to see: "We get near this bend in the road and he told me to hold out my hands. Then he rubbed them together with his and I looked down and see they got blood on them. Told me to take and rub it all over me . . . say that was a way of cleaning myself" (9). This is the blood of àṣẹ, the power to make things happen. Africana women's menstrual cycles result in natural endowments of both àṣẹ and Àjẹ́, the ability to do and undo, create and destroy. Africana women do not need to cut themselves to access their blood of power, but men do.

After Bynum bathes in his personal elixir, his spiritual eyes open: "Turn around that bend and everything look like it was twice as big as it was. The trees and everything bigger than life! Sparrows big as eagles!" (9). When the spiritual realm impresses itself upon a human being, there may be any number of visible results. The ojú inú, spiritual eyes, may burst forth causing the eyes to bulge. One's eyes may roll backward. One's vision may be altered. When Malidoma Somé returns from the spiritual realm, he finds that things he ordinarily would not have noticed increase exponentially in size to make him aware of their presences.[12] Bynum's experience is similar to Somé's. With his ojú inú open, Bynum beholds the power in everything, including John:

> I turned around to look at this fellow and he had this light coming out of him. I had to cover up my eyes to keep from being blinded. He shining like new money with that light. He shined until all the light seemed like it seeped out of him and then he was gone and I was by myself in this strange place where everything was bigger than life. (9)

John goes light years beyond the transfiguration of Jesus that is described in Matthew 17:1–9, because rather than just looking radiant, John shares his glory. The shining that "can pass on to anybody" enters Bynum and bestows upon him the mantle and obligations of Divinity.

Bynum's second guide on his journey to deification is his father, who appears with a massive mouth and huge hands. The size of Bynum's father's hands and mouth appears to reflect the magnitude of the Healing Song that he is obliged to carry and share. As a divine healer of two heads and two worlds, Bynum's father knows that healing can take many forms. While Bynum is not physically ill, he is not whole. In order to ensure his own, his son's and his people's continuity, Bynum's father sings to him a song of identity and destiny that situates Bynum within the continuum of the Ancient Immortals and arms him with the tools of holistic evolution. Bynum's father tells him that the shiny man is He Who Goes Before and Shows the Way: "Said there was lots of shiny men and if I ever saw one again before I died then I would know that my song had been accepted and worked its full power in the world and I could lay down and die a happy man. A man who done left his mark on life. On the way people cling to each other out of the truth they find in themselves" (10).

During his search for the shiny man, Bynum drops the jewels that can help members of his community and members of Wilson's audience find shining people or find themselves shining. While Bynum clearly articulates the path to divinity, the message is encoded; it is a cipher. Selig does not have the appropriate spiritual, cultural, or moral foundation to decode the cipher, and he asks Bynum, "Well, how is that the Secret of Life? I thought you said he was gonna show you the secret of life?" (10). Wilson knows that this is the statement that the majority of his audience will make upon hearing Bynum's revelation. Like the true African two-headed doctor he is, Bynum's answer to Selig, and Wilson's audience, leaves the quest for knowledge up to the questioner: "Oh, he showed me alright. *But you still got to figure it out. Can't nobody figure it out for you.* You got to come to it on your own. That's why *I'm* looking for the shiny man" (10–11, emphasis added). With the last sentence, Bynum reiterates the fact that Selig is no more than a signified tool; the search for the shiny man is Bynum's responsibility, and it is his passion.

Robert Johnson is the quintessential shining man, but his luminosity has been obfuscated by the shadow of the Caucasian boogeyman (the devil). Stokes serves as both exorcist and agent of restoration, because he, like Bynum, is an elder with two heads. Bynum is initiated into his divinity by the shiny man, and he is shown the foundation of his inheritance and his path of divine actualization by his father. Similar to Bynum and innumerable Pan-African wisdom workers, Stokes reveals that while the foundation of his power is genetic endowment, he had to meld his inheritance with acquired wisdom:

> See, my grandmama was a healer. Ma Ruth was her name. Had the gift and the Black Wisdom from the olden days. And I ain't just talking about motherwit when I say Black Wisdom. And ain't talking about slavery when I say olden days. Ma Ruth had it but it

took me a long time; but I got it now. Had to wander off down a lot of blind alleys, but I got it now. (7)

Stokes may have lost his eyesight, but, to paraphrase John Henrik Clarke, he has gained insight that has the depth of ages.[13] Indeed, like Djigui of *Yeelen*, Stokes' spiritual vision is so overwhelming that it permanently supplants his material vision. Stokes' vision helps him to read the minds of members of his audience who have been miseducated not only about Robert Johnson but also about Africana spiritual systems and Africana history. Consequently, Stokes makes it clear that African spiritual powers and technologies are not synonymous with "mother wit" and that African history does not begin with slavery.

Ma Ruth and Stokes are seers, protectors, and healers in the same vein as Bynum and his father. Ma Ruth has Ọ̀rọ̀, Power of the Word, and similar to Bynum's father's Healing Song, Ma Ruth heals with stories (8). Ma Ruth can also dismantle oppressors. Georgia reveals that no one knows the limits of the powers of Stokes and Ma Ruth:

> I ain't seen all he can do, but I know I don't want to get on his bad side. He can see more from inside then most can from out. And he told me a story how his grandmama did a white woman for slapping her: put some of that mess on her, and all I know is Miss What's her name laid there for six solid days, couldn't move nothing but her eyes. And when she did get up wasn't a hair no where on her body. (19)

Ma Ruth keeps the cornerstones of self-defense, self-preservation and self-protection intact by passing her myriad powers on to her grandson so that he, like Bynum, can protect and enliven the divinity of others.

While Robert does not boast a guiding biological father or grandmother, he has access to a university filled with two-headed doctors in his community's "hoodoo negroes" who are not tied to land owned by an oppressor and who are not raped yearly by cotton or other cash crops. The "hoodoo negroes" comprise a perfect school for Robert to master both the guitar and his power. Robert studies with, listens to, and plays and moves with his elders. And he practices: "Till I got so I could slip that slide so to make it talk to me like a best buddy; *(Demonstrates.)* hum and howl like the wind whining across a headstone; *(Demonstrates.)* squall like a freight train flying across the midnight silver moon—*(Demonstrates.)* or moan like a woman, touched low, slow and deep down to her soul" (20).

Binding what clings costs Bynum part of himself, and Robert's talent also exacts a serious spiritual toll. He describes how at times in the midst of a rocking juke there will be a person sitting stock still absorbing Robert and his music: "I know that that somebody looking is getting more than just the fun and good times of what I'm doing. Something in it is touching more than their feet. It's done got inside them. And they holding me responsible for driving away their trouble or heartache" (21). Robert is very much the diviner, and his lyrics and wrenching harmonies speak directly to the souls of his listeners. E. Bolaji Idowu asserts that babaláwo, rather than charging exorbitant fees, traditionally would "spend [themselves] in the service to the community."[14] In a manner similar to Bynum and Stokes, Robert effectively spends himself in his communities, and, in the process, he exerts so much dynamism that he captivates friends, fans, fiends, and foes that span multiple generations.

From the era of slavery to Civil Rights wars that spanned from 1950s to the 1980s, African Americans readily offered refuge and safety to African Americans who were fleeing the Ku Klux Klan, night riders, sheriffs, mayors, plantation owners, police, patterrollers, and any number of other United States' terror organizations and terrorists. Consequently, it is not surprising that Robert could stumble into Georgia Mayberry's Colored Jook Joint and find protection from Kimbrough. Robert also establishes immediate spiritual bonds with Georgia and Stokes. With Georgia, Robert makes love and may very well have produced his heir. Robert's bond with Stokes is established in a subtle gesture that many would overlook. After Stokes discusses his and his grandmother's power, he turns his attention to Robert's guitar. Robert says, "I'm particular. I don't let just anybody touch my guitar" (8). But Stokes is not just "anybody," and Robert knows this: "ROBERT very deliberately takes the instrument from its case, moves to STOKES, *kneels before him and using both hands presents it to STOKES*. STOKES takes it and 'senses' it with his hands before returning it" (8, emphasis added). Robert presents the guitar to Stokes in the manner identical to that with which a person presents a gift to her elder in Yoruba culture—stationed on the knees and presenting with both hands. Following the binding ritual, Robert, Stokes, and Georgia, a unified trio, celebrate with an impromptu celebration that can best be described as juba.

That both *JTCG* and *RJTD* include some manner and mention of juba is an indication of the importance of this ritual to the plays, to the playwrights, and to Africana culture.[15] In African America, the classic juba is a holistic ceremony that is similar to African ring shouts. The participants dance in a counter-clockwise circle, and each participant exhibits his or her unique dance stylings while remaining at one with the unified whole. With its focus on exultation and originality, juba may be a recreation of or an homage to the movement of the planets around the Sun. While it is most recognizable in its classic form, juba is not limited to one style or manifestation. Juba takes whatever shape its participants find necessary to invoke Deities, offer praise, lament, re-member, wail, and exalt. Just as the crossroads is the site where all entities, forms, and forces gather, all emotions and expressions converge in juba.

Given the purpose of juba and the energies it invokes, it is fitting that Herald Loomis snaps when someone mentions the Holy Ghost during the ritual. Herald stuns the celebrants with his queries:

> What's so holy about the Holy Ghost? You singing and singing. . . . You singing for the Holy Ghost to come? What he gonna do, huh? He gonna come with tongues of fire and burn up your woolly heads? You gonna tie onto the Holy Ghost and get burned up? What you got then? Why God got to be so big? Why he got to be bigger than me? How much big is there? How much big you want? (52)

Loomis' reaction to and critical analysis of Christianity and its myths and realities reveal a struggle similar to that various members of the Nation of Islam faced when they began acknowledging their divinity. Loomis' queries are also reflective of the observations of jazz innovator Sun Ra who asserts in broadsides titled "MESSAGE TO THE SPOOK. . . .," "THE BIBLE WAS NOT WRITTEN FOR NEGROES!!!!!!!," and "Jacob in the Land of U.S." that African Americans are, in fact, Holy Ghosts.[16] As Loomis concludes his demystification of the Christian Holy Ghost, he unzips his pants so that he can show and prove that his endowments are not only tangible but also that they are grander and more potent than those of any ghost.

What, you may ask, does Herald Loomis' penis have to do with divinity. The answer is: Everything!

In addition to being the storehouses of existence, the genitals house profound spiritual energies that open the doors to scientific, philosophical, and even architectural inventions. The tomb of Ramses VI boasts artwork that depicts the monarch standing in diagonal profile with his arms extended over his head and his erect penis at its zenith. A serpent is stationed at a 90 degree angle from the back of Ramses' head to his feet. The triangle that the serpent and Ramses form is the source of the theorem erroneously associated with Pythagoras. Pythagoras founded his brotherhood in 529 BCE, but the 3-4-5 triangle and "golden section" geometry had been in use in Kemet since at least 1143 BCE.[17]

When touring the temples of Kemet it is evident that the genitals were respected and celebrated as essential gateways of existence and numinescence. It also becomes clear, when observing the fact that someone chiseled away the image of Ramses' erect penis, that alien cultures, such as those of the Christians and Muslims who invaded Kemet, do not enjoy a healthy respect for the genitals or the blissful organic process through which many Gods and humans are conceived. But the holistic knowledge of the Kemites could not be chiseled away; it flourishes in Herald Loomis, and it is highlighted in the climax of Clarence Cooper, Jr.'s short story, "Not We Many."

After David and Famat of "Not We Many" discover God through Ax Muslim mathematics, David does what Herald Loomis attempts to do, which is also what his Kemetic ancestors did millennia before him: He shares his discovery with the Africana community. Before he introduces the Harlem masses to and initiates them into their divinity, David describes to them his own spiritual struggle, which is similar to Herald's, and his disillusionment with Islam because he finds it duplicates the enslaving, patriarchal, egotistical destructions as Christianity. David's disenchantment with Islam and his quest for truth lead him to the discovery of the true identity of God. In the vein of Allah, the Father, who founded the Five Percenters, David charges the masses to embrace the tools of their divinity as well as the identity of the Divine: "I pointed my finger at the black belly of the crowd. 'Take your genitals in hand, you Great Deceiver, for they are the crown of Him Who was, Who is, Who *will* be — to the end of eternity!'"[18]

The revelation that is the climax for David and his Harlem audience is merely the rising action for Herald. Being enslaved for seven years because he was ministering to gamblers taught Loomis a valuable lesson: He will not participate in binding anyone else to an agent or agency of oppression. After Herald finishes questioning the size, significance, relevance, and existence of the Caucasian God, the African Gods invoked by the juba embrace Loomis and usher him into the womb of re-membering:

> I come to this place . . . to this water that was bigger than the whole world. And I looked out . . . and I seen these bones rise up out the water. Rise up and begin to walk on top of it. [. . .] Walking without sinking down. Walking on top of the water. [. . .] A whole heap of them. They come up out the water and started marching. (53)

After the bones sink into the water, they wash up on land and are covered with the flesh of humanity. Loomis makes an important observation; he notes that the beings who stroll forth from Yemǫja's belly are "[j]ust like you and me! . . . They black. Just like you and me. Ain't no difference" (54). The "you and me" in question are not merely Herald and Bynum or even the characters in the play; August Wilson is speaking to his intended audience, his peers, his ancestors, his Gods. Bynum further emphasizes the Bones People's curvilinear reincarnating nature when he notes, "They walking around here now. Mens. Just like you and me. Come right up out the water" (56). Through Herald and Bynum's "oracular utterance," Wilson's text and characters become mirrors that reflect the history, genealogy, and destiny of every member of his intended Africana audience who holds or beholds his play. The audience members are the Bones People, the ancestors, the survivors, the Gods.

What Loomis beholds and becomes through the re-membering power of water recurs in numerous literary works in scenes that involve water, human forms, and the moanings of a multitude. Bynum has his water-born revelation when his father's spirit visits him, as Bynum recalls, "Then he carried me further into this big place until we come to this ocean. Then he showed me something I ain't got words to tell you. But if you witness it, you done seen something there" (10). Bynum withholds details about what he sees because he will direct Loomis to bear witness for both of them as part of Loomis' transformation. What Bynum and Herald see are the Africans who did not survive the Middle Passage re-membering themselves to those who made it through.

August Wilson describes the Ethiopic Ocean as "the largest unmarked graveyard in the world."[19] Toni Morrison dedicates *Beloved* to *"Sixty Million / and more,"* in homage to those ancestors who made a home in that ocean by force or by choice. With Wilson's and Morrison's observation and reverence, a clearer picture of the scope of the most monumental tragedy in the world is revealed. The murders and unceremonious burials that occurred over and over in the Ethiopic are part of the curvilinear collective unconscious and consciousness of all Africana peoples because contemporary Africana people are reincarnations of these ancestors and all are seeking to be re-membered.

Before she journeys to the other side, Ma Ruth re-members Stokes to the power, tragedy, and triumph of his ancestors:

> [S]omething called me back just as she was dying. They lead me in the room. Tell me she can't talk. I reached and find her hand. She said my name clear as day. And I said, "Yes'm." And felt what I first thought was a death tremor running through her to me, least that's what I thought it was at first. . . . I don't know how long it took me to come to. But look like I heard drumming and waves of water and people moaning. Moaning and creaking. And them drums—like the sound of Ma Ruth's chair rocking on that porch. Rocking and drumming. And moaning and water waves—(25)

Stokes does not get to finish his recollection because Kimbrough interrupts him! However, in her spiritual-autobiographical tome, *Jambalaya*,

Luisah Teish offers a richly detailed account of an experience she had as a child that is similar to those of Loomis, Bynum, and Stokes:

> There under the bed was an undulating, sinewy, mass of matter as brown as the waters of the muddy Mississippi River. . . . The brown was taking forms, humanoid but undistinguishable by gender. They were getting higher, showing heads with eyes, bellies, legs, outstretched arms, and I was getting closer to the bed. My face, now only a few inches from the sheet returned to the other side of my head, and as my body descended I looked at these brown humanoids towering over me. I seemed to shake uncontrollably, my muscles moved about as if I had no bones. I opened my mouth, screamed but the sound was made only inside my head. The brown-folk seemed to take a deep breath as my body settled on the mattress. They touched me and their matter slipped into my muscles and ran through my veins.[20]

Teish later learns that these entities are her ancestors who were introducing Teish to both her lifework and the persistence of their memories and power.

Toni Cade Bambara makes numerous references to submerged, emerging, and waiting ancestors in her literature. In *The Salt Eaters*, Velma re-members herself to the mud mothers, who are the originators of life and keepers of time; in "Broken Field Running," the elders sing lamentations for the ancestors who have become "bones bleaching in the briny deep" of the Ethiopic Ocean.[21] Ama Ata Aidoo writes of Anowa, who dreams she is Asase Yaa, the Great Mother, who births multitudes only to see lobster-red Caucasians emerge from the roiling Ethiopic to dash, smash, and devour her progeny.[22] In one of the most powerful scenes in cinema, Julie Dash's *Daughters of the Dust* confirms that everything said to have happened on Igbo Landing occurred: Some Igbo walked on water back to Africa, some Igbo found a home in the ocean, and other Igbo planted roots of permanence and power in the United States.[23]

The work of re-membering and reclaiming occurs in August Wilson's play *Gem of the Ocean* and Henry Dumas' short story "Ark of Bones." Each of these texts includes a discussion of a body of water that boasts a magnificent edifice where the bones of drowned and lynched African ancestors are gathered, embraced, and re-membered to the Africana collective and its consciousness.[24] These bones also constitute the building blocks of Pan-African reparations. The root of the word reparations is "repair," and these artistic tributes involving Bones People and a womb of water help mend fragmented psyches, heal spiritual wounds, and make amends for various crimes including the crime of willful forgetfulness.

In the case of Herald Loomis, the most pressing repairs concern his soul's bones, as they are incapable to enabling his legs to stand or his hands to feel (56 and 77). The diagnosis of the Dagara elders would be that Herald's *Sìè* (spirit) is not in his body.[25] His spirit appears to be just outside of his body, waiting for Herald to reformulate and reconstitute his Self. Until Herald is whole, his Sìè will be an outside observer, and Loomis' legs will not stand up; or to put it another way, Herald cannot access his power or direct his destiny. Bynum knows the spiritual confusion in which Herald is mired and the revelations that await them both. So Bynum, as brother of Èṣù, the Divine Linguist, Mediator, and Trickster, situates himself close to the Earth with Herald and crawls with and talks his charge through the endless ocean of continuity.

One of the most effective tools that Bynum uses to guide Loomis to his divinity is his name. When Bynum says, "Then what happened, Herald Loomis?" (54); "The breath coming into you, Herald Loomis" (55); and "They walking, Herald Loomis. They walking around here now" (56), the name "Herald" becomes a command. Similar to the way Madame Koto of Ben Okri's *The Famished Road* whips Azaro's mother with her name until she is revivified,[26] Bynum charges Herald with the power and promise resident in his name. That Bynum is using Herald's name as a spiritual tool for healing and galvanization is evident in the fact that, similar to Yoruba king-makers who use ìtàn ipọnri only at sacred times and in sacred spaces because of the names' powers, Bynum only challenges and charges Herald with his name when Herald is on the threshold of numinescence.

Robert is in full command of his bones, and he is as comfortable with his divinity as he is with his penis—he totes both with a relaxed swagger. Because of his lyrical and musical talents and his ability to signify, Robert made his mark upon the world long before Kimbrough came to the Delta. By contrast, Herald Loomis is unable to signify because psychologically he bears the mark of his enslaver. Bynum continues the process of initiating Herald into himself by singing the song that he is marked by:

> They tell me Joe Turner's come and gone
> Ohhh Lordy
> They tell me Joe Turner's come and gone
> Ohhh Lordy
> Got my man and gone (67)

According to the Thirteenth Amendment to the United States' Constitution, slavery is illegal—except as a punishment for a crime. Caucasians made sure that the very law that "freed" enslaved Africans was written to justify and facilitate their enslavement in perpetuity. As soon as slavery was "abolished" African Americans found that they could be arrested for anything or for nothing at all: "Intent" to steal was a punishable offense.[27] If neoenslavers could not conjure a charge to justify arrest, they used the same tactics that their enslaving progenitors used in Africa—they simply abducted African Americans. Once arrested, the African Americans became part of a "virtual penitentiary" called the convict lease system.[28]

Thanks to the concerted efforts of police officers, mayors, governors, and plantation owners, not only did slavery thrive in America despite its abolition, but because its abolition gave birth to a model of oppression firmly rooted in capitalism, neoslavery became wildly profitable for individual plantation owners as well as for states that used convict labor for government projects. Because the monetary values attached to enslaved Africans were nullified with "abolition," the convict lease system made it convenient for the state to literally work men, women, and children to death and simply arrest new laborers as necessary. The system was so brutal that there is no record of a convict living out a ten year sentence. I must reemphasize here that Caucasians designed the convict lease system exclusively for African Americans.[29]

The song Bynum sings to summon Herald's Siè is the actual song recorded by W. C. Handy in 1916 that African American women in Memphis would sing in the wake of Joe Turney's departure. Joe Turney was the brother of Pete Turney, who was the governor of Tennessee from 1893 to 1897. Pete may have been the governor, but his brother eclipsed him in notoriety: Joe Turney, the man for whom the blues song and August Wilson's play are named, created his own personal convict lease system. He would organize gambling parties for African American men, arrest them for gambling, and enslave them so that his plantation could flourish off of free labor. Convict leasing spanned from roughly 1868 to 1928.[30] Joe Turney and many other profiteers enjoyed at least sixty years of free African labor and expansive wealth thanks to the abolition of slavery.

The song "Joe Turner's Blues" is significant because it provides another example of how the empowered blood and ancient methodology of the djeli survived in African America and were used to document significant historical events. The women of Memphis make clear their significance as the blood of their community, for, were it not for them harnessing Ọ̀rọ̀, the Power of the Word, through their lamentations, the tragedies that they and their men suffered would have been just another forgotten atrocity. But the women sang, W. C. Handy transcribed, and August Wilson continued the re-membering process by writing his play. Wilson compounds the significance of Òrò by centering his work of recovery and discovery on a man who has forgotten his song and is unable to signify. As Bynum surmises, "Now, I can look at you, Mr. Loomis, and see you a man who done forgot his song. Forgot how to sing it. A fellow forget that and forget who he is. Forget how he's supposed to mark down life" (71).

Loomis was caught by Joe Turner in 1901 and released in 1908. Turner followed the biblical model of enslavement and kept the captives seven years and released them on his birthday. Bynum, Seth, and Herald try to understand what compelled Turner to capture and enslave so many Africana men. Loomis muses that although Joe Turner called him worthless, "worthless is something you throw away. Something you don't bother with. I ain't seen him throw me away. . . . So I must got something he want. What I got?" (73). Seth reasons that Turner wanted Loomis' labor, but Loomis disputes this in the light of the obvious: "I can look at him and see where he big and strong enough to do his own work. So it can't be that. He must want something he ain't got" (73). It is Bynum who reveals the truth:

> What he wanted was your song. He wanted to have that song be his. He thought by catching you he could learn that song. Every nigger he catch he's looking for the one he can learn that song from. Now he's got you bound up to where you can't sing your own song. Couldn't sing it them seven years 'cause you was afraid he would snatch it from under you. But you still got it. You just forgot how to sing it. (73)

Joe Turner, not unlike the greedy Pemba of Mande mythistory and the Jew character who steals the soul-piece, is so attracted to the melody of Africana song and the glow of the Africana shine that he hears and sees but cannot control or own that he steals and enslaves Africans in his attempt to obtain what will always elude him. Similarly, Kimbrough leaves his home and job and risks his life in hopes and finding, demystifying, and remystifying a force that he cannot comprehend. While it is tempting to compartmentalize these men and their attacks on Africana people, history, and power, Turner, Kimbrough, and Selig are fictional representations of actual persons who have devoted their lives to profiting off of Africana labor, soul power, and divinity.

Jesus and Satan: Identical Forms, Functions, and Objectives

To the Western mind titillated by issues regarding Africana men, sexuality, artistic ability, and devils, the myth of Robert Johnson selling his soul to the devil to become a master musician is attractive. In the Africana ethos it is ludicrous. When Georgia hears the myth she signifies, "So, he sold his soul to the devil, so he could pick the guitar and chase some tail" (13): One certainly needs no satanic assistance to undertake these endeavors. Stokes follows Georgia's assessment with wisdom from Ma Ruth:

> My grandmama say the white folks the one started that talk about the devil. She say wasn't no devil in Africa till the white folks took him with them in the first empty slave ships they took over there. She say white folks ended up with us, and we ended up with the devil. (13)

It is important to reiterate here that there is no devil or inherently evil entity in traditional African cosmology. Belief in such a figure would stymie knowledge acquisition, self-actualization, and community evolution. Caucasian missionary colonizers sought to associate African Gods of myriad powers, such as Èṣù, the Trickster and Divine Linguist, with the Judeo-Christian devil to disconnect Africans from their Gods and from their cultures, powers, and numinosity. Missionary colonizers are still working to achieve this goal, and they are not working alone. Their minion labor feverishly in every field in which Africana creativity thrives to replace the wisdom of the creators with the devils of the takers. Kimbrough comes to represent every racist Africanist, blues aficionado, ethnomusicologist, and historian whoever turned his myopic mind to ponder and poised his agenda-bogged pen to write about Africana arts, science, and culture.[31]

During his long-awaited interrogation of Robert, Kimbrough pumps his subject for proof of an evil pact. Kimbrough's insistence is reminiscent of that of Traynor, the Elvis-inspired singer of Alice Walker's short story "1955." Traynor makes millions recording one of Gracie Mae's songs, and unlike many historical Caucasian "artists" he plies her with extravagant gifts. Traynor hopes to accomplish two things with his largess: compensate Gracie Mae for the song that made him famous and move her to tell him what "his" signature song means. Gracie Mae, relishing her power as creator and definer, keeps her wisdom within. Traynor goes to his grave a wealthy and obese sham.

Kimbrough is much more aggressive with Robert and demands, "What did you give to get what you have?" to which Robert responds, "I started with nothing, so I didn't have nothing to give up" (33). When Kimbrough asks Robert where his songs come from, Robert reveals his creative praxis: "They just come. No one place or time. Be like a fire, they bubble and boil from inside. I take them see if they'll please the people" (36). The truth is too mundane for Kimbrough. It is not sensational enough; so he tries again:

> The question is, how you are able to grasp
> intuitively ideas my students
> fail to understand with intense tutoring.
> Is it because you suffered while I was
> cradled in an ivied ivory tower?
> The answer I want is should I footnote
> your "creations" in the Book of Riddles
> as the effect of a freak alignment
> of the stars? and fly back to my Northeast nest. (38)

The depth of African wisdom systems is beyond the comprehension of the Western-educated Kimbrough. However, Kimbrough knows that because he is part of the vanguard of professional miseducators and indoctrinators he can twist his ignorance of Johnson into a publishable and profitable lie.

The power of the African American man's song is magnificent. As Omowale avers in *Look What the Done to My Song*, musicians are Gods with the ability to divine what is needed and then "space out whitey. . . . Drive the cracker mad with abstractions, put righteous voodoo on his ass. Musicians can control the spirits, remember."[32] As if he hears Omowale's call, Robert composes a song, or, more precisely, casts an ẹsẹ Ifá (divination verse), or, equally accurate, constructs a cipher just for Professor Kimbrough.

Robert describes himself going to the crossroads out of casual curiosity to "see what old Satan got to say" (39). The devil, who is an "ordinary white man in a suit and tie" (39), tells Robert how the simplistic ritual works, but Robert refuses to begin the rite and give the devil his guitar. Robert knows it is not possible to get something for nothing, and, what is more important, he knows that no Caucasian man would or could do anything worthwhile for him—from dying on a cross to granting him with knowledge of his own birthright. Robert realizes that the mythmaker is one with the myth: Not only is the devil not a supernatural entity, but there is no difference between the devil and the Caucasian enslavers, rapists, lynchers, and convict leasers and lessees who planted, plucked, and picked Robert's father and millions more Africana men as "clean as a hound's tooth" (20). The devil Robert encounters is not the cool brother in *Mules and Men*; this racist n-word-slinging entity is another Kimbrough, a twin of Joe Turner.

Because Johnson refuses to take part in the ritual, his interaction with the devil becomes a meeting of equals. Similar to High John and Jack, the Africana culture heroes who entered into contests of wills and intelligence with Devil, Robert and the Caucasian devil square off in a blues showdown. During the battle, Robert learns to do what his ancient forebears did—harness his creative resources and access the divinity waiting within:

> I was slipping back to the beginning of all mankind, but I kept on playing, knowing it was all stood between me and losing my soul. But I kept on playing—But then little by little, from somewhere, I don't know, from me mostly—I thought. But maybe not. Look like something told me to walk them four corners from point to point and I did. Then kitty corner. Then round and round. And that's what I done. And something else come to me and say, "Bob, the best way to get ahead is to go back where you started." And I reckon that's when I took the Devil by surprise. (40)

Robert states throughout the play that he is a student of Son House, Willie Brown, and other musicians; however, he becomes the master of his destiny when he stops referencing his mentors and summons his own artistic truth.

Robert plays himself to the origin of time and finds himself standing at the crossroads where he must take with his soul the same journey that Carlos Moore took with his eyes. Robert enters the crossroads and is joined by Èṣù. The pair walks through the four stages of existence—birth, life, death, rebirth—and are joined by BaKongo Gods as they catalyze the four moments of the Sun.[33] Once fortified by Yoruba and BaKongo Gods and powers, Robert hears He Who Goes Before and Shows the Way tell him to return to his source; at the same time, he hears soul singer D'Angelo advise him from the future to "remember what you already know."[34] Robert pulls his power from the Womb of Existence where creation and consciousness spring. When Robert accesses and plays his truth, his guitar becomes a history text with facts so stunning that they shame the devil.

While Robert and Bynum are not technically Five Percenters, they are clearly at one with that way of life, and they do, in fact, try to teach their "devils." Robert diagnoses Kimbrough's ailment: "You lost and down low and you want to get found and rise up. You was drawed to me by my blues, admit the truth and shame the Devil. Get out that nightmare. Quit being a coward and a hypocrite" (44). Kimbrough's cure is to admit that Robert is not merely equal or superior to Shakespeare, but that Robert is a God and a member of a vast consortium of Deities. However, Kimbrough refuses to acknowledge either his own or the Africana man's truths, genealogies, and identities. Kimbrough takes comfort and seeks recourse in the myth of "white" superiority and dismisses Africana divinity as "nigger mumbo jumbo" (44).

Kimbrough is a professor: This term signifies one who professes to be an expert in a particular field, but there is a difference between one professing to have expertise and one actually having it. The word "professor" also moves one to consider the hot air expended in professing—often only for the sake of professing—as opposed to the laborious efforts involved in creating, building, and elevating. Perhaps, the most important thing about Kimbrough's occupation is that he thinks that his profession, ethnicity, and economic status all confer upon him a superiority that magically grants him the ability to instantly interpret Africana culture despite the fact that he does not even have a rudimentary understanding of Africana philosophy, art, or wisdom systems. In this, Kimbrough is reminiscent of the Caucasian "Africanist" who, often from the comfort of his armchair, claims to be an expert or specialist on Africa . . . the *whole* continent. (By contrast, while many are needed, the academic world boasts few "Europeanists" and "Caucasianists."[35])

The Western educational scheme is dependent upon and necessarily fuels myopic and racist assertions with extraordinary ease because information (or indoctrination) in the lecture hall often flows unidirectionally. As a case in point, "Professor" Kimbrough, as resident Africanist, cannot and will not be taught—not by the likes of his "subject," Robert Johnson. Kimbrough is completely resistant to education and growth; righteousness is out of the question. Consequently, rather than humble himself, acknowledge his superiors, and exorcise his devil, he projects his evil outward so that it can infect and infest others' minds and souls: "Robert Johnson? My research proves that he was in league with Satan from the age of seventeen. . . . And evil did swarm around his lust swollen, Satan stolen soul. That explains his unnatural insights and musical mastery, that and that alone" (45). After professing with aplomb and reifying lies via publication, the professor who knows and cares the least becomes mythmaker-in-chief.

Despite its nonsensical nature, some Caucasians are avid, even rabid, defenders of the lie associated with Johnson. In their level-headed study, *Robert Johnson: Lost and Found*, Barry Lee Pearson and Bill McCulloch reveal that when they discussed their intention to demystify the legacy of

Johnson they were greeted with profound disappointment by individuals who have enormous cultural, creative, and economic investments in the "romantic fantasy" that was created to hijack the history of Robert Johnson.[36] The authors attribute the campaign of disinformation's success to "ignorance and economics: white ignorance about African American traditions and culture and the desire to find ways to market Johnson's music to new generations of mostly white blues fans long after Johnson's death."[37] Pearson and McCulloch go on to assert that "[t]he crowning result of all this was reverse alchemy. Valuable information about Johnson was debased, distorted, or just ignored; a counterfeit story line emerged in which Johnson was cast as a twentieth-century Faust, relinquishing his soul and perhaps his sanity in an unholy trade for musical knowledge."[38]

Africana peoples have too many skills, talents, and teachers to need a Faustian myth to make do. But dislocated and struggling to survive in a nation that fosters in its citizens belief in such entities including, but by no means limited to, Santa Claus, the Tooth Fairy, and the Easter Bunny, the humble glow of Africana divinity is routinely overlooked by masses who are dazzled by department store glitter.[39]

While many people have the ability to shine, the distractions of this world are such that very few people exist in a state of enlightenment and liberation in which they actually do shine let alone promote luminosity in others. Bynum, employing the methodology of the Five Percent, has been patiently leading his emergent shiny man to the doorway of divinity for years; from the time he bound Martha Pentecost (formerly Loomis) to her daughter Zonia, Bynum has been summoning the God within Herald. After swimming with him in the sea of rememory and singing in the key of liberation Herald's song of oppression, Bynum walks Herald to the threshold of revelation and tells him that he has the power to free himself: "You binding yourself. You bound onto your song. All you got to do is stand up and sing it, Herald Loomis. It's right there kicking at your throat. All you got to do is sing it. Then you be free" (91).

Before Herald can liberate himself, Martha tries to reconvert him to Christianity. Her attempt to re-enslave him to religion triggers one of the most resonant exchanges in literature:

> MARTHA: ". . . .The Lord is my shepherd I shall not want. He maketh me to lie down in green pastures. He leads me beside the still water. He restoreth my soul. He leads me in the path of righteousness for His name's sake. Even though I walk through the shadow of death—"
> LOOMIS: That's just where I be walking!

MARTHA: "I shall fear no evil. For Thou art with me. Thy rod and thy staff, they comfort me."
LOOMIS: You can't tell me nothing about no valleys. I done been all across the valleys and the hills and the mountains and the oceans [. . . .] And all I seen was a bunch of niggers dazed out of their woolly heads. And Mr. Jesus Christ standing there in the middle of them, grinning. [. . .] He grin that big old grin . . . and niggers wallowing at his feet. [. . .] Great big old white man . . . your Mr. Jesus Christ. Standing there with a whip in one hand a tote board in another, and them niggers swimming in a sea of cotton. And he counting. He tallying up the cotton. "Well, Jeremiah . . . what's the matter, you ain't picked but two hundred pounds of cotton today? Got to put you on half rations." And Jeremiah go back and lay up there on his half rations and talk about what a nice man Mr. Jesus Christ is 'cause he give him salvation after he die. Something wrong here. Something don't fit right! (91–93)

As an eighty-fiver, Martha wants Herald to resume a slave's status, exchange Joe Turner's shackles for Jesus', and abandon his song and his divinity. However her recitation of the 23rd Psalm triggers an epiphany that moves Herald beyond man and beyond prophet. As he betters every biblical scripture that Martha recites with his own existentialist truth, Herald realizes that his history began before the Bible was even imagined. Herald does not need to study anyone else's book: He is The Text. He does not need to sing any oppressor-penned hymns: He came from the womb with his own song of self-sufficiency. He does not need to pray; for, like Zora Neale Hurston,[40] Herald is the answer to his prayers. And he does not need the blood of Jesus. Herald knows that that blood is fortified by the bodies and minds of millions of innocent Africans sacrificed on Christianity's altar to slavery and submission.

Herald Loomis's epiphany about Jesus is similar to the wisdom shared by Sun Ra who argues that

> NEGROES ARE WORSHIPPING A GOD THAT HAS NOT SAVED THEM ACCORDING TO THE SALVATION THAT THE WHITE MAN HAS ENJOYED AS RULER OF THE WHOLE EARTH. A GOD OF POWER COULD HAVE SAVED THE NEGRO LONG AGO BUT NEGROES ARE WORSHIPPING A GOD THAT WILL NOT SAVE THEM, AS IT IS WRITTEN "JESUS CHRIST, THE SAME YESTERDAY, TODAY AND FOREVER." IF JESUS DOES NOT CHANGE THEN THE NEGRO WILL NEVER BE FREE AS LONG AS HE WANTS A GOD OF THAT KIND.[41]

Sun Ra and Herald Loomis discern that the Jesus concept is designed to maintain the status quo for Caucasians and ensure the perpetual enslavement of Africana worshippers of Christianity. The facts that no biblical figure or scripture offers a condemnation of slavery and that the institution of slavery is supported by Christianity buttresses the assertions of Herald and Sun Ra that the Jesus concept offers Africana people a salvation that is tantamount to eternal servitude. What is more, from both Sun Ra's and Herald's perspectives, Africana adherents of Christianity are supporters of their own perpetual oppression. The concept of salvation through Jesus, even in its glorified sense, is revealed to be as preposterous as waiting for death to enjoy life or to be free, and it is as duplicitous as the notion that one can have one's sins white-washed or rinsed away with a private confession or some ritual recitations rather than one having to make amends for the atrocities one has committed, make reparations for the lives one has ruined.

When comparing Jesus in *JTCG* to the devil in *RJTD* it becomes clear that these figures are indistinguishable. While at the outset the twinning of these figures appears incongruous, the oneness of Jesus and Lucifer, a oneness that is celebrated in their shared home in the Evening Star, is essential to Christianity. Jesus and the devil not only work together but they are also so interdependent that one makes no sense and cannot exist without the other. The devil was created to terrorize people into adhering to Christianity; the construct of Jesus was created to "save" people from the fictions of devil, hell, sin, and damnation. While the devil appears to be the ultimate psychological terrorist in this carrot-and-stick scheme, the Jesus construct is arguably more pernicious than that of the devil. As Sun Ra and Herald Loomis both stress, belief in Jesus requires a disavowal of facts, history, and logic, and such belief necessarily compromises or altogether destroys one's spiritual and technological foundations and potential. One must subjugate the multifaceted, responsible, and empowered self and forgo the arduous process of developing one's identity and divinity and embrace a construct that was created to foment hypocrisy; spiritual and physical destruction; and physical, mental, sexual, and economic slaveries.

Herald realizes that rather than "save" him, Jesus forged and secured slavery's shackles around his limbs and mind. In fact, Herald experienced hells much worse than those described in the Bible *because* he was a good Christian. With experiential knowledge as opposed to belief guiding him, Herald shuns the savior of slavery and chooses the path of ancient African Gods who came to Earth equipped with the tools of holism, evolution, and immortality to be exercised with balance, harmony, and propriety in this lifetime. Herald anoints himself with his own blood and becomes the liberated and liberating "GOD OF POWER" to whom Sun Ra refers. Herald's patient Siè reunites with his body, and the man stands tall on ancient bones. Like his guide, Bynum, Herald luxuriates in the wealth derived from Hoodoo economics, for while Herald does not have one dollar, he is "shining like new money" with riches no accountant can tally (94).

. . .

Stokes, Herald, and Bynum in literature and Robert Johnson in life and literature are descendants of the ancient Bachwezi of East Africa. Their numinosity is so great it bursts forth from their bodies in an uncontainable juba of light, sound, and power.[42] Most important, and as further evidence of the proliferation of the Bachwezi, the shining of these men illuminates the realities and possibilities that exist for all who come into contact with them–whether through the empowered ink and whispering pages of their texts or through the mind-altering melodies of their songs. We, too, can travel inside ourselves and re-member forgotten odes to our Gods; we too can experience exponential soul expansion at the crossroads; we can live lives that are so profound that when our physical bodies are laid to rest we are honored with three different graves, as is the case with Robert Johnson. When we join the ancestors, we may find people at our graves, praying to us and "ask[ing] for the right direction," as pilgrims do at one Robert Johnson's graves.[43]

Indeed, we may find that there is no death to fear at all, because, as the Yoruba know, immortality is the result of a perfect and complete existence, and the Eternal Immortals do not need diamonds to shine.

CHAPTER FIVE

"Meet Me In Another World":[1] The Middle Passages Within Walter Mosley's *47*, Amos Tutuola's *My Life in the Bush of Ghosts*, and Malidoma Somé's *Of Water and the Spirit*

> "What else could it be, this work, this colossus, of three men and a woman, all of them huge, giants, chained together, heads bowed and broken, all blinded and tragic, as if the greatest humiliation had been heaped on their bodies. And yet how they shone, these beings, as if they were gods, unconquerable even by the vilest suffering. How they shone."
> ~ Ben Okri, *Starbook*

> "Why should you die to go to heaven? The Earth is already in space"
> ~ Killah Priest, "B.I.B.L.E."

In organized religions, paradises and heavens are described as places of luxury, laziness, and unlimited bliss where entrants float on clouds, play harps, and relax . . . forever. This type of place might make sense for people who have been branded, enslaved, beaten, raped, defiled, and worked like mules. But why would any other people envision or look forward to such an afterlife? With an idle mind being the devil's workshop, how does the Christian concept of heaven reconcile itself with the evil of eternal idleness? Given that Jesus needs the devil like the concept of freedom needs slavery, perhaps it all makes sense in a particular worldview. Speaking of worldviews, since, as Killah Priest observes in the epigraph above, the Earth is in space,[2] where, indeed, is heaven and its raging opposite hell?

In Africana cosmology, the purpose of existence is to evolve to higher intellectual and spiritual levels individually and collectively. This work does not begin or end with death because there is no death in the Africana worldview. The body is sloughed off and whether or not one acquires a new body, the soul continues its work of knowledge sharing, trial overcoming, crossroads walking, and wisdom gathering. From the Africana perspective, the afterlife is an inexhaustible university, and this paradise is the wisdom seeker's dream.

This chapter will explore the curvilinear curricula of the spiritual realm as detailed in Amos Tutuola's *My Life in the Bush of Ghosts* (*My Life*), Walter Mosley's *47*, and Malidoma Somé's *Of Water and the Spirit*. These books portray the spiritual realm as being as real as the terrestrial realm; and rather than offering a bliss-filled escape, the spiritual realm provides the protagonists of these books with complex and confusing challenges that further their intellectual, moral, and spiritual developments.

47, *My Life*, and *Of Water and the Spirit* come from dissimilar genres: young adult fiction, fiction, and autobiography, respectively. But these texts address many of the same issues in similar ways. Each narrative explores the infinite intricacies of the spiritual realm and complex examples of love between human and spiritual beings. Each book offers uniquely contextualized elucidations of the diverse African technologies and skills detailed in chapter one of this book. Each text also focuses on the importance of the acquisition and application of holistic knowledge. While all of the protagonists enjoy rich connections with the spiritual realm and its beings, they all have blind spots in their spiritual vision. Somé's eyes have been blinded by Western indoctrination; Forty-seven has been brainwashed to believe that the world is inhabited only by "masters" and "niggers"; and after living in the bush for twenty-four years and having assimilated so much that he is nearly a full ghost, Tutuola's protagonist cannot find his way back to the terrestrial realm.

In addition to their various trials, the protagonists of each of these books are considered Gods at some point during their sojourns. Their inherent divinity and the purposeful application thereof are essential to their self-actualization because all the protagonists' journeys into the spiritual realm are mission-related: Tutuola's protagonist is fleeing war and chaos; Somé is struggling to regain his soul and become a whole man; and Forty-seven is responsible for saving the universe. Perhaps the most important issue that these texts share is that each protagonist is struggling to liberate himself from very specific and stultifying types of slavery. Amos Tutuola sheds light on the impact of slavery and neoslavery on the continental African psyche and spirit. Somé's autobiography details the components essential in making a modern-day slave and the arduous passage that leads from slavery to a liberated illuminated self. Forty-seven must reap, on a plantation whose cash crop is oppression, a harvest of cosmic power.

Journey to the Drinking Gourd

While his book certainly appeals to readers of all ages, Walter Mosley wrote *47* specifically for young adults. Mosley is cognizant of the damage being done to tender psyches and hungry minds by the images, occupations, and preoccupations that spew from the global media, and he offers, as an alternative, an alter-narrative (or altar-narrative) that has multigenerational impact and depth and that offers rich, complex, and vibrant arcs of expression.

Mosley frames his work with a setting that situates the audience within the book's curvilinear sphere. The book's eponymous protagonist is an Immortal. Forty-seven is the same age that he was in 1832, and nearly two centuries of existence have left him untouched. When discussing African and cosmic technology, such as that used to endow Forty-seven with eternal youthfulness, Mosley leaves his audience no room to concoct fantasies about "black magic," "witchcraft," or any other fictions of the Western imagination. In the preface, Forty-seven defines Tall John's power as a science and technology similar to that which brought airplanes, radios, and submarines into existence. The difference is that, similar to the Africana elders I discuss in chapter one, Tall John's science is so advanced that it "seems like magic even today."[3] Forty-seven reveals that, similar to wisdom recipients of Igbo, African American, BaKongo, and Dagara origin, he made a promise not to discuss the science that he wields. However, Forty-seven shares his experiences not only because he knows that most people have been trained to discredit and mock what they do not understand, cannot control, and cannot profit from but also because he has information that can positively impact the world.

While many Gods enter the world through the divine womb, some Gods enter the Earth from the spiritual realm, and others enter from the Cosmos. Tall John's intergalactic arrival would be recognized as customary in numerous Africana cosmologies, including those of the BaKongo, Yoruba, Dogon, and Dagara; in the book of Ezekiel; and in the lyrical scriptures of OutKast, Lord Jamar, and Parliament Funkadelic. Tall John shows up at the Corinthian plantation and is described as being about 14 years of age and having copper-toned or brass-hued skin. In reality, Tall John is approximately 3000 years old; and while he is associated with the Continent, Tall John reveals that he is from "beyond Africa."

That Africana people are "Sun People," to use Andre 3000's expression, is given additional resonance by Tall John who travels from

Elle to Earth in a "Sun Ship" and who harnesses the Sun's rays for power, for life, and to charge his many technological implements. Tall John uses solar power to fuel a technological device similar to Imí Òṣùmàrè, the sacred serpent's stone. Like Dagara and Yoruba masters of spiritual technology, John has the ability to "jump," or cover miles in seconds, and he can fly. Tall John can harmonize vibrations that can put an entire plantation to sleep and awaken only certain inhabitants, and he can coo to vicious dogs and render them docile.

One of Tall John's most important powers, a skill that is becoming increasingly rare in the 21st century, is his ability to feel and empathize. Tall John, unlike many human beings, especially those who have been repeatedly traumatized or regularly exposed to violence, has not been desensitized to pain. In fact, his sensory perception is so keen he could be considered an empathy. When he and Forty-seven walk past "the hanging tree," Tall John falls down and writhes in the same agony felt by victims who were tortured and killed on the tree (88–89). This is a resonant example of the force of rememory. A term introduced by Sethe, the protagonist of Toni Morrison's *Beloved*, rememory is the spiritual pain, the historic incidents, the vicious realities that continue thriving long after the actual acts have ended.[4]

While Tall John's technology, linguistic dexterity, and spiritual powers mark him as divine, when the enslaved Africans of the Corinthian plantation begin making the obvious connections between High John the Conqueror and Tall John, the latter makes it plain that while High John's spirit may have passed through him, he is not the divine liberator; Forty-seven is. Tall John says of Forty-seven: "He might not know it yet, but this boy is destined for greatness. If you stick close enough to him you might jes' find yourself wearing the chains of freedom" (85). Tall John's seemingly contradictory statement is a reference the incredible responsibilities that the Gods have. Tall John exhibits the self-effacement necessary for one God to recognize and erect another as he humbles himself before Forty-seven and praises him because it prepares his miseducated charge for self-actualization.

The duty of Five Percenters is to civilize the deaf, dumb, and blind eighty-five percent of the world and help them to acknowledge and accept their Divinity. Such mentoring is also the work of Tall John, whose first order of business is to deconstruct and destroy Forty-seven's slave mentality. Tall John's mantra is "neither master nor nigger be." Tall John does not bother to elaborate on the fallacy of "nigger," but he tells Forty-seven, "Never say master. . . . Not unless you are looking inward or up beyond the void" (48). Tall John's philosophical wisdom riddles the untutored ears of Forty-seven, but it reflects the ethos of the Nation of

Gods. When looking inward, one will be traveling into the Self to connect with one's inherent numinosity. When looking into the Universe, one will find one's Self reflected eternally in the Cosmos and connecting with what Tall John calls "the great mind."

Tall John's mantra helps Mosley's audience better appreciate the impact that language has on one's concepts of self and other as well as on aesthetics and self-actualization. Language offers its users an ability to defile and condemn or to inspire and empower that is routinely taken for granted. Tall John's mantra is a reminder that when people analyze the language that they use, especially the terms that they use to define themselves, and decide to liberate themselves from linguistic subjugation and dehumanization, the path toward full personal and social liberation becomes illuminated.

Many Africana peoples have been defined by the odious term "nigger" and, subsequently, have been taught to hate themselves—from their physical features to their souls. The visibly identifiable hallmarks of Africa, those dominant genotypic traits that express themselves in phenotypic glory, have made purveyors of bleaching creams and hair straighteners and plastic surgeons immeasurably wealthy. The ever-popular language of self-hatred that inundates nearly every form of "entertainment" in Africana communities, from playing the dozens to the sick spectacle of reality television shows, has provided media executives and their heirs generations of wealth to enjoy. The roots of the denigration of Africa and Africans lie in the ideology that uses difference to justify exile and perpetual enslavement, and these roots found rich soil in American plantations where physical differences were used to further rationalize social stations.

As is typical of a mental slave, Forty-seven considers the oppressor's Caucasian daughter, Eloise, to be "the most beautiful person in the world," and he dismisses Eighty-four as "black and ugly with nappy hair and liver lips" (106). The same technology that Malidoma Somé's grandfather Bakhye uses to protect his community, Tall John activates to teach Forty-seven to associate himself and his people with beauty, correctness, and perfection. While Forty-seven gazes at his reflection in a placid pond, Tall John summons the image of Forty-seven's Big Mama Flore, and Forty-seven weeps over the beauty of her visage. Tall John reminds his friend that Big Mama has the same rich melanin, outstanding hair, voluptuous lips, and ashy elbows as Eighty-four, Forty-seven, and nearly all the other enslaved Africans. The tutorial at the pond has such an impact on Forty-seven that he has a revelation that is as resplendent as his African features: He asks Tall John, "Are you a angel?" The always self-effacing God immediately turns the light of divine recognition onto Forty-seven: "All of my people . . . my whole race says a prayer for you every night. They have given you their blessings and their hope. A black-skinned, nappy headed child who was born into slavery and who shall ride into the greatest battle in the history of the world" (107).

Under Tall John's tutelage, Forty-seven's horizon of possibility expands exponentially. At one point when the duo is running from enslavers and their dogs, Tall John grabs Forty-seven's wrist and they fly: "We moved quickly through the trees. My legs were pumping as fast as they could go but it didn't feel as if I were touching the ground with my feet" (49). During this flight, which evokes the flights of High John de Conqueror as described by Hurston, Tall John laughs and is revitalized and restored. Tall John takes Forty-seven on an ecological tour and also teaches the child to be a full, laughing, joyous, adventurous participant in the world. After the lessons in life, laughter, and botany, Tall John transports Forty-seven and himself directly to overseer Tobias and his "six slave-hating bloodhounds." Tall John uses juxtaposition to reveal not only how inhumane enslaving oppressors are but also how irrelevant they are. Similar to High John the Conqueror, Tall John does not run from trouble; he confronts his enemies with an arsenal that includes disarming trickery, cosmic weaponry, and his inherent divinity and superiority.

Depending on the dictates of their profession, wisdom workers carry tools and medicines for divination, uncrossing, protection, destruction, and much more in various types of pouches. The contents of such bags are so powerful the Yoruba call them *àpo ìkà*, wicked bags. African Americans call such containers Hoodoo bags and nation sacks. The term nation sack indicates the possession and galvanization of one's spiritual identity, geography, and genealogy. A nation sack comprises one's spiritual I.D.: It houses one's unique implements, protectors, and activators. Nation sacks are worn on the body near the heart and groin where the elements they contain, which may include coins, John the Conqueror Root, and hair, charge and are charged by the bearer's body.[5] The nation sack is a concealed empowerer, and the Hoodoo bag is an overt storehouse of power. Hoodoo bags are larger than nation sacks because in addition to containing elements and activators of one's spiritual force, Hoodoo bags also hold implements such as sea shells, bones, earth, tortoise shells, playing cards—whatever speaks to the soul of the diviner and facilitates divination, healing, and the galvanization of power. F. J. Jackson witnessed a Hoodoo bag displaying its wicked power and gave the following testimony: "I seen a root man take his bag an in it wuz needles an pins an grabeyahd dut an sulphuh an rusty nails, an he made it *crawl*."[6]

Tall John's àpo ìkà is a shiny yellow bag filled with a plethora of technological devices, and he shares his tools and powers with Forty-seven. When being locked in a sunless tomb has drained Tall John's spirit, he instructs Forty-seven, "Find my yellow bag and study its contents. Certain items therein will speak to you. . . . And after a while you will have a nagging feeling at the back of your mind. And soon you will know how to go about using that thing" (149–150).

Many Africana elders found no human vessels worthy of sharing sacred knowledge so they took their wisdom with them when they entered the spiritual realm. Tall John, however, has found a sound vessel. Forty-seven will properly store and apply the wisdom that Tall John shares with him, and he will add new lessons, skills, and powers to his cosmic nation sack. But Forty-seven's most powerful weaponry is contained within the nation sack of his soul. As Tall John informs him, "You, Forty-seven. You are the promise. Your blood is capable of great power, your heart is free from hatred, and your mind dares to consider new ways" (96).

Tall John mentors Forty-seven in the same way that Bynum guides Herald Loomis in August Wilson's *Joe Turner's Come and Gone*. The power of song that connects Bynum to Herald and Herald to his Divinity is what leads Tall John to Forty-seven. In a passage directly reminiscent of Bynum's relationship with Herald Loomis in *Joe Turner's Come and Gone*, Tall John describes Forty-seven's song as both a form of identification and a path to deification: "I could sense you, hear your music among all of the music that men make with their blood. . . . Every living being has their own song thrilling through the strings that hold them together. I knew your song. . . . And once I knew you were here I had to meet you to make sure that you were up to the task" (110).

In "High John de Conquer," Zora Neale Hurston describes High John taking enslaved Africans on a flight through time and space so that they can acquire their unique songs of survival, power, and divinity. After visiting Hell, where John is elected High Chief Devil, he leads the dislocated Africans to heaven where Ole Maker crafts for them a tune that has no words because each individual has to mold the song to fit his or her identity and destiny.[7] In an identical manner, Tall John takes Forty-seven on a cosmic tour with the goal of helping Forty-seven better understand Tall John, the struggle, the universe, and his relationship to each of them so that Forty-seven can properly harness the power of his song.

While Forty-seven is sleeping and his pineal and pituitary glands are open and his melatonin is flowing, Tall John transports him to Elle. In addition to it being facilitated by sleep, it is significant that the astral journey begins at the base of a tree, for trees are spiritual avatars and portals. The significance of trees is apparent in the early African American "arbor churches," the sacred groves found throughout Pan-Africa, and the *poteau-mitan*, or center post, of Voodoo praise houses. The poteau-mitan, which is the portal of the Gods, is a sacred tree cut, carved, and erected indoors.

Tall John cannot return to Elle physically, but thanks to arboreal portals, he can travel there spiritually and take a companion along. On their astral visit, the pair is able to interact with everyone and everything they encounter. John tells Forty-seven that he can journey to Elle whenever he wants because when he thinks about home the great mind transports him there. He goes on to reveal that "[b]ehind all of existence there is one great mind. And every single living, thinking being is a part of that mind. Once you learn to connect with it you can always return to a place or a thought that you once had" (117). While some consider the great mind concept to be thinly veiled Christianity,[8] the great mind has much more in common with the Africana concepts of rememory and re-membering.

In addition to revealing how easily wisdom-keepers can access the spiritual realm, one of Tall John's objectives for taking Forty-seven to Elle is to introduce his charge to the universe's adversaries. The Calash were once part of Tall John's people, but a split occurred millennia ago that rendered the Calash both inherently incomplete and also willing to do anything to control and destroy those who are whole. Tall John reveals that "after they split off from our race, [the Calash] developed a taste for the small trace of spirit that makes its way into our bodies. They suck out the energy and souls of sentient beings for their sustenance. But they're greedy; they yearn to obtain the Upper Level where they can feast on the God-Mind" (143). The Calash's lust for the soul and soul power that they lack places them in a class with Joe Turner, Kimbrough, and the Jew character of the "Song of the Soul-Piece." The mentally and physically malformed and melanin deficient Calash also appear to be Mosley's fictionalized recasting the Nation of Islam's well-known Yacub mythistory. The controversial account describes Yacub as an ancient scientist who grafted the dominant genes and melanin out of Africans and created an aberrant albino race. These entities were banished to the Caucasus Mountains and became known as Caucasians. The Calash, like Yacub's creations, are locked in a never-ending but never-to-be-fulfilled quest for completion of themselves and destruction of the Gods.

It is fitting that the Calash adopt the earthly forms of Caucasian enslavers and oppressors. *47* would have had greater intricacy if the Calash had also taken on African bodies. The sell-out/Uncle Tom construct would have been an easy fit, and Tall John and Forty-seven's struggle against the enemy would certainly have been more complex. However, Mosley is cognizant of the stultification, misery, and emptiness that writhe in the breasts of self-hating sellouts. No matter how their viciousness manifests itself, they are not the architects of destruction; they are the most damaged victims of the destroyers. The albinism of the Calash and the lack of melanin in their Caucasian hosts are not coincidental: Mosley seems to be making a powerful point about the Caucasian ethos, aesthetic, and cultural and political directive; but his view is not racist. Tall John tells Forty-seven that everyone, including Eloise, Tobias, and Wall, the leader of the Calash, is part of the great mind; and they are all part of the cycle of continuity. The machinations of the Calash, Soma, Pemba, Massa, and the Jew character are also cyclical because they are essential to holistic education, actualization, and deification. It is the struggle against enemies of progress and agents of oppression that prepares anointed and appointed human beings to assume the responsibilities of Divinities.

Recognizing and manifesting one's divinity can be a dangerous process, especially when one is constantly bombarded with missiles of self-doubt and self-hatred from one's own mind. When Tobias throws Tall John and Forty-seven into the Tomb as punishment for saving Eloise, Forty-seven regresses. Rather than focusing his rage on the racist ingrate, Forty-seven turns on his friend and declaims, "But you a niggah, man. . . . An' ain't no niggah gonna ever speak to a white man wit'out givin him his proper due" (140–141). Rather than being allies in the struggle against a common foe, Tall John and Forty-seven often face off in a battle of ideologies as Tall John struggles to help Forty-seven recognize his divinity while Forty-seven parrots the rhetoric of his Caucasian oppressors. That Forty-seven undertakes the work of his oppressors in their absence is the clearest indication that the process of turning a human being into a slave is progressing.

Consciousness raising is an arduous task, but the trials that Tall John exposes Forty-seven to and the lessons that he teaches him help him to become a Warrior God in the tradition of Ògún, Oya, Sàngó, and Nyabinghi. Tall John informs his charge that while Wall has might, Forty-seven has majesty: "You know how to survive against forces much greater than you. You are the teacher and I am the dunce. Without you there can be no future for anyone" (142).

While Tall John appears to be the wisdom worker in their relationship, he respects the fact that Forty-seven also has knowledge to share, and he positions himself to receive and Forty-seven to dispense that wisdom because that transference is crucial to Forty-seven's growth.

For example, Forty-seven teaches Tall John that individual survival is a precursor to extinction. Rather than enjoy a personal escape from slavery, Forty-seven returns to Corinthian to battle the Calash and save his friends and family. Harriet Tubman made thirteen trips from America to Canada because her individual freedom was not only meaningless, it was blasphemous. Forty-seven teaches Tall John what Tubman knew: Freedom only has power when it was magnified by a collective of liberated minds, bodies, and souls. Forty-seven teaches Tall John that while he may be the universe's hero, all life is holy.

As mentor and mentee meld, it becomes apparent that Tall John and Forty-seven are ẹnikejì. Their doubling is even apparent in the numerological breakdowns of their names and designations. The four and the seven of Forty-seven equal eleven; the letters in Tall John's name also add up to eleven. In numerology, the number eleven can represent either the number eleven or the number two because $1 + 1 = 2$. In numerology, the number two indicates "support, cooperation, a follower, receptive."[9] Eleven is considered a "master number" indicative of a higher state of evolution; eleven signifies a person who is "extremely spiritual, high strung, visionary, sensitive."[10] Both Tall John and Forty-seven have the characteristics of twos and elevens at various times in their lives, and the pair's twinning becomes so intricate and entwined that by the end of the novel they literally become one.

Eighty-four, both the character and number, is also rich with numerological symbolism and significance. The numerological breakdown of eighty-four is $8 + 4 = 12$, and $1 + 2 = 3$. As a three, Eighty-four is that third force who is essential to spiritual completion. Tall John calls Eighty-four "Tweenie," which reflects the fact that she stands between, mediates, and provides balance. Not only does Tweenie love Tall John, but she is a true sister of the struggle for both Forty-seven and Tall John. Eighty-four saves them from death in the tombs by killing overseer Stewart, and she becomes a literal force of support as Forty-seven leans on her while she physically carries Tall John out of the tomb. Tweenie represents the complete manifestation of the trinity. Similar to the Yoruba Gods Onílẹ̀, Ọ̀ṣun, and Odù, Tweenie is that indispensable female power who balances male forces and is essential to world rotation and harmonization. She is not a subjugated female who stands behind great men; as her name indicates, she stands shoulder to shoulder with and bolsters her complements.

The restorative power and strength of woman is essential to *47*, but the most significant bond is that shared by brothers. Tall John and Forty-seven's relationship is further concretized when Tall John infuses Forty-seven with his cha, which is Divinity distilled:

I am going to perform a ritual that my people have been doing since before any man walked on the earth. . . . I am going to put my cha into yours. You will still be you but you will begin to know everything I know and everything my people have known. You will have power that no human being has ever dreamed of. And with that knowledge and that power you will save the world. (169)

Tall John's cha is a flaming light that surrounds his head as does an aura: The Kemites would call it Khu, "the shining part of man."[11] Tall John places the "living light" of his cha on Forty-seven's chest: "As the light filled me I had the desire to fly, to rise above the world and see the oceans and the continents. Continents? How did I know about continents? I wondered. How did I know the names of oceans and constellations and phrases in languages both human and inhuman?" (170). While Forty-seven's experience may seem to be the stuff of science fiction, Africana history—from testimonies in *Drums and Shadows* and *The American Slave: A Composite Autobiography* to Rebecca Jackson's autobiography, *Gifts of Power*[12]—offers evidence of individuals receiving and granting what could be called instant education. However, the description of the cha and Tall John's transference of it into Forty-seven finds its closest equivalent in the shiny man conferring spiritual enlightenment and divinity on Bynum Walker in *Joe Turner's Come and Gone*.

Tall John gives Forty-seven the "child" of his cha, and this sentient force "will grow to be a full soul within Forty-seven" (171). Having received the cha, Forty-seven will no longer age physically, but he will grow in wisdom. Feeling the "little creature of light" shining and growing within him, Forty-seven has an epiphany: "It was as if the hero that I always wanted to be in my heart was set free by my friend and now I would never be a nigger again" (172). With this realization, Forty-seven becomes more than a man; he becomes an immortal Divinity filled with knowledge of his cosmic role and purpose and the tools necessary to fully manifest his destiny.

"This is What Hatred Did"

In discussions about Africa and slavery, the African American experience often takes center stage. In specialized studies, the Africans of Brazil, Cuba, Surinam, Mexico, France, Britain, and other lands are highlighted, but few people, including African scholars, acknowledge the trauma that continental Africans endured as they returned from fishing, hunting, farming, or selling wares at the market only to find their wives, husbands, daughters, fathers, sons, brothers, and sisters had been abducted and dragged across the Continent by factors to factories where Caucasians systematically undertook the work of attempting to turn human beings into slaves. In addition to this, after the trafficking of human beings on international waters had allegedly been abolished, Africans had the privilege of being enslaved, dispossessed, and oppressed on African soil by Caucasian colonizers and neocolonizers.

Imagine the rage and discombobulation one would feel at being enslaved or being a refugee in the very land one calls home. When home is besieged by wars and human life is commoditized for capitalist gain, where is a son of the soil to flee? This is the dilemma of the unnamed narrator and protagonist of *My Life*, whose earliest recollections are of a homeland fragmented by war:

> There were many kinds of African wars and some of them are as follows: general wars, tribal wars, burglary wars and the slave wars which were very common in every town and village and particularly in famous markets and on main roads of big towns at any time in the day or night. These slave-wars were causing dead luck to both old and young of those days, because if one is captured, he or she would be sold into slavery for foreigners who would carry him or her to unknown destinations to be killed for the buyer's god or to be working for him.[13]

Tutuola's protagonist lives in a western Nigerian environment that is similar to that of Olaudah Equiano, who was born in eastern Nigeria in 1745 at the height of the trans-Atlantic exile and enslavement of Africans. Enslavers and their wars, raids, and kidnappings of human beings were so rampant that Equiano and his sister's childhood games included climbing trees to lookout for and sound an alarm about the coming of raiders who "took those opportunities of our parents' absence, to attack and carry off as many as they could seize."[14] The events in Equiano's and Tutuola's narrators' environments are disturbingly similar, but there is an important difference—Tutuola's narrator makes seemingly anachronistic references to radios, televisions and other contemporary devices. While some scholars have expressed doubts that Tutuola could have set his novel during the 1954 date of publication,[15] he certainly could have.

In the early 1800s, many Caucasian-run nations outlawed the trafficking of Africans on international waters, but that did not stop Caucasians from kidnapping and trafficking Africans.[16] Similarly, throughout the 1800s, various Caucasian-controlled nations claimed to have abolished slavery, but few actually did. America's lust for oppression is apparent in its thirteenth constitutional amendment which both abolishes and legalizes slavery. What is more, by declaring slavery a legal punishment for a crime, America guaranteed itself the "right" to enslave—and also contain, destroy, and profit from—certain peoples forever.

While pondering the concept of slavery in perpetuity, it is important to note that in the contemporary era, freedom narratives such as *Restavec* (1998) by Jean-Robert Cadet;[17] *Slave, My True Story* (2003) by Mende Nazer; *Escape from Slavery* (2003) by Francis Bok; as well as exposés by such media organs as MSNBC Investigates and BBC; and general news reports of people enslaved in the Sudan, England, America (Detroit, Texas, San Francisco) Italy, South Korea, Thailand, England, Niger, Russia, and Nigeria, to name but a few nations, are so common they fail to stir national interest, let alone international outrage. Consequently, when in *My Life* Tutuola's protagonist reveals that when he was captured "the slave trade was still existing" (167), the conscientious reader is forced to ask, *which* "slave trade?" *My Life* was written by Tutuola in the 1950s and was published in 1954. While the setting is not specified, given the slavery that I witnessed in Nigeria in the middle and late 1990s and the slavery that my Nigerian colleagues furtively and tearfully described having witnessed during their childhoods, the 1850s or 1950s (or 1980s or 2000s, for that matter) could easily serve as the setting for this novel. Tutuola forces his readers to admit the gargantuan scope of the most egregious betrayal of humanity in this world.

Tutuola wraps the neat Western literary construct of a "setting" into a confounding riddle, and, by doing so, he accomplishes many goals in an adroit fashion. He reveals the curvilinear scope of enslavement and the unending quests for liberation that accompany it. With the projection of his protagonist into the spiritual realm, Tutuola is able to reveal the ways by which the spiritual and material realms exist in a state of interdependent superimposition. By folding the world's ẹnikejì upon itself, Tutuola is able to use the spiritual realm as a tutorial of existence for his protagonist and for his audience as well. The most significant feature of Tutuola's curvilinear setting is that it offers a powerful testimony about the psychological impact of slavery on continental Africans.

The fact that slavery had a tremendous impact on Tutuola's life, consciousness, artistry, and worldview is most obvious in *My Life*, but the impact is also apparent in the work for which he is most well-known, *The Palm-Wine Drinkard*. In describing the "Unknown Man's Beauty," Father of the Gods muses, "As this gentleman came to the market on that day, if he had been an article or animal for sale, he would be sold at least for £2000 (two thousand pounds)."[18] This is a stunning assessment made all the more so because it is offered without guile or agenda. This is simply a manner of "appreciating" "value" for Tutuola as well as his protagonist. The ease and rapidity with which the unknown gentleman is associated with a commodity and commoditized—most tellingly in pounds sterling!—is clearly indicative of a people who have been deeply and permanently altered by both the Caucasian commercialization of African humanity and Caucasian chattel slavery.

Despite the popular and bizarre notion that Africans took a nonchalant "out of sight; out of mind" approach to their lost kin, the psychological trauma wrought by slavery left indelible scars on the Pan-African spirit and psyche. Tutuola, who could be using his literature as a tool for personal and community truth telling and healing, reinforces for his audience the fact that re-membering is as essential to sentient beings as breathing.

In *My Life*, the protagonist's odyssey begins when war breaks out in his village and he and his adolescent older brother are left to fend for themselves. In the midst of chaos, the protagonist finds protection under the canopy of a tree that he calls the "FUTURE SIGN," which may be a manifestation of the Àṣúrín tree of Àjẹ́, which is the tree of all possibilities.[19] Throughout his life in the bush, trees will mark transitions and offer opportunities of various types for the protagonist. Under the "FUTURE SIGN" tree he follows the path of Tall John and Forty-seven and enters the spiritual realm; but unlike Mosley's protagonists, Tutuola's protagonist travels whole—body and spirit—into the spirit realm.

The streets of heaven are rumored to be paved with gold. That gold may very well be the spoils from the enslavement of human beings. The first sight the protagonist sees in the Bush is a house that is bedecked with a gleaming gold door. The child enters the home and arrives at the crossroads where capitalism births oppression. Behind the gold door, Tutuola's protagonist finds three more doors—one gold, one silver, one copper—that are associated with three ghosts of the same metals. The copper ghost, from its hue to the cuisine that so entices the narrator, appears to represent African enslavers. The golden ghost with roast fowl and baked bread most likely represents Arabs, who, unable to find the source of African gold, began stealing and enslaving East Africans in 800 CE and West Africans in 1500 CE. Europeans' mouths were electrified by sugar cane, and enslaving Africans on sugar plantations became an effective way for them to satisfy their cravings. Consequently, the silver ghost with a tell-tale cake in the oven appears to symbolize Europeans.

Contemporary discussions about trans-Atlantic exile and enslavement rely heavily on the Africans-sold-Africans theme. Not only does this myth ignore the tragic and monumental losses that continental Africans suffered, but also, attempting to equate debt peonage, in which a debtor provides labor for a mutually agreed upon time in lieu of cash payment for a debt or other similar labor relationships, with chattel slavery, which reduces human beings to objects in perpetuity, is ridiculous.

Before the arrival of Arabs and Caucasians to the African continent, chattel slavery and fomenting wars for the sole purpose of creating war captives who could be enslaved and exiled were unheard of as was declaring war on people because of their worldview or spiritual system. When one reads the contemporary autobiographies of Mende Nazer, Malidoma Somé, and Francis Bok, to name but a few, and examines their Nuba, Dagara, and Dinka societies, it is clear that slavery makes no sense in these lands. In societies where everyone shares love, labor, triumphs, and tragedy; where everyone one is considered kin; where everyone is invited to dine; where education and spirituality are integral aspects of existence, and, most important, where money has little or no importance, slavery is not only anathema, but it is revealed to be beyond barbaric.

Caucasian enslavers made barbarism the norm in Africa. They went to work all over the Continent to foment war, generate conflict, and steal people—African divinity, knowledge, and skills being such invaluable resources. Caucasians did not discriminate between northern, southern, central, eastern, or western Africans or those living on African islands because they understood that African genius has one source and is well-distributed around the Continent.

In addition to stoking hostilities and fomenting wars, Caucasian enslavers used myriad means—including, lying, tricking, conning, and abducting—to procure Africans. In her historical novel, *Red River*, Lalita Tademy reveals that the source of her surname is Tatamee, her thrice-over great-grandfather, who was born in Alexandria, Egypt. In the 1700s, Caucasians sailors asked him if he would like to sail with them to various lands while working to pay his passage. Tatamee agreed and never placed his feet on African soil again: He was brought to America and enslaved. But he never forgot his roots, and he would not let his progeny forget either.[20] When discussing his home, Tatamee would display his hand with his fingers outstretched so that he could re-member his progeny to the Nile—the waterway of their souls—and its fertile delta.

There is no honest way to convince a person to submit to slavery, so enslavers were creative in their ruses to lure Africans onto their ships. Tatamee gives but one example; Robert Pickney describes how Caucasians tricked Africans onto ships with the promise of trinkets and baubles.[21] Phoebe Gilbert's grandfather, Calina, was a boy playing on the beach with other children. Sailors hoisted a bright red cloth to attract the children, and when the children approached the boat, "[D]uh mens comes off boat an ketch um, an wen duh old folks come in frum duh fiels dey ain no chillum in village. Dey's all on boat. Den dey brings um yuh."[22] Hannah and her aunt were digging peanuts when they were attacked by two Caucasian men. The rogues took Hannah and her aunt to a place in the woods where they had secreted other abductees. The Caucasians forced Hannah and the abductees into sacks and transported them to a vessel bound for America.[23] Caucasian enslavers offered a woman named Hettie a three-day trip to America. Rumors about the jaunt spread and ignited excitement, and Hettie and many of her friends boarded the tragedy-bound vessel.[24]

Such horrific accounts as these inspired songwriter Randy Newman to write "Sail Away" in 1972. The lyrics constitute an enslaver's pitch, and the mocking tone, the lies, and never-to-be fulfilled promises of the lyrics contrast with the sorrow of the reality as Newman sings,

> In America you'll get food to eat
> Won't have to run through the
> jungle And scuff up your feet
> You'll just sing about Jesus and drink wine all day
> It's great to be an American[25]

The claims of Newman's singing enslaver, including the following, "In American every man is free / To take care of his home and his family,"[26] never came to fruition; they were not meant to. Likewise, Tutuola's protagonist is not allowed to choose which meal to eat or even which dazzling enslaver to follow. As soon as he attempts to make a choice, the ghosts blind the child in a contest of mesmerism.

The ghosts' relationship to the narrator differs from that of the shiny man and Bynum and Tall John and Forty-seven in that the ghosts are not endowing the child with spiritual gifts. They recognize that the child has something much more valuable than their mineral wealth or x-ray eyes. He is the child of the Sun, a divine human rich with the melanin of perfection: He is God. The ghosts' desire to possess the child is so great that they begin fighting amongst and destroying themselves.

Tutuola's "smelling-ghost" has excited much interest as one of the more grotesque entities in literature. He has a body that is "full of excreta, urine, and also wet with the rotten blood of all the animals that he was killing for his food" (29). The smelling-ghost, whose body provides a home for vermin and snakes, is actually the embodiment of the horrific "factories" that industrious Caucasians factors built to turn human beings into slaves. The screams of the enslaved spiraled from the stones walls of these factories and echoed for miles while the stench of murder, rape, destitution, and lack of any type of sanitation in these dungeons rode the wind. When the smelling-ghost tosses the protagonist into his Hoodoo sack of horrors, which is filled with rotten blood, mosquitoes, snakes, and centipedes, the smelling-ghost morphs into the Middle Passage that so many millions of Africans sailed after exiting the factories.

As the terrestrial representation of the horrific water-way connecting Africa to African America, it is fitting that the smelling-ghost's spirit wafts into another monumental work of literature. Toni Morrison's respect for Tutuola's art is revealed in subtly encoded scenes in *Beloved*. The meaning of Beloved's recollection that "the men without skin bring us their morning water to drink" becomes clear when Tutuola's protagonist describes the smelling-ghost giving him urine to drink.[27] Similar to Tutuola's protagonist, Beloved is bitten by rats and forced to wallow in feces and vomit. Beloved's journey is so abominable that she and her fellow captives do not wish to go to the spirit realm or to be reincarnated and return to Earth. They wish to put an end to the atrocity that is existence and "die forever."[28] But Beloved survives, at least three times, and so does Tutuola's protagonist.

As if giving the young African an idea of the horrors to which Africans of the Itànkálè were subjected, the smelling-ghost subjects the narrator to myriad forms of humiliation and abuse: The child is used as a stool when the ghost needs a place to sit; he is made to sleep on the floor without any cover; and he is forced to live in and on the filth of his captors. Because he is in the Bush of Ghosts, the protagonist is subjected to additional outrages. With the smelling-ghost having stored him in his sack, the protagonist becomes not only part of the smelling-ghost's spiritual paraphernalia, he becomes the àṣẹ, the galvanizing force, or the nickel, to quote a Robert Johnson lyric, that powers the ghost's nation sack.[29] The smelling-ghost shows off his spiritual prowess by turning the child into a monkey, a lion, a horse, a cow, and a camel. After placing the narrator on display before his family and friends and mocking the child, the oppressor realizes how useful the child can be and turns him into a camel and rents him out. The child's trials are similar to those faced by enslaved Africans in the Americas, who, as Baby Suggs of *Beloved* recalls, "got rented out, loaned out, bought up, brought back, stored up, mortgaged, won, stolen or seized."[30]

Tutuola's accounts are also comparable to those of the recent victims of slavery in the Sudan. In his autobiography *Escape from Slavery* Francis Bok describes how, during his enslavement which began in 1986, he is made to sleep with animals, is fed rotten food, and is called *jedut*, which means maggot, by his Arab enslavers.[31] Similar to Tutuola's protagonist being displayed and splayed, Bok reveals that when he is introduced to his enslaver's children, they create a song in his honor, *"abeed, abeed, abeed,"* which means "slave, slave, slave," and beat him with glee.[32] When the seven-year-old boy asks his enslaver why he treats him like an animal, after several days of cogitation, Giemma replies, *"[B]ecause you ARE an animal."*[33]

Bok uses the concept of his dehumanization to his benefit and enacts an ingenious and simple method of escape. Because his principal job is to graze Giemma's cows, he simply grazes them farther and farther from Giemma until he is free. Unlike Bok, Tutuola's protagonist is not called dehumanizing names because his enslaver literally dehumanizes him by turning him into various animals. However, Tutuola's protagonist also uses his dehumanization to liberate himself.[34] The child uses the smelling-ghost's own technology to turn himself into a cow, and he runs away.

Tutuola's protagonist comes to learn many lessons about slavery's link with sadism. After successfully transforming himself back into a human being, the child crawls into a log to sleep, but the log is home of a snake. When a homeless ghost sees the child in the log, he traps him inside. When the ghost knocks on the log, the snake begins tormenting the child, who cries. Human cries are like music to the ghosts, so the log becomes a boom-box of sorts, a radio of agony, and the homeless ghost is the deejay. The closest equivalent to the rapture the ghosts' find in the sorrowful wailing of this child is the ecstasy that the blues elicits in certain "aficionados," as is evident in Joe Turner of *Joe Turner's Come and Gone* and Kimbrough of *Robert Johnson: Trick the Devil*.

Rather than playing harps and floating on clouds, Tutuola's protagonist finds himself struggling to overcome obstacles more stultifying than those he would have faced anywhere on Earth; and, in addition, he must master the worldview, terrain, mores, culture, and ethos of ghosts. Rather than adjusting to mere culture shock, he must pull from within and without the wisdom and wiles to master life in another dimension. It is important to note that at no time does the protagonist pray for deliverance or ask assistance from any God. Similar to Niánankoro, Zora Neale Hurston, and High John the Conqueror, the protagonist uses his intellect, skills, and inherent divinity to overcome each obstacle he faces.

Unlike Caucasian-controlled countries that are structured on perpetual slavery and racism, there is unfettered upward mobility in the Bush. Tutuola's protagonist marries a ghost, and this union is an important milestone for the narrator and the novel because the brutality of slavery ends with this relationship.[35] Tutuola also appears to relax, and he interjects intertextual nods into his narrative. His protagonist's wedding guests include Skulls, the Invincible and Invisible Pawn, and Father of the Gods, all of whom first appear in Tutuola's *The Palm-Wine Drinkard* (62; and see also 107 and 111). With these intertextual shouts-out, Tutuola is decades ahead of rappers. The author also debunks the "out of sight; out of mind" myth, as the protagonist's marriage does not last because he misses his family and resumes his journey home.

The narrator's enslavement is over, but with his desire to return home, his trials, triumphs, and lessons continue. In one instance he is awakened by an army of ghosts who shake him down from a tree and give him a brutal physical inspection. This inspection could be an initiation because following the examination the protagonist is made privy to the one of the most coveted technological devices: Imí Òsùmàrè, which Hurston calls the serpent's diamond of diamonds. The protagonist describes his experience with Òsùmàrè's earthly emissaries:

> I saw about a thousand snakes which almost covered me, although they did not attempt to bite me at all. . . . The biggest and longest among these snakes which was acting as a director for the rest vomited a kind of coloured lights from his mouth on to the floor of this room. These lights shone to every part of the room and also to my eyes, and after all of the snakes saw me clearly through the lights then they disappeared at once with the lights and then the room became dark as before. (67)

Immediately following this experience, the protagonist finds his body trapped inside a pitcher, and he has a huge head which is his only accessible extremity. The protagonist has become the embodiment of the Yoruba Òrìsà Orí, which is one's literal head as well as the God who directs one's destiny. Just as Yoruba spiritualists worship Orí, the pitcher-protagonist is stationed at the crossroads, not unlike Èsù the Trickster, and worshipped as a God.

It is said that human beings create their Gods; ghosts logically invert this theory and make the human protagonist their Deity. With his actual deification, Tutuola's protagonist learns what members of the Nation of Gods know—being a God is not easy. The protagonist must suffer receiving blood sacrifices, being adorned according to the tastes of the town's chief ancestor, and being plied with tobacco and liquor. Once the God begins smoking and drinking, his inhibitions fall and he expresses himself fully: "So at this time I forgot all my sorrow and started to sing the earthly songs which sorrow prevented me from singing since I entered this bush" (74). The protagonist sings what can only be described as soul music, and his songs have the same effect across the Ethiopic Ocean. The narrator inspires so much jubilation among the ghosts that they begin to boogie and hold what African Americans would call juba and what the narrator calls a "gala day." The celebration is so inspiring that the King of the Bush of Ghosts asks the chief ancestor to bring the protagonist-God for a visit. The chief uproots a cocoanut tree and installs the pitcher-protagonist-God at its crown. The chief adorns everyone with feathers, and the chief, the God, the tree, and everyone fly to the 20th town of ghosts. The juba concludes with a feat that is well-known among the Yoruba: The chief ancestor commands the cocoanut tree to bend down. The tree bends as ordered, and the ancestor removes the pitcher-God from its apex.

The complexities of the Gods and ghosts in the Bush are endless, and the "flash-eyed mother" offers ample evidence of this. The mother is stationed in the center of the town and appears to be immobile. She has innumerable heads on her body, a huge mouth, and eyes that shoot fire. Similar to the versatility of apeta, the mother can use her eyes to ignite firewood, illuminate the town, or obliterate adversaries. The flash-eyed mother extends the comforts of her town and her protection to the protagonist. He stays in her village three years, and when a warrant is issued for his arrest, the mother replies, "I am ready for war or for any consequence" (107). After centuries of sitting, the mother stands and marches to war on behalf of the protagonist. The protagonist's impressive vertical ascent in the Bush is most evident in his relationship with the flash-eyed mother and the fact that rather than being used, abused, and pursued, he becomes, as the chapter's title indicates, "an aggressor for Ghosts." After their successful battle, the narrator realizes he has almost become a "full ghost." But his longing for his mother moves him to continue his journey.

In an account very similar to Òrìṣà Oya meeting Olúkòsì Ẹ̀pẹ́,[36] the protagonist meets a woman he calls the "Super Lady," and this oríkì fits her. Similar to Anyanwu in Octavia Butler's *Wild Seed*, the Super Lady can transform herself into any number of animals including an antelope, a python, and a tiger. She possesses the "power of lights," and with a technology akin to Imí Òṣùmàrè, she can illuminate her home with lights that shine like diamonds and are natural sources of electricity; indeed, she keeps her cold drinks on ice.

Another example of intertextuality between *My Life* and *Beloved* surfaces in the Super Lady's bedroom. Her boudoir is so lavishly decorated and adorned with such powerful implements and objects that her husband is stunned. After his enslavement, long treks, sleeping in trees, and being exposed to elements; after having been turned into an animal and having been treated like various animals; and after becoming a God and a ghost aggressor, he feels that he is too wild to enter her room and that he is unworthy of resting on her fine bed. His wife solves the problem by gently pushing him onto the bed and wrapping her body around his until he relaxes. This tender moment is revisited in *Beloved* when Paul D stumbles into Wilmington, Delaware and meets a woman who is the owner of a pristine bed with sheets and pillows: "Soil, grass, mud, shucking, leaves, hay, cobs, seashells—all that he'd slept on. White cotton sheets had never crossed his mind."[37] Paul D makes as much love to the sheets as he does to the woman.

Morrison recasts textual offerings from Tutuola, and Tutuola embraces and revises offerings from Yoruba divination verses, history, and folklore. Various Yoruba divination verses describe women founding and thriving in gender-exclusive towns. Because women carry the principle life and the power of existence in their beings, men wage war on the women to force them to return. No force or weaponry—human or Divine—can defeat the women. They live ensconced in peace and power until a humble God, in some versions Ọṣun in others Ọrúnmìlà, approaches the women with a charming display of reverence and persuades them to reunite with men.[38]

Yoruba history also describes a group of women living in a gender-exclusive settlement outside of the historic Oyo Empire. Rather than attack them, king Ṣàngó and the women of Oyo herald the divinity and majesty of these women:

> Other traditions collected in Ọ̀yọ́ say that Ṣàngó looked upon the women in Bàrà with great reverence for he is reported as prostrating for them. These women shaved their heads clean like men; they did not wear the bùbá, (the Yoruba women's upper blouse), and the upper part of the wrapper they put on were tied to the body just above the breasts, the lower part touching the ground. Whenever they happened to leave Bàrà people treated them with awe. Whenever they visited the market, they looted any foodstuff they wanted, and whenever they visited the palace, palace women on their approach, pour water on the ground, shouting that their 'fathers' had come to visit them. Whatever these women demanded would be brought out with respect.[39]

In *My Life* there is also a town inhabited by empowered women. The Super Lady informs her husband that after the women were betrayed by their husbands they left them and founded a town where women marry women. Similar to the women of Bara, the women in *My Life* live in harmony and no attempts are made to drag these women from their sanctuary. The casual and wholly nonjudgmental manner in which this information is both conveyed and received in *My Life* and the recurrence of female-exclusive towns in Yoruba myth, history, and fiction, reveal the diversity, flexibility and dynamism of both gender and gender issues in the traditional Yoruba ethos and worldview.

The protagonist and his super wife enjoy great wealth, and as they travel to and explore various lands it becomes clear that every encounter and episode holds a lesson for the protagonist, his audience, or both. The couple traverses "Loss or Gain Valley," and after losing their expensive clothes and jewelry and gaining another couple's rags, the narrator introduces the African dilemma tale into his narrative and asks his audience how to cross the valley "without any loss except gain" (133).[40] The narrator also offers a critique of human-spiritual relationships and how to ruin them: After four years of wedded bliss, the narrator jokingly tells his wife that "earthly people are superior to the ghosts and ghostesses or all other creatures" (133). As did Oya before her,[41] the Super Lady shape-shifts into an animal form and drives the bigot from her home.

While his marriage ends, the protagonist's journey continues, and he has amassed sufficient skills and contacts to effectively navigate life in the spiritual realm. Some of his most important resources are his relatives. His son with the Super Lady saves him from a sentence of sixteen years' hard labor, and he is reunited with a cousin in Dead's Town. Making the concept of a "novel" literal and giving his narrative a new level of audience engagement, the narrator uses Tutuola's book as match-making vehicle for his cousin's eligible children. The narrator asks the reader, "So do you like to marry one of them? If it is so, please, choose any and only one of these numbers—733, 744, 755, 766 and 777, 778 respectively so that his or her picture may be sent to you" (153). From shouts-out, to a dating service, to dilemma texts, Tutuola exhibits an adroit ability to seamlessly marry seemingly disparate genres of literature and orature and various modes of discourse. Tutuola has been ridiculed by many and is a source of shame for some,[42] but in creating an interactive text before the concept of interactivity existed, Tutuola is genius.

Tutuola also includes a unique version of the popular Pan-African Talking Skull text. The introduction to the text is a recasting of a popular trope in African orature, that of two powerful entities who enter into a shape-shifting battle. Malidoma Somé's autobiography offers a version of such a battle as does Souleymane Cisse in *Yeelen*. In Tutuola's version, the battle ensues when a wisdom-worker asks the protagonist if they can share technologies; the protagonist refuses, and the shape-shifting battle begins. The protagonist loses the battle and is forced to reveal the contents of his wicked bags. However, because the protagonist is truly a two-headed doctor, boasting both ghost knowledge and human knowledge, he emerges from the battle as more than a conqueror. He kills an animal and sets its skull on the ground. His adversary thinks the skull is a Deity, and he bows before it, offers it the spiritual implements he finagled from the protagonist, and then runs off to tell the king that the "ground has head and eyes" (160). The protagonist reclaims his tools and the skull and watches as his antagonist is killed for lying. The talking skull did not even have to speak for the man's big mouth to kill him.

Tutuola's respect for gender balance is evident in all his works, and *My Life* is no exception. The shape-shifting battle is the final test of masculine cunning and power. His final test with a female powerbroker comes from a ghost who is covered in sores and crawling with maggots. The power of saliva to cure, kill, and bless is well known in Pan-Africa, and this ghost wants the protagonist to lick her sores because human saliva will cure her. As an incentive, she opens her palm and reveals images of his family. By referring to her as the "Television-handed Ghostess" Tutuola describes the accuracy and clarity of this ancient African technology in modern Western terms. After seeing his family in the palm of her hand but learning that he must lick her sores to be reunited with them, the protagonist is in such a quandary that he titles the chapter, "Hard to say 'No' and Hard to say 'Yes.'" However while watching her high definition hands, he sees his mother use a particular leaf to cure a baby's sore. He is able to find that leaf and cure the Television-handed Ghostess who sends him back to the FUTURE SIGN tree and the terrestrial world where he is promptly enslaved.

There is a tremendous difference between a slave and a human being who is enslaved. The protagonist is the latter. He consistently refuses to attempt any servile duties or to exhibit any manner of bestial behavior: He will not work like an animal, eat like an animal, or behave like one whether he is in human or animal form. He simply rejects a slave's status on every level. He also does not refer to any of his earthly or ghostly oppressors as "master"; he calls them "boss" which indicates that even though he receives no payment for his labor, he considers himself an employee. No matter the working conditions, the protagonist remains the master of his destiny and identity.

The contributions that *My Life* makes to *Beloved* resurface when the protagonist notices a scar on his latest boss' head. This scar is as much a revelation to the protagonist as Beloved's scar is to Sethe. Beloved is not only marked by a scar created by the ultimate protection, but her mind is also marked with a song that Sethe composed for and sang to her children. When Beloved sings this song, Sethe knows Beloved is her daughter returned. The protagonist and his brother also composed original songs before they were separated. When the protagonist observes that his boss' scar is identical to that of his brother, the protagonist sings one of their childhood compositions. The song serves as a form of shared identification that cannot be forged, stolen or lost, and it is the protagonist's ultimate liberator. The protagonist is reunited with his mother and brother, and he learns that all of them had been enslaved; in fact, his mother had been worked as hard as a man. Perhaps she had an oppressor who, like Joe Turner of the play *Joe Turner's Come and Gone*, used the Bible as a guide, for her enslaver set her free in her eighth year of captivity. While all three family members suffered the horrors of slavery, because they were enslaved in Africa and not condemned to a life of perpetual slavery and eternal racist oppression, as would be the case in America, for example, all three lived to enjoy freedom, reunification, and prosperity.

Tutuola closes what I like to call his *phenomenovel* with a succinct indictment: "This is what hatred did" (142). The most obvious manifestation of hatred is that of slavery—of *any* kind. There is no "good" or "tolerable" form of slavery, and this is evident in the fact that the protagonist's brother, despite having been enslaved, becomes part of the cycle of oppression and unwittingly brutalizes his own brother. The institution of slavery, no matter when or where it is enacted—from 6th century Greece, to 19th century Nigeria, to 21st century America—fosters nothing but depravity, devastation, and hatred.

Slavery is not the only hatred that Tutuola's protagonist indicts. The vicious relationships that are born of and fostered by patriarchal inadequacy and the abhorrence for equality and the avarice that fuels capitalism and war-mongering at the expense of communality and humanity are other hatreds that impact the protagonist. Another important hatred is that which led colonizers and neocolonizers to create Nigeria and more than fifty other àbíkú African countries whose rotational failures provide endless luxury, bounty, and power to a selfish few. The racism that targets the shine of the Divine for either cooptation or extermination and the rage produced by an internal deficiency that seeks to obliterate the perfection it can never attain are other destructive hatreds.

These hatreds are logical outgrowths of this racist capitalistic era; however, one should consider them to be tricksters that test wills and skills, for these and other hatreds can provide those who conquer and refuse to perpetuate them with unimaginable rewards. As Tutuola's protagonist confirms: "Hatred sometimes brings good luck to one who is abhorred or hated" (142). Àṣẹ.

Making Friends with the Self

Malidoma Somé's autobiography *Of Water and the Spirit* offers a revealing and complex portrait of the spiritual realm, and that portrait underscores the spirit realm's impact on human evolution and cosmic expansion. As Somé reveals:

> I had heard that we usually come to Earth from other planets that are more evolved and less in need of mediation. Our errand on this planet is informed by a decision to partake in the building of the Earth's cosmic origin, and to promote awareness of our celestial identity to others who are less evolved. Our elders taught that some of the universe's inhabitants were as much in need of help as others had the need to help them. This Earth was one of many places where those who needed help could easily become recipients of it.[43]

Because understanding is born of experience, perhaps Somé needed to be thrown into a social-cultural hell that could only have been wrought by hatred to understand his errand on Earth.

When he was four years old, Somé was kidnapped, with his father's approval, by a Jesuit priest called Father Maillot. Somé's father, like so many Africans, struggled with Christian indoctrination and terrorism to the extent that he lost his first wife and four children to death because he refused to honor his ancestors (33–35). He rebuilt his life by alternately observing his Dagara customs and Christianity, but he passed the gift of religious terrorism on to Somé by allowing Maillot to abduct and confine him in a mission. With his captivity, Somé becomes the very thing that Tutuola's protagonist fears becoming—a literal sacrifice to a capricious Christian God.

While their methodologies differ, the goals of Tutuola's protagonist's abusers, Forty-seven's enslavers, and Somé's oppressors are identical: They seek to destroy the humanity of these males and turn them into malleable tools ripe for religious, economic, sexual, and/or cultural exploitation. The vicious and violent abuses to which Tutuola's and Mosley's protagonists are subjected are facilitated by geographic dislocation. However, the curtain on Somé's theater of the absurd rises on the only land he has ever known. Somé, like thousands of African children, spent his formative years imprisoned in one of many missions Christians built in Africa. At the Jesuit mission and seminary, Somé is completely divested of his culture, language, identity, and community. The French language is literally beaten into the children, and the Catholic religion is used to rape their souls. In addition to violent religious and cultural indoctrination, Somé is a victim of sexual terrorism as he is repeatedly molested by Father Lamartin and possibly by older boys in the seminary. Somé and his young peers are assailed by an unending avalanche of atrocities, but because the best slave is one whose mind is controlled, one of the most pernicious aspects of the racist imperialist Caucasian colonial "crusade" is the damage done to the African psyche.

The central topic of the children's educational training in the seminary is the concept of Europe, with a special emphasis on France, and the glorious gifts Caucasians have given, or have forced on, the world. The seminary's training never extends to African cultures, languages, or contributions to the world because, from the colonizers' perspective, African cultures, languages, and contributions to the world do not exist. In the work of miseducation, the Jesuits show themselves to be master spin doctors. Somé comes to the realization that

> Utilizing the white man's violent philosophy, even the terrible commerce of slavery became comprehensible—justifiable even. In our history books there were illustrations of ships full of slaves heading west. All of this sounded unreal to me until some of the students who came from the coast confirmed having heard stories from their grandfathers about people who were deported and never returned. (112)

In his attempt to find some explanation for the Caucasian domination of so many lands that belong to other peaceful peoples, Somé realizes that the Caucasian "brought a kind of meanness that no one could face because it made no sense to anyone, and eventually he took over because no one loved blood and killing more than he did" (112).

While the Caucasians are the architects of religious, geopolitical, and economic oppression, it is the African running dog of neocolonialism, Father Joe, who lashes out most violently against Somé. Father Joe distinguishes himself by being the stereotypical African who expresses a bottomless hatred for Africa and Africans. Individuals like Joe are important tools in the machinery of slavery, colonialism, corruption, and general oppression, as Somé muses:

> Religious colonialism tortures the soul. It creates an atmosphere of fear, uncertainty, and general suspicion. The worst thing is that it uses the local people to enforce itself. Our teachers were Black, from the tribe, yet they were our worst enemies. The question I often asked myself in later years, when I thought about how Black nationals are leading our country, is whether a person schooled in an atmosphere of such abuse can actually lead with compassion, justice

and wisdom. My experience was not uncommon. Today, Africa's leaders are mostly people who were educated in this manner. Is it surprising that there is so much instability in so many African countries? (95)

Self-hatred and self-destruction have taken such firm holds that some African people argue that draconian violence is necessary to govern the unruly masses, and the practice of literally whipping people into compliance routinely begins with childhood floggings and continues into adulthood in some African countries.

To better understand the difference between the learned depravity that many consider to be not only normal but vital and essential to childrearing and state governance and a balanced approach to familial and civic relationships that is grounded in reciprocity, one need only study Somé's relationship with his grandfather Bakhye. Because Bakhye has determined that Somé is his brother reincarnated, Bakhye respects and shares knowledge with Somé just as he did with his brother. Rather than beat his progeny into submission, demand that he be seen and not heard, or rely on the edict of parental hypocrisy that demands, "Do as I say, not as I do," Bakhye is literally nourished by Somé's questions, assertions, and observations. Somé's words are the soul food that Bakhye needs to fortify his spirit and prepare for life in the spiritual realm, and Bakhye's wisdom prepares Somé to survive and thrive on Earth. Bakhye walks with, talks with, learns from, and teaches Somé as a friend would a beloved friend. Bakhye never raises his hand to Somé for any reason because his child-rearing and child-loving tools are so effective and complete, violence is not only unnecessary it is unthinkable.

Bakhye shares his knowledge and technology freely with his grandson. Somé watches his grandfather protect the community's crops using a spiritually-charged pot of water for surveillance. He sees his grandfather heal and feed community members. Bakhye teaches Somé how to understand the language of chickens and how to control his body and prepare his mind to receive spiritual edification. Somé witnesses such feats as his grandfather walking home from hospital, and his elders cooking Bakhye's final supper satulmo, upside down on the ceiling, and his grandfather eating this spiritually-prepared last meal all *after* Bakhye had technically died (46–50). Before Somé is kidnapped, Bakhye tells him that he has been designated to study with Caucasians and learn their ways. He tells Malidoma that he will "never come back whole" from his journey in the Western world and this will cause him and the community great suffering and frustration (40). He also tells his progeny, "Many ambushes await you. But my spirit will stand by your side" (40).

In clear contrast to the gentle divinity with which Bakhye molds his progeny are the Jesuits whose pedagogy is rooted in spine-splitting violence. As protective in the afterlife as in life, Bakhye's spirit soothes his grandchild after his first brutal caning at the mission. When the African youths create a play at the seminary, Somé invokes and becomes his grandfather. When the students are tasked with decorating a processional, memories of Bakhye move Somé to depict an elder wisdom keeper at work and emblazon the processional path with the truth that "GOD IS IN EVERY MAN" (134). When Somé finally liberates himself from the seminary only to find himself terrified and lost on the road to freedom, a huge bird with a soft "familiar" body picks him up and flies him to a safe location (143–144). This bird is ever-present Bakhye, and his method of transportation recalls the experience of African American culture hero Jack who hitches a ride on a bald eagle to visit the Devil, the Igbo relationship with the bird Ayolo, and the African Americans who sing, "This crow, this crow gonna fly tonight!" and then take wing.[44]

Bakhye could easily have carried Somé home, but Somé's lengthy trek includes character-building lessons. In addition to preparing his mind for his return home, the arduous journey prepares his body and psyche for the rigors of initiation. In the Dagara community, one of the purposes of initiation is to enable the individual to witness wisdom and power in their most raw, tangible, and multitudinous forms so that he can fully integrate his mind, body, soul, spirit, and self with that of the community, world, and Cosmos to ensure personal, communal and universal evolution. At the initiation there are no computer-driven contraptions, no passages to study or recite, and no dates to memorize. There are no fees, and there is no jewelry—the youths do not even wear any clothing. All the initiates need to successfully traverse this crossroads is a mind that is at peace and in tune with the material and spiritual worlds. But what makes the initiation a fact of life for traditional Dagara people is what would make it nearly impossible for Westerners; for the things that Western belief says are impossible, Dagara elders undertake with ease. Rather than engaging in an impassioned armchair analysis of how something might be accomplished or why something could never be done, the Dagara simply *do*.

The Dagara elders understand why Dagara and Caucasian educational systems are so different. They find that Caucasians "are empty inside. Someone who does not have an inside cannot teach anyone anything" (177). This assessment elucidates the truth of Somé's "education" at the seminary, for what do imperialists, robber barons, colonizers, enslavers, and rapists have to teach those they imprison, rob, colonize, enslave, and rape? Furthermore, as one reads Somé's book one is forced to question the relevance of Western education and the veracity of its teachings. One begins to wonder, after being indoctrinated for so many years, what type of individual does the modern Western educational system produce? Somé's Dagara elders determine that Western captivity and indoctrination killed the fertile living part of Somé's mind and replaced it with "something dead that does not like to confront anything having to do with life" (179).

When he is unable to free his mind and fully enter the initiation rites, Somé, himself, realizes the veracity of his elders' assessment of Caucasians and how they have damaged him. A true Westernized academician, Somé attacks a holistic and living experience with analytical dissection, skeptical inspection, and hypothesis testing:

> I became conscious of an overwhelming urge to analyze and intellectualize everything I was seeing and experiencing. This impulse to question was cold and purposeless. I was tired of getting nowhere in my thoughts, tired of being constantly defeated in my understanding. I felt trapped, caught inside a stone wall, trying uselessly to break out. But I didn't know where I would be if I escaped. (200)

Somé's elders realize that Western education has damaged his ability to hear, behold, and know. By witnessing the damage done to Somé, the elders gain insight about Caucasian culture's truth, and they muse, "Can it be that the white man's power can be experienced only if he first buries the truth? How can a person have knowledge if he can't see?" (209). If it is necessary to bury truth in order to experience power, then what one is experiencing is not power but a lie rooted in oppression. Furthermore, that the elders connect sight to knowledge is profoundly important because African philosophers and wisdom keepers make it clear that knowledge and wisdom are not the products of years of academic study, book learning, and memorization. They are living forces that literally become part of one's being, one's existence.[45]

In African wisdom systems, the modes by which one acquires knowledge are empirical and include, but are not limited to, physical and spiritual and exoteric and esoteric acts of seeing, touching, ingesting, feeling, hearing, and becoming. Thus, rather than the Western mandate of forcing belief through indoctrination, in the African ethos, the information, itself, interacts with individuals viscerally and spiritually. Through this process, information becomes living knowledge that is part of a person's being. The relationship that persons have with knowledge is interactive, and when knowledge and its human partner work together harmoniously, the result is wisdom.

As Somé comes to learn, the ability to see involves more than the physical act of seeing objects in the terrestrial plane. In order to truly see, one's spiritual eyes must be open and one must be receptive to and respectful of what one beholds. The ability to truly hear is also a profound process. In "Identity and the Artistic Process in Yorùbá Aesthetic Concept of Ìwà," Rowland Abiodun reveals that in Yoruba language, the word *ìlutí* literally means the ability to hear well, but it signifies such qualities as "obedience" and "understanding."[46] A person with ìlutí is one who is both capable and worthy of receiving wisdom. Abiodun reveals that the qualities of ìlutí are not only essential for persons who are seeking wisdom but also, "when considering the efficacy of an *Òrìṣà* (deity), *Oògùn* (traditional medicine), or a work of art (*iṣẹ́ ọnà*)," the Yoruba look to Gods, medicines, and creations that are able to literally respond to one's needs and are, thus, "alive" and "efficacious."[47] Rather than the fossilized construct of the Western world, in the African worldview, knowledge is a reciprocally giving, interactive, living, eternally expanding, ever-relevant force.

When one is able to behold and become knowledge and develop wisdom in the ways of the African Ancients, one's relationship with everything in one's environment deepens and widens, and one becomes privy to information and conversations from which others are excluded. The significance of being able to exchange knowledge holistically is not only appreciated and articulated in African wisdom systems; it is also stressed by William Wordsworth who, in the poem "The Tables Turned," offers a clear elaboration of the destructive nature of Western education: "Our meddling intellect / Mis-shapes the beauteous forms of things: — / We murder to dissect."[48] The system that necessitates the murder of life and burial of truth in order to obtain information is a system that is actually anti-life and anti-knowledge.

Despite the fact that Somé personally knows the cold, hypocritical, surgically-destructive nature of Western "knowledge," his indoctrination that what lies there is superior, universal, and true is so thorough that it continues to pervert his thoughts and control his manner of thinking even when his miseducators are worlds away from him.

In order to become an interactive knowledge sharer, Somé must first acknowledge that everything that he learned in school and the ways that he was taught to learn are designed to impede the acquisition of true knowledge. When Somé is able to escape the prison of pseudo-intellectualism, he catches up to a self who is at one with his Dagara culture and who had been patiently awaiting his return. After being re-membered to himself and the living knowledge that is his inheritance,

Somé fully comprehends the differences between the living power of African wisdom systems and Western academic education:

> The techniques of indigenous learning were revealing themselves before my eyes, sweeping away my preconceived notions of how learning was accomplished. The contrast between this state of mind and what I had been accustomed to at the seminary was the same as the difference between liquid and solid. It seemed to me that Dagara knowledge was liquid in the sense that what I was learning was living, breathing, flexible, and spontaneous. What I was learning made sense only in terms of relationship. It was not fixed, even when it appeared to be so. . . . By contrast, I could see that the Western knowledge I had been given had the nature of a solid because it is wrapped in logical rhetoric to such a degree that it is stiff and inflexible. The learning one gets from a book, from the canons of the written tradition, is very different from the knowledge that comes from within, from the soul. (203–204)

The two forms of knowledge and modes of education that Somé compares produce completely different types of people with sharply divergent views on and relationships with the world and the Cosmos. Whereas the Western educational scheme demands uniformity and conformity in the memorization and parroting of information, education among the Dagara is specific to the individual's needs, goals, identity, and destiny. The dissimilarity in the modes and products of education also reflects the disseminators of information. The typical Western "educator" is an individual who—stationed in a static hall and armed with a curriculum of irrelevance—demands that his students commit to memory and to their existence the prejudices, propaganda, predilections, and superstitions of Caucasia. By contrast, the knowledge facilitators among the Dagara include one's elders, one's ancestors, one's selves, one's soul, and also flora, fauna, the Earth, and the Cosmos. Indeed the universe and its multitudinous inhabitants prove to be some of Somé's most scintillating instructors.

Space is not an empty vacuum; space is teeming, throbbing with life. The stars are not inanimate objects. The worlds that appear to earthlings as stars are organisms, like the Earth and the Sun, that give life to innumerable entities, and the stars boast all of the diversity of the lives they produce. It is because of their life and soul that the stars reach, teach, and speak to the star in Somé, and when his shining reunites with its source, waves of nostalgia for the most ancient of couplings crash through his being. Somé's empirical knowledge about his relationship to the Cosmos may be unbelievable to most Westerners; however, one of the West's most lauded astronomers, Carl Sagan, echoes Somé's sentiments. In his PBS series titled "The Shores of the Cosmic Ocean," Sagan argues that it is natural that humanity is drawn to the Cosmos: "We long to return, and we can, because the cosmos is also within us. We're made of star stuff. We are a way for the cosmos to know itself."[49] While most Westerners can only undertake "observations from afar" to quote Lord Jamar, the Dogon, Dagara, Igbo, Bachwezi, Kushites, Kemites, and their progeny, including Lord Jamar and Malidoma Somé, boast intimate knowledge of and relationships with the universe.

The cosmic knowledge that Somé experiences during initiation is a precursor to the eternal dynamism that is the reward of the Kemites. In an ancient Kemetic Pyramid Text of King Pepi, Nwt, the God of the Sky, welcomes Pepi after his earthly duties are completed and transforms him into an "indestructible star within [her]."[50] Long before Pepi rejoined Nwt, the Kemetic God Ausar returned to Nwt's cosmic womb of creation so that he could be reconceived and "come as Orion."[51] It seems that the transformation that follows deification is *constellization*—becoming a star, planet, nebula or galaxy. Lord Jamar celebrates his constellization during this lifetime and informs his audience that he is the Sun whose family consists of "a constellation of stars."[52] Likewise, Rakim Allah describes himself as a reincarnated God who anticipates not only aligning "with the stars" in constellization but also returning to Earth after death and resurrection to continue his most significant work.[53]

As Somé's expansive network of wisdom sharers guides him through initiation, it becomes clear that they are reacquainting Somé with an infinitude of existence that is comprised of a continuum of his historical, ancient, and cosmic lives, powers, and possibilities. During his initiation, Somé is truly—to paraphrase D'Angelo yet again—remembering what he already knows so that he can complete the mission assigned him in his present life. The emotions that Somé experiences during his brief reunions and reunifications are comparable to those that move Beloved to seek to meld her entire being with Sethe's forever. The "join" Beloved desires to have with her mother is the perfect unification of all aspects of one's being—mental, physical, cosmic, spiritual, sensual, sexual, intellectual—with one's source. Somé experiences a complete, stunning, and soul-deep love with many entities during his initiation, and they leave him grieving and yearning and groping for muchlessmore.

The profundity, paradox, and passion that cosmic reunification elicits in Somé are also found in Mosley's *47*. When Forty-seven travels through the Cosmos and becomes one with both Tall John and the universe, his reunion with and knowledge of his source and home seamlessly morph into a cavernous sense of isolation and desolation:

> The star I was heading for became as big as the sun. It was a wide field of fire that sang with power and majesty, but I wasn't afraid. I slipped through the white flames of the star and came to a place that was pure and red. It was hot but there was a place right in the middle of the star that was black and cold. I/John dove into the center of the blackness and suddenly I/John was somewhere else. I/John was far, far away from my home, and lonely. I/John would never be home again. All of my people were far behind me while I/John would find star after star traveling so far away from my home that it would be as if there was no home for me, anywhere.
>
> I woke up crying for that loneliness. (207)

In a passage that may well have inspired Mosley's description, Somé describes his relationship with the beckoning stars:

> I wanted to join with the stars way up there in the infinite spaces of the cosmic realm. There was the night and there was the bush and there was me. Nothing else mattered. I did not even notice that I had been crying quietly until the stars became blurred.
>
> My tears were the language of the longing that I felt to merge with the stars. They sent a message to them, sharing something I could never express in human terms, and I felt the sky accept my tears as a response to their attention. The bright scintillating lights came closer and closer until I could see only a few of them. The closer they got, the bigger and brighter they became. The stars brought the day to me, their day, pulsating, breathing the stuff that keeps the cosmos in order. (216)

Somé realizes that the various stars throughout the Cosmos, and the Cosmos itself, are all his sentient sources of Self; they are all his ẹnikeji, and they are his home. However, concurrent with Somé's and Forty-seven's knowledge of the ecstasy of the ultimate reunion is the realization that celestial unification must be indefinitely postponed until their terrestrial obligations are fulfilled.

The overwhelming oneness and loneliness that knowledge of their celestial selves brings Somé and Forty-seven is also described by Kelis in her song "Little Star." In the song's video, Kelis is a star who, caught between constellization and humanization, muses on her duality, her astronomical origins, and her earthly responsibilities:

> There is nothing special about me
> I am just a little star

If it seems like I'm shining it's probably
A reflection of something you already are[54]

These lyrics recall the Dagara revelation that from the spiritual realm, human beings look like stars and shine. Echoing the Dagara elders and Somé's personal relationship with the stars, Kelis informs her audience that any glow they perceive as coming from her is also coming from inside of them: "When deep inside you feel the darkest / That is where I can always be found."[55] The lyrics provide confirmation that the celestial divinity that Kelis embodies thrives inside of everyone, and it awaits acknowledgment and activation.

The Yoruba hold that individuals must find their orí (destiny) and manifest it in this lifetime to attain immortality. Discovering one's destiny is difficult in and of itself, but imagine how devastating it would be to know your purpose but not be able to fulfill it. This conundrum is expressed by Kelis when she sings, "I plan on being much more than I am but that's in due time / But until then I'm guilty, and being human's my crime."[56] While struggling through the crossroads, Kelis receives encouragement and affirmation from a galactic Cee-Lo Green who watches her progress from the stars and sings:

> It's surprising how inspiring
> It is to see you shining
> 'Cause in the dark of night
> You're all I can see
> And you sho look like a star to me[57]

Somé's "crime" is similar to Kelis': He has succumbed to humanity when Divinity is his destiny. Initiation reacquaints him with his cosmic identity and destiny and infuses him with a love whose fierceness only the Gods can comprehend.

Initiation also introduces Somé to the innumerable terrestrial entities who watch and assist often oblivious human beings. Following his ecstasy in the stars, Somé has an experience with a tree that is beyond rapturous and calls into question the concept of "love" as it is produced and consumed in the West. It is with what he refers to as a flash in his spirit, a force so profound Robert Farris Thompson named his book after it, that Somé sees a woman where a tree had been. She is tall; she wears a black veil; and she is green: "[T]his green was the expression of immeasurable love" (221). And her love is soul altering:

> The sensation of embracing her body blew my body into countless pieces, which became millions of conscious cells, all longing to

reunite with the whole that was her. If they could not unite with her, it felt as if they could not live. Each one was adrift and in need of her to anchor itself back in place.... We exploded into each other in a cosmic contact that sent us floating adrift in the ether in countless intertwined forms. In the course of this baffling experience, I felt as if I were moving backward in time and forward in space. (221)

Somé asserts that if human beings were to experience this type of consciousness-embracing, soul-expanding, curvilinear love on a regular basis they would not be able to function or survive. Love fills and feels all aspects of Somé's being, and the complement to the holistic orgasms he experiences with the green lady is the knowledge that she pours into the core of his being. While Somé endeavors to describe the sensory impact of her embrace for his audience, he refuses to share the green lady's wisdom to ensure that it will continue to live within him. He is as protective of her words as the Yoruba are of their ipọnri.

Somé's rapturous experiences continue when he travels through the Cosmos to visit one of his former homes. In *The Palm-Wine Drinkard*, Father of the Gods Who Can Do Everything in this World travels to the spiritual realm and visits many towns including one inhabited by red people. During his initiation, Somé also visits a land of red people, and there he re-members to his consciousness the work he did with them in a former life. Although he is separated from the red people by an invisible barrier, when he touches the barrier the people experience "a delirium of bliss" (228). This ecstasy is as utilitarian as that he experiences with the stars and the green lady for Somé uses his electrifying touch to infuse three baby girls with divinity. It becomes clear that for many millennia Somé has been undertaking the work of the Gods, which is to create more and more Gods.

During one of his most formidable challenges, Somé travels—body and soul—into the core of the spiritual realm to visit the Mother of Power. With so much at stake and so much healing to do on Earth, the elders issue stern warnings against being mesmerized by the magnificence of the spiritual realm and attempting to stay there: "Those who want to live a serious life go there and come back. Those who don't want to live a serious life go there—but don't come back" (234). While spiritual and material beings readily cross into one another's realms and share knowledge, one cannot satisfactorily live in the other's realm. Dagara elders inform their charges that an eternity in limbo awaits the frivolous: "If you stay in that world without going through your life and death here, the people there will only acknowledge you as a ghost, just the way we deal with ghosts here in this world" (234).

The elders' caveats help to shed light on the sightings of spirits and otherworldly figures. Some of these entities could be ancestors who seek to assist their relatives in a manner similar to Bynum's father who visits his son and gives him his song. Spirits could also be figures from other times or worlds who are observing and attempting to share knowledge. Some forms could be human souls who have lost their way. The protagonist of *My Life in the Bush of Ghosts* reveals how difficult it can be to return from the spiritual realm; but for many, a return is impossible. Indeed, Dagara diviners can interact with humans who are lost in the spirit world, but they cannot offer them a route of return. The consequences of failing initiation are much more profound than failing one's qualifying or comprehensive examinations. Initiation is a trial for the complete being—body, mind, and soul. It is preparation for eternal existence that is so complete that it makes Western accomplishments, like obtaining a Ph.D., appear hollow, a window dressing at best and a deviation from the divine at worst.[58]

The Dagara elders' technological advances include implements that open a portal into the space-time continuum. Technology that is unbelievable to Westerners is a normal and, indeed, necessary in Dagara society, for every Dagara male must enter the space-time continuum to truly know his identity and destiny.

The first sensations Somé's feels upon entering the portal are freezing and falling. Following this, he witnesses Khu and Cosmos at work: "Slowly like dawn breaking, I began to see light. At first it was like aurora borealis, shot with areas of dark and ones of extreme luminescence—rays of such intensity they made me think of the cosmos in expansion or a cosmogony in progress" (242). The lights are so dazzling they would have blinded him if he were gazing on these wonders with his physical eyes, but he is using his spiritual eyes. In fact, he has no physical eyes or body. He holds tightly a bundle of light lines, even though he has no hands. He tries to hold his breath but finds there is no breath to hold. He has been completely transformed into energy.

Having been returned to pure soul power, Somé can behold the source of the world's force as she laughs, breaths, births, and vibrates life:

> The space beneath me was terrifying. It was violent, as if it were a volcano in action, and there was no end to it. I was not surprised by the endlessness—I had expected something like this from the beginning when I had seemed to fall very far and fast, but the volcanic action was not very reassuring. The bundles of light wires ended in the volcano, as if they were fed by the power coming out of it. Like a living entity, the volcano opened and closed periodically. (244)

The living energy that Somé visits and interacts with may also be that which the Kemites channeled.

In *The Giza Power Plant: Technologies of Ancient Egypt*, engineer Christopher Dunn states that "[s]cientists believe that the Earth is analogous to a giant dynamo, with convection currents of charged molten metal circulating in the Earth's core."[59] Dunn goes on to describe how the Kemites harnessed this dynamo and its magnetic fields and energies to generate electricity. The Dagara, as did the Kemites and Kushites and as do the Yoruba, Igbo, BaKongo, and other Africana peoples, access and channel the Earth's power to activate various tools and technologies, but for the Dagara initiates, bearing witness to the dynamo itself in its habitat is a phenomenal teaching tool.

While watching the volcano reciprocally give and take lines of light to and from the world, Somé realizes that this force is alive. In language similar to Tall John's description of the "great mind," Somé describes the volcano as a "vast intelligence" who knows he is present and is curious about him (244). Somé also notes where this sentient power is stored and how it is distributed. He sees and struggles to decipher "cosmic hieroglyphics," and he is entranced by a mountain that could have inspired the Kemites to construct the pyramids, encase them in gleaming limestone, and cap them with electrum: "Nothing had ever looked more beautiful than this living mountain crowned with gold and luminescent sapphires and all kinds of precious metals. Every bit of it pulsed with motion and life" (245). The mountain is the mother of the soul-piece, and it dazzles Somé's eyes and summons his soul with its song. As he drifts closer to the resplendent edifice he sees a door open and finds a person gazing at him. The person is huge and his eyes are protruding fireballs, like the Bachwezi.

When Somé emerges from the portal, tongues of fire lick at his body which undergoes transformation from energy to light to human entity. Somé discovers that he must reacquaint himself with terrestrial existence. He must retrain his limbs to transport his body, and he finds that he is still seeing through spiritual vision: "A termite that I was about to crush under my bare foot suddenly grew enormous, as if to make me notice it. As soon as I changed the direction of my foot, it became small again. I saw a spider's web, and the spider grew huge just in time for me to avoid running into it. . . . The horizon of reality had increased exponentially" (246). The magnification that comes with Somé's spiritual vision is similar to that described by Bynum in *Joe Turner's Come and Gone* when during his initiation he finds that "everything was twice as big as it was" from trees to sparrows to his father's hands and mouth. Somé's and Bynum's experiences in the spiritual realm act as rebirths that allow them to see things as infants do and to be humbled by the diverse powers of the world.[60] What is more, by traveling into the portal and beholding the soul of the world, Somé understands his relationship to all of the world's souls. Because he is the product of and dependent on all that exists in the world and universe, Somé gains cognizance of and respect for the sovereignty, interconnectedness, and dynamism of all matter, all forms, all forces. Somé is the jewel on the mountain, the delicate web of a spider; he is a nebula in a galaxy, the termite building a hill, the stone being smoothed in a roiling riverbed, the initiate and the elder; Somé is the son of the Mother Cell who became two who became All.

Of Water and the Spirit encourages Westernized persons to reevaluate their presumed superiority to flora and fauna and the antediluvian, geocentric, backward belief, embraced by Western scientists, astronomers, and astrophysicists, that posits, most bizarrely and contrary to readily observable proof, that space is a vacuum and that the Earth is the only planet—the only thing in the entire Cosmos—that sustains life. Somé's autobiography elucidates the fact that everything that produced and sustains the Earth and everything that the Earth produces and sustains is alive—including the Earth itself, the Cosmos in which the Earth exists, and all matter. If the Earth and its earth and other matter were devoid of life, they could not support and foment life.

The living Earth does not merely exist; it has a soul and spirit that is vibrant, powerful, magnetic. For proof of the Earth's life one need only ponder floods, volcanoes, hurricanes, tsunamis, tornadoes, a growing dandelion, air, or an atom. One finds other examples of the Earth's consciousness in African orature and literature. The protagonist of *My Life* has a dramatic encounter with the living Earth when he runs over a swath of communicative land. The Earth feels the protagonist's every step and she cries out in pain (84–85). Similarly, a Yoruba praisesong to Onílẹ̀, the Earth Mother Deity intones, "Don't let us step on you wrongly / . . . / Don't let us step on you Ilẹ̀ (Earth) / Where it will cause you injury."[61] References to a sentient Earth occur in Africana literatures because of the cognition that Earth sustains human life with its life.

Africana technicians, scientists, and physicians harness the abundant healing powers of the living Earth. In addition to the well-known and readily accessed power resident in dirt from graves, Africans of Sierra Leone and Georgia bury sick or weak humans and animals in the Earth for three days to cure ailments and strengthen limbs.[62] During initiation, Somé and his peers are buried up to their necks as part of the process of knowing and becoming (258–262). The empowering and healing ancestral and magnetic properties within the Earth are also, logically, found in the planet's flora.

Igbo dibia know that for every ailment there is a cure waiting in the Earth's medicine chest and that the medicines in nature can never be exhausted. Somé discovers another fact that Igbo dibia know: The Earth's flora and fauna long to share their healing wisdom with worthy human beings. After his journey to the Source, Somé gains the ability to truly see flora: "I could see the different personalities of the trees and larger plants. Even their roots were visible to me. Some appeared as a vast network growing out in all directions, others were simply a single tubercle on top of which stood the plant erect and content. I saw the medicine and the healing power in all of them" (263).

Communicating with and understanding flora and fauna is a staple for Africana spiritualists. In *Mules and Men*, Dr. Duke teaches Hurston that "John de Conqueror must be gathered before September 21st. Wonder of the World Root must be spoken to with ceremony before it is disturbed, or forces will be released that will harm whoever handles it. Snakes guard other herbs and roots and must not be killed."[63] Plants communicate with each other and with fauna, including knowledgeable human beings. In *After God is Dibia*, John Umeh confirms, "Those who understand know that herbs talk, particularly at certain hours in the night."[64] Herbs that can speak can also, logically, hear and respond. Umeh discusses Chief Eze-Onwaneti who, before seeking medicines from the Earth, invokes and honors flora with the following invocation:

> Herbal grass please answer my call
> For my father used you in marrying my mother
> Herbal grass please answer my call
> For my father used you in begetting me[65]

By heralding flora as the source of his existence, Eze-Onwaneti can rely on their communication and assistance as surely as he can rely on that of his parents. Somé realizes his connection with flora when he hears plants hum and vibrate to him: "The plants around me were all glowing violet, and the trees kept moving their branches as if they were noticing my presence. I was happy to be noticed that way. I knew nature loved me and I was happy to love nature back" (262). Only in a relationship rooted in reciprocal respect, admiration, and love can wisdom flow between flora and fauna without encumbrance.

The spirit that the Dagara call Sìè, that the Yoruba call Orí, that the Kemites call Ba, and that the Igbo call Chi is not limited to human beings. Somé comes to see, know, and communicate with the souls of the Earth and its flora and fauna and to understand that they have always been in communication with his own Sìè. Communications, interactions, and knowledge acquisition between souls occurs at all times. Similar to Carrie Nancy Fryer whose ancestors taught her cures in her dreams, when Somé is asleep he continues learning and being challenged. In one dream a white bull confronts Somé and chants "you, you, you" while spraying spit in his face (250). African Americans call such apparitions "shadows," and so prevalent are shadows that they are paid homage in the title of the book *Drums and Shadows*. These apparitions test, prepare, and mark human beings in life, as with Somé, and in literature, as is the case with Freddie in Toni Morrison's *Song of Solomon* who is also marked by a white bull.[66] Saliva can be used to mark, cure, bless, and/or curse as necessary in traditional Africana pharmacology. The white bull that marks and blesses Somé with words and saliva is actually one of the elders who guides Somé through his initiation. Even though the initiation is not over at this point, the elders understand that Somé will succeed in his initiation and in the fulfillment of his destiny. The bull's saliva and invocation represent the elders' acceptance and recognition of Somé.

Somé's final task during initiation is to journey into the underworld. He enters a cave and finds a shepherd who is two feet tall and appears to also be in possession of Imí Òṣùmàrè. The shepherd uses light to guide animals who feed during the night to avoid human beings whose poaching has endangered their species. Somé also receives a visit from an important friend. When he was a child, Somé chased a rabbit in hopes of killing and eating it. Instead of catching the rabbit, Somé found himself staring at a tiny shining elder: "All around him there was a glow, a shiny rainbow ring, like a round window or portal into another reality. Although his body filled most of that portal, I could still see that there was an immense world inside it" (18). As a child, Somé gets a glimpse of the world to which he will travel as an adult jumping though the space-time continuum. The tiny elder sitting on the threshold of two worlds is one of the spiritual beings the Dagara call Kontombili. For eons the Kontombili have revealed wisdom, technology, and science to the Dagara. The ability to enter the space-time continuum, to harness sunlight, to use water to see events occurring miles away, and many more skills, are technologies the Dagara learned from the Kontombili.

As does the shiny man in *Joe Turner's Come and Gone*, the tiny shining man goes before to show Somé the way during his childhood. The shining elder tells Somé that the rabbit is Somé's brother and that the rabbit has a mother and family who love him just as Somé does. Despite the lesson he learned as a child and all his has learned since then, during his mission to the underworld, Somé loses focus and tries to catch and eat the rabbit. The rabbit, very much in the vein of his African American "Brer," looks at Somé and says, "You still do not get it, man. After all these years here you are again, eager to hurt me" (268). Despite his lack of focus at this crossroads, Somé is sent forward to meet his selves.

It is important to note how patient every entity is with Somé. He is never dismissed or given up on. Everyone and everything from the elders, to rabbits, to bulls, to stars, to shiny men warn, tease, embrace, teach, shock, reprimand, cajole—whatever is necessary, save violence—to remember Somé to the divine and dynamic power that is his inheritance.

Upon entering the underworld, Somé receives a painful reminder to open his mind and let the world educate him. Somé is accosted by a puling and screaming so intense it makes his ears bleed. His thoughts are creating the cacophony. While Western educators lament the death of critical thought in the classroom, Somé must turn off his "critical-thinking mechanism" in order to receive "the speech of silence" (272–273). This incident may intimate the damage done to the human body, psyche, and soul by Western analytics. It is only when Somé relinquishes control in every form that he is guided toward the same type of portal that Tall John, Forty-seven, and Tutuola's protagonist accessed. The huge tree, crowned with leaves that shine, introduces Somé to every terrestrial life he has ever lived.

Somé's former earthly existences reveal the inextricable bond that unites Pan-Africanism with the continuum of the eternal, for Somé is every African: He is the pyramid builder, the stone-city erector, and the great migrator. Somé is the language fashioning, literature writing, number creating, civilization starting, sacred oath swearing, sacred oath breaking African. He is the son of the soil who speaks with and through all life forms; he is the chosen one who heals, harms, kills, learns, loses, and loves and who has been doing so since the birth of this planet. While knowledge of all of his former lives provides him with essential and elemental tools necessary for him to manifest his destiny, Somé's existence prior to his present life is a study of lessons in continuity, power, technology, gender, and spiritual-material transposition and exposition.

Prior to his present existence, Somé was his great-grandfather, Sabare. One day while hunting, Sabare enters into a shape-shifting battle with an entity whose original form is that of a literal white female (not to be confused with a Caucasian) whose breasts hang down her back and who has three eyes. She hails from another dimension and lives in a land where women dominate every aspect of society. The men of the society are kept naked, are half the size of women, and are excluded from women's power and knowledge. Apparently the benefits of living in this land outweigh the position men must assume therein because Sabare marries the woman, and they enjoy a fruitful relationship. When after a long absence his family begins making funeral preparations for him, Sabare returns home on a white steed that is moving so quickly that its hooves barely touch the ground. Sabare tells his sons to abandon their plans to hold his funeral because he is not dead. He has "shifted to the other side of existence without going through the door of death" (27). Sabare states that this shift will benefit the family as he can protect them more effectively from the spirit realm. He tells them, "Whenever you need me, say these words. . . ." (27). Bakhye does not tell Somé the sacred words; perhaps because Somé is Sabare, he does not need to.

From shape-shifting battles, to successfully shifting to the "other side," to marriages to super ladies, Sabare's life evinces striking parallels to that of the protagonist of *My Life*. Sabare's experiences also confirm the veracity of the assertions of Djigui of *Yeelen*, the Dagara elders, Somé, himself, and Killah Priest, that death is not a prerequisite for a sojourn in the spiritual realm. It is important to note that unlike individuals who lose their way and get trapped in other dimensions, the fluidity of his existence is such that Sabare is able to guide and protect his loved ones, and the assistance he provides his family is identical to the support that Bakhye provides Somé from the spiritual realm.

Because of his stunning arrival and revelations, his family wants more information from Sabare, and Bakhye and his brother ask Sabare to stay a few days and discuss his new life and talk to the family about his decision. Sabare's refusal is almost violent. In full consonance with Pan-African injunctions against discussing certain sacred names, flora, signs, and technologies, Sabare commands, "No more should be said or the thread will be cut between you and me" (27). Telling them to be content with his spiritual protection, Sabare mounts his steed, which is his transformed wife, and literally flies up through the troposphere into the stratosphere and beyond: "We watched him get on his horse and ride away. After he had gone a very short distance, he and the horse began mounting up into the sky. Stunned, we watched them rise higher, then vanish" (27). Even though they are surrounded by a loving healthy family and community and have Sabare's assurance of spiritual guidance, Bakhye and his brother must have been as astounded and devastated as Ryna was when she watched her mother Theresa turn, levitate, and fly away.[67]

It is ironic that Sabare's downfall (pardon the pun) is the result of his desire to learn more about the rulers of his adopted world. Sabare is so intrigued by the powerful women that he spies on one of their ceremonies and is caught and sentenced to death. On the day of his execution, his wife tells him that he will be reincarnated as his own progeny. Sabare's "death" is actually a relocation into a womb. While in the womb, Sabare is questioned by Bakhye about his purpose and intentions, as the Dagara query the unborn just before they arrive. Shortly after revealing his identity and mission, Sabare is reborn and named Malidoma Somé.

Sabare and Somé both find themselves inextricably bound to but forever outside of their earthly homes, and both find it is their destiny to make friends with strangers and/or enemies. Indeed, the name Malidoma means "be friends with the stranger/enemy." However, before Somé can assist enemies and strangers, he must befriend himself. His Jesuit captors sought to remove every trace of Dagara culture, language, history, and spirituality from him; their goal was to irreparably sever him from his identity. Thanks to the Jesuits, Somé becomes a stranger to himself, and he becomes his village's enemy. The Dagara initiation helps Somé slough off the damning ways of his oppressors and reunite with the core of his being. Every stage, lesson, and trial of initiation introduces Somé to another aspect of his ancient self and the intergalactic relationships he forged eons ago.

Somé's initiation, his "date in the bush" with "all the gods," "all the trees," and "the Kontomblé" is, most of all, an education in himself (295–296). The successful initiates sing of the comprehensive knowledge they have been re-membered to:

> It was all in me.
> I was the room and the door.
> It was all in me.
> I just had to remember.
> And I learned that I lived
> Always everywhere.
> I learned that I knew everything.
> Only I had forgotten. (296)

The Dagara's is a complete and whole education that far outstrips what any Westernized educational institution can offer. And rather than having a diploma to hang on his wall or a certificate of chieftaincy, after completing initiation, Somé has 360° of soulpower with which to navigate this life and all others. It is also important to note that whereas university tuition rates are always rising and many modernized African spiritualists charge exorbitant fees for their services, no money is exchanged between Somé and his community wisdom keepers. Money is not only irrelevant to the wisdom that they share but the introduction of money into the circle of pure power would be an abomination. True wisdom, knowledge, and understanding are priceless, and true wisdom workers do not seek to debase divinity with dollars.

. . .

In the African ethos the spiritual realm is an intriguing, dangerous, fantastic place. It may not boast the eternal idleness of the Christian heaven, but it has much more character, intricacy, flavor, and complexity. Additionally, and this will be disheartening to those who shun learning, growing, and developing, the spiritual realm is where all questions are answered by issues and entities that lead to yet more startling and confounding questions. The cycle of knowledge acquisition is unending as are the gifts that the universe and its various forms, figures, and forces have to give. What is more, the dimensions, textures, complexities, and galaxies in the Cosmos are as innumerable as our thoughts. In the words of a Dagara elder:

> Our minds know better than we are able and willing to admit the existence of many more things than we are willing to accept. The spirit and the mind are one. . . . *Nothing can be imagined that is not already there in the outer and inner worlds.* Your mind is a responder; it receives. *It does not make things up. It can't imagine what does not exist.* The blessing is that you are your mind. That is also a curse. (253–254, emphasis added)

From the minds and experiences of Walter Mosley, Amos Tutuola, and Malidoma Somé come magnificent "heavens" that are extraordinarily dynamic and filled with Gods who are just like you and me—with the same powers, fears, responsibilities, tragedies and triumphs. That these three books of disparate genres, written by three very different authors in different eras for different reasons envision similar spiritual realms, cosmic entities, and spiritual missions is not a coincidence. Perhaps these authors are allied in the goal of accelerating the process by which we finally "catch up with [ourselves]" in this realm so that we are properly prepared—intellectually, technologically, spiritually, and morally—for the rigors of life in the next world.

CHAPTER SIX

The Saline Solutions and Winged Revolutions of
Toni Cade Bambara and Toni Morrison

"You never really know a person until you've eaten salt together."
~ Toni Cade Bambara, *The Salt Eaters*

"My meaning is specific: it is about black people who could fly."
~ Toni Morrison, on *Song of Solomon*

Toni Morrison supported the art of many Africana writers in her position as the first African American editor at Random House, and her respect for those artists is evident in the intertextual homage she pays them in her works. Her graceful re-membering of the song, scars, and well-made bed of Amos Tutuola's *My Life in the Bush of Ghosts* into *Beloved* offer rich examples. It is also important to note that the blue silk wings of *Song of Solomon's* Robert Smith actually made an earlier flight of equally paradoxical success in John McCluskey's *Look What They Done to My Song*.[1] But Toni Morrison's bond with Toni Cade Bambara is a sisterhood of unique dimension in literary history.

Morrison edited and supported Bambara's first Random House offerings, and when Bambara joined the ancestors in 1995, Morrison shepherded to posthumous publication a collection of essays and short stories titled *Deep Sightings and Rescue Missions* (1996) and Bambara's haunting historical novel *Those Bones Are Not My Child* (1999). Bambara and Morrison worked together to make sure that no one forgot that the victims of the Atlanta Child Murders have not yet received justice, and they collaborated to ensure the continuation of the struggle through their art.

While only a privileged few could have been in the presence of these powerhouses when they shared laughter, fried fish, and discussed plots,[2] the entire world has access to the resonant intertextual conversations and meditations that speak within and across the leaves of Morrison's and Bambara's literature.

In Bambara's *The Salt Eaters*, Porter revises his life so completely that Western status means nothing to him. He pulls a page from the wisdom book of Africana elders and devotes his life to mastering the ability to become invisible. When Porter is murdered, Fred Holt, his best friend, plunges into astral abysses and dreams of murder and suicide until he has an epiphany: He whispers to the wind, "Porter, are you there?" and Porter confirms his invisible and eternal presence. Fred is the literary sibling of Nell Wright who learns that her "dead" friend Sula Peace also rides the wind. At the close of the Morrison's novel *Sula*, Nell feels the energy of her friend's wry sass and whispers, "Sula?" and the winds and leaves chuckle her response.

In *Beloved*, Sethe spins and circles while trying to tell Paul D why and how she saved her daughter from schoolteacher; similarly, in *The Salt Eaters*, Velma spins, rotates, and crashes as she struggles with the psychological imbalance brought on by post-traumatic stress disorder. When Velma and Sethe tire of grinding salt like circling hawks, they land, re-member the wisdom of Braziel Robinson, and invite their second selves, their ẹnikejì, to conference.[3] When Beloved returns from the other side at her mother's request, the misunderstandings, accusations, apologies, ecstasies, and desires of the pair are so intense that this world cannot contain both Beloved and Sethe. For Velma, the second self is Barbara "Sweetpea" Watson, the jaded, sassy, ex-activist who has gone on to seemingly better things. But Barbara's judgmental defeatist comments— "And still into the same idealistic nonsense," "You honestly think you can change anything in this country," and "Thank god I got out of here in time"—serve as a rich fuel supply for a depleted Velma, whose replies to Barbara—"we're all still here"; "I want to learn to grow, to become. . ."— root a floating Velma back into the community and the struggle.[4]

Morrison and Bambara recover the dismembered and discredited ways of knowing, doing, and understanding that are crucial to the African ethos and its continuity. They infuse ancient wisdom and technologies such as invisibility, spiritual doubling, and immortality into their art because this wisdom and these technologies are Africana peoples' eternal inheritance. The infinite relevance of these tools is evident in their distinct applications in Morrison's and Bambara's literature. Perhaps the richest examples of intertextual spiritual technology in the art of Bambara and Morrison occur in their explorations of masculine magnificence, especially as it relates to the phenomenon of human flight, the technologies that facilitate flight, and the impact of flight on the evolution of Africana individuals, communities, and consciousness.

This chapter will examine the impact that salt has on both flight and Africana divinity. Following a spiritual-historical examination of the impact of salt on divinity and flight, this exposition will focus on the nexus of divinity, salt, and power that undergirds the philosophies and fuels the actions of certain characters in Bambara's short story "Broken Field Running" and in her novel *The Salt Eaters* and in Milkman of Morrison's *Song of Solomon*. Bambara and Morrison use salt differently in their literary cuisine, but both use it expertly to achieve specific textual and extratextual outcomes. Using the works of Morrison and Bambara, along with data from Africana spiritual systems, this chapter debunks long-standing myths about the impact of salt on human flight and illuminates the complex relationship between salt, divinity, and divine technology.

"The Salt Trails of a People"

The relationship between salt and physical flight is one of the most storied and misunderstood in the Pan-African world.[5] Many Africana spiritualists and scholars of Africana studies argue that salt prevents flight. This theory is born largely of the testimonies of African Caribbeans that are documented in such studies as Monica Schuler's *Alas, Alas, Kongo* and Lorna McDaniel's *The Big Drum Ritual of Carriacou*. Despite the fact that the salt-inhibits-flight testimonies come from rather narrow geographic regions, the theory that once Africans ate salt they were unable to fly has become widely accepted.

The problem with the theory that salt prevents flight is that salt is vital to human existence. Salt is present in semen, breast milk, and vaginal fluid. While in the uterus, the fetus frolics and develops in a warm and sterile cocoon of salt-enriched fluids. Not only is salt essential to the human body's ability to heal cuts and bruises, but without salt the human body cannot sustain itself. In "A Bicultural Approach to Salt Taboos," Thomas W. Neumann describes how the human body reacts to salt deficiency: "The salt-depleted individual feels tired and unwell and may suffer from hand, foot, or limb cramps. His working efficiency tends to drop, his judgment suffers, and he may overestimate the passage of time. . . . The penultimate response, short of death, is mental derangement."[6]

Salt is necessary for existence, and Africans have enjoyed harmonious relationships with the mineral for eons. However, when Caucasians entered the African world bearing the gift of subjugation, they used salt as a tool to formalize, solidify, and eternalize oppression. In *Mothering Across Cultures: Postcolonial Discourse*, Angelita Reyes discusses the concern among Central Africans, including the BaKongo, that "eating salt would convert them to European Christianity and deprive them of their African mystic abilities."[7] When Catholic priests learned of the spiritual rationale behind these Africans' avoidance of salt they went beyond salting baptismal waters; they started making Africans eat what they called "the salt of God."[8] In this way, priests attempted to literally season Africans with Caucasian religious and ideological oppression.

The Central Africans that Reyes discusses originally had harmonious, healthy, and organic relationships with salt that were conducive to every aspect of their existence. The salt that they ingested was likely limited to that found naturally in their environments, which provided them with the optimum biochemical balance. It was easy for these Africans to determine that Caucasians' unnatural and destructive worldview, which moved them to exploit, enslave, or destroy Africans, was facilitated by the Caucasian manipulation of salt. These Africans logically shunned both Caucasians and their salt.

It is because of Caucasians that, for millions upon millions of Africans around the world, salt conjures images of the Middle Passage and its accompanying death and desolation. In addition to the high salt content of the ocean, Caucasian seamen used salt as a food preservative, and they forced Africans to ingest heavily salted foods so that they could survive the Middle Passage.[9] Once Africans arrived in the lands of oppression, enslavers used salt to estimate their value. In Mexico, medical inspectors thought that the salt content of sweat was related to blood pressure, so they would lick the chins of enslaved Africans who had survived the Middle Passage to determine the salt content of their sweat and their suitability for servitude.[10] Caucasians were also known to whip Africans until the blood pooled under their feet and then rub both salt and pepper into their victims' wounds to simultaneously heal the wounds and compound the agony.[11] In myriad and macabre ways, commoditized salt was the enslaver's essential ally.

While, to my knowledge, there are no documented African proscriptions against ingesting indigenous terrestrial salt, such as halite, there are numerous discussions of Africans from landlocked regions being debilitated by the salt that emanates from the ocean. In Uwem Akpan's short story "Fattening for Gabon" Paul, a child from the desert of northern Nigeria who has been trafficked to the coast for enslavement, suffers "seasickness" from simply smelling the salt-rich winds that blow off of the Ethiopic Ocean.[12] Similarly, Emmanuel Dongala's novel *The Fire of Origins* describes African laborers from Chad and Ubangi not only as having severe gastrointestinal aliments because they are unused to eating foods with high salt content, but also as being convinced that if they so much as see the ocean they will die. The salt content in the air of semicoastal Congo-Brazzaville is so high that Djibril begins suffocating long before he sees the ocean.[13] In the case of Djibril, salt prevents *life*—making flight irrelevant.

Bodies of water are perfect repositories of paradox and plentitude. Life and death recur there cyclically, and despite being the intentional and unintentional dumpsters for assorted waste products, rivers and seas cleanse themselves with every rhythmic wave. Given salt's preservative qualities, it is only natural that bodies of salt water would preserve and foment the seas' cycles of existence, death, and renewal. But as it relates to salt taboos and Dongala's and Akpan's descriptions, it could very well be the case that the salty sea itself, as an overwhelming and overwhelmed organic preservative of paradox, is working with the spirits of the millions of unceremoniously buried African ancestors who are, themselves, preserved in the ocean, to warn Africans not yet tainted to avoid the coast, avoid the sea for oblivion there waits.

The ocean's warning and threat to Africans appear to be as enduring as the ocean itself. Over two centuries after human trafficking on international waters was outlawed, Akpan describes an "At-sea Orientation" for contemporary enslaved children that includes learning to survive being placed overboard if the ship is searched and also drinking salt water twice a day so that if the ship runs out of fresh, the children can survive on salt water. It is the height of irony that these contemporary Africans are taught to preserve their lives—and ensure their enslavement—by ingesting the salt bequeathed to the sea courtesy of their ancestors.[14] In the discussion of salt in the African ethos, the *source* of the salt is just as if not more important than the chemical's properties.

Perhaps the most important aspect of the theory that salt prevents flight is that it provides an excellent way to explain why there are so few Flying Africans today. However, even if it were possible for people to abstain from intentionally ingesting salt orally, they would still absorb the mineral by eating foods that are natural sources of salt. If they are a coastal or island-dwelling people, they would ingest salt by simply breathing. Being conceived and nurtured *in vitro* in salt-balanced amniotic fluid also presents a problem, as does the fact that humans must ingest salt in order to live. It is simply not possible for human beings to not consume any salt at all and also fly or do anything else. Considering this, it could be the case that some Africans refused to consume salt so that they could die. With an earthly death, one could fly metaphorically from the horrors of the plantation and join one's ancestors. But because the focus of this analysis is not the flight of the soul but a technology used by living Africana people in the past and the present, we must discard the salt-prevents-flight/abstain-from-salt-and-fly theories because they are not plausible.

As is apparent in the testimonies discussed in chapter one of this book and in chapter two of *Our Mothers, Our Powers, Our Texts*, Africana peoples of the Continent and Ìtànkálẹ̀ discuss myriad methods of flight. In *The Autobiography of a Runaway Slave*, Esteban Montejo goes into elaborate detail about various African ethnic groups' unique flying styles and facilitators. Montejo extols the flying skills of the Musundi Congolese, and his assessments are buttressed by Daniel Kanza. The premiere issue of Kanza's *Kongo Dieto* newspaper includes an important analysis of the ways by which the Belgians and their concept of "independence" spiritually and technologically cripple the BaKongo and make them dependent on primitive, ecologically destructive, profit driven Caucasian products. In addition to the Belgians preventing the BaKongo from making vehicles because indigenous developments would reveal the obsolescence and inadequacy Caucasian modes of transportation, Kanza argues that Belgian missionaries "saw that the power of our elders exceeded their own, so they sought a way to burn all the charms in Mbanza Kongo and substitute the images of the saints."[15]

It is significant that long after the period of trans-Atlantic exile and enslavement ended, the BaKongo were using their indigenous technologies—including the ability to fly and to reconstitute matter—to escape colonization and persecution and to protect their Divinity. Kanza discusses the diverse technological abilities of the BaKongo which enabled them to use mundane items, such as knives and mats, and the Kodya, which is a large snail shell and "symbol of Kongo nationalism," to transport entire communities to safety:

> Then the chief called Ne Kongo took his Kodya and his sword Lulewu and fled with his following, the people of Kongo. On their journey the Kodya demonstrated many marvels. They crossed rivers on little things, for example, the clan Mbamba Kalunga crossed the River on a knife blade; others, on a raffia mat, or in the Kodya itself. In short, the Kodya had and has enormous power.[16]

The struggles and strategies of the BaKongo provide confirmation of and contextualization for the feats discussed in chapter one, including the abilities of African Americans to use common tools to facilitate flight and such Igbo skills as ikwu ekili, igho, and ndena. The skills of the BaKongo are also similar to those used by Father of the Gods Who Could Do

Anything in this World and other characters in Tutuola's *The Palm-Wine Drinkard* and *My Life in the Bush of Ghosts*.[17] In both life and literature, these skills and technologies are used for personal, community, and political purposes, and, unlike Caucasian products and industries, African technologies are in no way tied to capitalism: Such an association would be senseless.

The ease with which Ne Kongo is able to transform and transport his nation is most germane to this discussion, for if the theory that salt inhibits flight were valid, Ne Kongo's transformation and relocation of entire communities would have been impossible. Indeed, Kanza makes clear in the second issue of *Kongo Dieto* that the impediment to BaKongo technology was not salt but Caucasians: "Our elders knew how to make iron tools, guns, and many other things, but when [the Caucasians] came to steal our freedom, the old [skills] disappeared."[18] Myriad technologies—from iron working to artillery, from bi-location to flight—which were used for community evolution and elevation, were destroyed so that destructive capitalist Caucasian technology could dominate and delimit African life, mobility, and power.

Although human flight is most often associated with fleeing oppression in the Western hemisphere, this African technology was in use long before the concept of slavery was invented, and it is still in use today. Continental African wisdom workers, especially hunters, continue to use flight for such practical purposes as traveling long distances, avoiding death, attending important meetings, and transporting heavy objects and quarry. In his discussion of ikwu ekili, Umeh describes how a dibia named Ugwumba lights a piece of firewood that is connected by strings to various farm animals. Ugwumba throws the blazing wood into the air, takes his son's hand, catches the blazing wood and everything—father, son and animals—is transformed into a blazing comet of white light.[19] Spiritually-enlightened and cosmically-empowered Africans of various ethnic groups and occupations enjoy meals well-seasoned with salt and other spices and continue to utilize the technology that makes it possible for them to transport themselves, other individuals, and animate and inanimate objects—including salt.

Two of the reasons that salt has a delimited role in certain neo-African communities are Christianization and a misunderstanding of African rituals and customs. While it is true that certain ritual meals are cooked without salt, it is not the case that salt is not used for any rituals other than cleansing and banishing evil. It is also not the case that salt prevents spiritual entities (wanted or unwanted) from entering certain spaces and places. If a liberal sprinkling of salt were all it took to rid the world of evil and evildoers, life would be different: Given that the concept of evil is subjective, if salt destroyed evil, there may not be any human life at all.

Traditional Yoruba cosmology and pharmacology do not place restrictions on salt. In *Ewé: The Use of Plants in Yoruba Society*, Pierre F. Verger documents the use of salt in numerous works including establishing an open air market, attracting apprentices, acquiring nice clothes, making someone obey you, acquiring wealth, winning wars, being well spoken of when absent, reducing the stature of a tall man, making rain fall, rendering a man impotent, killing the lover of one's wife, keeping one's wife from dying, being clairvoyant, protecting one from evil, protecting one from sudden death, and helping one conceive a child.[20] Salt is used in multitudinous capacities among the Yoruba and many other African peoples as well.

In Africana spiritual systems, the pineal gland is considered to be the spring and storehouse of spiritual enlightenment and shining. In Igbo cosmology, the pineal gland, or seat of the third eye, is called *akpa uche* and is symbolized by a "miniature cone of moulded salt."[21] The *nganga* (wisdom keeper and diviner) of the BaKongo has innumerable technological devices, and one of the most important is the progenitor of African American goofer dust: *Mungw'a basenzi*, which literally means "indigenous salt," consists of white ashes from a cadaver.[22] Mungw'a basenzi not only reveals how the Earth obtained some of its most potent salt, but also how living persons can harness the literal "salt of the earth"—which is the salt of both their ancestors and themselves—to work wonders.

While a common supposition is that the ancestors shun salt and that salt should not be used on shrines, in sacrifices, or in ceremonies for the ancestors, one of the key elements of the elaborate Ìjùmú Yoruba burial ritual called Orò Imọlẹ̀ includes the ancestor's surviving relatives tasting salt that is positioned beside a bundle of sacred ancestral cloths. The family tastes the salt because

> As the salt is sweet, so also will you have a sweet (peaceful) life.
> Your father's head will . . . pray for you.
> As soon as we taste the salt, the father will commence . . . his
>   journey to the spirit world.[23]

The Ìjùmú ritual reflects salt's multifaceted significance, from its ability to "sweeten," or make appetizing, meals, to its ability to "sweeten," or make worthwhile, life. The ability of salt to add flavor to existence is especially important because the tasting of salt unifies the surviving relatives and grounds them on the Earth while simultaneously signaling to the ancestor that his cosmic existence and duties as a divine guide and protector of his terrestrial kin have begun.

The rich relationship between salt and Divinity is everywhere apparent in Yoruba culture. Shrines for Ajé Saluga, the God of Prosperity, include copious amounts of salt. Yemọja is the Great Mother and the Mother of Waters. As the vaginal fluid of the Earth,[24] she is manifest in the Ethiopic Ocean and all the world's waters—salt and fresh: It would be both illogical and impossible for Yemọja to shun salt! Yemọja is one of the principal Gods of Àjẹ́, and neither she nor any celestial or terrestrial Àjẹ́ has a salt taboo. Indeed, as the literal and spiritual Mothers of Existence, Àjẹ́ created this world and everything in it, including salt. In order to successfully sustain existence, Àjẹ́ must maintain the perfect salt balance in their bodies, in their wombs, in their offspring, and in the world.

Astral and physical flight are the signature forces and modes of travel of Àjẹ́, and Àjẹ́ travel wherever they like after eating whatever they like, including foods seasoned with salt. Indeed, one of Àjẹ́'s favorite dishes, and the one that is regularly offered to them for sacrifice, is àkàrà, ground and deep fried black-eyed bean fritters that are seasoned with salt and red and black pepper whether for human or spiritual consumption.

To make the relationship between Àjẹ́ and salt even more vivid, worshippers of Òṣun, the Yoruba God of sensuality, fertility, and abundance, proudly herald her as the "leader" of Àjẹ́, and they use a profound simile to describe their Mother's power and their own:

> My *Òṣun* of healing waters, one who is as effective as salt.
> When we are as effective as salt in using the healing waters,
> When I am *àjẹ́*, I am as effective as salt,
> I proudly grow long arms and hands for dancing.[25]

In Yoruba cosmology, salt is clearly not considered negative and does not have a harmful impact on divinity, spirituality, or technology—quite the opposite.

Òṣun has many daughters across the Ethiopic Ocean who are also as "effective as salt." In the late 1930s Zora Neale Hurston studied under Mother Catherine, also known as Mother Seal. Mother Seal's sanctuary, as described by Hurston, features many of the same totems and animals that symbolize and are used to worship Òṣun, including 365 polished brass lamps; red, white, and blue banners emblazoned with images of serpents; and an array of cockatoos, parrots, and canaries. At the center of all is Mother Seal, who presides over her domain while holding "a box of shaker salt in her hand like a rod of office."[26] When Hurston falls to her knees before the Mother and states her desires, Mother Catherine announces: "Thank God. Do y'all hear her? She come here lookin for wisdom. *Eat de salt, daughter, and get yo mind with God and me.* You shall know what you come to find out. I feel you. I felt you while you was sitten in de chapel. Bring her a veil."[27]

At the outset, Mother Seal's use of salt appears to be identical to that of enslaving Catholic priests, but her respect for her multiethnic congregation and the knowledge with which she uplifts them is clearly in consonance with the philosophies of Elijah Muhammad, Malidoma Somé, Toni Cade Bambara, and Hurston's own treatise on religion. Mother Seal's sermons include the following wisdom:

> There is no hell beneath this earth. God wouldn't build a hell to burn His earth.
> There is no heaven beyond dat blue globe. There is a between-world between this brown earth and the blue above. So says the beautiful spirit.
> When we die, where does the breath go? Into trees and grass and animals. Your flesh goes back to mortal earth to fertilize it. So says the beautiful spirit.
> Our brains is trying to make something out of us. Everybody can be something good.
> It is right that a woman should lead. A womb was what God made in the beginning, and out of that womb was born Time and all that fills up space. So says the beautiful spirit.[28]

Like her African sisters of Àjẹ́, Mother Seal is a God, and she knows it, and Hurston confirms this fact: "It is evident that Mother Seal takes her stand as an equal with Christ."[29] But Mother Seal's focus is not on being believed in, worshiped, or adored. Similar to the BaKongo use of Mungw'a basenzi, Mother Seal uses salt and her influence as catalysts to spark her congregation's spiritual consciousness, to harmonize its relationship to the Earth and the universe, and to galvanize its collective energy and divinity.

Rather than having an irrational fear of or place a prohibition on the mineral, spiritual and terrestrial Gods use salt's properties in ways most efficacious to their needs and to those of their communities; and what is true in life is apparent in literature. In Toni Morrison's *Beloved*, one of the last images of the eponymous protagonist before her fragmentation is that of a divine daughter-ancestor sucking on a salt rock in an attempt to solidify her terrestrial existence so that she can finalize the "join" with her mother.[30] Beloved's use of salt and its impact on her divinity can be contrasted to that of Makandal as depicted in Nalo Hopkinson's *The Salt Roads*. The fictional Makandal is based on the historical François Makandal, the revolutionary leader who used his knowledge of flora and fauna to kill hundreds of oppressors in the nation now known as Haiti. In Hopkinson's novel, Makandal stops eating salt so that his divinity and liberatory technologies can become magnified.[31] Beloved is a Deity who sucks salt to preserve her fragile humanity whereas Makandal only eats "fresh" to expand his numinosity; however, salt does not compromise Beloved's divinity or her immortality, and abstinence from salt does not destroy the intricacy and potency of Makandal's humanity. Beloved's and Makandal's relationships with salt emphasize the fact that, rather than a one-taste-for-all measure, the use of salt in Africana life and literature is directly related to the needs, politics, directives, and desires of an individual and/or a community, and this is especially true when the individual and/or community are on the verge of lift-off.

Bambara's short story "Broken Field Running" offers some of the richest elucidations of the roles of salt in the lives and in the flights of both spiritual and human beings. The short story follows nation-building activists, Dada Lacey and Ndugu Jason, as they walk their adolescent charges home from school in freezing weather. Lacey is so miserable she appears to be living the lyrics of Gil Scott-Heron's song "Winter in America." As a Sun person languishing in "the land of snow," Lacey is so exhausted by the unending and unfulfilled struggle to achieve freedom, justice, and equality that she yearns to simply fly away. Her wish triggers a profound rememory from the days when the community's freedom school was founded.

Lacey recalls jewel-dropping history lessons by Wade "Granddaddy" Sanderson, Fess Newton, and Miz Surrentine on the origins and original identity of certain Africans. According to Sanderson, some Africans arrived on the Continent in a manner similar to that of Tall John of Walter Mosley's *47*: "When we came to Africa, hear me now. I say when we came to Africa on the mother ship. . . . I say when we came to Africa, we could fly. You heard me. We could fly."[32] Sanderson goes on to state that Ezekiel witnessed the divine Africans' arrival on Earth in a vehicle that Tall John, Elijah Muhammad, and George Clinton would all recognize. Clinton would call it the vehicle the Mother Ship; Ezekiel, equating it with objects of his era, calls the vessel a wheel.

According to the Bible, Ezekiel watches as a whirlwind becomes four creatures, and each one has four faces and four wings. All of these entities are described as shining with the same complexion as Jesus, Tall John, and The RZA: "[T]hey sparkled like the colour of burnished brass" (Ezekiel 1:4–7). This magnificent multitudinous entity, who boasts a wheel of eyes within a wheel of eyes, presents Ezekiel with the book of knowledge, which Ezekiel, in the ways of the African wisdom workers,[33] eats so that the knowledge becomes one with his being.

The entity that Ezekiel witnesses is similar to a manifestation of Ọya, the Yoruba God of Transformation. Her chief symbols are the same whirlwind and lightning that accompany Ezekiel's wheel. Ọya's visage is so stupendous that it must not be seen; correspondingly, Ezekiel sees an awesome force that he cannot adequately define or describe. Ọya is known as Áàjálayé, the Winds of the World, and the word *áàjà* of Áàjálayé is defined as both a "whirlwind" and a spirit that is "said to carry persons into the wilderness for from three to nine years to instruct them in magic and all kinds of medicines."[34] Because of Ezekiel's reluctance, the cosmic sojourners use a different methodology to educate him: They make him ingest knowledge, and then they fly him to Telabib and place him on the path of his destiny.

Although the Bible fails to mention what becomes of the divine and flying Africans that Ezekiel encounters, Sanderson finds their fates to be much more important than that of Ezekiel because they are the progenitors of many contemporary Africana people. While some descendants of these cosmic travelers were born with the ability to fly, and they continue to soar about the Earth and the universe, the majority of their descendants are earthbound because, according to Sanderson, "we ate too much salt." Sanderson elaborates on the chemical, biochemical, and geological connections and reactions that are essential for human flight, and he avers, "Can't mess with too much salt cause it throws things out of proper balance. . . . And when the forces were all in balance, we were at the center of the field. The electro mag-net-tic field. . . . Gravity? Don't be tellin me about no somesuch gravity. That ain't nuthin. We could fly" ("Broken Field Running," 53).

This all sounds like great fodder for a "magical realist" tale until one ponders how the Dagara are able to prepare a meal, seasoned with salt, on a ceiling or how the Kemites were able to *perfectly* cut and place limestone and granite stones and slabs weighing from 2.5 to over 200 tons for the construction of the Great Pyramid of Kufu, not to mention all the other pyramids and temples in East Africa. If one gets lost in the maze of lies that Hollywood and history books have woven about the pyramids and is unable to see anything but historically and ethnically inaccurate and propaganda-ridden "Jewish slaves," then it may be helpful to look to Homestead, Florida and Edward Leedskalnin's Coral Castle. Leedskalnin, weighing approximately 100 pounds and standing five feet tall, was able to quarry, cut, transport, and position coral slabs and monuments that weighed from 30 to 300 tons.[35]

In *Magnetic Current*, his 51-page disquisition, Leedskalnin argues that everything on the Earth is a magnet and that the chief magnets governing the Earth are the North and South Poles. The poles constitute a "cosmic force" that holds "together this earth and everything on it."[36] Leedskalnin "believed that electricity and magnetism were two aspects of the basic energy force that powers the universe"; he called the force "magneticity."[37] Leedskalnin found that once one is able to control the magneticity of matter, one can control matter: Gravity becomes irrelevant. Leedskalnin used his knowledge to create a magnetic generator for which he applied but was refused a patent. It is thought that he used this generator to move multi-ton objects and to generate electricity on his property.

Leedskalnin, who likened his technology to that used by the Kemites to build the pyramids,[38] is one of many people around the world who used ancient and fundamental knowledge of physics and science to levitate objects. Many centuries before Leedskalnin was born, an Arabic historian named Abu Hasan Ali Al-Masudi observed the Kemites using magnetism to move massive stone blocks, and Tibetan Monks were described as using acoustic resonance to move huge boulders.[39] In *The Giza Power Plant*, Christopher Dunn offers impressive evidence that the Great Pyramid, which is erected at the geographical center of the world, was built to generate electricity by harnessing the magnetic, seismic, and microwaves of the Earth.[40] When Granddaddy Sanderson waxes prophetic about Africans being the very center of the world's "electro mag-net-tic field" it appears he knows exactly what he is talking about.

Despite the fact that tuition rates skyrocket annually, education is free. One need not pay tuition, let alone go into debt, to be educated—Malidoma Somé's initiation is proof of this. Granddaddy Sanderson in "Broken Field Running" shares his knowledge without charge; his goal is not to profit off of but to educate, inspire, and literally uplift his community. Edward Leedskalnin was an immigrant from Latvia, and he was not a rich or Western educated man. It goes without saying that the Tibetan monks are not a wealthy group, and the Kemite Empire reached its apex before either capitalism or slavery existed. Indeed, the ancient achievements of the Kushites, the Kemites, the Igbo, the Dagara, the BaKongo, the Dogon, and other groups around the world, make it clear that social progress, architectural masterworks, technological advances, and scientific discoveries were most prevalent and impressive *before* the advents of slavery, capitalism, organized religion, and Western pseudoscience and primitive technology.

Western science, which has been globalized and sold to the world as factual and empirical, is actually the reification of the patriarchal,

Christocentric, capitalistic, and egomaniacal prevarications of the Caucasian ethos. Western science is no more than Western superstition packaged, commoditized, and mandated for world consumption. Before obvious truths that disprove the veracity and validity of Western science, its keepers fall mute. Acknowledging the obvious—including the facts that space is not a vacuum, that the Cosmos is teeming with life, and that the Earth's ancient inhabitants had profound astrophysical knowledge—would expose the inadequacy, backwardness, and destructive nature of Caucasian/European/Western philosophy, technology, and science. Rather than appearing to be the vanguard of technological, philosophical, and astrophysical advances and advancement, the devolutions born of Western thought and machinations—which are designed to keep the world's inhabitants ignorant and dependent—would be clear. However, because Western anti-science, anti-human, and anti-life policies, products, and predilections have been mandated and adopted as universal norms, many inhabitants of the modern world will continue to regress and view the world and Cosmos with the wisdom and insight of a Neanderthal. That such myopia and ignorance have suffused nearly all parts of the world is not surprising given that paleogeneticists have determined that "[t]he only modern humans whose ancestors did not interbreed with Neanderthals are apparently sub-Saharan Africans."[41]

Despite deliberate impediments, Western science is coming closer to understanding and harnessing the technologies effortlessly mastered by the Ancients. In 1997, scientists at the High Field Magnet Laboratory of Radboud University of Nijmegen in the Netherlands "levitated a small frog over a very powerful superconducting electromagnet. . . [I]t worked because of the diamagnetic properties of water, protein and DNA in the frog's body."[42] In addition to revealing that another group of scientists successfully enacted diamagnetic levitation in 1939, in discussing why they were able to levitate the frog, the researchers at Radboud give an explanation that is remarkably similar to Leedskalnin's elaboration on how to harness magneticity.[43]

In 2010, engineers at Switzerland's Laboratory of Thermodynamics in Emerging Technologies, published their research on how they were able to use acoustic levitation "to make liquid droplets and small solid objects float in the air and merge into each other on command."[44] Rather than bask in adulation, Dimos Poulikakos, engineer and senior author of the study, offered an important observation: "Levitation is an old story. . . . It was really discovered 100 years ago."[45] Although one would need to add several millennia to Poulikakos's century for accuracy, it is important that Poulikakos, and the scientists at the High Field Magnet Laboratory, acknowledge that levitation is not a new technology. From the origins of existence until now, African scientists have been using acoustic resonance to move objects and have been catalyzing the natural diamagnetic properties in flora and fauna, including human beings, to facilitate flight.

American scientists could be leading the Western world in the resuscitation of the technologies of the Ancients if the United States had granted Leedskalnin a patent for his generator. To understand why he was denied a patent one need only imagine a world without capitalism and taxes. Needless to say, a country founded on slavery, genocide, usurpation, and the oppression of the masses for the wealth of a few, could not support the unfettered empowerment that Leedskalnin's technology promised. So Leedskalnin left wisdom seekers a monument of genius, the shell of his generator, and many encoded clues.[46]

Like the magnetic currents that move through all matter and space, wisdom continues its curvilinear journey through space, time, and the human mind. Fess Newton becomes a conduit for the transmission of ancient wisdom in "Broken Field Running" as he joins Sanderson with a "fast-talking explanation of gravity, replete with positive and negative poles. Salt as a conductor. Too much as an inhibitor" ("Broken Field Running," 54).

Newton's argument is in consonance with Leedskalnin's findings and with certain fauna's biological responses to salt. When seabirds ingest too much salt, they excrete it through their nasal glands. Frogs and tadpoles are able to metabolize and excrete salt as necessary. Human beings also have ways of attaining optimal biochemical balance as Somé learns when he prepares to enter the space-time continuum. The Dagara elders make Somé and the other initiates run for hours under the hot Sun before they enter the portal. It could be the case that the initiates are made to excrete excess salt through sweat to ensure the safety and success of their journeys. As Newton seeks to explain, the optimum level of salt facilitates human flight as well as the transformation of the human body into pure energy.

Sanderson and Newton make it clear that it is not salt that keeps Africans from flying but "too much" salt. Granddaddy Sanderson's detailed explication also reveals that the types of salt ingested contribute to the grounding of Africans: "I was saying that we could fly, but we got messed around with all that salt. Salt treks, salt trails, all those mother's tears, all those bones bleaching in the briny deep, all that sweat. Digging in the earth we became the salt of the earth. Couldn't pay us a salt, so they paid us a salary. Same thing. Too much salt—" ("Broken Field Running," 54). Sanderson's ability to connect Gods with ancestors with salt and Africana technology places him within the continuum of African philosophers.

Sanderson also exhibits his knowledge of etymology with an analysis of the roles that salt and capitalism play in stymieing the contemporary Africana community. Salary has its root in the Latin *sal* which means salt. The salt of the Earth sweating into the earth and being paid literally in kind (sal, salary, salt) is a cycle of destruction, a masterful manipulation. In using the mineral elements of the self to destroy the Self, the toxicity of capitalism to spiritual, technological, and cosmic elevation becomes apparent.

Sanderson expands his elegant elucidation and further articulates the profound impact that salt—in its many forms and manifestations—has on Africana peoples and powers:

> The salt trails of a people . . . crisscrossing tracks down the road of history. And sometime they're scooped up like so much dust so we leave no trace. Scooped up to leave a lie in its place. And when you scoop a people's salt tracks up, you can lay em down somewhere else and misdirect the traffic. Or you can plunk down the whole bunch of salt and it be a stumbling block sure. Or you get it all sold back to you. . . . Sure. They scoop em up, distill the stuff to crystals and sell ourselves back to us for seasoning so we can sweat some more. Seasoning. Did you hear me? ("Broken Field Running," 55)

Hurston describes High John the Conqueror as treading "sweat-flavored clods" as he strides from plantation to plantation fomenting liberation. Sanderson's exposition reveals that the salt that crumbled under High John's feet, the salt that Africana people have invested in America—the collective toil, tears, stress, blood, and struggle poured by force and by choice from 1526 until today into a land with an unslakable thirst for oppression—serves one primary purpose: to derail, detour, and divest Africana people from and of their divinity. Sanderson offers a final assessment that reflects the African American paradox: "We salt eaters" ("Broken Field Running," 56).

The Caucasian oppressors' manipulation of salt has been so confusing, corrupting, and lethal to Africana people that the only equivalent of such destruction can be found in the ocean. Following Sanderson's pronouncement, Miz Surrentine sings, "I know why the Ethiopic is so salty, Lawd" ("Broken Field Running," 56). The Ethiopic Ocean is salty because of the millions of Africans who sway in its watery bosom. In "Little Salt Won't Kill Yuh," Meredith Gadsby reveals one source of the Ethiopic Ocean's salt and soul:

> Perhaps the first incidence of sucking salt in the collective Black diasporic experience occurred on the Middle Passage, among

enslaved Africans, men and women, who chose the salt rather than to endure bondage in a foreign land. Some also chose to throw their children overboard for the same reason. In this case, salt sustains/preserves the spirit against degradation.[47]

The original revolutionary act of sucking salt that Gadsby describes devolved into the most monumental tragedy in world history, as the number of Africans who entered the Ethiopic Ocean—both of their own volition and thanks to the ruthlessness of their enslavers—is far larger than those who survived the Middle Passage. Indeed, oppressors packed Africans into vessels of horror in such a way that profits would be maximized and innumerable deaths would be inevitable.

The elders of "Broken Field Running" invoke the Africans who give even deeper significance to the name "Ethiopic Ocean":

> "They sleep in the deep, sated with salt."
> "How many you suspect? How many?" the call.
> "Many thousands gone," the reply. "Many thousands gone."
> ("Broken Field Running," 56)

The elders undertake a deft revision of Ezekiel's dry bones vision by exchanging parable with reality. The bones of the ancestors bleaching in the briny deep comprise the foundation of an ancient and organic regeneration process. Those submerged ancestors awaken when summoned and stroll from the waters into life and literature. They speak to and through Herald Loomis, Bynum, and Stokes. They become an Ark upon which sails the literary mastery of Henry Dumas. They become a City erected by the charged ink of August Wilson. Those forgotten ancestors, always waiting and ever-ready for their invocation, once remembered, become re-membered to the perfectly preserved eternally resurrecting continuum.

While Sanderson's conclusion, "We salt eaters," is far from celebratory and in this context it signifies a misled, confused, unhealthy people who have been misdirected from their destiny, Sanderson is aware that the technology of flight is as well preserved as the àṣẹ of the ancestors. This technology is part of Africana history and divinity, and, according to Sanderson, this technology awaits purposeful application and activation: "All I'm saying is we got grounded. Ain't been measuring our wingspan too much lately, as you'll notice. But we sure as hell got to rise above this here mess. We got to fly" ("Broken Field Running," 54–55). Sanderson makes it clear that it is imperative for Africans to claim their birthright and obtain and maintain the optimum biological, chemical, and spiritual balance necessary for holistic elevation and evolution.

Lacey returns from her epiphanic rememory to a freezing present with few rewards. The revolution that warrior-activists have worked to manifest "in our lifetime" remains elusive, and Lacey is beginning to lose hope. She muses: "Children waiting to grow up, spread out, leap forward, soar. When? All the babies on the way. When? Ancestors bleaching in the deep. When? Conditions been ripe. When?" ("Broken Field Running," 66). Lacey is suffering the initial stages of the post-traumatic stress disorder that incapacitates Velma Henry in Bambara's aptly titled novel *The Salt Eaters*.

Velma Henry has dedicated her life to the struggle for equality, liberation, and elevation; however, decades of stress and feelings of impotence before the hydra that is American oppression lead Velma to abandon the battle for freedom and seek personal peace instead: "So she would be light. Would go back to her beginnings in the stars and be starlight, over and done with" (*The Salt Eaters*, 19). That Bambara's knowledge of her own and this Earth's origin is identical to the wisdom of Kemite, Nubian, Dogon, Igbo, Dagara, and Yoruba cosmologists is evident in Velma's acknowledgement of her Source. But Velma cannot, at this time, rejoin Nwt and embed herself in the warmth of the galactic womb. The name Velma means "Protector," and Velma is the protective soul and unifying force of her community. The contributions she will make in Claybourne will have global repercussions; consequently, for Velma to choose personal gratification over the struggle for community elevation is not only selfish, it is also a breach of the cosmic laws of reciprocity and responsibility.

In the Caribbean, Velma Henry's conundrum would be understood as a salt-born paradox. Meredith Gadsby finds that the expression "sucking salt" has both a conventional meaning of suffering hardship and an encoded political meaning that signifies a "preparedness to persevere and fight."[48] Velma Henry stands at the crossroads of these definitions as she has sucked so much salt (endured so much hardship) as a general on the frontlines of the liberation battle that she has decided to stop "sucking salt"—she has lost the will to fight. Having slit her wrists and stuck her head in a gas oven, Velma appears to have entered the last stages of salt deficiency syndrome.

The novel is centered on a healing session in which the goal is to persuade Velma to eat salt, regain her spiritual-biochemical balance, and continue the liberation struggle. Velma is so salt deprived that she is nearly floating over the stool on which she sits in the Southwest Community Infirmary. Throughout the healing session she flies off astrally and sails through windows and crashes into tabby walls as she journeys into her past to revisit the freedom marches, rallies, and showdowns with showbiz politicians and brothers with god complexes who revel in their own glory but refuse the burden of divine responsibilities.

Velma's guide to recovery is wisdom keeper Minnie Ransom, who is assisted by her spirit guide, Old Wife. The trio is encircled by a collective of twelve elders called the Master's Mind, who is surrounded by a seeking, curious, skeptical, prayerful community. Throughout the healing session, Minnie Ransom probes Velma with variations of the following query: "Are you sure, sweetheart, that you want to be well?" "Cause wholeness is no trifling matter. A lot of weight when you're well" (*The Salt Eaters* 3, 10).

Ransom's inquiries and assertions are significant because if Velma is as sick as 85% of the populace, she can enjoy the oblivion of being what the Five Percent refer to as "deaf, dumb, and blind," which is the equivalent of being socially dead. If Velma chooses wellness, she is choosing to fully manifest her destiny as a poor righteous teacher, and she is obligated to invest her entire being in the struggle for the liberation and elevation of her people: This is the weight to which Ransom refers, and it is a weight only the Gods can bear.

While Velma floats and flounders with salt deficiency, her husband Obie has the opposite problem. He is suffering from over-consumption of salt, and he is so physically and spiritually bloated that he is on the verge of disintegration. Ahiro, the Japanese masseuse, diagnoses Obie's condition and prescribes

> A good cry man. Good for the eyes, the sinuses, the heart. The body needs to throw off its excess salt for balance. Too little salt and wounds can't heal. Remember Napoleon's army? Those frogs were dropping dead from scratches because their bodies were deprived of salt. But too much— (*The Salt Eaters*, 164)

Ahiro concludes his assessment with a pantomime of the flow of life struck down in hypertensive agony. Obie does not engage in a soul-balancing cry in the course of the novel, and his unhealthy, draining, counterrevolutionary concept of "love" constitutes both an annoyance and an additional problem for an overwhelmed Velma. While he recognizes that Velma is the unifier of the community and that it would take at least eight women to replace her, Obie has no idea how to be an effective complement for such a force.

While Velma seeks to permanently rejoin the stars and Obie staggers about leaving salt crystals in his wake, their son Jabari possesses the chemical and spiritual balance that they lack. Campbell, the self-effacing waiter whose independent study of physics leads him to the realization that the Serpent God Damballah is the first law of thermodynamics, watches as Jabari strains to propel his bike up a hill: "It looked as though any minute the boy's jeans would tear, his shirt rip, his clothes pop off and fly up like the kites the kids were writing notes to God on and releasing on the day before festival" (*The Salt Eaters*, 174). Jabari is his own thermodynamic reservoir of power; he, himself, is a letter to and from the Gods.

In his essay, "The Burden of Liberty: Choice in Toni Morrison's *Jazz* and Toni Cade Bambara's *The Salt Eaters*," Derek Alwes makes an interesting assertion: "For Bambara, there are only two choices available in any consideration—the right one and the wrong one—and the right one always involves subordinating individual freedom to the needs of the larger community."[49] Alwes' claim is validated by both Sophie Haywood, who is disgusted with her goddaughter Velma for undertaking such a retrogressive act as attempting suicide, and Jabari, for even if his garments are ripped from his body and fly as freely as butterflies, *he* will not fly away: Jabari will remain a grounded community intermediary who translates for the masses the ciphers of the Divine. In the context of *The Salt Eaters*, Alwes is correct: The "right" choice is to eat salt, remain grounded, and continue the work of collective liberation until *everyone* can rise and shine. This is the decision that Velma must make. This is the decision that Bambara writes to move her audience to make. Acting as a literary Mother Seal, Bambara enjoins her intended audience to *be* salt eaters—and remain catalyzing, committed, eternal forces of elevation and evolution.

Although Alwes sees Bambara's directive as one that seeks to "falsify and betray the possibilities available to us,"[50] he has overlooked the butterslick complexity and multiplicity of Doc Serge, who is pimp, hustler, hospital administrator, "Sweet Bear," and philosopher. Serge is not limited to any one occupation or designation because he is the owner and master of all destinies, and the depth and breadth of his identity is born of his divinity, as his sermon-on-the-self reveals:

> "I am one beautiful and powerful son of a bitch," he told himself. "Smart as a whip, respected, prosperous, beloved and valuable. I have the right to be healthy, happy and rich, for I am the baddest player in this arena or any other. I love myself more than I love money and pretty women and fine clothes. I love myself more than I love neat gardens and healthy babies and a good gospel choir. I love myself as I love The Law. I love myself in error and in correctness, waking or sleeping, sneezing, tipsy, or fabulously brilliant. I love myself doing the books or sitting down to a good game of poker. I

love myself making love expertly, or tenderly and shyly, or clumsily and inept. I love myself as I love The Master's Mind," he continued his litany, having long ago stumbled upon the prime principle as a player—that *self-love produces the gods and the gods are genius*. (*The Salt Eaters*, 137, emphasis added)

Sula drops the knowledge that "[n]othing in this world loves a black man more than another black man,"[51] and Serge provides a rich affirmation of this, for he loves his Selves to the fullest. Serge's self-love does more than bolster his ego; it is a divine catalyst that reciprocally charges and is charged by his biochemical balance. Serge is so together he can fly, but, like Jabari, he would not fly away because he is a testament to the power and bliss that come from embracing divinity's dynamism along with its profound responsibilities.

Doing the Impossible with Ease

Expressions and applications of divinity are as diverse as their wielders. There are many methods of human flight, and the political, spiritual, cosmological, and cultural consequences and repercussions of flight are equally multitudinous. The African worldview is holistic, and just as certain persons must remain grounded in and assist in the liberation and elevation of their communities, so too are there persons whose responsibilities include using their technological and spiritual abilities to literally rise above oppressive forces and liberate both themselves and the horizons of others via the spectacle of human flight. Toni Morrison's *Song of Solomon* explores the divergence and convergence of these two imperatives through Guitar, who is the ultimate community activist, and Milkman, who is descended from the ascendant Flying Africans. Through Milkman and Guitar and Shalimar and Jake, Morrison elucidates the complementary revolutionary praxes of both those who can fly and those who are earthbound.

Macon Dead the III, affectionately known as Milkman, and Guitar Bains have a relationship similar to that of Forty-seven and Tall John in that they are beyond brothers. Milkman is the younger of the pair, and, as his name intimates, he is spoiled and pampered. His name is symbolic of the crossroads he will straddle for years because Milkman is a grown man whose maturity is delayed due to a decadence born of wealth. Guitar is the wizened elder, protector, and educator of the pair who acts as brother, teacher, and life-guide for his friend and who serves as Milkman's gateway to family, consciousness, and manhood.

One of the most significant acts that Guitar undertakes is introducing Milkman to his relatives, and the relationships that Milkman develops with his cousin Hagar and aunt Pilate are some of the most powerful and complex in literature. Because of the nature of the bond he shares with Milkman, Guitar also develops connections with Pilate and Hagar that are as compelling as they are complex. For example, when Milkman psychologically destroys Hagar and leaves her hollow eyed and empty hearted, it is Guitar who gathers the pieces of the woman and places them in the arms of her mothers.

Guitar offers the reader a prismatic portrait of masculinity that is drawn by equal portions of circumstance and choice: With the horrific death of his father, Guitar became a man when he was a child, and as a man who takes a vow to have no children, Guitar directs his passions paternally and holistically to individuals in need and through his work as one of the community's seven premier freedom fighters.

While Milkman and Guitar could not be closer brothers, their life trajectories could not differ more. Guitar peaks early and becomes, along with Sethe from *Beloved*, one of the most intense, resolute, and misunderstood characters in literary history. But as Guitar's arc of self-actualization plateaus, Milkman, who coasts in neutral for decades, jets into a trajectory of power that catapults him straight through manhood and into divinity.

The foundation of Milkman's divinity is his earliest known progenitor, Shalimar, the Flying African. Because of Milkman's provenance, it is fitting that Robert Smith's fluttering wings usher him into the world and mark him with their promise. Indeed, the spectacle of velvet rose petals on snow, a praisesong wrapped in a quilt, and an African draped in blue silk is so dazzling that even the Caucasian characters associate this confluence of power with Africana Divinity and the influence of Father Divine.[52] The power of human flight marks Milkman both *in vitro* and well over a century before his conception: That power's promise is his Orí, his Divine Guide, and it is his orí, his destiny. However, Mr. Smith's apparent lack of success seems to confirm Western theories regarding physics. With his birthright—human flight—seemingly denied him, Milkman reconciles himself to living the life of social death that is signified by his surname and that is endemic of upper-middle-class America.

Milkman's journey through life is marked by indolence, ego-boosting bravado, and bourgeois complaints until he is convinced that stealing a horde of gold from Pilate will impart depth and clarity to his amorphous self. Guitar, whose next assignment with the Seven Days is expensive and calls for him to blow up a church and kill four Caucasian girls in response to the 1963 bombing of the 16th Street Baptist Church in Birmingham, Alabama, is much more eager than the wealthy Milkman to obtain the gold, but Guitar is able to inspire in his friend feelings equal to the task. After conceiving and aborting a series of plans and plots, a frustrated Guitar charges: "You got a life? Live it! Live the motherfuckin life! Live it!" (183).

Milkman receives a thunderbolt of testosterone through his friend's words which create a chemical reaction:

> Milkman's eyes opened wide. He tried hard not to swallow, but *the clarion call in Guitar's voice filled his mouth with salt.* The same salt that lay in the bottom of the sea and in the sweat of a horse's neck. A taste so powerful and necessary that stallions galloped miles and days for it. It was new, it was delicious, *and it was his own.* All the tentativeness, doubt, and inauthenticity that plagued him slithered away without a trace, a sound. (183, emphasis added)

Bynum and Herald of *Joe Turner's Come and Gone* find that the powers necessary to save, cleanse, and deify are resident within their bodies, and the same is the case with Milkman. Guitar's Ọrọ catalyzes Milkman's *internal* salt reserves. The sodium and chloride necessary to galvanize Milkman's electromagnetic field of power are inherent within his being.

In the passage above, Morrison makes the gentlest of references to the salt that bleaches the bones that rest in the briny deep. Later in the novel, when she invokes the smell of ginger from Accra, Ghana, and the curvilinearity of Milkman meeting his grandfather Jake and obtaining his inheritance from Shalimar (aka Solomon), it is clear that Bones People are strolling through the leaves and lives of *Song of Solomon*, just as they do in *The Salt Eaters*. *Song of Solomon's* most obvious Bones Person is Pilate; she is the glue who binds all seemingly disparate textual entities. Other Bones People are Shalimar, who signifies the destiny that Milkman will embrace, and Jake, the novel's key guide and trickster.

In a most understated way, Jake encapsulates the brilliance, tragedy, and triumph of Africana spiritual and physical existential technology. Jake flies three times in *Song of Solomon*, and each flight has a different catalyst and methodology. Jake's first flight is at the beginning of his life when Shalimar, his Flying African father, tries to take his infant son with him when he flies home to Africa. Had Shalimar not dropped Jake, *Song of Solomon* would be a very different novel. When Jake falls to the ground his life path takes him from Shalimar, Virginia to Danville, Pennsylvania. Jake also takes a name that is the product of a drunken Caucasian clerk, and he turns complete inconsideration into high praise: Jake becomes "Macon Dead, the magnificent," a man who can create a home of abundance from a wilderness. Racist, jealous, cowardly, lazy Caucasians seeking to reap what Jake has sown shoot him, and Jake flies "five feet into the air." After guiding his grandson to Shalimar (both the man and the land), Jake undertakes his third flight at the end of the novel as a bird who unites his Ba with the Ba of Pilate (336).

In addition to offering the reader literal and figurative forms of flight to ponder, Jake, Pilate, and Shalimar force Morrison's audience to acknowledge that immortality, not death, is the norm in the Africana ethos. Pilate is steadfast in her assertion that her father is alive, not only because Jake defies the cliché of being "dead and buried" by routinely visiting and guiding Pilate after he is shot, but also because Pilate literally heralds Jake as the Eternal Immortal that he is. In addition to her conscious acts of remembering her father, Pilate unknowingly ensures Jake's destiny and immortality when she enfolds his skeleton in the grass green sack and takes him everywhere she goes. With no idea of the trinity she is consecrating, Pilate creates of her father a nation sack to the nth degree by stationing him in a position of ascendant supremacy in her home. When Milkman robs Pilate of her nation sack, he inadvertently releases Jake's spirit. The irony of meeting his grandson through theft leads Jake to sigh and then station himself behind Guitar so that he can bear witness to the revelations that unfold alongside the folly and also lead his progeny to the threshold of divinity (186).

Jake provides ample evidence of his immortality; and by doing so, he makes a mockery of his given\taken name, "Dead." Macon Dead is at one with the "dead" speaker of the ancient Kemetic Coffin Text[53] and Malidoma Somé's grandfather, Bakhye, who makes it clear that to be "dead" is to experience life without limits. When Bakhye appears to Somé prior to his initiation, Somé is shocked at his grandfather's manner of address and asks, "Grandfather—you speak French?" To which his elder replies, "Of course I do. I'm dead."[54] What the Kemetic utterance does for the soul and what Bakhye does for Somé is what Jake does for Pilate and Milkman: offer divine speech, whisper clues, and provide protection so that destiny and divinity can be fully manifest.

Jake lives not only because his daughter feeds his soul with power but also because he must provide essential assistance to his progeny to ensure continuity. When Milkman arrives in Danville, Pennsylvania, he has no idea how to begin his search for Jake's farm, the Butler home, or the gold, so Macon Dead III unwittingly stops, talks to, and gets assistance from Macon Dead I, also known as Jake (227). With his appearance in Danville, Jake is one of the Bones People who is, to quote Bynum from *Joe Turner's Come and Gone*, "walking around here now. . . . Just like you and me."[55] Milkman does not know that the tall elder with the old fashioned clothes is his progenitor, in fact Milkman is so poorly raised that, similar to Somé when he leaves the seminary,[56] he does not even know how to properly greet his elders. But Jake sends his son forward to the farm, into the cave, and deeper within himself.

References to salt abound in *The Salt Eaters*. There are buildings and walkways made of the African invention called tabby, which is a mixture of crushed oyster shells, lime, water, and ash, that is used to construct buildings that are nearly indestructible. Sophie and her husband Dolphy make tabby; and, as a result, their legs are often adorned with rings of salt. At the beginning of the healing session, Velma ponders "the difference between eating salt as an antidote to snakebite and turning into salt, succumbing to the serpent" (8). It is most telling that, when her healing is nearing completion, Velma wonders, since there are no cows in Claybourne, "What in hell could anybody do with a saltlick in the middle of the LaSalle project anyway" (260). The saltlick that appears to be out of place fits Bambara's objective—it provides the community and its activists with a way to stay balanced, grounded, and dedicated to the struggle for complete liberation.

While salt is liberally sprinkled throughout *The Salt Eaters*, it only flows from or within Milkman three times in *Song of Solomon*. When Guitar issues his charge, Milkman tastes salt and the absurdities begin. When Milkman arrives at the foot of the hill of the cave in Danville, salt water floods into his mouth. He is so excited he can barely contain himself. But there is no gold in the cave. The gold that Milkman seeks is inside of him; it is as intrinsic an aspect of his being as the salt that flows in his blood, semen, and his mouth when the right stimuli are provided. Morrison uses only a soupçon of salt symbolism in her novel, and Granddaddy Sanderson, Fess Newton, and Toni Cade Bambara would concur that Morrison's use of salt fits her objective, which is to galvanize Milkman's power.

Milkman's search for gold moves him closer to the Ethiopic Ocean, further into his history, and deeper into himself. Because he has stretched his boyhood into his thirties and is self-centered, arrogant, and disconnected from and disaffected by his people, Milkman must be initiated into his culture and into his own identity. The initiation begins when, during his search for the gold, he undertakes physical labors that are more rigorous than collecting rents and having sex. But Milkman's consciousness and character, skewed by decades of unearned privilege and wealth, also need molding. While Jake excuses his progeny's lack of etiquette, Fred Garnett is insulted when Milkman offers to pay him for a ride and a soda, and when he arrives in Shalimar, Virginia, Milkman's lack of home training nearly gets him killed. After a bloody brawl, Milkman is so angry that "If he'd had a weapon, he would have slaughtered everybody in sight" (269). The irony is that he is almost killed by and fantasizes about massacring his own blood kin.

Milkman's desire to destroy an entire town because of his own shortcomings and shortsightedness is played out every day in Pan-African nations and Africana neighborhoods as countless Africana people devastate and decimate members of their communities with the same gun and Bible that Caucasian enslavers and colonizers used to enslave and slaughter Africans. The murder rates of such American "Chocolate Cities" as Washington, D.C., New Orleans, Chicago, and Philadelphia (nicknamed "Killadephia"), and the wars that rage with unimaginable ferocity all over the African continent are indicative of the disaster that occurs when a people are misdirected by salt trails and forced to ingest their own salt or the salt of another culture or that of an oppressor's God: Rather than salt being used to preserve culture and power and to facilitate perseverance in the fight against oppression, misdirection leads the salt of the Earth to love their enemies and massacre themselves.

W. D. Fard made the important observation that 85% of the world is easily led in the wrong direction and difficult to lead in the right direction. The veracity of Fard's assertion is evident in the majority of rap songs that enjoy heavy rotation in commercial media, as many of them revel in murder. Most relevant to this chapter and book, in "Tha Heat," which was recorded in 2004, Lil Wayne chants, "I shoot your arm leg leg arm head."[57] With these lyrics, Lil Wayne not only rejects being civilized and embracing the God in himself, but he also threatens to annihilate Gods. He is oblivious to the fact that by destroying the Allah in another he is obliterating his own divine potential. With his lyrics, Lil Wayne effectively puts Milkman's sentiments about his Virginia kin to a pistol-popping soul-killing beat. Lil Wayne is not alone: 85% of the rap produced the 21st century stands of evidence of the fact that the number of political activists, healers, and spiritually aligned wisdom workers is at an all-time low.

The job of loving, protecting, defending, and preparing one's people is easily the most dangerous, thankless, and important of vocations. As is apparent in the work of the Seven Days of *Song of Solomon* and the activists of *The Salt Eaters*, holistic love is not a game. Malidoma Somé states that human beings would not be able to function if they experienced the ever-climactic tidal wave that is holistic love. Some people are blessed to experience such ecstasy for short time, as does Somé. But most human beings never experience anything more than the West's "sham polish" show of romance, to borrow a phrase from Hurston, beneath which there is nothing. What is more, some people find themselves trapped in a "graveyard love." While Morrison highlights this early 20th century blues expression in *Song of Solomon* and imbues it with political dynamism in *Beloved*, John McCluskey may be the first writer to introduce the term to the literary world. In *Look What They Done to My Song*, Swine defines "graveyard love" in the simplest of terms: "She'd rather see me in the graveyard than with another woman."[58]

One might hypothesize that some Africana people have developed graveyard loves for their own people for they would rather see a brother or sister spiritually or physically dead than shining, building, creating, or flying. Then there are others—the Robert Smiths, the Henry Porters, the Sethes, the Pilates, the Guitars, and the Seven Days—who know that we are sublime and who refuse to see us lynched, beaten, raped, incarcerated, seasoned, burned alive, demoralized, or demonized. So many warriors— Angela Davis, Toni Cade Bambara, Marcus Garvey, Fela Anikulapo Kuti, Toni Morrison, El Hajj Malik El Shabazz, Patrice Lumumba, Assata Shakur, Zora Neale Hurston, W. E. B. Du Bois, Ayi Kwei Armah, Thomas Sankara, Ngugi wa Thiongo, George Iwilade, and so many more—have given and are giving their lives to Africana glory.

Living a life guided by a full, unfettered, and decidedly political love, especially when it is not appreciated or reciprocated, can be devastating. Velma grows so distraught that she attempts to return to the stars long before her time. Robert Smith, who is a member of *Song of Solomon's* Seven Days, buckles under the weight of loving his people and begins selecting the perfect shade of blue silk. Henry Porter, also a member of the Seven Days, urinates, weeps, and begs for a woman in his attempt to ease the weight of the responsibility of saving and preserving the salt of the Earth:

> Tears streamed down his face and he cradled the barrel of the shotgun in his arms as though it were the woman he had been begging for, searching for, all his life. "Gimme hate, Lord," he whimpered. "I'll take hate any day. But don't give me love. I can't take no more love, Lord. I can't carry it. Just like Mr. Smith. He couldn't carry it. It's too heavy. Jesus, *you* know. You know all about it. Ain't it heavy? Jesus? Ain't love heavy? Don't you see, Lord? Your own son couldn't carry it. If it killed Him, what You think it's gonna do to me? Hun? Hun?" (26)

The dilemma of the Gods is clear in this passage: Porter has embraced his responsibility, as a God should, and he finds the weight of love to be as all-consuming, mind-blowing, and heavy as the love Somé experiences with the green lady. While Porter cries out for help, because he is a God, he will have to answer his own prayer. And he does: after a stabilizing cry, he slips into the sleep of the innocent. Years later, after he wakes up to a woman's love, he releases more salt in his semen-rich efforts to bond with First Corinthians. Porter finds a love that is lighter and more manageable than the weighty love, generations deep, that revolution and resistance offer him.

> *Yes*
> *Warriors need rest too*
> *and sometimes*
> *the poetry of tender kisses on the jaw*

Guitar, with his horizon-wide shoulders, lives a solitary life filled with purpose, meaning, and a single-minded devotion to his people. The intensity of Guitar's passion is reflected in his vision which eventually narrows to the point that he becomes convinced that Milkman has betrayed him. Guitar vows to run Milkman "as long as there is ground" (297), which means he chooses to stop determining his own destiny in hopes of destroying Milkman's. Guitar develops a graveyard love for his brother, and, like Hagar before him, he makes Milkman's life and death his personal (pre)occupation.

While Guitar is deviating from divinity, Milkman is being introduced to it. Milkman joins a hunting party in Shalimar and finds he is unable to keep up with men twenty years his senior. While resting against a sweet gum tree Milkman undertakes self-analysis and admits that he is selfish, inconsiderate, and shallow. This honest evaluation helps him begin to comprehend how a male becomes a man, and it opens him up in other ways. In addition to better understanding himself, masculinity, and humanity, Milkman forges relationships with the Earth and flora and fauna. Milkman begins to comprehend what Africana Ancients and elders know: Multitudinous visible and invisible entities on this Earth and beyond it are touching us, communicating with us, challenging us, and impacting our lives. After initiating himself into the Earth as a son of the soil, Milkman engages in a conversation with a tree who is yet another manifestation of Jake: "Down either side of his thighs he felt the sweet gum's surface roots cradling him like the rough but maternal hands of a grandfather. Feeling both tense and relaxed, he sank his fingers into the grass. He tried to listen with his fingertips, to hear what, if anything, the earth had to say" (279). With Jake and Onílè, the Mother of the Earth, guiding him, Milkman is able to save his life by surrendering to Life and reveling in a holistic love for everything, even the Africana men who seek to kill him (278).

Following the hunt, Milkman is not only welcomed by and humbled before his kin in Shalimar, but he also emerges, like Malidoma Somé, as an initiate who knows true power because he has surrendered to it. Rather than writhing with ennui or submitting to the urges of his penis, Milkman strolls the earth with the confidence and direction of a Sun of Man. Confirmation of Milkman's successful initiation into manhood is evident in his cooking, scrubbing, cleaning, and loving alongside Sweet. His revelations continue as he acknowledges the lives he has narrowed and ruined. But even painful admissions add dimension to his awakening consciousness and knowledge of self, for Milkman's relationship with Hagar echoes Shalimar's union with Ryna. The more Milkman learns about himself, the more his unformed identity attains cohesion; eventually, he finds his face to mirror that of his earliest known progenitor, Shalimar, a man so brilliant that he has the eternal admiration of every citizen in his eponymous town. Shalimar's flight is the quintessential juba, for his glorious ascension and deification could not have occurred unless he left everybody behind, including and especially Jake, to celebrate, lament, mourn, and exalt.

When Milkman hears Shalimar's history in song and implants that information into his being, the chemical reaction that the Bachwezi, Herald Loomis, and Nianankoro experience begins in Milkman. His soul expands from the core of his being; it envelops his skin and celebrates its host's revelation. The internal shining of what Morrison calls the "ancient properties" begins to grow and glow in Milkman: "He ran back to Solomon's store and caught a glimpse of himself in the plate-glass window. He was grinning. His eyes were shining. He was as eager and happy as he had ever been in his life" (304). Milkman is no longer fragmented and unfinished. Not only is he whole, complete, and perfect, but his divinity is surging forth.

Morrison shows numinosity's range through Milkman and Pilate. Milkman, who has an abundance of material things, must surrender them all in order to come into full possession of a divinity that grants him everything. Pilate, who appears to have nothing, is rich with the jewels of a poor righteous teacher, not unlike Bynum Walker, Bakhye, and traditional dibia, babaláwo, and iyaláwo. As further evidence of the understanding and interconnectedness of the Gods, after Guitar shoots her, Pilate expresses a sentiment that only a member of the Seven Days can truly appreciate: "I wish I'd a known more people. I would of loved 'em all. If I'd a knowed more, I would a loved more" (336). Even when headed for the next life, Pilate remains focused on offering yet more love and completely spending herself in service to her community. Although she boasts no empowering sermon-to-the-self, Pilate evinces the same enduring numinescence as Doc Serge. Also like Serge, Pilate gives the gifts of self-love, correction, direction, Godliness, and genius to all who come in her path. As further proof that there is no death, the end of Pilate's human existence results in the release of her Ba which joins that of her father in flight.

By having Pilate echo the Seven Days' philosophy, Morrison reminds her audience of the inherent interdependence and interconnectedness of these seemingly disparate characters and their callings. While it is easy to label Guitar a villain, he is not. He is Milkman's ẹnikejì, and he is essential to Milkman's evolution. Guitar is the catalyst who ensures the divinity and immortality of the Deads. Without Guitar's charge, Milkman would not have tasted the salt of potential and possibilities. If Guitar had not shot Pilate, the only woman Milkman truly loves, Milkman would not have the impetus to fly. Indeed, one of the most magnificent and significant things about Milkman's flight is that his friend, brother, and twin is there to witness it. Guitar, as his name makes wondrously clear, is both instrumental to Milkman's rapture and he is the instrument upon which the Song of Solomon is played. Milkman's destiny, flight, and life are linked with Guitar's like sodium bonds with chloride.

During his initiation, Somé had to sweat out excess salt before entering the portal to the spiritual realm; Milkman releases excess salt by crying just before he flies. This is the third occasion during which salt flows within or out of Milkman in *Song of Solomon*, and these tears, the first Milkman sheds since infancy, provide him with the spiritual balance necessary to begin the transformation into light. Some power wielders combine flora and fauna and words of power to fly. Others need only tap into the Self to access power: Milkman, boasting what Brother J would call "Godly genes," is one of the latter.[59]

When he flies, Milkman is "bright as a lodestar" (337), and he is indistinguishable from the Dagara initiate returning from the spiritual realm and the Igbo dibia transforming into light via ekili. With his flight, Milkman becomes one with the Divine and Shining. He becomes the Yoruba God, Odùduwà, who is a star shooting across the sky. Milkman is Sirius B, the Dogon's "Dark Star," giving birth to the Earth. He is High John the Conqueror taking wing. He is the BaKongo prenda of seven stars entering the pot of continuity. Milkman is the Truth.

. . .

Bambara and Morrison offer their audiences two related but distinct explorations of Africana divinity, human flight, and the spiritual-chemical utilization of salt. In some respects the political and social directives of Morrison and Bambara mirror those of Milkman and Guitar at their most evolved. While some might wish to polarize these perspectives, it is important to note that each writer is holding a mirror up to a multifaceted collective Self: One mirror reflects Gods using communality, activism, and dedication to transform humanity and destroy the inhumane; the other reflects the complex journey from mundane humanity to manifest Divinity. But it is not necessary for the audience to choose one self to develop or one reflection to admire. The manifestations and applications of African spiritual technologies and methodologies are infinite and provide the Africana community with endless options for expansion. One can be a jetsetter giving and taking healing tools to and from material and spiritual realms like Malidoma Somé. One can be as divine as Sun Ra, as multifaceted as Doc Serge, or as devoted as Guitar. One can become as humble before one's own divinity as Milkman.

Perhaps the most important issue to acknowledge when reading their works is the reason that Morrison and Bambara, two of the world's most important literary talents, dedicated some of their deepest art to numinosity and the phenomenon of human flight: They know the power of their ink; they know the powers in their audience.

CHAPTER SEVEN

**Warriors, Writers, Revolutionaries:
Africana Secret Societies and Spiritual-Political
Imperatives in the Literature of Ayi Kwei Armah,
Toni Morrison, Ishmael Reed, and Ngugi wa Thiong'o**

> ". . . [B]ehind all political and cultural warfare
> lies a struggle between secret societies."
> ~ Ishmael Reed, *Mumbo Jumbo*
>
> "Fuckin' with G-O-D can be a deadly game."
> ~ Mood featuring Sunz of Man,
> "Illuminated Sunlight"

Toni Cade Bambara reveals that the novel *The Salt Eaters* was born of an important observation:

> I was trying to figure out as a community worker why political folk were so distant from the spiritual community—clairvoyants, mediums, those kind of folks, whom I was always studying with. I wondered what would happen if we could bring them together as Bookman brought them together under Toussaint, as Nan brought them together in Jamaica. Why is there that gap? Why don't we have a bridge language so that clairvoyants can talk to revolutionaries?[1]

The divide that Bambara describes and spent her life bridging is the result of Africana peoples succumbing to the Western desire to bifurcate, compartmentalize, and, most of all, discredit African spiritual technologies which are inherently political and have always facilitated revolutionary goals.

The African worldview is holistic: The spiritual, the cosmological, the political, the medicinal, the metaphysical, the scientific, and the physical are one. However, with physical and mental slavery colonization and neocolonialism, and imperialism, indoctrination, and globalization deployed to prevent Pan-African uprisings and African unity, many Africana movements and institutions were crushed. While it is the case that numerous Africana organizations remain compartmentalized, there are spiritual-political revolutionary writers and warriors and writer-warriors who catalyze and coalesce the holistic weaponry of the Ancients with contemporary needs, objectives, and agendas. Those writers and revolutionary works are the focus of the chapter.

This analysis begins with two of Ayi Kwei Armah's masterworks: *Two Thousand Seasons* and *Osiris Rising*. *Two Thousand Seasons* is rooted in the ancient and original African ethos and worldview that is simply and logically referred to as "the way." The historical novel depicts the monumental conflicts that arise when those who adhere to the way and manifest holism, reciprocity, and balance encounter peoples whose worldviews are rooted in usurpation, destruction, and depravity. A logical and elegant outgrowth of and complement to the way is defined in *Osiris Rising* as the companionship of the ankh. The companionship is a secret and sacred society devoted to the protection and elevation of Africana life; and, in addition to its similarities with Kemetic, Yoruba, and Akan sacred institutions, the society of the ankh has many literary siblings. Two of the ankh's sister societies in African America that I analyze are the Seven Days, which is the secret society featured in Toni Morrison's *Song of Solomon*, and Jes Grew, which is the signifying force of Ishmael Reed's *Mumbo Jumbo*, a labyrinthine historical novel that offers an encyclopedic elucidation of the ancient and curvilinear struggles between African sacred societies and Divinities and Judeo-Christian instruments of destruction.

It is often the case that the Africana people who extol their divinity most exuberantly are ten percenters. For example, the notorious Joseph-Désiré Mobutu, who ruled the Democratic Republic of Congo (formerly Zaïre) from 1960 to 1997, commemorated his rise to power in 1972 by changing his name to Mobutu Sese Seko Nkuku Ngbendu Wa Za Banga, which means "The all-powerful warrior who, because of his endurance and inflexible will to win, goes from conquest to conquest, leaving fire in his wake."[2] That title was insufficient: Mobutu was also known as "Savior of the People" and "Supreme Combatant."[3] Rulers like Mobutu come to epitomize antidivinity for many.

Ngugi wa Thiong'o calls out political demigods and their sycophants in his satirical masterpieces *Matigari* and *Wizard of the Crow*. Both novels follow the struggles of revolutionary-spiritualist warriors, or grassroots Gods, who embrace the ancient, holistic, spiritual-political revolutionary principles of African sacred and secret societies because these organizations' understated power, flexibility, and capacity for evolution make them the perfect apparatuses for fighting an international conglomeration of ever-morphing foes.

The Only Way

Ayi Kwei Armah's *Two Thousand Seasons* (*Seasons*) reveals the depth, breadth, complexities, and resolve that form the foundation of the African warrior consciousness. While *Seasons* is a novel, it is rooted in three powerful sources. *Seasons* offers the reader a literary exploration of the extensive research of Senegalese historian Cheikh Anta Diop, specifically his book *The Cultural Unity of Black Africa: The Domains of Patriarchy and of Matriarchy in Classical Antiquity*, which examines the matrilineal structure of traditional African societies and their holistic and gender-balanced ethos. Another source that informs *Seasons'* artistic milieu and political consciousness is Anoa, the ancient Divine Mother of the Akan people who acts as revolutionary muse for the author and moral compass for the characters. The third influential force is the power of history.

Seasons recounts an ancient migration of African people from the eastern region of the Continent, across a fertile land that eventually desiccated and became the Sahara, to Africa's western coast. The community settles in a lush land that they name Anoa out of respect to their guiding God. Anoa could be any number of African nations, and to emphasize the fact of African unity, Armah uses Akan, Wolof, Igbo, Yoruba, Hausa, Xosha, Kikuyu, and Zulu names and words throughout the narrative. Armah also stresses the importance of communality in *Seasons*. The narrator, for example, is simply a member of the community, the collective. The name, age, gender, and lineage of the narrator are not given so that the audience can focus on the power, politics, betrayals, and liberations that impact the whole.

The whole with which *Seasons'* author and narrator are concerned is not limited to the historical confines of the novel but encompasses the entire Pan-African world at all times. The eternal immediacy of the novel becomes apparent in the Prologue, which constitutes a revolutionary treatise that speaks directly to and warns the Africana listener/reader: "Springwater flowing to the desert, where you flow there is no regeneration. The desert takes. The desert knows no giving. . . . Springwater flowing to the desert, your future is extinction."[4] Armah is making points on both metaphorical and literal levels, for, in the novel, the desert represents Arabs and death. The narrator posits that only an entity accustomed to thievery, devolution, and desiccation can live in an environment where even the land has no sense of reciprocity and only consumes. The narrator goes on to offer a stunning exposition of the Arabs' relationship to the desert:

> The desert was made the desert, turned barren by a people whose spirit is itself the seed of death. Each single one of them is a carrier of destruction. The spirit of their coming together, the purpose of their existence, is the spread of death all over the world. . . . They have wiped the surface barren with their greed. They have dug deep to take what the earth needed for itself to stay fertile earth. They have taken everything within their reach, things that made the earth good, and they have put nothing back but hard, dead things in place of life destroyed. (*Seasons*, 7)

Seasons exists as a timeless interweaving of literary, metaphorical, and literal tragedies, for while *Seasons* was published in 1973, Springwater has continued its headlong rush to its death in the Sahara's burning sands where thousands die every year.

In 2008 Alfred Kofi and a group of friends left Ghana to seek their fortunes in Libya. Arabs set up the young men, robbed them, and left them to die in the desert. Kofi and his countrymen wandered in the Sahara for four days. While Kofi escaped the Sahara, his companions remain in the desert, for each one died of thirst there. Kofi was forced to drink his own urine to survive, and so precious a commodity was it, he could not bear to share it without risking his own life. Kofi's experience forever altered his body, psyche, and soul, making him an unwilling messenger of truth: The spirit of his best friend, whose body is buried in the Sahara's dunes, visits Kofi in his dreams and begs him to tell his parents what happened to their son. Kofi has not yet summoned the courage to reveal the truth.[5]

If Springwater is reduced to drinking its own urine to survive in the desert, what perils would Springwater face when riding salty waves West? *Season's* narrator issues a warning that reveals the gruesome truth behind the glorified concept of Manifest Destiny:

> Hau, people headed after the setting sun, in that direction even the possibility of regeneration is dead. There the devotees of death take life, consume it, exhaust every living thing. Then they move on, forever seeking newer boundaries. Wherever there are living remnants undestroyed, there lies more work for them. Whatever would direct itself after the setting sun, an ashen death lies in wait

for it. . . . a pale extinction awaits them among the destroyers. (*Seasons*, xi)

Kingsley Ofusu knows the West's unquenchable thirst for death. In 1992 he, his brother Albert, and seven other Africans sneaked aboard a ship bound for France. When the Russian crew discovered the stowaways, they killed them—one by one—and tossed their bodies into the sea. Ofusu, the only person fortunate enough to survive, lived to watch his life dramatized in the film *Deadly Voyage*.[6] Despite all he suffered, Ofusu and tens of thousands of other youths continue to risk their lives to seek success in the West.[7] Believing that they will be able to turn a nightmare relationship of epic imbalances into a capitalist's dream of luxury, the majority end up adding more salt, blood, and bones to those of their ancestors already bleaching in the briny deep.

When one considers the international appeal the word "nigger" has gained, the bloody bling that shines on fragmented mortals, and the fact that once-revolutionary forms of art have been hegemonized and co-opted, the following queries asked in *Seasons'* Prologue are more difficult to answer now than they were in 1973:

How have we come to be mere mirrors to annihilation? For whom do we aspire to reflect our people's death? For whose entertainment shall we sing our agony? In what hopes? That the destroyers, aspiring to extinguish us, will suffer conciliatory remorse at the sight of their own fantastic success? The last imbecile to dream such dreams is dead, killed by the saviors of his dreams. (*Seasons*, xiii)

The eternal relevance of Armah's art and the perniciousness of two thousand seasons of concerted genocide are evident in the fact that a new generation is posing Armah's queries to its contemporary audience. African American hip hop group Reflection Eternal introduces their aptly titled song "2000 Seasons" with the proceeding quotation from Armah. While Reflection Eternal's song, like the songs of Killarmy, Sunz of Man, Rakim Allah, Gravediggaz, and other conscious hip hop artists, offer their audiences chastisement, analysis, and solutions, the lurid lure of savagery continues to attract and entrap the masses.

While the lyrics of rappers reach millions and facilitate the Gods' struggles to "civilize the savage[s]," Armah reminds wisdom-workers that many eighty-fivers are not merely deaf, dumb, and blind; they are socially dead and unimaginably dangerous. As it relates to those Zora Neale Hurston would call "slave ships in shoes,"[8] Armah's narrator has this advice:

> Leave them in their graves. Whatever waking form they wear, the stench of death pours ceaseless from their mouths. From every opening of their possessed carcasses comes death's excremental pus. Their soul itself is dead and long since putrefied. Would you have your intercourse with these creatures from the graveyard? Go to them then, and speak your message to long rotted ash. (*Seasons*, xiii)

In the midst of the socially dead, those devoted to destruction, and those left dancing in their chains, are the Africans who have not lost their minds, focus, or knowledge of the way. *Seasons* is written for them:

> You hearers, seers, imaginers, thinkers, rememberers, you prophets called to communicate truths of the living way to a people fascinated unto death, you called to link memory with forelistening, to join the uncountable seasons of our flowing to unknown tomorrows even more numerous, communicators doomed to pass on truths of our origins to a people rushing deathward, grown contemptuous in our ignorance of our source, prejudiced against our own survival, how shall your vocation's utterance be heard? (*Seasons*, xi)

With this charge, the monumental investments and the extraordinary perils of revolutionaries are clear. Loving one's people to life is arduous, dangerous, and shows few immediate rewards. Revolutionaries must communicate truths to the deaf, pump life into the damned. They must find ways to detour and waylay those who have traded the glow of their souls for dime store gewgaws and lead them to the power of their destiny and divinity. Revolutionaries must do what is nearly impossible, and this is why so many are both Divine and often deeply misunderstood.[9]

Chapter one of *Seasons* begins with a simple statement: "We are not a people of yesterday" (*Seasons*, 1). The narrator goes on to establish the fact that the foundations of African existence predate the concept of "ancient." With the narrator's elucidations, the reader becomes aware of the fact that Africans had built and expanded civilizations; charted celestial calendars; harnessed waters; sailed the globe; created medicine, agriculture, philosophy, algebra, mathematics, geometry; and erected pyramids and temples eons before the concepts of Europe or Arabia or their citizens existed.

As it relates to the Caucasians and Arabs who now inhabit some parts of Africa, in "The African World and the Ethnocultural Debate" Wole Soyinka warns his audience against having a "saline consciousness" and assuming that everyone and everything on the African continent (enclosed by the salty seas) is African and that everything beyond its oceanic barriers is not African.[10] Armah concurs with Soyinka, and he makes sure his audience is not fooled by redundant and slyly deprecating talk of "black Africans," unnecessary and divisive designations like "sub-Saharan Africa," and specious arguments that assert that "black Americans are not African": "That we the black people are one people we know. Destroyers will travel long distances in their minds and out to deny you this truth. We do not argue with them, the fools. Let them presume to instruct us about ourselves. That too is in their nature" (*Seasons*, 3).

African unity is as important to the evolution of Africa as the concept of African fragmentation is to the academic neocolonizers who style themselves "Africanists." It is imperative for the latter to replace originators and creators with invaders and colonizers, but Armah's narrator speaks simple truths with clarity: "This land is ours, not through murder, not through theft, not by way of violence or any other trickery. This has always been our land. Here we began. Here we will continue even after death the thousand seasons' scattering and the thousand seasons' groping. . . ." (*Seasons*, 4).

An issue that is central in all of Armah's novels is the fact that the African woman is the foundation of life, the force of existence, and the source of power. *Seasons* carefully details the differences in African matriarchal and patriarchal systems, and it is clear which of the two foments egoism, vanity, and violence. The "time of men" constitutes a tag-team of vicious patriarchs who do anything to obtain and maintain power. The patriarchal era culminates in a "festival of annihilation" in which the men are either killed or they are exhausted by having killed so many (*Seasons*, 9). The women rebuild the community and reinstitute the way, and their era brings fertility, abundance, and prosperity.

During the matriarchal era, a series of prophets utter dire warnings. Two seers foretell flames and carnage. Three more prophets foresee nearly interminable journeys at the end of which is perpetual slavery. Anoa's utterance follows these five. The Anoa are a lineage of divine revolutionary liberators who reincarnate cyclically to guide, prophesy, and avenge. One of the first Anoas

> brought the wrath of the patriarchs on her head. . . by uttering a curse against any man, any woman who would press another human being into her service. This Anoa also cursed the takers of services proffered out of inculcated respect. It was said she was possessed by a spirit hating all servitude, so fierce in its hatred it was known to cause those it possessed to strangle those—so many now—whose joy it was to force the weaker into tools of their pleasure and their laziness, into creatures dependent upon their users. (*Seasons*, 14)

Another Anoa, this one a master hunter, prophesizes two thousand seasons of destruction. She details a catalogue of deaths—physical and spiritual—and the destruction of entire nations. She foresees conflagrations, labor camps, and "bodies driven to exhaustion for no purpose of their own" (*Seasons*, 16). Anoa envisions "souls stranded away from all the waters of the spirit fit to give them life," and she witnesses the horrors of the Middle Passage and those who do not survive the crossing: "That voice told of saltwater washing over thousands upon thousands of our dead" (*Seasons*, 16).

These atrocities are, in part, the result of the way having been forsaken. The way involves living in consonance with the seven Kemetic "keys of human perfectibility": reciprocity, balance, justice, truth, harmony, propriety, and order.[11] The way is rooted in pragmatic agrarian production and equitable trading practices. The way's foundation is what Diop describes as "harmonious dualism" between the sexes. As the narrator reveals, "The way is not the rule of men. The way is never women ruling men. The way is reciprocity. The way is not barrenness. Nor is the way this heedless fecundity. The way is not blind productivity. The way is creation knowing its purpose, wise in the withholding of itself from snares, from destroyers" (*Seasons*, 17). However, instead of insisting on reciprocity, Africans exhibit a "generosity of fools" that gives glories in exchange for garbage. The welcoming of predators and destroyers, the proffering of gifts, the exchange of human beings for baubles, the allocation of land for factories dedicated to the destruction of humanity, and the hopes that Africans would be treated with respect, dignity, and courtesy by peoples unworthy of their consideration are all condemned by Anoa.

The first people to attack the way and the Anoa are Muslim Arab "predators." In direct opposition to the balance manifest in traditional African spiritual systems, Islam is described in *Seasons* as a system of physical and ideological domination built on the cornerstones of racism, slavery, and hypocrisy. Armah's narrator asserts that the centrality of slavery to Islam is evident in the names of the faithful; for example, the name Abdallah is translated in *Seasons* as "slave of a slave-owning god" (*Seasons*, 36). In Arabic, *abd* means "male slave," *abda* means "female slave," and *abeed* means "slaves"; *abdul* means "slave" or "servant." Abdallah literally means "slave to Allah," and Armah's point has even more resonance when one understands that the many Muslim names that begin with "abd" or "abdul"—such as Abdul-Aziz, Abdul-Razak, Abdul-Rahim—signify that their bearers are slaves to and/or servants of various manifestations of Allah (*aziz*, "victorious," *razak*, "sustainer," *rahim*, "all merciful").

By contrast, the Nation of Gods rejects the religion of Islam and embraces the way of life of I.S.L.A.M.: I Self Lord Am Master. The Gods do not take Muslim names because they are not Muslims and cannot submit to any God or religion. The names they adopt—such as Righteous Allah, Justice, Power Infinite Allah—indicate their divinity and equality with any and every Allah or God. When comparing typical Muslim names to Nation of God names, the impact that naming has on identity, way of life, destiny, and divinity is as evident as the Sun.

In addition to analyzing how Muslim names and Islam promote slavery and subjugation, *Seasons'* narrator asserts that certain Arabic linguistic concepts, similar to certain English terms, are rooted in racism and dehumanization: "We [Africans] with our way were all condemned, *our very colour turned into the predators' name for evil*" (*Seasons*, 39, emphasis added). The Arabic word "kaffir," which is translated as "infidel," is widely treated as being synonymous with the word "black" and has been subjected to similar linguistic and cultural devaluations and political manipulations as the word "black." However, "kaffir" has an interesting etymology. The *American Heritage Dictionary of the English Language* reveals that kafir "is the present participle of *kafara*, to deny, be skeptical."[12] The relationship between kafara and kafir reveals how a peoples' logical and intelligent questioning and rejection of an alien worldview and their refusal to negate their sources of self for the dictates of an alien other are perverted by that alien other into a mark of opprobrium that is used to justify genocide under the banners of jihad and holy war.

Similar to the word "kafir," the Arabic word "abd" and its variants (abdul, abda, abeed) are used to signify and, more importantly, conflate the words "slave," "black," and "African." Contemporary African freedom narratives reveal the perniciousness and power that racist linguistic reification continues to enjoy. Francis Bok's ordeal reveals the extremes of linguistic and physical oppression under Islam. While Bok is initiated into slavery with the mocking cry, "*abeed, abeed, abeed*," after his indoctrination appears to be complete, Giemma, Bok's enslaver, decrees that Bok must become a Muslim. Giemma gives Bok the Muslim name "Abdul Rahman," which means "servant of the compassionate one."[13] The compassion of Allah notwithstanding, Bok's new identity is still a signifier of slavery through both the name "Abdul" and actual slavery, as Giemma continues to beat Bok, treat him like an animal, and threaten to amputate his legs if he tries to escape.

By using the resplendence of melanin as the basis of their sociopolitical attacks, Caucasian and Arab oppressors have accomplished three important goals: the justification of the institutionalization and internationalization of African enslavement, exile, raping, and lynching; the disassociation of Africans from African empires, inventions, and achievements; and the misappropriation of Africa's vast mineral, agricultural, and intellectual resources for the fortification of Arab and Caucasian nations and economies. It is most important to acknowledge that Arab and Caucasian enslavers and usurpers did not have to negotiate around their religions to rationalize their treatment of Africans: The religions of Islam Judaism, and Christianity, themselves, justify and facilitate slavery and all of its attendant savageries.

Organized religions have proven themselves to be faithful, flexible, and indispensable allies of enslavers, especially when the persons to be subjugated are Africans. For example, although it is not permissible for a Muslim to enslave another Muslim, when the target of enslavement is an African, the construct of kaffir/black is used to negate religious affiliation. This is apparent with Bok, above, and with Mende Nazer, the Muslim author of *Slave, My True Story*. One of the first things enslaver Rahab does is rename Nazer. She calls her abda, as if that were her name, but the term she most enjoys calling Nazer is *yebit*, which means "girl worthy of no name."[14] After attempting to strip the child of her name and her identity, Rahab attacks Nazer's religious convictions. When she finds Nazer praying, Rahab quips, "Islam isn't for black people like you."[15] Rahab conflates the adjective "black" with inherent slavery and subhumanity; with this logic, Mende's "blackness" prevents her from being considered a "true" Muslim. In actuality, Rahab has a few shades less melanin than Mende; outside of Sudan, both females would be considered "African" or "Black." In the Sudan, Rahab uses Nazer's richer melanin along with Islam to brand Mende as inherently condemned and eternally damned.

As if avenging in-advance the tragedies that would befall Nazer, Bok, and countless other Africans enslaved by Arabs in the 20th and 21st centuries while punishing their own oppressors and defilers, the women of *Seasons*, guided by the Anoa who curses and strangles to death enslavers, find inventive ways to free themselves of the Arabs who are raping and enslaving them. In the novel, Arabs celebrate Eid al-Fitr by gorging themselves on food, alcohol, and drugs. The finale of the festival is an orgy featuring African women. In one of literature's most triumphant passages, the women come prepared for their tormentors. Hussein is stabbed in the spine during his attempt to suck dates from women's vaginas. Faisal and his askari lover are impaled on the same spear while they are having sex. While Hassan has women stimulating his penis, fingers, toes, and tongue, another women sticks a funnel into his anus and pours a mixture of boiling honey and oil into the cavity. Suffice it to say that the women kill their Arab oppressors in ways that the men are best able to appreciate.

The Arab "predators" offer a tutorial in oppression that prepares the Anoa for the European "destroyers." Assisting the destroyers in their mission are African rulers who are labeled "ostentatious cripples." Dazzled by the power wielded by the Caucasians, the patriarchal braintrust of Anoa establishes a system of governance to support their flashy and morally-bankrupt leaders. The egalitarianism of the way is replaced with a patriarchal monarchy, and each king discussed in *Seasons* boasts his own unique degeneracy. The nadir of patriarchal rule is marked with the coronation of Koranche, who arrives at the following conclusion about himself *vis-à-vis* his peers: "These people can walk naked and not be ashamed. . . . they give more than they receive. I, the king, I only know how to take. They are full vessels overflowing. I am empty. In place of a bottom I have a hole" (*Seasons*, 73). The king finds the answer to his problem is not to improve himself and find a way to impart some luster on his genetically and socially determined dullness but to attempt to destroy the members of his community who shine.

Throughout suffering enslavement at the hands of Koranche and his depraved son and then liberating themselves and continuing the war to rid Anoa of its Caucasian destroyers and psychotic African sycophants, the Anoa collective remains a united front dedicated to ensuring the restoration of the way for Africa and Africans.

The war for liberation, unification, and elevation against a multi-national collective of enemies that begins in *Seasons* continues after the book's lyrical coda and finds its way into the leaves of Armah's *Osiris Rising*. Written over two decades after *Seasons* and set approximately three centuries after *Seasons'* conclusion, *Osiris Rising* focuses on a collective of contemporary keepers of the way who use their knowledge of a painful past and confounded present to illuminate the path to an eternally whole and liberated self and society. The society of the ankh is both a formalized elaboration of the way and it is an articulation of the timeless way of life of the Kushites and Kemites and of sacred and secret Pan-African societies, such as the Ògbóni society of the Yoruba.

In Yoruba history and cosmology, Ẹdan is the God of Justice who came to Earth to rid the inhabitants of Ile-Ife of liars, traitors, thieves, and rogues. After Ẹdan successfully cleansed the town, she made all inhabitants—both genders and all ages—swear an oath that included the following statement: "If you are guilty of treachery, you will die / If you steal, you will die / If you are disloyal, you will die."[16] In this way, the entire nation was initiated into Ògbóni and bound by its sacred oaths.

Ògbóni is an institution that "ensures all round fertility, peace, orderliness and concord" by enforcing the elemental laws of the Earth and punishing violators of those laws.[17] Members of Ògbóni are not analogous to police officers or soldiers. Their authority is not predicated on power trips, racism, oppression, or capitalism; it comes from the ultimate authorizing agent: The Mother of All, who is also The Law. Similar to the Akan reverence of Great Mother Anoa, members of Ògbóni confirm that they are all the children of the same mother, and their sacred handshake symbolizes that they nursed at the breast of the same mother.[18] That Mother is the God Ẹdan, who is the daughter of the Great Mother, Onílẹ̀, the Owner of the Earth, who is also known as Ìyá Ayé (literally, Mother of the Earth).

Contentious matters such as land disputes and accusations of theft and murder are all brought before Ògbóni and Òrìṣà Ẹdan. The most important issues that they adjudicate are those that involve the spilling of blood on the Earth, which is an abomination. But whether an infraction is formally brought before Ògbóni or not, Ẹdan is cognizant of it. She is aware of everything that occurs because she is everywhere. Ẹdan is known as Ọmọ Onílẹ̀, which means the Child of the Mother of Earth, and her oríkì is Child Who Is Perfectly Positioned All Over the Earth.[19] Yoruba geology and cosmology reveal that the Earth is sentient, and not only does she feel pain but she also beholds everything. Unlike the allegedly blinded eyes of American justice, Ẹdan's eyes never close. Because her eyes are always open, Ẹdan witnesses every single act. As justice personified, Ẹdan "hastens to pass judgment on people," and she "uses honesty to scatter the possessions of the wicked."[20] She easily disposes of violators because, as the Child of the Mother of the Earth, Ẹdan has abundant space to literally "[swallow] dubious people whole."[21] With Ẹdan's all-seeing eyes, Ìyá Ayé's constantly revolving wheel of reciprocity, and Ògbóni and Àjẹ́ enforcing laws and instituting balance, it is not possible to trespass the laws of Ẹdan and Ìyá Ayé and escape punishment.[22]

Ẹdan and the Ògbóni society ensure quality of life and full self-actualization and deification; they are analogous to both Anoa and the way and to the Kemetic God Maat and her "keys of human perfectibility." That these three Gods and their social instruments are focused exclusively on protecting and enhancing life is evident in their iconography. Ankh is a Kemetic word that means life, and the ankh resembles an anthropomorphic human figure. The penis finding oneness within the vagina and undertaking its role in the work of creation is also symbolized in the ankh. The ankh represents the unification of the male and female, the spiritual and material, the mind and body—which makes it a perfect symbol for *Osiris Rising*.

The cyclic, spiritual, and material rejuvenation that the ankh signifies is also reflected in the brass images of Ẹdan and the *akuaba* fertility dolls of the Akan peoples of Ghana. The akuaba doll, with its disproportionately large head and with its arms perfectly outstretched at 180°, is remarkably similar to the ankh. Òrìṣà Ẹdan of Yoruba cosmology is often depicted as a male and female pair whose heads are connected by a chain. Some representations of Ẹdan, similar to the elegance of the ankh, represent a male and female joined at their backs or one entity who encompasses both genders and all powers. The Ẹdan is the elegant encapsulation of the comprehensive divinity and power of Yoruba law, and her powers are diverse. The linked masculine-feminine icon of Ẹdan can be separated and used to send encoded messages, to energize the human body, and to heal illnesses.[23] But no matter how Ẹdan is employed, what may appear to be a pair—two figures connected by a chain—is one and is heralded as Ìyá: Mother.[24]

The ankh, akuaba, and Ẹdan are such powerful symbols and boast such diverse and essential uses that they have all been carried by human beings and Gods from ancient times to the present. Kemetic Divinities are often depicted holding ankhs, which signifies their guardianship over existence. Akan women who wish to bear children carry akuaba dolls in anticipation of the lives they will nurture one day. In Yoruba nations, members of Ògbóni carry Ẹdan around their necks to signify their relationship to the Great Mother, and they invoke her when swearing oaths, meting justice, and undertaking other serious acts that protect the vitality and ensure the growth of society. The ankh, Ẹdan, and akuaba dolls have similar meanings and fulfill similar purposes, and the Gods represented by these symbols, the human beings who carry them, and the children born of them are one. Because the fact of existence is meaningless without the assurance that one can live a purposeful and empowered life and reach one's full potential, the guardians of existence take their duties very seriously.

The society of the ankh in *Osiris Rising* is dedicated to protecting African life and furthering holistic African values and ethics. The society opposes hierarchical class and caste systems, and, most important, the organization is "a resurrection of an ancient Egyptian sacred society sworn against slavery."[25] By revealing the origin of the companionship of the ankh, Armah arms his readers with a powerful liberatory truth. Because Caucasian pseudo-academic neo-enslavers and their African running dogs have created and strive to maintain a mythical "Africa" in which African women conveniently gave birth to "slaves" instead of human beings (as if African parents thought no more of their progeny than enslavers did) and in which "Africans" casually and conveniently "sold Africans," it is difficult for many people to conceive of Africans fighting against slavery. However, innumerable Africans dedicated their lives to not only the abolition of the institution but to the necessary obliteration the enslavers.

The Anoa and the companionship of the ankh are part of a grand continuum of African warriors against slavery that includes King Nzinga Mbemba of the Kongo; Queen Nzinga Mbande of the Ndongo; the Africans of Palmares, Brazil, including Acotirene, Zumbi, and Ganga Zumba; Queen Nanny and the Maroons of Jamaica; Denmark Vesey and Nat Turner of African America; Boukman, Toussaint L'Ouverture, and Jean Jacques Dessalines of Haiti; and the Knights of Liberty, a secret society conceived by African American Moses Horton in 1844 that boasted more than forty-seven thousand members who were prepared to fight to the death to end slavery.[26] There are also millions of unknown abolitionists who cleared paths for liberation using such tools as arson, poison, pick axes, boiling vats of lye, and the setting Sun.

The Sereer peoples of Senegal and The Gambia may be Armah's direct source of inspiration. As James F. Searing reveals in "'No Kings, No Lords, No Slaves': Ethnicity and Religion among the Sereer-Safèn of Western Bawol, 1700–1914," the Sereer ethnic groups collectively refused to be ruled by any king, governor, or overlord. The Sereer also would not enslave others, and they refused to be enslaved. Their rejection of all forms of oppression and enslavement included their refusal to convert to Islam. The Sereer defended their autonomy by living in the fortified enclaves provided by nature and with firearms.[27] When aggressors entered their domains seeking to capture, dominate, or enslave them, the Sereer executed them. French missionary Abbé Boliat describes the Sereer's protection and defense of their inalienable human rights as fundamental: "They only want to be free and independent, and they regard slavery as a crime. They don't want kings or emperors, they only want to be able to govern themselves through their elders, without ever accepting any foreign domination."[28] Rather than participate in criminality or pray for deliverance from criminals, the Sereer fought, and their battles infuse the pages of both *Two Thousand Seasons* and *Osiris Rising*.

It is profoundly important to recognize that the fight against slavery commenced with enslavement. Through *Osiris Rising*, Armah forces his audience to acknowledge the centuries-long wars that Africans have waged, and continue to wage, against those who would depopulate, enslave, colonize, and mystify Africa's shining Suns. Similar to Ògbóni's position on bloodshed,[29] the Anoa and the companionship of the ankh "forbid the shedding of human blood—except in the execution of slavers"; what is more, the society's "purpose was to detect, judge and execute any native who traded in slaves, be it with whites or with other natives" (*Osiris Rising*, 177).

In addition to working to rid Africa of abomination and the abominable, the society also strives to preserve the holistic African worldview and consciousness. Tete, the society's historian, describes the companionship of the ankh as a many-millennia-old way of life that stands as "an ellipse of life linking future with past through intelligent work in the present" (*Osiris Rising*, 261). As Tete reveals, an egalitarian collective of "the most inventive people of the age: astronomers, scientists, builders, scribes, artists, keepers of the calendar, dedicated knowledgeable people averse to life in palaces" poses a threat to monarchies, dictatorships and democracies:

> The companionship risked attack from those ambitious to dominate others. For it respected no social hierarchies, only the fellowship of shared ideas and work. Those whose power was based on force and fraud quickly enough understood that this society of intelligence and work, this society of life, the companionship of the ankh, would end their rule if it survived. They tried to destroy it. The companionship protected itself, survived, died and was reborn, and learned that under harsh conditions secrecy—invisibility, an invisibility compatible with effectiveness—was the condition of survival. (*Osiris Rising*, 262)

As is the case in *Seasons*, in *Osiris Rising* prophets of consciousness arise periodically to "utter gentle truths to power and instructions, prophecies, warnings" (*Osiris Rising*, 263). When African rulers, intoxicated by their self-spun mythology and bloated on another culture's lies, acquiesce in the destruction of the people, the society of the ankh stands and defends:

> Those who formed the secret companionship of the ankh, then, began with a vow never themselves to engage in the lucrative trade in death brought here by Arabs and Europeans. Secondly, the companionship swore to protect the African people against the white slavers and their African partners, where necessary by killing the killers of people. The immediate outcome of the secret society's work, the sudden death of several white traders on this coast, was not the end of slavery. Instead, the slavers created security systems to protect themselves and their African helpers. Now the killers'

helpers stopped boasting of their profits from the slave trade. They proclaimed their kinship with all Africans, called themselves authentic. But the secret society saw through their game. The hidden slave suppliers, called factors, also began dying sudden quiet deaths. (*Osiris Rising*, 264)

The work of the companionship of the ankh is the actualization of the Rastafarian call to arms, "Nyabinghi," which means "death to all oppressors." This expression has its origin in East Africa with Queen Nyabinghi, who was a powerful ruler of the Bashombo states of northern Rwanda, eastern Kongo, and southwestern Uganda.[30] So influential was she that, upon her transition from the material to the spiritual realm, Nyabinghi went from being a woman to being a God to being a spiritual system and a way of life. Nyabinghi's transformation and proliferation are logical, as she is protector *par excellence* of her people. Markedly similar to Anoa, Nyabinghi is also a cyclic intergenerational force who inhabits the spirits and bodies of select individuals and leads them to war against oppression and oppressors. Muhumusa of Uganda, who played a prominent role in the Ugandan war against the British, is said to have been guided by the spirit of Nyabinghi.[31]

Just as Nyabinghi enjoys constant revivification in life, lyrics, and literature, Armah makes it clear that the ankh, the Anoa, and the ancient African trinity of Aset, Ausar, and Heru are not isolated anomalies relegated to the past but are dynamic immortal forces who influence the political imperatives of Africans of both the Continent and the Ìtànkálẹ̀. The companionship of the ankh, as a timeless source of political consciousness and activism, is a seminal organization and symbol, but Armah deepens the relevance of the society by invoking and recasting the Kemetic Netcherw (Gods) Ausar and Aset in his novel.

The protagonist of *Osiris Rising* who is charged with traveling to the home of the companionship of the ankh, joining the society, and continuing its life-giving and community-empowering work is Ast. Historically, Ast, also known as Aset, is praised as the "Oldest of the Old. She was the Goddess from whom all becoming arose."[32] In addition to creating all of the Gods, Aset is the inventor of agriculture, which is the world's oldest profession. The Greek name for Aset is Isis. The Kemetic name for Osiris, for whom the novel *Osiris Rising* is named, is Ausar. Ausar is "The Lord of Perfect Blackness" and the guardian of eternity and everlasting life. Fittingly, in *Osiris Rising*, Ast's companion is Asar, the premiere spiritual, political, academic activist. Ast and Asar become members of a contemporary companionship of the ankh that fights against a new generation of ostentatious cripples who oversee modern methods of enslavement that include political and economic corruption, terrorism and social destabilization, and academic miseducation.

It is ludicrous to think that the same parties who made it illegal for Africana people to read and write, as was the case in the United States under the institution of slavery, and who enslaved, colonized, and oppressed Africans, would offer Africana people an education that serves Africana needs and objectives. Ast and Asar are cognizant of the fact that our education is our responsibility and that if Africana teachers have comprehensive knowledge of self and a curriculum that is grounded in African history, literatures, philosophies, science, mathematics, and languages—as opposed to Caucasian supremacist propaganda—then the students those teachers educate will understand that "the intelligent life is not the hunt for dollars and privilege but the struggle to liberate the continent from criminals" (*Osiris Rising*, 77).

In their effort to revolutionize and make relevant the Teacher's College of Manda, Ast and Asar work with a group of progressive colleagues and an eager student body to replace the Caucocentric curriculum with a comprehensive Africentric one. Stressing the connection between literature and life, Armah includes the complete detailed proposal and curriculum in *Osiris Rising*, and, by doing so, he places in our hands the tools necessary to create the types of academic institutions we need: This is revolutionary writing at its most relevant.

Asar has devoted his life to the struggle, and the curriculum revision is the latest in a long line of revolutionary sociopolitical projects that make him a prime target for neutralization. The neutralizer-in-chief is Seth Spencer Soja: Deputy Director of Security and the running dog of neocolonial oppressors. Soja is also a reincarnation of Set, the mythistorical brother and nemesis of the God Ausar. Seth's goal is to complete the ancient circle by killing Asar. However, when Seth shoots him, Asar's body explodes into "fourteen starry fragments" (*Osiris Rising* 305). Like Faro, Èṣù, and Allah, the Father, Asar does not die; his physical division leads to spiritual multiplication. The God of Everlasting Life will be reborn in fourteen more Gods who will continue the work of revising the curricula of our schools, refocusing the directions of our minds, ensuring the health of our bodies, and expanding the horizons of our souls.

The God Who Works on Sabbath Day

After Caucasians passed laws forbidding the trafficking of human beings on international waters, Caucasians simply started enslaving Africans in Africa. The Africans who resisted and refused to be enslaved and colonized were slaughtered. So many people were killed in the Congo under Leopold II's colonial administration that an American missionary declared that "if the natives were to rise and sweep every white person on the Upper Congo into eternity, there would still be left a fearful balance to their credit."[33] That missionary could have given the same assessment while viewing the lynched bodies of Africans in America, because after African Americans fought for and won emancipation, Caucasians began fertilizing American soil with African blood with the assistance of the convict lease system, chain gangs, and the Red Summers, Red Winters, Red Springs, and Red Autumns that have gone on for Red Decades: turning millions of African Americans into ancestors before their times.

No other people in the world have seen so many of their kin butchered, raped, defiled, and used as macabre community decorations and been counseled to turn the other cheek; wait on the lord; sing, sit, and march; or forgive and forget as have African Americans. However, long before propagandists made masochistic nonviolence the mandate, before the cameras started rolling, and before "We Shall Overcome" was composed, some organizations were quietly and methodically instituting balance. One example of a society devoted to ensuring the quality of Africana life and the ability of Africana people to live, shine, and enjoy the world that they were created to explore is the Seven Days.

The Seven Days' philosophy melds and evolves the tenets of the way, Ògbóni, and the companionship of the ankh to fit the needs of Africans surviving in Jim Crow Era America. A small society working for the benefit of the Africana whole, the Seven Days works to institute balance, harmony, and, most important, justice through reciprocity. Similar to the way of the Anoa and the companionship of the ankh, it may be the case that the Seven Days is based on an actual group. When asked about the inspiration for the Seven Days during a 2001 C-SPAN interview, Toni Morrison offered a veiled but profound revelation: "The origin of the Seven Days was based on rumor. I always heard that there was an organization of Black men who were avengers, and they were anonymous, and they ran around doing what the Seven Days did. . . . It was a very popular rumor. . ."[34] Morrison developed the whispered exploits of these warriors into the fictional Seven Days. Given that *Song of Solomon* is set in Detroit, which is where W. D. Fard began building his Nation, it could very well be the case that the historical Seven Days organization, if it did, indeed, exist, inspired lesson ten of "Lost-Found Muslim Lesson No. 1."

Song of Solomon describes the society as being founded in 1920 in response to the Red Summer of 1919, during which hundreds of innocent

African Americans, especially servicemen, were lynched by mobs of racist Caucasian cowards.[35] It is not clear when Guitar joins the organization, but he is a member in 1955 when Emmett Till was lynched. In an explication similar to Tete's description of the companionship of the ankh, Guitar explains the Seven Days to Milkman:

> There is a society. It's made up of a few men who are willing to take some risks. They don't initiate anything; they don't even choose. They are as indifferent as rain. But when a Negro child, Negro woman, or Negro man is killed by whites and nothing is done about it by *their* law and *their* courts, this society selects a similar victim at random, and they execute him or her in a similar manner if they can. If a Negro was hanged, they hang; if a Negro was burnt, they burn; raped and murdered, they rape and murder.[36]

The Bible asserts that after creating the world, the Christian God rested on the seventh day. As the Sunday man of the Days, Guitar Bains undertakes his life's work, one of the most important jobs in this world, on the Christian sabbath. Racism, barbarism, and wickedness never take a sabbatical, and like Julius Lester and Gloria Naylor, Morrison, through Guitar, offers a stunning critique of a God who relaxes while others suffer, fight, and die for justice.[37] One might say that Guitar and the Days are the Gods who do the work that another God does not care to do.

The reciprocal justice enacted by the Seven Days is a direct response to American injustices. With a ruthlessness that tutored both Hitler and the creators of apartheid, America works unceasingly to deny its Africana citizens justice, human rights, and the elemental right of existence. That these are inherent inalienable rights that cannot be doled out, granted, or taken away is irrelevant to imperialists who seek to completely disenfranchise African Americans and Africana people around the world. It is important to note that the atrocities that African Americans have suffered have also been visited on Africans in the Congo, Haiti, Nigeria, Ghana, France, Cuba, Brazil—wherever Africana people live, their human rights and humanity have been and continue to be violated with impunity.

Fela Anikulapo Kuti is the legendary and immortal Pan-African warrior-spiritualist-artist who is known for attacking corruption and oppressors. While he is known simply as "Fela," so remarkable a man is he that, as an example of the prevalence of African divinity, since his death he has been deified and is now Òrìṣà Olufela Anikulapo Kuti. In his classic song "Beasts of No Nation," Fela reveals that he does indeed possess the perspicacity of the Gods when he laughs at the concept of Caucasian world leaders and organizations holding meetings and deciding to give, or "dash," Africana peoples human rights. He informs the "animals in human skin" of a fundamental fact of which they, given their constitution, are obviously unaware: "Human rights na my property / So, therefore, you can't dash me my property."[38]

While "Beasts of No Nation" is as evenhanded as Armah's *Seasons* in its attacks on corrupt leaders of all ethnicities, it is clear that the natally alienated beasts leading the herd of oppressors are Caucasian. Guitar asserts that Caucasians are as "unnatural" as the atrocities they commit, and, given the title and lyrics of his song, Fela would agree. However, Fela informs his audience that he did not christen Caucasians beasts; he is merely quoting South Africa's P. W. Botha, who threatened Africans who were fighting against apartheid that "[t]his uprising will bring out the beast in us."[39] P. W. Botha is not alone in harboring and routinely unleashing an inner beast; Fela reveals that Botha has well-known allies:

> Botha na friend to Thatcher and Reagan
> Botha na friend to some other leaders too
> And together dem want dash us human rights
> Animals want dash us human rights
> Animal can't dash me human rights
> Animal can't dash us human rights[40]

While some people may very well be beasts of no nation and others may resign themselves to an evolution from apes and Neanderthals, the Gods know both their identity and that of their oppressors. In his analysis of issues regarding Africana peoples and inalienable rights, Sun Ra focuses not on the machinations of "beasts" but on the inherent divinity of Africana peoples. In an exposition titled "THE BIBLE WAS NOT WRITTEN FOR NEGROES!!!!!!!," Sun Ra asserts that Africana people are spiritual beings, and while human beings may seek equal rights and protections under the law, "THERE ARE NO LAWS IN THE CONSTITUTION GUARANTEEING THE EQUALITY OF . . . SPIRITUAL BEINGS . . . TO MEN WHO ARE CREATED EQUAL."[41] Fela moves his audience to ponder the depths to which Africana Gods have sunk if thirty years after Sun Ra's polemic they are to accept a gift of human rights from an international collective of animals.

As if educated by the same logic that tutored Fela and Sun Ra, the Seven Days' warriors do not grovel, march, beg, or wait for what is theirs to be given. Despite being locked out of the American justice system, the members of the Seven Days know that justice is an inherent right and that they have the authority to enforce their rights and administer justice as well:

Where's the money, the state, the country to finance our justice? You say Jews try their catches in a court. Do we have a court? Is there one courthouse in one city in the country where a jury would convict them? There are places right now where a Negro still can't testify against a white man. Where the judge, the jury, the court, are legally bound to ignore anything a Negro has to say. What that means is that a black man is a victim of a crime only when a white man says he is. Only then. If there was anything like or near justice or courts when a cracker kills a Negro, there wouldn't have to be no Seven Days. But there ain't; so we are. And we do it without money, without support, without costumes, without newspapers, without senators, without lobbyists, and without illusions! (160)

When a person's inalienable rights have been breached, suspended, or negated, it is the responsibility of that individual to do everything in his power to ensure those rights are restored. The warriors of Ògbóni, Anoa, Nyabinghi, and the society of the ankh have familiarity of terrain, access to the criminals, and spaces of support that make it possible for them to capture and execute violators. The Seven Days is only a fraction of a fragmented, geographically dislocated, terrorized people who have no legal voice or authority and whose enemies abound. Unable to kill or prosecute the actual murderers, the Seven Days enacts restoration through covert reciprocity to ensure the balance of the Earth, as Guitar explains: "Any man, any woman, or any child is good for five to seven generations of heirs before they're bred out. So every death is the death of five to seven generations. You can't stop them from killing us, from trying to get rid of us. And each time they succeed, they get rid of five to seven generations. I help keep the numbers the same" (154). Whereas with lesson number ten of "Lost-Found Lesson No. 1," one has fulfilled one's responsibilities after killing four "devils," the Seven Days is a timeless force, and its members have eternal obligations: The men undertake their work of balance as long as imbalance exists.

With Guitar's elucidation it becomes clear that the Seven Days' philosophy is at one with the way and is rooted in the eternal cosmic and terrestrial laws of reciprocity. The Seven Days' philosophy is also in consonance with the seven cardinal virtues of Maat and the tenets of such sacred African societies as Àjẹ́ and Ògbóni. Evidence of shared philosophy is also apparent in the Seven Days' organizing principles: "Numbers. Balance. Ratio. And the earth, the land . . . . The earth is soggy with black people's blood. And before us Indian blood. Nothing can be done to cure them, and if it keeps on there won't be any of us left and there won't be any land for those who are left. So the numbers have to remain static" (158). With their prime directive being to avenge innocent victims and institute balance after abomination, the Seven Days' members are clearly Ẹdan's expertly placed progeny who continue to ensure that violators of Onílẹ̀'s laws are introduced to oblivion.

Because they are protected by the same shield of invisibility as the society of the ankh, no one knows exactly when the Seven Days began or if it ended. The longevity of the society rests in its secrecy and exclusivity. The society consists of "always seven and only seven" members. They carry no insignia and undertake no prideful recapitulation of events. Their methodology is simple: If an African American is killed on a Monday and the justice system turns a blind eye, the man whose day for enacting vengeance is Monday selects a Caucasian victim; whispers, "Your day has come"; and kills the Caucasian in the same manner that the African American was killed. The avenging Day notifies the group upon completion of his assignment. Other than this, as with Ògbóni, "The eyes may see; the ears may hear; the mouth remains silent."[42]

The ankh, the akuaba doll, and Ẹdan all represent life, and there is no greater threat to life than the slavery, castration, lynching, rape, decimation, and genocide that characterizes racists' historical and contemporary interactions with Africana peoples. But while the ignorant may assume that the Seven Days is motivated by a hatred of Caucasians and their ghastly racist behavior, they are incorrect. The organization is inspired by the greatest force of all—love for the collective Self. As Guitar explains, "What I'm doing ain't about hating white people. It's about loving us. . . . My whole life is love" (159). Ralph Story offers an apt comparison for the love of which Guitar speaks: "'Love' for the Seven Days is like the love of one solider for a countryman who has died in combat. It forces the reader to consider black people as if they have been engaged in a protracted struggle against superior and unpredictable adversaries."[43] I do not agree that racist terrorists are "superior" foes; those who are superior do not need to oppress and terrorize others. However, I concur with Story's corollary assertion that a war has been and is being waged.

Story's analysis echoes the lyrics of Killarmy and Sunz of Man, who repeatedly remind their audiences of the on-going war, and Wade Noble's likening the African experience in America to a hostage crisis. To illustrate the veracity of Story's, Killarmy's, and Noble's points, one need only view the evidence provided by the festivals and photo shoots that Caucasians organized around the charred, bullet-riddled, castrated, dangling bodies of Africana people and the responses to those attacks by such historical organizations as the Deacons for Defense (originally known as the Deacons for Defense and Justice), which was founded by African Americans in Jonesboro, Louisiana. In addition to having been inspired by the existence of armed Africana militias in Mississippi and Alabama, the Deacons for Defense motivated other communities to do what is most logical: embrace the second amendment to the Constitution and take up arms and defend themselves. It is fitting that many of the members of the fictional Seven Days and many members of historical defense organizations, like the Deacons for Defense, acquired the skills and strategies necessary to defend their communities while fighting in the United States' military.

While African Americans have been miseducated, programmed, and coerced into believing that loving their enemies and practicing nonviolence—even in the face of unconscionable atrocities, savagery, and barbarism—is the only way to inspire sociopolitical revolution and obtain equal rights, the reality is that violent social injustices, usurpations, and deprivations have always been and will always be met with armed resistance. Despite one of the most protracted disinformation campaigns in history, many African Americans living in the Jim Crow South were no different from any other oppressed group in using every available means to defend and protect themselves.[44] Africana life, literature, and lyrics provide myriad examples of organized and effective armed resistance. While they are not fixtures of world or American history or Black History Month, Nathaniel "The Prophet" Turner, Robert F. Williams' militant NAACP, the Black Panther Party, Assata Shakur, the Black Liberation Army, Republic of New Africa, and countless other groups and individuals devoted their lives to Africana defense, protection, and liberation. In addition to the books discussed in this chapter, Sam Greenlee's *The Spook Who Sat By the Door*, John A. Williams' *Captain Blackman*, and Jeff Stetson's *Blood on the Leaves* are novels that not only reveal shrouded histories but also serve as instruction manuals for revolutionaries-in-waiting.

Stetson's novel is especially relevant to this discussion for it answers Milkman's query to Guitar: "Why don't you just hunt down the ones who did the killing?" (155). *Blood on the Leaves* introduces the reader to Professor Martin Matheson whose popular course on "unpunished civil rights 'war criminals'" who lynched African Americans in the 1960s spawns both a list of perpetrators and a new millennium avenger who kills lynchers in the way of the Seven Days—in the same manner in which they slaughtered Africana innocents.[45] When Matheson is tried for murder, he reveals himself to be a mastermind who uses the same skewed "justice" system that liberates Caucasian killers to orchestrate his exoneration.

In the realm of music, hip hop duo dead prez's song "I Have a Dream Too" offers a stunning response to the contemporary lynchings of African Americans. The song opens with African American men turning drive-by shootings into revolutionary acts as they patrol the streets and kill police officers in retaliation for the unjustified murder by the police of an African American child. The song ends with a tribute to revolutionary heroes of various ethnicities, including Mutulu Shakur, Leonard Peltier, George Jackson, Assata Shakur, and Bunchy Carter, as well as such organizations as Uhuru, the Black Liberation Army, the Zapatistas, and the Mau Mau.[46]

While the Seven Days is one of the most misunderstood societies in literature, it stands as an important link connecting ancient African organizations with contemporary Pan-African revolutionaries, societies, and imperatives. The fact that every aspect of the Days' existence is devoted to ferreting out injustice and instituting order underscores the global and cosmic significance of their work. They cannot see omnisciently or act with omnipotence as can Ẹdan, so they peruse the newspapers and scan their radios for trespasses against the laws of existence. The men cannot marry or have children; their humble jobs provide life's necessities, including artillery. They receive no thanks for their gifts and sacrifices because instituting the way, protecting Africana existence, and ensuring the balance of Ẹdan is both reward enough and a necessity for, as Guitar avers, "It's not about you living longer. It's about how you live and why. It's about whether your children can make other children. It's about trying to make a world where one day white people will think before they lynch" (160).

While the country that Guitar kills to heal in the 1950s and 1960s remains hazardous to Africana health, one could argue that the Seven Days' success is evident in the fact that Caucasians are no longer the ethnic majority in America. However, Guitar makes an important assertion: "Nothing can be done to cure them." Indeed, rather than undertake self-inspection and analysis, Caucasians' responses to their dwindling numbers have ranged from founding scores of new and resuscitating traditional Caucasian American terror organizations who are stockpiling arms in preparation for a long-awaited "race war," to attempting to classify certain human beings as "illegal" and refusing them (yes) human rights and human recognition, to killing and incarcerating as many Africana and Chicano citizens as possible, to attempting to legislate the patriarchal control of women's wombs.

Just as the struggle is unending so too might it be the case that the Seven Days is still actively balancing imbalances. Guitar reveals the organization's sources of strength: "Time and silence. Those are their weapons, and they go on forever" (155). The philosophies and motivations of the Seven Days certainly survive in groups like dead prez. M-1 and stic.man of dead prez are Gods whose music epitomizes the devotion of revolutionary Divinities. In the song "I'm A African," stic.man describes the group's art as "natty dread lock / fuck-a-cop hip hop" as well as a "socialist movement" to which one can "bounce."[47] In the song "Fucked up," stic.man and M-1 reveal that they can relate to all stages and aspects of the struggle as they describe lives that evolve from submersion in the original staples of Milkman's young adulthood—partying and drinking—to the purpose and empowerment that defines Guitar's political directive and direction: "I used to have a thing for cognac / Nowadays I train for combat."[48] With this couplet, dead prez reminds its audience that the world's longest undocumented war is still being waged and that the Pan-African allies are in need of recruits.

"Writin' Is Fightin'"[49]

During the Great Migration, African Americans risked their lives to leave a South that was smoldering with the remains of their roasted kin, but they arrived in the North to find rope, fire, tar, and feathers awaiting them and Caucasian mobs amassed to drive all Africana people out of town.[50] Despite these pan-American horrors, African Americans dug in, planted new roots, and reached into their souls and brought forth innate intellect, music, poetry, business acumen, visual artistry, and literary creativity along with pride, resilience, and courage. Consequently, the Great Migration of African Americans from the South to the North resulted in the Harlem Renaissance, the Roaring Twenties, and the Jazz Age.

Jazz, often spelled "jass," is an African word that signifies sex, dance, music, and holistic harmonic vibration. Boogie-woogie, which is a genre of jazz, comes from the Bantu expression *mbuki-mvuki*, which means, "I take off (in flight), I shuck off (all clothing that hinders my performance)."[51] The first definition of boogie-woogie adds another layer of depth to the transformation undertaken in the Crow Song and Milkman's glorious flight; the second definition harkens back to the eras when Africana people reveled in the fact that their melanin signifies complete perfection.

That blues and jazz are truly "seminal" African genres of American music is logical: Jazz is the linguistic cognate of the words jism and jizz, and these words are derived from the KiKongo word *dinza*, "to discharge one's semen, to come."[52] The obvious references to sex and virility in these African words, and others like "booty" and "poontang," are indicative of a people who honor the Gods' responsibility to create life. Yemọja represents the force of the survival of Africana peoples; indeed, she is the first Òrìṣà who was invoked and praised by the Yoruba who survived the Middle Passage.[53] Racists strive to associate Africana peoples with slavery and to enslave them in perpetuity, but Yemoja and her progeny know that no condition is permanent; they know that Africana people must continue to bring new life into the world to correct historic imbalances. There are Gods who are awaiting rebirth, and copulation is a crucial part of the wonderful work of becoming and returning.

The creative and sexual virility and abilities of Africans enraged some Caucasians and delighted and entranced others during the Jazz Age. *Mumbo Jumbo* is set in this appropriately named era, and it is a perfect example of jazz literature. Some passages can be read, but others must be heard. And like any great jazz album, each listen/read offers new nuances, unexplored changes, and fresh insights. One of the most important jazz-inspired elements of *Mumbo Jumbo* is the book's signature force. Swinging music, freedom of expression, and sex gave rebirth to a concept that had been patiently awaiting another opportunity to get on up and get down, and that force is Jes Grew: Jes Grew is the irresistible tune of the unprintable text;[54] it is the soundtrack of the ankh; it is the promise of Ògbóni; it is the penis greeting the vagina; quite simply, it is Life.

The term Jes Grew is steeped in jazz-inspired creative power. The expression is actually an answer to a question about the origins of African American folk songs. Because Africans do not come from a tradition where art is created for its own sake or to be commoditized, no one can document the sources of such songs as "Uncle Bud," "Halimuhfack," and "Sweet Home Chicago"—and no one needs to because art is communal property. Accordingly, versions and verses of songs can change from region to region and singer to singer. When discussing the bawdy southern classic, "Uncle Bud," Zora Neale Hurston stated that the song developed through "incremental repetition."[55] Had she not been making a professional recording, she might have simply said, "Uncle Bud 'jes grew.'" But "jes grew" is a deceptive phrase because songs, dances, and Gods do not spontaneously generate. As is apparent with High John, there is always a source. The source of the Jes Grew that enlivens hosts in *Mumbo Jumbo* is mumbo jumbo.

The definition for mumbo jumbo that Reed attributes to *The American Heritage Dictionary of the English Language* is incorrect. Mumbo jumbo is not a "'magician who makes the troubled spirits of ancestors go away': ma-ma, grandmother+gyo, trouble+mbo, to leave."[56] *The American Heritage Dictionary* does not offer this erroneous definition in its third edition. Identical to the power and reverence of Ẹdan, Nyabinghi, and Anoa, it is the Mother, or "ma-ma," of Mama Dyumbo who protects, empowers, and eradicates,[57] and the Mother of Jes

Grew's Text is Aset who is the Mother of the Gods. Because Reed's legendary issues with empowered women are evident in *Mumbo Jumbo* and *The Last Days of Louisiana Red* and are addressed by Reed, himself, in *Reckless Eyeballing* and other works, one wonders if he uses the erroneous definition of mumbo jumbo intentionally in this very male-centered novel to promote Africana patriarchal supremacy or if Reed uses the erroneous definition to further complicate the motivation of Jes Grew while subtly reminding his audience not to trust the other's definitions of the self. Given Reed's complexity, both suppositions may be correct.

Reed also misleads his readers about one of the sources of the phrase "jes grew." When asked about her origin, Topsy of Harriet Beecher Stowe's *Uncle Tom's Cabin* does not say she "jes grew." She says, "I spect I grow'd."[58] What may appear to be an inconsequential semantic alteration becomes an issue of profound importance when one is discussing the name of the Mother of Powers.

In *The Signifying Monkey: A Theory of African-American Literary Criticism*, Henry Louis Gates Jr. argues that Reed is encoding a narrative within a narrative.[59] In addition to literary layering, Reed is challenging his audience to question and probe *everything*—even the information that he, the textual architect, presents. All meanings, signs, assumptions, definitions, quotations, and truths must be investigated. Gates describes Papa LaBas as *Mumbo Jumbo's* "chief sign reader."[60] However, while LaBas' name indicates that he is a manifestation of Ẹlẹ́gbà, when considering Reed's erroneous definition of "mumbo jumbo" and his misquoting Topsy, it is clear that Reed is the Trickster-in-Chief who tosses decoys, "errors," and mystifications wrapped in demystifications to discern just how deeply his audience is willing and/or able to see.

Revolutionizing the concept of a novel, *Mumbo Jumbo* is a work of "fiction" that also contains a partial bibliography, footnotes, illustrations, and photographs. *Mumbo Jumbo* is easily one of the most intellectually and politically astute books ever written, and Reed expects intellectual rigor from his audience. The reason he cites sources and encourages members of his audience to look up information for themselves is because *Mumbo Jumbo* is not merely a novel about Papa LaBas' search for Jes Grew's Text. It is also a history book about a little-known but profoundly important war. In addition to these, similar to Jethro sending HighJohn on a quest to find the Lost Book of Hoodoo in Arthur Flowers' *De Mojo Blues*, Reed is sending his audience on a mission to discover political and historical truths. The real detective work begins when one finishes reading *Mumbo Jumbo* and begins consulting the sources in Reed's bibliography and footnotes.

The novel, proper, depicts the struggle between those who desire to destroy Jes Grew and those who seek to excite it. The persons who wish to destroy the force are a hydra of Caucasian American secret societies that all have the same directive and objective—to dominate the world and force everyone to follow their worldview and ethos. Reed calls them Atonists in honor of Akhenaton, the Kemetic ruler who forced his entire nation to worship only one God: Aton, the Sun God. On the Atonists' lowest rung are the police, led by Schlitz of Yorktown and Curator/Commissioner Biff Musclewhite. On the next rung is the Wallflower Order (those who cannot dance and who despise those who can) led by robber baron Walter "the sphinx" Mellon. At the apex of the Eurocentric forces is Hierophant 1. The featured defenders of Atonism are Hinckle Von Vampton and Herbert Gould, who are members of the Knights Templar. At the same time that the aforementioned wage war against Jes Grew on American soil, the United States is invading Haiti, the first free Africana nation in the Western Hemisphere. With this two-pronged assault, the Atonists hope to eradicate African Gods and the African revolutionary imperative in the West, if not everywhere.

In contrast to the cornucopia of Caucasian power-wielders, the Jes Grew Carriers are few and they are headed by PaPa LaBas and Black Herman. LaBas is a Hoodoo man extraordinaire who "carries Jes Grew in him like most other folk carry genes" (23). Seemingly unlike Èṣù Ẹlẹ́gbára, his versatile, sensual, cunning, mischievous namesake, PaPa LaBas moves slowly, and his followers tease him for being old fashioned. However, he is merely following the advice of Èṣù and taking the time to examine all sides of all issues.[61] LaBas also listens closely to what appears to be cacophonous chaos because as the director the Mumbo Jumbo Kathedral he knows there is sense in nonsense—*everything* has meaning.

From his name to his powers, Black Herman is a recasting of Ausar, The Lord of Perfect Blackness. The fictional Black Herman is also a projection of the historical gentleman-magician of the same name who so thrilled Sun Ra's mother that she named her son after him.[62] Black Herman lived from 1892 to 1934, and he was a true Pan-African. Not only did he state that he was of Zulu origin, but one of his skills is reminiscent of Igbo powers. He would let audience members tie and bind him and then he would demonstrate how "[i]f the slave traders tried to take any of my people captive, we would release ourselves using our secret knowledge."[63]

In 1932 Black Herman launched his Buried Alive act, which evokes the immortal powers of Kemet. He would bury a woman six feet underground for six hours and then exhume her alive and well. When he incorporated himself into the act he became Ausar:

> A few days before a major performance, Black Herman would sell tickets for the public to come to a plot of ground near the theater he called "Black Herman's Private Graveyard". They could view his lifeless body and even check for a pulse—nothing. The audience would then see Black Herman's body placed in a coffin and into the grave. The night of the show, another audience was invited to attend as the body was exhumed. They saw the coffin get dug up, opened, and Black Herman would emerge, alive and well. He would then walk to the theater, and the audience usually followed.[64]

Because of his Ausarian ability to defy death and be buried and resurrected, in *Mumbo Jumbo*, Black Herman is called the Human Seed.

In their quest to find Jes Grew's text, Black Herman and LaBas ally with Haitian Voodoo houngan Benoit Battraville, who is a recasting of an historical figure of the same name (spelled Batraville) who led the 1918 rebellion against the United States' occupation of Haiti and its attempt to enslave Haitians.[65] There are also nods to the Nation of Islam and the Prince Hall Masons through Abdul Sufi Hamid and Buddy Jackson, respectively. Hamid and Jackson are also restyled historical figures, and while they are minor characters, they are essential to the book. Papa LaBas bears the name, analytical ability, and versatility of Èṣù Ẹlẹ́gbára, but the actual tricksters of *Mumbo Jumbo* are Jackson and Abdul. The religious and craft-oriented beliefs of Abdul and Buddy Jackson, respectively, place them on the line that separates consciousness-raisers from destroyers, or Five Percenters from eighty-fivers and ten-percenters. Jackson's and Hamid's relationships with the Text are indicative of their duality: Jackson receives Jes Grew's text from Hinckle Von Vampton, but rather than follow Von Vampton's instructions, Jackson gives the book to Abdul Sufi Hamid, who is the only character with the linguistic mastery to translate Medu Netcher, the language of the Kemites, into English.

The Text that Jes Grew seeks also boasts a historical counterpart. The Text consists of the holistic wisdom of the Africans of Nubia and Kemet. These medicinal, spiritual, philosophical, artistic, architectural, linguistic, cultural teachings were written by the Kemetic God Djhuiti (whom the Greeks misnamed Thoth). Djhuiti is the God of "wisdom, science, medicine, magic, measurement, mathematics," and his knowledge and teachings adorn, inspire, and instruct from ancient sacred scrolls as well as colonnaded temples.[66] Most relevant to *Mumbo Jumbo* and Jes Grew is the fact that Djhuiti compiled "the wisdom of ancient Egypt" into forty-two books, and, according to Manly P. Hall, "[T]he Romans – and later the Christians – realized that until these books were eliminated they could never bring the Egyptians into subjugation."[67]

Jes Grew's Text, which is also called the Book of Thoth, is, historically, the ancient Book of Djhuiti, and it has always proven problematic for Atonists of Islamic, Jewish, and Christian faiths. According to Muslims, Islam's Qur'an is the "ultimate truth"; Caucasian Jews consider themselves to be the "chosen people"; and Christians assert that they have the one and only way, truth, and life. When religious ideology is steeped in claims of supremacy, exceptionalism, and exclusivity, it is necessary to substantiate those claims. Purveyors of organized religions found the ownership, control, and/or destruction of the holistic texts of Kemet to be essential to the growth of their faiths. While some non-African scholars such as Herodotus acknowledged their African sources and admitted having studied in Africa, others drank deeply the waters of African wisdom and then cemented or poisoned the well so that they could present themselves as founts of knowledge.

After Christians studied and copied the medical, scientific, architectural, mathematical, and philosophical wisdom of the ancient Kemetic scrolls housed in the Library of Alexandria in 391 CE, the Christian emperor Theodosius decreed that "all that was ancient was pagan and therefore sinful," and he ordered his men to burn the library and its contents.[68] But Theodosius could not stop Jes Grew from growing. After Jes Grew reconstituted itself following the Christian razing, it encountered the Muslim General Amr. In 640 CE, after Amr and his men raped the Library and University of Alexandria of texts, Amr is credited with having said the following: "If the library contains what is not in the Koran, it is false. If it contains what is already in the Koran, then it is superfluous. Burn it."[69] But Amr's conflagration could not stop the shining and growth of African wisdom. In *Mumbo Jumbo*, Jes Grew rebirths itself again and boogies into Abdul's hands. Abdul follows the pattern of his Atonist forebears: He translates the Text, and, after noting the passages helpful to his cause, he declares it vile and heretical and burns it. Given this, the book *Mumbo Jumbo* is more than just a historical novel; it is the indestructible ẹnikejì of the Book of Djhuiti. Not only does *Mumbo Jumbo* protect and project the essence of the wisdom of the Text, but it also encourages the recreation of those ancient African powers documented by Djhuiti and the consecration of new powers, books, arts, and technologies.

The Text and the Jes Grew Carriers are not the only curvilinear forces at work. The Atonists also reconstitute themselves cyclically, and in addition to fighting Jes Grew and its carriers and hoping to find and destroy the Book of Djhuiti, the Atonists are struggling with the rise of three influential Africana sacred societies: the Prince Hall Masons, the Nation of Islam, and the Mu'tafikah. Reed does not delve deeply into the Masonic and Islamic organizations because they involve Africans struggling to obtain entry into societies and systems that are African in origin but have been debased by aliens. Buddy Jackson reveals that Africana Freemasons discovered that "the Masonic mysteries were of a Blacker origin than we thought" and that the Caucasian masons' "mysteries" are actually misunderstood and distorted tenets of African wisdom systems (194). It is most telling that the Templar's God Baphomet (who bears a striking resemblance to the Mason's Divinity, the African master architect, Nimrod) makes several cameo appearances in the book as the "ugly nigger doll" that Von Vampton worships with reverence, rigor, and orgasmic ceremony (22, 55, and 61).

Cognizant of the ability of Africans to create organizations that speak specifically to their political and spiritual needs, Reed crafts his own secret society. Mu'tafikah is a multicultural collective of which former Mumbo Jumbo Kathedral minister Berbelang is a leader. As a contraction of Berber language or a pun on "babble," the name "Berbelang" constitutes an intratextual nod to the phrase "mumbo jumbo" and serves as another intimation that what appears to be nonsensical prattle has great depth, meaning, and power to those who understand. The term Mu'tafikah also has alternate meanings: the term intimates what the society has in store for Atonist robber barons and culture vultures. But in addition to reminding one of the word "motherfucker," Mu'tafikah, is an Arabic term that relates to an event that is well-known in Islamic and Judeo-Christian folklore. As Reed notes in *Mumbo Jumbo* (15), in the Qur'an, Mu'tafikah refers to the inhabitants of Sodom and Gomorrah, and while Allah allowed Lot and his unnamed wife to leave, "al-Mu'tafikah He destroyed."[70]

The Mu'tafikah of *Mumbo Jumbo* has nothing in common with the residents of Sodom and Gomorrah. Like the Seven Days, Mu'tafikah works in a covert manner for balance, order, justice, and reciprocity. Even its lair reflects its sociopolitical motivation. Mu'tafikah meets in the basement of a three-story building: on the first floor is a store that sells religious paraphernalia; the second floor houses a gun shop; the third floor is home to an advertising agency that specializes in soap accounts. Reed informs his audience that "[i]f Western History were a 3-story building . . . it would resemble this little architectural number" (82). Reed is signifying on the Caucasian methodology of mandating an ideology or way of life, killing those who refuse to submit, and attempting to launder history of the genocides, rapes, and lynchings they have committed in their lust to conquer. By stationing the Mu'tafikah in the basement of this iconic building, Reed reveals that the forces of the Ancients are still alive and are covertly enacting retribution through various spiritual and political revolutions and revolutionaries. In a more aggressive sense, Reed implies that some revolutionary acts involve "sticking it to the man" in the rear, no less.

When Caucasians attacked, enslaved, decimated, and colonized the various peoples of the world, they also stole innumerable treasures from their victims. In addition to wondering what the very people that they derided as savage, filthy, primitive, and subhuman could possibly have created that Caucasians would admire or desire, one must ponder why Caucasians not only placed prices on these priceless artifacts but also continue to imprison and display their pilfered booty in museums, which Reed astutely labels "Art Detention Center[s]." Mu'tafikah liberates these stolen treasures and returns them to their rightful owners:

> On the table lies a Nimba mask made of Guinea wood they've seized from a private collection belonging to a society woman on Park Ave. . . . "Tam" a Nigerian musician and writer will return 5,000 masks and wood sculpture to Africa. He had begun by lifting a Benin bronze plaque with leopard from the Linden-Museum in Stuttgart, Germany. Before museum heads could warn their continental colleagues of his presence in Europe, he and his aides, posing as innocuous exchange students, had repatriated masks and figures—carried to Europe as booty from Nigeria, Gold Coast, Upper Volta and the Ivory Coast—from where they were exhibited in the pirate dens called museums located in Zurich, Florence, England and in a private collection in Milan. (83)

What the Anoa and the society of the ankh do for Africans, and what the Seven Days does for African Americans, Mu'tafikah does for world's creators and their cultural artifacts. The group liberates Kemetic statues, gigantic Olmec heads, and seated Buddhas in addition to thousands of other ancient sacred works. Reed's idea of liberating these creations and repatriating them to their creators is so logical and necessary that one wonders why Mu'tafikah hasn't become an international call to arms and why there aren't Mu'tafikah cells around the world undertaking this important work.

The historic Benin Empire of Nigeria would certainly appreciate the assistance of Mu'tafikah. They have been demanding the return of treasures "illegally taken by the British during the Benin Massacre of 1897" for decades.[71] Yusuf Abdallah Usman, director general of Nigeria's National Commission for Museums and Monuments made his position clear in the following statement: "Without mincing words, these artworks are heirlooms of the great people of the Benin Kingdom and Nigeria generally. They form part of the history of the people. The gap created by this senseless exploitation is causing our people untold anguish, discomfort and disillusionment."[72] The British and American looters have not, at the time of this publication, responded to the request to return the stolen artifacts.

The Ethiopians' demand for the return of an ancient 100 ton tekhen was more successful, but the return reveals how African creative genius is treated by non-African thieves. Just as tekhens (also known as obelisks) pierce the landscape of Egypt from the ruins of Kemet, they also abound in Ethiopia as reminders of the grand Nubian Empire. The tekhen represents both the life-giving rays of the Sun and the fecund and fertilizing penis, and Kushite tekhens that boast a rounded apex are especially penile in appearance. During its brief occupation of Ethiopia from 1936–1941, Italy stole the tekhen of Axum.[73] When Italians stole the monument they were acting out on a grand scale the climax of American lynching bees: the excision and display of the African penis. Although the United Nations ordered the Italians to return the tekhen in 1947, they refused. After nearly 70 years, Italy finally returned the monument. As a testament to their penis-envy and creative, political, and architectural impotence, before they returned the icon to Ethiopia in 2005, the Italians reenacted the lynching finale: They cut the phallus into three sections and sent them back to Africa one piece at a time.[74]

An unacknowledged pathology provides the impetus for many crimes, including the international theft and misappropriation of African artifacts; the continued displacement of these treasures based on the thieves' assertions that they own them or are better able to care for them; the improper display and use of these artifacts; the proffering of stolen, colonized, and usurped artifacts as gifts, as many Arab rulers have given Kemetic artifacts to Europeans; and the raiding, looting, and defiling of graves, tombs, and temples, as has occurred in Egypt for centuries and continues in the 21st century, especially during the "Arab Spring" uprising. Because the masterpieces in question do not represent the labors, loves, genius, achievements, tragedies, ancestors, triumphs, and Divinities of Caucasians or Arabs, but those of Africans, unimaginable and unconscionable atrocities are committed. Mu'tafikah is an attempt to address and redress in literature these on-going international crimes.

Although Berbelang is described as being at odds with Papa Labas over Jes Grew, Berbelang and the Mu'tafikah are political-spiritual siblings and facilitators of Jes Grew. Just as Jes Grew is seeking its text, so too are the members of Mu'tafikah seeking their texts and the righteous restoration of their ancient liturgies. Their goals are to facilitate a material-spiritual rebirth that will "see the gods return and the spirits aroused" and "conjure a spiritual hurricane which would lift the debris of 2,000 years from its roots and fling it about" (88). The 2,000 year old debris in this case is Christianity.

Mu'tafikah is an egalitarian multicultural collective. The North American branch consists of Berbelang, who is African American; Fuentes, who is Mayan; and Yellow Jack, who is Chinese. Leadership of the group is rotational with an individual Mu'tafikah leading the group for three months and organizing the work of liberation. By juxtaposing the diversity of the art liberators and liberated artifacts to the Pan-African union of Labas, Black Herman, and Battraville, Reed reveals the interconnectedness of various Gods, spiritual systems, and cultures. When one considers the ancient knowledge sharing that took place among Africans, Asians, and Native Northern, Southern, and Middle Americans, and the fact that these ethnic groups have all been assaulted, enslaved, and colonized by Caucasians, it is logical that members of these groups would unite. However, Berbelang does not appear to truly understand the depth and direction of the struggle, because he is convinced that Mu'tafikah must ally with Caucasians, and, to this end, he forces Thor Wintergreen on the group.

In a scene that may well have inspired the exchange between Robert Johnson and Kimbrough, Berbelang uses the construct of Faust to explain the Caucasian worldview. Berbelang describes Caucasians as not having authentic original spiritual systems, philosophies, sciences, technologies, and arts, and because of that lack, they misappropriate and misuse the wisdom systems of others. What Marimba Ani would term the way of Yurugu,[75] Berbelang calls "bokorism," and he is intent on purging the bokor from the soul of Wintergreen (91).

Wintergreen reveals his dependence on the construct of "white supremacy" through his refusal to critically analyze himself or his culture. Thor whines, "Why would you give me such responsibility? I'm just 1 man. Not Faust nor the Kaiser nor the Ku Klux Klan. I am an individual, not a whole tribe or nation" (92). Thor is the only Mu'tafikah who refuses to examine the motivations, accomplishments, and setbacks of his ethnic group; he is the only Mu'tafikah who eschews ethnic identification. This Mu'tafikah seeks to transcend his ethnic group's historical and contemporary depravities and usurpations by sheathing himself in a cloak of imaginary "whiteness."

The New World gave Caucasians of the Old World the opportunity to flee grinding poverty, unimaginably prolific diseases and plagues, ethnic oppression, lifelong prison sentences, slavery, serfdom, and much more destitution. The America that Caucasian immigrants created on the graves of Native Americans and on the backs of Africans also provided Caucasians with the opportunity to forget their pasts and ethnicities and conceal their identities in the glorifying fiction of "whiteness" which granted them the additional benefit of oppressing those deemed "non-white."

The muddy truths and checkered complexities that underlie the would-be ethnicity- and culture-free concept of "whiteness" are laid bare in *Mumbo Jumbo*, when Biff Musclewhite, the curator for the Center of Art Detention, is captured by Mu'tafikah and held in exchange for the liberation of one of the colossal African stone heads for which the Olmec people are famous. Musclewhite uses his time in captivity to raise Thor's consciousness about their shared objectives.

> I know you look down on me because I come from one of the European countries under domination by stronger Whites than my people. We were your niggers; you colonized us and made us dirt under your heels. But in America it's different. There is no royalty in the European sense. Only money counts. Guggenheim, Astor, Ford, Carnegie . . . people you would spit on if you had them home in Europe. We're saving our dough and soon we will be able to purchase our own heraldry cheap and then maybe our values will be your values. (112)

In addition to revealing the rigidity of pre-"white" Caucasian tribalism and casteism, Musclewhite's explication of the Caucasian ethos confirms that the mythical constructs of "whiteness" and capitalism are designed to complement and advance one another for the benefit of Caucasians.

Despite his and Wintergreen's glaring class, ethnic, and cultural differences, Musclewhite inspires unity through the myth of the necessity of "whiteness" and by appealing to Thor's vanity as the paragon of "whiteness": "You are all we had. Against them. Against the Legendary Army of Marching Niggers against the Yellow Peril against the Red Man" (112). Musclewhite's speech is an elaboration of the founding principles of the Caucasian ethos and worldview. When he speaks, Johann Blumenbach, Cecil Rhodes, P. W. Botha, Margaret Sanger, King Leopold II, and hordes of other enslavers, oppressors, and garden variety racists nod their heads in agreement.

Musclewhite is the spokesman-in-chief for the most far-reaching secret society of all, so-called Western Civilization. What Musclewhite and his historical and contemporary clansmen are struggling to protect is the fact that they have no civilization, no culture, and no philosophy to protect. Musclewhite confirms that Berbelang's real threat lies in the fact that "he is aware of his past and has demystified ours. Son, this is a nigger closing in on our mysteries and soon he will be asking our civilization to 'come quietly'" (114).

It is Papa Labas who unmasks the masquerade that is Western Civilization, and he does this by journeying through time and space to Kemet and the origins of the ancient struggle between the Gods and the Atonists. Using the Greek names, perhaps to discern how deeply his audience is willing to search and re-search, *Mumbo Jumbo* details the ascension of Ausar and the destructive jealousy of his brother, Set. The significance of Ausar, the Lord of Perfect Blackness, to Africana masculine magnificence is evident in the fact that both Armah and Reed invoke this ancient God to frame their evolutionary art and inspire holistic revolution.

The extended dénouement of *Mumbo Jumbo* reveals the source of the various Pan-African orature that feature Èṣù, Yurugu, Pemba and Faro, the soul-piece and the Jew, and Djigui and Soma by depicting the ancient conflict that distinguishes the inherently divine from the inherently deficient. *Mumbo Jumbo* reveals that Jes Grew is of ancient origin and is harnessed by Osiris whose artistic and cosmic powers are unifying forces in Kemet. Set, Osiris' jealous brother, is similar to King Koranche of *Two Thousand Seasons* in that he also boasts a void instead of a solid foundation. Set, also like Koranche, channels his creative impotence destructively. Capitalizing on Osiris' nickname "Seedman," in reference to his sensual and spiritual prowess, Set challenges his brother to prove his fertilizing power and become a "Human Seed" who can be "planted in the Nile and then spring from the waters" (165).

Before describing Ausar's betrayal, Reed, riffing with Ivan Van Sertima's groundbreaking study *They Came Before Columbus*, offers a glimpse of one of the ways that African wisdom came to suffuse the globe and the galaxy. Osiris travels to Teotihuacan and poses for a portrait that will become one of the famous Olmec heads; following this, he shares wisdom with a contingent of international and intergalactic beings; and, before returning to Kemet, he masters the art of burial and resurrection. Confident in his power and divinity, Osiris allows himself to be buried, but before he is able to rise on the eighth day, Set's minions dig up Osiris and hack his body into fourteen pieces. Set hopes that by destroying Osiris he will be able to dominate the world and creation, but, like Pemba, Yurugu, and the Jew character who steals the soul-piece, Set renders himself eternally impotent and deficient.

Historically, Ausar's immortalization is the result of the devotion and foresight of Ast who collected the pieces of her husband's body so that she could memorialize him. The only piece she could not recover was his penis. Ast enclosed the thirteen pieces she found into a hollow tree, and the tree sprang to life as evidence of Ausar's immortality. This tree, itself, became the missing fourteenth piece, as it evolved into a phallic tribute to Ausar's immortality that gave birth to the tekhens that have stimulated East and West African empires for eons.

The tekhens that aroused the envy of European thieves and whose immensity dwarfed Arab invaders symbolize the majesty, might, and eternally resurrected perfection of the African penis and African masculine genius. It is ironic that the tekhens that Europeans stole and that Arabs could not wait to excise and exile, stand today as tributes to African penile power, creativity, and fecundity in America, Turkey, Poland, Israel, and France. England and Italy were so fascinated that they excised and erected several tributes to the African penis, including one that serves as the showpiece and focal point of Vatican City. Furthermore, it is not mere coincidence that the centerpiece of America's tell-tale "thirteen original colonies" is a knock-off tekhen known as the Washington Monument. Thanks to the envy of his enemies, Ausar's penis stands as a global icon of eternal Black priapic power.

Because Seth's attempts at destroying Ausar resulted in the God's immortalization and proliferation, the Atonists undertake cyclic attempts to destroy, dilute, or distort Africana Gods and powers. Moses is arguably the most successful destroyer discussed in *Mumbo Jumbo*. Rather than a great law giver, Moses is described as a forerunner of Joe Turner. He schemes and plots and tricks his way into Jethro's life so that he can find the secrets and power of African song. When Moses thinks he has Joe Turnered all he needs from his father-in-law and is prepared to return to Egypt, Jethro tells him, "1 day when you return . . . you can take a trip to Koptos where there is in existence the Sacred Book said to have been written by Thoth himself" (177). Moses creates a ruse so that he can learn how to obtain the Text. Jethro warns him that, because of the phase of the moon, the book will not yield holistic balanced information, only "a few things about converting rods to snakes; simple bokor tricks, the rest will be so awful that you will wish you had never known The Work" (179). But Moses, to turn a phrase with Hurston, lusts after power. Before he leaves for Koptos, Moses tosses Jethro a "copyright fee for the junk" he taught him (179). With this act, Moses becomes the archetype of the notorious music moguls who have grown wealthy using contracts and copyrights to pimp and then impoverish artists.

While Moses' feats are glorified in the Bible and have been idolized by Hollywood, *Mumbo Jumbo* relegates his acts, and those of Jesus as well, to the realm of "simple bokor tricks," at best. At worst, their machinations, misappropriations, and misapplications of African wisdom and technology are genocidal (185–186). Through *Mumbo Jumbo*, Reed encourages his audience to compare biblical "tricks" to African science and technology to better understand true power, its rightful wielders, and its purposeful applications. Reed also impresses upon his audience the fact that objects thought to be inanimate can be both sentient and divine. The Text knows much more than Moses ever will. It has a mind of its own and its own designs and destinies. Indeed, when Abdul burns the Text, the Text and Jes Grew do not actually dissipate; like Ausar, Faro, and Allah, the Father, the Text and Jes Grew sink into sacred leaves, empowering ink, whispering winds, and open minds where they inseminate, regenerate, and proliferate forever.

The Pure and Resurrected Warriors

In the African American secret societies described by Toni Morrison and Ishmael Reed women are not included or are irrelevant. While some of the Seven Days' members establish remarkably empowering connections with women, they cannot have romantic relationships or establish families due to the nature of their work and the focus needed to manifest holistic sociopolitical love. All of the women in *Mumbo Jumbo* are caricatures. Isis can be found "blushing" because she is going to receive Osiris' "rod of authority." On the flipside of this two-dimensional depiction, Isis is a man-eating shrew ostensibly suffering from premenstrual syndrome. Earline goes from being a puppet who pines and whines uselessly for Berbelang to being a host for Erzulie, a hip-swinging home-wrecking God who can only be tamed by Black Herman's "magnificent joint," to borrow a phrase from Morrison. However, just as sure as Shrines of the Black Madonna, which honor the bond between Ast and Heru, can be found all over the world, including the lands being eternally stimulated by Ausar's penis, no holistic, progressive revolution can occur without joint male-female respect, understanding, and cooperative work.[76]

Ngugi's *Matigari* centers on cooperative revolutionary struggle within a gender-balanced collective. The novel begins with the eponymous protagonist preparing to return to his home after finally killing the British usurper, Settler Williams. Harriet Tubman realized that her individual freedom meant nothing: She needed a free family and community to rejoice with her, so she made thirteen trips from America to Canada to bring a nation to glory. Similarly, Matigari realizes that he cannot have a homecoming without his family: "We shall all go home together. We shall enter the house together. We shall light the fires together. After all, the struggle was for the house, wasn't it? A home . . .

a shelter . . . with children playing on the verandah in the open air . . . Sharing what little we have. . . ."[77] Matigari has no idea that the world has completely changed since he chased Williams into the woods, and that rather than morally bankrupt settlers, it is modernization, globalism, and "progress" that are determinedly destroying African civilization.

Matigari finds the children he longs to embrace competing with dogs and vultures as they sift through a landfill in search of food, bits of bones, string, and defunct electronic devices. The children are orphans whose parents were killed while fighting the war of liberation. Forced to raise, feed, and protect themselves, many of the orphans excel at theft, violence, and viciousness. In this brave new African world, which is fully infected with the ills of Western society, it is logical that adults are the enemies of children, and when Matigari crosses an invisible boundary bordering the children's territory, the orphans pummel him with stones.

After he killed Settler Williams, Matigari buried his AK 47 under a tree and girded himself with the belt of peace. When the children's stones draw his blood and tears, Matigari's instinct is similar to Milkman's, he reaches for a weapon, but also like Macon Dead III, Matigari has no weapon other than his Arm-Leg-Leg-Arm-Head. After re-membering that his antagonists, whom he might have killed had he been armed, are *his* children, Matigari begins to comprehend how complicated the struggle has become, and he realizes that he must evolve his weaponry and divinity to address new needs and atrocities.

Matigari bonds with the orphan Mũriũki and together they meet Ngarũro wa Kĩrĩro, a labor organizer and activist who enlightens Matigari as to the current economic and industrial struggle the community is facing. Matigari ma Njirũũngi means "the patriots who survived the bullets" and Ngarũro wa Kĩrĩro means "wiping your tears away." Through the names of the characters, alone, Ngugi is transmitting a powerful cipher to his audience. Matigari tells Ngarũro wa Kĩrĩro to tell everyone that Settler Williams and his African lackey, John Boy, are dead and that Matigari ma Njirũũngi has returned from the hills to reclaim his home. Ngarũro is not aware that Matigari is in a time warp after having been isolated in the hills and battling Settler Williams for decades, he understands Matigari's message to be a revolutionary code that he takes to the masses who prepare to re-determine their destinies.

Having found his children and his brethren, Matigari seeks his sistren, his wives, his daughters. When he finds them, he finds epic devastation. The assertion that prostitution is the oldest profession in the world is the most protracted and demented lie ever uttered. While Caucasians may brag about having erected economies between their women's thighs, not all of the peoples of the world thought or think so little of women. The world's first civilizations, Nabta Playa, Nubia, Kitara, and Kemet, structured their societies on agriculture and philosophical, cosmological, and spiritual enlightenment, as is evidenced in ancient pyramids, temples, universities, agrarian advances, and astronomical calendars. What is more, women in these and the majority of African societies were, and still are, in many cases, rightly revered as Gods because of their essential roles in creation.

The demented minds that created prostitution and promoted it as a viable way of life are the same ones that created the concepts of Christianity, slavery, lynching, currency, copyright, and capitalism. These sick individuals have infected nearly everyone on the globe with their economic, social, and mental diseases. Because one of the primary objectives of Caucasian slaveries and consumerisms is to reduce the inherently divine Africana woman to a commodity all around the world, including and especially in Africa,[78] Matigari finds his female complement quickly. In fact, she propositions him.

After Gũthera asks him if he is a wife-beater or if he will need to sell his wife's land to afford her charms, Matigari exclaims, "Can't you see that I am old enough to be your father?" Gũthera's response enlightens Matigari about the society that sprang up while he was fighting in the forests:

> These days it does not matter whether it's your father or your son, whether it's your brother or your sister. The most important thing is money. Even if a boy like this one came to me with money in his pocket, I would give him such delights as he has never dreamt of. . . . The only people I have sworn never to have anything to do with are policemen. (*Matigari*, 24)

The "civilization" brought by Caucasian colonizers is an interesting one indeed. For the right price, Gũthera, a community mother, would have sex with Mũriũki, her community son, and such debasements are so rampant in this society that they fail to raise an eyebrow, let alone stir outrage. It is through the debasement of Gũthera and Mũriũki that one gains a clear understanding of the cost of globalization and modernization to African women and children.

Both Gũthera and Mũriũki are the progeny of freedom fighters. Mũriũki's father was a Matigari who was killed in the war. Similar to the French racists who burn Africans and Arabs out of their homes,[79] Mũriũki's mother was killed when their landlord set their house on fire because she could not pay the rent. Gũthera's father was the type of person Toni Cade Bambara would have admired: He was both a priest and a revolutionary: He stored his bullets in his Bible. When the police discover that he is a Matigari, the superintendent arrests Gũthera and tells her, "You are carrying your father's life between your legs" (*Matigari*, 29). Gũthera, a devout Christian, must choose between two commandments: honor thy father and mother and thou shall not commit adultery. (The reduction of Maat's Forty-Two Admonitions into ten commandments is more evidence of the destructive work wrought by Moses' theft and his misunderstanding of the Book of Djhuiti.[80]) When Gũthera tells the superintendent that she must honor her "Father, Creator of heaven and earth" and not commit adultery, the officer kills her father.

Gũthera is trapped by a religion that offers her no viable choice, and because she does not have a revolutionary ideology, she has neither plan nor protection. Ngugi highlights the importance of teaching children practical and revolutionary principles as opposed to religious beliefs. Oppression is not kind enough to wait until a child has come of age. As is illustrated in Carlos Diegues' film *Quilombo*, children must be armed with mental, spiritual, and martial weaponry and arts. Gũthera has no skills, weaponry, or artistry, and with her earthly father slain, she turns to her heavenly father for directions on how to feed and clothe her young siblings: He is silent. Gũthera is forced to undertake the labor that her colonizers and neocolonizers prepared for her: prostitution. However, she opens the Bible, a book often thought to be closed, and inscribes therein her own eleventh commandment: Gũthera vows to never take a police officer as a sexual client. Although she later breaks her commandment to liberate an incarcerated Matigari, the commandment is *hers* to keep or break. Gũthera, and Gũthera alone, is the author of her destiny and the legislator of her laws.

In his 17 February 2002 Saviour's Day Speech, Minister Louis Farrakhan observes that Caucasians change the spirit of everyone and everything they encounter.[81] Empires are transformed into sprawling ghettos; mothers are reduced to whoredom; children become scavengers; fathers are little more than drones. Air that was fresh and crisp is weighted with waves of static and virulent strains of diseases that only the maddest of scientists could concoct. After European colonizers vacate a land, they leave cadres of "ostentatious cripples," to quote Armah, to continue enforcing their agenda and to ensure the permanence of neocolonization. Consequently, Matigari finds that although he killed Settler Williams and John Boy, he must now grapple with their sons.

As if he were trained beside Malidoma Somé's antagonist Father Joe in the school of self-hatred, John Boy, the well-trained running dog of imperialism, is much more ferocious an adversary than his master. A self-styled *"African Anglophile and proud of it,"* Boy is so oppressor-oriented that the motto of his family coat of arms is "Destroy Terrorists"—the "terrorists" in question are African freedom fighters (*Matigari*, 86, emphasis in the original). Boy is part of a network of oppressors that includes the police, African and Caucasian robber barons, and the entire government, including corrupt ministers and the head of state. The only difference between the Atonists of *Mumbo Jumbo* and the oppressors of *Matigari* and *Wizard of the Crow* is ethnicity, which gives the chant "Nyabinghi" even more resonance and relevance.

In his timeless "Message to the Grassroots" speech, El Hajj Malik El Shabazz describes the "house Negro" as "loving the master more than the master loved himself";[82] this is true of African Anglophiles. Because their love for their masters is predicated on their hatred of themselves, neo-house Negroes are especially vicious to other Africans, and they are often the ringleaders of the terrorism and domination essential to African subjugation. It is telling that in *Matigari*, the Minister of Truth and Justice calls a meeting to deal with the threat posed by Matigari, and citing Caucasian American advances in the selective distribution of justice, the Minister creates a judicial body that will dispense "instant justice." One of the chief members of the court of instant justice is Hooded Truth and Justice: an African man wearing a Ku Klux Klan hood and robe. In fact, all of the judges, attorneys, and commissioners wear ties with KKK emblazoned on them.

The Ku Klux Klan's legacy is more far-reaching than its grand wizards might imagine. Lynching, the instant justice that became the Klan's calling card in African American communities, has grown in popularity in many crippled neocolonial nations. Instant justice is also known as extrajudicial killing because, in actuality, no form of justice is involved. Similar to the KKK's attacks against African Americans, a person is accused of a crime and summarily lynched while titillated spectators watch. The Klan's original purpose was to terrorize the African American population, banish them from towns and prevent them from starting businesses, integrating schools, and voting. Lynchings were America's favorite national pastime from the 1860s until the 1960s, when African Americans embraced the Second Amendment and began defending themselves. Since that time, lynchings have largely been outsourced to the police who are free to kill Africana people with impunity.

Although the Klan popularized barbarity, the origins of instant justice and its methods of administration predate the Klan. Lynching, public whipping, drawing and quartering, burning at the stake, and death via cradle, iron maiden, interrogation chair, impalement, saw, and breaking on the wheel are just a few of the classic methods by which Medieval Christian Caucasians would torture some individuals while entertaining others.[83] The fact that Christian Caucasians not only imagined but actually industrialized the manufacture of such unthinkably horrific devices of torture is incredible. As perhaps their signature contribution to world "civilization," Caucasians took their passion for pain and their extraordinary tools of torture with them and used them to "teach" the various world peoples whom they colonized.

That many Africana people are excellent students of their oppressors is evident in the contemporary African use of Caucasian methods of torture. During the era of apartheid, the African National Congress used "necklacing," placing a tire filled with gasoline around the neck of a person and burning them alive, to punish people who were accused of spying or other counterrevolutionary offenses. In Nigeria, "weti-weti," a concept similar to necklacing, is employed: A person accused of stealing is caught, beaten, doused in petrol and burned alive. One need only shout, "Thief! Thief!" for the masses to gather their truncheons, petrol, tires, and cameras. It is rarely the case that explanation or expiation can save the person branded thief because punishing thieves is not the objective.

Similar to the victims of the Klan, victims of extrajudicial killings around the world need not have committed any crime at all. Jealousy, envy, and hatred of one's self and lot in life fuel the fires of immolation. This was certainly the case for Tekena Elkanah, Chidiaka Biringa Lordson, Ugonna Obuzor, and Lloyd Michael Toku, four college students who were tortured and lynched in Aluu, Nigeria in 2012. When one sees the images of these naked students alive and either struggling to explain themselves to or being methodically humiliated by their captors and when one knows the students' purpose and backgrounds, it becomes clear that the fury unleashed on them is not punishment for actual or perceived crimes, it is the murderers' rage at their miserable lives and destinies; it is self-hatred, inadequacy, jealousy, and eternal internal defeat projected outward with a savagery that only a Christian Klansman or priest can appreciate.

While extrajudicial killings are labeled "jungle justice" by some individuals, this custom does not originate in any "jungle." Correctly linking community lynching to racism, corruption, and injustice, Fela Anikulapo Kuti describes such murders as not only "wrong" but also "very un-African."[84] In traditional African societies, thievery was punished with complete community ostracism not with a gruesome orgy of torture. To find the origin of "necklacing" and "weti-weti" one must look to Caucasian history—from the "trials" of "witches" to the lynchings of African Americans. To better understand the Klan's gift to Africa, including shared methodology and torture-induced ecstasy, compare the tragic photographs, postcards, trade cards, and mementos of African American lynching victims framed by proud grinning Caucasian men, women, and children to the videos and photos of the Aluu community lynching Elkanah, Lordson, Obuzor, and Toku.[85]

In addition to organizing spectacles of annihilation, those who seek to destroy Africana divinity and Divinities have also taken pains to prevent life from forming at all. In *Mumbo Jumbo*, after Set destroys Osiris' body he tries to eradicate everything the Netcher represents: "He outlawed Dancing. . . . Next he banished Music. And then as his mind deteriorated he banned Fucking. And later even Life itself" (173). In *Matigari*, the Minister of Truth and Justice shows himself to be a geographical and geopolitical neighbor and brother of Set. The Minister bans for eternity a song praising Matigari and decrees: "No song, no story, or play or riddle or proverbs, mentioning Matigari ma Njirũũngi will be tolerated" (*Matigari* 59). The Minister of Truth and Justice understands the connection between creative expression and inspired procreation, and with a proposition that mirrors Set's ban, he is prepared to sever that connection:

> I have been told that women around here have been singing that they will give birth to more Matigari ma Njirũũngi. Are you drunk with this Matigari ma Njirũũngi? The KKK government has said that the main cause of poverty is the fact that women breed like rats. . . . I shall get the USA to establish one of those open air birth-control clinics where women can have their wombs closed. No more children for the poor! . . . . Pregnancies are the result of evil and wild desires. I shall ask the government to ban dreams and desires of that kind for a period of two years. Fucking among the poor should be stopped by a presidential decree!" (*Matigari*, 100)

The United States, the world leader in preemptive genocide, offers the Minister a renowned role model: He will tailor to fit his society the methodology of Margaret Sanger, the founder of Planned Parenthood, who advocated the sterilization of African American women.[86] While Sanger sought to obliterate Africans in America, the Minister hopes to ensure the birth of a nation of slaves, lackeys, and sell-outs.

Despite the Minister's decrees and decrying, Matigari Ma Njirũũngi becomes a self-fulfilling and self-proliferating prophecy. Not only does he survive the bullets of Williams and Boy, but his powers lead the community to first compare him to Jesus and later to understand that he is the Messiah. The people of this African country are not surprised by Matigari's divinity because they know their history: "Where is the oldest church in the world? In Ethiopia, Africa. When he was a baby, where did he flee to? Egypt, Africa. What has happened before can happen again"

(*Matigari*, 67). It is important to note that Messiah Matigari, like High John the Conqueror, is a collective God who encompasses and includes all the peoples. The community begins to use the title Matigari Ma Njirũũngi in its proper collective sense to include everyone: "Whomever dares touch that woman will know who we really are, we, Matigari Ma Njirũũngi!" (*Matigari*, 67).[87]

Through the inclusiveness of the term "Matigari Ma Njirũũngi" and the novel's opening poem, which encourages the reader to set the events in the land and era of his or her choosing, Ngugi extends an invitation to members of his textual community and his actual audience. The qualifications necessary to enter the continuum of divine revolutionaries are knowledge of self and knowledge of the self's unlimited revolutionary and evolutionary potential. Ngugi encourages his Africana audience to do what Matigari does: embrace, reclaim, erect, protect, and develop revolutionaries and revolution. Ngugi's objective is clearly elucidated through the names of his characters: Gũthera means "Pure" and Mũriũki means "Resurrected." The divine triumvirate established by Ausar, Aset, and Heru is intact, as Gũthera, Mũriũki, and Matigari form a trinity of sacred power as the Pure and Resurrected Patriots Who Survived the Bullets. Consequently, the end of *Matigari* returns to the beginning, as the cycle, like the struggle, continues but with more warriors, more consciousness, and more determination.

Wizard of the Crow continues the revolutionary weaving spun in *Matigari*. The action takes place in the fictional nation of Aburĩria, but by applying the logic of the opening poem of *Matigari*, the reader can find Aburĩria reproduced in any number of nations. *Wizard of the Crow* extends other lines drawn in *Matigari*. While the audience only hears about His Excellency Ole Excellence, the head of state in *Matigari*, the reader has full access to the Ruler, as the head of state of Aburĩria is called. The access Ngugi grants the reader is so complete that we get to see how the Ruler's pregnancy is conceived and what he gives birth to. The pregnant male ruler is only the tip of the satirical iceberg toward which Ngugi steers his reader; the audience is also granted intimate knowledge of the president's cabinet, most of whom take advantage of the wonders of plastic surgery.

Machokali, the Minister of Foreign Affairs, has had his eyes increased to the size of light bulbs to symbolize his ability to see all and report to the Ruler. Silver Sikiokuu, the Minister of State, has had his ears surgically expanded to enhance his ability to eavesdrop for the Ruler. In their competition for the title of number one snitch, Machokali and Sikiokuu are aided by Big Ben Mambo. Mambo was deemed unfit for the military because of his diminutive stature, but he held on to his dream and had his tongue elongated to better echo the Ruler's commands to soldiers and threats to enemies. The elongation was over successful and left Mambo with a long drooling tongue that hung from his mouth like a dog's; so he had his lips stretched to cover his tongue. The Ruler rewarded Mambo's self-directed deformation by crowning him Minister of Information (one can only imagine hearing a speech from this mouth). These grotesque yes men are surrounded by a host of sellouts, struggling police officers, commissioners, inspectors, "reformed" revolutionaries, and greedy businessmen, such as Titus Tajirika, the president of Eldares Modern Construction and Real Estate.

Matigari's union with Gũthera and Mũriũki is essential to *Matigari*, but Matigari, the masculine principle, is the guiding force of the work. *Wizard of the Crow* features three revolutionary movements and the force behind each one is Woman. The Movement of the Voice of the People (MVP) is a secret society composed of revolutionary women, and their leader is the redoubtable Nyawĩra, the outspoken intellectual and warriors' warrior who has committed class suicide.[88] Rather than use her education and potential to rise to independent heights and amass personal wealth, Nyawĩra devotes her life to grassroots frontline revolutionary struggle. A true revolutionist, whose name in English means "hard-working," Nyawĩra uses her job at Eldares Construction to gain inside information about the plans of Aburĩria's leaders. Acting as Titus Tajirika's secretary also places her in the path of Kamĩtĩ, her complement and the novel's protagonist.

Kamĩtĩ is a miseducated directionless youth who is introduced in the novel in a state remarkably similar to that of Velma Henry of *The Salt Eaters*: He has crawled onto a mountain of garbage and has allowed his soul to fly free. As his spirit floats above Aburĩria, Kamĩtĩ wonders if he should allow his body to be crushed along with the trash or if he should reenter his body and continue existing. While Kamĩtĩ decides to rejoin his body and live, like all too many Africana men and women with Western college educations, Kamĩtĩ's life is bereft of purpose, meaning, and employment. Kamĩtĩ decides to go to the Paradise Hotel and beg for a living. With this decision, Kamĩtĩ joins a growing class that also serves as a symbol of a familiar African paradox: beggars in the midst of plenty.

The leaders of Aburĩria have no interest in the struggles of the masses. Similar to the U.S. politicians who are masters of pork barrel politics, the ministers of Aburĩria focus on concocting ridiculous and expensive schemes to line their pockets while displaying their devotion to the Ruler. Machokali proposes a birthday gift that will allow the Ruler to "call on God daily to say good morning or good evening or simply how was your day today, God? The Ruler would be the daily recipient of God's advice."[89] This updated tower of Babel is called Marching to

Heaven. Not to be outdone, Sikiokuu proposes the construction of a luxury spaceship to permit the Ruler to travel throughout the Cosmos and mine the riches therein.

In a critique of the dynamics of international political begging, Machokali and Sikiokuu have invited the leaders of the Global Bank to Aburĩria's Paradise Hotel so that they can beg for money for Marching to Heaven. The impoverished community converges on the Paradise to solicit alms from the political beggars who are begging international benefactors for money. Ngugi moves his audience to ponder an important query: When one has a hotel in "paradise" and has the means to create what one needs, for what does one need beg?

Ousmane Sembene, the father of African cinema, asserts that foreign aid and charity are ruinous to both nations and individuals. Sembene argues that the person who survives on alms will "end up losing all sense of real life, not being able to accomplish anything for himself. . . . he is a monster among us; all he says is thanks, thanks, thanks."[90] Similarly, in some cases, whole nations expect, beg for, and wait for monies to flow from abroad rather than solve their own problems. One could easily argue that charity actually contributes to the impoverishment of people and nations. Sembene goes on to ask, "How many millions of dollars the U.S. has handed Africa for thirty-five years, and where is the money? Where are the results of those investments?"[91] That money marched to heaven along with the guilt of those who enjoy vast wealth as a result of the enslavement of Africans in both the traditional and neocolonial senses. Indeed, one of the benefits of charity is that it assuages guilty feelings without righting wrongs or repairing what has been destroyed. Charity directed to Africa has the added advantage of making Africans appear to be stuck in a time warp of helplessness, backwardness, and ignorance when, in fact, African resources and genius remain the backbone of the world.

Ironically, Kamĩtĩ's decision to beg leads him to the vocation designed for his inherent and inherited skill set. Kamĩtĩ creates Wizard of the Crow as a ruse to deflect the police's attention from him and Nyawĩra, who staged a beggars' protest at the Paradise. However, the ploy introduces Kamĩtĩ to his destiny as a wisdom worker. Kamĩtĩ becomes the Wizard of the Crow, and his first client is his pursuer, Constable Arigaigai, who is also the trickster and narrator of the novel. Arigaigai describes to rapt audiences the Wizard's ability to use a mirror to capture and destroy one's enemies. He also reveals that the Wizard can take the form and voice of a man or a woman. Through Arigaigai's oratorical prowess, Nyawĩra and Kamĩtĩ become entwined as the dual gendered Deity, "Sir Madam Wizard of the Crow," and they establish a sacred society that is founded on the elemental building blocks of creation and civilization—a man and a woman.

A mirror and knife are Kamĩtĩ's spiritual-technological implements of choice, and his methodology is simple. Kamĩtĩ has his client envision his enemy. If the client does not know exactly who the villain is it does not matter. Whatever shape takes form in his client's mind, Kamĩtĩ can see in his mirror. When Kamĩtĩ scratches the image in the mirror with his knife, the enemy is destroyed. The Wizard's scratching methodology is comparable to both Yoruba and BaKongo divination. The Sanza Player of Aime Cesaire's *A Season in the Congo* declares himself to be the "Scratching spur!": "In the sand of falsehood I scratch. Spur, I scratch! Down to the truth I scratch. . . . The cock of divination."[92] William Bascom finds that the scratching methodology is an intrinsic aspect of Yoruba divination: "The name Ifa is interpreted as meaning scraping, because he 'scrapes' sickness and other evil away from those who are afflicted."[93]

Kamĩtĩ's use of a mirror to interact with souls is also similar to the Pan-African technology that the Yoruba call apeta, that the Egbo refer to as "shadow calling," and that the Dagara honor as Pintul. In *The Sanctified Church*, Zora Neale Hurston details how a mirror and a gun are used to kill a community predator, and her data corresponds to that of Kimbwandende Kia Bunseki Fu-Kiau, who describes how a *nganga* (diviner) uses a *sènso* or "televisor pot" to determine the identity of a violator and kill him: "The nganga took the knife appropriate for the practice and knocked it on the head of the kidnapper whose shadow was radiating within the sènso. At once the clear water was transformed (changed) into blood, the enemy of the community is unmistakably hit."[94] Fu-Kiau goes on to discuss the possibility of using the sènso pot to kill the world's numerous despots.

Wizard of the Crow's methodology is as fluid and versatile as that of his historical progenitors; in addition to banishing evil, he can use his mirror to project clients into their desired states of being. When Titus Tajirika is selected to be the first chairman of the Marching to Heaven Building Committee, he becomes the recipient of so many bribes that he cannot effectively hide or manage all the money. Astonished by the literal financial avalanche and the possibilities that await him, Titus loses the ability to do anything other than stand before his mirror and bark, "If. . . . If only." Titus has acquired "white ache": He is immobilized by wondering what his life would be like "if only" he were Caucasian. The Wizard uses his mirror to project Titus and his wife Vinjinia into their dream. When they see what their lives would be like as homeless destitute Caucasians, their "white ache" is sent into remission.

Harnessing the flexibility of spirit image technology, *Wizard of the Crow* exposes and heals delicate and damaged human psyches. Kamĩtĩ reveals that rather than using the mirror to eradicate reprobates, he takes a different approach: "I punish evil itself, not the evil ones. I am a healer. I heal wounded bodies and troubled souls" (*Wizard of the Crow*, 293). While using image projection to kill, as described by Fu-Kiau and Hurston, is an important defense strategy, Kamĩtĩ's technique is equally important. Balancing political, spiritual, economic, social, personal, and cosmic imbalances is a delicate task. And while it is necessary for many people to die in order for justice, balance, propriety, and order to be restored, so many individuals have given themselves over to corruption and are contributing to destruction, that if all destroyers were slain, there would be few people on the Earth. Furthermore, such a simplistic solution as destroying all of the destroyers is not acceptable in the realm of the Gods.

The battles, struggles, intricacies and vicissitudes of existence are essential to existence. This is why the prayer of "Ole Nigger" in African American folklore to "kill all the white folks," no matter how heinous and vile they are, will not be answered.[95] "Ole Nigger" must find within himself the tools of High John the Conqueror and apply them to liberate and transform himself from Ole Nigger to God. Similarly, while Nianankoro can see his father in the spiritually charged water, he cannot kill him through that medium. The only way that Nianankoro can self-actualize is by honing his skills through struggle and harnessing the infinite powers that reside within him. Kamĩtĩ's methodology is firmly rooted in the paradigm of revolutionary Africana praxis, for rather than destroying "evil doers" and leaving "evil" free to thrive, Kamĩtĩ focuses on destroying the mentalities that foment slavery, capitalism, self-hatred, prostitution, corruption, social inequities, and "white ache." Perhaps the most important outgrowth of the Wizard's methodology is the facilitation of self-disclosure and self-analysis: Once the "evil" is eradicated there are no more scapegoats or excuses; the only choices left the client are to consciously revert to wickedness or to strive to evolve and elevate.

The Wizard's divinations are designed to change minds, alter destinies, and expand consciousnesses intratextually, intertextually, and extratextually, and the novel encourages the application of African spiritual technology for personal, political, and social liberation. Contrary to Bambara's lament, Ngugi depicts the relationship between spiritualists and revolutionaries and enemies of progress to be intricately layered and meticulously laced. Indeed, *Wizard of the Crow*'s mirror reveals that the enemies of his clients are those selfsame clients who seek out and wait days to receive the wisdom of the dual-gendered Wizard. The images that are conjured in the mind and destroyed in the mirror are the clients' reflections of themselves as their own agents of internal and external devastation. By destroying that fragmented and sick self, the Wizard seeks to provide the catalyst for a whole and healthy being to grow. Wizard of the Crow operates in a manner similar to Olódùmarè and the African American God in taking a nonjudgmental stance and providing the client the means and materials to re-determine her own destiny as she chooses.

While Kamĩtĩ's work is politically motivated, his spiritual gifts and technologies are a genetic inheritance, and like both Malidoma Somé and Milkman of *Song of Solomon*, Kamĩtĩ is led by the spirit of his grandfather. Kamĩtĩ's father describes the wisdom and technology of his progenitors:

> Not only were they healers, but some had the gift of seeing things hidden from ordinary eyes. Some could even fly like birds. Consider your grandfather, Kamĩtĩ wa Kĩenjeku, from whom you take your name! He sometimes found himself atop a mountain impossible for humans to climb or floating in the middle of a lake though he did not know how to swim. (*Wizard of the Crow*, 294)

In addition to him boasting many of the skills that I discuss in chapter one, Kamĩtĩ's grandfather was also a Matigari, and he used his knowledge of flora to heal and empower the other Matigari during the battle against the colonizers. True to the African ethos, rather than die, Kamĩtĩ wa Kĩenjeku joined the immortals and continues the struggle, as Kamĩtĩ's father reveals: "The British shot him dead one day, but his body was never found. Some maintain that he is still alive and that his spirit hovers over Aburĩria, ensuring that the truth of our past endeavors shall never be forgotten" (*Wizard of the Crow*, 294).

With his father granting him the gift of his grandfather's ìtàn (history) and knowledge of his ipǫnri (sacred identity), Kamĩtĩ has an illuminated path to his orí (destiny) and to his Divinity. To ensure his son does not stray from the path, Kamĩtĩ's father informs him of the universal African spiritualist's law: "You cannot use the gift to acquire earthly riches beyond the clothes you wear, the food you eat, and the house in which you live" (*Wizard of the Crow*, 295). This is the same law that traditionally guided all Africana spiritualists but is today ignored by many.

Jesuit indoctrination had calamitous cultural, psychological, and spiritual impacts on Malidoma Somé; and Kamĩtĩ is similar to Somé in that his Eurocentric university education left him a fragmented useless being immersed in garbage. Despite his recovery and finding his purpose as Wizard of the Crow, Kamĩtĩ suffers another psychological breakdown. He decides to remove himself and his spiritual gifts from the rancid politicos, beggars, and lovelorn who, with money reeking of deceit in hand, camp on the Wizard's doorstep. When Kamĩtĩ abandons the shrine for a simple life in the forest fortified by herbs and protected by the stars, Nyawĩra leaves the "new-millennium Buddha" and continues a warrior's unending work. Unlike Kamĩtĩ, Nyawĩra is not confounded by the useless information spewed in Western educational institutions. She needs no conscientization. She does not gravitate toward revolution; she is its catalyst. While Kamĩtĩ ponders the stars, Nyawĩra and the MVP foment revolution.

While African women are routinely portrayed as voiceless, helpless, hopeless beings (an image created to generate charitable donations and foreign aid), in reality, African women are inherently and profoundly empowered. The African female body, itself, is a power station of immense magnitude. Àjẹ́, the spiritual power inherent in Africana women that is resident in and magnified by the womb, manifests itself in myriad ways. One of its most well-known and politically-charged manifestations is that a woman can destroy a man by cursing him while revealing to him her naked body. In various parts of Africa, if a man has committed an especially heinous act, like beating a pregnant woman, community women strip him naked, remove their own clothing and "sit on" him—press their vaginas and buttocks all over the man's body and face—to remind him of his origin and the ties that bind all women and mothers. Another powerful weapon is for a woman to slap an offending man with a blood-rich menstrual cloth.[96] Because Woman is the only God who reproduces both herself and her complement (man), the vagina, breasts, menses, and womb are obvious reminders to men that women control their destinies. A woman's vagina is the literal doorway of life and her womb and breasts are the life-support system of humanity. As effortlessly as she provides and sustains life, a woman can use her breasts and vagina to usher despicable men into oblivion.

In "Politicisation of the Female Breasts," Kehinde Oyetimi describes the female body as a catalyst of revolution and an essential and guiding force in Yoruba politics: "Monarchs who have lost their political and social relevance were cursed with the exposure of the female breasts, in protest. The breasts of such women were weapons of social and political change."[97] The political power of the breasts is majestically harnessed in Dani Kouyate's film *Sia: Dream of the Python*; similarly, the symbolic power of the vagina provides the climax of Akinwumi Isola's play *Madam Tinubu*.[98]

In contemporary African life, women continue to use their cosmic-biological powers to effect change. In the spring of 2003, six hundred women from the Nigerian Delta, took over Chevron-Texaco's Escravos terminal trapping seven hundred employees for a week. The women demanded many things for their communities including the correction of river erosion, clean water, electricity, and schools and health clinics. Chevron agreed to their terms.[99] In Liberia, Leymah Gbowee, Janet Johnson Bryant, and Sugars Cooper, exhausted with a war that had lasted over a decade, united with community women. After a sex strike, the women's collective took their case to the African Union. After watching heads of state and war-mongers swirl about in flowing robes and designer suits, Gbowee staged a sit-in and threatened to curse the political fashion show with her raw Àjẹ́. The threat of her curse alone was enough to move the men to action: Charles Taylor, Liberia's head-of-state, resigned, was incarcerated, and was found guilty of several counts of war crimes and crimes against humanity. Ellen Johnson Sirleaf was elected president of Liberia in 2005 and was reelected in 2011.[100] Perhaps inspired by the successes of their Liberian sisters, in 2012, the female activists of Togo's "Sauvons Le Togo" ("Let's Save Togo") organized a sex strike and followed that effort with genital cursing in their struggle to end the reign of the Gnassingbé dynasty which has been in power since 1967.[101]

Ngugi also offers an example of the African woman's power to devolve destinies in a scene that showcases women's organic strength in a most compelling manner. A nationwide fundraiser for Marching to Heaven features a presentation of tens of thousands of Aburĩrian women: "From the platform it appeared as if the formations had no beginning and no end, or rather it was one movement with the end and the beginning being the multitude" (*Wizard of the Crow*, 250). The women stop, point to the Ruler, and demand he free his wife Rachel. Then the women turn, and with their backs to the Ruler, Global Bank officials, and foreign dignitaries, they offer a gesture recognized worldwide: "All together we lifted our skirts and exposed our butts to those on the platform, and squatted as if about to shit en masse in the arena. Those of us in the crowd started swearing: MARCHING TO HEAVEN IS A PILE OF SHIT! MARCHING TO HEAVEN IS A MOUNTAIN OF SHIT! And the crowd took this up" (*Wizard of the Crow*, 250). Nyawĩra reveals that this ritual protest has its roots in Aburĩrian history, for her ancestors, when completely fed up with corruption, would actually defecate to make it plain that "they could no longer take shit from a despot" (*Wizard of the Crow*, 250).

The politically-exposed breasts and vaginas intimate not only death but also eventual regeneration so that the miscreant in question can be reborn, remothered, and retrained. Politically-charged buttocks and feces are presented to violators who are beyond redemption. While this particular political shaming act can be and often is undertaken by men as well as women, no Aburĩrian men join the women in their protest. Ngugi appears to be specifically highlighting the courage of women in the face of tyrannical and terroristic misogynists. Furthermore, with his use of feces as a symbol of corrupt dictators and dictatorships, Ngugi can be heard chanting with Òrìṣà Fela the conclusion of Fela's scathing hit song, "I.T.T. (International Thief Thief)."

"I.T.T." is a stunning cultural-political indictment. The song begins with Fela swearing before the Òrìṣà that he is about to speak the truth and that he has both seen with his own eyes and has academically studied the facts he will share. Fela then launches into an exposition on precolonial African sanitation practices:

> Long, long, long, long time ago
> African man we no dey carry shit
> We dey shit inside big big hole
> For Yorubaland na "Shalanga"
> For Igboland na "Onunu-insi"
> For Hausaland na "Salunga"[102]

Fela goes on to list numerous African ethnic groups and the indigenous names of their pit latrines. Fela's lengthy exposition on the similarities of Pan-African waste disposal is significant because when Europeans came to Africa, they brought and enforced the method of sanitation that fit their culture:

> Na European man, na him dey carry shit
> Na for them culture to carry shit
> During the time dem come colonize us
> Dem come teach us to carry shit[103]

Fela reveals that after Europeans stole, kidnapped, exiled, and enslaved Africa's shining Suns, they made mentally and physically colonized continental Africans carry vats of economic, psychological, and actual shit.

As it relates to the literal practice, "carrying shit" refers to "night soil" labor. The term and the occupation originate in England and involve men carrying huge vats of human feces that have been collected throughout the day. Carrying fecal matter is one of many "civilizing" practices that Caucasians forced on South American, African, and Asian nations. This labor is so debilitating that not only are night soil men shunned long after they have deposited the containers of waste because even after bathing the stench remains with them, but in some nations they are nicknamed "tiger men" because when the waste drips down the side of the bucket and slides down the face, the acids streak the skin. If the waste drips into the eye, the eye can be blinded permanently.[104]

As does Ngugi in *Wizard of the Crow*, Fela extends his scatological critique to the contemporary political sphere where corrupt Africans and Caucasians work together to rape African nations of their wealth, power, culture, and integrity through inflation, embezzlement, bribery, and other "white collar" thefts of billions of dollars and naira (Nigerian currency) that devastate the masses and leave infrastructures so dilapidated and poverty so complete that human beings are forced to carry feces on their heads in their struggle to survive. In "I.T.T.," Fela describes how an African of questionable repute will travel to Europe to beg for and receive grants for construction, waste management, and other projects. But rather than use the monies as intended and develop African industries and infrastructures, the monies go to ego-building schemes, such as a chieftaincies and Marching to Heaven.

In "I.T.T." Fela accuses two notable Nigerian leaders of corruption and profiteering: Moshood K. O. Abiola and Olusegun Obasanjo. Obasanjo ruled Nigeria as a military dictator from 1976 to 1979 and as a democratically elected president from 1999 to 2007. Abiola held various high positions, including Chief Financial Officer of International Telephone and Telegraph from 1969 to 1988. Fela deliberately uses the acronym of the telecommunications company, I.T.T., to attack Abiola's character. After calling out the two primary people who give the song its meaning, Fela concludes his song chanting, "We done tire to carry any more of dem shit." This sentiment is exactly that expressed by the MVP in Aburîria. Fela wrote "I.T.T." in 1979, but, in many African and Asian nations, human beings continue to literally carry feces through cities at night, just as the masses bear the burdens of the figurative shit of debts owed by their countries to the World Bank and International Monetary Fund.

Fela created a political organization called Movement of the People to organize and inspire the masses to wake up, rise up, and fight for their rights. Similarly, in *Wizard of the Crow*, the women of the Movement of the Voice of the People signify on the Ruler while inspiring the masses to initiate a holistic revolution. While armed struggle is a necessary aspect of revolutionary resistance, it is not the only aspect. Fela and the women of *Wizard of the Crow* make it known that politically-charged songs, truth telling, and even feces can be sites of phenomenal power. In addition to being Ngugi's nod of respect to Fela, his courageous brother of the struggle, *Wizard of the Crow* is a book about the revolutionization of revolution, and it appears that the first step is to rid one's self, mind, and nation of metaphorical and literal shit.

Coprological expositions in life, lyrics, and literature serve as powerful reminders of the fact that enslavement and oppression can take one to incomprehensible lows, but even in the bottom of the filthiest abyss, one can find and harness tools of unimaginable power. In *Wizard of the Crow*, when Titus Tajirika is imprisoned, the most powerful torture tactic employed by his captors is a passive-aggressive one: They refuse to empty his waste bucket. After seven days of accumulated filth and funk laced with paranoia, Titus uses his bucket of feces as a weapon. Claiming that he has a bucket filled with bloody AIDS-infected feces, Titus parlays a meeting with his captor, Silver Sikiokuu, the Minister of State. When he arrives at Sikiokuu's office, Titus, with bucket of shit in hand, trips and showers the room and everyone and everything in it with his feces: No matter how they scrub, they cannot remove the stains. Titus successfully negotiates his release with an overwhelming bargaining chip.

When they become cognizant of their influence and apply it purposefully, the would-be dregs of society will find themselves liberated, elevated, and celebrated. This is the lesson offered by Titus and by Nigerian author Ben Okri, who, in the novel *Dangerous Love*, details the redemption of a night soil man. In a most pungent passage, Okri describes a group of night soil men converging on a neighborhood:

> Then, like figures emerging from the semidarkness of a curious nightmare, he saw them. Buckling under the weights of brimming nightsoil buckets. . . . They staggered to the waiting lorries, rested a while, went into the various compounds light and came out again weighted.
>
> The place stank. People fled from them. People hurried. They ran, covering their noses, averting their eyes. The nightsoil men moved clumsily, their knees trembling, their backs arched. They grunted. The buckets they carried were often too full and things slithered down and took their place amongst the accumulated rubbish on the streets. There were no flies around.[105]

Okri masterfully depicts the inconceivable. Not only are the loads ridiculously heavy and unwieldy, but everyone is tormented by the transfer of human waste from homes to lorries to the treatment site: Even flies cannot stand the stench.

As is typical of capitalist societies, the people most victimized are the ones working the hardest, and in the midst of his struggle to perform his unimaginable chore, a night soil man becomes the target of children who verbally abuse and throw rocks at him. The fact that he is being taunted and ridiculed by children while he is disposing of their feces leads the night soil collector to exert his power and humanity in the simplest way:

> With the awkward and sometimes wicked dignity that comes with such labours, the nightsoil man struggled, snorted, and then deposited the bucket right in front of the elders, in admonishment for the bad training of their children. The effect was staggering. . . . The elders, the neighbors, the women around, screamed and howled. . . .
>
> When the commotion died down a little a delegation, consisting of the parents of the naughty children, was sent to the man. They stood a good distance from him and begged him, in the name of the gods and ancestors, to carry his infernal deposit from their living places. The nightsoil man stared at them, his eyes quietly contemptuous. He didn't even bother to acknowledge their pleas. . . .
>
> The women went and sought and dragged out the offending children and they were flogged mercilessly in public. The rest of the delegation pressed on with their entreaties. . . . The eldest amongst them prayed for the nightsoil man to become wealthy, successful, to have a happy life with good health. But the nightsoil man, seemingly offended by such excessive prayer, stood away from them, surveying the whole scene with blazing indifferent eyes.
>
> The delegation went away and, after a short conference, they came back again. They had collected some money, which they hoped would appease his anger. He looked at the amount of money they offered. It was ten Naira. With an insulted expression on his face, he turned his head away. The delegation trundled off again, conferred heatedly and come back with the money doubled. But it was only after they had pleaded for another fifteen minutes, after they had got the children to kneel in front of him and beg his forgiveness, and after they had raised the money to thirty Naira, that he condescended to acknowledge their request.[106]

In this lengthy but important passage, the elders initially keep their distance from the night soil man; however, the power of his protest so exalts the night soil man that it is he who stands apart from and looks with scorn upon the offending community. By the end of his exceptional protest, the gap between the haves and have-nots has vanished, making it clear that human beings are interdependent and intimately connected: The king is no more important than the night soil man; the queen is no better than the community's crack whore. It is with this knowledge that entire nations, as opposed to a select few, elevate.

Even though the nature of his job calls for a horrendous adjective to precede the fact, the night soil man is, in fact, a *man*—one whose work is so important that the community would be riddled with fatal diseases if he were to revolt. He appears to be the most lowly, but even with his monstrous loads, he is indispensable and divine. The single moment of power described by Okri can be expanded and duplicated until nations implement the technology necessary to eradicate night soil work. Indeed, with the simple logical premise that "[e]ngaging people to carry human excreta on their heads is degrading and cruel," Ghanaian attorney Nana Adjei Ampofo is fighting to get the Ghanaian Supreme Court to outlaw the night soil waste disposal system.[107]

With an equally logical approach, Wizard of the Crow undertakes the work of purging long-impacted wickedness from the bowels Aburĩria. The respect the Wizard elicits and his-her necessity to the nation is evident in the fact that despite copious references to angels, evil, and evildoers, which reveal the impact of Christianity on Aburĩria, citizens of all religions and sociopolitical ranks, including the Ruler, seek out the Wizard. As the citizens confront their personal evils, shortcomings, enemies, and hopelessness in the mirror, psychological and political shifts occur that make it difficult to determine who the "real" enemies are. This is because no condition is permanent: Human beings are always changing—always undergoing revolution and/or devolution, as the case may be. *Wizard of the Crow* is not a fairytale in which evil is facilely vanquished; it cannot be. However, the novel does carefully detail the intricacies, nuances, absurdities, devastating gains, and fortunate losses that line the path of existence.

Ngugi is part of a collective of African warrior-artists whose works are wrought for life's sake and who are cognizant of the fact that if the source of human life, the African woman, is not protected and respected, then all that she produces and sustains is in jeopardy. Given the slander, humiliation, and devaluation to which Africana women are subjected globally, it is not at all surprising to find that the most vulnerable people in the world are Africana girls. Artists like Ngugi, Armah, and Sembene use their art to reverse the anti-life tide that is drowning Africana daughters.

Moolaadé, the last film Sembene made, centers on Collé Ardo who revolutionizes her society by protecting four girls who refuse to be circumcised. Although female genital circumcision is promoted as "tradition" and a "purification" rite, it is actually designed to protect and expand patriarchal domination by excising the female genitalia, including and especially that kernel of concentrated power known as the clitoris.[108]

In the documentary that chronicles the making of *Moolaadé*, Sembene challenges the need for female genital excision by making a stunning comparison:

> We are in 2004; out of some 54 states of the African Union, more than 38 still practice female circumcision. Why? I don't know! Origins? I don't know! *But why cut a woman's clitoris? Why not cut off the head of a man's penis?* But *Moolaadé* is not just about female circumcision[;] it's about the liberation of our societies, the freedom of our people.[109]

With *Moolaadé*, Sembene returns his audience to the queries that Ngugi raises about female circumcision in his 1965 novel *The River Between*. In their book and film Ngugi and Sembene, respectively, make it clear that Africans do not need Western aid or assistance to end female circumcision. Indeed, Westerners routinely exacerbate problems— especially those that they create—with their political agendas, myopia, unconscious and conscious racism, arrogance, and ignorance. Sembene stresses the fact that the only saviors that Africans need are Africans, themselves: "As far as I am concerned, politically speaking, cinema allows me to show my people their predicaments so they take responsibility; they hold their destiny in their hands. Nobody other than ourselves can solve our problems."[110]

Collé Ardo is not the only protector in *Moolaadé*; the film also features a heroic character who earned the ironic nickname Mercenaire (Mercenary) because he stood up for the rights of his fellow Africans soldiers who were victims of racial discrimination. Mercenaire is the only person who defends Collé when her husband publicly flogs her, and this carefully woven character outright accuses Ibrahim Doucoure and his father of pedophilia for preparing to have an adult Ibrahim marry an eleven-year-old child named Fily. Mercenaire, and Sembene through him, puts African male elders on notice that the defiling and delimiting of Africana daughters must stop.

Armah also takes African men to task for allowing their lust and greed to destroy the lives of the youths they should be protecting. *Two Thousand Seasons* describes the relationship of Brafo and Ajoa who are, respectively, seventeen and fifteen and preparing to unite their lives when they are interrupted by Brafo's father who wants to possess Ajoa. His sense of entitlement becomes so virulent and violent that the couple must flee their community to escape his wrath (*Seasons*, 5). The narrator of *Seasons* also rails against Jonto, the African lecher with "a spirit caught straight from the white predators from the desert" (*Seasons*, 64). Jonto rapes animals as well as children: "He loved particularly the tender arseholes of boys not yet in the thirtieth season. Some he had oiled for ingress but in his happiest moods he dispensed with oil, preferring as lubricant the natural blood of each child's bleeding anus as he forced his entry" (*Seasons*, 65).

With their critiques of aberrant patriarchy, Armah, Sembene, and Ngugi join Alice Walker, Ntozake Shange, and Toni Morrison, who were censured and even branded "castrating bitches" because they spoke long-known truths about the culture of patriarchal pedophilia in their efforts to protect and empower all Africana peoples, especially those who are the most important and the most vulnerable.

Ngugi attacks the culture of pedophilia in *Wizard of the Crow* through the concept of the "bed-maker." Because of his status, the Ruler has more "bed-makers" than any other person. But it is not the number of conquests that bothers his wife Rachel but the ages of his victims:

> You know that I have not complained about all those women who make beds for you, no matter how many children you sire with them. But why schoolgirls? Are they not as young as the children you have fathered? Are they not really our children? You father them today and tomorrow you turn them into wives? Have you no tears of concern for our tomorrow?" (*Wizard of the Crow*, 6)

From the African communal perspective, the Ruler is no better than the Caucasian American enslavers who thought nothing of raping African women and then raping their own daughters and sons conceived in rape.[111]

The Ruler does not bother to excuse his actions because, like the enslaver, his power is his justification; but he does punish his wife for querying him. He imprisons her in a house that is suspended in time to replicate the moment when Rachel issued her query. It is this imprisonment and abuse that the Movement of the Voice of the People protests, but it is important to note that Rachel is the first person to tire of carrying the Ruler's shit. She speaks out for herself and for all the daughters and mothers of the nation. By doing so, Rachel becomes both outcast and icon, and she becomes the soul of the Movement for the Voice of the People.

The women of T. Obinkaram Echewa's historical novel *I Saw The Sky Catch Fire* take on the British colonizers and their minion with elemental liberation tools—the pestles that help them feed their nation and the vaginas that brought the nation into being.[112] In Ben Okri's *Infinite Riches*, one wife's search for her imprisoned husband creates a river of Woman-Power so strong that jail and prison doors open before them, and the cells cough up their starving, suffering, unjustly-incarcerated husbands.[113] Throughout *Wizard of the Crow*, Aburĩrian women unite and become a sacred society of justice that stuns and silences rulers and chastises abusive husbands.

Titus Tajirika encounters the power of Woman after he beats his wife. While Sir Wizard uses a mirror to divine and heal, Madam Wizard summons the Aburĩrian equivalent of the Yoruba ẹgbẹ́ Àjẹ́ (collective of spiritually empowered Mothers) to assist Vinjinia. Madam Wizard and her collective kidnap and interrogate Tajirika. During his trial, Titus insists that his wife be called to testify because she will clear him. Because Àjẹ́ are the keepers of balance, order, and justice, they grant Titus' request. Vinjinia recants and tells the women that her husband did not beat her. The sensitivity and integrity of Ngugi are apparent in his including this scene which so many battered women and men enact routinely as a result of public and private shame and terrorism.

Like most victims of abuse, Vinjinia learns that her silence will only guarantee her future cruelties. Titus tells her, "You did well. Anything else and the last beating would have paled in comparison with the one I would have given you tonight" (*Wizard of the Crow*, 437). This threat motivates Vinjinia to speak truth to power, and Titus is sentenced to receive as many blows as he gave Vinjinia. Before the beating begins, a woman with a machete warns Titus, "[I]f you ever appear before us again, you will not leave here with your penis dangling between your legs" (*Wizard of the Crow*, 439). Ngugi offers stunning example of the original African sacred society—that of the Mothers, and he emphasizes the elemental power that Africana women wield. After his chastisement, Titus and Vinjinia reconcile, and so intense is their passion that nature suspends its animation in their honor. Titus offers proof that growth is possible, and, for many, it need not come after a beating.

Titus is a compelling character whose intricacies, vulnerability, and unassuming nature endow him with a fluidity that makes him appear to be peripheral when he is actually central to the action and intrigues. Throughout the novel Titus has the set-backs and growth spurts that are indicative of a human being who is alternately astounded by, bullied by, befuddled by, and lusting after various illusions of power. Titus clumsily vacillates from one political faction to another, until he finds a way to meld and marry binary oppositions and make duality his physical and political ally: "Tajirika had discarded the glove used to cover his right hand. To the wonderment of his guests, his right arm and left leg were white, his left arm and right leg black" (*Wizard of the Crow*, 752). Either the psychological white-ache that struck Titus earlier has manifested itself physically or he has followed the lead of the other Ministers and taken a hint from Johann Blumenbach and has started treatments to remove his melanin. To the military police, with the stereotypical hatred-of-the-self-adoration-of-the-other complex, Titus' chessboard body marks him not only for rulership, but for deification. The first decree the newly christened and crowned Emperor Titus Whitehead issues is for the police to kill the Ruler.

Although the head of state changes, the state of the union remains the same. To combat the new era of corruption that Whitehead will bring to Aburĩria before he is squeezed and popped, the MVP ally with the Aburĩrian People's Resistance. This third secret society is a holistic army that specializes in defense, medicine, healing, education, social revolution, and spiritual elevation—just as Bambara had envisioned. Nyawĩra is the chairperson for the MVP and the commander in chief of the Resistance, and if she needs to don the cloak of Wizard again to save her people, she will because the tools in her nation sack are innumerable. Nyawĩra is the driving force at the center of all three secret societies because she is the consummate revolutionary. She is the curvilinear intergenerational force that is manifest in the Anoa, the Mu'tafikah, the Seven Days, and Ògbóni.

Kamĩtĩ is a profoundly important character because he reveals the psychological battles that many revolutionaries fight. Kamĩtĩ is an effective complement and balance for Nyawĩra not because of his doubts and vulnerabilities but because he analyzes and addresses them honestly and uses the knowledge he gains to continue treading the path toward full self-actualization. Kamĩtĩ, himself, becomes a mirror who reveals human beings' enormous potential for growth, and he also reflects the fact that Man desperately needs and is dependent on the divine catalyzing fire of Woman.

. . .

Grounded in reverence for the source of life and united in the struggle not only for a fully actualized existence but for an ever-evolving one, revolutionary Africana secret societies and their members arise, work, and return to the Earth only to be regenerated and rebirthed.

The Anoa, Ògbóni, companionship of the ankh, Mu'tafikah, Matigari ma Njirũũngi, Movement of the People, Movement of the Voice of the People, and the Seven Days share many of the same objectives, methodologies, and properties. None of these organizations exhibits a conflict between spiritual and political objectives because the spiritual and political are integral, essential, inextricably linked components of the Africana ethos: They are the cornerstones upon which civilizations have been and will be built, and they are sacred chests that hold the tools that are needed to repair the ruptures of the world.

In his attempt to understand why Africans who were enslaved and exiled in the Americas embraced Yoruba Gods like Ṣàngó, Ògún, Èṣù, Ọya, and Ifá and "braved the threat of excommunication" to participate in the "liberating communion of social upheaval" with the avenging Òrìṣà, Wole Soyinka became privy to a truth cherished by displaced Africans: "African gods, they knew, were revolutionary deities."[114]

The revolutionary Deities of Africa are at work in all of the books explored in this chapter. The Gods include not only Ẹdan, Ògbóni, Aset, Ausar, and Set, but also the Anoa, Nyabinghi, Guitar, Ast, Papa LaBas, Black Herman, Matigari, and Sir Madam Wizard of the Crow. These characters do not glorify themselves for their egos' sake, and they do not refer to themselves as Gods. They simply do the essential nation-building, truth-telling, oppressor-killing, future-ensuring work that Gods must do. What is more, the authors of these works are not writing to merely entertain the masses. They craft characters who can motivate their readers and move them to manifest their divinity. These artists and works of art ensure that the circle of divinity from ancient to modern eras and from literature to life remains unbroken.

If we were to ask the African Gods if they are, in fact, revolutionary Deities they would respond, "Yes, *we* are" with a "we" that is inclusive of us. The role of the reader is of the utmost importance: The companionship of the ankh cannot kill all the enslavers; the Seven Days is only seven men strong; the problems of Aburĩria were not solved within the leaves of *Wizard of the Crow*, and Jes Grew is waiting patiently for the opportunity to reemerge, boogie, and blossom. This is where you come in: As a recipient of the Word, you are now obligated to act. With knowledge having been shared with you, you now become responsible for its activation, actualization, and proliferation. With the simple act of reading you have become initiated into the sacred and secret societies sworn to educate, liberate, and elevate. Congratulations!

Grab your AK 47s, Black Cat Bones, High John the Conquer Roots, grenades, tobies, goofer dust, and Kevlar: It is nation time, and we are running . . . late.

360°

> "Ye *are* gods"
> ~ Psalms 82:6

> "You can never defeat the Gods!
> Impossible for you to defeat the Gods!"
> ~ Wu-Tang Clan, "Impossible"

A reconsideration of the tools of analysis and a reevaluation of the goals of the artistry and artists are necessary to truly comprehend the profundity, paradox, and power of some of the most influential wordsmiths and works in the world. Three elements that are essential to the elucidation of Africana masculine magnificence are understanding, equality, and cipher. These principles are indispensable independently, but when united and interpreted through Supreme Mathematics, they constitute 360°, which signifies completion, perfection, and continuity.

The need for grounding analyses in understanding, equality, and cipher transcends ethnic, cultural, and artistic lines and is evident in published studies, reviews, and even graffiti. A desk at Fisk University in Nashville, Tennessee is covered in tags, symbols, and signs from such organizations as the Nation of Gods, the Black Gangster Disciples, the Crips, the Bloods, and the Vice Lords. In the midst of the numerous identifications and proclamations someone has written, "You can't mix gangs with religion!" That individual did not get it. It is not that these institutions cannot be mixed; it is that they are inextricably bound.

The need for respectful understanding, recognition of equality, and the ability to cipher struck me again when I was conducting research on continuity in Africana signs, symbols, and material arts in the southern United States and met an African American Ifá priest who lived in Chicago. I asked him if he ever reached out to and interacted with members of the Black Gangster Disciples, whose iconography evinces clear references to Yoruba Gods and spiritual systems. The disgust that filled the priest's face was palpable. He dismissed them as rouges and reprobates who were not worthy of existence let alone sharing knowledge. "But they are your sons!" I exclaimed, hoping to inspire in him a sense of understanding. The priest sucked his teeth and retorted, "They ain't no sons of mine."

This "priest" didn't get it. If he had deigned to converse with the "gang members" he so disparaged, he may very well have found that many of those seemingly lowly youths have impressive degrees of wisdom, knowledge, and understanding—and more integrity and character than any religious grandstander. Most importantly, as a priest, especially of Ifá, those often forgotten youths are truly his responsibility: They are his and all our destiny.

So-called gang members and gangs deserve more careful consideration. Organizations that are dismissed as gangs are, in many cases, reformulated African secret societies that are built on formidable political, spiritual, economic, intellectual, and revolutionary foundations. Attempts at compartmentalizing, separating, and devaluing come from Caucasian cultures with myopic one-dimensional modes of thought and from the desire of some Caucasians to use the shifting concept of criminality to absolve themselves and their organizations of monumental crimes while fragmenting and destroying organized Africana peoples and movements. However, members of certain Africana organizations make misidentification easy when they adopt Western mores, morals, and methodologies—such as drive-bys, extortion, and indiscriminate community mayhem—and exhibit behavior identical to well-known and long-standing enemies of Africana existence. In other words, the Ku Klux Klan does not need to drive through Africana communities with a massive cross on a red pick-up truck with "Dixie" blaring from the truck's horn looking for a victim to lynch when Bloods with Jesus piece medallions swinging round their necks and crosses tatted on their arms are rolling in a '64 blasting "Tha Heat" with guns cocked in preparation to shoot up a family reunion.

In addition to problems born of cultural confusion, self-hatred, the absence of knowledge of self, and the globalization of Western amorality, American authorities have convinced multitudes to view the world with the Western objectifier's solipsistic gaze that criminalizes Africana victims and ignores or supports individual, national, and international crimes committed by or under the auspices of Caucasians.

Some African Americans interviewed in the late 1800s and early 1900s understood the role-reversal that was occurring, and they combated it with simple truths. Shang Harris, for example, put the concept of criminality into proper context: "Dey talks a heap 'bout de niggers stealin'. Well, you know what was de fust stealin' done? Hit was in

Africy, when de white folks stole de niggers, jes' like you'd go get a drove o' hosses and sell 'em."[1] A Gullah preacher's sermon of truth inquired of his congregation how, if Caucasians did not steal, did millions of Africans wind up enslaved in America?[2] African American school children in Louisville, Kentucky in 1866 declared in unison that the only difference between them and Caucasians was that the latter had "MONEY" that they had stolen from them.[3] The children are right about stolen wealth. According to historian Kevin Shillington, West Africa's Golden Empires of Ghana, Mali, and Songhai are the source of the world's gold standard: "[O]ver two-thirds of the gold circulating in Europe and North Africa in the 14th century originated from these three West African Empires."[4] When Europeans and Arabs could no longer steal gold from Africans, they began stealing Africans so that they could profit from the priceless gifts of African intellect, ingenuity, and divinity.

Through the mythmaking of plantation spin doctors, including overseers, priests, and planters, the thefts of which oppressors were guilty—the most ghastly and gargantuan in world history—were simply ignored or they were repackaged as arduous expressions of agape love. James Mellon's *Bullwhip Days: The Slaves Remember: An Oral History* includes a series of "recollections" about "Africa" by African Americans who had been enslaved. The "Africa" that Chaney Mack, Mary Johnson, and Tony Cox recall is mired in godlessness, savagery, cannibalism, and filth.[5] One gets the impression that Mack, Johnson, and Cox all ran into the arms of their enslavers and chained themselves into the hulls of the ships to escape African abomination.

These plantation "memories" are actually evidence of a powerful concerted indoctrination scheme designed by Caucasians to make enslaved Africans feel that lashings; rapings; feasts of pig intestines, tails, brains, and tripe; feet cracked by sub-zero weather; watching one's child be auctioned off; watching one's man be sent to sire; and watching the overseer outrage a daughter were better than *anything* that Africa had to offer; and that industrialized, generalized, institutionalized racism and unimaginable interminable suffering were Christian blessings. As Tony Cox opines: "If we hadn't been brung over an' made slaves, us an' us chillum dat is being educated an' civilized would be naked savages back in Africa, now."[6] Generations of such lies as these made loving and suffering for one's enemy appear to be logical. In addition to acting as a comforting consolation prize, anti-African indoctrination had the added benefit of making dislocated Africans loathe the Continent and their Continental counterparts. Anti-African conditioning has been so successful that one can find Africana peoples in this era who are disgusted at the very mention of Africa and who are completely ignorant of Africa's rich and influential past and its contemporary depth, power, and complexity.

Implanted plantation "memories" do not include recollections of the organized, immeasurably wealthy, and peaceful empires of Ghana, Mali, and Songhai, which dazzled Caucasians and Arabs. Plantation indoctrination makes no mention of the architectural might that led to the construction of the most perfect edifices in the world which were encased in gleaming limestone and capped in electrum. Africans are not associated with the university education that they founded and disseminated. The philosophies, Gods, astronomical knowledge, technologies, and beautifications that they developed and the iron-working, gold-giving, literature-loving, rap-spitting Africans, themselves, were erased and replaced with one-dimensional props and propaganda. Alien definitions moved Africa and Africans from center to margin: After eons of building, writing, creating, shaping, pontificating, and philosophizing, Africans went from being inherently divine to being erroneously defined. Doctors became witchdoctors; mothers morphed into witches before they gave birth to anonymous slaves; sacred speech was translated as "boolah boogah boo"; the perfection of melanin was twisted into the curse of Ham; defending and avenging armies were headhunters and savages before they became gangs and thugs, Crips and Bloods.

American authorities insist that the Nation of Gods as a "gang," and *The Five Percenters* offers an insightful discussion of the successful legal battles the Gods have fought to show and prove their divinity, manifest their righteous way of life, and ensure and secure their rights even while incarcerated.[7] The denigration of Africana movements, philosophies, and struggles is not new: The Black Panthers, Deacons for Defense, and El Rukns/Black P. Stone Rangers were all discredited and dismissed as gangs, mobs, and thugs. However, using the criteria of Caucasian American authorities, the police are nothing more than a gang: They are color coded, territorial, and they routinely visit violent and vicious attacks on others for no just cause or to further the cause of Caucasian supremacy. The same can be said for the Ku Klux Klan, the CIA, and the FBI, especially under the administration of J. Edgar Hoover.[8] The armed forces of the United States is easily the most violent and lethal gang in the world. In fact, the military industrial complex is run with the type of hierarchical rigidity and blind obedience that is often attributed to gangs. All of these American organizations can be classified as gangs, but they are not maligned or even justly prosecuted for their crimes because they are all in service to the United States of America.

By anointing the solipsistic "self" as superior while denigrating and fomenting nationwide and international campaigns of dehumanization against the "other," it becomes easy, justifiable, even necessary to slaughter the "other": After all, they are just _____ (insert desired epithet: "thugs," "pagans," "blacks," "niggers"). It is important to avoid solipsism and a perspective that privileges a group because they wear sheets or suits or sport metal stars on their clothes: This is especially important for Africana peoples in America, because a people who accept the definitions foisted upon them by their enemies are a people damned.

Many of the African American organizations that are casually condemned today are the products of both ancient African secret societies and one of the world's longest wars. The war for liberation that was waged in America from the 1920s to 1980s gave birth to many Africana organizations. The NAACP, the Student Nonviolent Coordinating Committee, the Southern Christian Leadership Conference, the Congress for Racial Equality, the Deacons for Defense (and Justice), the Black Panther Party (for Self-Defense), the Nation of Islam, the Black Liberation Army, the Republic of New Africa, and MOVE, among many others, battled against American oppression and oppressors and for Africana liberation and self-determination.

These groups made impressive strides in the war and forged political bonds with oppressed peoples of all ethnicities all over America and the world. These organizations provided invaluable community services, such as free legal counsel, Freedom Schools, armed protection and defense, testing for Sickle Cell Anemia, and prisoner visitation programs. All Americans can thank the Black Panther Party for community health care clinics and gardens and for schools' free breakfast programs. These Africana organizations were so successful, influential, and necessary that America's government-approved gangs—the police, the CIA, and the FBI with its Counter Intelligence Program—infiltrated and destroyed many of these organizations and murdered, drove into exile, or incarcerated many revolutionaries.

In 1968, Fred Hampton, the dynamic deputy chairman of the Illinois chapter of the Black Panther Party, introduced Jose "Cha Cha" Jimenez to the power of revolutionary politics while they were incarcerated. Upon his release from prison, Jimenez transformed the Young Lords from a street gang into a revolutionary organization and an off-shoot of the Black Panther Party.[9]

The Young Lords comprised the Puerto Rican contingent of Fred Hampton's multicultural revolutionary Rainbow Coalition. Hampton understood that there is consonance and fluidity between revolutionary organizations and so-called gangs because these societies often boast similar objectives, struggles, and agendas and they share a common enemy. Fred Hampton's multicultural collective of freedom fighters, which included Native Americans, Asians, Puerto Ricans, Caucasians, Mexicans, and African Americans, was so empowered and effective that the FBI and Chicago police officers organized a gangland-style lynching to destroy Hampton, his positive works, and the dynamic potential of inner-city Chicago.

Fred Hampton was not the only person to acknowledge and successfully harness the power resident in urban Africana youths and communities and to intimidate American authorities in the process. In 1959 Jeff Fort founded the Blackstone Rangers, which later became known as the Black P. Stone Rangers, in Chicago. While American authorities define the organization as a gang, the Black P. Stone Rangers have always been aligned with Black nationalist politics and urban youth empowerment; this focus is represented in the signature symbol of the Stones, a pyramid with 21 stones, and the organization's colors, which are the red, black, and green of African liberation.[10] Perhaps as another indication of the influence and utilization of African wisdom-systems, particularly those of the Igbo, Lance Williams asserts that Jeff Fort was widely known as Angel because "he used to do mysterious kinds of things like disappearing acts and other things. He was like that. You know[,] he was very elusive and that's how come the Feds couldn't catch him cause he played games with who was who and where he was and you would think he was in one place and he wouldn't actually be there."[11]

As the Stones' community involvement and political consciousness expanded, the organization and its leader transformed. Jeff Fort, inspired by the wisdom of Noble Drew Ali, the founder of the Moorish Science Temple of America, became known as Caliph Abdullah Malik, and the Blackstone Rangers became the El Rukn Tribe of the Moorish Science Temple of America. "El Rukn" means "the foundation" in Arabic,[12] which makes it an appropriate translation for "Blackstone"; and "Malik" means leader, king, chief—a perfect title for the architect of the El Rukn Nation.

Malik began forging bonds with Libyan head of state Muammar al-Qaddafi, who had shown himself to be a devoted Pan-African freedom fighter and formidable ally to many Africana leaders and revolutionary organizations for many decades. Indeed, Qaddafi's last known revolutionary effort, before his savage ouster and lynching in 2011, was his support of the South Sudanese in their successful bid for independence.[13] An El Rukn delegation visited Libya in 1986, and the potential of an El Rukn–Libyan alliance terrified United States' authorities who targeted Malik and the El Rukn Nation for neutralization.

Chicago's Angel was setup and incarcerated, but the complex model of activism of both the Black P. Stone Rangers and the El Rukns continued to thrive through those organizations and in two other Chicago societies, the Black Gangster Disciples and the Conservative Vice Lords.

The Vice Lords, El Rukns, and Black P. Stone Rangers are part of the "People Nation," but more than merely distinguishing themselves from the "F.O.L.K.S. Nation" of the Black Gangster Disciples, the term "People" is a reference to their divinity. In *The Almighty Black P Stone Nation*, Lance Williams reveals that "Vice Lord leadership in the Illinois Department of Corrections interpreted Qur'anic references to 'my people' as meaning the righteous ones of Allah."[14] Making clear their commitment to the righteous people of Allah, the Vice Lords, an organization allied with the El Rukns – Black P. Stone Rangers, undertook community development projects in Chicago in the 1960s and 1970s that are still widely acclaimed, and their efforts have been chronicled in numerous books, including David Dawley's classic *A Nation of Lords*.

Because the concept of "Allah's people" is inclusive of all Africana peoples and organizations, Malik reached out to Larry Hoover, the head of the Supreme Gangster Nation, to offer him a position within the Stones and to create an expansive network by merging their organizations. While Hoover declined Fort's offer, Hoover had goals of his own that were similar to those of the Stones. Larry Hoover and David Barksdale united their separate organizations, the Supreme Gangster Nation and the Black Disciples, respectively, in 1966 to form the Black Gangster Disciples (BGD). Rod Emery reveals that the BGDs launched a series of development projects to including opening a gas station and two restaurants, organizing "community clean-up programs," and enforcing "school truancy policies."[15]

Emery also discusses how the BGDs worked with the Vice Lords, the Black P. Stone Rangers, Jesse Jackson's Operation Breadbasket, and other activist organizations to protect and empower the Africana community:

> The Business Men's Association assisted us in obtaining centers for the organization. The first to open was on 63rd and Normal Streets and 61st and Halstad Streets, out of which David Barksdale operated a free breakfast program for the community. Another center was located at 6th and Halsted Streets, out of which Larry Hoover operated a free lunch program to feed the needy children in the community. . . . We became active in community issues and got involved with the Reverend Jesse Jackson and Operation Breadbasket. We formed the LSD Coalition, which as an acronym

for Lords, Stones and Disciples. We marched and picketed the "Red Rooster Grocery Store" which was a large food chain that contribute[d] primarily to the black community. We were successful in shutting down the Red Rooster chain and stopped the selling of bad meat to the black community.[16]

The work of these organizations, both independently and collectively as the LSD Coalition, is akin to the nation-building efforts of the Black Panther Party. As further evidence of these societies' influence and significance, in an essay titled *"21st Century V.O.T.E.,"* Greg Donaldson reveals that "[a] convoy of Rangers, Vice Lords, and Disciples helped escort Martin Luther King through the howling white mobs in Marquette Park [Chicago] in 1966."[17] King would never have trusted his protection and defense to mere "street gangs."

As the war between Africana revolutionaries and American agents of oppression intensified, freedom fighters were assassinated, incarcerated, firebombed, and lynched. Survivors understood that given the weaponry, ruthlessness, and expansiveness of America's sanctioned gang network, freedom fighting was lethal. Gang banging, however, was deemed an acceptable American vocation because it demanded that Africana people direct their rage, intensity, and firepower away from their enemies and within their communities. Revolution became an afterthought as communities were inundated with drugs, materialism, extortion, racketeering, pimping, prostitution, and gambling—the classic mainstays of America's urban economies.

Cognizant that America's path of success for inner city Africana youths leads either to the penitentiary or to the cemetery, King Hoover, as he came to be heralded, returned to his activist roots in full and completely revamped his organization in the 1990s. Hoover redefined the "GD" of "BGD" (Black Gangster Disciples) to represent "Growth and Development"; and with the 21st Century V.O.T.E. movement, the GDs were poised to use their electoral power to dominate Chicago politics. However, similar to the way America has refused to acknowledge the transformation of the Caucasian-hating Malcolm X into the globally enlightened El Hajj Malik El Shabazz, Hoover and the GD movement were mocked, criticized, and vilified—not because their goals were ridiculous, but because their potential and power were stunning.

The attempts of the El Rukns, Vice Lords, Black Gangster Disciples, Nation of Gods, and other organizations to reshuffle and cut the ever-stacked deck that is American politics, business, and economics are routinely maligned and misunderstood. However, comprehending the complexity of these organizations is essential to gauging the proliferation of power and the true scope of masculine magnificence, because these African American community organizations are reconceptualizations of ancient African secret societies, and their African underpinnings are evident in myriad ways. In addition to the obvious work of protecting and defending their communities, enforcing codes of conduct, and exerting political power, the African heritage of African American organizations abounds in verbal displays, visual arts and symbols, and ritual handshakes and hand signs.

During the Black Power era, intricate "soul shakes" or "daps" punctuated Africana greetings, and soul-rich handshakes can be found throughout Africana life and literature. In Vodun ceremonies in Ghana, when the Gods arrive they greet Vodunsi with powerful and resounding handshakes.[18] In *Mumbo Jumbo*, Black Herman, LaBas, and Buddy Jackson "exchange the ancient Black handshake, the vulva embracing the phallus."[19] The handshake of the Seven Days calls for one Day to enclose the hand of another Day in his two hands, signifying secrecy, protection, and covert power. Perhaps the Seven Days and the Jes Grew carriers are dislocated Ògbóni members, for the primary hand sign of Ògbóni is the left fist placed over the right fist with both thumbs concealed. This hand sign signifies "secrecy and covenant";[20] it could also represent the vagina embracing the penis, the unification of the forces of life. Further ensuring the circle of life, the Ògbóni handshake signifies that all its members nursed at the breast of the one Great Mother.

In the Africana community one can often say more with one's body than one can with one's mouth as Africana non-verbal communicative signs are rich with esoteric meaning and Pan-African significance. Robert Farris Thompson finds that the BaKongo use "*tuluwa lwa luumbu*, arms crossed on the chest to symbolize self-encirclement in silence,"[21] and this pose retains its meaning in African American communities. BGDs and Five Percenters both cross their right arms over their left. Raekwon of Wu-Tang Clan refers to this stance as "Black power at itself."[22] Similarly, "Roof of the world" is the accolade Brother J of X Clan uses to describe himself as he sits "cross-legged, right over left."[23]

Some signs are clear and unmistakable, like the Black Power fist. Some signs may signify one thing to the general public but have an encoded meaning that relates to specific tenets of a secret society. The Virginia Tourism Corporation discovered this in 2007 when it launched its "Virginia is for Lovers" campaign which featured individuals making a heart sign with their hands. After the commercials began to air, state officials were informed that that hand sign is used by Black Gangster Disciples: The sign signifies eternal love for all brothers and sisters of the struggle.

For millennia, Africana people have used hand signs to communicate effectively and silently. The character Eli of Julie Dash's film *Daughters of the Dust* offers a study of the intricacy and fluidity of this African mode of communication. The Black Gangster Disciples, who define "stacking" as "telling a story with hand signs,"[24] reveal that the poetry, complexity, and impact of the original African mode of expression is well-preserved by the BGDs. Hand signs are commonly used to reveal one's affiliation with a particular organization or way of life, as is the case with the BGD heart symbol and the Ògbóni sign. Hand signs can also be used to communicate one's thoughts, deeds, or needs: An elder from Alabama taught me how she could indicate to her relatives that she was in trouble without uttering a sound.

In many respects, contemporary African American secret societies are cultural repositories for various ancient African customs. So-called gang members have been pouring libation, religiously, to the collective power of the ancestors long before it became a fad in elite gatherings. Like many ancient African secret societies, members of African American societies have codified sacred speech, and they have intricate iconography and insignia. The F.O.L.K.S. Nation's six point star, pitchforks, and winged heart and the People Nation's five point star, crescent moon, eye of Allah, and pyramid all have African antecedents. When rendered in elaborate tags, Black Gangster Disciple and Vice Lord signs are remarkably similar to Voodoo *ve ve* (spiritual writing) and *nsibidi* writing of the Egbo secret society of Eastern Nigeria. Just as the Egbo, Ògbóni, Seven Days, Nation of Islam, Deacons for Defense, and other organizations protect their members and communities, so too do the F.O.L.K.S. Nation and People Nation offer security for some and sure death for others.

It is important to understand *all* that has come before. When analyzed comprehensively, it becomes apparent that Africana sacred and secret societies and their members are some of the most potent vessels of potential revolutionary change. I know this to be true because when pondering Toni Cade Bambara's observation of the rift dividing spiritualists and revolutionaries, I think back to the first organization that made it clear to me that the artistic, cultural, political, spiritual, and revolutionary were inherently connected—The Black Gangster Disciples.

My Midwest hometown was one of the fertile areas that the BGDs seeded. I grew up immersed in the language, iconography, and philosophy of the F.O.L.K.S. Nation. When visiting relatives in Mississippi, the state where Caliph Abdullah Malik, King David Barksdale, and King Larry Hoover were born, I was reunited with cousins from Joliet, Illinois who were F.O.L.K.S. and who disseminated

F.O.L.K.S.' philosophy and iconography as they traveled Interstate 55. However, the F.O.L.K.S. Nation extends far beyond the Midwest; it is nationwide. Every stateside university I have taught at (Mississippi, California, Ohio, Tennessee, and Louisiana) has shown ample evidence of having been attended by F.O.L.K.S., and I have had the honor and pleasure of building with male and female students who were F.O.L.K.S., People, and Gods: They have been some of the most disciplined, respectful, and deepest students I have shared knowledge with.

The BGDs also boast an impressive international presence, not only due to the success of King Hoover's Growth and Development initiative, but also due to F.O.L.K.S. who are in the military, who are entrepreneurs, and who are scholars. When I first traveled to Ghana in 1995, my right hand and traveling companion was a F.O.L.K.S.-affiliated brother from Chicago. When I returned to Ghana a year later, my Ghanaian friends were excited to introduce me to another brother from Chicago. When I revealed I was from Illinois, the brother's first question to me was, "You F.O.L.K.S.?"

The BGDs is truly a secret society with its own oaths, pledges, literature, language, and laws; and it boasts its own alphabetic and numeric definitions and designations, just as the Five Percenters have the Supreme Mathematics and Alphabet. Furthermore, with such laws as "[y]ou are to never say that you 'sleep.' Sleep is a form of death to us. Our Third Eye is forever open, so therefore we rest, but never sleep"; instructions on how to enter the Lost Pyramid; and descriptions of their cosmic home as being "[i]n the sky beyond the North Star,"[25] it is clear that BGD codes and ciphers evince a deep knowledge of Africana cosmology and ontology that is in consonance with that of the Kemites, Igbo, Dogon, Nubians, and BaKongo. While it is highly likely that BGD semiology inspired and is inspired by that of the Five Percenters and the Prince Hall Freemasons, Ifá cosmology and iconography also emerge as possible sources of BGD signs.

One of the most empowering signifying forces in Yoruba cosmology is Òrò. As Rowland Abiodun elucidates in "Verbal and visual metaphors: mythical allusions in Yoruba ritualistic art of Orí," Òrò has at least three definitions: It is "word and the spoken word"; it is "a matter, that is something that is the subject of discussion, concern or action"; additionally, Òrò is "power of the word."[26] Yoruba orature reveals that at the dawn of creation, Olódùmarè, made a force that was comprised of wisdom (ogbón), knowledge (ìmò), and understanding (òye), and this force is Òrò. Ancient orature describes Òrò's characteristics and recounts its arrival on Earth:

Ọrọ, the cause of great concern for the wise and
    experienced elders.
It sounds *kù* (making the heart miss a beat).
Kẹ̀ (as a ponderous object hitting the ground).
Gì (making the last sound before silence)
The Ọrọ that drops from the elderly
Is stupendous.
It was divined for Ọrọ-Ọrọ-Ọrọ
Who did not have anyone to communicate with.
And started groaning.[27]

Ẹlà is the "wise and experienced" Deity who interpreted and revised Ọrọ's profound utterances so that human beings could comprehend them.[28] Consequently, Ẹlà became both the mediator between Ọrọ and humanity and the "embodiment of wisdom, knowledge and understanding in all their verbal and visual forms."[29] These forms include proverbs, curses, visual arts, prayers, dance, literature, coded messages, cosmic signs—all forms of spiritual, communal and artistic expression.

Ẹlà and Ọrọ's influence is ubiquitous in Africana life, lyrics, and literature; indeed, Ọrọ's three components constitute the first three formulae of the Supreme Mathematics, and they form the foundation of the most iconic BGD symbol. Three points of the BGD's six point star signify wisdom, knowledge, and understanding. The other three points represent love, life, and loyalty. One could say that when Họọ united with rọ and became Ọrọ, the spoken word's physicality and cosmic energy united with wisdom, knowledge, and understanding to foment love, life, and loyalty. When viewing the star complete with symbols, what emerges is a sign that signifies balanced holistic existence, verbal and visual artistry, and political protection and power.

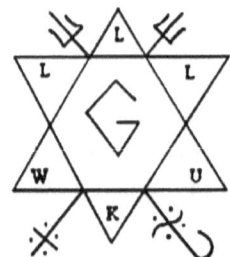

BGD symbol drawn by author

Many people associate the six point star with the Seal of Solomon or Star of David, but that is not all it signifies. In addition to heralding the biblical African Israelites, the six point star memorializes slain BGD founder David Barksdale. The BGD's six point star also has ties to

Yoruba cosmology. In some Yoruba traditions, the six point star represents Odùduwà, who is described as a dark star who fell from the Cosmos to the Earth.[30] Known as the Pot of Origins and the Womb of Existence, many Yoruba herald Odùduwà as the Mother of Creation.[31] Odùduwà's name has also been translated as "oracular utterance created existence,"[32] and oracular utterance is Ọ̀rọ̀.

The influence of Ọ̀rọ̀ on the Disciples is evident in their representation of the components of Ọ̀rọ̀ in the star's six points and in the act of "spitting literature," which involves exhibiting one's knowledge and undertaking the ritual recitation of codes and laws on demand. Just as a BGD must be able to spit literature, the Gods must know the mathematics of a given day, for Gods will commence a cipher or challenge one another by demanding, "What's today's mathematics, Sun?" The Five Percenters' curriculum and the Disciples' literature must be committed to memory, committed to consciousness, committed to one's Self, for they comprise the foundations of their members' holistic existence.[33] While many are quick to dismiss their members as illiterate and ignorant, with the BGDs' respect for literature and the Gods' reverence for mathematics, it is clear that these societies champion the acquisition of holistic wisdom and knowledge of self: It is also evident that nations of youths the world over gravitate to and master these organizations' intricate curricula because the lessons relate to, inspire, and empower them.

In addition to the similarities in their uses of Power of the Word and in their words of empowerment, the Disciples and Ògbóni also have great reverence for the power of silence. The Ògbóni law which demands secrecy no matter what the eyes see or the ears hear corresponds with one of the BGD's laws: "Silence and Secrecy — No member is to discuss any matter [or] function to anyone who is not an outstanding member of this organization."[34] Ògbóni was instituted to balance the Earth and to ensure honesty, integrity, and righteousness and to rid Ile-Ife of traitors, liars, thieves, and the like. The Disciples also have laws to ensure integrity and concord: A BGD must not steal from or disrespect a fellow member, rape is not allowed, and no member can engage in addictive drug use. Members must be educated and "have some form of diploma or be participating in educational programs."[35] The prophets of Anoa and the society of the ankh killed anyone who would enslave another person or profit off of slavery. As if modifying the laws of Anoa and the society of the ankh for America's predatory nihilistic environment, the BDGs are forbidden from extorting "any funds or favor from any member or non-member."[36] It is significant that the law against exploitation is extended to everyone. This law offers a clear indication as to the character of this organization and its members.

The pitchforks stationed at the top of the star are a key BGD symbol and hand sign. In the Ifá spiritual system, the pitchforks symbolize Èṣù, the Yoruba Trickster God who is also the Divine Linguist and Mediator. Stationed at actual and metaphysical crossroads and wielding the power to facilitate or confound communication, Èṣù, who is erroneously associated with the Judeo-Christian devil, is the perfect tutelary Deity for the BGDs who are sometimes called the "Devil's Disciples," a nickname befitting their often dubious roles in the community.

The association with Èṣù brings to mind the famous orature about two friends who live across the road from each other and are so close that they swear that nothing can ever make them fight or destroy their friendship.[37] Èṣù hears this oath and decides to test the bond. He dresses elegantly and tops his outfit with a magnificent two-toned crown. He mounts a gallant steed and parades down the road that separates the friends. After seeing this spectacle, the friends meet to discuss the stranger. They rave about his luxurious clothes but disagree about the color of his hat. One friend swears the hat is red; the other claims it is blue. This disagreement becomes an argument which escalates into a fight. Before the friends kill each other, Èṣù appears and shows them his two-toned hat. He admonishes them to swear oaths only with the greatest care and to always examine all sides of an issue.

Èṣù must be amazed at how easily his progeny can be convinced to destroy each other over colors or arbitrary territorial markers today. Having forgotten that we are one Divine Nation, have nursed at the breast of the Great Mother, and have emerged from the infinite depths of her womb to tote, often unconsciously, the nation sacks of all, too many Africana people have converted the "G" of God into the sign of the gangster, as they specialize in dividing, conquering, and destroying the Self.

The F.O.L.K.S. vs. People divide is an American example of a Pan-African dilemma. This rift is a cousin of the horrific wars that spread like cancer across Africana countries and communities and destroy or disfigure everyone unfortunate enough to have been born in particular places at certain times. The vicious acts of hacking off limbs, ears, and noses; burning people alive; and shooting people in the spine so that they are disabled for life is not our intended destiny; it is the demented self that we have settled for after centuries of living in the land of the diseased and in the home of the depraved. The degeneracy in which we are mired is part of the two thousand seasons of atrocities Anoa foresaw, and it is no respecter of position, title, or origin.

In his keynote address to the Wilberforce Conference on Nigerian Federalism, Peter P. Ekeh presents astonishing historical information about the Oyo Empire of the Yoruba and its unintended globalization:

> [F]or several centuries Oyo managed a splendid political system which was remarkable for the way it balanced power between the *Alafin*, the King of Oyo, and representative assemblies, the *Oyo Mesi*. Oyo's political system has especially appealed to students of the political sociology of ancient Africa because it achieved an uncanny system of accountability in which noblemen of the *Ogboni* Chamber as well as the King of Oyo, the Alafin, were fully answerable for their public behaviors. Such a tradition was manifest in the famous institution of royal suicides by which the King of Oyo was compelled to commit suicide if his acts of governance were gravely abusive of the public interest. It was the ultimate expression of the norm of accountability in ancient Africa.
>
> All these remarkable achievements were ruined when Oyo plunged itself into the Atlantic slave trade, becoming a major source of supply of captives for the evil trade. Slave raids into neighboring ethnic groups could not satisfy the demands for captives[;] it was a matter of time before the violence of the slave raids turned inwards, as members of many non-royal groups became victims of the slave trade. As violence begot violence, Oyo imploded in a fierce civil war in the early part of the nineteenth century.
>
> .... Soldiers from an Oyo satellite town, ruled by a *Bale*, a feudal lord, were pressed by their leader into the civil war. They lost. Rather than being taken as prisoners of war, as it would be the case in previous normal times, they were now sold into the slave trade. Six of these soldiers—all grades of them: general, horsemen, foot soldiers, and of different ages—found themselves as slaves in a Caribbean sugar plantation. One afternoon, as they labored in the field, three new slaves were brought in to join them. One of the ex-soldiers looked up to observe these new labor recruits. He then cried out: "Oh no, oh no, oh my God: It is the Bale himself." The others joined him in this emotional recognition of their ruler back home in Yorubaland and Oyo nobility and commoner, all now slaves, wept together at the fate of their fallen ruler and their fallen civilization. None of them knew of the fate that had befallen their wives and children and relatives at home. But each of them had paid a heavy price for the mismanagement of Oyo's public affairs.[38]

Through the fall of the Baálẹ̀ and his warriors and priests one sees the avenues through which Ògbóni members and iconography traveled to the

Western Hemisphere. One can also compare the fate of the Baálẹ̀ and his council to the fates of such leaders as Fred Hampton, Mutulu Shakur, Assata Shakur, Caliph Abdullah Malik, Mumia Abu Jamal, and King Larry Hoover who were assassinated, exiled, or sold into the modern-day slavery of the prison industrial complex.

King Hoover's Growth and Development Movement, which gave many of Chicago's youths direction and purpose, was all but obliterated when Hoover was silenced by cruel, unusual, and unjustifiable Supermax incarceration in 1997. Rather than young people building alliances across organizations and involving themselves in community uplift, American politics, and social empowerment,[39] Chicago's rudderless youths have turned the Windy City into one of the most dangerous places in the world.

Young adults in Chicago—like many young people across America—are now driven by a uniquely American nihilism and culture of destruction that seems to be sated only with pointless, remorseless, senseless slaughter. Jeff Williams of Chicago's Ceasefire organization asserts that, rather than youth organizations or even "gangs," Chicago is beset with "cliques" that will kill for little or no reason: "It can range from somebody stepped on a shoe, to a guy swerving in the street, somebody got wet with a water gun and didn't want to get wet with a water gun. . . . Anything could spark at any given time."[40]

The desire to murder for the sake of murdering is not restricted to Africana youths; this pathology has stricken Americans of all ethnicities and economic classes; however, because African Americans are disproportionately affected by homicide—whether through death, destitution, or incarceration[41]—America's politicians and law enforcement agencies are reluctant to solve a problem that is both expeditious and profitable for them. Indeed, with the assassination of Fred Hampton and the neutralization of King Hoover and Caliph Abdullah Malik, it is clear that Chicago officials worked with federal agents and agencies to *create* the problem. What is more, to further the agenda of genocide, hospitals in certain Chicago neighborhoods have stopped treating victims of gunshot wounds; other hospitals have decided or have been forced to close rather than save Africana lives.[42]

With Chicago's big shoulders in a state of collapse, perhaps the city's only hope lies in the revolutionary awakening that follows a monumental tragedy: That was certainly the root of change in South Central Los Angeles, California.

As a result of Hollywood's glamorization of "black-on-black crime," in the late 1980s early 1990s the Disciples and Vice Lords were eclipsed in prominence by the Crips and Bloods, organizations that originated in California and spread throughout America. Warfare between Crips and

Bloods internationalized the concept of killing over colors. As further evidence of the rejection of communality and understanding, Crips and Bloods turned popular terms of endearment—"cuz," short for cousin, and "blood," which had previously unified Africana peoples, especially African American men fighting in Vietnam—into codes that could result in murder simply for being uttered. The hatred that Crips and Bloods learned to have for one another, similar to that dividing the Disciples and Vice Lords, was fueled by their struggle for currency and control of the drug trade. This struggle is endless, because America's soul is owned by capitalism and its body is sustained by drugs: As KRS-One astutely observes, "Illegal business controls America."[43]

In 1991, the Crips and Bloods were busy anointing their communities with blood, splattered brains, and intestines when the images of a gang of Los Angeles police officers beating Rodney King for sport, exercise, and fun were broadcast internationally. The gratuitous brutality the officers unleashed against their defenseless victim stunned everyone. The images of the officers being acquitted threw South Central Los Angeles into a righteous rage. Awakened by America's sanctioning of casual, brutal, racist violence, the Crips and Bloods negotiated a truce in 1992.

In 1994, a collective of Crips and Bloods formed the Oakland, California Youth Organizing Committee (YOC) to solidify their unity and further their goals. After participating in a three-day summit that failed to acknowledge or address the root causes of Africana rage, destitution, and nihilism, the YOC queried the U.S. government about its dubious intentions towards Africana youths:

> We have got some problems with the program of the summit. Why is violence only equated with black-on-black, youth-on-youth violence? Isn't hunger also violence? Isn't being cut off welfare violence? .... What about the role of the police? ... Surely police terror plays some role in the violence on our streets. We don't think it's accidental the summit left this out.[44]

The YOC makes astute points: What could be more violent than the Klan terror of the Reconstruction and Jim Crow eras seamlessly morphing into contemporary and "legal" police terror? What is more, when the terrorism enacted by the police does not result in deaths, it is netting new slaves for America's thriving prison industrial complex. In addition to these threats, homelessness, HIV/AIDS epidemics, dying wages, and clawing hunger threaten the lives of the majority of American citizens.

In a most cruel irony, with Africana labor having successfully built, clothed, and fed Caucasian America by force, the progeny of those who were enslaved are maneuvered out of the sphere of productive labor and, thus, out of existence. As the YOC asserts, "High technology with its robots and computers replaces jobs. There aren't going to be too many jobs for young people like us. We charge the government—federal, state and local—with a deliberate policy of criminalizing the [Africana] youth to keep us out of the job market."[45] Looking at America's incarceration and unemployment rates in the 21st century, the YOC correctly prophesied a tragedy.

Refusing Jesse Jackson's plea for pacifism in the face of "three strikes and you're out" legislation and prisons bulging with lost, and often innocent, Africana lives, the YOC states they will follow the agenda of El Hajj Malik El Shabazz: "We propose to use any means necessary . . . the days of begging on [the government's] good intentions are over."[46] Recalling the foundation of justice and reciprocity established by Ògbóni, the society of the ankh, and the Seven Days, but tailoring ancient paradigms to fit the ever-morphing dimensions of Caucasian supremacy, the YOC states its ultimate aims:

> We'll match Clinton's 100,000 cops with 100,000 generals. They can be found among our gangs and our posses, our teenage mothers, in the high schools, on the street corners and in the prisons. We've got our crews and we know how to work together. . . . We're living this capitalism; all it offers is unemployment, hunger, homelessness, welfare cuts, epidemics, drugs and police terror to guarantee we shut up. *Our vision is a whole new society . . . and we can't stop, because the system has declared us the enemy.*[47]

This is a phenomenal acknowledgment of potential and holistic strength; it is a statement of purpose from a people cognizant that they are at their nadir but aware that they can uplift themselves and clear a path to true freedom. The "whole new society" YOC envisions has yet to be born, as its would-be builders are often its most destructive impediments. But that world will be born when its builders recall how to reclaim their lost selves, trust their best selves, and resurrect their submerged Gods.

. . .

It is not easy being God. You may find, as did Ṣàngó, that your abuse of power results in the death of your favorite brother. You may get intoxicated while making human beings and fashion people with deformities, as did Ọbàtálá. You may find yourself slaughtered and hacked to pieces by your brother, as was the case with Ausar, Èṣù, and Faro. You, Gods, might find yourselves joining the thousands of African Americans whose bodies were used to decorate trees and enrich

American rivers because their inherent powers and promise outshone the vapidity of their oppressors. Or, like Patrice Lumumba, you may be so blindingly resplendent that your killers soak the remains of your burned and butchered body in sulfuric acid in hopes of obliterating even the memory of your majesty.

You Gods may find yourselves nodding from heroin or chained to cocaine because your genius is so profound few can understand it—ask Bird, Lady, and Gil. You may find yourself adored by millions but hating your pharaohnic reflection. So suffering from "white ache," you amputate God's own nose and bleach the Creator's Khu out of sight. Ask Mike what it is like to be the young, gifted, and Black poster child for the persistence of white supremacy. You may find yourself celebrating the fact that you are your community's biggest gangbanger, drugslanger, childkiller. Yes, rather manifesting a God's destiny you may find yourself becoming the American Dream, which is the African Nightmare.

It is not easy being God, but no struggle is more worthwhile. King Ṣàngó became instantly immortalized and deified in Yorubaland, and he sailed the Middle Passage to foment wars for liberation. Today he is not only one of the most revered Pan-African Gods, but Ṣàngó has gone on to star in Haile Gerima's *Sankofa* and Carlos Diegues' *Quilombo*. Ọbàtálá's inebriation resulted in the magnificent diversity of humanity and the recognition of the divinity in all creation. The killing and scattering of Ausar, Èṣù, and Faro resulted in these Deities being multiplied and dispersed all over the Earth for the benefit of humanity. If you listen to Charlie Parker, Billie Holiday, and Gil Scott-Heron you will know that Khu shines through no matter what you do. Divinity is in your genes as is genius God the arms, legs, legs, arms heads that you shoot in ignorance will be reincarnated through you God waits in every mirror looking at and longing for you too God it isn't easy but that is who we are and what we must do God.

Africana artists access and activate the untapped and boundless numinosity of their communities. They select, resurrect, and project forgotten and discredited sources of self, profiles of power, redemptions songs, cosmic philosophies, pragmatic methodologies, and political strategies to construct ways of creating, interpreting, and manifesting Africana masculine magnificence that foment depth, growth, and a concept of Self that is as familiar as one's reflection and as expansive as the Cosmos. The works of art analyzed in this book double as timeless instruction manuals on how to burnish the soul until it gleams like the life-giving Sun, on how to harness infinite powers from ancient and contemporary wisdom keepers, on how to be holy books again, transform prayers into planets, and master the skill of conceiving and birthing the waiting worlds within. The artists featured in this book, and many more, fashion art that guides their audiences past stereotype, hypocrisy, destitution, and myth straight to the recognition of their rightful identities as the True and Living Gods, as the lost and found Deities, as the patient Divinities who Abbey Lincoln gathers in her arms, anoints with her tears, and ushers to immediate restoration with her stunning revelation:

> Where are the African Gods?
> Did they leave us on our journey over here?
> Where are the African Gods?
> Will we know them when they suddenly appear?
> The ones dismissed with voodoo, rock and roll, and all that jazz
>   and jungle mumbo-jumbo and the razzmatazz?
> Where are the African Gods who will save use from this misery and
>   shame?
> Where are the African Gods?
> Will we find them while we pray in Jesus' name?
> Where are the African Gods who live and set us free?
> We are the African Gods, you know...
> We are!
> You and me.[48]

NOTES

Acknowledgments

[1] Sly & the Family Stone, "Somebody's Watching You," *Stand!* (Epic 1969), LP; and Sly & the Family Stone, "Thank You (Falettinme Be Mice Elf Agin)," *Greatest Hits* (Epic 1970) LP, respectfully and respectively.

Cipher

[1] Anthony T. Browder, *Nile Valley Contributions to Civilization: Exploding the Myths*, volume one (Washington, D. C.: Institute of Karmic Guidance, 1992), 31.
[2] Browder, *Nile Valley Contributions to Civilization*, 19; and see Shirley Better, *Institutional Racism: A Primer on Theory and Strategies for Social Change*, second edition (Lanham, MD: Rowman and Littlefield, 2007), 4.
[3] Browder, *Nile Valley Contributions to Civilization*, 19.
[4] Nell Irvin Painter, "Why Are White People Called 'Caucasians'?" Collective Degradation: Slavery and the Construction of Race, Proceedings of the Fifth Annual Gilder Lehrman Center International Conference at Yale University (November 7–8, 2003), 23 <http://www.yale.edu/glc/events/race/Painter.pdf> accessed 12 November 2011.
[5] Quoted in Browder, *Nile Valley Contributions to Civilization*, 33.
[6] For more information on "black's" logical connotations see, Joe Pinkster, "The Financial Consequences of saying 'Black' vs. 'African American,'" *The Atlantic* 30 Dec 2014 <http://www.theatlantic.com/business/archive/2014/12/the-financial-consequences-of-saying-black-vs-african-american/383999/> accessed 30 December 2014.
[6] Toni Morrison, *Beloved* (New York: Plume, 1988), 190.
[7] Stephen Hagan, "If you're white, you're right" *Online Opinion* 25 May 2006 <http://www.onlineopinion.com.au/view.asp?article=4490> accessed 09 November 2011.
[8] Gurleen Grewal, *Circles of Sorrow, Lines of Struggle: The Novels of Toni Morrison* (Baton Rouge: Louisiana State University Press, 2000), 6; and Malcolm X and Alex Haley, *The Autobiography of Malcolm X* (New York: Ballantine, 1964), 459.
[9] Quoted in Ivan Van Sertima, *Egypt Revisited* (Edison, NJ: Transaction, 1989), 44.
[10] Browder, *Nile Valley Contributions to Civilization*, 128; and field research in Egypt, Valley of the Kings, 2003.
[11] Quoted in Browder, *Nile Valley Contributions to Civilization*, 138.
[12] Quoted in Browder, *Nile Valley Contributions to Civilization*, 139.
[13] Browder, *Nile Valley Contributions to Civilization*, 48–49.
[14] Runoko Rashidi, "The Great University of Sankore at Timbuktu: A Brief Note," *The Global African Presence* 2002 <http://www.cwo.com/~lucumi

/timbuktu.html> accessed 12 November 2011; and *The Manuscripts of Timbuktu*, director, Zola Maseko (SABAC, 2009).
[15] Quoted in Cheikh Anta Diop, *The African Origin of Civilization: Myth or Reality* (Chicago: Lawrence Hill, 1974), 28.
[16] Browder, *Nile Valley Contributions to Civilization*, 31–32; and "Pope Felix V," 25 Most Evil People of the 15th Century, *One-Evil* <http://one-evil.org/people/people_15c_Felix_V.htm> accessed 09 November 2011.
[17] Orlando Patterson, *Slavery and Social Death: A Comparative Study* (Cambridge: Harvard University Press, 1982), 13.
[18] Toni Morrison, *Tar Baby* (New York: Quality Paperback Book, 1981), 305.
[19] E. Black, "The Three Virtual Intentional Communities Of God In A Body In Real Time (1868–2008)," *Alternative Considerations to Jonestown and Peoples Temple* 25 January 2009 <http://jonestown.sdsu.edu/AboutJonestown/ JonestownReport/Volume10/Black.htm> accessed 11 November 2011; and Michael Muhammad Knight, *The Five Percenters: Islam, Hip Hop and the Gods of New York* (Oxford: Oneworld, 2007), 12.
[20] Carlton D. Pearson, Religion Panel, Harlem Book Fair, *Book TV: C-SPAN*, 17 July 2010.
[21] Carlton D. Pearson, *God is Not a Christian, Nor a Jew, Muslim, Hindu. . . : God Dwells with Us, in Us, Around Us, as Us* (New York: Atria, 2010), 123.
[22] Pearson, *God is Not a Christian, Nor a Jew, Muslim, Hindu*, 123.
[23] Pearson, *God is Not a Christian, Nor a Jew, Muslim, Hindu*, 124.
[24] Johnson's written and audio report is available online: <http://www.npr.org/templates/story/story.php?storyId=5614846.> accessed 15 November 2011.
[25] Molara Ogundipe, "The Sacred and the Feminine: An African Response to Clément and Kristeva," in *The Sacred and the Feminine: Imagination and Sexual Difference*, edited by Griselda Pollock and Victoria Turvey-Sauron, (New York: I. B. Tauris, 2008), 96.
[26] Henry John Drewal and Margaret Thompson Drewal, *Gẹlẹdẹ Art and Female Power Among the Yoruba* (Bloomington: Indiana University Press, 1983), xxxii, 14, 102, 219.

1. Divinity and Divine Technology in the African Continuum

[1] Rowland Abiodun, "Identity and the Artistic Process in Yorùbá Aesthetic Concept of Ìwà," *Journal of Cultural Inquiry* 1:1 (December 1983): 23, 14.
[2] Miriam Lichtheim, *Ancient Egyptian Literature: Volume I: The Old and Middle Kingdoms* (Berkeley: University of California Press, 1973), 132, italics are retained from the original.
[3] Lichtheim, *Ancient Egyptian Literature*, 132.
[4] Lichtheim, *Ancient Egyptian Literature*, 133.

[5] "Heka," *Encyclopedia of African Religion*, volume one, edited by Molefi K. Asante and Ama Mazama (Thousand Oaks, CA: Sage, 2008), 312.
[6] Quoted in Laird Scranton, *The Science of the Dogon: Decoding the African Mystery Tradition* (Rochester, VT: Inner Traditions, 200), 84.
[7] Rowland Abiodun, "Verbal and visual metaphors: mythical allusions in Yoruba ritualistic art of *Orí*," *Word and Image, A Journal of Verbal/Visual Enquiry* 3:3 (1987): 252–253.
[8] Flora Lugard Shaw, *A Tropical Dependency: An Outline of the Ancient History of the Western Sudan with an Account of the Modern Settlement of Nigeria* (London: James Nisbet and Co., 1905), 221.
[9] Quoted in Browder, *Nile Valley Contributions to Civilization*, 139.
[10] Shaw, *A Tropical Dependency*, 220.
[11] "Nubian/Egyptian Gods and Goddess," *Dignubia* <http://www.dignubia.org/bookshelf/goddesses.php> accessed 9 May 2012.
[12] Browder, *Nile Valley Contributions to Civilization*, 58.
[13] "Lineage of the Nubian Rulers," *Dig Nubian* <http://www.dignubia.org/bookshelf/rulers.php?rul_id=00007&ord=> accessed 9 May 2012.
[14] Browder, *Nile Valley Contributions to Civilization*, 222. Heru-em-akhet is known to Westerners as The Sphinx, which means "The Strangler" and to Arabs as "Abu Hol," which means "The Father of Terror." These erroneous identifications reveal how little these outsiders understand Kemet and how quickly they supplanted African wisdom with alien ignorance.
[15] Browder, *Nile Valley Contributions to Civilization*, 222.
[16] Browder, *Nile Valley Contributions to Civilization*, 222.
[17] Browder, *Nile Valley Contributions to Civilization*, 78.
[18] Hatshepsut, "Speech of the Queen," in *Daughters of Africa*, edited by Margaret Busby (New York: Pantheon, 1992), 12.
[19] Hatshepsut, "Speech of the Queen," 14.
[20] John S. Mbiti, *African Religions and Philosophy*, second edition (Portsmouth, New Hampshire: Heinemann, 1969), 177.
[21] Mbiti, *African Religions and Philosophy*, 177–178.
[22] Naja Nzumafo, "The Ikom Monoliths of Nigeria" 08 August 2011 <http://camericans-atcam.blogspot.com/2011/08/ikom-monoliths-of-nigeria.html> accessed 24 August 2011; Keith Nicklin and Jill Salmons, "Cross River Art Styles" *African Arts* 18:1 (Nov 1984), 29; and Babatunde Lawal, "The Present State of Art Historical Research in Nigeria: Problems and Possibilities," *The Journal of African History* 18:2 (1977): 215.
[23] Teresa N. Washington, *The Architects of Existence: Àjẹ́ in Yoruba Cosmology, Ontology, and Orature* (Oya's Tornado, 2014).
[24] Teresa N. Washington, *Our Mothers, Our Powers, Our Texts: Manifestations of Àjẹ́ in Africana Literature*, revised and expanded edition (Oya's Tornado, 2015), 13, 15.
[25] The title of John Anenechukwu Umeh's two volume study, *After God is Dibia*, is inspired by this truism.

[26] Jen Pliya, "The Watch-Night," in *Jazz and Palm Wine*, edited by Willfried F. Feuser (Essex, London: Longman, 1981), 89.

[27] Zora Neale Hurston, *Mules and Men* (1990; reprint, New York: Harper Perennial, 1935), 195.

[28] Quoted in Olufemi Taiwo, "Òrìṣà: A Prolegomenon to a Philosophy of Yorùbá Religion," in *Òrìṣà Devotion as World Religion: The Globalization of Yorùbá Religious Culture*, edited by Jacob K. Olupona and Terry Ray (Madison: University of Wisconsin Press, 2008), 97, emphasis is as is quoted by Taiwo.

[29] Cornelius O. Adepegba, "Associated Place-Names and Sacred Icons of Seven Yorùbá Deities: Historicity in Yorùbá Religious Traditions," in *Òrìṣà Devotion as World Religion: The Globalization of Yorùbá Religious Culture*, edited by Jacob K. Olupona and Terry Ray (Madison: University of Wisconsin Press, 2008), 107.

[30] Wande Abimbola, *Ifá: An Exposition of Ifá Literary Corpus*, second edition (Brooklyn: Athelia Henrietta Press, 1997), 114.

[31] Abiodun, "Verbal and visual metaphors," 257.

[32] Abiodun, "Verbal and visual metaphors," 257.

[33] Abiodun, "Verbal and visual metaphors," 257.

[34] Adepegba, "Associated Place-Names and Sacred Icons of Seven Yorùbá Deities," 107.

[35] Quoted in Pierre Fatumbi Verger, *Articles*, volume one, translated by Christophe Brunksi (Montclair, NJ: Black Madonna Enterprises, 2007), 11.

[36] Stephen W. Boston, "And God Said..." *The Reluctant Messenger* <http://reluctant-messenger.com/and-God-said.htm> accessed 22 May 2011.

[37] Malidoma Somé, *Of Water and the Spirit: Ritual, Magic and Initiation in the Life of an African Shaman* (New York: Penguin Compass, 1994), 232–233.

[38] Somé, *Of Water and the Spirit*, 20.

[39] Lenell Harris, personal communications, Rienzi, MS, 1996; and Zora Neale Hurston, *Mules and Men* (New York: Harper Perennial, 1935), 127–128.

[40] George P. Rawick, editor, *The American Slave: A Composite Autobiography*, volume XIII, Georgia Narratives, part four (Westport: Greenwood, 1941), 262.

[41] Gabriel Bannerman-Richter, *The Practice of Witchcraft in Ghana* (Elk Grove, CA: Gabari, 1982), 41.

[42] John A. Umeh, *After God is Dibia*, two volumes, volume two (London: Karnak House, 1999), 41.

[43] Barry Hallen and J. Olubiyi Sodipo, *Knowledge, Belief and Witchcraft* (1986; reprint, Stanford: Stanford University Press, 1997), 110–111.

[44] Washington, *Our Mothers, Our Powers, Our Texts*, 16, 53.

[45] Drewal and Drewal, *Gẹlẹdẹ*, 251.

[46] William Bascom, *Sixteen Cowries: Yoruba Divination from Africa to the New World* (Bloomington: Indiana University Press, 1980), 231.

[47] Rawick, *American Slave*, Georgia Narratives, volume XII, part one, 339.

[48] Rawick, *American Slave*, Georgia Narratives, volume XII, part one, 337.

[49] Rawick, *American Slave*, Georgia Narratives, volume XII, part one, 337. Fryer's methodology is similar to that of Igbo mothers who chant "Uso, Uso, Uso" while strengthening their children's limbs. Flora Nwapa, *Efuru* (London: Heinemann, 1966), 34.

[50] Margaret Washington Creel, "Gullah Attitudes towards Life and Death," *Africanisms in American Culture*, edited by Joseph E. Holloway (Bloomington: Indiana University Press, 1990), 87.

[51] Rawick, *American Slave*, Georgia Narratives, volume XII, part one 337. This corrects the impression that Fryer uses a grave to cure her daughter in Teresa N. Washington, "Nickels in the Nation Sack: Continuity in Africana Spiritual Technologies," *The Journal of Pan African Studies* 3:5 (2010): 8.

[52] Zora Neale Hurston, *Sanctified Church* (New York: Marlowe and Co. 1981), 20–21.

[53] Roland Steiner, "Braziel Robinson: Possessed of Two Spirits," 378.

[54] George P. Rawick, *From Sunup to Sundown* (Westport: Greenwood, 1972), 49.

[55] Browder, *Nile Valley Contributions to Civilization*, 91.

[56] Browder, *Nile Valley Contributions to Civilization*, 91; see also Washington, *Our Mothers, Our Powers, Our Texts*, 60–61.

[57] Lichtheim, *Ancient Egyptian Literature*, 165.

[58] Lichtheim, *Ancient Egyptian Literature*, 165–169.

[59] Babatunde Lawal, *The Gèlèdé Spectacle* (Seattle: University of Washington Press, 1996), 261.

[60] Lawal, *The Gèlèdé Spectacle*, 262.

[61] Emefie Ikenga Metuh, *God and Man in African Religion: A Case Study of the Igbo of Nigeria* (London: Geoffrey Chapman, 1981), 69.

[62] Lawal, *The Gèlèdé Spectacle*, 261.

[63] Rochelle Williams, "I Wore No Veil... I Have No Caul," unpublished essay, Grambling State University 2007, 1.

[64] Williams, "I Wore No Veil... I Have No Caul," 3.

[65] Toni Morrison, *Home* (Alfred A. Knopf: New York, 2012), 131.

[66] Williams, "I Wore No Veil... I Have No Caul," 4.

[67] Sharen Rawls, personal communication, Grambling State University, 2007. 68 Rawick, *American Slave*, Kentucky Narratives, volume XVI, part one, 91.

[69] Lenell Harris, telephone interview, 2004.

[70] Rawick, *American Slave*, Georgia Narratives, volume XII, part one, 338.

[71] Georgia Writers' Project, *Drums and Shadows* (Athens: University of Georgia Press, 1940), 3.

[72] See Flora Nwapa, *Efuru* (London: Heinemann, 1966), 29–30.

[73] Lawal, *The Gèlèdé Spectacle*, 260n9.

[74] Beloved, of Toni Morrison's novel *Beloved* is very much the àbíkú, the child born to die who returns bearing the marks given by her mother. See also Chinua Achebe *Things Fall Apart* (London: Heinemann, 1958), 54–55.

[75] Lawal, *The Gèlèdé Spectacle*, 237.

⁷⁶ Lawal, *The Gẹ̀lẹ̀dẹ́ Spectacle*, 263.
⁷⁷ Ousmane Sembene, "Tribal Scars or The Voltaique," *Tribal Scars and Other Stories* (1962; reprint, London: Heinemann, 1974), 102–117; Georgia Writers' Project, *Drums and Shadows*, 71; and Morrison, *Beloved*, 61.
⁷⁸ Joseph Holloway and Winifred K. Vass, *The African Heritage of American English* (Bloomington: Indiana University Press, 1993), 87.
⁷⁹ My mother called me "Ba," in addition to many other love-filled and spirit-rich names, all throughout her life.
⁸⁰ This example of ritual protective naming is taken directly from my maternal forebears, all of whom have sacred names that appear on their birth certificates but are never used. Indeed, my father had no idea what my mother's "legal"/sacred name was!
⁸¹ Quoted in Drewal and Drewal, *Gẹlẹdẹ*, 271n4.
⁸² Quoted in Drewal and Drewal, *Gẹlẹdẹ*, 271n4.
⁸³ Rowland Abiodun, "Àṣẹ: Verbalizing and Visualizing Creative Power through Art," *Journal of Religion in Africa* 24:4 (Nov 1994): 311–312.
⁸⁴ Toni Morrison's *Song of Solomon* (New York: Plume, 1977, 329–30) gives a powerful elaboration on the relevance of African naming practices for both human beings and places. In addition to discussing African names and naming practices, chapter four of Joseph Holloway and Winifred K. Vass' *The African Heritage of American English* (Bloomington: Indiana University Press, 1993) elucidates African geographic place names in the United States.
⁸⁵ *Song of Solomon* provides a perfect example with the character "Guitar."
⁸⁶ Field research in Christian Village, Legon, Ghana, 1995.
⁸⁷ Quoted in Drewal and Drewal, *Gẹlẹdẹ*, 5.
⁸⁸ Moses A. Makinde, *African Philosophy, Culture and Traditional Medicine* (Athens, OH: Center for International Studies, 1988), 88, 89. For an African American variant in fiction, see Toni Morrison's *Home* in which community women administer to Ycidra a "permanent cure. The kind beyond human power," after her womb is defiled. The capstone of the permanent cure for Ycidra to be "sun-smacked," which is to open her vagina unto the inestimable healing power of the Sun (124-125).
⁸⁹ Somé, *Of Water and the Spirit*, 170.
⁹⁰ Umeh, *After God is Dibia*, volume two, 132.
⁹¹ Esteban Montejo, *The Autobiography of a Runaway Slave* (London: Bodley Head, 1968), 131.
⁹² Georgia Writers Project, *Drums and Shadows*, 154.
⁹³ Georgia Writers Project, *Drums and Shadows*, 154.
⁹⁴ Georgia Writers Project, *Drums and Shadows*, 145.
⁹⁵ Lorna McDaniel, *The Big Drum Ritual of Carriacou: Praisesongs in Rememory of Flight* (Gainesville: University Press of Florida, 1998), 81. In Haile Gerima's film *Sankofa*, characters Mona/Shola and Nunu both make journeys through time and place with the assistance of buzzards. *Sankofa*, directed by Haile Gerima (Mypheduh, 1993), VHS.

[96] Montejo, *Autobiography of a Runaway Slave*, 30.
[97] Zora Neale Huston, "Crow Dance," *Speak So You Can Speak Again*, edited by Lucy Anne Hurston, companion CD (New York: Doubleday, 2004).
[98] Jonathan Tatum, personal communication, Grambling State University, 2010.
[99] Umeh, *After God is Dibia*, volume two, 33.
[100] Umeh, *After God is Dibia*, volume two, 33.
[101] Hallen and Sodipo, *Knowledge, Belief and Witchcraft*, 108.
[102] Bascom, *Ifa Divination*, 111, 412–415.
[103] Wande Abimbola, *Sixteen Great Poems of Ifá* (n.p.: UNESCO, 1975), 331; see also 226.
[104] Umeh, *After God is Dibia*, volume one, 131.
[105] Umeh, *After God is Dibia*, volume one, 131.
[106] Georgia Writer's Project, *Drums and Shadows*, 79, 81.
[107] Montejo, *Autobiography of a Runaway Slave*, 43–44.
[108] Quoted in Robert Farris Thompson, *Flash of the Spirit: African and Afro-American Art and Philosophy* (New York: Vintage, 1983), 123.
[109] Quoted in Thompson, *Flash of the Spirit*, 124.
[110] The images NASA recorded are compelling and have raised many questions that remain unanswered. It is interesting to note that NASA stopped broadcasting live images from space when citizens began demanding information about the apparent forms, figures, and forces active in the universe. See <http://www.youtube.com/watch?v=lBIrANSMihg>, <http://www.youtube.com/watch?v=buWBonjaVT4&feature=related>, <http://www.youtube.com/watch?v=_62WWGLzynY&feature=related> all accessed 8 January 2012.
[111] Somé, *Of Water and the Spirit*, 237. Somé's experiences are comparable to the theories David Faige offers in "What Would It Feel Like To Travel in Time," in *Time/Space Continuum—A Thesis*, 2006 <http://www.west.net/~ke6jqp/spacetime/spacetime4.html> accessed 19 July 2009.
[112] Somé, *Of Water and the Spirit*, 52.
[113] Umeh, *After God is Dibia*, volume two, 211–212.
[114] Georgia Writers' Project, *Drums and Shadows*, 7
[115] Georgia Writers' Project, *Drums and Shadows*, 7.
[116] Georgia Writers' Project, *Drums and Shadows*, 31; and C. L. Adeoye, *Ìgbàgbọ́ àti Ẹ̀sìn Yorùbá* (Ibadan: Evans Bros., 1985), 304–307.
[117] Umeh, *After God is Dibia*, volume two, 211.
[118] See Washington, *Our Mothers, Our Powers, Our Texts*, 88–89.
[119] Bannerman-Richter, *The Practice of Witchcraft in Ghana*, 29.
[120] Lawrence Levine, *Black Culture and Black Consciousness: Afro-American Folk Thought from Slavery to Freedom* (Oxford University Press, 1977), 74.
[121] Umeh, *After God is Dibia*, volume two, 212. In Cheikh Oumar Sissoko's film *Guimba the Tyrant*, the character Siriman gives a wonderful example of ibi iboo, and other technologies that I discuss in chapter one, in action. *Guimba the Tyrant*, directed by Cheikh Oumar Sissoko (2005; Kino, 1995), DVD.

[122] Ayo Opefeyitimi, "Women of the World in Yoruba Culture," Unpublished paper, 1993, 13; and Umeh, *After God is Dibia*, volume two, 212.
[123] Umeh, *After God is Dibia*, volume two, 109.
[124] Umeh, *After God is Dibia*, volume two, 109.
[125] Umeh, *After God is Dibia*, volume two, 109.
[126] "Àfẹ̀rí," *A Dictionary of the Yoruba Language*, part two, 8. I have replaced "ẹ̃" with "ẹ̀ẹ́" to better represent the word.
[127] Georgia Writers' Project, *Drums and Shadows*, 20.
[128] Georgia Writers' Project, *Drums and Shadows*, 24.
[129] Rawick, *The American Slave*, Georgia Narratives, volume XIII, part four, 262.
[130] Georgia Writers' Project, *Drums and Shadows*, 58.
[131] Hurston, *Mules and Men*, 220–221.
[132] Somé, *Of Water and the Spirit*, 68.
[133] Pierre F. Verger, *Ewé: The Use of Plants in Yoruba Society* (Sao Paulo: Odebracht, 1995), 347.
[134] Verger, *Ewé*, 347.
[135] Somé, *Of Water and the Spirit*, 263.
[136] Umeh, *After God is Dibia*, volume two, 132.
[137] Bass, "Mojo," 385–386.
[138] "Plants can talk, say scientists," Mail Online, *Daily Mail* <http://www.dailymail.co.uk/news/article-112942/Plants-talk-say-scientists.html> accessed 3 August 2012. See also Joseph Scheppach, "The Latest News from Brother Tree and Sister Flower," *Facts are Facts* <http://www.facts-are-facts.com/magazin/5_research_human_greenery.ihtml> accessed 3 August 2012.
[139] Umeh, *After God is Dibia*, volume two, 132.
[140] Umeh, *After God is Dibia*, volume two, 132.
[141] Carlos Moore, *Pichón: A Memoir: Race and Revolution in Castro's Cuba* (Chicago: Lawrence Hill, 2008), 50.
[142] Moore, *Pichón*, 12.
[143] Robert Farris Thompson, *Flash of the Spirit*, 109.
[144] Thompson, *Flash of the Spirit*, 109.
[145] Moore, *Pichón*, 12.
[146] Moore, *Pichón*, 13.
[147] Moore, *Pichón*, 13.
[148] Roland Steiner, "Braziel Robinson: Possessed of Two Spirits," in *Mother Wit from the Laughing Barrel*, edited by Alan Dundes (1973; reprint, Jackson: University of Mississippi Press, 1990), 378.
[149] Bass, "Mojo," 382.
[150] Luisah Teish, *Jambalaya: The Natural Woman's Book of Personal Charms and Practical Rituals* (New York: Harper San Francisco, 1988), 196.
[151] Awolalu, *Yoruba Beliefs and Sacrificial Rites*, 175.
[152] Rawick, *The American Slave*, Georgia Narratives, volume XIII, part four, 254.

[153] Washington, *Our Mothers, Our Powers, Our Texts*, 20, 23–24.
[154] Browder, *Nile Valley Contributions to Civilization*, 91.
[155] Awolalu, *Yoruba Beliefs and Sacrificial Rites*, 49.
[156] Georgia Writers' Project, *Drums and Shadows*, 204n11c.
[157] See Thompson, *Flash of the Spirit*, 142–145.
[158] Eben Sheba, "Ààlè: A Deterrent Symbol and Communication device among the Ikale Yoruba of Nigeria," *Ifẹ̀* 7 (1999), 10–13.
[159] Field research in the southern United States, 2001 and 2003.
[160] Awolalu, *Yoruba Beliefs and Sacrificial Rites*, 79.
[161] Georgia Writers' Project, *Drums and Shadows*, 20–21.
[162] Georgia Writers' Project, *Drums and Shadows*, 21.
[163] Ayanna Gillian, "Yoruba Religion: The Cornerstone of Society," *Roots Women* 10 April 2003 <www.rootswomen.com/ayanna/articles/10042003.html> accessed 12 August 2007. See also Rowland Abiodun, "Àṣẹ: Verbalizing and Visualizing Creative Power through Art," 314.
[164] Thompson, *Flash of the Spirit*, 117–131.
[165] Umeh, *After God is Dibia*, volume two, 75.
[166] Umeh, *After God is Dibia*, volume two, 75.
[167] Rawick, *The American Slave*, Georgia Narratives, volume XIII, part three, 218–219.
[168] Mbiti, *African Religions and Philosophy*, 175–176.
[169] Verger, *Ewé*, 391.
[170] Bass, "Mojo," 382.
[171] Bill Nye, "Ask Bill Nye," Online posting, 2007, Columns: Clouds <http://encarta.msn.com/encnet/Features/Columns/?article=BNClouds> accessed 16 February 2008; and SOARS (Seeding Operations and Atmospheric Research) "SOARS Pioneers Cloud Seeding with Milled Salt," 2005, *just-clouds* <http://www.just-clouds.com/SOAR_pioneers_cloud_seeding_milled_salt.asp> 16 February 2008.
[172] Awolalu, *Yoruba Beliefs and Sacrificial Rites*, 78.
[173] Hurston, *Mules and Men*, 280.
[174] Lenell Harris, personal communications, Rienzi, MS, 2000.
[175] Hurricane G featuring Rishi, "No More Prisons," *No More Prisons* (Raptivism, 1999).
[176] Verger, *Ewé*, 335.
[177] Verger, *Ewé*, 335.
[178] Hurston, *Mules and Men*, 224.
[179] Hurston, *Mules and Men*, 275.
[180] Hurston, *Mules and Men*, 225; for another variant, see Hurston, *Mules and Men*, 275.
[181] Awolalu, *Yoruba Beliefs and Sacrificial Rites*, 78–79.
[182] Hurston, *Mules and Men*, 218.
[183] Hurston, *Mules and Men*, 220.

[184] Verger, *Ewé*, 307.
[185] Verger, *Ewé*, 367.
[186] Bass, "Mojo," 384.
[187] Verger, *Ewé*, 309.
[188] Verger, *Ewé*, 309.
[189] Hurston, *Mules and Men*, 188.
[190] Hurston, *Mules and Men*, 189.
[191] Verger, *Ewé*, 417.
[192] Hurston, *Mules and Men*, 219, 226. For other examples of "running feet" see Rawick, *Georgia Narratives*, volume XIII, part two, 283.
[193] Umeh, *After God is Dibia*, volume two, 121.
[194] Umeh, *After God is Dibia*, volume two, 134.
[195] Makinde, *African Philosophy, Culture and Traditional Medicine*, 97.
[196] Quoted in Makinde, *African Philosophy, Culture and Traditional Medicine*, 96.
[197] P. Amaury Talbot, "The Egbo Secret Society," in *A Treasury of African Folklore: The Oral Literature, Traditions, Myths, Legends, Epics, Tales, Recollections, Wisdom, Sayings, and Humor of Africa*, edited by Harold A. Courlander (1976; reprint, New York: Marlowe & Co., 1996), 272.
[198] David Pratten, *The Man-Leopard Murders: History and Society in Colonial Nigeria* (Bloomington: Indiana University Press, 2007), 43.
[199] Somé, *Of Water and the Spirit*, 24.
[200] "Àkàtàmpó," *A Dictionary of the Yoruba Language*, part two, 27; and see Cromwell Osamaro Ibie, *Ifism: The Complete Works of Orunmila*, volume one (Lagos: Efehi, 1986), 179.
[201] Somé, *Of Water and the Spirit*, 41.
[202] Somé, *Of Water and the Spirit*, 25 and Malidoma Somé, lecture, Grambling State University, February 2007.
[203] Hurston, *The Sanctified Church*, 36.
[204] Rawick, *The American Slave*, volume XVI, Kentucky Narratives, 36.
[205] Rawick, *The American Slave*, volume XVI, Kentucky Narratives, 35.
[206] Awo Fa'lokun Fatunmbi, *Ìwa-pèlé: Ifá Quest* (Bronx: Original, 1991), 84–85.
[207] Fatunmbi, *Ìwa-pèlé: Ifá Quest*, 84.
[208] E. Bolaji Idowu, *Olódùmarè: God in Yorùbá Belief* (1962; reprint, New York: Wazobia, 1994), 34–35.
[209] Hurston, *The Sanctified Church*, 34.
[210] Rawick, *The American Slave*, Kentucky Narratives, volume XVI, 36; and Montejo, *The Autobiography of a Runaway Slave*, 131.
[211] Umeh, *After God is Dibia*, volume one, 209.
[212] Umeh, *After God is Dibia*, volume one, 134.
[213] Umeh, *After God is Dibia*, volume one, 209.
[214] P. Amaury Talbot, "The Egbo Secret Society," 271.

2. High John and His Conquering Suns

[1] For further elucidation, please see Teresa N. Washington, "*Mules and Men* and Messiahs: Continuity in Yoruba Divination Verses and African American Folktales," *Journal of American Folklore* 125:497 (2012): 263–285. This article was a chapter in an earlier draft of this book.
[2] Hurston, *Mules and Men*, 158, 4, 96–97, respectively.
[3] Osamaro Ibie, *Ifism: The Complete Works of Orunmila*, volume one (Lagos: Efehi, 1986), 170–171, 176, respectively.
[4] Washington, *Our Mothers, Our Powers, Our Texts*, 94–97.
[5] Julius Lester, "How The Snake Got His Rattles," *Black Folktales* (New York: Grove Weidenfeld, 1969), 44.
[6] Hurston, *Mules and Men*, 47 and 155, respectively.
[7] Hurston, *Mules and Men*, 31–34.
[8] Hurston, *The Sanctified Church*, 55, emphasis added.
[9] Hurston, *Mules and Men*, 119 and 160–161, respectively.
[10] Hurston, *Mules and Men*, 164–165.
[11] History's most well-known Mansa is Mansa Musa, the emperor who earned the nickname The Golden One when he showered the citizens of Cairo, Egypt with so much gold during his legendary hajj to Mecca in 1324 that it took the Egyptian economy years to recover. History's least known but arguably most significant Mansa is Abubakari II, who equipped two fleets of hundreds of ships in 1310 CE and 1311 CE and successfully sailed from Mali to the Americas. See Ivan Van Sertima, *They Came Before Columbus* (New York: Random House, 1976).
[12] Holloway and Vass, *The African Heritage of American English*, 142; and Eric Charry, *Mande Music: Traditional and Modern Music of the Maninka and Mandinka of Western Africa* (Chicago: University of Chicago Press, 2000), 107n30.
[13] Ousmane Sembene gives a powerful discussion of slavery and jaam in "An Interview with Ousmane Sembène by Sada Niang," in *Ousmane Sembene: Dialogues with Critics and Writers* edited by Samba Gadjigo, Ralph H. Faulkingham, Thomas Cassirer and Reinhard Sander (Amherst: University of Massachusetts Press, 1993), 104. See also Holloway and Vass, *The African Heritage of American English*, 142; and David Dalby, "Americanisms That May Once Have Been Africanisms," in *Mother Wit from the Laughing Barrel: Readings in the Interpretation of Afro-American Folklore* edited by Alan Dundes (Englewood Cliffs, N.J.: Prentice Hall, 1973), 139.
[14] Levine, *Black Culture and Black Consciousness*, 127.
[15] "Promises of Freedom," in *Crossing the Danger Water*, edited by Deirdre Mullane (New York: Anchor, 1993), 251.
[16] Holloway and Vass, *The African Heritage of American English*, 147.
[17] Hurston, *The Sanctified Church*, 70.

[18] Abiodun, "Verbal and Visual Metaphors," 253–254.

[19] Kola Abimbola, "Yoruba Diaspora," *Encyclopedia of Diasporas: Immigrant and Refugee Cultures Around the World*, volume two, edited by Melvin Ember, Carol R. Ember, Ian Skoggard (New York: Springer, 2004), 322; and Zora Neale Hurston, *Tell My Horse* (1938; reprint, New York: Harper and Row, 1990), 114.

[20] Hurston, *The Sanctified Church*, 69–70.

[21] Hurston, *The Sanctified Church*, 69–70.

[22] Hurston, *The Sanctified Church*, 70–71.

[23] Hurston, *The Sanctified Church*, 71.

[24] Hurston, *The Sanctified Church*, 71.

[25] I find it appalling but telling that the texts of the three major organized religions include numerous verses detailing how to be "good" slaves and "good" oppressors and offering numerous enslaving techniques, rules, and rationales. In their wholehearted sanctioning of slavery, it is clear that these are the words of morally bankrupt capital-driven men masquerading as "God"—either that or the "Gods" issuing these decrees are not worthy of worship. Also disturbing is the fact that no commandment, savior, or prophet offers any condemnation of slavery in these religions. See "What the Old Testament Says About Slavery," R*eligious Tolerance.org* <http://www.religioustolerance.org/sla_bibl1.htm>; "Slavery in the Bible," *Evil Bible* <http://www.religioustolerance.org/sla_bibl1.htm>; "What the Quran Says About Slavery," *The Skeptics Annotated Quran* <http:// skeptics annotatedbible.com/quran/says_about/slavery.html>; "What the Bible Says About Slavery," *The Skeptic's Annotated Bible* <http://skeptics annotatedbible .com/says_about/slavery.html> all accessed 18 November 2012. It is important to note that Hurston's praisename for Africana people "Aunt Hagar's Children" is rooted in the theory that Africana people are descendants of Hagar, the Kemite who was enslaved by Sarai and was forced to submit to rape by Abram and bear Ishmael (Genesis 16).

[26] Hurston, *Mules and Men*, 72.

[27] Mbiti, *African Religions and Philosophies*, 175.

[28] Hurston, *Mules and Men*, 88–89.

[29] Walker, *The Color Purple*, 177.

[30] Zora Neale Hurston, *Every Tongue Got to Confess* (New York: Harper Collins, 2001), 76.

[31] Levine, *Black Culture and Black Consciousness*, 46.

[32] Washington, *Our Mothers, Our Powers, Our Texts*, 18, 281–282.

[33] Lemuel A. Johnson, "The Inventions of Paradise: The Caribbean and the Utopian Bent," *Poetics Today* 15:4 (Winter 1994): 707; Reginald McKnight, "Palm Wine," in *Speak My Name: Black Men on Masculinity and the American Dream*, edited by Don Belton (Boston: Beacon, 1995), 182; and Washington, *Our Mothers, Our Powers, Our Texts*, 166.

[34] Amos Tutuola, *The Palm-Wine Drinkard* (Boston: Faber and Faber, 1952), 194.

[35] Hurston, *Mules and Men*, 164.

[36] Tutuola, *The Palm-Wine Drinkard*, 16.
[37] Hurston, *Mules and Men*, 164.
[38] Hurston, *Mules and Men*, 42, 89, and 82, respectively.
[39] Hurston, *The Sanctified Church*, 71–72.
[40] Thompson, *Flash of the Spirit*, 131.
[41] Ntozake Shange, *for colored girls who have considered suicide/when the rainbow is enuf: a choreopoem*, in *Totem Voices: Plays from the Black World Repertory*, edited by Paul Carter Harrison (New York: Grove Press, 1989), 274.
[42] Zora Neale Hurston, *Dust Tracks on a Road* (1996; reprint, New York: Harper Perennial, 1942), 216.
[43] Hurston, *Dust Tracks on a Road*, 217.
[44] Hurston, *Dust Tracks on a Road*, 226.
[45] Toni Morrison, *Tar Baby* (1981; reprint, New York: Quality Paperback Book Club, 1987), 305.
[46] Kim Powers, "An Interview with August Wilson," in *Conversations with August Wilson*, edited by Jackson R. Bryer and Mary C. Hartig (Jackson: University of Mississippi Press, 2006), 9. Wilson makes this point and others similar to it in the majority of his interviews and many of his plays. In an interview with Bill Moyers in the same volume, Wilson credits Amiri Baraka with introducing him to the logic that one's God should resemble one's self (77).
[47] *John Henrik Clarke: A Great and Mighty Walk*, directed by St. Claire Bourne (Black Dot Media, 1996).
[48] Black, "The Three Virtual Intentional Communities Of God In A Body In Real Time (1868–2008)"; and Knight, *The Five Percenters*, 12.
[49] Knight, *The Five Percenters*, 12.
[50] Knight, *The Five Percenters*, 13.
[51] Quoted in Knight, *The Five Percenters*, 13.
[52] Michael A. Gomez, *Black Crescent: The Experience and Legacy of African Muslims in the Americas* (Cambridge: Cambridge University Press, 2005), 210.
[53] Hurston, *Mules and Men*, 124n6.
[54] Gomez, *Black Crescent*, 210–211.
[55] Gomez, *Black Crescent*, 211.
[56] "Our Ten Commandments," *Universal Hagar's Spiritual Church Association* <http://www.uhsca.org/Commandments.html> accessed 23 September 2011.
[57] "Our Creed," *Universal Hagar's Spiritual Church Association* <http://www.uhsca.org/Commandments.html> accessed 23 September 2011.
[58] Walker, *The Color Purple*, 178.
[59] "Our Founder, *Universal Hagar's Spiritual Church Association* 2011 <http://www.uhsca.org/Commandments.html> accessed 23 September 2011.
[60] Quoted in Gunnar Myrdal, *An American Dilemma: The Negro Problem and Modern Democracy*, volume two (1944; reprint, New York: Harper and Row, 2009), 747.
[61] Constantine Francis Chassebeuf de Volney, *The Ruins of Empires* (1890; reprint, Baltimore: Black Classic Press, 1991).

[62] Knight, *The Five Percenters*, 16.
[63] Knight, *The Five Percenters*, 16.
[64] Richard Brent Turner, *Islam in the African-American Experience* (Bloomington: Indiana University Press, 2003), 88.
[65] Turner, *Islam in the African-American Experience*, 88.
[66] Knight, *The Five Percenters*, 16.
[67] Drew Ali, *The Holy Koran of the Moorish Science Temple of America Circle 7 Koran*, 1927 *hermetic* <http://hermetic.com/moorish/7koran.html> accessed 17 March 2013.
[68] Ali, *The Holy Koran of the Moorish Science Temple of America Circle 7 Koran*.
[69] Ali, *The Holy Koran of the Moorish Science Temple of America Circle 7 Koran*.
[70] Ali, *The Holy Koran of the Moorish Science Temple of America Circle 7 Koran*.
[71] Ali, *The Holy Koran of the Moorish Science Temple of America Circle 7 Koran*.
[72] Knight, *The Five Percenters*, 21.
[73] Quoted in Knight, *The Five Percenters*, 29.
[74] C. M. Bey, *Clock of Destiny*, volume I (1947; reprint, Cleveland: R V Bey Publications, 1973), 57.
[75] Knight, *The Five Percenters*, 29.
[76] Bey, *Clock of Destiny*, 57.
[77] Rahsmariah V. Bey, *She Redeems* (New York: R V Bey Publications, 2005), 2. Bey and El are the names that members of the Moorish nation adopt to signify their identity and nationality. The names do not necessarily signify a biological or marital relationship.
[78] Bey, *She Redeems*, 2.
[79] R. V. Bey, "Return of the Matriarch," *R V Bey Publications* <http://www.rvbeypublications.com/id78.html> accessed 01 October 2011.
[80] Fard was known by many names during his many lives. He understood and effectively harnessed the flexibility and fluidity inherent in naming.
[81] Elijah Muhammad, "I Want To Teach You," *Our Savior Has Arrived, Nation of Islam Settlement No. 1* <http://www.seventhfam.com/temple/books/our_saviour/saviour10.htm> accessed 31 July 2008.
[82] Elijah Muhammad, *The Theology of Time* (Phoenix, AZ: Secretarius MEMPS, 2006), 133.
[83] Quoted in Louis E. Lomax, *When the Word is Given. . .* (New York: Signet, 1963), 108–109.
[84] Knight, *The Five Percenters*, 73.
[85] Malcolm X and Alex Haley, *The Autobiography of Malcolm X* (1973; reprint, New York: Ballantine, 1965), 185.

[86] X and Haley, *The Autobiography of Malcolm X*, 185.
[87] X and Haley, *The Autobiography of Malcolm X*, 215.
[88] X and Haley, *The Autobiography of Malcolm X*, 217.
[89] X and Haley, *The Autobiography of Malcolm X*, 239.
[90] X and Haley, *The Autobiography of Malcolm X*, 217.
[91] X and Haley, *The Autobiography of Malcolm X*, 217.
[92] X and Haley, *The Autobiography of Malcolm X*, 217.
[93] X and Haley, *The Autobiography of Malcolm X*, 217.
[94] X and Haley, *The Autobiography of Malcolm X*, 340–341.
[95] Abdul Noor, *The Supreme Understanding: The Teaching of Islam in North America* (Lincoln, NE: Writers Club Press, 2002), 120.
[96] X and Haley, *The Autobiography of Malcolm X*, 415.
[97] Malcolm X, "The Ballet or the Bullet," 12 April 1964 *American Radio Works* <http://americanradioworks.publicradio.org/features/blackspeech/mx.html> accessed 05 June 2013.
[98] "Manning Marable's *Malcolm X* Panel: 23 Jul 2011" C-Span Video Library <http://www.c-spanvideo.org/program/Marabl> accessed 23 July 2011.
[99] "Manning Marable's *Malcolm X* Panel."
[100] Wakeel Allah, *In the Name of Allah: A History of Clarence 13X and the Five Percenters* (Atlanta: A Team, 2007), 96–104.
[101] W. D. Fard Muhammad, "Lost Found Muslim Lesson No. 2," in *The Supreme Wisdom Lessons*, 20 February 1934 *The Nation of Islam.org* <http://www.thenationofislam.org/muslimlessontwo.html> accessed 19 December 2007.
[102] C. O. Adepegba, *Yoruba Metal Sculpture* (Ibadan: Ibadan University Press, 1991), 2; and quoted in Supreme Understanding Allah, et. al., *Knowledge of Self: A Collection of Wisdom on the Science of Everything in Life* (Atlanta: Supreme Design Media, 2009), 23.
[103] Fard Muhammad, "Lost Found Muslim Lesson No. 2."
[104] Clarence Cooper, Jr., "Not We Many," in *Black* (1997; reprint, Edinburg: Payback Press, 1963), 305.
[105] Cooper, "Not We Many," 318–319.
[106] Umeh, *After God is Dibia*, volume one, 130–131.
[107] Cooper, "Not We Many," 319.
[108] Cooper, "Not We Many," 322.
[109] Allah, *In the Name of Allah*, 153, emphasis in the original.
[100] Allah, *In the Name of* Allah, 142; and W. D. Fard Muhammad, *The Supreme Wisdom Lessons*, 20 February 1934 *The Nation of Islam.org* <http://www.thenationofislam.org/supremewisdom.html.html> accessed 15 September 2013.
[111] Felicia Miyakawa, *Five Percenter Rap: God Hop's Music, Message, and Black Muslim Mission* (Bloomington: Indiana University Press, 2005), 29.
[112] De La Soul featuring Red Man, "Oooh!" *Art Official Intelligence: Mosaic Thump* (Rhino, 2000).

[113] Miyakawa, *Five Percenter Rap*, 29.
[114] "Supreme Mathematics," Nation of Gods and Earths/Five Percent FAQ (frequently asked questions), *Black Apologetics* <http://www.blackapologetics.com/fivepercentfaq.html> accessed 31 July 2008.
[115] In an interview with Wakeel Allah, Minister Akbar Muhammad of the Nation of Islam discusses how shocked and angered he was to see Allah, the Father, smoking a cigarette while addressing the Parliament. See "The true history of the Muslims coming to the first 5% parliament and debating Clarence 13X," *You Tube* <http://www .youtube.com/watch?NR=1&v=fwSdfr1AJBk> accessed 15 November 2011.
[116] Knight, *The Five Percenters*, 110.
[117] Knight, *The Five Percenters*, 108, 111.
[118] Knight, *The Five Percenters*, 97.
[119] Quoted in Allah, *In the Name of Allah*, 129.
[120] Quoted in Miyakawa, *Five Percenter Rap*, 21.

3. "I Call My Brother Sun 'Cause He Shine Like One"

[1] My knowledge of the fundamentals of rap helped me to learn Yoruba and memorize ęsę Ifá, which are rhythmic and often rhyming verses that display the linguistic mastery of the Yoruba language and the significance of tonality. The similarities between rap and the ęsę Ifá made it easy for me to convert the verses into songs, raps, and chants for memorization. My love of hip hop and my understanding of the relationship between these genres of orature helped me to understand ìtàn, oríkì, and ęsę Ifá, and they gave me a great appreciation for the depth, intricacy and beauty of the Yoruba language.
[2] For Museveni's original rap, see "Museveni Another Rap Freestyle" at <http://www.youtube.com/watch?v=B3fSwwPArqo&NR=1> accessed 24 October 2012. For the remix see "PRESIDENT YOWERI MUSEVENI You want another Rap 2010" at <http://www.youtube.com/watch?v=3BjOHc_R0PA> accessed 24 October 2012.
[3] Ogundipe, *The Sacred and the Feminine*, 95.
[4] Ogundipe, *The Sacred and the Feminine*, 96.
[5] August Wilson, "Preface," *King Hedley II* (New York: Theatre Communications Group, 2000), x.
[6] Holloway and Vass, *The African Heritage of American English*, 142.
[7] Siga Jallow and Babacar M'bow, "Griots/Griottes of West Africa," in *Encyclopedia of the African Diaspora: Origins, Experiences, and Culture*, edited by Carole Elizabeth Boyce Davies (Santa Barbara: ABC-CLIO, 2008), 479.
[8] Ogundipe, *The Sacred and the Feminine*, 96.
[9] Rowland Abiodun, "Àşę: Verbalizing and Visualizing Creative Power through Art," 311.
[10] Knight, *The Five Percenters*, 56.

[11] The RZA, *The Wu-Tang Manual* (New York: Penguin, 2005), 43.
[12] Jay Z, "Heaven," *Magna Carta... Holy Grail* (Roc Nation, 2013), CD.
[13] Jay Z, "Run the Town," *The Blueprint 3* (Roc Nation, 2009), CD.
[14] De La Soul featuring Red Man, "Oooh!"
[15] AZ featuring The RZA, "Whatever Happened (The Birth)," *Wu Chronicles* (Wu-Tang Records, 1999), CD.
[16] Poor Righteous Teachers, "Butt Naked Booty Bless," *Holy Intellect* (Profile/Arista, 1990), LP.
[17] Eric B and Rakim, "No Competition," *Follow the Leader* (UNI/MCA, 1988), CD.
[18] Lord Jamar, "I.S.L.A.M.," *The 5% Album* (Babygrande, 2006), CD.
[19] Lord Jamar, "Supreme Mathematics," *The 5% Album* (Babygrande, 2006), CD.
[20] Lomax, *When the Word is Given...*, 48.
[21] Killarmy, "Universal Soldiers," *Silent Weapons for Quiet Wars* (Priority/EMI, 1997), CD.
[22] Killarmy, "Last Poet," *Dirty Weaponry* (Priority, 1998), CD.
[23] Killarmy, "Allah Sees Everything," *Dirty Weaponry* (Priority, 1998), CD.
[24] Knight, *The Five Percenters*, 150.
[25] See also Sun Ra, *The Wisdom of Sun Ra*, compiled by John Corbett (Chicago: White Walls, 2006), 125.
[26] William Bascom, *Sixteen Cowries*, 459; and John Mason, *Orin Òrìṣà*, 314.
[27] Gil Scott-Heron and Brian Jackson, "Winter in America," *Winter in America* (1974; reissue, Tvt, 1998), LP.
[28] Goodie Mob, "Black Ice (Sky High)," *Still Standing* (LaFace, 1998), CD.
[29] Wade W. Nobles, "African American Family Life: An Instrument of Culture," in *Black Families*, edited by Harriette Pipes McAdoo, third edition (Thousand Oaks, CA: Sage, 1997), 85.
[30] William Loren Katz, *Black Indians: A Hidden Heritage* (New York: Atheneum, 1997), 22.
[31] See also Gregory Allan, "Silent Weapons for Quiet Wars: An Introduction Programming Manual," *The Lawful Path* <http://www.lawfulpath.com/ref/sw4qw/> accessed 18 August 2011.
[32] Gravediggaz, "Dangerous Mindz," *Wu-Chronicles: Chapter II* (Wu-Tang Records, 2001), CD.
[33] Gravediggaz, "Dangerous Mindz.
[34] Bob Marley and Peter Tosh, "Get Up, Stand Up," *Legend: The Best of Bob Marley and the Wailers* (1973; Def Jam, 2001), CD.
[35] Marley and Tosh, "Get Up, Stand Up."
[36] Mutabaruka, "Mutabaruka on Religious HardTalk," part two of eleven, *Youtube* <http://www.youtube.com/watch?v=GzZYAZ3ngKk&NR=1> accessed 12 August 2011.
[37] Mutabaruka, "Mutabaruka on Religious HardTalk," part one of eleven, *You Tube* <http://www.youtube.com/watch?v=IdAXGmYRSlY> accessed 12 August 2011.

[38] Mutabaruka, "Mutabaruka on Religious HardTalk," part two of eleven.
[39] Ismael AbduSalaam, "The RZA: Do the Knowledge (Tao of the Wu)," part 1, *All Hip Hop* 15 October 2009 <http://allhiphop.com/stories/reviewsbooks/archive/2009/10/15/21979105.aspx> accessed 16 August 2011. For the etymology of "religion" and its relationship to the words "bind" and "rely," see "religion," *The American Heritage Dictionary of the English Language*, third edition, (New York: Houghton Mifflin, 1992), 1525.
[40] Ismael AbduSalaam, "The RZA: Do the Knowledge (Tao of the Wu)."
[41] Sun Ra, *The Wisdom of Sun Ra*, 5–6.
[42] Sun Ra, *The Wisdom of Sun Ra*, 77, emphasis in the original.
[43] W. Kim Heron, "Space is Still the Place," *Metro Times* 6 June 2007 <http://www.metrotimes.com/editorial/story.asp?id=10582> accessed 18 January 2008.
[44] Heron, "Space is Still the Place."
[45] Goodie Mob, "Fighting," *Soul Food* (LaFace, 1995), CD.
[46] Goodie Mob, "The Experience," *Still Standing*, (LaFace, 1998), CD.
[47] Goodie Mob, "The Experience."
[48] Goodie Mob, "The Experience."
[49] Goodie Mob, "The Experience," emphasis in the original.
[50] Hurston, *Mules and Men*, 96–97; Ibie, *Ifism*, 170, 171; and William Bascom, *Ifa Divination* (Bloomington: Indiana University Press, 1969), 431, 437, 441.
[51] Gravediggaz, "The Night the Earth Cried," *The Pick, the Sickle, and the Shovel* (BMG Records, 1997), CD. In the song's video, The RZA shows himself to be a master of the African sciences and technologies that I discuss in chapter one. See "Gravediggaz - THE NIGHT THE EARTH CRIED (1997) dir. The RZA" <http://www.youtube.com/watch?v=5VFkgfhRljE> accessed 20 January 2014.
[52] One of my students did his research paper on the Nation of Gods and its influence on his sibling, who recognized and embraced his destiny and divinity as a God after hearing "The Night the Earth Cried."
[53] Knight, *The Five Percenters*, 96–97.
[54] Knight, *The Five Percenters*, 111, 112.
[55] Knight, *The Five Percenters*, 128.
[56] Quoted in Allah, *In the Name of Allah*, 202.
[57] Knight's deeds and actions raise questions about his motivations regarding the Five Percent. My suspicions were initially aroused when I noted in *The Five Percenters* what appeared to be Knight's attempt to bait Gods into conferring divinity on Caucasian men. Rather than seeking wisdom, Knight appeared to be motivated by the typical oppressors' desire to infiltrate, conquer, and obliterate. I was also jarred by one of Knight's glib references to Allah, the Father, and the overall tone of his discussion of the Five Percent in "The Five Percenters: between Afrocentrism and Islam," which he presented at the Fourth Annual Prince Alwaleed Bin Talal Islamic Studies Conference, *Expressions of Islam in*

Contemporary African American Communities at Harvard University, 7-8 April 2012 <http://vimeo.com/41310986> accessed 13 June 2013. Given the foregoing, I was not surprised when, in February 2013, after having a disagreement via internet with certain Gods about their views on homosexuality, Knight published an essay titled "Lifting Up My Skirt" and used a symbol of the Five Percent Nation that he desecrated for his essay's graphic art. Knight declared in that article that he and the Five Percent Nation were "breaking up" (Michael Muhammad Knight, "Lifting Up My Skirt," *Vice* <http://www.vice.com/read/lifting-up-my-skirt> accessed 13 June 2013). The level of provocation, unwarranted disrespect, and opportunistic grandstanding that Knight generated in this exchange (which is comparable to the *modus operandi* of Hinckle Von Vampton of Ishmael Reed's *Mumbo Jumbo*), left me with the impression that after gaining attention by promoting himself as The Caucasian Five Percenter and reaching his desired heights in Caucasian society, Knight no longer needed to use the Gods as his stepping stone. Knight tellingly went from plastering his stated affiliation on the title of a book, *Why I Am A Five Percenter*, in 2011 to stating that he was merely a "friend of this [Five Percent] community" in January 2013 (M. M. Knight, "What I Learned from the Five Percenters," *Vice* <http://www.vice.com/read/what-i-learned-from-the-five- percenters> accessed 7 July 2013). It speaks volumes that rather than simply leave the Nation, Knight, in the tradition of his forebears (see my discussion of Emperor Theodosius and General Amr p. 286), felt compelled to attempt to disgrace and destroy it. For a similar but more concentrated example of racist culture-vulture behavior, see Thomas Morton's revival of *Tarzan* and *Heart of Darkness* in "Senegalese Laamb Wrestling," "Fighting Chances," *Vice*, episode 8, *HBO* 31 May 2013. I think it is significant that Knight and Morton both work for *Vice*.

[58] David Hunter, "Blue-Eyed Devil: An Interview with Michael Muhammad Knight," *KGB Bar Lit Magazine* <http://www.kgbbar.com/lit/non_fiction/blue_eyed_devil_an_interview_with_michael_muhammad_knight> 11 August 2011.

[59] Fard Muhammad, "Lost-Found Muslim Lesson No. 1," in *The Supreme Wisdom Lessons*, The Nation of Islam <http://www.thenationofislam.org/lostfoundlesson.html> accessed 19 July 2013.

[60] Fard Muhammad, "Lost-Found Muslim Lesson No. 1."

[61] Fard Muhammad, "Lost-Found Muslim Lesson No. 1."

[62] Fard Muhammad, "Lost-Found Muslim Lesson No. 1."

[63] Fard Muhammad, "Lost-Found Muslim Lesson No. 1."

[64] Fard Muhammad, "Lost-Found Muslim Lesson No. 1."

[65] RZA as Bobby Digital, "Terrorist," *Bobby Digital in Stereo* (Gee Street, 1998), CD.

[66] RZA as Bobby Digital, "Terrorist."

[67] Boston, "And God Said…"

[68] Gravediggaz, "Twelve Jewelz," *The Pick, the Sickle, and the Shovel* (BMG Records, 1997), CD.

[69] X Clan, "Grand Verbalizer, What Time Is It?" *To the East Blackwards* (4th and B'Way, 1990), audiocassette.
[70] Davey D, "Interview with Brother J of X-Clan," *Davey D's Hip Hop Corner: Antithug* <http://www.daveyd.com/interviewbrotherj.html.> 15 November 2007.
[71] X Clan, "Do It Like You?!," *Mainstream Outlawz* (Suburban Noize 2009), CD.
[72] X Clan, "Grand Verbalizer, What Time Is It?"
[73] Dark Sun Riders featuring Brother J, "Dark Sun Riders Firmly Handle This," *The Seeds of Evolution* (Polygram, 1996), CD.
[74] Gravediggaz, "Dangerous Mindz," *Wu-Chronicles: Chapter II* (Wu-Tang Records, 2001), CD.
[75] Gravediggaz, "Dangerous Mindz."
[76] Gravediggaz, "Dangerous Mindz."
[77] Gravediggaz, "Dangerous Mindz."
[78] Gravediggaz, "Dangerous Mindz."
[79] Ayi Kwei Armah, *Two Thousand Seasons* (London: Heinemann, 1973), 1.
[80] Rakim, "Guess Who's Back," *The 18th Letter* (Universal, 1997), CD.
[81] Rakim, "Guess Who's Back."
[82] Wakeel Allah, "It's Been A Long Time: Interview with Rakim Allah," *The A Team's Blog, My Space* 23 January 2007 <http://www.myspace.com/allahteam/blog/221128665> accessed 20 October 2012.
[83] Rakim, "Guess Who's Back."
[84] Browder, *Nile Valley Contributions to Civilization*, 87.
[85] X Clan, "Grand Verbalizer, What Time Is It?"
[86] Knight, *The Five Percenters*, 214. One example of the flag that Prince Allah Cuba describes can be seen at <http://allahteam.blogspot.com/> accessed 26 August 2012.
[87] Quoted in Mamady Keita and Uschi Billmeier, *A Life for the Djembé: Traditional Rhythms of the Malinke* (1999; reprint, Uhlstadt-Kirchhasel, Germany: Arun, 2004). 112. See also Marcel Griaule and Germaine Dieterlen, *The Pale Fox*, translated by Stephen C. Infantino (1965; Chino Valley, AZ: Continuum, 1986), 53n23.
[88] Babatunde Lawal, "*À Yà Gbó, À Yà Tó*: New Perspectives on Edan Ògbóni," *African Arts* 28:1 (Winter, 1995): 45.
[89] Lawal, "*À Yà Gbó, À Yà Tó*," 45.
[90] See Babatunde Lawal, *The Gẹ̀lẹ̀dẹ́ Spectacle: Art, Gender, and Social Harmony in an African Culture* (Seattle: University of Washington Press, 1996), 39, 71, 74, and 97.
[91] Lord Jamar, "Supreme Mathematics"; and Knight, *The Five Percenters*, 220–221.
[92] X Clan, "Wiz Degrees," *Mainstream Outlawz* (Suburban Noize 2009), CD.
[93] X Clan, "Wiz Degrees."
[94] X Clan, "Do It Like You?!"
[95] X Clan, "Wiz Degrees."

[96] X Clan, "Wiz Degrees."
[97] X Clan, "Wiz Degrees."
[98] X Clan, "Primetime Lyrics," *Mainstream Outlawz* (Suburban Noize 2009), CD.
[99] X Clan featuring Medusa, "Keys To Ur City," *Mainstream Outlawz* (Suburban Noize, 2009), CD.
[100] X Clan featuring Medusa, "Keys To Ur City."
[101] Erykah Badu, "On and On," *Baduizm* (Kedar/Universal Labels, 1997), CD.
[102] Erykah Badu, "On and On," *Baduism*.
[103] Erykah Badu, "On and On," *Live* (Kedar/Universal, 1997), CD.
[104] Erykah Badu, "On and On." *Baduizm*.
[105] Digable Planets, "9th Wonder," *Blowout Comb* (Capitol, 1994), CD.
[106] JR, "'The Re-Birth of Mec': Choppin' it up with Ladybug Mecca, formerly of Digable Planets," *Davey D's Hip Hop Corner* <http://www.daveyd.com/interviewmeca.html> accessed 20 June 2009.
[107] C. M. Bey, *Clock of Destiny*, volume I, 5.
[108] Nas, "Warrior's Song," *God's Son* (Ill Will, 2002), CD.
[109] Wu-Tang Clan, "Wu-Gambinos," *Wu-Chronicles* (Priority, 1999), CD.
[110] Mood and Sunz of Man "Illuminated Sunlight," *Doom* (TVT/Blunt, 1997), CD.
[111] Wu-Tang Clan, "Sunlight," *8 Diagrams* (SRC/Universal Motown, 2007), CD.
[112] Lord Jamar, "The Sun," *Deep Space/The Corner, The Streets* (Babygrande, 2006), CD.
[113] Lord Jamar, "The Sun."
[114] Peter Morton-Williams, William Bascom, and E. M. McClelland, "Two Studies of Ifa Divination. Introduction: The Mode of Divination," *Africa: Journal of the International African Institute*, 36:4 (Oct. 1966): 423.
[115] Digable Planets, "9th Wonder," *Blowout Comb* (Capitol, 1994), CD.
[116] "C Know the Doodlebug (@ceeknowledge) on Twitter," *Twitter* <https://twitter.com/ceeknowledge> accessed 22 February 2013.
[117] Lord Jamar, "Deep Space," *The 5% Album* (Babygrande, 2006), CD.
[118] Lord Jamar, "Deep Space."
[119] "UFO Files: UFOs and the White House" (History Channel, 2005), television.
[120] Martyn Stubbs is a Canadian who was employed at a cable television station. His interest in astronomy and his job provided him with the opportunity and equipment to film the live raw feed of NASA's space walks and journeys to the international space station. The footage Stubbs recorded was also broadcast live on C-SPAN. Many people, including Stubbs, documented interesting occurrences on nearly every broadcast. So much interest was generated by the activity and active participants of "space" that NASA stopped live-feed broadcasts. Thanks to Stubbs, everyone has the ability to view and analyze NASA's recordings and better appreciate Earth's position as one small part of an infinite system of organic dynamism. See *The Secret NASA Transmissions: 'The Smoking Gun'*, directed by Graham W. Birdsall, Quest Publication, 2001. See also

<http://www.snagfilms.com/films/title/the_secret_nasa_transmissions> accessed 24 March 2011.

[121] Lord Jamar, "Deep Space."

[122] Thomas G. Brophy, *The Origin Map: Discovery of a Prehistoric, Megalithic, Astrophysical Map and Sculpture of the Universe* (Bloomington: iUniverse, 2002); and see "Magical Egypt III" Descent 1, 2, 3 *You Tube* <http://www.youtube.com/watch?v=dWMKMT4CCJI> and <http://www.youtube.com/watch?v=C4nB3RyrrgY&feature=related>, and <http://www.youtube.com/watch?v=huXAqcVeQWA&feature=related>, respectively, accessed 29 June 2009.

[123] Christopher Dunn, *The Giza Power Plant* (Rochester VT: Bear and Company, 1998); and Browder, *Nile Valley Contributions to Civilization*, 105–111.

[124] "In Search of . . . Dark Star," producer, Alan Landsburg, (History Channel, 1979), television.

[125] Umeh, *After God is Dibia*, volume one, 37.

[126] Umeh, *After God is Dibia*, volume two, 37.

[127] Sly & The Family Stone, "Everybody is a Star," *Greatest Hits* (Epic, 1970), LP.

[128] Earth, Wind & Fire, "Keep Your Head to the Sky," *To The Sky* (Columbia, 1973), LP; and "Shining Star," *That's the Way of the World* (Columbia, 1975), LP.

[129] Somé, *Of Water and the Spirit*, 199.

[130] Quoted in Allah, *In the Name of Allah*, 198.

[131] Ishmael Beah, *A Long Way Gone: Memoirs of a Boy Soldier* (New York: Sarah Crichton, 2007), 92.

[132] Somé, *Of Water and the Spirit*, 54.

[133] Henry Olela, "The African Foundations of Greek Philosophy," *African Philosophy*, edited by Eze Emmanuel Chukwudi (Malden, MA: Blackwell, 1998), 47.

[134] Marimba Ani, *Yurugu: An African-Centered Critique of European Cultural Thought and Behavior* (Trenton: Africa World Press, 1994), 466.

[135] Quoted in Ani, *Yurugu*, 466.

[136] Ani, *Yurugu*, 466.

[137] Anthony Browder, *Nile Valley Contributions to Civilization*, 48–49.

[138] Kihura Nkuba, "Africa: The Bachwezi Were Egyptians," *All Africa* 5 April 2008 <http://allafrica.com/stories/200804070661.html> accessed 29 June 2009; and "The Bachwezi," *Ugandan Travel Guide* <http://www.ugandatravelguide.com/bachwezi.html> accessed 29 June 2009.

[139] For a better understanding of the underworld and the manner by which it can be accessed, see the discussion of Malidoma Somé's initiation in chapter five.

[140] Kihura Nkuba, "Africa: The Bachwezi Were Egyptians."

[141] Basil Davidson, *The Lost Cities of Africa*, revised edition (New York: Little Brown, and Company, 1959), 17.

[142] Charles Q. Choi, "Strange! Human Glow in Visible Light," *Live Science* 22 July 2009 <http://news.yahoo.com/s/livescience/20090722/sc_livescience/strange humansglowinvisiblelight> 22 July 2009.
[143] Choi, "Strange! Human Glow in Visible Light."
[144] Cornelia Walker Bailey, *God, Dr. Buzzard, and the Bolito Man: A Saltwater Geechee Talks about Life on Sapelo Island, Georgia* (New York: Anchor, 2000), 192.
[145] Ben Okri, *Infinite Riches* (London: Phoenix, 1998), 46.
[146] Okri, *Infinite Riches*, 54.
[147] Okri, *Infinite Riches*, 54.
[148] Okri, *Infinite Riches*, 54.
[149] Okri, *Infinite Riches*, 58.
[150] Okri, *Infinite Riches*, 58.
[151] Killarmy featuring Sunz of Man, "Wake Up," *Wu-Chronicles* (Priority, 1999), LP.
[152] Killarmy featuring Sunz of Man, "Wake Up."
[153] Killarmy featuring Sunz of Man, "Wake Up."

The Bridge: Shining Lords of the Singing Soul-Piece

[1] Hurston *Mules and Men*, 3–4.
[2] Washington, "*Mules and Men* and Messiahs," 267–270.
[3] Hurston *Mules and Men*, 4.
[4] For mythistories featuring Èṣù see Thompson, *Flash of the Spirit*, 21. For the Dogon mythistory that features Yurugu, see Griaule and Dieterlen, *The Pale Fox*. For orature featuring the Kemetic Deity Ausar, see Browder, *Nile Valley Contributions to Civilization*, 97.
[5] Aguibou Y. Yansane, "Cultural, Political, and Economic Universals in West Africa," in *African Culture: The Rhythms of Unity*, edited by Molefi K. Asante and Kariamu W. Asante (Trenton: Africa World Press, 1985), 58.
[6] *Yeelen*, directed by Souleymane Cisse (Kino, 1987), VHS.
[7] *Yeelen*.
[8] *Yeelen*.
[9] *Yeelen*.
[10] *Yeelen*.
[11] Georgia Writers Project, *Drums and Shadows*, 27. Bailey provides a more recent historical account of Scip Bell of Georgia using what the Yoruba call ààlè to suspend the animation of a child thief in *God, Dr. Buzzard, and the Bolito Man*, 190–191. For an example in cinema, see *Bintou*, Dir. Fanta Nacro in *Mama Africa: She's in Your Soul* (Fox Lorber, 2000).
[12] *Yeelen*.

[13] Aguibou Y. Yansane, "Cultural, Political, and Economic Universals in West Africa," 58.
[14] *Yeelen*.
[15] John A. McCluskey, *Look What They Done to My Song* (New York: Random House, 1974), 3; emphasis retained from the original.
[16] McCluskey, *Look What They Done to My Song*, 3; emphasis retained from the original.
[17] McCluskey, *Look What They Done to My Song*, 3; emphasis retained from the original.
[18] McCluskey, *Look What They Done to My Song*, 16.
[19] McCluskey, *Look What They Done to My Song*, 108, 203.
[20] McCluskey, *Look What They Done to My Song*, 236, emphasis added.
[21] McCluskey, *Look What They Done to My Song*, 250, emphasis added.
[22] McCluskey, *Look What They Done to My Song*, 108.
[23] Arthur R. Flowers, *De Mojo Blues: De Quest of HighJohn de Conqueror* (New York: Ballantine, 1985), 68–69.
[24] Flowers, *De Mojo Blues*, 69.
[25] Flowers, *De Mojo Blues*, 69.
[26] Flowers, *De Mojo Blues*, 100.
[27] Flowers, *De Mojo Blues*, 130–131.
[28] Flowers, *De Mojo Blues*, 178.
[29] Flowers, *De Mojo Blues*, 212.
[30] Flowers, *De Mojo Blues*, 220.
[31] Flowers, *De Mojo Blues*, 224.
[32] Zora Neale Hurston, "High John de Conquer," in *Zora Neale Hurston: The Complete Stories* (New York: Harper Perennial, 1995), 148.
[33] Patricia R. Schroeder, "Rootwork: Arthur Flowers, Zora Neale Hurston, and the 'Literary Hoodoo' Tradition," *African American Review* 36:2 (Summer, 2002), 271.
[34] Flowers, *De Mojo Blues*, 241.

4. Resurrecting the Shining Self

[1] Hedy Weiss, "Devil looks past Faustian bargain of Johnson saga," *Chicago Sun-Times* 6 July 2005 *Find Articles* <http://findarticles.com/p/articles/mi_qn4155/is_20050706/ai_n14830463> 28 December 2007.
[2] Note the rancor of Jonathan Abarbanel's review of *RJTD* in *Windy City Times*, *Theater Review* 7 July 2005 <http://www.windycitymediagroup.com/gay/lesbian/news/ARTICLE.php?AID= 8837> 29 December 2007.
[3] August Wilson, *Joe Turner's Come and Gone* (New York: Plume, 1998), 1, 2. All subsequent references are to this edition and will be given parenthetically in the text.

[4] Levine, *Black Culture and Black Consciousness*, 56–57.
[5] Piet Meyer, "Divination among the Lobi of Burkina Faso," in *African Divination Systems: Ways of Knowing*, edited by Philip M. Peek (Bloomington: Indiana University Press, 1991), 93.
[6] Meyer, "Divination among the Lobi of Burkina Faso," 93–94; emphasis added. E. Bolaji Idowu offers a powerful elaboration on the babaláwo's ethical obligations in *Olódùmarè*, 79–80.
[7] The "Arab Spring," which began in 2011, inspired the American "Occupy" movement in which fed up Americans occupied Wall Street and other American financial and economic meccas to protest the pyramid scheme of capitalism that has left the American masses suffering in abject poverty, homelessness, foreclosure, food insecurity, job insecurity, and/or unemployment while a handful of robber barons enjoy wealth so vast their children's children's children will not be able to spend it all. In apparent cognizance of the fact that money, currency, and capitalism are enslaving myths, some of Occupiers were photographed burning dollar bills. See Maura Judkis, "Occupy's Most Controversial Art: Burning Money, Saints in Suits," *The Washington Post* 17 October 2011 <http://www.washingtonpost.com/blogs/arts-post/post/occupys-most-controversial-art-burning-money-saints-in-suits/2011/10/17/gIQAhUPnrL_blog.html > accessed 22 October 2012.
[8] Washington, *Our Mothers, Our Powers, Our Texts*, 22–25.
[9] Bill Harris, *Robert Johnson: Trick the Devil*, in *The National Black Drama Anthology*, edited by Woodie King, Jr. (New York: Applause, 1995), 5. All subsequent references are to this edition and will be given parenthetically in the text.
[10] *"Can't You Hear The Wind Howl?" The Life and Music of Robert Johnson*, directed by Peter Meyer (Winstar, 1998), DVD.
[11] *"Can't You Hear The Wind Howl?" The Life and Music of Robert Johnson*.
[12] Somé, *Of Water and the Spirit*, 246.
[13] *John Henrik Clarke: A Great and Mighty Walk*.
[14] Idowu, *Olódùmarè*, 79.
[15] Stokes mentions "juba" specifically on page 25.
[16] Sun Ra, *The Wisdom of Sun Ra* 74–75, 77, 89–90, emphasis in the original.
[17] Browder, *Nile Valley Contributions to Civilization*, 128.
[18] Cooper, "Not We Many," 334, emphasis in the original.
[19] Wilson, "Preface," *King Hedley*, x.
[20] Teish, *Jambalaya*, 5.
[21] Toni Cade Bambara, *The Salt Eaters* (New York: Vintage, 1980), 110, 115, 255, 259; and Toni Cade Bambara, "Broken Field Running," in *The Sea Birds are Still Alive* (New York: Vintage, 1977), 56.
[22] Ama Ata Aidoo, *Anowa* in *Dilemma of a Ghost and Anowa* (Essex: Longman, 1985), 106.
[23] *Daughters of the Dust*, directed by Julie Dash, (1991; New York: Kino, 2000), DVD.

[24] August Wilson, *Gem of the Ocean* (New York: Theatre Communications Group, 2006); and Henry Dumas, "Ark of Bones," in *Echo Tree: The Collected Short Fiction of Henry Dumas*, edited by Eugene B. Redmond (Minneapolis: Coffee House, 2003), 9–22.

[25] Some, *Of Water and the Spirit*, 186.

[26] Ben Okri, *The Famished Road* (New York: Double Day, 1991), 57.

[27] "Chain Gangs," History's Mysteries (History Channel, 2000), television.

[28] "Chain Gangs," History's Mysteries.

[29] "Chain Gangs," History's Mysteries.

[30] "Convict Lease System," *Digital History* 23 November 2011 <http://www.digitalhistory.uh.edu/database/article_display.cfm?HHID=214> accessed 23 November 2011.

[31] See Barry Lee Pearson and Bill McCulloch, *Robert Johnson: Lost and Found* (Champaign, IL: University of Illinois Press, 2003), 50.

[32] McCluskey, *Look What They Done To My Song*, 94.

[33] Teish, *Jambalaya*, 129–130; and Thompson, *Flash of the Spirit*, 108–111.

[34] D'Angelo, "Africa," *Voodoo* (Virgin, 2000), CD.

[35] The only scholar to date who has undertaken a comprehensive in-depth elucidation and analysis of Caucasian culture is Marimba Ani, the author of the masterwork *Yurugu*.

[36] Pearson and McCulloch, *Robert Johnson*, ix; see also 62–64.

[37] Pearson and McCulloch, *Robert Johnson*, 3.

[38] Pearson and McCulloch, *Robert Johnson*, 4.

[39] I do not think it mere coincidence that parents and entire societies fill children's impressionable minds with myths about entities that are purely fictitious and reward belief in these fictions with material goods and money and then associate the fictional entities and capitalist gains with religion and fictitious religious figures. This system is so widespread that parents in America are accused of depriving their children if they refuse to lie to and indoctrinate them. Truth-telling children and parents are considered pariahs in many communities. On a related note, I find it intriguing that Westernized parents, in particular, are often the first ones to lie to and visit violence (justified as discipline) on their children.

[40] Hurston, *Dust Tracks on a Road*, 226.

[41] Sun Ra, *The Wisdom of Sun Ra*, 90, emphasis in the original.

[42] Davidson, *The Lost Cities of Africa*, 17.

[43] Robert Johnson has three graves: one in Money, MS; one in Morgan City, MS; and one in Quito, MS. The one in Quito is adorned with money, guitar picks, shot glasses, and a beer can as evidence of people having poured libation for and having prayed to Robert Johnson. At the top of the headstone is a divining rod with "Ask for the right direction" emblazoned on it (author's field research, Mississippi, 2003).

5. "Meet Me In Another World"

[1] Prince and the Revolution, "Girls and Boys," *Parade* (Paisley Park, 1986), LP.
[2] Killah Priest, "B.I.B.L.E.," *The GZA, Liquid Swords* (Geffen/MCA, 1997), CD.
[3] Walter Mosley, *47* (New York: Little, Brown, and Co., 2005), ii. All subsequent references are to this edition and will be given parenthetically in the text.
[4] For a full elaboration of the force of rememory, see Washington, *Our Mothers, Our Powers, Our Texts*, 236–241.
[5] In "Come on in My Kitchen," Robert Johnson sings about how he violated his lover by taking the last nickel from her nation sack. *Robert Johnson: The Complete Recordings*, disk one (1937; Sony 1990).
[6] Georgia Writers' Project, *Drums and Shadows*, 102.
[7] Hurston, *The Sanctified Church*, 75–77.
[8] See *47*, Book Review, *Kirkus Reviews*. 73:9 (2005): 542.
[9] Carole Kennedy, *Psychic: Awakening the Power Within You* (Chicago: Contemporary Books, 1988), 347.
[10] Kennedy, *Psychic*, 347.
[11] Henry Olela, "The African Foundations of Greek Philosophy," in *African Philosophy*, edited by Eze Emmanuel
Chukwudi (Malden, MA: Blackwell, 1998), 47.
[12] Rebecca Jackson, *Gifts of Power: The Writings of Rebecca Jackson, Black Visionary, Shaker Eldress*, edited by Jean McMahon Humez (Amherst: University of Massachusetts Press, 1981), 220.
[13] Amos Tutuola, *My Life in the Bush of Ghosts* in *The Palm-Wine Drinkard and My Life in the Bush of Ghosts* (1954; reprint, New York: Grove, 1984), 17–18. All subsequent references are to this edition and will be given parenthetically in the text.
[14] Olaudah Equiano, "from *The Interesting Narrative of the Life of Olaudah Equiano, or Gustavus Vassa, the African*," in *Crossing the Danger Water*, edited by Deirdre Mullane, (New York: Anchor, 1993), 8–9.
[15] Laura Murphy, "Into the Bush of Ghosts: Specters of the Slave Trade in West African Fiction," *Research in African Literatures* 38:4 (Winter 2007): 144–145.
[16] See Washington *Our Mothers, Our Powers, Our Texts*, 106–107.
[17] See the moving exposé on slavery in Haiti and interview with Cadet conducted by Sanjay Gupta of CNN at <http://www.cnn.com/video/#/video/world/2009/07/21/iyw.gupta.haiti.slavery.lo ng.cnn?iref=videosearch> accessed 09 August 2009.
[18] Amos Tutuola, *The Palm-Wine Drinkard* (1953; reprint, New York: Grove, 1984), 202.
[19] Pierre F. Verger, *Articles*, volume one, translated by Christophe Brunski (1995; reprint, Montclair, NJ: Black Madonna Enterprises, 2007), 126–129.
[20] Lalita Tademy, *Red River* (New York: Warner 2007), 105–107.
[21] Georgia Writers Project, *Drums and Shadows*, 105.
[22] Georgia Writers Project, *Drums and Shadows*, 164.

[23] Georgia Writers Project, *Drums and Shadows*, 163.
[24] Georgia Writers Project, *Drums and Shadows*, 181.
[25] Randy Newman, "Lyrics—Sail Away," *RandyNewman* <http://www.randynewman.com/tocdiscography/disc_sail_away/tocdiscography/disc_sail_away/lyricssailaway#sailaway> accessed 31 December 2007.
[26] Randy Newman, "Lyrics—Sail Away."
[27] Toni Morrison, *Beloved* (1987; reprint, New York: Plume, 1988), 210.
[28] Morrison, *Beloved*, 211.
[29] Robert Johnson, "Come On In My Kitchen."
[30] Morrison, *Beloved*, 23.
[31] Francis Bok, *Escape from Slavery* (New York: St. Martins, 2003), 24, 55–56.
[32] Bok, *Escape from Slavery*, 17–18.
[33] Bok, *Escape from Slavery*, 46.
[34] For examples see Georgia Writers' Project, *Drums and Shadows*, 31; and Adeoye, *Ìgbàgbọ́ àti Ẹ̀sìn Yorùbá*, 304–307.
[35] In her article, "Into the Bush of Ghosts," Murphy makes the erroneous assertion that "[i]n each of the novel's episodes, the narrator is bound to a ghost through his labor, for which he is held captive" (148). She repeats this erroneous assertion with a few qualifications in her book *Metaphor and the Slave Trade in West African Literature* (Athens: Ohio University Press, 2012), 65.
[36] See Washington, *Our Mothers, Our Powers, Our Texts*, 168–170.
[37] Morrison, *Beloved*, 131.
[38] William Bascom, *Sixteen Cowries*, 413–419; and Ibie, *Ifism*, 48.
[39] S. O. Babayemi, *Egúngún Among the Ọ̀yọ́ Yoruba* (Board Publications: Ibadan, 1980), 20. Tone marks of Bàrà have been altered for consistency.
[40] My answer to the dilemma is that those who seek to gain at "Loss or Gain Valley" must arrive there without any clothing or material possessions whatsoever.
[41] See Washington, *Our Mothers, Our Powers, Our Texts*, 165–170.
[42] Chinua Achebe writes of the feelings that Tutuola engenders in some readers in "Work and Play in Tutuola's The Palm-Wine Drinkard," in *Hopes and Impediments: Selected Essays* (New York: Anchor Doubleday, 1988): 100–112.
[43] Malidoma Somé, *Of Water and the Spirit* (New York: Penguin, 1994), 232–233. All subsequent references are to this edition and will be given parenthetically in the text.
[44] Hurston, *Mules and Men*, 47–53; Umeh, *After God is Dibia*, volume two, 33; and Huston, "Crow Dance," respectively.
[45] Washington, *Our Mothers, Our Powers, Our Texts*, 109–110.
[46] Rowland Abiodun, "Identity and the Artistic Process in Yorùbá Aesthetic Concept of Ìwà," *Journal of Cultural Inquiry* 1:1 (December 1983): 25.
[47] Abiodun, "Identity and the Artistic Process in Yorùbá Aesthetic Concept of Ìwà," 23.
[48] William Wordsworth, "The Tables Turned" (1789) *The Poetry Foundation* <http://www.poetryfoundation.org/poem/174826> accessed 14 February 2013.

⁴⁹ Carl Sagan, "The Shores of the Cosmic Ocean," *PBS* 28 September 1980 <http://www.englishdaily626.com/discovery_channel.php?005> accessed 01 December 2011.
⁵⁰ Lichtheim, *Ancient Egyptian Literature*, 44.
⁵¹ Lichtheim, *Ancient Egyptian Literature*, 45.
⁵² Lord Jamar, "Deep Space."
⁵³ Rakim, "Guess Who's Back."
⁵⁴ Kelis, "Little Star," *Kelis Was Here* (LaFace, 2006), CD.
⁵⁵ Kelis, "Little Star."
⁵⁶ Kelis, "Little Star."
⁵⁷ Kelis, "Little Star."
⁵⁸ African technology is so complete that it makes attaining excellence in Western education as simple as opening one's eyes . . . literally. Ishmael Beah in *A Long Way Gone*, Toyin Falola in *A Mouth Sweeter Than Salt* (270), and Malidoma Somé in *Of Water and the Spirit* all discuss being given medicines that enhance the brain's ability to memorize, process, and store information. Beah states that during scholastic examinations he was able to visualize his notes and read the information they contained (51). Somé states that he could read the answers to questions in the auras of his professors (5–6).
⁵⁹ Christopher Dunn, *The Giza Power Plant: Technologies of Ancient Egypt* (Rochester, VT: Bear and Company, 2004), 127.
⁶⁰ I am appreciative of Ayanna Ivory-Lindsey for the observation that Bynum's vision is akin to that of an infant.
⁶¹ Washington, *Our Mothers, Our Powers, Our Texts*, 41.
⁶² Bailey, *God, Dr. Buzzard, and the Bolito Man*, 204–206 and 306–307.
⁶³ Huston, *Mules and Men*, 223.
⁶⁴ Umeh, *After God is Dibia*, volume two, 132.
⁶⁵ Umeh, *After God is Dibia*, volume two, 133.
⁶⁶ Toni Morrison, *Song of Solomon* (1977; reprint, New York: Plume, 1987), 110.
⁶⁷ Georgia Writers Project, *Drums and Shadows*, 145.

6. Saline Solutions and Winged Revolutions

¹ McCluskey, *Look What They Done to My Song*, 5–6.
² For more on this powerful relationship, read Valerie Boyd, "'She was just outrageously brilliant': Toni Morrison Remembers Toni Cade Bambara" in *Savoring the Salt: The Legacy of Toni Cade Bambara*, edited by Linda Janet Holmes and Cheryl A. Wall (Philadelphia: Temple University Press, 2008), 88–99.
³ See Washington, *Our Mothers, Our Powers, Our Texts*, 239.
⁴ Toni Cade Bambara, *The Salt Eaters* (New York: Vintage, 1980), 261. All subsequent references are to this edition and will be given parenthetically in the text.

[5] While this discussion may seem bizarre to the uninitiated, the topic of Flying Africans and the role that salt plays in flight is a subject that is vigorously debated in academic circles. During the 2002 African Literature Association conference in San Diego, a group of African, African American, and Caucasian scholars discussed these issues after listening to a paper presented on them. Indeed, this chapter has its roots in that lively discussion.

[6] Thomas W. Neumann, "A Biocultural Approach to Salt Taboos: The Case of the Southeastern United States," *Current Anthropology* 18:2 (June 1977): 292.

[7] Angelita Reyes, *Mothering Across Cultures: Postcolonial Discourse* (Minneapolis: University of Minnesota Press, 2001), 43.

[8] Reyes, *Mothering Across Cultures*, 43.

[9] McDaniel, *The Big Drum Ritual of Carriacou*, 79–80.

[10] Henry Louis Gates Jr., "Mexico & Peru: A Hidden Race," *Black in Latin America* (Inkwell Films, 2011).

[11] Works Projects Administration, *The Project Gutenberg EBook of Slave Narratives: A Folk History of Slavery in the United States From Interviews with Former Slaves* (1941), page 28, 2 December 2009 <http://www.gutenberg.org/files/30576/30576-h/30576-h.htm> accessed 9 May 2013.

[12] Uwem Akpan, "Fattening for Gabon," *Say You're One of Them* (New York: Back Bay Books, 2008) 94.

[13] Emmanuel Dongala, *The Fire of Origins*, translated by Lillian Corti (Chicago: Lawrence Hill Books, 2001), 98.

[14] Akpan, "Fattening for Gabon," 156–157.

[15] Wyatt MacGaffey, "The West in Congolese Experience," in *Africa and the West: Intellectual Responses to European Culture*, edited by Philip D. Curtin (Madison, University of Wisconsin Press, 1972), 59.

[16] Quoted in Wyatt MacGaffey, "The West in Congolese Experience," 59.

[17] Amos Tutuola, *The Palm-Wine Drinkard*, 221–223, 252, 286, 294.

[18] Quoted in Wyatt MacGaffey, "The West in Congolese Experience," 59.

[19] Umeh, *After God is Dibia*, volume one, 42.

[20] Verger, *Ewé*, 323, 325, 349, 371, 381, 391, 397, 421, 427, 435, 443, 449, 277.

[21] Umeh, *After God is Dibia*, volume two, 73.

[22] Simon Bockie, *Death and the Invisible Powers* (Bloomington: Indiana University Press, 1993) 68.

[23] Olawole Francis Famule, "Art And Spirituality: The Ijumu Northeastern – Yoruba Egúngún," dissertation, University of Arizona, 2005, 144 <arizona.openrepository.com/arizona/.../1/azu_etd_1372_sip1_m.pdf> accessed 3 January 2013.

[24] Fatunmbi, *Ìwa-pèlé: Ifá Quest*, 124.

[25] Diedre Badejo *Ọṣun Ṣèègèsí: The Elegant Deity of Wealth, Power, and Femininity* (Africa World Press, 1996) 25.

[26] Hurston, *The Sanctified Church*, 24.

[27] Hurston, *The Sanctified Church*, 24, emphasis added.

[28] Hurston, *The Sanctified Church*, 26.
[29] Hurston, *The Sanctified Church*, 27.
[30] Toni Morrison, *Beloved* (New York: Plume, 1988), 261.
[31] Nalo Hopkinson, *The Salt Roads* (New York: Time Warner, 2003), 68–69.
[32] Toni Cade Bambara, "Broken Field Running" in *The Sea Birds are Still Alive* (New York: Vintage, 1977), 53. All subsequent references are to this edition and will be given parenthetically in the text.
[33] See Bascom, *Ifa Divination*, plate 20B.
[34] "*Àájà*," *A Dictionary of the Yoruba Language* (Ibadan: University of Ibadan Press, 1991), part two, 23.
[35] "Mystery at Coral Castle," *Baltic Tourism Directory: Florida Coral Castle - Ed Liedskalnins - Korallu Pils - The Latvian Connection* 12 June 2009 <http://www.baltictourism.info/2009/06/florida-coral-castle-ed-liedskalnins.html> accessed 31 July 2009.
[36] Edward Leedskalnin, *Magnetic Current* (Homestead, FL: Rock Gate, 1945), 2–3.
[37] "Artifacts: Coral Castle," *Mysterious World* Winter 2003 <http://www.mysteriousworld.com/Journal/2003/Winter/Artifacts/> accessed 31 July 2009.
[38] Dunn, *The Giza Power Plant*, 109.
[39] "Ancient Secrets and Mysteries of Levitation," *The Unexplained Mysteries* <http://theunexplainedmysteries.com/levitation-secrets.html> accessed 31 July 2009.
[40] Dunn, *The Giza Power Plant*, 109–208.
[41] Charles Choi, "The real question: Who didn't have sex with Neanderthals? Sub-Saharan Africans only modern humans whose ancestors did not interbreed with them," *NBC News* 1 November 2012 <http://www.msnbc.msn.com/id/49642484/ns/technology_and_science-science/t/real-question-who-didnt-have-sex-neanderthals/> accessed 24 November 2012.
[42] "Diamagnetic Water," *Wonder Magnet* 2003 <http://wondermagnet.com/diamagh2o.html> accessed 31 July 2009; and "The Frog that Learned to Fly," High Field Magnet Laboratory, Radboud University Nijmegen, *Archive.is* 15 September 2012 <http://archive.is/UnQr> accessed 15 July 2013.
[43] "The Frog that Learned to Fly."
[44] Nada Bjelobrk, Daniele Foresti, Marko Dorrestijn, Majid Nabavi, and Dimos Poulikakos*, "Contactless transport of acoustically levitated particles," *Applied Physics Letters* 97:161904 (2010) <https://edit.ethz.ch/ltnt/publications/Journal/Journal/pubimg/2010_Bjelobrk1.pdf> accessed 16 July 2013; and Alan Boyle, "Engineers juggle objects with levitating sound waves," NBC News Science, *NBCNews* 15 July 2013 <http://www.nbcnews.com/science/engineers-juggle-objects-levitating-sound- waves-6C10643299> accessed 15 July 2013.
[45] Boyle, "Engineers juggle objects with levitating sound waves."

[46] Leedskalnin begins *Magnetic Current* with the following cipher:

> This writing is lined up so when you read it you look East, and all the description you will read about magnetic current, it will be just as good for your electricity.
> Following is the result of my two years experiment with magnets at Rock Gate, seventeen miles Southwest from Miami, Florida. Between Twenty-fifth and Twenty-sixth Latitude and Eightieth and Eighty-first Longitude West. (Leedskalnin 1).

Another cipher presented by Leedskalnin is that of the "Sweet Sixteen," which does not represent a lost love but a found technology.

[47] Meredith Gadsby, "Little Salt Won't Kill Yuh: English Licks and Two Generations of Migrating Subjects," *Migrating Words and Worlds: Pan-Africanism Updated*, African Language Association Annual No. 4, edited by E. Anthony Hurley, Joseph McLaren, and Renee Larrier (Trenton: African World Press, 1998), 55.

[48] Meredith Gadsby, *Sucking Salt: Caribbean Women Writers, Migration, and Survival* (Columbia: University of Missouri Press, 2006), 133.

[49] Derek Alwes, "The Burden of Liberty: Choice in Toni Morrison's *Jazz* and Toni Cade Bambara's *The Salt Eaters*," *African American Review* 30:3 (Autumn 1996): 354.

[50] Alwes, "The Burden of Liberty," 364.

[51] Toni Morrison, *Sula* (New York: Plume, 1973), 104.

[52] Toni Morrison, *Song of Solomon* (1977; reprint, New York: Plume, 1987), 6. All subsequent references are to this edition and will be given parenthetically in the text.

[53] Lichtheim, *Ancient Egyptian Literature*, 132–133.

[54] Somé, *Of Water and the Spirit*, 192.

[55] August Wilson, *Joe Turner's Come and Gone*, 56.

[56] Somé, *Of Water and the Spirit*, 151.

[57] Lil Wayne, "Tha Heat" *Tha Carter* (Cash Money Records, 2004), CD.

[58] McCluskey, *Look What They Done To My Song*, 72.

[59] Dark Sun Riders featuring Brother J, "Jewels of Evolution," *The Seeds of Evolution* (Polygram, 1996), CD.

7. Warriors, Writers, Revolutionaries

[1] Bambara, *The Salt Eaters*, 234–235.

[2] Michela Wrong, *In The Footsteps of Mr. Kurtz: Living on the Brink of Disaster in Mobutu's Congo* (New York: Harper Perennial, 2002), 4.

[3] Hassan B. Sisay, "Africa: A Democracy Conundrum?" *The Patriotic Vanguard* 7 December 2011 <http://www.thepatrioticvanguard.com/spip.php?article6310> accessed 6 May 2012.

[4] Ayi Kwei Armah, *Two Thousand Seasons* (Ibadan: Heineman, 1973), xi. All subsequent references are to this edition and will be given parenthetically in the text.
[5] Jenny Cuffe, "Surviving a Desert 'Nightmare,'" *BBC News Online* 7 January 2008 <http://news.bbc.co.uk/2/hi/programmes/7154722.stm> 9 January 2008.
[6] *Deadly Voyage*, directed by John McKenzie (HBO Films, 1996), television.
[7] Nick Davis, "The Cruellest Voyage," *The Guardian* 2 December 2007 <http://www.guardian.co.uk/world/2007/dec/03/immigration.uk> accessed 19 April 2013.
[8] Hurston, *Dust Tracks on a Road*, 87.
[9] *Lumumba, la mort du prophete*, directed by Raoul Peck (Velvet Films, 1992), DVD; and *A Huey P. Newton Story* by Roger Guenveur Smith, directed by Spike Lee (Urban Works, 2001), DVD are two powerful, spiritual, curvilinear films that emphasize the divinity, struggles, and complexities of these revolutionaries.
[10] Wole Soyinka, "The African World and the Ethnocultural Debate," in *African Culture: The Rhythms of Unity*, edited by Molefi K. Asante and Kariamu W. Asante (Trenton: Africa World Press, 1985) 19.
[11] Browder, *Nile Valley Contributions to Civilization*, 82.
[12] "Kaffir," *The American Heritage Dictionary of the English Language*, 980.
[13] Bok, *Escape from Slavery*, 17–18 and 54.
[14] Mende Nazer, *Slave: My True Story* (New York: Public Affairs, 2003), 139.
[15] Nazer, *Slave*, 172.
[16] Adeoye, *Ìgbàgbọ́ àti Ẹ̀sìn Yorùbá*, 339–340.
[17] A. P. Anyebe, *Ògbóni: The Birth and Growth of the Reformed Ògbóni Society* (Lagos: Sam Lao, 1989), 28.
[18] Anyebe, *Ògbóni*, 21.
[19] Adeoye, *Ìgbàgbọ́ àti Ẹ̀sìn Yorùbá*, 341.
[20] Adeoye, *Ìgbàgbọ́ àti Ẹ̀sìn Yorùbá*, 359–360.
[21] Adeoye, *Ìgbàgbọ́ àti Ẹ̀sìn Yorùbá*, 359–360.
[22] For a full discussion of Ògbóni and its relationship to Àjẹ́ see chapter four of Washington, *The Architects of Existence*.
[23] Babatunde Lawal, "Ejiwapo: The Dialectics of Twoness in Yoruba Art and Culture," *African Arts* (Spring 2008), *Find Articles* <http://findarticles.com/p/articles/mi_m0438/is_1_41/ai_n24327210/> accessed 9 February 2012.
[24] Babatunde Lawal, "Ejiwapo."
[25] Ayi Kwei Armah, *Osiris Rising* (Popenguine: Per Ankh, 1995), 131. All subsequent references are to this edition and will be given parenthetically in the text.
[26] "Moses Dickson (1824–1901)," *Black Past* <http://www.blackpast.org/?q=aah/dickson-moses-1824-1901> accessed 02 May 2010. See also Ralph Story, "An Excursion into the Black World: The 'Seven Days' in Toni Morrison's *Song of Solomon*," *Black American Literature Forum* 23:1 (1989): 152.
[27] James F. Searing, "'No Kings, No Lords, No Slaves': Ethnicity and Religion among the Sereer-Safèn of Western Bawol, 1700–1914," *The Journal of African History* 43:3 (2002): 415.

[28] Quoted in Searing, "'No Kings, No Lords, No Slaves,'" 412–413.
[29] Peter Morton-Williams, "The Yoruba Ògbóni Cult," *Africa: Journal of the International African Institute* 30:4 (Oct 1960): 366.
[30] Randall M. Packard, "Chiefship and the History of Nyavingi Possession among the Bashu of Eastern Zaire," *Africa: Journal of the International African Institute* 52:4 (1982): 67.
[31] See Washington, *Our Mothers, Our Powers, Our Texts*, 58; and Mary E. M. Kolawole, *Womanism and African Consciousness* (Trenton, NJ: Africa World Press), 46.
[32] Barbara J. Walker, *The Woman's Encyclopedia of Myths and Secrets* (San Francisco: Harper San Francisco, 1983), 453. For a deeper analysis of Ast and her significance please see Washington, *Our Mothers, Our Powers, Our Texts*, 58–61.
[33] Quoted in Chinweizu, *The West and the Rest of Us* (New York: Vintage, 1975), 64.
[34] "In-depth with Toni Morrison," *Book-TV: CSPAN*, 4 February 2001 <http://www.c-spanvideo.org/program/162375-1> accessed 2 May 2013.
[35] For examples, see "Negro Veteran Lynched for Refusing to Doff Uniform," in *100 Years of Lynching*, edited by Ralph Ginzburg (1962; reprint, Baltimore: Black Classic Press, 1988), 118.
[36] Toni Morrison, *Song of Solomon* (1977; reprint, New York: Plume, 1987), 154–5; emphasis is retained from the original. All subsequent references are to this edition and will be given parenthetically in the text.
[37] In Julius Lester's recasting of the folktale "How The Snake Got His Rattles," God tells Brer Rabbit that he will not be answering any prayers from 1960 to 1970. This decade was a time of turbulent struggle for freedom that saw many Africana leaders assassinated (*Black Folktales* (New York: Grove Weidenfeld, 1969), 51). For Naylor's signification on God, see Washington, *Our Mothers, Our Powers, Our Texts*, 122.
[38] Fela and Egypt 80, "Beasts of No Nation," *Beasts of No Nation/ODOO* (Fak Ltd., 1989), CD.
[39] Fela and Egypt 80, "Beasts of No Nation."
[40] Fela and Egypt 80, "Beasts of No Nation."
[41] Sun Ra, *The Wisdom of Sun Ra*, 90.
[42] Adeoye, *Ìgbàgbọ́ àti Ẹ̀sìn Yorùbá*, 341.
[43] Ralph Story, "An Excursion into the Black World: The 'Seven Days' in Toni Morrison's *Song of Solomon*," *Black American Literature Forum* 23:1 (1989): 154–155.
[44] See Annelieke Dirks, "Between Threat and Reality: The National Association for the Advancement of Colored People and the Emergence of Armed Self-Defense in Clarksdale and Natchez, Mississippi, 1960–1965," *Journal for the Study of Radicalism* 1:1 (2007): 71–98.

[45] Jeff Stetson, *Blood on the Leaves* (New York: Warner Books, 2004), 19.
[46] Dead Prez, "I Have a Dream Too," *RBG: Revolutionary But Gangsta* (Sony, 2004), CD.
[47] Dead Prez, "I'm A African," *Let's Get Free* (Relativity, 2000), CD.
[48] Dead Prez, "Fucked Up," *RBG: Revolutionary But Gangsta* (Sony, 2004), CD.
[49] Ishmael Reed, *Writin' Is Fightin': Thirty-Seven Years of Boxing on Paper* (New York: Atheneum, 1988).
[50] See *Banished: How Whites Drove Blacks Out of Town in America*, directed by Marco Williams (Two Tone Productions/Center for Investigative Reporting, 2007), DVD.
[51] Holloway and Vass, *The African Heritage of American English*, 95.
[52] Thompson, *Flash of the Spirit*, 104.
[53] John Mason, *Orin Òrìṣà* (Brooklyn: Yoruba Theological Archministry, 1992), 308.
[54] Reed, *Mumbo Jumbo*, 11 and 211.
[55] Zora Neale Hurston, "Uncle Bud," *Speak So You Can Speak Again*, edited by Lucy Anne Hurston, companion CD (New York: Doubleday, 2004).
[56] Ishmael Reed, *Mumbo Jumbo* (1972; reprint, New York: Scribner, 1996), 7. All subsequent references are to this edition and will be given parenthetically in the text.
[57] "Mumbo jumbo," *From Juba to Jive: A Dictionary of African-American Slang*, edited by Clarence Major (New York: Penguin, 1994), 313.
[58] Harriet Beecher Stowe, *Uncle Tom's Cabin* (1852; reprint, New York: Norton, 1994), 210.
[59] Henry Louis Gates, Jr. *The Signifying Monkey: A Theory of African-American Literary Criticism* (New York: Oxford University Press, 1988), 227.
[60] Gates. *The Signifying Monkey*, 223.
[61] See the conclusion of this book for a discussion of the orature about Èṣù encouraging the examination of all sides of an issue.
[62] Yvonne P. Chireau, "Black Herman's African American Magical Synthesis," *Cabinet* 26 (2007) <http://www.cabinetmagazine.org/issues/26/chireau.php> accessed 6 May 2012.
[63] "Black Herman," *Magic: The Science of Illusion*, 2000 *California Science Center* <http://www.magicexhibit.org/story/story_blackHerman.html> accessed 18 January 2008.
[64] "Black Herman," *Magic: The Science of Illusion*.
[65] "Profile: Benoit Batraville," *History Commons* <http://www.historycommons.org/entity.jsp?entity=benoit_batraville> accessed 28 July 2012.
[66] Browder, *Nile Valley Contributions to Civilization*, 193.
[67] Quoted in Browder, *Nile Valley Contributions to Civilization*, 193.
[68] Browder, *Nile Valley Contributions to Civilization*, 141.

[69] Browder, *Nile Valley Contributions to Civilization*, 174.
[70] Ehsan Yar-Shater, editor, *The History of Al-Tabari*, translated by William M. Brinner (New York: State University of New York Press, 1987), 124; and Muhammad Taqui-ud-Din Al-Hilali and Muhammad Muhsin Khan, *Interpretation of the Meanings of the Noble Qur'an in the English Language* (Riyadh, Saudi Arabia: Maktaba Dar-es-Salaam, 1993), 827.
[71] Tambay A. Obenson, "Nigeria Demands Return of Looted Benin Artifacts From Boston's Museum of Fine Arts," *Shadow and Act* 23 July 2012 <http://blogs.indiewire.com/shadowandact/nigeria-wants-museum-of-fine-arts-boston-to-return-trove-of-benin-artifacts> 30 July 2012.
[72] Obenson, "Nigeria Demands Return of Looted Benin Artifacts From Boston's Museum of Fine Arts"; and "Boston's Museum Of Fine Arts Urged To Return Looted Artifacts To Nigeria," *Huffington Post* 20 July 2012 <http://www.huffingtonpost.com/2012/07/20/bostons-museum-of-fine-ar_n_1690062.html#s1165130> accessed 27 April 2013.
[73] "I saw them steal our obelisk," *Meskel Square* 10 April 2005 <http://www.meskelsquare.com/archives/2005/04/i_saw_them_stea_1.html> accessed 30 July 2012.
[74] "Rome obelisk set for African return," *BBC News Online* 8 November 2003 <http://news.bbc.co.uk/2/hi/europe/3252283.stm> 7 July 2008.
[75] Marimba Ani, *Yurugu, An African-Centered Critique of European Cultural Thought and Behavior* (Trenton: Africa World Press, 1994).
[76] Browder, *Nile Valley Contributions to Civilization*, 97, 190; and Vincenzina Krymow, "Black Madonnas: Still Black and Still Venerated," *The Mary Page*, University of Dayton, *udayton* July 1998 <http://campus.udayton.edu/mary/resources/blackm/blackm.html> accessed 1 August 2012; "Black Madonnas, "Christian Mystery Schools, cults, Heresies," *Encyclopedia of the Unusual and Unexplained* <http://www.unexplainedstuff.com/Religious-Phenomena/Christian-Mystery-Schools-Cults-Heresies-Black-madonna.html> accessed 03 April 2012.
[77] Ngugi wa Thiong'o, *Matigari* (Trenton: African World Press, 1998) 9. All subsequent references are to this edition and will be given parenthetically in the text.
[78] For an in-depth discussion of this important issue see the conclusion of Washington's *The Architects of Existence*. See also *Faraw! Mother of the Dunes*, directed by Abbdoulaye Ascofare (1997; ArtMattan 2007).
[79] Catherine Zemmouri, "Paris fire relatives blame government," *BBC News Online* 26 September 2005 <http://news.bbc.co.uk/2/hi/europe/4189840.stm>, accessed 24 July 2009; and "Immigrants in Paris: Dreams go up in flames," UN-Habitat: State of the World's Cities 2006/7 <http://ww2.unhabitat.org/mediacentre/documents/sowcr2006/SOWCR%2015.pdf> accessed 24 July 2009. Israeli attacks on Africans in 2012 bear a chilling similarity to French attacks. See "Israel denies African migrants' rights, says US," *BBC News*

Online 25 May 2012 <http://www.bbc.co.uk/news/world-middle-east-1821 0133> accessed 17 June 2012.

[80] See Browder, *Nile Valley Contributions to Civilization*, 91–92.

[81] Louis Farrakhan, "Saviour's Day Speech," C-SPAN Video Library 17 February 2002 <http://www.c-spanvideo.org/program/168761-1> accessed 22 March 2013.

[82] Malcolm X (El Hajj Malik El Shabazz) "Message to the Grassroots," 1963 *American Rhetoric* <http://www.americanrhetoric.com/speeches/malcolmx grassroots.htm> 12 January 2008.

[83] "Most Painful 20 Torture Devices in History," *Reading Shouts* 12 May 2008 <http://readingshouts.wordpress.com/2008/05/12/most-painful-20-torture-devices-in-the-history/> accessed 26 November 2012.

[84] *Fela Kuti – Music is the Weapon*, directed by Jean-Jacques Flori, Stéphane Tchalgadjieff (Universal Import, 1982), DVD.

[85] See James Allen, et al., *Without Sanctuary: Lynching Photography in America* (Santa Fe: Twin Palms, 2000) and "4 UNIPORT Students Were Killed Yesterday in Portharcort [sic]," *You Tube* 6 Oct 2012 <http://www.youtube.com/watch?v=PCU7WwV3zOE&bpctr=1351966407> accessed 02 November 2012. Viewer discretion is advised as both the book and video contain horrifying images.

[86] Citizens Commission on Human Rights, *Psychiatry's Betrayal: In the Guise of Help* (Los Angeles: Citizens Commission on Human Rights, 1995), 6.

[87] One of my most moving memories as a professor is of teaching *Matigari* at Obafemi Awolowo University in Nigeria and at the conclusion of the discussion the students were chanting in unison, "We are the sons and daughters of Matigari!"

[88] Maulana Karenga, "The African Intellectual and the Problem of Class Suicide: Ideological and Political Dimensions," in *African Culture: The Rhythms of Unity*, edited by Molefi Asante and Kariamu Welsh Asante (Trenton: Africa World Press, 1990), 92.

[89] Ngugi wa Thiong'o, *Wizard of the Crow* (New York: Pantheon, 2006), 16. All subsequent references are to this edition and will be given parenthetically in the text.

[90] Mamadou Niang, "Still the Fire in the Belly: The Confessions of Ousmane Sembene," in *Ousmane Sembène: Interviews* (Jackson: University Press of Mississippi, 2008), 186.

[91] Niang, "Still the Fire in the Belly," 186.

[92] Aime Cesaire, *A Season in the Congo* in *Kuntu Drama: Plays of the African Continuum*, edited by Paul Carter Harrison (New York: Grove 1974), 151.

[93] Bascom, *Ifa Divination*, 107.

[94] Kimbwandende Kia Bunseki Fu-Kiau, *African Cosmology of the Bântu Kôngo: Tying the Spiritual Knot: Principles of Life and Living* (New York: Athelia Henrietta Press, 1980), 123–126.

[95] Hurston, *Mules and Men*, 89.
[96] See Washington, *Our Mothers, Our Powers, Our Texts*, 133–134.
[97] Kehinde Oyetimi, "The politicisation of the female breasts," *Tribune* 12 September 2010 <http://tribune.com.ng/sun/features/2038-the-politicisation-of-the-female-breasts> accessed 25 November 2011,
[98] *Sia: Dream of the Python*, directed by Dani Kouyate (ArtMattan, 2002), DVD; and Akinwumi Isola, *Madam Tinubu: The Terror in Lagos* (Ibadan: Heinemann, 1998).
[99] "Shell, Chevron, and Elf all Quit Nigerian Delta," *SRi Media: Corporate Governance News* 24 March 2003 <http://www.srimedia.com/artman/publish/article_466.shtml> accessed 15 March 2004.
[100] *Pray the Devil Back to Hell*, directed by Gini Reticker (Passion River, 2009).
[101] "Togolese women turn their back (sides) on police," *France 24* 29 August 2012 <http://observers.france24.com/content/20120829-togolese-women-protesters-turn-back-sides-police-lome-sauvons-le-togo-sex-strike-faure-gnassingbe> accessed 10 October 2012.
[102] Fela Anikulapo Kuti, "I.T.T.," *I.T.T.-International Thief Thief* (Kalakuta, 1979), LP.
[103] Fela Anikulapo Kuti, "I.T.T."
[104] *Brazil: An Inconvenient History*, directed by Phil Grabsky (Seven Arts, 2000), DVD; and see Jonah Fisher, "The Unsung Heroes of Wajir," *BBC News Online* 25 October 2004 <http://news.bbc.co.uk/2/hi/africa/3764556.stm> accessed 12 January 2008.
[105] Ben Okri, *Dangerous Love* (London: Phoenix, 1996), 266.
[106] Okri, *Dangerous Love*, 267–268.
[107] "Move to End Ghana Night Soil Work," *BBC News Online* 20 January 2006 <http://news.bbc.co.uk/2/hi/africa/4631834.stm> accessed 25 January 2008.
[108] Rowland Abiodun, "Woman in Yoruba Religious Images," *African Languages and Cultures* 2:1 (1989): 11; and see chapter two of Washington, *The Architects of Existence*.
[109] *The Making of Moolaadé*, directed by Samba Gadjigo, in *Moolaadé* (New Yorker, 2004), DVD, emphasis added.
[110] *The Making of Moolaadé*.
[111] Alice Walker's *The Color Purple* offers an example of such depravity when Squeak meets with her uncle to save Sofia (90–95).
[112] See Washington, *Our Mothers, Our Powers, Our Texts*, 113–140.
[113] Okri, *Infinite Riches*, 21–24.
[114] Soyinka, "The African World and the Ethnocultural Debate," 18.

360°

[1] Quoted in *Bullwhip Days: The Slaves Remember: An Oral History*, edited by James Mellon (New York: Grove, 1988), 49.

[2] Levine, *Black Culture and Black Consciousness*, 123–124.
[3] Levine, *Black Culture and Black Consciousness*, 123–124.
[4] Kevin Shillington, *History of Africa*, revised edition (Hampshire, England: Palgrave Macmillan, 1995), 94.
[5] *Bullwhip Days: The Slaves Remember: An Oral History*, 50–51.
[6] *Bullwhip Days: The Slaves Remember: An Oral History*, 51.
[7] Knight, *The Five Percenters*, 160–176.
[8] It is telling that the FBI and J. Edgar Hoover, the Disciples and King Larry Hoover, and the Black P. Stone Rangers and Caliph Abdul Malik have all been featured on BET's "American Gangster" documentary series.
[9] *All Power to the People: The Black Panther Party and Beyond*, directed by Lee Lew-Lee (Electronic News Group, 1996), television; and "Jose (Cha-Cha) Jimenez," *National Young Lords* <http://nationalyounglords.com/?page_id=15> accessed 20 March 2012.
[10] Lance Williams, "The Almighty Black P. Stone Nation: Black Power, Politics, and Gangbanging," lecture given at UIC School of Public Health, transcribed 18 October 2001, revised by Lance Williams, 12 February 2002. <http://www.uic.edu/orgs/kbc/ganghistory/UrbanCrisis/Blackstone/lance.htm> accessed 25 November 2011; and Natalie Y. Moore and Lance Williams, *The Almighty Black P Stone Nation: The Rise, Fall, and Resurgence of an American Gang* (Chicago: Lawrence Hill, 2011), 35.
[11] Lance Williams, "The Almighty Black P. Stone Nation."
[12] Natalie Y. Moore, "Muammar Qaddafi's Chicago Connection," *The Root* 16 March 2011 <http://www.theroot.com/views/muammar-gaddafi-and-el-rukns?page=0,1> accessed 26 November 2011.
[13] Muammar al-Qaddafi's support of Africa and his political and cultural identification as an African, as opposed to an Arabic, leader contributed in large part to his horrific lynching in 2011. His Africanity is evident not only in his support of African unity and his reverence of African martyrs, but in the fact that he supported the African citizens of Libya who lived in the town of Tawergha, the only Libyan city with a majority African population. Arab Libyans, largely of Misrata, used the civil war as an excuse to enact genocide and ethnic cleansing of the Africans of Tawergha. All 35,000 residents have been killed or driven out of Tawergha; the town is completely abandoned and the Arabs of Misrata have sworn to kill any African citizen who tries to return. Arab Libyans are also hunting unarmed African Libyans in refugee camps and killing them. The objective of the Arabs is revealed in the slogan of the Misrata brigade, which states that it exists *"for purging slaves and black skin."* Here, again, melanin is equated with slavery and being an inherent infidel, an imaginary status used to justify actual genocide. "Ethnic cleansing, genocide, and the Tawergha," *Human Rights Investigations* 26 September 2011 <http://humanrightsinvestigations.org/2011/09/26/libya-ethnic-cleansing-tawargha-genocide/> accessed 2 August 2012.

[14] Natalie Y. Moore and Lance Williams, *The Almighty Black P Stone Nation*, 21.
[15] Rod Emery, "The History of the Gangster Disciples – In Their Own Words," <http://gangresearch.net/ChicagoGangs/BGD/bgdnhistory.html> accessed 26 November 2011.
[16] Rod Emery, "The History of the Gangster Disciples – In Their Own Words."
[17] Greg Donaldson, "*21st Century V.O.T.E.*," *gangresearch* <http://www.gangresearch.net/ChicagoGangs/BGD/vote21.html> accessed 6 May 2013.
[18] Field research, Christian Village, Legon, Ghana, 1995.
[19] Reed, *Mumbo Jumbo*, 192.
[20] Babatunde Lawal, "À Yà Gbó, À Yà Tó," 43.
[21] Robert Farris Thompson, "Kongo Influences on African-American Artistic Culture," in *Africanisms in American Culture*, edited by Joseph E. Holloway (Bloomington: Indiana University Press, 1990), 158.
[22] "Bling'd: Blood Diamonds and Hip Hop," directed by Raquel Cepeda (Djali Rancher Productions and VH1 2007).
[23] X Clan, "Funkin' Lesson," *To the East Blackwards* (4th and B'Way, 1990), audiocassette.
[24] "Growth and Development," Parts 1–12 <http://peperonity.com/go/sites/mview/growthanddevelopment?act=0110-2169368-1276842830_13c03> accessed 18 June 2010.
[25] "Growth and Development."
[26] Abiodun, "Verbal and visual metaphors," 252.
[27] Abiodun, "Verbal and visual metaphors," 252–253 (punctuation is retained from the original).
[28] Abiodun, "Verbal and visual metaphors," 253.
[29] Abiodun, "Verbal and visual metaphors," 255.
[30] Thompson, *Flash of the Spirit*, 115.
[31] Lawal, *The Gẹ̀lẹ̀dẹ́ Spectacle*, 39.
[32] Modupe Oduyoye, "The Spider, the Chameleon, and the Creation of the Earth," in *Traditional African Religion in West Africa*, edited by I. A. Akinjogbin (Accra: Asempa, 1983), 383.
[33] DJ Cyrus, "Fake Thug Rappers Need to Read This Here," *My Space* 11 June 2007 <http://blogs.myspace.com/index.cfm?fuseaction=blog.view&friendId=177960506&blogId=274832403> accessed 2 August 2009. For literature spitting in a different context, see Hurston *Mules and Men*, 47, 84, 85. In Hurston's work, spitting literature is a form of opening ritual invocation. For the BGDs, spitting literature can be an opening ritual invocation, a confirmation, or a challenge.
[34] "Follow and Obey the Laws the Kings Set," *Tha Gangsta Disciples Homepage & Webring* <http://www.angelfire.com/folk/gangstaz/index.html> accessed 17 November 2007.
[35] "Follow and Obey the Laws the Kings Set," *Tha Gangsta Disciples Homepage & Webring*.
[36] "Follow and Obey the Laws the Kings Set," *Tha Gangsta Disciples Homepage & Webring*.

[37] This orature is the source of the African American folktale, "How a Loving Couple Was Parted" (Hurston, *Mules and Men*, 165–168).
[38] Peter P. Ekeh, "A Case for Dialogue on Nigerian Federalism," A Keynote Address To The Wilberforce Conference On Nigerian Federalism, 1997 <http://www.waado.org/nigerian_scholars/archive/pubs/wilber4.html> accessed 23 December 2007.
[39] Please see Donaldson, "*21st Century V.O.T.E.*"
[40] Scott Simon, "Gang Violence Smolders on Hot Chicago Streets," *NPR* 28 July 2012 <http://www.npr.org/2012/07/28/157454927/gang-violence-smoulders-on-hot-chicago-streets> accessed 2 March 2013.
[41] Joseph E. Logan, Sharon G. Smith, and Mark R. Stevens, "Homicides – United States, 1999-2007," *Morbidity and Mortality Weekly Report* 60:01 (14 January 2011): 67–70 <http://www.cdc.gov/mmwr/preview/mmwrhtml/su6001 a14.htm> accessed 6 May 2013.
[42] Lauren Petty and Alexandria Fisher, "Gang Members: We Deserve to be Saved, Keep Hospital Open," *NBC Chicago* 04 June 2013 <http://www.nbcchicago.com/news/health/South-Side-Hospital-Ordered-to-Move-Patients-209906611.html> accessed 11 June 2013; and "Gangs and Oil," *Vice*, Episode 9, HBO, 07 June 2013.
[43] Boogie Down Productions, "Illegal Business," *By All Means Necessary* (Jive, 1990), audiocassette.
[44] Oakland, California Youth Organizing Committee, "Youth Speak Out," *Global Africa Pocket News* 1:7 (1994): 20.
[45] Oakland California Youth Organizing Committee, "Youth Speak Out," 20.
[46] Oakland California Youth Organizing Committee, "Youth Speak Out," 21.
[47] Oakland California Youth Organizing Committee, "Youth Speak Out," 21, emphasis added.
[48] "Abbey Lincoln: 40 Years Later," *Nothing But a Man*, 40th Anniversary Special Edition (DuArt 2004), DVD.

BIBLIOGRAPHY

Abarbanel, Jonathan. Rev. of *Robert Johnson: Trick the Devil*, by Bill Harris. *Windy City Times, Theater Review.* 7 July 2005. 29 December 2007 <http://www.windycitymediagroup.com/gay/lesbian/news/ARTICLE.php?A ID=8837>.

Abbey Lincoln: 40 Years Later. In *Nothing But a Man.* Dir. Michael Roemer. 40th Anniversary Special Edition. Cinema V, 2004. DVD.

AbduSalaam, Ismael. "The RZA: Do the Knowledge (Tao of the Wu)." Part 1 of 2. *All Hip Hop.* 15 October 2009. 16 August 2010 <http://allhiphop.com/stories/reviewsbooks/archive/2009/10/15/21979105.a spx>.

Abimbola, Wande. *Sixteen Great Poems of Ifá.* UNESCO, 1975.

Abimbola. Kola. "Yoruba Diaspora." *Encyclopedia of Diasporas: Immigrant and Refugee Cultures Around the World.* Vol. 2. Eds. Melvin Ember, Carol R. Ember, and Ian Skoggard. New York: Springer, 2004. 317–326.

Abiodun, Rowland. "Àṣẹ: Verbalizing and Visualizing Creative Power through Art." *Journal of Religion in Africa* 24:4 (Nov 1994): 309–322.

-----. "Identity and the Artistic Process in Yorùbá Aesthetic Concept of Ìwà." *Journal of Cultural Inquiry* 1:1 (December 1983): 13–30.

-----. "Verbal and Visual Metaphors: Mythical Allusions in Yoruba Ritualistic Art of Orí." *Ifẹ̀: Annals of the Institute of Cultural Studies* (1985): 3–38.

Achebe, Chinua. "Work and Play in Tutuola's *The Palm-Wine Drinkard.*" *Hopes and Impediments: Selected Essays.* New York: Anchor Doubleday, 1988. 100–112.

-----. *Hopes and Impediments.* New York: Anchor Books, 1988.

-----. *Things Fall Apart.* London: Heinemann, 1958.

Adeoye, C. L. *Ìgbàgbọ́ àti Èsìn Yorùbá.* Ibadan: Evans Bros., 1985.

Adepegba, Cornelius O. "Associated Place-Names and Sacred Icons of Seven Yorùbá Deities: Historicity in Yorùbá Religious Traditions." In *Òrìṣà Devotion as World Religion: The Globalization of Yorùbá Religious Culture.* Ed. Jacob K. Olupona and Terry Ray. Madison: University of Wisconsin Press, 2008.

-----*Yoruba Metal Sculpture.* Ibadan: Ibadan University Press, 1991.

Aidoo, Ama Ata. *The Dilemma of a Ghost and Anowa.* 1965. London: Longman, 1987.

Akpan, Uwem. "Fattening for Gabon." *Say You're One of Them.* New York: Back Bay Books, 2008. 37–172.

Ali, Drew. *The Holy Koran of The Moorish Science Temple of America.* 1927. 18 March 2013 <http://hermetic.com/moorish/7koran.html>.

All Power to the People: The Black Panther Party and Beyond. Dir. Lee Lew-Lee. Electronic News Group, 1996. Television.

Allah, Supreme Understanding, et al. *Knowledge of Self: A Collection of the Wisdom on the Science of Everything in Life.* Atlanta: Supreme Design Media, 2009.

Allah, Wakeel. *In the Name of Allah: A History of Clarence 13X and the Five Percenters*. Atlanta: A-Team Publishing, 2001.

Allan, Gregory. "Silent Weapons for Quiet Wars: An Introduction Programming Manual." *The Lawful Path*. 18 August 2011 <http://www.lawfulpath.com/ref/sw4qw/>.

Alwes, Derek. "The Burden of Liberty: Choice in Toni Morrison's *Jazz* and Toni Cade Bambara's *The Salt Eaters*." *African American Review* 30:3 (Autumn 1996): 353–365.

The American Heritage Dictionary of the English Language. Ed. Anne H. Soukhanov. 3rd ed. New York: Houghton Mifflin, 1992.

"Ancient Secrets and Mysteries of Levitation." *The Unexplained Mysteries*. 31 July 2009 <http://theunexplainedmysteries.com/levitation-secrets.html>.

Ani, Marimba. *Yurugu: An African-Centered Critique of European Cultural Thought and Behavior*. Trenton: Africa World Press, 1994.

Anikulapo Kuti, Fela and Africa 70. "I.T.T." *I.T.T. – International Thief Thief*. Kalakuta, 1979. LP.

Anikulapo Kuti, Fela and Egypt 80, "Beasts of No Nation," *Beasts of No Nation/ODOO*. Fak Ltd., 1989. LP.

Anyebe, A. P. *Ògbóni: The Birth and Growth of the Reformed Ògbóni Society*. Lagos: Sam Lao, 1989.

Armah, Ayi Kwei. *The Healers*. Oxford: Heinemann, 1978.

-----. *Osiris Rising*. Popenguine: Per Ankh, 1995.

-----. *Two Thousand Seasons*. Oxford: Heinemann, 1973.

"Artifacts: Coral Castle." *Mysterious World*. Winter 2003. 31 July 2009 <http://www.mysteriousworld.com/Journal/2003/Winter/Artifacts/>.

Awolalu, J. Omosade. *Yoruba Beliefs and Sacrificial Rites*. Essex: Longman, 1979.

AZ featuring The RZA. "Whatever Happened (The Birth)." *Wu Chronicles*. Wu-Tang Records, 1999.

Babayemi, S. O. *Egúngún among the Ọ̀yọ́ Yoruba*. Ibadan: Board Publications, 1980.

"The Bachwezi." *Ugandan Travel Guide*. 29 June 2009 <http://www.ugandatravelguide.com/bachwezi.html.>

Badejo, Diedre. *Ọṣun Ṣẹ̀ẹ̀gẹ̀sí: The Elegant Deity of Wealth, Power, and Femininity*. Africa World Press, 1996.

Badu, Erykah. "On and On." *Baduizm*. Kedar/Universal, 1997. CD.

-----. "On and On." *Live*. Kedar/Universal, 1997. CD.

Bailey, Cornelia Walker. *God, Dr. Buzzard, and the Bolito Man: A Saltwater Geechee Talks about Life on Sapelo Island, Georgia*. New York: Anchor, 2000.

Bambara, Toni Cade. "Broken Field Running." In *The Sea Birds Are Still Alive*. Vintage: New York, 1977. 43–70.

-----. *The Salt Eaters*. New York: Random House, 1980.

Banished: How Whites Drove Blacks Out of Town in America. Dir. Marco Williams. Two Tone Productions/Center for Investigative Reporting, 2007. DVD.

Bannerman-Richter, Gabriel. *The Practice of Witchcraft in Ghana.* Elk Grove, California: Gabari, 1982.

Bascom, William. *Ifa Divination: Communication Between Gods and Men in West Africa.* Bloomington: Indiana University Press, 1969.

-----. *Sixteen Cowries: Yoruba Divination from Africa to the New World.* Bloomington: Indiana University Press, 1980.

Better Shirley. *Institutional Racism: A Primer on Theory and Strategies for Social Change.* 2nd edition. Lanham, MD: Rowman and Littlefield, 2007.

Bey, C. M. *Clock of Destiny.* Vol. I. 1947. Cleveland: R V Bey Publications, 1973.

-----. *Clock of Destiny.* Vol. II. 1947. Cleveland: R V Bey Publications, 1973.

Bey, R. V. "Return of the Matriarch." *R V Bey Publications* 1 October 2011 <http://www.rvbeypublications.com/id78.html>.

-----. *She Redeems.* New York: R V Bey Publications, 2005.

Bjelobrk, Nada Daniele, Foresti, Marko Dorrestijn, Majid Nabavi, and Dimos Poulikakos*. "Contactless transport of acoustically levitated particles." *Applied Physics Letters* 97: 161904 (2010). 16 July 2013 <https://edit.ethz.ch/ltnt/publications/Journal/Journal/pubimg/2010_Bjelobrk1.pdf>.

Black, E. "The Three Virtual Intentional Communities Of God In A Body In Real Time (1868–2008)." *Alternative Considerations to Jonestown and Peoples Temple.* 25 January 2009. 11 November 2011 <http://jonestown.sdsu.edu/AboutJonestown/JonestownReport/Volume10/Black.htm>.

"Black Herman." *Magic: The Science of Illusion.* California Science Center. *Magic Exhibit* 2000. 18 January 2008 <http://www.magicexhibit.org/story/story_blackHerman.html>.

Bling'd: Blood Diamonds and Hip Hop. Dir. Raquel Cepeda. Djali Rancher Productions and VH1, 2007. Television.

Bockie, Simon. *Death and the Invisible Powers: The World of Kongo Belief.* Bloomington: Indiana University Press, 1993.

Bok, Francis. *Escape from Slavery.* New York: St. Martins, 2003.

Boogie Down Productions. "Illegal Business." *By All Means Necessary.* Jive, 1990. Audiocassette.

Boston, Stephen W. "And God Said…" *The Reluctant Messenger.* 22 May 2011<http://reluctant-messenger.com/and-God-said.htm>.

Boyd, Valerie. "'She was just outrageously brilliant': Toni Morrison Remembers Toni Cade Bambara." In *Savoring the Salt: The Legacy of Toni Cade Bambara.* Eds. Linda Janet Holmes and Cheryl A. Wall. Philadelphia: Temple University Press, 2008. 88–99.

Boyle, Alan. "Engineers juggle objects with levitating sound waves." NBC News Science. *NBC News.* 15 July 2013. 15 July 2013 <http://www.nbcnews.com/science/engineers-juggle-objects-levitating-sound-waves-6C10643299>.

Brazil: An Inconvenient History. Dir. Phil Grabsky. Seven Arts, 2000. Television.

Brophy, Thomas G. *The Origin Map: Discovery of a Prehistoric, Megalithic, Astrophysical Map and Sculpture of the Universe.* Bloomington: iUniverse, 2002.

Busia, Abena, P. A. "Parasites and Prophets: The Use of Women in Ayi Kwei Armah's Novels." In *Ngambika: Studies of Women in African Literature*. Eds. Carole Boyce Davies and Anne Adams Graves. Trenton: Africa World Press. 1986. 89–113.

"Can't You Hear The Wind Howl?" The Life and Music of Robert Johnson. Dir. Peter Meyer. Winstar, 1998.

"Chain Gangs." *History's Mysteries*. The History Channel, 2000.

Charry, Eric. *Mande Music: Traditional and Modern Music of the Maninka and Mandinka of Western Africa*. Chicago: University of Chicago Press, 2000.

Chinweizu. *The West and the Rest of Us*. New York: Vintage, 1975.

Chireau, Yvonne P. "Black Herman's African American Magical Synthesis." *Cabinet Magazine*. 26 (2007). 6 May 2012<http://www.cabinetmagazine.org/issues/26/chireau.php>.

Choi, Charles. "The real question: Who didn't have sex with Neanderthals? Sub-Saharan Africans only modern humans whose ancestors did not interbreed with them." *NBC News*. 1 November 2012 <http://www.msnbc.msn.com/id/49642484/ns/technology_and_science-science/t/real-question-who-didnt-have-sex-neanderthals/>.

Choi, Charles Q. "Strange! Human Glow in Visible Light." *Live Science*. 22 July 2009 <http://news.yahoo.com/s/livescience/20090722/sc_livescience/strangehumansglowinvisiblelight>.

"Convict Lease System." *Digital History*. 23 November 2011 <http://www.digitalhistory.uh.edu/database/article_display.cfm?HHID=214>.

Cooper, Jr., Clarence. "Not We Many." In *Black*. Edinburg: Payback Press, 1963.

Courlander, Harold A. ed. *A Treasury of African Folklore: The Oral Literature, Traditions, Myths, Legends, Epics, Tales, Recollections, Wisdom, Sayings, and Humor of Africa*. New York: Marlowe and Company, 1996.

-----. *A Treasury of Afro-American Folklore: The Oral Literature, Traditions, Recollections, Legends, Tales, Songs, Religious Beliefs, Customs, Sayings and Humor of Peoples of African Descent in the Americas*. New York: Crown Publishers, 1976.

Cuffe, Jenny. "Surviving a Desert 'Nightmare.'" *BBC News Online*. 7 January 2008. 9 January 2008 <http://news.bbc.co.uk/2/hi/programmes/7154722.stm>.

D'Angelo. "Africa." *Voodoo*. Virgin, 2000. CD.

Dalby, David. "Americanisms That May Once Have Been Africanisms." *Mother Wit from the Laughing Barrel: Readings in the Interpretation of Afro-American Folklore*. Ed. Alan Dundes. Englewood Cliffs, N.J.: Prentice Hall, 1973. 136–140.

Dark Sun Riders featuring Brother J. "Dark Sun Riders Firmly Handle This." *The Seeds of Evolution*. Polygram, 1996. CD.

-----. "The Jewels of Evolution," *The Seeds of Evolution*. Polygram, 1996. CD.

Daughters of the Dust. Dir. Julie Dash. 1991. New York: Kino, 2000. DVD.

Davey D. "Interview with Brother J of X Clan." *Davey D's Hip Hop Corner: Antithug.* 15 November 2007 <http://www.daveyd.com/interviewbrotherj.html>.

Davidson, Basil. *The Lost Cities of Africa.* Rev. edition. New York: Little Brown, and Company, 1959.

Davies, Nick. "The Cruellest Voyage." *The Guardian.* 2 December 2007 <http://www.guardian.co.uk/world/2007/dec/03/immigration.uk>.

De La Soul featuring Red Man. "Oooh!" *Art Official Intelligence: Mosaic Thump.* Rhino, 2000. CD.

dead prez. "Fucked Up." *RBG: Revolutionary But Gangsta.* Sony, 2004. CD.

-----. "I Have a Dream Too." *RBG: Revolutionary But Gangsta.* Sony, 2004. CD.

-----. "I'm A African." *Let's Get Free.* Relativity, 2000. CD.

-----. "They Schools." *Let's Get Free.* Relativity, 2000. CD.

Deadly Voyage. Dir. John McKenzie. HBO Films, 1996. Television.

"Diamagnetic Water." *Wonder Magnet.* 2003. 31 July 2009 <http://wondermagnet.com/diamagh2o.html>.

Dictionary of the Yoruba Language. Ibadan: University of Ibadan Press, 1991.

Digable Planets. "9th Wonder." *Blowout Comb.* Capitol, 1994. CD.

Diop, Cheikh Anta. *The African Origin of Civilization: Myth or Reality.* Chicago: Lawrence Hill, 1974.

-----. *The Cultural Unity of Black Africa.* 1959. Chicago: Third World Press, 1963.

Dirks, Annelieke. "Between Threat and Reality: The National Association for the Advancement of Colored People and the Emergence of Armed Self-Defense in Clarksdale and Natchez, Mississippi, 1960–1965." *Journal for the Study of Radicalism* 1:1 (2007): 71–98.

DJ Cyrus. "Fake Thug Rappers Need to Read This Here." *My Space.* 11 June 2007. 2 August 2009 <http://blogs.myspace.com/index.cfm?fuseaction=blog.view&friendId=177960506&blogId=274832403>.

Donaldson, Greg. "*21st Century V.O.T.E.*" *Gang Research.* 6 May 2012 <http://www.gangresearch.net/ChicagoGangs/BGD/vote21.html>.

Dongala, Emmanuel. *The Fire of Origins.* Trans. Lillian Corti. Chicago: Lawrence Hill Books, 2001.

Drewal, Henry John and Margaret Thompson Drewal. *Gẹlẹdẹ: Art and Female Power among the Yoruba.* Bloomington: Indiana University Press, 1983.

Dumas, Henry. "Ark of Bones." In *Echo Tree: The Collected Short Fiction of Henry Dumas.* Ed. Eugene B. Redmond. Minneapolis: Coffee House, 2003.

Dundes, Alan, ed. *Mother Wit from the Laughing Barrel.* Englewood Cliffs: Prentice Hall, 1973.

Dunn, Christopher. *The Giza Power Plant: Technologies of Ancient Egypt.* Rochester, VT: Bear and Company, 2004.

Earth, Wind & Fire. "Keep Your Head to the Sky." *To The Sky.* Columbia, 1973. LP.

-----. "Shining Star." *That's the Way of the World.* Columbia, 1975. LP.

Ekeh, Peter P. "A Case for Dialogue on Nigerian Federalism." A Keynote Address To The Wilberforce Conference On Nigerian Federalism. 1997. 23 December 2007 <http://www.waado.org/nigerian_scholars/archive/pubs/wilber 4.html>.

Emery, Rod. "The History of the Gangster Disciples – In Their Own Words." 26 November 2011 <http://gangresearch.net/ChicagoGangs/BGD/bgdnhistory.html>.

Encyclopedia of African Religion. Vol. 1. Eds. Molefi K. Asante and Ama Mazama. Thousand Oaks, CA: Sage, 2008.

Encyclopedia of the African Diaspora: Origins, Experiences, and Culture. Ed. Carole Elizabeth Boyce Davies. Santa Barbara: ABC-CLIO, 2008.

Equiano, Olaudah. From *The Interesting Narrative of the Life of Olaudah Equiano, or Gustavus Vassa, the African*." In *Crossing the Danger Water*. Ed. Deirdre Mullane. New York: Anchor, 1993. 8–19.

Eric B and Rakim. "No Competition." *Follow the Leader*. UNI/MCA, 1988. LP.

Faige, David. "What Would It Feel Like To Travel in Time?" *Space-Time Continuum—A Thesis*. 2006. 19 July 2009 <http://www.west.net/~ke6jqp/spacetime/spacetime4.html>.

Fard Muhammad, W. D. "Lost Found Muslim Lesson Number One." In *Supreme Wisdom Lessons. The Nation of Islam*. 20 February 1934. 19 December 2007 <http://www.thenationofislam.org/muslimlessonone.html>.

-----. "Lost Found Muslim Lesson Number Two." In *Supreme Wisdom Lessons. The Nation of Islam*. 20 February 1934. 19 December 2007 <http://www.thenationofislam.org/muslimlessontwo.html>.

Fatunmbi, Awo Fá'lokun. *Ìwa-pèlé: Ifá Quest: The Search for the Source of Santería and Lucumí*. Bronx: Original, 1991.

Fisher, Jonah. "The Unsung Heroes of Wajir." *BBC News Online*. 25 October 2004. 12 January 2008 <http://news.bbc.co.uk/2/hi/africa/3764556.stm>.

Flowers, Arthur. *De Mojo Blues: De Quest of HighJohn de Conqueror*. New York: Ballantine, 1985.

"Follow and Obey the Laws the Kings Set." *Tha Gangsta Disciples Homepage & Webring*. 17 November 2007 <http://www.angelfire.com/folk/gangstaz/index.html>.

Franklin, John Hope and Loren Schweninger. *In Search of the Promised Land*. New York: Oxford University Press, 2006.

"The Frog that Learned to Fly." High Field Magnet Laboratory. Radboud University Nijmegen. *Archive* 15 September 2012. 15 July 2013 <http://archive.is/UnQr>.

Fu-Kiau, Kimbwandende Kia Bunseki. *African Cosmology of the Bântu-Kôngo: Tying the Spiritual Knot: Principles of Life and Living*. New York: Athelia Henrietta Press, 1980.

Gadsby, Meredith. "Little Salt Won't Kill Yuh: English Licks and Two Generations of Migrating Subjects." In *Migrating Words and Worlds: Pan-Africanism Updated*. African Literature Association Annual No. 4. Eds. E. Anthony Hurley, Joseph McLaren and Renee Larrier (Trenton: African World Press, 1998), 53–72.

-----. *Sucking Salt: Caribbean Women Writers, Migration, and Survival*. Columbia: University of Missouri Press, 2006.
Gates, Jr., Henry Louis. "Mexico & Peru: A Hidden Race." *Black in Latin America*. Inkwell Films, 2011. DVD.
-----. *The Signifying Monkey: A Theory of African-American Literary Criticism*. New York: Oxford University Press, 1988.
Georgia Writer's Project. *Drums and Shadows: Survival Studies Among the Georgia Coastal Negroes*. Athens: University of Georgia Press, 1940.
Gerima, Haile. *Sankofa*. Mypheduh. 1993. VHS.
Gillian, Ayanna. "Yoruba Religion: The Cornerstone of Society." 10 April 2003. 12 August 2007 <www.rootswomen.com/ayanna/articles/10042003.html>.
Ginzburg, Ralph, ed. *100 Years of Lynching*. Baltimore: Black Classic Press, 1962.
Gomez, Michael A. *Black Crescent: The Experience and Legacy of African Muslims in the Americas*. Cambridge: Cambridge University Press, 2005.
Goodie Mob. "Black Ice (Sky High)." *Still Standing*. LaFace, 1998. CD.
-----. "Fighting." *Soul Food*. LaFace, 1995. CD.
-----. "The Experience." *Still Standing*. LaFace, 1998. CD.
Gravediggaz. "Dangerous Mindz." *Wu-Chronicles: Chapter II*. Wu-Tang Records, 2001. CD.
-----. "The Night The Earth Cried." *The Pick The Sickle, and the Shovel*. BMG Records, 1997. CD.
-----. "Twelve Jewelz." *The Pick, the Sickle, and the Shovel*. BMG Records, 1997. CD.
Grewal, Gurleen. *Circles of Sorrow, Lines of Struggle: The Novels of Toni Morrison*. Baton Rouge: Louisiana State University Press, 2000.
Griaule, Marcel and Germaine Dieterlen. *The Pale Fox*. Trans. Stephen D. Infantino. 1965. Chino Valley, Arizona: Continuum, 1986.
"Growth and Development." Parts 1–12. 18 June 2010 <http://peperonity.com/go/sites/mview/growthanddevelopment?act=0110-21693681276842830_13c 03>.
Hagan, Stephen. "If you're white, you're right." *Online Opinion*. 25 May 2006. 9 November 2011 <http://www.onlineopinion.com.au/view.asp?article=4490>.
Hallen, Barry and J. Olubiyi Sodipo. *Knowledge Belief and Witchcraft*. 1986. Stanford: Stanford University Press, 1997.
Harris, Bill. *Robert Johnson: Trick the Devil*. In *The National Black Drama Anthology*. Ed. Woodie King, Jr. New York: Applause, 1995. 1–46.
Hatshepsut. "Speech of the Queen." In *Daughters of Africa*. Ed. Margaret Busby. New York: Pantheon, 1992.
"Helping Haiti's Child's Slaves." *CNN*. 21 July 2009. 9 August 2009 <http://www.cnn.com/video/#/video/world/2009/07/21/iyw.gupta.haiti.slavery.long.cnn?iref=videosearch>.
Heron, W. Kim. "Space is Still the Place." *Metro Times*. 6 June 2007. 18 January 2008 <http://www.metrotimes.com/editorial/story.asp?id=10582>.

Herskovits, Melville J. and Frances S. Herskovits. *Dahomean Narrative: A Cross Cultural Analysis*. Evanston: Northwestern University, 1958.
Holloway, Joseph E. and Winifred K. Vass. *The African Heritage of American English*. Bloomington: Indiana University Press, 1993.
Hopkinson, Nalo. *The Salt Roads*. New York: Time Warner, 2003.
A Huey P. Newton Story. Dir. Spike Lee. Urban Works, 2001. Television.
Hunter, David. "Blue-Eyed Devil: An Interview with Michael Muhammad Knight." *KGB Bar Lit Magazine*. 11 August 2011 <http://www.kgbbar.com/lit/non_fiction/blue_eyed_devil_an_interview_with_michael_muhammad_knight>.
Hurston, Zora Neale. "Crow Dance." *Speak So You Can Speak Again*. Ed. Lucy Anne Hurston. Companion CD. New York: Doubleday, 2004.
-----. *Dust Tracks on a Road*. 1942. New York: Harper Perennial, 1996.
-----. *Every Tongue Got to Confess*. New York: Harper Collins, 2001.
-----. "High John de Conquer." *Zora Neale Hurston: The Complete Stories*. New York: Harper Perennial, 1995.
-----. *Mules and Men*. 1935. New York: Harper Perennial, 1990.
-----. *The Sanctified Church*. New York: Marlowe & Co., 1981.
-----. "Uncle Bud." *Speak So You Can Speak Again*. Ed. Lucy Anne Hurston. Companion CD. New York: Doubleday, 2004.
Ibie, Cromwell Osamaro. *Ifisim: The Complete Works of Orunmila*. Vol. 1. Lagos, Efehi, 1986.
Idowu, E. Bolaji. *Olódùmarè: God in Yoruba Belief*. 1962. New York: Wazobia, 1994.
"In Search of . . . Dark Star." Prod. Alan Landsburg. *History Channel*. 1979. Television.
"Immigrants in Paris: Dreams go up in flames." *UN-Habitat: State of the World's Cities*. 2006/7. 24 July 2009 <http://ww2.unhabitat.org/mediacentre/documents/sowcr2006/SOWCR%20 15.pdf>.
"In-depth with Toni Morrison." *Book-TV*: *CSPAN*. 4 February 2001 <http://www.c-spanvideo.org/program/162375-1>. Television.
Isola, Akinwumi. *Madam Tinubu: The Terror of Lagos*. Ibadan: Heinemann, 1998.
"Israel denies African migrants' rights, says US." *BBC News Online*. 25 May 2012. 17 June 2012 <http://www.bbc.co.uk/news/world-middle-east-18210133>.
Jackson, Rebecca. *Gifts of Power: The Writings of Rebecca Jackson, Black Visionary, Shaker Eldress*. Ed. Jean McMahon Humez. Amherst: University of Massachusetts Press, 1981.
Jay Z. "Heaven." *Magna Carta . . . Holy Grail*. Roc Nation, 2013. CD.
-----. "Run the Town." *The Blueprint 3*. Roc Nation, 2009. CD.
John Henrik Clarke: A Great and Mighty Walk. Dir. St. Claire Bourne. *Black Stars*. Black Dot Media, 1996. Television.
Johnson, Christopher. "God the Black Man and the Five Percenters." *NPR*. 4 August 2006. 15 November 2011 <http://www.npr.org/templates/story/story.php?storyId=5614846.>.

Johnson, Lemuel A. "The Inventions of Paradise: The Caribbean and the Utopian Bent." *Poetics Today* 15:4 (Winter 1994): 685–724.

Johnson, Robert. "Come on in My Kitchen." *Robert Johnson: The Complete Recordings*. Sony, 1990. CD.

J. R. "'The Re-Birth of Mec': Choppin' it up with Ladybug Mecca, formerly of Digable Planets." *Davey D's Hip Hop Corner*. 20 June 2009 <http://www.daveyd.com/interviewmeca.html>.

Karenga, Maulana. "The African Intellectual and the Problem of Class Suicide: Ideological and Political Dimensions." In *African Culture: The Rhythms of Unity*. Eds. Molefi Asante and Kariamu Welsh Asante. Trenton: Africa World Press, 1990.

Katz, William Loren. *Black Indians: A Hidden Heritage*. New York: Atheneum, 1997.

Kelis. "Little Star." *Kelis Was Here*. LaFace, 2006. CD.

Kennedy, Carole. *Psychic: Awakening the Power Within You*. Chicago: Contemporary Books, 1988.

Khan, Muhammad Muhsin and Muhammad Taqi-ud-Din Al-Hilali. *Interpretation of the Meanings of the Noble Qur'an in the English Language*. Riyadh, Saudi Arabia: Maktaba Dar-es-Salaam, 1993.

Killarmy. "Allah Sees Everything." *Dirty Weaponry*. Priority, 1998. CD.

-----. "Last Poet." *Dirty Weaponry*. Priority, 1998. CD.

-----. "Universal Soldiers." *Silent Weapons for Quiet Wars*. Priority/EMI, 1997. CD.

Killarmy featuring Sunz of Man. "Wake Up." *Wu-Chronicles*. Priority, 1999. CD.

Knight, Michael Muhammad. *The Five Percenters: Islam, Hip Hop and the Gods of New York*. Oxford: Oneworld, 2007.

Kolawole, Mary E. M. *Womanism and African Consciousness*. Trenton, NJ: Africa World Press, 1996.

Lawal, Babatunde. "*À Yà Gbó, À Yà Tó*: New Perspectives on Edan Ògbóni." *African Arts* 28:1 (Winter, 1995): 36–49, 98–100.

-----. "Ejiwapo: The Dialectics of Twoness in Yoruba Culture." *African Arts. Free Online Library*. 2008. 15 January 2012 <http://www.thefreelibrary.com/Ejiwapo%3A+the+dialectics+of+twoness+in+Yoruba+art+and+culture.-a0175443008>.

-----. *The Gèlèdé Spectacle: Art, Gender, and Social Harmony in an African Culture*. Seattle: University of Washington Press, 1996.

-----. "The Present State of Art Historical Research in Nigeria: Problems and Possibilities." *The Journal of African History* 18:2 (1977): 193–216.

Layiwola, Dele. "Womanism in Nigerian Folklore and Drama." *African Notes* XI:1 (1987): 26–33.

Leake, Jonathan. "Oceans charge up new theory of magnetism." *Times Online*. 14 June 2009. 7 June 2010 <http://www.timesonline.co.uk/tol/news/science/article6493481.ece>.

Leedskalnin, Edward. *Magnetic Current*. Homestead, FL: Rock Gate, 1945.

Lester, Julius. *Black Folktales*. New York: Grove Weidenfeld, 1969.

Levine, Lawrence. *Black Culture and Black Consciousness: Afro-American Folk Thought from Slavery to Freedom*. Oxford University Press, 1977.

Lichtheim, Miriam. *Ancient Egyptian Literature: Volume I: The Old and Middle Kingdoms*. Berkeley: University of California Press, 1973.

Lil Wayne. "Tha Heat." *Tha Carter*. Cash Money Records, 2004. CD.

Logan, Joseph E., Sharon G. Smith, and Mark R. Stevens. "Homicides – United States, 1999-2007." *Morbidity and Mortality Weekly Report* 60:01 (14 January 2011): 67–70. 6 May 2013 <http://www.cdc.gov/mmwr/preview/mmwrhtml/su6001a14.htm>.

Lomax, Louis E. *When the Word is Given...* New York: Signet, 1963.

Lord Jamar. "Deep Space." *The 5% Album*. Babygrande, 2006. CD.

-----. "I.S.L.A.M." *The 5% Album*. Babygrande, 2006. CD.

-----. "The Sun." *Deep Space/The Corner, The Streets*. Babygrande, 2006. CD.

-----. "Supreme Mathematics." *The 5% Album*. Babygrande, 2006. CD.

Lumumba, la mort du prophete. Dir. Raoul Peck. Velvet Films, 1992. DVD.

MacGaffey, Wyatt. "The West in Congolese Experience." *Africa and the West: Intellectual Responses to European Culture*. Ed. Philip D. Curtin. Madison, University of Wisconsin Press, 1972. 49–74.

Major, Clarence, ed. *From Juba to Jive: A Dictionary of African American Slang*. New York: Penguin, 1994.

Makinde, Akin Moses. *African Philosophy, Culture and Traditional Medicine*. Athens: Ohio University Center for International Studies, 1988.

The Making of Moolaadé. Dir. Samba Gadjigo. *Moolaadé*. Dir. Sembene Ousmane. New Yorker, 2004. DVD.

"Manning Marable's *Malcolm X* Panel: 23 Jul 2011." *C-Span Video Library*. 23 July 2011 <http://www.c-spanvideo.org/program/Marabl>.

The Manuscripts of Timbuktu. Dir. Zola Maseko. SABAC, 2009. DVD.

Marley, Bob and Peter Tosh. "Get Up Stand Up." *Legend: The Best of Bob Marley and the Wailers*. Def Jam, 2001. CD.

Mbiti, John S. *African Religions and Philosophy*. 2nd edition. Portsmouth, New Hampshire: Heinemann, 1969.

McCluskey, John. *Look What They Done to My Song*. New York: Random House, 1974.

McDaniel, Lorna. *The Big Drum Ritual of Carriacou: Praisesongs in Rememory of Flight*. Gainesville: University Press of Florida, 1998.

McKnight, Reginald. "Palm Wine." In *Speak My Name: Black Men on Masculinity and the American Dream*. Ed. Don Belton. Boston: Beacon, 1995. 182–196.

Mellon, James, ed. *Bullwhip Days: The Slaves Remember: An Oral History*. New York: Grove, 1988.

Metuh, Emefie Ikenga. *God and Man in African Religion: A Case Study of the Igbo of Nigeria*. London: Geoffrey Chapman, 1981.

Meyer, Piet. "Divination among the Lobi of Burkina Faso." *African Divination Systems: Ways of Knowing*. Ed. Philip M. Peek. Bloomington: Indiana University Press, 1991. 91–100.

Miyakawa, Felicia. *Five Percenter Rap: God Hop's Music, Message, and Black Muslim Mission*. Bloomington: Indiana University Press, 2005.

Montejo, Esteban. *The Autobiography of a Runaway Slave*. London: Bodley Head, 1968.

Mood and Sunz of Man. "Illuminated Sunlight." *Doom*. TVT/Blunt, 1997. CD.

Moolaadé. Dir. Ousmane Sembene. New Yorker, 2004. DVD.

Moore, Natalie Y. "Muammar Qaddafi's Chicago Connection." *The Root*. 16 March 2011. 26 November 2011 <http://www.theroot.com/views/muammar-gaddafi-and-elrukns?page=0,1>.

Moore, Natalie Y. and Lance Williams. *The Almighty Black P Stone Nation: The Rise, Fall, and Resurgence of an American Gang*. Chicago: Lawrence Hill, 2011.

Morrison, Toni. *Beloved*. New York: Plume, 1988.

-----. *Home*. New York: Alfred A. Knopf, 2012.

-----. *Sula*. New York: Plume, 1973.

-----. *Tar Baby*. 1981. New York: Quality Paperback Book Club, 1987.

Morton-Williams, Peter, William Bascom, and E. M. McClelland. "Two Studies of Ifa Divination. Introduction: The Mode of Divination." *Africa: Journal of the International African Institute* 36:4 (Oct. 1966): 406–431.

"Moses Dickson (1824–1901)." *Black Past*. 02 May 2010 <http://www.blackpast.org/?q=aah/dickson-moses-1824-1901>.

Mosley, Walter. *47*. New York: Little, Brown, and Co., 2005.

"Move to End Ghana Night Soil Work." *BBC News Online*. 20 January 2006. 25 January 2008 <http://news.bbc.co.uk/2/hi/africa/4631834.stm>.

Muhammad, Elijah. "I Want To Teach You." *Our Savior Has Arrived. Nation of Islam Settlement No. 1*. 31 July 2008 <http://www.seventhfam.com/temple/books/our_saviour/saviour10.htm>.

Murphy, Laura. "Into the Bush of Ghosts: Specters of the Slave Trade in West African Fiction." *Research in African Literatures* 38:4 (Winter 2007): 141–152.

-----. *Metaphor and the Slave Trade in West African Literature*. Athens: Ohio University Press, 2012.

Mutabaruka. "Mutabaruka on Religious HardTalk." Parts 1 and 2 of 11. *You Tube*. 12 August 2011 <http://www.youtube.com/watch?v=GzZYAZ3ngKk&NR=1>.

Myrdal, Gunnar. *An American Dilemma: The Negro Problem and Modern Democracy*. 1944. Vol. 2. New York: Harper and Row, 2009.

"Mystery at Coral Castle." Baltic Tourism Directory: Florida Coral Castle - Ed Liedskalnins - Korallu Pils - The Latvian Connection. Baltic Tourism. 12 June 2009. 31 July 2009 <http://www.baltictourism.info/2009/06/florida-coral-castle-ed-liedskalnins.html>.

Nas. "Warrior's Song." *God's Son*. Ill Will, 2002. CD.

Nazer, Mende. *Slave: My True Story*, New York: Public Affairs, 2003.

Neumann, Thomas W. "A Biocultural Approach to Salt Taboos: The Case of the Southeastern United States. *Current Anthropology* 18:2 (June 1977): 289–308.

Newman, Randy. "Lyrics--Sail Away." *Randy Newman*. 31 December 2007 <http://www.randynewman.com/tocdiscography/disc_sail_away/tocdiscogra phy/disc_sail_away/lyricssailaway#sailaway>.
Ngugi wa Thiong'o. *Matigari*. Trenton: African World Press, 1998.
-----. *Wizard of the Crow*. New York: Pantheon, 2006.
Niang, Sada. "An Interview with Ousmane Sembene by Sada Niang." In *Ousmane Sembene: Dialogues with Critics and Writers*. Eds. Samba Gadjigo, Ralph H. Faulkingham, Thomas Cassirer and Reinhard Sander. Amherst: University of Massachusetts Press, 1993. 87–108.
Nicklin, Keith and Jill Salmons. "Cross River Art Styles." *African Arts* 18:1 (Nov 1984): 28–43, 93–94.
Nkuba, Kihura. "Africa: The Bachwezi Were Egyptians." *All Africa*. 5 April 2008. 29 June 2009 <http://allafrica.com/stories/200804070661.html>.
Nobles, Wade W. "African American Family Life: An Instrument of Culture." In *Black Families*. 3rd edition. Ed. Harriette Pipes McAdoo. Thousand Oaks: Sage, 1997.
Noor, Abdul. *The Supreme Understanding: The Teaching of Islam in North America*. Lincoln NE: Writers Club Press, 2002.
"Nubian/Egyptian Gods and Goddess." *Dig Nubia*. 9 May 2012 <http://www.dignubia.org/bookshelf/goddesses.php>.
Nwapa, Flora. *Efuru*. London: Heinemann, 1966.
Nye, Bill. "Ask Bill Nye." *Columns: Clouds. Encarta*. 2007. 16 February 2008 <http://encarta.msn.com/encnet/Features/Columns/?article=BNClouds>.
Nzumafo, Naja. "The Ikom Monoliths of Nigeria." 08 August 2011. 24 August 2011 <http://camericans-atcam.blogspot.com/2011/08/ikom-monoliths-of-nigeria.html>.
Oakland, California Youth Organizing Committee. "Youth Speak Out." *Global Africa Pocket News* 1:7 (1994): 20.
Oduyoye, Modupe. "The Spider, the Chameleon and the Creation of the Earth." In *Traditional Religion in West Africa*. Ed. E. E. Ade Adegbola. Accra: Asempa, 1983. 374–388.
Ogundipe, Molara. "The Sacred and the Feminine: An African Response to Clément and Kristeva. In *The Sacred and the Feminine: Imagination and Sexual Difference*. Eds. Griselda Pollock and Victoria Turvey-Sauron. New York: I. B. Tauris, 2008. 88–110.
Okri, Ben. *Dangerous Love*. London: Phoenix, 1996.
-----. *Infinite Riches*. London: Phoenix, 1998.
-----. *The Famished Road*. New York: Double Day, 1991.
Olela, Henry. "The African Foundations of Greek Philosophy." In *African Philosophy*. Ed. Eze Emmanuel Chukwudi. Malden, MA: Blackwell, 1998. 43–49.
Opefeyitimi, Ayo. "Women of the World in Yoruba Culture." Unpublished paper. Obafemi Awolowo University, 1993.
"Our Creed." *Universal Hagar's Spiritual Church Association*. 23 September 2011 <http://www.uhsca.org/Commandments.html>.
"Our Founder." *Universal Hagar's Spiritual Church Association*. 23 September

2011 <http://www.uhsca.org/Commandments.html>.
"Our Ten Commandments." *Universal Hagar's Spiritual Church Association*. 23 September 2011<http://www.uhsca.org/Commandments.html>.
Oyetimi, Kehinde. "The politicisation of the female breasts." *Tribune*. 12 September 2010. 25 November 2011 <http://tribune.com.ng/sun/features/2038-the-politicisation-of-the-female- breasts>.
Packard, Randall M. "Chiefship and the History of Nyavingi Possession among the Bashu of Eastern Zaire." *Africa: Journal of the International African Institute* 52:4 (1982): 67–86, 90.
Painter, Nell Irvin. "Why Are White People Called 'Caucasians'? Collective Degradation: Slavery and the Construction of Race." Proceedings of the Fifth Annual Gilder Lehrman Center International Conference at Yale University. 7–8 November 2003. 12 November 2011 <http://www.yale.edu/glc/events/race/Painter.pdf>.
Patterson, Orlando. *Slavery and Social Death: A Comparative Study*. Cambridge: Harvard University Press, 1982.
Pearson, Barry Lee and Bill McCulloch. *Robert Johnson: Lost and Found*. Champaign, IL: University of Illinois Press, 2003.
Pearson, Carlton D. *God is Not a Christian, Nor a Jew, Muslim, Hindu. . . : God Dwells with Us, in Us, Around Us, as Us*. New York: Atria, 2010.
Pliya, Jean. "The Watch-Night." In *Jazz and Palm Wine*. Ed. Willfried F. Feuser. Essex, London: Longman, 1981.
Poor Righteous Teachers. "Butt Naked Booty Bless." *Holy Intellect*. Profile/Arista, 1990. Audiocassette.
"Pope Felix V." 25 Most Evil People of the 15th Century. *One-evil*. 9 November 2011 <http://one-evil.org/people/people_15c_Felix_V.htm>.
Powers, Kim. "An Interview with August Wilson." *Conversations with August Wilson*. Eds. Jackson R. Bryer and Mary C. Hartig. Jackson: University of Mississippi Press, 2006. 3–11.
Pratten, David. *The Man-Leopard Murders: History and Society in Colonial Nigeria*. Bloomington: Indiana University Press, 2007.
Pray the Devil Back to Hell. Dir. Gini Retiker. Fork Films, 2008. DVD.
"Promises of Freedom." In *Crossing the Danger Water*. Ed. Deirdre Mullane. New York: Anchor, 1993. 251.
Public Enemy. "Welcome to the Terrordome." *Fear of a Black Planet*. Def Jam/Columbia, 1990. Audiocassette.
Rakim. "Guess Who's Back." *The 18th Letter*. Universal, 1997. CD.
Rashidi, Runoko. "The Great University of Sankore at Timbuktu: A Brief Note." *The Global African Presence*. 2002. 12 November 2011 <http://www.cwo.com/~lucumi/timbuktu.html>.
Rawick, George P., ed. *The American Slave: A Composite Autobiography*. Vols. 2–17. Westport: Greenwood Press, 1972.
-----. *From Sundown to Sunup: The Making of the Black Community*. Vol. 1 *The American Slave: A Composite Autobiography*. Westport: Greenwood Press, 1972.

-----. *God Struck Me Dead*. Vol. 19. *The American Slave: A Composite Autobiography*. Westport: Greenwood Press, 1972.
-----. *The Unwritten History of Slavery*. Vol. 18. *The American Slave: A Composite Autobiography*. Westport: Greenwood Press, 1972.
Reed, Ishmael. *Mumbo Jumbo*. 1972. New York: Scribner, 1996.
Religion Panel. Harlem Book Fair. *Book TV: C-SPAN*. 17 July 2010. Television.
Reyes, Angelita. *Mothering Across Cultures: Postcolonial Discourse*. Minneapolis: University of Minnesota Press, 2001.
"Rome obelisk set for African return." *BBC News Online*. 8 November 2003. 7 July 2008 <http://news.bbc.co.uk/2/hi/europe/3252283.stm>.
The RZA. *The Wu-Tang Manual*. New York: Penguin, 2005.
RZA as Bobby Digital. "Terrorist." *Bobby Digital in Stereo*. Gee Street, 1998. CD.
Sagan, Carl. "The Shores of the Cosmic Ocean." *PBS*. 28 September 1980. 1 December 2011 <http://www.englishdaily626.com/discovery_channel.php?005>.
Searing, James F. "'No Kings, No Lords, No Slaves': Ethnicity and Religion among the Sereer-Safèn of Western Bawol, 1700–1914." *The Journal of African History* 43:3 (2002): 407–429.
Sembene, Ousmane, "Tribal Scars or The Voltaique." In *Tribal Scars and Other Stories*. 1962. London: Heinemann, 1974.
Schroeder, Patricia R. "Rootwork: Arthur Flowers, Zora Neale Hurston, and the 'Literary Hoodoo' Tradition." *African American Review* 36:2 (Summer 2002): 263–272.
Scott-Heron, Gil and Brian Jackson. "Winter in America." *Winter in America*. 1974. Tvt, 1998.
Scranton, Laird. *The Science of the Dogon: Decoding the African Mystery Tradition*. Rochester, VT: Inner Traditions, 2006.
Shange, Ntozake. *for colored girls who have considered suicide/when the rainbow is enuf: a choreopoem*. In *Totem Voices: Plays from the Black World Repertory*. Ed. Paul Carter Harrison. New York: Grove Press, 1989. 223–274.
Shaw, Flora L. *A Tropical Dependency: An Outline of the Ancient History of the Western Sudan with an Account of the Modern Settlement of Nigeria*. London: James Nisbet and Co., 1905.
Sheba, Eben. "Aale: A Deterrent Symbol and Communication device among the Ikale Yoruba of Nigeria." *Ifẹ* 7 (1999): 10–13.
"Shell, Chevron, and Elf all Quit Nigerian Delta." *SRi Media: Corporate Governance News*. 24 March 2003. 15 March 2004 <http://www/srimedia.com/artman/publish/article_466shtml>.
Shillington, Kevin. *History of Africa*. Rev. edition. Hampshire, England: Palgrave MacMillan, 1995.
Sia: The Dream of the Python. Dir. Dani Kouyate. ArtMattan, 2002. DVD.
Simon, Scott. "Gang Violence Smolders on Hot Chicago Streets," *NPR*. 28 July 2012. 2 March 2013 <http://www.npr.org/2012/07/28/157454927/gang-violence-smoulders-on-hot-chicago-streets>.

Sisay, Hassan B. "Africa: A Democracy Conundrum?" *The Patriotic Vanguard*. 7 December 2011. 6 May 2012 <http://www.thepatrioticvanguard.com/spip.php?article6310>.

Sly & The Family Stone. "Everybody is a Star." *Greatest Hits*. Epic, 1970. LP.

-----. "Somebody's Watching You." *Stand!* Epic, 1969. LP.

-----. "Thank You (Falettinme Be Mice Elf Agin)." *Greatest Hits*. Epic, 1970. LP.

SOARS (Seeding Operations and Atmospheric Research). "SOARS Pioneers Cloud Seeding with Milled Salt." *just-clouds*. 2005. 16 February 2008 <http://www.just-clouds.com/SOAR_pioneers_cloud_seeding_milled_salt.asp>.

Somé, Malidoma Patrice. *Of Water and the Spirit: Ritual, Magic and Initiation in the Life of an African Shaman*. New York: Penguin Compass, 1994.

Soyinka, Wole. "The African World and the Ethnocultural Debate." In *African Culture: The Rhythms of Unity*. Eds. Molefi K. Asante and Kariamu Welsh Asante. Trenton: Africa World Press, 1990. 13–38.

Steiner, Roland. "Braziel Robinson: Possessed of Two Spirits." In *Mother Wit from the Laughing Barrel*. Ed. Alan Dundes. 1973. Jackson: University of Mississippi Press, 1990. 377–379.

Stetson, Jeff. *Blood on the Leaves*. New York: Warner Books, 2004.

Story, Ralph. "An Excursion into the Black World: The 'Seven Days' in Toni Morrison's *Song of Solomon*." *Black American Literature Forum* 23.1 (1989): 149–158.

Stowe, Harriet Beecher. *Uncle Tom's Cabin*. 1852. New York: Norton, 1994.

Sun Ra. *The Wisdom of Sun Ra*. Comp. John Corbett. Chicago: White Walls, 2006.

"Supreme Mathematics." Nation of Gods and Earths/Five Percent FAQ (frequently asked questions). *Black Apologetics*. 31 July 2008 <http://www.blackapologetics.com/fivepercentfaq.html>.

Swedenburg, Ted. "Islam in the Mix: Lessons of the Five Percent." 15 November 2011 <http://comp.uark.edu/~tsweden/5per.html>.

Tademy, Lalita. *Red River*. New York: Warner 2007.

Taiwo, Olufemi. "Òrìṣà: A Prolegomenon to a Philosophy of Yorùbá Religion." *Òrìṣà Devotion as World Religion: The Globalization of Yorùbá Religious Culture*. Ed. Jacob K. Olupona and Terry Ray. Madison: University of Wisconsin Press, 2008.

Talbot, P. Amaury. "The Egbo Secret Society." *A Treasury of African Folklore*. Ed. Harold Courlander. New York: Marlowe and Co., 1996. 270–278.

Teish, Luisah. *Jambalaya: The Natural Woman's Book of Personal Charms and Practical Rituals*. New York: Harper Collins, 1985.

Thompson, Robert Farris. *Dancing Between Two Worlds: Kongo-Angola Culture and the Americas*. New York: Caribbean Cultural Center, 1991.

-----. *Flash of the Spirit*. New York: Vintage, 1983.

-----. "Kongo Influences on African-American Artistic Culture." *Africanisms in American Culture*. Ed. Joseph E. Holloway. Bloomington: Indiana University Press, 1990. 148–184.

"The true history of the Muslims coming to the first 5% parliament and debating Clarence 13X." *YouTube*. 15 November 2011 <http://www.youtube.com/watch?NR=1&v=fwSdfr1AJBk>.
Turner, Richard Brent. *Islam in the African-American Experience*. Bloomington: Indiana University Press, 2003.
Tutuola, Amos. *The Palm-Wine Drinkard and My Life in the Bush of Ghosts*. 1954. New York: Grove, 1994.
-----. *The Palm-Wine Drinkard*. Boston: Faber and Faber, 1952.
"UFO Files: UFOs and the White House." *History Channel*. 2005. Television.
Umeh, John A. *After God is Dibia*. 2 vols. London: Karnak House, 1999.
Van Sertima, Ivan. *Egypt Revisited*. Edison, NJ: Transaction, 1989.
-----. *They Came Before Columbus*. New York: Random House, 1976.
Verger, Pierre Fatumbi. *Ewé: The Use of Plants in Yoruba Society*. Sao Paulo: Odebrecht, 1995.
-----. "The Rise and Fall of the Worship of Ìyàmi Òṣòròngà (My mother the sorceress) Among the Yoruba." *Articles*. Vol. 1. Trans. Chris Brunski. 1965. Montclair, N.J.: Black Madonna Enterprises, 2007.
Volney, Constantine-Francis Chassebeuf. *The Ruins of Empires*. 1890. Baltimore: Black Classic Press, 1991.
Walker, Barbara J. *The Woman's Encyclopedia of Myths and* Secrets. San Francisco: Harper San Francisco, 1983.
Washington Creel, Margaret. "Gullah Attitudes towards Life and Death." In *Africanisms in American Culture*. Ed. Joseph E. Holloway. Bloomington: Indiana University Press, 1990. 69–97.
Washington, Teresa N. *The Architects of Existence: Àjẹ́ in Yoruba Cosmology, Ontology, and Orature*. Oya's Tornado, 2014.
-----. "*Mules and Men* and Messiahs: Continuity in Yoruba Divination Verses and African American Folktales." *Journal of American Folklore*. 125:497 (2012): 263–285.
-----. *Our Mothers, Our Powers, Our Texts: Manifestations of Àjẹ́ in Africana Literature*. 2005. Revised and expanded edition. Oya's Tornado, 2015.
Weiss, Hedy. "Devil looks past Faustian bargain of Johnson saga." *Chicago Sun-Times*. Find Articles. 6 July 2005. 28 December 2007 <http://findarticles.com/p/articles/mi_qn4155/is_20050706/ai_n14830463>.
Williams, Lance. "The Almighty Black P. Stone Nation: Black Power, Politics, and Gangbanging." Lecture. UIC School of Public Health. 12 February 2002. 25 November 2011 <http://www.uic.edu/orgs/kbc/ganghistory/UrbanCrisis/Blackstone/lance.htm>.
Williams, Rochelle. "I Wore No Veil. . . I Have No Caul." Unpublished essay. Grambling State University, 2007.
Wilson, August. *Gem of the Ocean*. New York: Theatre Communications Group, 2006.
-----. *Joe Turner's Come and Gone*. New York: Plume, 1998.
-----. *King Hedley II*. New York: Theatre Communications Group, 2000.
Wrong, Michela. *In The Footsteps of Mr. Kurtz: Living on the Brink of Disaster in Mobutu's Congo*. New York: Harper Perennial, 2002.

Wu-Tang Clan. "Wu-Gambinos." *Wu-Chronicles*. Priority, 1999. CD.

-----. "Sunlight." *8 Diagrams*. SRC/Universal Motown, 2007. CD.

X, Malcolm (El Hajj Malik El Shabazz). "Message to the Grassroots." *Teaching American History*. 10 October 1963. 6 June 2013 <http://teachingamericanhistory.org/library/document/message-to-grassroots/>.

-----. "The Ballet or the Bullet." *American RadioWorks*. 12 April 1964. 5 June 2013 <http://americanradioworks.publicradio.org/features/blackspeech/mx.html>.

X, Malcolm and Alex Haley. *The Autobiography of Malcolm X*. 1964. New York: Ballantine, 1992.

X Clan. "Do It Like You?!" *Mainstream Outlawz*. Suburban Noize 2009. CD.

-----. "Funkin' Lesson." *To the East Blackwards*. 4th and B'Way, 1990. Audiocassette.

-----. "Grand Verbalizer, What Time Is It?" *To the East Blackwards*. 4th and B'Way, 1990. Audiocassette.

-----. "Primetime Lyrics." *Mainstream Outlawz*. Suburban Noize 2009. CD.

-----. "Wiz Degrees." *Mainstream Outlawz*. Suburban Noize 2009. CD.

X Clan featuring Medusa. "Keys To Ur City." *Mainstream Outlawz*, Suburban Noize, 2009. CD.

Yansane, Aguibou Y. "Cultural, Political, and Economic Universals in West Africa." *African Culture: The Rhythms of Unity*. Eds. Molefi K. Asante and Kariamu W. Asante. Trenton: Africa World Press, 1985. 39–68.

Yar-Shater, Ehsan, ed. *The History of Al-Tabari*. Trans. William M. Brinner. New York: State University of New York Press, 1987.

Yeelen. Dir. Souleymane Cisse. 1987. Kino, 2003. DVD.

Zemmouri, Catherine. "Paris fire relatives blame government." *BBC News Online*. 26 September 2005. 24 July 2009 <http://news.bbc.co.uk/2/hi/europe/4189840.stm>.

Personal Communications

Harris, Lenell. Personal communications. Rienzi, MS, 1996.

Ivory-Lindsey, Ayanna. Personal communication. Grambling State University, 2011.

Rawls, Sharen. Personal communication. Grambling State University, 2007.

Somé, Malidoma Patrice. Lecture. Grambling State University, February 2007.

Tatum, Jonathan. Personal communication. Grambling State University, 2009.

INDEX

47 (Mosley), 13, 182–192, 213, 236

Abiodun, Rowland, 23, 33, 103, 211, 329
After God is Dibia (Umeh), 39, 41, 63, 142, 220
Àjẹ́, 10, 11, 22,–23, 26, 27, 29, 32, 45, 47, 55, 63, 74, 78, 147, 163, 195, 234–235, 236, 238, 268, 277, 307, 308, 316
Akpan, Uwem, 229, 230
Akuaba, 269–270, 278
Ali, Noble Drew, 65, 86–89, 115, 116, 117, 324
Allah, the Father, 12, 65, 92, 93–100, 103, 105, 106, 118, 131, 144, 168, 273, 294, 325
Ani, Marimba, 132, 290
Anikulapo Kuti, Fela, 252, 275, 276, 299, 309–310
Ankh, 118, 258, 267–272, 274, 275, 277, 278, 282, 288, 317, 331, 336
Armah, Ayi Kwei, 14, 20, 120, 252, 257, 258–274, 276, 292, 297, 313, 314
Àṣẹ, 19, 33, 34, 39, 44, 50, 57, 73, 84, 98, 103, 157, 163, 198, 205, 242
Aset, 6, 21–22, 118, 272, 283, 301, 318
Ausar, 6, 21, 73, 99–100, 107, 117, 119, 135, 148, 213, 272–273, 284–285, 292–294, 301, 318, 336, 337
Ax Muslim mathematical equations, 94–96, 186
Ayolo, 37–38, 209

Ba, 28, 29, 33, 34, 47, 50, 81, 132, 157, 220, 248, 254

Bachwezi, 131, 132, 133, 134, 181, 218, 254
Badu, Erykah, 10, 12, 101, 125–127
Bakhye (*Of Water and the Spirit*), 25, 59, 60, 186, 208–209, 223, 249, 251, 254
BaKongo, 17, 36, 39, 45, 50, 56, 63, 176, 184, 218, 229, 231–232, 233, 235, 238, 255, 304, 327, 329
Bambara (people), 19, 138–142, 144, 170
Bambara, Toni Cade, 14, 172, 226–228, 235, 236, 243, 245, 250, 252, 255–258, 296, 305, 317, 328
Berbelang (*Mumbo Jumbo*), 287, 289–290, 294
Bey, C. M., 65, 87, 127
Bey, R. V., 87–88, 127
Big Sixteen (*Mules and Men*), 77–78
Black Gangster Disciples (BGD), 325–334
Black Herman, 110, 284, 285, 290, 294, 318, 327
Black P. Stone Rangers (El Rukns), 322, 324–326
Bok, Francis, 194, 196, 198–199, 265–266
"Broken Field Running" (Bambara), 14, 228, 237–243
Bynum (*Joe Turner's Come and Gone*), 13, 153–157, 161–165, 166, 168–169, 171–173, 176, 178, 181

Caul, 27–30
Cipher, 1, 2, 4, 9, 10, 96–99, 103, 105, 123, 125–127, 136, 143, 164, 175, 245, 295, 319, 329, 331

Convict Lease System, 162, 172, 176, 266, 274
Cooper, Jr. Clarence, 94–96, 168

D'Angelo, 176, 213
De La Soul, 10, 98, 105, 118
De Mojo Blues: De Quest of HighJohn de Conqueror (Flowers), 12, 137, 142, 144–148, 283
dead prez, 279, 280–281
Devil (Trickster), 67–68, 69, 71–72, 78, 112, 115, 176, 188, 209
Djigui (*Yeelen*), 138–141, 158, 165, 223, 292
Dunn, Christopher, 218, 238

Earth, 17, 24, 28, 32, 38, 39, 40, 44, 45, 47, 48, 61, 66, 67, 73, 71, 79, 81, 89, 93, 95, 99, 101, 109, 110, 112, 119–131, 134, 135, 153, 171, 179, 181, 182, 184, 188, 199, 206, 208, 212, 213, 216, 218, 219, 233–236–240, 243, 251, 252, 253, 255, 260, 267, 268, 277, 305, 317, 329, 331, 337
Eighty-four (*47*), 186, 191
El Hajj Malik El Shabazz (Malcolm X), 3, 34, 90–92, 94, 111, 252, 298, 326, 336
Escape from Slavery (Bok), 194, 198
Èṣù Ẹlẹ́gbára, 17, 67, 73, 117, 283, 284, 285

Fard, W. D., 12, 88–89, 90, 92, 93, 96, 111, 114–115, 118, 251, 274
Faro and Pemba, 138, 273, 292, 294, 336, 337
Father Divine, 9, 12, 65, 82, 247
Father Jehovia, 9, 82

The Father of the Gods Who Can Do Anything in this World (*The Palm-wine Drinkard*), 99, 126, 194, 200, 217, 231
Five Percenters (see Nation of Gods)
Flowers, Arthur, 12, 137, 144, 147, 148, 283

Gadsby, Meredith, 241–242, 243
Garvey, Marcus, 12, 85–86, 90, 115, 118
"Get Up, Stand Up" (Marley and Tosh), 109
The Giza Power Plant, (Dunn), 218, 238
Goodie Mob, 12, 108, 111
Gottehrer, Barry, 113
Gravediggaz, 12, 108–109, 112, 116, 146, 261
Guitar Bains (*Song of Solomon*), 246–248, 249, 250, 252, 253, 254–255, 256, 275–281, 318

"High John de Conquer" (Hurston), 73–79, 137, 187–188
High John the Conqueror, 12, 13, 53–54, 65–79, 101, 103, 104, 107, 112, 119, 139, 143, 147, 148, 151, 162, 176, 185, 187, 188, 199, 220, 241, 255, 282, 305
High John the Conqueror Root, 48, 53, 74, 79, 318
Holy Ghost, 66, 110, 167
Hoodoo and Whodo(?), 54, 56–57, 60, 145–147, 153, 154, 156, 158, 165, 181, 187, 283
Hurley, George, 12, 82–85, 89, 106
Hurston, Zora Neale, 12, 25, 28, 36, 37, 42–43, 53–54, 56, 59, 62–63, 65, 67–69, 73, 75, 79–82, 83, 84, 93, 99, 121, 137, 137, 147–148, 160, 179, 187, 188, 199, 200, 220, 234–235, 241, 252, 261, 282, 293, 304, 305

I.S.L.A.M., 97, 105, 110, 115, 265
Imí Òṣùmàrè, 62–63, 185, 200, 201, 222

Jake (*Song of Solomon*), 246, 248–249, 250, 253, 254
Joe Turner's Come and Gone (Wilson), 13, 134, 151–181, 188, 192, 199, 205, 218, 248, 249
John (Trickster) (See High John the Conqueror)
Johnson, Robert, 13, 151, 152, 158, 160–163, 164, 165, 174, 177–178, 180, 181, 198
Juba, 166–167, 168, 183, 201, 254

Ka, 19, 28, 81, 132
Khu, 132–133, 136, 137, 158, 192, 217, 337
Killarmy, 12, 106, 108, 135, 261, 278
Kimbrough (*Robert Johnson: Trick the Devi*l), 158–161, 162, 166, 170, 172, 174, 175, 176, 177, 189, 199, 201, 290
Knight, Michael M., 9, 113, 114, 122, 357n57
Ku Klux Klan, 75, 166, 290, 298, 300, 320, 322

Leedskalnin, Edward, 237–240
Lincoln, Abbey, 338
Lindsay, Michael V., 113
Look What They Done to My Song (McCluskey), 12, 137, 142, 144, 148, 226, 251
Lord Jamar, 9–10, 105–106, 115, 123, 128–129, 130, 184, 213

Makinde, Moses Akin, 35, 58
Maat, 268, 277, 297
Matigari (Ngugi), 14, 258, 294, 301, 306, 317
McCluskey, John, 12, 137, 142, 144, 226, 251

Mecca (Digable Planets), 127, 126
Milkman (*Song of Solomon*), 228, 246–256, 275, 279, 281, 295, 306
Miyakawa, Felicia, 9, 97, 98
Montejo, Esteban, 36, 39, 63, 231
Moon, 39, 45, 46, 58, 82, 94, 95, 122–124, 134, 165, 293, 328
Moore, Carlos, 45, 151, 176, 297
Moorish Science Temple of America (MSTA), 86, 87–89, 324
Morrison, Toni, 3, 13, 30, 81, 126, 152, 169, 185, 198, 202, 221, 226–228, 236, 245, 246, 248, 250, 251, 254, 255, 256, 257, 258, 274, 275, 294, 315
Mu'tafikah (*Mumbo Jumbo*), 287–290, 291, 317
Muhammad, Elijah, 65, 88–90, 92, 95, 106, 110, 111, 115, 127, 148, 235, 236
Mules and Men (Hurston), 28, 53, 67, 75, 80, 81, 103, 137, 176, 220
Mumbo Jumbo (Reed), 14, 257, 258, 282–294, 298, 300, 327
Mutabaruka, 109–110
My Life in the Bush of Ghosts (Tutuola), 13, 182, 183, 192–205, 217, 219, 223, 226, 232

Nabta Playa, 6, 130, 296
Namoratunga, 130, 139
Nation of Gods (also, Nation of Gods and Earths), 10, 92–100, 103–136, 139, 143, 185, 200, 264, 319, 322, 326
Nation of Islam, 89–91, 93, 95, 100, 107, 111, 114–115, 169, 191, 285, 287, 323, 328
Nation sack, 48, 144, 187–188, 198, 249, 317, 332
Nianankoro (*Yeelen*), 138–142, 148, 149, 199, 254, 305

Night soil, 309–313
Nobles, Wade, W., 108, 279
"Not We Many" (Cooper), 94–96, 168
Nubia (also Kush), 5, 6, 10, 20, 41, 48, 68, 70, 121, 122, 130, 131, 133, 243, 285, 289, 296, 329
Nyabinghi, 107, 116, 190, 272, 277, 282, 298, 318

Ògbóni, 122, 267-269, 270, 274, 277, 278, 282, 317, 318, 327, 328, 331, 333, 336
Osiris Rising (Armah), 14, 258, 267–273
Òṣùmàrè, 61–63, 185, 200, 201, 221
Our Mothers, Our Powers, Our Texts (Washington), 10, 231
Oya, 27–28, 63, 201, 203, 237, 238, 317

The Palm-wine Drinkard (Tutuola), 77, 126, 194, 200, 216, 231
Papa Labas (*Mumbo Jumbo*), 283–285, 289, 292
Pilate (*Song of Solomon*), 247–249, 254
Poor Righteous Teachers (rap group), 10, 105
"Poor righteous teachers" (description), 93, 108, 157, 244, 254
Power of the Word (including Òrò and Hu), 18–19, 35, 39, 44, 73, 103, 104, 121, 145, 165, 173, 329, 331
Prenda, 39–40, 63, 144, 256

Raap (also Rab, Wolof Gods), 10, 102, 105
Rakim, 10, 12, 105, 120–121, 213, 261

Reed, Ishmael, 1, 14, 257, 258, 282–283, 287–288, 290, 292, 293–294
Robert Johnson: Trick the Devil (Harris), 13, 151–181
Rutherford Selig (*Joe Turner's Come and Gone*), 154–156, 156–157, 159, 162, 164, 173
The RZA, 9, 12, 104, 105, 109, 110, 116–117, 119, 128, 146, 236

Salt, 6, 13–14, 51–52, 56, 71, 170, 226–256, 257, 260, 261, 262, 264, 302
The Salt Eaters (Bambara), 14, 170, 226–228, 243–246, 248, 250, 251, 252, 302
Seven Days (*Song of Solomon*), 247, 251–253, 254, 258, 274–281, 287–289, 294, 311, 317, 318, 327, 328, 336
Shalimar (*Song of Solomon*), 246–248, 250, 253–254
Shine, Shining, 5, 7, 10, 12, 13, 18, 43, 46, 49, 50, 64, 69, 75, 78, 99, 100, 111, 128, 130,131–136, 137–140, 148, 151–158, 161–164, 173, 178, 181, 188, 192, 197, 201, 205, 212, 215, 221–222, 245, 254, 255, 261, 262, 267, 270, 274, 286, 309, 337
Shiny Man, 154–157, 162–164, 178, 192, 197, 221
Slave, My True Story (Nazer), 195, 267
Somé, Malidoma, 13, 25–26, 35, 40, 43, 44, 59, 63, 132, 134, 163, 182, 183, 186, 196, 203, 206–225, 235, 238, 249, 251–252, 255, 256, 297, 306
Song of Solomon (Morrison), 14, 221, 226, 228, 246–256, 274–281, 287–289, 294, 311, 317, 318, 327, 328, 336

"soul-piece," 12, 67, 137–138, 173, 189, 218, 292
Sun, 5, 12, 21, 42, 45, 46, 48, 49, 56, 65, 77, 81, 90, 94, 95, 99, 101, 108, 111, 113, 118, 120, 122–124, 127–130, 132, 133, 135, 139, 143, 146, 148, 151, 167, 176, 184, 197, 212, 214, 221, 236, 240, 253, 260, 270, 284, 289, 309, 331, 337
Sun Ra, 103, 110–111, 144, 167, 179–180, 181, 256, 276, 284
Sunz of Man, 10, 12, 128, 135, 257, 261, 278
Supreme Alphabet, 96–97, 104, 105, 107, 329
Supreme Mathematics, 95–97, 98, 101, 103, 104, 105, 106, 107, 120, 125, 319, 329, 330

Tall John (*47*), 184–192, 195, 197, 218, 222, 236, 246
Tekhen, 6, 21, 289, 293
Tutuola, Amos, 13, 77, 183, 193–205, 206, 222, 225, 226, 231

Two Thousand Seasons (Armah), 14, 121, 258, 259–267, 270, 292, 314, 332
Umeh, John A., 35, 38, 39, 41, 44, 45, 51, 63–64, 220, 232
Universal Hagar's Spiritual Church Association (UHSC), 83–85, 106, 220

Vice Lords, 319, 325, 326, 334

Of Water and the Spirit (Somé), 13, 25, 35, 134, 182, 183, 206–225
Wilson, August, 13, 82, 102, 134, 151–181, 242
Wizard of the Crow (Ngugi), 14, 258, 298–318

X Clan, 10, 117–118, 121, 124–125, 327

Yeelen (Cisse), 12, 137–142, 158, 165, 203, 223

Teresa N. Washington is the author of *The Architects of Existence: Àjẹ́ in Yoruba Cosmology, Ontology, and Orature*; *Manifestations of Masculine Magnificence: Divinity in Africana Life, Lyrics, and Literature*; and *Our Mothers, Our Powers, Our Texts: Manifestations of Àjẹ́ in Africana Literature*. She is also the editor of *The African World in Dialogue: An Appeal to Action!* Dr. Washington's analyses are published as chapters in *Harold Bloom's Modern Critical Interpretations: Toni Morrison's <u>Beloved</u>: New Edition*; *Yemoja: Gender, Sexuality, and Creativity in the Latina/o and Afro- Atlantic Diasporas*; *Èṣù: Yoruba God, Power, and the Imaginative Frontiers*; and *Step into a World: A Global Anthology of the New Black Literature*. Her articles have been published in many noted journals, including the *African American Review*, the *Journal of American Folklore*, *FEMSPEC*, and the *Journal of Pan African Studies*.

MORE "BOOKS TO BLOW YOUR MIND" FROM ỌYA'S TORNADO!

Ah Jubah! A PleaPrayerPromise (a novel)
Asiri Odu, author
ISBN: 9780991073047 (pbk); also available as a Kindle Book

Six Pan-African collectives organize to unite warring gangs, exterminate "good old boys," turn tables—and barrels—on trigger-happy cops, and heal victims of genital excision, rape, and sodomy. Want a blueprint for complete elevation and liberation? Check out the novel *Ah Jubah!* It's a revolution in ink.

The African World in Dialogue: An Appeal to Action!
Teresa N. Washington, editor
ISBN: 9780991073078 (cloth); 9780991073061 (pbk); 9780991073085 (ebook)

In this contemporary anthology, elders, warriors, scholars, artists, and activists address some of the most significant political, cultural, and social issues facing the African world. What is more, they offer viable solutions to facilitate progress, evolution, and elevation.

The Architects of Existence: Àjẹ́ in Yoruba Cosmology, Ontology, and Orature
Teresa N. Washington, author
ISBN: 9780991073016 (pbk); 9780991073030 (cloth)

The Architects of Existence is the companion to Teresa N. Washington's *Our Mothers, Our Powers, Our Texts: Manifestations of Àjẹ́ in Africana Literature*, and it is the only book-length exposition of the power of Àjẹ́ and the African Gods and Divine Mothers who own and control this power in Yoruba cosmology and ontology.

Manifestations of Masculine Magnificence: Divinity in Africana Life, Lyrics, and Literature
Teresa N. Washington, author
ISBN: 9780991073009 (pbk); 9780991073023 (cloth)

Teresa N. Washington uses a compelling historical and spiritual foundation as a lens by which to analyze the proliferation of humanodivinity in contemporary Africana life, in some of the deepest lyrics ever spit and in some of the richest literature ever written.

Our Mothers, Our Powers, Our Texts: Manifestations of Àjẹ́ in Africana Literature
Teresa N. Washington, author
ISBN: 9780991073054 (pbk)

Using orature and historical documents, this book explores Àjẹ́'s forces and figures throughout the African continuum. From this rich foundation, Teresa N. Washington analyzes the impact and influence of Àjẹ́ in the contemporary literature of Africana writers. Ọya's Tornado is proud to publish the revised and expanded edition of Washington's groundbreaking study!

Ọya's Tornado books are also available wherever fine books are sold!
Visit us at www.oyastornado.com

www.ingramcontent.com/pod-product-compliance
Lightning Source LLC
Chambersburg PA
CBHW031402290426
44110CB00011B/234